Policing Perspectives

An Anthology

Larry K. Gaines
*California State University
at San Bernardino*

Gary W. Cordner
Eastern Kentucky University

Roxbury Publishing Company
Los Angeles, California

Library of Congress Cataloging-in-Publication Data

Gaines, Larry K.
  Policing Perspectives: An Anthology
  [edited by] Larry K. Gaines, Gary W. Cordner
    p. cm.
    Includes bibliographical references and index.
    ISBN 1-891487-04-3 (acid-free paper)
    1. Police—United States. 2. Police. I. Gaines, Larry K. II. Cordner, Gary W.
  HV8138.P675 1999
  363.2'0973—dc21   97-39253
                                                                              CIP

Policing Perspectives: An Anthology

Publisher and Editor: Claude Teweles
Copy Editors: Sacha Howells and Robert Watrous
Assistant Editor: Dawn VanDercreek
Production Assistant: David Massengill
Typography: Synergistic Data Systems
Cover Design: Marnie Deacon Kenney

Printed on acid-free paper in the United States of America.
This paper meets the standards for recycling of the Environmental Protection Agency.

ISBN 1-891487-04-3

Roxbury Publishing Company
P.O. Box 491044
Los Angeles, California 90049-9044
Tel: (213) 653-1068 • Fax: (213) 653-4140
Email: roxbury@crl.com

Table of Contents

Introduction

Everyone knows at least a little about policing, perhaps from personal experiences or those of friends and relatives, or from a few chance observations, and especially from that fountain of all true knowledge, television. We all know that police carry guns and can arrest people and write tickets. We suspect that they have other powers as well. Most of us must find police work rather intriguing—how else to account for all those police TV shows and movies, not to mention the shelves full of novels termed "police procedurals." In truth, many people probably have conflicting thoughts and emotions about policing, a mixture of fascination, curiosity, fear, suspicion, awe, respect, and even hate. Needless to say, some people have themselves suffered at the hands of police, and some groups, particularly minority groups, have suffered disproportionately. The police are sort of a necessary evil, even in a free society, but not one we all completely trust.

The general public's lack of trust could be countered by statistical evidence. In fact, study after study has demonstrated that police officers are attracted to their work primarily out of a desire to help other people. Also, study after study has found that most police work is fairly mundane, that a lot of it has to do with keeping the peace and providing services, and that police officers use their coercive powers less than we might think. In the past decade or so, the advent of community policing has probably put an even happier face on day-to-day police work, improved relations between the police and the public, and earned the police higher marks in terms of public confidence and satisfaction.

However, policing will never completely shed its taint or stigma. Commitment to service and happy faces notwithstanding, these are still ultimately the men and women who can take us to jail, take away our children, search our homes in the middle of the night, or write us a ticket for going three miles over the speed limit. We will also always suspect them of some type of corruption, at least a little, whenever our kids or neighbors know of drug dealers who seem to be impervious to arrest. If nothing else, who will promise never to tell stories about how many patrol cars they saw parked at the local donut shop?

These are truths to be regretted by those who practice policing or study the police, but also ones that need to be appreciated and understood. The contents of this anthology, 32 chapters in all, address many facets of policing and discuss many issues underlying the function of the police in a free and pluralistic society. The first section of four chapters directly focuses on the function of the police, including the police role, the centrality of coercive force in police work, the question of whether policing could be privatized, and the curiously American police institution of the elected sheriff. The second section delves more into the history of policing in the U.S. and other countries, including the little-known role of slave patrols, the development of the detective, and the tendency to wax overly nostalgic about "the good old days" of American policing.

The effectiveness of police strategies and programs is examined in the third section of the book, including traditional strategies and the currently popular tandem of community policing and problem-oriented policing. The fourth section looks more at police work as performed by individual officers, including patrol and detective work, how officers learn their craft, and how they adapt to their unique role. The fifth section focuses on some of the more problematic aspects of reactive and proactive policing—handling domestic disputes, handling people with mental illness, controlling gangs, and wrestling with the endemic problem of drug abuse.

Police work poses ethical issues and sometimes outright ethical dilemmas for its practitioners—these are examined in the sixth section along with several forms of unethical, deviant, and outright illegal police behavior, including drug corruption, lying, and sexual violence against women. Ways of controlling these types of misconduct, and of managing police organizations generally, are presented in the seventh section of the anthology. While the focus of this book is more on police work and police behavior, it is also important to consider, albeit briefly, some of the issues and problems associated with police administration.

The final section offers a look at several contemporary issues facing the police, including brutality, the use of deadly force, the increasing militarization of policing, and the plight of female police officers.

These situations represent just the tip of the iceberg, of course, of serious issues and problems that confront policing today and that will arise, or resurface, in the years to come. While our inability to solve or eliminate all the shortcomings and problems associated with policing may seem frustrating, and it certainly does frustrate police executives and reformers alike, it is a false expectation anyway. Policing is destined to be always controversial and problematic precisely because of its core function—the use of coercive authority against certain citizens, on behalf of the state—and because police are ultimately judged against subjective criteria of reasonableness, fairness, and justice that are always evolving and constantly undergoing debate in political and social arenas. It is for these reasons that the study and practice of policing are so interesting and challenging. ✦

Acknowledgements

The editors would like to thank the following reviewers for their comments on the manuscript:

William Doerner (Florida State University)

Ronald Hunter (Jacksonville State University)

Robert Little (University of Northern Alabama)

Richard Lumb (Northern Michigan University)

Peter Manning (Michigan State University)

Dennis Payne (Michigan State University)

Roy Roberg (San Jose State University)

Gerald Williams (Institute for Law and Justice) ✦

Part I

The Function of the Police

Introduction

The role and function of the police have long been the subject of both hot debate and reasoned, scholarly analysis. This is a subject of some interest to many citizens, as they contemplate the legitimacy of police intrusion into their everyday lives (e.g., traffic stops), the quality and responsiveness of routine police services (e.g., quieting noisy neighbors), and the effectiveness of the police in controlling serious crime. Many citizens have wildly distorted views of the police role, of course, thanks in large part to the popular media, especially television and movies. As a result of these distorted perceptions, citizens' expectations of what the police can deliver and accomplish are often quite exaggerated. This situation poses serious difficulties for the police, particularly if they are committed to notions of public service and customer satisfaction.

In some ways, the function of the police has changed little over the past 150 years. Now, as then, police are expected to maintain order and prevent crime. Among their duties, police still respond to emergencies, chase criminals, enforce the law, keep an eye on kids and drunks, and patrol in order to create a sense of "omnipresence," just as they did in London and New York in the 1840s. Citizens still look to the police as a symbol of stability and order and protection against crime and criminals. The police are still separated from ordinary citizens by uniforms, weapons, and the authority to use force on behalf of the state.

In other ways, though, police functions have changed. Most police are in cars now, and they spend much more of their time "handling calls" than they did 100, or even 20, years ago. Police technology has changed dramatically, as have the legal and administrative constraints on police use of authority and discretion. Police officers are much better educated and trained than their forebears, and much more likely to be women and members of minority groups. Traffic control and drug enforcement are two significant aspects of policing today that were given much lower priority in the early years of organized policing (although "traffic" control of horses, wagons, and carts was a real headache for 19th-century urban police officers).

Historians and social scientists have been seriously examining the role and function of the police for the last 30 years. When their research began in the 1960s, the popular view of policing emphasized the dramatic crime fighting and law enforcement features of the work. Not surprisingly, perhaps, the historians revealed that early policing had been much more focused on peace keeping, order maintenance, and general services than the dominant 1960s-era popular conception. Similarly, the social scientists discovered that what police officers were really doing in contemporary po-

1

licing was much more mundane than the image projected through television and movies. The cumulative effect of this research was to challenge the dramatic crime-fighting picture of policing and to offer an alternative that de-emphasized law enforcement and emphasized service as the central feature of the police role.

The first two readings in this section tackle these issues head on. From them you should derive a fuller and deeper understanding of the police function as well as an appreciation for the dilemmas that confront policing in a free society. The last two readings discuss important topics related to the role of the police: (1) whether policing, which we have traditionally thought of as a government activity, can be privatized, and (2) the distinctive features of that uniquely American police institution, the county sheriff. ✦

1

Dilemmas of Police Administration

James Q. Wilson

James Q. Wilson was one of the first scholars to look closely at the police. In this article, adapted from his pioneering book Varieties of Police Behavior, *Wilson addresses several basic questions about the police, including: (1) What is the true nature of the police function? (2) How do police organizations control their members, who exercise so much discretionary authority? (3) Which measures for reforming the police hold the most promise? As you read this article, which was first published in 1968, ask yourself how much has changed in the last 30 years and how much remains the same.*

You will notice some outdated language in this article, written three decades ago. For example, African Americans are referred to as Negroes, and police officers are repeatedly identified as men or patrolmen (which they almost all were in 1968). Please remember that Wilson was using the accepted terminology of the time and that he certainly intended neither disrespect nor exclusion by his word choice.

Policy making for the police is complicated by the fact that, at least in large cities, the police department is an organization with at least two objectives, one of which produces conflict and the other of which cannot be attained.[1] The dilemmas facing police administrators arise out of their inability to obtain agreement on what constitutes satisfactory performance of the first objective, and their difficulty in finding a strategy which would permit the realization of the (agreed-upon) second objective. (There are, of course, additional objectives which a police department serves—providing certain nonpolice services and handling large-scale disorders, for example.)

Objectives

The first objective I call *order maintenance*—the handling of disputes, or behavior which threatens to produce disputes, among persons who disagree over what ought to be right or seemly conduct or over the assignment of blame for what is agreed to be wrong or unseemly conduct. A family quarrel, a noisy drunk, a tavern brawl, a street disturbance by teenagers, the congregation on the sidewalk of idle young men (especially in eccentric clothes or displaying an unconventional demeanor)—all these are cases in which citizens disagree as to whether or how the police should intervene. If the police do intervene, one party or another is likely to feel harassed, outraged, or neglected. Though a law may have been broken, as with an assault inflicted by a husband on his wife, the police do not perceive their responsibilities as involving simply the comparing of a particular behavior to a clear legal standard and making an arrest if the standard has been violated. For one thing, the legal rule is, in many order-maintenance cases, ambiguous. A "breach of the peace" implies a prior definition of "peace," and this is a matter on which persons commonly disagree. For another thing, even when the legal standard is clear enough—as with an assault—the "victim" is often not innocent (indeed, he may have called for the police because he was losing a fight he started) and thus the question of blame may be to the participants more important than the question of "guilt" and they will expect the officer to take this into account. Finally, most order-maintenance situations do not result in an arrest—the parties involved wish the officer to "do something" that will "settle things," but they often do not wish to see that settlement entail an arrest. And in any case the infraction is likely to be a misdemeanor and thus, in many states, the officer cannot make a valid arrest unless the illegality was committed in his presence or unless the victim is willing to sign a complaint. As a result, the officer cannot expect a judge to dispose of the case; the former must devise a substantive solution for a disorderly event which the latter will never hear of.

The second objective is *law enforcement*—the application of legal sanctions, usually by means of an arrest, to persons who injure or deprive innocent victims. A burglary, purse snatch, mugging, robbery, or auto theft are usually crimes committed by strangers on persons who did not provoke the attack. Though there is, in these matters, a problem of finding the guilty party, once guilt is established there is no question of blame. For almost all such law-enforcement situations, the officer is expected to either make an arrest or act so as to prevent the violation from occurring in the first place. His task is the seemingly ministerial and technical act of either apprehending or deterring the criminal. The difficulty is that the officer lacks the means—the information, primarily—to apprehend or deter more than a very small fraction of all criminals. Leaving aside murder, rape, and aggravated assault—in which a high proportion of suspects are known or even related to their victims—few major crimes such as burglary and robbery that are of primary concern to the citizen are "cleared by arrest." In 1965 only 38 percent of all *known* robberies and 25 percent of all *known* burglaries were cleared by arrest, and even that figure is artificially high. The household victimization study done by the National Opinion Research Center for the President's Commission on Law Enforcement and Administration of Justice[2] showed that in 1965 there were over three times as many burglaries and 50 percent more robberies than were reported to and recorded by the police; thus, the adjusted clearance rates are only about 8 percent for burglary and 24 per cent for robbery. But even those figures may be too high, for, as Skolnick points out, there are often strong organizational pressures leading detectives to induce arrested burglars and robbers to "cop out" to as many offenses as possible in order to boost the clearance rate.[3]

There is, of course, no way to measure the number of crimes prevented by police activity, but the number is not likely to be large. Crimes of passion that occur in private places (many, if not most, murders, rapes, and serious assaults are in this category) probably happen at a rate independent of the nature or intensity of police activity. Crimes of stealth, such as burglary and many forms of larceny, may in unknown ways be affected by police activity, but the effect is probably not great—no city, whatever its police strategy, has been able to show any dramatic reversal in the rising rates of reported thefts. There is some evidence that certain kinds of street crimes—muggings, purse snatches, holdups of taxi and bus drivers, and the like—can be reduced by very intensive police patrol, the use of officers disguised as cabbies or lady shoppers, the formation of citizen auxiliaries, and the like. But even with these crimes, which surely are the ones most disturbing to the average person, two problems exist. First, no one is confident that what appears to be a reduction is not in fact a displacement of crime (to other places or to other forms of crime), or that if a reduction genuinely occurs it will persist over time.[4] And second, the kinds of police activities apparently best adapted to suppressing street crime—intensive patrols, close surveillance of "suspicious" persons, frequent street stops of pedestrians and motorists, and so on—are precisely those most likely to place the police in conflict with important segments of the community—primarily with persons who because of their age, race, or social class are regarded (and, as far as the evidence goes, correctly regarded) as most likely to commit criminal acts. In short, in the one aspect of law enforcement where there may be opportunities for substantial deterrence, the police are obliged to act in a way which, like their actions in order-maintenance situations, is most likely to bring them into conflict with the citizen.

The dilemmas of police administration arise out of the difficulty confronting a chief who seeks policies which can guide his men in performing the order-maintenance function and a technique which will prove efficacious in serving the law-enforcement function. The conflict over how the police should behave in order-maintenance cases results from differing expectations as to the appropriate level of public or private order and differing judgments over what constitutes a just resolution of a given dispute. In a homogeneous community, where widely shared norms define both the meaning of order and the standards of justice (who is equal to whom and in what sense), the police role is comparatively simple. But where the community, usually because of differences of class or race, has no common normative framework, the police have no reliable guides to action and efforts to devise such guides will either be halfhearted or sources of important public controversy. The conflict that arises over the performance of the law-enforcement function, on the other hand, arises out of the lack of any technique by which crime can be reduced significantly and without incurring high costs in terms of other values—privacy, freedom, and so forth. The dispute about the law-enforcement function is, unlike the dispute over order-maintenance, not over ends but over means.

Criticisms

Organizations to which society gives tasks that cannot be performed to the satisfaction of society suffer not only certain frustrations but some fundamental administrative problems as well. The criticisms directed at the police are well known and often sound, but conditions giving rise to these criticisms are frequently not well understood by the critic. For example, police departments are frequently charged with hiring unqualified personnel, suppressing or manipulating crime reports, condoning the use of improper or illegal procedures, using patrol techniques that create tensions and irritation among the citizens, and either over-reacting (using too much force too quickly) or under-reacting (ignoring dangerous situations until it is too late) in the face of incipient disorder. All of these criticisms are true to some extent, though the extent of the deficiencies is often exaggerated. But let us concede for the moment that they are all true. Why are they true?

Explanations vary, but commonly they are some variation on the "bad men" theme. Unqualified, unintelligent, rude, brutal, intolerant, or insensitive men, so this theory goes, find their way (or are selectively recruited into) police work where they express their prejudices and crudeness under color of the law. Though a few of the commanding offi-

cers of the department may try to improve matters, on the whole they are ineffective. At best they invent paper palliatives—empty departmental directives, superficial community relations programs, one-sided internal disciplinary units—which do little more than offer a chance for issuing favorable, but misleading, publicity statements about the "new look." And at worst, the theory continues, such administrators exacerbate tensions by encouraging, in the name of efficiency or anti-crime strategies, various techniques, such as aggressive preventive patrol, that lead to the harassment of innocent citizens. The solution for these problems is, clearly, to hire "better men"—college graduates, Negroes, men who can pass tests that weed out "authoritarian" personalities, and the like. And those on the force should attend universities, go through sensitivity training, and apply for grants to develop "meaningful" community relations programs.[5]

Some critics go even further. Not only do the police fail to do the right thing, they systematically do the wrong thing. Not only do the police fail to prevent crime, *the police actually cause crime*. Not only do the police fail to handle riots properly, *the police cause riots*. Presumably, things might improve if we had no police at all, but since even the strongest critics usually recognize the need for the police under some circumstances, they are willing to permit the police to function provided that they are under "community control"—controlled, that is, by the neighborhoods (especially Negro neighborhoods) where they operate. If police departments are at best a necessary evil, filled with inept or intolerant men exploiting the fact that they are necessary, then the solution to the problem of abuse is to put the police under the strictest and closest control of those whose activities they are supposed to regulate.

The view taken in this paper is quite different from at least the more extreme of these arguments. If all big-city police departments were filled tomorrow with Negro college graduates and placed under the control of the neighborhoods they are supposed to control, most of the problems that exist today would continue to exist and some in fact might get worse. The crime rate would not go down;

indeed, owing to police timidity about making arrests among people who have a voice in their management, it might go up marginally. Police involvement in conflict and disorder would have no happier outcomes, because most disorder—family or neighbor quarrels—does not involve the community nor would the community necessarily have any better idea how to resolve it than do the police now. Perceived police abuse and harassment might decline in the neighborhood, but since each neighborhood would have its own police, the amount of abuse and harassment perceived by a person from one neighborhood entering a different neighborhood (say a Negro entering a white area, or vice versa) might increase. The conflict between neighborhood residents who want more police protection (small businessmen, home-owners, older people) and those who want less (teenagers, transients, young men hanging on street corners) would remain and the police would tend, in the eyes of one group, to serve the standards of the other.

There would, of course, be some improvements. The police might have better information about the neighborhood if they were controlled by it and thus, in the event of large-scale disorders, be able to distinguish more accurately between solid citizens and trouble makers. They might also be more alert to the customs of the area and thus prepared to tolerate behavior (street-corner gatherings, loud noises) which the neighborhood tolerates, even though in other places such behavior might be regarded as breaches of the peace. And college-educated men might display more civility in routine encounters, handling incidents more impersonally and people more politely.

But it is difficult to say that such gains would be more than marginal. Some police departments (such as those on the West Coast) already have large numbers of men with some college training, but these departments (Oakland and Los Angeles, for example) are frequently criticized by Negroes for being "too tough," "too impersonal," "gung ho," and the like. (There may be no causal relation between police education and Negro criticism, but it is possible that while college men are more civil, they also have a stronger sense of duty.) It is not clear that departments with large numbers of Negroes patrolling Negro areas have experienced less community tension than departments with few Negroes, or that in any given encounter a Negro officer behaves much differently from a white one. This is not an argument against hiring Negro police officers; on the contrary, there are in my view compelling reasons for having as many as possible patrolling Negro areas. But their value would, in my opinion, be primarily symbolic (no less important for that!) and their presence would not make substantially easier the policy-making or administrative problems of the police. Nor are the consequences of different patrol and community relations policies clear. Some departments (San Francisco, Chicago) have made a major community relations effort, but they seem to fare no better than those (such as Philadelphia or Albany) with a "get tough" policy. Departments which use aggressive preventive patrol and have strict traffic enforcement policies (such as Los Angeles) produce criticism and experience disorders, but so do departments (such as Boston) which are less aggressive or strict. Though there are these differences in police practices,[6] it is not clear how they affect the management of order, the enforcement of laws, or the maintenance of good community relations.

Nature of Police Function

The difficulty in managing the police arises, in my view, less from the quality of men recruited or the level at which authority is exercised and more from the nature of the police function. Mental hospitals provide a useful comparison to the police in this regard. Like the police, they are regarded as essential; like the police, they are routinely and repeatedly condemned for failures and inadequacies. The indictment of such institutions found, for example, in Ivan Belknap's book, has become commonplace.[7] The appalling conditions to be found in hospital wards, the apparent callousness and brutality of the staff, the denial of rights and privileges, the shortage of qualified psychiatric and medical staff, and (equally important) the inability of such professional staff as exists to control the practices of the hospital—all these circumstances have been described, and the accounts are no doubt in large measure correct. Repeated efforts at reform have been made. Budgets have been increased, hospitals have been reorganized, better-qualified personnel have been sought, staff services have been increased, and volumes of research have been published. And yet each decade sees essentially the same lamentable conditions exposed and the same indignation unleashed. With the failure of successive reform efforts, the prescriptions have become more radical. At first the need was thought to be for "better men" and "more money." Then the attack shifted to the professional staff itself—doctors and others were charged with "causing" mental illness, or at least retarding its elimination. The hospital was administration-centered; it should become patient-centered.[8]

In an incisive review of the literature on mental hospitals, Perrow concludes that the reason for the failure of reform has not been bad men or low budgets or improper organization or incompetent management (though all of those things may exist); the central problem is that we do not know how to cure mental illness. The problem is not one of ideology, but of technology. The hospitals are given a task they cannot perform, yet they must try to perform it, for the alternative (doing nothing) seems even worse.[9] The most important recent improvement in mental hospital care was the result of an advance in medical technology—the development of tranquilizer drugs. Changes in organization, leadership, and in the men recruited to hospital tasks have rarely produced significant or lasting results from the patient's point of view. To be sure, some hospitals manage to treat the inmates humanely—these are often small, heavily staffed hospitals with patients who can afford the high costs of such facilities. Bestial practices can be eliminated, but it costs a lot of money and requires large concentrations of scarce talent. But even in these circumstances, the improvement in the mental health of the patient does not seem to be much greater than whatever improvement occurs in less intensive (and less expensive) programs.[10]

The parallel with the police is striking. Abusive practices or indifference to citizen needs can be eliminated, but it typically requires a community that (like the intensive-treatment hospital) is small, expensive, and cooperative. In short, it requires a middle- or upper-middle class suburb. Some advocates of community control over the police argue that it is the close supervision of the police by the suburban community that accounts for the good relations between police and citizens to be found there; if one duplicates those political conditions in the central city—if one, in short, "suburbanizes" the central-city neighborhoods—comparable improvements in police-citizen relations will occur. My research suggests that it is not the decree or kind of control that produces this effect in the suburbs, it is the class composition of the community. In a homogeneous, middle-class suburb there is relatively little public disorder; consequently the police rarely need intervene in situations of high conflict, and thus rarely need become parties to conflict. When the chief law enforcement problem involves crimes of stealth (burglary and larceny) rather than street crimes (assaults, robberies, muggings), the police need not practice aggressive preventive patrol or otherwise keep persons on the streets under close surveillance; accordingly, it is rare for a suburban resident walking the streets at night to feel he is being "harrassed." Finally, a socially homogeneous middle-class area provides the police with relative unambiguous cues as to who should be regarded as a "suspicious person" and thus who should be made the object of police attention. Teenagers hanging around a suburban ice-cream parlor late at night or a Negro in the back alley of an all-white residential community would be viewed suspiciously by the police and citizenry alike. Though this suspicion may be, in the particular case, unjust to the teenagers or the Negro, acting on the basis of it does not bring the police into conflict with the community. (But though an affluent suburb may provide the conditions that reduce the likelihood of police-citizen conflict or of police abuses of their authority, it does not provide the conditions that make the management of such disorder as exists or the prevention of such crimes as occur any easier. In short, high-status communities permit the police to solve their ideological but not their technological problems.)

The policy implications of this argument are clear, though gloomy. Substantial and lasting improvements in police-community relations are not likely until and unless there is a substantial and lasting change in the class composition of the central city population—i.e., until the street-crime rate and the incidence of public disorder in the central cities becomes closer to that in the middle-class suburbs. Only then will it be possible to reduce substantially the police-community tension generated by practices like aggressive preventive patrol and the use of gross indicators such as race and apparent class as clues to criminal potential.

Racial Complication

Race complicates the issue, of course, and renders it more explosive. A black person is more likely to be regarded as lower-class or otherwise suspicious than a white person, and thus a law-abiding and peaceful Negro is more likely to be treated as if he were potentially lawless and disorderly than an equivalent white person. Innocent Negroes so treated will naturally feel a deep sense of injustice. It is sometimes argued that this would not happen if police officers were not prejudiced. No doubt many officers are prejudiced (indeed, one study indicates that the vast majority are) and this prejudice may make matters worse.[11] But the crucial point is that large numbers of innocent Negroes would still be treated in (to them) unjust ways even if all policemen were entirely free of race prejudice so long as a disproportionate number of Negroes are lower-class. Violent crime and disorder are predominantly (though not exclusively) lower-class phenomena;[12] Negroes are disproportionally (though far from exclusively) lower-class; a black skin, therefore, will continue to be a statistically defensible (though individually unjust) cue that triggers an officer's suspicion.

Among the consequences of this generalization will be continued police suspicion of blacks and continued Negro antagonism toward the police. The point is perhaps more easily understood if we examine other cues to which police respond and other forms of prejudice which they may have. Young people commit a disproportionate share of many kinds of crime, especially crimes against property. Being young is therefore a statistically useful cue to an officer who is scanning a population in search of persons more likely than others to commit, or to have committed, a crime. In addition, it is quite possible that the police have "youth prejudice"—that is, they may impute to young people even more criminality than in fact they possess, just as officers having race prejudice impute to Negroes more criminality than in fact they display. But if all officers were cured of "youth prejudice," young people would still be singled out for special attention and suspicion. The difference, of course, is that young people outgrow their youth, while Negroes cannot outgrow their blackness.

The best evidence that race prejudice is not the crucial factor can be found in the behavior of Negro police officers. There has been no systematic study of such men, but my observations suggest that black policemen are as suspicious and tough in black neighborhoods as white officers. Indeed, in the long run Negroes have an advantage over youth. It may be possible to improve the class position of Negroes so that the crime rates found among them will be no higher (and perhaps even lower) than the rates found among whites. Then there will be no reason, other than prejudice, why an officer would treat a Negro differently from a white. By contrast, there is probably no way even in principle to reduce greatly the criminogenic properties of youth and therefore no way even in principle to make the police less suspicious of young people.

If the fundamental problem is one of class (admittedly greatly complicated by the problem of race), what can a police administrator do in the short run while he waits for society somehow to solve the class problem? If the point of view presented here is correct, not a great deal. But since even marginal gains are desirable when conditions are (or are widely thought to be) deplorable, it is worth considering palliatives however slight may be their benefits.

First, the police should recognize clearly that order maintenance is their central function—central both in the demands it makes on time and resources and in the opportunities it affords for making a difference in the lives of the citizens. Hunting criminals both occupies less time (at least for the patrolmen) and provides fewer chances for decisive action. How well disputes are settled may depend crucially on how competent, knowledgeable, and sensitive the police are; how fast the crime rate mounts is much less dependent on the level and nature of police activity. (As will be argued below, other than by reducing the size of the lower class the best way society can affect the crime rate may be through the court and correctional systems rather than through the police.)

Order-Maintenance Function

A police department that places order maintenance uppermost in its priorities will judge patrolmen less by their arrest records and more by their ability to keep the peace on their beat. This will require, in turn, that sergeants and other supervisory personnel concern themselves more with how the patrolmen function in family fights, teenage disturbances, street corner brawls, and civil disorders, and less with how well they take reports at the scene of burglary or how many traffic tickets they issue during a tour of duty. Order maintenance also requires that the police have available a wider range of options for handling disorder than is afforded by the choice between making an arrest and doing nothing. Detoxification centers should be available as an alternative to jail for drunks. Family-service units should be formed which can immediately assist patrolmen handling domestic quarrels. Community-service officers should be available to provide information, answer complaints, and deal with neighborhood tensions and rumors.

Patrolmen who are given the order-maintenance function will obviously require a great deal of information about their beats—more than can be obtained by riding around in a patrol car or rotating frequently among several beats. Obtaining this knowledge will be made easier by the decentralization of the patrol function so that local commanders deal with local conditions subject to general policy guidelines from the police administrator. This decentralization need not always take the form of proliferating precinct station houses—these facilities, as traditionally used for mustering the watch, jailing prisoners, and keeping records, are expensive. Many of them, indeed, were built in a period when patrolmen, like firemen, slept in when they had night duty. Smaller, less elaborate, and more numerous "store-front" police offices scattered throughout central-city neighborhoods might prove more effective and less expensive. Officers assigned to a particular neighborhood ought to remain in that area for long periods of time, rather than experience frequent rotation among neighborhoods. An even more radical experiment might be to assess the value of having patrolmen actually live in certain key areas. For example, some officers might be encouraged, on a volunteer basis, to live in public housing projects. To make such an assignment more attractive and to increase the pay of the officer, he could be given the apartment rent-free or at a substantial discount.

Such decentralization of function requires the strengthening of the command system if it is not to produce inconsistent behavior, political intervention, and corruption. Supervisory officers, especially watch commanders, ought to have more authority to assign, direct, and evaluate their officers. Mechanical, fixed assignments and evaluation solely by written examinations decrease the possibility of inducing patrolmen to take seriously their order-maintenance function and lead them instead to emphasize following the safe routine, memorizing the penal code and departmental rule book, and "pushing paper"—filing reports, writing tickets, and so forth.

At the same time, if patrolmen are expected to devote themselves primarily to the most conflict-laden, unpleasant parts of their task, there must be rewards available that are commensurate with the burdens. At present, the major rewards open to the patrolman—promotion, higher pay, specialized duty—all take him out of the patrol force and place him in supervisory posts, criminal investigation, or headquarters staff units. If the patrol function is the most important and difficult job in the department, the best men ought to be rewarded for doing it well in ways that leave them in the patrol force and on the street. It should be possible to obtain substantial pay increases while remaining a patrolman, just as it is now possible to win higher salaries in the Federal Bureau of Investigation while remaining a special agent.

Getting good men to serve, not only in the police department, but in those police roles that are the most demanding, may produce only a marginal gain, but we are largely ignorant of how to achieve even that. Almost no systematic research has been done to define and measure those qualities characteristic of officers best able to keep the peace. Entrance examination in many states and cities may not measure any relevant quality other than (perhaps) general literacy, familiarity with a police handbook, or some knowledge of current events. Indeed, there is hardly any evidence that they measure even these traits very accurately. How—or indeed, whether—such tests can be more useful is a matter on which we know very little, and perhaps a modest amount of research would be in order (though I would not be surprised if such research turned out to be inconclusive).

Policy Statements

If able men are found and assigned to neighborhood patrol forces under conditions that will facilitate their understanding of neighborhood conditions and personalities and if they are rewarded for successful performance of the peace-keeping function, what in concrete terms will these men actually do? How, in short, does one keep the peace? Some have argued that police departments ought to develop and issue policy statements that will give some guidance to officers who must necessarily exercise wide discretion with respect to matters where legal codes contain few applicable rules.[13] To the extent this is possible, of course it should be done, and it is not being done at all in many departments. But it would be a mistake to assume that policies can be found that will provide meaningful guides to action in most situations of real or potential disorder. The most feasible rules perhaps are those which tell the patrolman what *not* to do—don't use racial epithets, don't hit a man except in self-defense, don't grasp a man's arm or shoulder unless it is necessary to complete an arrest or prevent violence, and so forth. But relatively few rules can be devised that tell a patrolman what he *should* do with quarreling lovers, angry neighbors, or disputatious drunks. This is not because the police have had little experience with such matters (on the contrary!) or even because they do know in a given case what to do (they may), but because so much depends on the particular circumstances of time, place, event, and personality. No psychiatrist would attempt to produce, much less use, a "how-to-do-it" manual for these cases, and he has the advantage of dealing with people at his leisure, over long periods of time, and in moments of relative calm. The best that can be done is to list "factors to be taken into account," but in the concrete case everything depends on *how* they are taken into account.

In the broadest terms, the patrolman in performing his order-maintenance function is neither a bureaucrat nor a professional, and thus neither increased bureaucratization nor increased professionalism will be of much value. He is not a bureaucrat in that he does not and cannot apply general rules to specific cases—there are no general rules, and thus his discretion is wide. (In performing his law-enforcement function, by contrast, he can act more nearly like a bureaucrat—the legal rules defining a crime are relatively unambiguous and the officer's discretion, especially if it is a serious crime, is narrow.) On the other hand, the patrolman is not a professional—there is no organized group of practitioners (as there is with doctors or physicists) who can impart to him by education certain information and equip him by apprenticeship with certain arts and skills that will make him competent to serve a "client" when the latter cannot be the sole judge of the quality of the service he receives. Nor do such external reference groups (professional societies) exist to certify that the patrolman is competent or to make him subject to a code of ethics and a sense of duty.

The patrolman is neither a bureaucrat nor a professional, but a member of a *craft*. As with more crafts, there is no generalized, written body of special knowledge; learning is by apprenticeship, but the apprenticeship takes place on the job rather than in an academy; the primary reference group from which the apprentice wins (or fails to win) respect are his colleagues on the job, not fellow members of his discipline wherever they may be; and the members, conscious of having a special skill or task, think of themselves as set apart from society and in need of restrictions on entry. But unlike other members of a craft—carpenters, for example, or journalists—the police work in an environment that is usually apprehensive and often hostile, and they produce no product (like a finished house or a well-written newspaper) the value of which is evident and easily judged.

An attempt to change a craft into a bureaucracy will be perceived by the members as a failure of confidence and a withdrawal of support and thus strongly resisted; efforts to change them into a profession will be seen as irrelevant and thus in great part ignored. Such gains as can be made in the way the police handle citizens are not likely to come primarily from either proliferating rules (i.e., bureaucratizing the police) or sending officers to colleges, special training programs, or human relations institutes (i.e., "professionalizing" the police). Instead, the most significant changes will be in organization and leadership in order to increase the officer's familiarity with and sensitivity to the neighborhood he patrols and rewarding him for doing what is judged (necessarily after the fact) to be the right thing rather than simply the "efficient" thing.

Law-Enforcement Function

These recommendations leave out of account the law-enforcement function of the police. This has been deliberate, partly because the crook-catching, crime stopping function is so often exaggerated. But obviously there is a law-enforcement function, and it is in any case hard to separate from the order-maintenance function. Law enforcement ideally should be organized differently from order maintenance, however. It is, for example, more suitably managed through centralized command structures, the issuance of explicit rules, and the specialization of tasks (burglary details, homicide details, traffic enforcement divisions, and so forth). Perhaps a police department should make the two functions even more separate than they are now. For example, there is some impressionistic evidence that such tactics worsen police-community relations.[14] Perhaps the roving patrol force should be composed of men different from those in the neighborhood patrol force, so that the tensions created by the former could be directed away from the role performed by the latter. Or perhaps intensive street patrol in a particular area could be done under the guidance of and on the basis of tactical intelligence furnished by neighborhood patrol officers who are best able to distinguish between innocent and suspicious behavior and between decent citizens and "bad actors."

But in crime prevention not too much should be expected of the police. I doubt that any deployment, any strategy, or any organizational principles will permit the police to make more than a slight or temporary reduction in the rate of most common crimes. As the police themselves are fond of saying, "we don't cause crime," and, as I would like to see them add, "we can't stop crime." They can and should make arrests and they can and should investigate suspicious circumstances. But I know of no police administrator who is optimistic that they can make more than marginal gains, however they behave. It would be well, therefore, not to "over-sell" proposed improvements in police manpower, organization, training, equipment, or tactics. Already too many citizens share the rather dangerous view that if only we "unleashed" the police we could "stop crime"—dangerous because if we act on that assumption we are likely to produce only frustrated expectations and deeper passions.

Indeed, it might be well if we shifted the focus of our legitimate concern to the behavior of those institutions that dispose of criminals once arrested—the courts and the correctional and probation systems. For all offenses other than the most trivial, the vast majority of the persons processed by these institutions are repeaters. According to one estimate, 87.5 percent of all persons arrested for nontraffic offenses have been arrested before.[15] The average person arrested will be arrested 7.6 times in his lifetime.[16] The problem of recidivism is obviously of the greatest importance—if we fail to induce a person after his first arrest to avoid crime, there is a strong chance we will have to arrest him six or seven more times; how many more times we *should* arrest him for crimes we do not learn of is anyone's guess. In the simplest cost-effective terms, a dollar invested in the right correctional program is likely to have a higher marginal product than a dollar invested in the right police program.

But what is the "right program"? Do we have a correctional technology capable of significantly reducing the recidivism rate? I am not sure we do, or that we ever will, but I suspect that we have not tried very hard to find out. There have been some promising experiments with community-based, heavily staffed programs in California, Utah, and New Jersey, but there appears to be little organized effort to repeat these experiments elsewhere, or if they are repeated to evaluate them rigorously, or if they are evaluated to institutionalize what we learn from them.[17] In our preoccupation with the crime problem, we have come to identify it either as wholly a "social" problem (which can only be solved in three or four generations by programs which might—no one quite seems to be sure how—eliminate the lower classes) or as a "police" problem which can be solved only by taking the "handcuffs" off the police and "cracking down." I am certainly not opposed to ameliorating social problems or to increasing public support for the police, but I would like to see at least an equivalent amount of attention given to improving the way existing institutions now manage the offenders who have already shown by their actions that antipoverty programs are yet to have a therapeutic effect, and by their appearance in court that they have not managed to escape the police.

Notes

1. This article is in part adapted from material [that appears] in my book-length study of the police, *Varieties of Police Behavior* (Cambridge, Mass.: Harvard University Press, 1968).

2. Philip H. Ennis, *Criminal Victimization in the United States*, a report to the President's Commission on Law Enforcement and Administration of Justice (Washington, D.C.: U.S. Government Printing Office, 1967), p. 13.

3. See Jerome H. Skolnick, *Justice Without Trial* (New York: John Wiley & Sons, 1966), pp. 167-181.

4. A "get-tough" policy by the police in Miami was reported to have led to a drop in street crimes, at least in one area of the city (*New York Times*, February 19, 1968). When off-duty police officers began to work as taxi drivers in New York City, there was a drop in the number of robberies and assaults against cabbies (*New York Times*, February 20, 1968). After the stories appeared, however, it was reported that these street crimes had begun to show an increase, though they had not yet risen to the level they attained before the counter-measures were adopted. We know very little about how great a reduction in crime is the result of criminal perceptions of police intent and how much the result of the direct consequences of police actions, nor have we tried (except in a very few cases) to measure the persistence of such improvement as does occur.

5. Various proposals for changing police practices are reported in the President's Commission on Law Enforcement and Administration of Justice *Task Force Report: The Police* (Washington, D.C.: U.S. Government Printing Office, 1967), p. xi, and the National Advisory Commission on Civil Disorders Report (Washington, D.C.: U.S. Government Printing Office, 1968), chap. 11.

6. Differences in patrol styles or strategies are described and to some degree explained in Wilson, *op. cit.*, chaps. 4-7.

7. Ivan Belknap, *Human Problems of a State Mental Hospital* (New York: McGraw-Hill, 1956). It is striking to note the similarities between Belknap's description of mental hospital attendants and my description of patrolmen in large cities—see especially Belknap, pp. 115, 116, 138, 152, 154, and 170.

8. See the excellent analysis in Charles Perrow's, "Hospitals: Technology, Structure, and Goals,"

in James G. March's, ed., *Handbook of Organizations* (Chicago: Rand McNally, 1965), pp. 916-946, and the accounts of certain "elite" hospitals practicing "milieu therapy" in W. Caudill's *The Psychiatric Hospital as a Small Society* (Cambridge, Mass.: Harvard University Press, 1958), R. N. Rapoport et al., *Community as Doctor* (London: Tavistock, 1960), and A. H. Stanton and M. S. Schwartz's *The Mental Hospital* (New York: Basic Books, 1954).

9. See Perrow, *op. cit.*, pp. 925, 926, 930, 934.

10. Rapoport et al., *op. cit.*, p. 208.

11. Donald J. Black and Albert J. Reiss, Jr., "Patterns in Police and Citizen Transactions," in *Studies of Crime and Law Enforcement in Major Metropolitan Areas*, a report to the President's Commission on Law Enforcement and Administration of Justice (Washington, D.C.: U.S. Government Printing Office, 1967), Vol. II, Section I, pp. 132-139. Observers working under the direction of Black and Reiss in Boston, Chicago, and Washington, D.C., reported that 72 percent of all white officers and 28 percent of all Negro officers volunteered "highly prejudiced" or "prejudiced" comments about Negroes. There was, however, no clear relationship between attitude and behavior: "A recurring theme in the observer's reports was the great disparity between the verbalized attitudes of officers in the privacy of the patrol car, and the public conduct of officers in encounters with Negroes and members of other minority groups" (p. 138). After observing police behavior, Black and Reiss conclude that "Policemen generally do not disproportionately behave aggressively or negatively toward Negroes," though they do "disproportionately behave amiably or positively toward white citizens" (p. 56).

12. A good summary of the evidence on the disproportionately lower-class origin of assaultive crime is Marvin E. Wolfgang's *Crimes of Violence*, a report to the President's Commission on Law Enforcement and Administration of Justice (1967), pp. 166-169. Additional evidence based on direct observation can be found in Walter B. Miller's "Violent Crimes in City Gangs," *Annals*, 364 (March 1966), 96-112, and "Theft Behavior in City Gangs," in Malcolm W. Klein's *Juvenile Gangs in Context* (Englewood Cliffs, N.J.: Prentice-Hall, 1967), p. 34.

13. See President's Commission on Law Enforcement and Administration of Justice, *Task Force Report: The Police* (Washington, D.C.: U.S. Government Printing Office, 1967), pp. 21-27.

14. Report of the National Advisory Commission on Civil Disorders (1968), chap. 11.

15. Ronald Christensen, "Projected Percentage of U.S. Population With Criminal Arrest and Conviction Records," in President's Commission on Law Enforcement and Administration of Justice, *Task Force Report*: Science and Technology (Washington, D.C.: U.S. Government Printing Office, 1967), Appendix J, p. 220.

16. Ibid., p. 227.

17. President's Commission on Law Enforcement and Administration of Justice, *Task Force Report: Corrections* (Washington, D.C.: U.S. Government Printing Office, 1967), chap. 4, especially pp. 38-39, 41-42.

2

The Functions of Police in Modern Society

Egon Bittner

In this classic piece, Egon Bittner discusses the origins of modern policing, identifies the source of some of policing's recurring crises (such as brutality, corruption, and discrimination), and presents what he sees as the core functions of policing—what distinguishes police business from other public and private activities. More than anything else, he argues, what separates the police from other institutions is their capacity and license to use force, including deadly force. In a way, this is just common sense and falls in that category of things that "everybody knows"—after all, who does not realize that the police have guns, sticks, handcuffs, and fast cars and the authority to use them against us? But the police perform other "public service" duties as well, leading many commentators to emphasize the similarities between police work and social work. Bittner warns us against this and similar analogies and urges us to keep the core function of policing squarely in mind. You should be warned, though, that he does so in a very rigorous and challenging style which you may find difficult—read this chapter slowly and carefully to get the full benefit.

Popular Conceptions About the Character of Police Work

The abandonment of the norm-derivative approach to the definition of the role of the police in modern society immediately directs attention to a level of social reality that is unrelated to the ideal formulations. Whereas in terms of these formulations police activity derives its meaning from the objectives of upholding the law, we find that in reality certain meaning features are associated with police work that are largely independent of the objectives. That is, police work is generally viewed as having certain character traits we take for granted, and which control dealings between policemen and citizens, on both sides. Though we are lacking in adequate evidence about these matters, the perceived traits we will presently discuss are universally accepted as present and the recognition of their presence constitutes a realistic constraint on what is expected of the police and how policemen actually conduct themselves. It is important to emphasize that even while some of these ideas and attitudes are uncritically inherited from the past they are far from being totally devoid of realism. In the police literature these matters are typically treated under either euphemistic or cynical glosses. The reason for this evasion is simple, the Sunday school vocabulary we are forced to employ while talking about any occupational pursuit as dignified, serious, and necessary forces us from dealing realistically with the facts and from being candid about opinion.

Among the traits of character that are commonly perceived as associated with police work, and which thus constitute in part the social reality within which the work has to be done, the following three are of cardinal importance.

1. Police work is a tainted occupation. The origins of the stigma are buried in the distant past and while much has been said and done to erase it, these efforts have been totally unsuccessful. Medieval watchmen, recruited from among the ranks of destitute and subject to satirical portrayals, were perceived to belong to the world of shadows they were supposed to contain.[1] During the period of the absolute monarchy the police came to represent the underground aspects of tyranny and political repression, and they were despised and feared even by those who ostensibly benefitted from their services. No one can say how much of the old attitude lives on; some of it probably seeps into modern consciousness from the continued reading of nineteenth century romantic literature of the Victor Hugo variety. And it cannot be neglected that the mythology of the democratic polity avidly recounts the heroic combat against the police agents of the old order. But even if the police officer of today did not evoke the images of the past at all, he would still be viewed with mixed feelings, to say the least. For in modern folklore, too, he is a character who is ambivalently feared and admired, and no amount of public relations work can entirely abolish the sense that there is something of the dragon in the dragon-slayer.[2] Because they are posted on the perimeters of order and justice in the hope that their presence will deter the forces of darkness and chaos, because they are meant to spare the rest of the people direct confrontations with the dreadful, perverse, lurid, and dangerous, police officers are perceived to have powers and secrets no one else shares. Their interest in and competence to deal with the untoward surrounds their activities with mystery and distrust. One needs only to consider the thoughts that come to mind at the sight of policemen moving into action: here they go to do something the rest of us have no stomach for! And most people naturally experience a slight tinge of panic when approached by a policeman, a feeling against which the awareness of innocence provides no adequate protection. Indeed, the innocent in particular typically do not know what to expect and thus have added, even when unjustified, reasons for fear. On a more mundane level, the mixture of fear and fascination that the police elicit is often enriched by the addition of contempt. Depending on one's position in society, the contempt may draw on a variety of sources. To some the leading reason for disparaging police work derives from the suspicion that those who do battle against evil cannot themselves live up fully to the ideals they presumably defend. Others make the most of the circumstance that police work is a low-paying occupation, the requirements for which can be met by men who are poorly educated. And some, finally, generalize from accounts of police abuses that come to their attention to the occupation as a whole.

It is important to note that the police do very little to discourage unfavorable public attitudes. In point of fact, their sense of being out of favor with a large segment of the society has led them to adopt a petulant stance and turned them to courting the kinds of support which, ironically, are nothing but a blatant insult. For the movement that is known by the slogan, "Support your local police," advocates the unleashing of a force of mindless bullies to do society's dirty work. Indeed, if there is still some doubt about the popular perception of police work as a tainted occupation, it will surely be laid to rest by pointing to those who, under the pretense of taking the side of the police, imply that the institution and its personnel are uniformly capable and willing to act out the baser instincts inherent in all of us.

In sum, the taint that attaches to police work refers to the fact that policemen are viewed as the fire it takes to fight fire, that they in the natural course of their duties inflict harm, albeit deserved, and that their very existence attests that the nobler aspirations of mankind do not contain the means necessary to insure survival. But even as those necessities are accepted, those who accept them seem to prefer to have no part in acting upon them, and they enjoy the more than slightly perverse pleasure of looking down on the police who take the responsibility of doing the job.

2. Police work is not merely a tainted occupation. To draw a deliberately remote analogy, the practice of medicine also has its dirty and mysterious aspects. And characteristically, dealings with physicians also elicit a sense of trepidated fascination. But in the case of medicine, the repulsive aspects, relating to the disease, pain, and death, are more than compensated by other features, none of which are present in police work. Of the compensatory features, one is of particular relevance to our concerns. No conceivable human interest could be opposed to fighting illness; in fact, it is meaningless to suppose that one could have scruples in opposing disease. But the evils the police are expected to fight are of a radically different nature. Contrary to the physician, the policeman is always opposed to some articulated or articulable human interest. To be sure, the police are, at least in principle, opposed to only reprehensible interests or interest lacking in proper

justification. But even if one were to suppose that they never err in judging legitimacy—a farfetched supposition, indeed—it would still remain the case that police work can, with a very few exceptions, accomplish something *for* somebody only by proceeding *against* someone else. It does not take great subtlety of perception to realize that standing between man and man locked in conflict inevitably involves profound moral ambiguities. Admittedly, few of us are constantly mindful of the saying, "He that is without sin among you, let him cast the first stone . . . ," but only the police are explicitly required to forget it. The terms of their mandate and the circumstances of their practices do not afford them the leisure to reflect about the deeper aspects of conflicting moral claims. Not only are they required to proceed forcefully against all appearances of transgression but they are also expected to penetrate the appearance of innocence to discover craftiness hiding under its cloak. While most of us risk only the opprobrium of foolishness by being charitable or gullible, the policeman hazards violating his duty by letting generosity or respect for appearances govern his decisions.

Though it is probably true that persons who are characterologically inclined to see moral and legal problems in black and white tend to choose police work as a vocation more often than others, it is important to emphasize that the need to disregard complexity is structurally built into the occupation. Only after a suspect is arrested, or after an untoward course of events is stopped, is there time to reflect on the merits of the decision, and, typically, that reflective judgment is assigned to other public officials. Though it is expected that policemen will be judicious and skill will guide them in the performance of their work, it is foolish to expect that they could always be both swift and subtle. Nor is it reasonable to demand that they prevail, where they are supposed to prevail, while hoping that they will always handle resistance gently. Since the requirement of quick and what is often euphemistically called aggressive action is difficult to reconcile with error-free performance, police work, by its very nature, is doomed to be often unjust and offensive to someone. Under the dual pressure to "be right" and to "do something," policemen are often in a position that is compromised even before they act.[3]

In sum, the fact that policemen are required to deal with matters involving subtle human conflicts and profound legal and moral questions, without being allowed to give the subtleties and profundities anywhere near the consideration they deserve, invests their activities with the character of crudeness. Accordingly, the constant reminder that officers should be wise, considerate, and just, without providing them with opportunities to exercise these virtues is little more than vacuous sermonizing.

3. The ecological distribution of police work at the level of departmentally determined concentrations of deployment, as well as in terms of the orientations of individual police officers, reflects a whole range of public prejudices. That is, the police are more likely to be found in places where certain people live or congregate than in other parts of the city. Though this pattern of manpower allocation is ordinarily justified by references to experientially established needs for police service, it inevitably entails the consequence that some persons will receive the dubious benefit of extensive police scrutiny merely on account of their membership in those social groupings which individual social comparisons locate at the bottom of the heap.[4] Accordingly, it is not a paranoid distortion to say that police activity is as much directed to who a person is as to what he does.

As is well known, the preferred targets of special police concern are some ethnic and racial minorities, the poor living in urban slums, and young people in general.[5] On the face of it, this kind of focusing appears to be, if not wholly unobjectionable, not without warrant. Insofar as the above-mentioned segments of society contribute disproportionately to the sum total of crime, and are more likely than others to engage in objectionable conduct, they would seem to require a higher degree of surveillance. In fact, this kind of reasoning was basic to the very creation of the police; for it was not assumed initially that the police would enforce laws in the broad sense, but that they would concentrate on the control of individual and collective tendencies towards transgression and disorder issuing from what were referred to as the "dangerous classes."[6] What was once a frankly admitted bias is, however, generally disavowed in our times. That is, in and of itself, the fact that someone is young, poor, and dark-complexioned is not supposed to mean anything whatsoever to a police officer. Statistically considered, he might be said to be more likely to run afoul of the law, but individually, all things being equal, his chances of being left alone *are supposed* to be the same as those of someone who is middle-aged, well-to-do, and fair-skinned. In fact, however, exactly the opposite is the case. All things being equal, the young-poor-black and the old-rich-white doing the very same things under the very same circumstances will almost certainly not receive the same kind of treatment from policemen. In fact, it is almost inconceivable that the two characters could ever appear or do something in ways that would mean the same thing to a policeman.[7] Nor is the policeman merely expressing personal or institutional prejudice by according the two characters differential treatment. Public expectations insidiously instruct him to reckon with these "factors." These facts are too well known to require detailed exposition, but their reasons and consequences deserve brief consideration.

In the first place, the police are not alone in making invidious distinctions between the two types.[8] Indeed the differential treatment they accord them reflects only the distribution of esteem, credit, and desserts in society at large. Second, because of their own social origins, many policemen tend to express social prejudices more emphatically than other members of society.[9] Third, policemen are not merely like everybody else, only more so; they also have special reasons for it. Because the preponderant majority of police interventions are based on mere suspicion or on merely tentative indications of risk, policemen would have to be expected to judge matters prejudicially even if they personally were entirely free of prejudice. Under present circumstances, even the most completely impartial policeman who merely takes account of probabilities, as these probabilities are known to him, will feel reasonably justified in being more suspicious of the young-poor-black than of the old-rich-white, and once his suspicions are aroused, in acting swiftly and forcefully against the former while treating the latter with reserve and deference. For as the policeman calculates risk, the greater hazard is located on the side of inaction in one case, and on the side of unwarranted action in the other.

That policemen deal differently with types of people who are thought always to be "up to something" than with people who are thought to have occasional lapses but can otherwise be relied upon to conduct their affairs legally and honorably, does not come as a surprise, especially if one considers the multiple social pressures that instruct the police not to let the unworthy get away with anything and to treat the rest of the community with consideration. But because this is the case, police work tends to have divisive effects in society. While their existence and work do not create cleavages, they do magnify them in effect.

The police view of this matter is clear and simple—too simple, perhaps. Their business is to control crime and keep the peace. If there is some connection between social and economic inequality, on the one hand, and criminality and unruliness, on the other hand, this is not their concern. The problem is not, however, whether the police have any responsibilities with regard to social injustice. The problem is that by distributing surveillance and intervention selectively they contribute to already existing tensions in society. That the police are widely assumed to be a partisan force in society is evident not only in the attitudes of people who are exposed to greater scrutiny; just as the young-poor-black expects unfavorable treatment, so the old-rich-white expects special consideration from the policeman. And when two such persons are in conflict, nothing will provoke the indignation of the "decent" citizen more quickly than giving his word the same credence as the word of some "ne'er-do-well."[10]

The three character traits of police work discussed in the foregoing remarks—namely, that it is a tainted occupation, that it recalls for peremptory solutions for complex human problems, and that it has, in virtue of its ecological distribution, a socially divisive effect—are structural determinants. By this is meant mainly that the complex of reasons and facts they encompass are not easily amenable to change. Thus, for example, though the stigma that attaches to police work is often viewed as merely reflecting the frequently low grade and bungling personnel that is currently available to the institution, there are good reasons to expect that it would continue to plage a far better prepared and a far better performing staff. For the stigma attaches not merely to the ways policemen discharge their duties, but also to what they have to deal with. Similarly, while it is probably true that moral naivete is a character trait of persons who presently choose police work as their vocation, it is unlikely that persons of greater subtlety of perception would find it easy to exercise their sensitivity under present conditions. Finally, even though discriminatory policing is to some extent traceable to personal bigotry, it also follows the directions of public pressure, which, in turn, is not wholly devoid of factual warrant.

The discussion of the structural character traits of police work was introduced by saying that they were independent of the role definitions formulated from the perspective of the norm-derivative approach. The latter interprets the meaning and adequacy of police procedure in terms of a set of simply stipulated ideal objectives. Naturally these objectives are considered desirable; more importantly, however, the values that determine the desirability of the objectives are also used in interpreting and judging the adequacy of procedures employed to realize them. Contrary to this way of making sense of police work, the consideration of the structural character traits was meant to draw attention to the fact that there attaches a sense to police work that is not inferentially derived from ideals but is rooted in what is commonly known about it. What is known about the police is, however, not merely a matter of more or less correct information. Instead the common lore consists of a set of presuppositions about the way things are and have to be. Thus, for instance, whatever people assume to be generally true of the police will be the thing that a particular act or event will be the

thing that a particular act or even will be taken to exemplify. If it is believed that police work is crude, then within a very considerable range of relative degrees of subtlety, whatever policemen will be seen doing will be seen as crudeness.

In addition to the fact that the normative approach represents an exercise in formal, legal inference, while the structural character traits reflect an approach of informal, commonsense practicality, the two differ in yet another and perhaps more important aspect. The normative approach does not admit the possibility that the police may, in fact, not be oriented to those objectives. Contrary to this, the sense of police activity that comes to the fore from the consideration of the character traits assigned to it by popular opinion and attitude leaves the question open.[11]

Since we cannot rely on abstract formulations that implicitly rule out the possibility that they might be entirely wrong, or far too narrow, and since we cannot depend on a fabric of commonsense characterizations, we must turn to still other sources. Of course, we can no more forget the importance of the popularly perceived character traits than we can forget the formulas of the official mandate. To advance further in our quest for a realistic definition of the police role, we must now turn to the review of certain historical materials that will show how the police moved into the position in which they find themselves today. On the basis of this review, in addition to what was proposed thus far, we will be able to formulate an explicit definition of the role of the institution and its officials.

The Cultural Background of the Police Idea

The police, as we know it today, is a creature of English society in the second quarter of the nineteenth century.[12] The location of origin reflects the fact that England was, at that time, further advanced along the path of development as an urban-industrial society than other states. In due course, the model was adopted everywhere else, albeit with modifications required by different traditions and different forms of political organization. In the United States the first modern police department was created by the State of New York for the city of New York, in accordance with recommendations made by a committee that was earlier sent to London to study the English model. Other American cities quickly acquired similar departments. Even though older forms of policing continue to exist, notably the office of the sheriff, and some new forms were added more recently, e.g., the Federal Bureau of Investigation, the municipal police department has been by far the most important way of doing police work in the United States since the turn of the century.

The most remarkable fact about the timing of the foundation of the modern police is that it is sequentially the last of the basic building blocks in the structure of modern executive government.[13] Military conscription, tax collection, economic and fiscal planning, social service, and a host of other administrative organs antedate the police by several generations. Even public education existed in a limited form in Prussia and in France long before Sir Robert Peel marshaled through Parliament the Bill establishing the Metropolitan Police of London. This seems strange because the absolute monarchies of the seventeenth and eighteenth century had ample reasons for creating the kind of institution that would furnish them with means for the continuous and detailed surveillance of citizens. Yet they did not develop such means, but relied on inherited methods of crime control and met such peacekeeping problems as they confronted by contingently mobilized means. The postponement of the creation of the police calls for an explanation and directs attention to the particular circumstances that surrounded it.[14]

In the years following the Peace of Vienna (1815), English society experienced what seemed to have been an alarming escalation of rates of criminality in her cities. Especially in the 1820's, the people of London were startled by a series of extremely brutal crimes of violence.[15] Though the country had a history of crime waves dating back to the beginning of the eighteenth century,[16] and resorted to a variety of means to control them, the idea of having a police force that would function as an arm of executive government was always strongly resisted. The main rea-son for the resistance was the fear that the existence of such a force would tip the balance of power in favor of the executive branch of government, leading ultimately to a suppression of civil liberties. Though these fears were never wholly allayed, the advocates of the police gained the upper hand in the debate when it became clear that the inherited methods were utterly incapable of handling the seemingly exploding crime problem. Furthermore, the aftermath of the Napoleonic wars brought forth a sequence of disastrous urban riots that had to be subdued by military force at great expense of life and property. This method of peacekeeping came to be viewed as inefficient as the old forms of crime control since the use of armed repression did not seem to have any noticeable deterrent effects, despite its unrestrained brutality. Reasoning along lines of efficiency was, of course, quite persuasive to a people that deliberately cultivated a spirit of hardheaded business rationality, and it would be easy to say that the police were finally accepted, despite many objections in principle, on grounds of considerations of sheer expediency. But there were other motives at work, too. The inherited methods of crime control and peace-keeping did not only fail in attaining the desired objectives, they were also perceived as incompatible with the ethos of a civil society. The corrupt and brutal thief-catcher extorting a pound of flesh from the wretch he accused of crimes and the yeomanry massacring mobs of hungry protesters in front of St. Peter's Cathedral harked back to a dark and despised past, and offended the sensibilities of a people who were at the threshold of a period of their national history they defined as the acme of civilization.

The sentiment that could not abide the more archaic forms of repressive control of deviance and disorder was an expression of cultural and ideological change initiated in the nineteenth century. It is best described as the rise of the sustained, and thus far not abandoned, aspiration of Western society to abolish violence and install peace as a stable and permanent condition of everyday life.[17] To be sure, the history of this aspiration is by and large a history of its failures and those who count only results may judge the avowals of nonviolence as a massive display of hypocrisy. No generation would be more justified in passing this judgment than ours, for the violence we have experienced is overwhelming by the standards of any age. Yet, there can be no doubt that during the past one-hundred-fifty years the awareness of the moral and practical necessity of peace took hold of the minds of virtually all people. The advocacy of warfare and violence did not disappear entirely, but it grew progressively less frank and it keeps losing ground to arguments that condemn it.

The yearning for peace is, of course, not a nineteenth century invention. But it happened only after the end of the Napoleonic wars that attempts were made to develop practical measures to bring its attainment within the orbit of practical possibility. More importantly perhaps, during the nineteenth century the structure of everyday life changed, especially in the cities, in ways indicating that people relied on the efficacy of the means that were available to secure freedom from violence, despite the fact that this reliance was demonstrably hazardous. Though these developments reflect the growth of humane sentiments, they derive more basically from a shift of values in which the virtues associated with material progress and assiduous enterprise gained ascendancy over the virtues of masculine prowess and combative chivalry.

Because the quest for peace has remained such a dubious enterprise, some of the efforts it inspired must be reviewed briefly. As will be shown, proper appreciation of these efforts furnishes the indispensable background for the understanding of the role of the police in modern society.[18]

At the international level, Europe enjoyed between 1815 and 1914 a period of historically unprecedented tranquility. The system of diplomatic consultations that controlled this state of affairs did not eliminate all belligerence and it failed completely in 1914, as did its successor, the League of Nations, in 1939. Remarkably, however, the lesson nations learned from these reversals did not lead to the abandonment of efforts, but, quite the contrary, to endeavors to form an even more binding commitment to worldwide peacekeeping through the United Nations Organization and through a variety of other regional treaty organizations.

At the level of internal governing, two developments are of particular importance. First, compliance with the demands of political authority became, after the beginning of the nineteenth century, less and less dependent on the direct presence of officials and on threats or the exercise of physical coercion, and more and more on voluntary performances of the governed. Indeed, it is the salient characteristic of modern authority implementation that it interposes distance between those who command and those who obey. It clearly makes a great difference, for example, whether taxes are collected by armed retainers or by means of written communications of demands. And it makes an equally great difference whether the recruitment of conscripts for military service is accomplished through the presence of armed might in villages or by means of mailed notices ordering eligible persons to report to induction centers. The threat of coercion is certainly not absent in modern forms of governing but its elaborate symbolization makes it more remote. The extent to which we have become accustomed to, and take for granted, the indirect ways of authority implementation and peaceful governing is perhaps best illustrated by the fact that the notorious "knock on the door," associated with totalitarian regimes, is generally viewed as the supreme political abomination.[19]

The second, even clearer indication of progressive avoidance of force in governing is evident in changes in the administration of justice. Up to the nineteenth century it was commonly taken for granted that the criminal process, from accusation, through inquiry and trial, to punishment, must properly involve the systematic mortification of defendants. Punishment for crimes meant death, mutilation, or physical pain. It is sufficient to point to the most obvious changes. The ordeal of inquisition has been entirely abandoned and its psychological forms are condemned. The atmosphere of the modern courtroom, with its emphasis on rationally argued proof and rebuttal—or even in its *sub rosa* dependence on plea bargaining—is profoundly inimical to the traffic of force between accused and accuser. Finally, modern punishment, with its emphasis on rehabilitation, partakes of the nature of an argument against evil. People are sent to prisons to persuade them to mend their ways, more than to suffer deprivation, at least in terms of the prevailing penal philosophy.[20] In fact, it would seem that the criminal process of today, at least in terms of its official script, seeks to dramatize the possibility of life without violence even under conditions where the imposition of coercive sanctions is the business at hand. Again, as in the case of international affairs, it is all too easy to show that reality often belies intentions, but surely it does make a difference whether some methods are used because they are viewed as just and proper or by way of subterfuge.

Parallel to the admittedly insufficient efforts to conduct the affairs of governing in a pacific manner are changes in the manner of conducting private affairs. After ages of unquestioned presence, weapons ceased to be a part of expected male attire in the nineteenth century. Though we are certainly not a disarmed people, especially in the United States, we do not ordinarily consider swords, daggers, and guns as necessary accoutrements in our dealings with others and we require special reasons for carrying them around. The relatively late survival of armed life in the American West is conspicuous by contrast, not only with conditions in Europe, but also in the densely populated urban areas of the eastern part of the United States. Aside from such occasional relics of the past, the use of physical force has all but vanished as an acceptable means for defending one's honor, and certainly as an effective way of advancing interest or gaining honor. Indeed, the vestigial survival of regular patterns of interpersonal violence are perceived either as indications of personal immaturity or as features of "lower-class culture."[21] As if we were not fully satisfied with banishing the private use of force from the pale of respectability, our canons of good taste, which also originate in the nineteenth century, require us not only to avoid belligerence but "bodiliness" in general. That is, we tend to suppress, conceal, or deny matters which, through their visceralness, are related to violence. This is under-

standable when one considers that candor about sex, pain, and death is typically associated with styles of life in which violence is a normal part of daily existence; they are found joined in some pre-literature cultures, in our medieval past, and in "lower-class culture." Even more remarkably, the recent history of medicine reveals some of these trends. Such violent remedies as bloodletting, purging, and cauterization started disappearing from *materia medica* before the full justification for their abandonment was available, and our efforts to devise anaesthetic procedures, that is procedures that would neutralize unavoidably inflicted pain, have reached a level of complexity requiring an entire medical specialty for its proper administration.

Clearly the foregoing discussion of the pacific tendencies contained in the past century and a half contains one-sided exaggerations. We have repeatedly indicated that it would be naive to view it as an epoch of peace. Indeed, there is some question whether the several generations wanted peace above all. The times were, after all, a period of revolution of both nationalist and social nature.[22] But it was not our intention to render a balanced picture of the recent past, but merely to highlight one aspect of it. Our main point is that the trend towards the achievement of peace is basically new in Western history, even as we admit it is continuously in danger of being overwhelmed by counter-tendencies.

One last comment is necessary before concluding the discussion of the importance of the ideal of peace and nonviolence in modern civilization. It is often said that our morality is based on precepts epitomized in the teachings of the Prince of Peace and on the humane wisdom of Socratic philosophy. Whatever the influence of these inspirations might have been, it appears that our quest for peace, such as it was and is, draws mainly on other sources. In the two thousand years since their announcement, neither religious faith nor humanistic concern led to even perfunctory efforts of practical implementation. The aspiration to peace that has finally led to some realistic steps towards its attainment derives from the lack-luster ethic of utilitarianism. According to its maxims we are directed to sacrifice the lesser and momentary interests of personal gratification for the benefit of the greater common good. The common good, however, is not advocated as an abstract ideal because within it is located the greater advantage of every individual. Accordingly, our desire to abolish violence is fundamentally based not on the belief that it is spiritually reprehensible, but on the realization that it is foolish. Forceful attack and the defense it provokes have an unfavorable input/output ratio; they are a waste of energy. A simple, hardheaded, business-like calculus of preference dictates that coercive force, especially of a physical nature, is at best an occasionally unavoidable evil. Jeremy Bentham, the leading prophet of this outlook, taught that even legal punishment was, in and of itself, mischievous and defensible solely in such minimal forms and measures as was necessary to contain those few who could not or would not see that their advantage too was on the side of cooperation rather than conflict.[23]

Though it is always hazardous to formulate estimates of historical necessity, it would seem to be exceedingly unlikely that the idea of the modern police could have arisen in any other cultural context except that described above. In any case, though some forms of policing existed in many different societies and many different time periods, none of these forms resembled our institution even remotely.

The Capacity to Use Force as the Core of the Police Role

We have argued earlier that the quest for peace by peaceful means is one of the culture traits of modern civilization. This aspiration is historically unique. For example, the Roman Empire was also committed to the objectives of reducing or eliminating warfare during one period of its existence, but the method chosen to achieve the *Pax Romana* was, in the language of the poet, *debellare superbos*, i.e., to subdue the haughty by force. Contrary to this, our commitment to abolish the traffic of violence requires us to pursue the ideal by pacific means. In support of this contention we pointed to the development of an elaborate system of international diplomacy whose main objective it is to avoid war,

and to those changes in internal government that resulted in the virtual elimination of all forms of violence, especially in the administration of justice. That is, the overall tendency is not merely to withdraw the basis of legitimacy for all forms of provocative violence, but even from the exercise of provoked force require to meet illegitimate attacks. Naturally this is not possible to a full extent. At least, it has not been possible thus far. Since it is impossible to deprive responsive force entirely of legitimacy, its vestiges require special forms of authorization. Our society recognizes as legitimate three very different forms of responsive force.

First, we are authorized to use force for the purpose of self-defense. Though the laws governing self-defense are far from clear, it appears that an attacked person can counterattack only after he has exhausted all other means of avoiding harm, including retreat, and that the counterattack may not exceed what is necessary to disable the assailant from carrying out his intent. These restrictions are actually enforceable because harm done in the course of self-defense does furnish grounds for criminal and tort proceedings. It becomes necessary, therefore, to show compliance with these restrictions to rebut the charges of excessive and unjustified force even in self-defense.[24]

The second form of authorization entrusts the power to proceed coercively to some specifically deputized persons against some specifically named persons. Among the agents who have such highly specific powers are mental hospital attendants and prison guards. Characteristically, such persons use force in carrying out court orders; but they may use force only against named persons who are remanded to their custody and only to the extent required to implement a judicial order of confinement. Of course, like everybody else, they may also act within the provisions governing self-defense. By insisting on the high degree of limited specificity of the powers of custodial staffs, we do not mean to deny that these restrictions are often violated with impunity. The likelihood of such transgressions is enhanced by the secluded character of prisons and mental institutions, but their existence does not impair the validity of our definition.

The third way to legitimize the use of responsive force is to institute a police force. Contrary to the cases of self-defense and the limited authorization of custodial functionaries, the police authorization is essentially unrestricted. Because the expression "essentially" is often used to hedge a point, we will make fully explicit what we mean by it. There exist three formal limitations of the freedom of policemen to use force, which we must admit even though they have virtually no practical consequences. First, the police use of deadly force is limited in most jurisdictions. Though the powers of a policeman in this respect exceed those of citizens, they are limited nevertheless. For example, in some jurisdictions policemen are empowered to shoot to kill fleeing felony suspects, but not fleeing misdemeanor suspects. It is scarcely necessary to argue that, given the uncertainties involved in defining a delict under conditions of hot pursuit, this could hardly be expected to be an effective limitation.[25] Second, policemen may use force only in the performance of their duties and not to advance their own personal interest or the private interests of other persons. Though this is rather obvious, we mention it for the sake of completeness. Third, and this point too is brought up to meet possible objections, policemen may not use force maliciously or frivolously. These three restrictions, and nothing else, were meant by the use of the qualifier "essentially". Aside from these restrictions there exist no guidelines, no specifiable range of objectives, no limitations of any kind that instruct the policeman what he may or must do. Nor do there exist any criteria that would allow the judgment whether some forceful intervention was necessary, desirable, or proper. And finally, it is exceedingly rare that police actions involving the use of force are actually reviewed and judged by anyone at all.

In sum, the frequently heard talk about the lawful use of force by the police is practically meaningless and, because no one knows what is meant by it, so is the talk about the use of minimum force. Whatever vestigal significance attaches to the term "lawful" use of force is confined to the obvious and unneces-

sary rule that police officers may not commit crimes of violence. Otherwise, however, the expectation that they may and will use force is left entirely undefined. In fact, the only instructions any policeman ever receives in this respect consist of sermonizing that he should be humane and circumspect, and that he must not desist from what he has undertaken merely because its accomplishment may call for coercive means. We might add, at this point, that the entire debate about the troublesome problem of police brutality will not move beyond its present impasse, and the desire to eliminate it will remain an impotent conceit, until this point is fully grasped and unequivocally admitted. In fact, our expectation that policemen will use force, coupled by our refusals to state clearly what we mean by it (aside from sanctimonious homilies), smacks of more than a bit of perversity.

Of course, neither the police nor the public is entirely in the dark about the justifiable use of force by the officers. We had occasion to allude to the assumption that policemen may use force in making arrests. But the benefit deriving from this apparent core of relative clarity is outweighed by its potentially misleading implications. For the authorization of the police to use force is in no important sense related to their duty to apprehend criminals. Were this the case then it could be adequately considered as merely a special case of the same authorization that is entrusted to custodial personnel. It might perhaps be considered a bit more complicated, but essentially of the same nature. But the police authority to use force is radically different from that of a prison guard. Whereas the powers of the latter are incidental to his obligation to implement a legal command, the police role is far better understood by saying that their ability to arrest offenders is incidental to their authority to use force.

Many puzzling aspects of police work fall into place when one ceases to look at it as principally concerned with law enforcement and crime control, and only incidentally and often incongruously concerned with an infinite variety of other matters. It makes much more sense to say that the police are nothing else than a mechanism for the distribution of situationally justified force in society. The latter conception is preferable to the former on three grounds. First, it accords better with the actual expectations and demands made of the police (even though it probably conflicts with what most people would say, or expect to hear, in answer to the question about the proper police function); second, it gives a better accounting of the actual allocation of police manpower and other resources; and, third, it lends unity to all kinds of police activity. These three justifications will be discussed in some detail in the following.

The American city dweller's repertoire of methods for handling problems includes one known as "calling the cops." The practice to which the idiom refers is enormously widespread. Though it is more frequent in some segments of society than in others, there are very few people who do not or would not resort to it under suitable circumstances. A few illustrations will furnish the background for an explanation of what "calling the cops" means.[26]

Two patrolmen were directed to report to an address located in a fashionable district of a large city. On the scene they were greeted by the lady of the house who complained that the maid had been stealing and receiving male visitors in her quarters. She wanted the maid's belongings searched and the man removed. The patrolmen refused the first request, promising to forward the complaint to the bureau of detectives, but agreed to see what they could do about the man. After gaining entrance to the maid's room they compelled a male visitor to leave, drove him several blocks away from the house, and released him with the warning never to return.

In a tenement, patrolmen were met by a public health nurse who took them through an abysmally deteriorated apartment inhabited by four young children in the care of an elderly woman. The babysitter resisted the nurse's earlier attempts to remove the children. The patrolmen packed the children in the squad car and took them to Juvenile Hall, over the continuing protests of the elderly woman.

While cruising through the streets a team of detectives recognized a man named in a teletype received from the sheriff of an adjoining county. The suspect maintained that

he was in the hospital at the time the offense alleged in the communication took place, and asked the officers to verify his story over their car radio. When he continued to plead innocence he was handcuffed and taken to headquarters. Here the detectives learned that the teletype had been canceled. Prior to his release the man was told that he could have saved himself grief had he gone along voluntarily.

In a downtown residential hotel, patrolmen found two ambulance attendants trying to persuade a man, who according to all accounts was desperately ill, to go to the hospital. After some talk, they helped the attendants in carrying the protesting patient to the ambulance and sent them off.

In a middle-class neighborhood, patrolmen found a partly disassembled car, tools, a loudly blaring radio, and five beer-drinking youths at the curb in front of a single-family home. The homeowner complained that this had been going on for several days and the men had refused to take their activities elsewhere. The patrolmen ordered the youths to pack up and leave. When one sassed them they threw him into the squad car, drove him to the precinct station, from where he was released after receiving a severe tongue lashing from the desk sergeant.

In the apartment of a quarreling couple, patrolmen were told by the wife, whose nose was bleeding, that the husband stole her purse containing money she earned. The patrolmen told the man they would "take him in," whereupon he returned the purse and they left.

What all these vignettes are meant to illustrate is that whatever the substance of the task at hand, whether it involves protection against an undesired imposition, caring for those who cannot care for themselves, attempting to solve a crime, helping to save a life, abating a nuisance, or settling an explosive dispute, police intervention means above all making use of the capacity and authority to overpower resistance to an attempted solution in the native habitat of the problem. There can be no doubt that this feature of police work is uppermost in the minds of people who solicit police aid or direct the attention of the police to problems, that persons against whom the police proceed have this feature in mind and conduct themselves accordingly, and that every conceivable police intervention projects the message that force may be, and may have to be, used to achieve a desired objective. It does not matter whether the persons who seek police help are private citizens or other government officials, nor does it matter whether the problem at hand involves some aspect of law enforcement or is totally unconnected with it.

It must be emphasized, however, that the conception of the centrality of the capacity to use force in the police role does not entail the conclusion that the ordinary occupational routines consist of the actual exercise of this capacity. It is very likely, though we lack information on this point, that the actual use of physical coercion and restraint is rare for all policemen and that many policemen are virtually never in the position of having to resort to it. What matters is that police procedure is defined by the feature that it may not be opposed in its course, and that force can be used if it is opposed. This is what the existence of the police makes available to society. Accordingly, the question, "What are policemen supposed to do?" is almost completely identical with the question, "What kinds of situations require remedies that are non-negotiably coercible?"[27]

Our second justification for preferring the definition of the police role we proposed to the traditional law enforcement focus of the role requires us to review the actual police practices to see to what extent they can be subsumed under the conception we offered. To begin we can take note that law enforcement and crime control are obviously regarded as calling for remedies that are non-negotiably coercible. According to available estimates, approximately one-third of available manpower resources of the police are at any time committed to dealing with crimes and criminals. Though this may seem to be a relatively small share of the total resources of an agency ostensibly devoted to crime control, it is exceedingly unlikely that any other specific routine police activity, such as traffic regulation, crowd control, supervision of licensed establishments, settling of citizens' disputes, emergency health aids, ceremonial

functions, or any other, absorb anywhere near as large a share of the remaining two-thirds. But this is precisely what one would expect on the basis of our definition. Given the likelihood that offenders will seek to oppose apprehension and evade punishment, it is only natural that the initial dealings with them be assigned to an agency that is capable of overcoming these obstacles. That is, the proposed definition of the role of the police as a mechanism for the distribution of non-negotiably coercive remedies entails the priority of crime control by direct inference. Beyond that, however, the definition also encompasses other types of activities, albeit at lower level of priority.

Because the idea that the police are basically a crimefighting agency has never been challenged in the past, no one has troubled to sort out the remaining priorities. Instead, the police have always been forced to justify activities that did not involve law enforcement in the direct sense by either linking them constructively to law enforcement or by defining them as nuisance demands for service. The dominance of this view, especially in the minds of policemen, has two pernicious consequences. First, it leads to a tendency to view all sorts of problems as if they involved culpable offenses and to an excessive reliance on quasilegal methods for handling them. The widespread use of arrests without intent to prosecute exemplifies this state of affairs. These cases do not involve errors in judgment about the applicability of a penal norm but deliberate pretense resorted to because more appropriate methods of handling problems have not been developed. Second, the view that crime control is the only serious, important, and necessary part of police work has deleterious effects on the morale of those police officers in the uniformed patrol who spend most of their time with other matters. No one, especially he who takes a positive interest in his work, likes being obliged to do things day-in and day-out that are disparaged by his colleagues. Moreover, the low evaluation of these duties leads to neglecting the development of skill and knowledge that are required to discharge them properly and efficiently.

It remains to be shown that the capacity to use coercive force lends thematic unity to all police activity in the same sense which, let us say, the capacity to cure illness lends unity to everything that is ordinarily done in the field of medical practice. While everybody agrees that the police actually engage in an enormous variety of activities, only a part of which involves law enforcement, many argue that this state of affairs does not require explanation but change. Smith, for example, argued that the imposition of duties and demands that are not related to crime control dilutes the effectiveness of the police and that the growing trend in this direction should be curtailed and even reversed.[28] On the face of it this argument is not without merit, especially if one considers that very many of those activities that are unrelated to law enforcement involve dealing with problems that lie in the field of psychiatry, social welfare, human relations, education, and so on. Each of these fields has its own trained specialists who are respectively more competent than the police. It would seem preferable, therefore, to take all those matters that belong properly to other specialists out of the hands of the police and turn them over to those to whom they belong. Not only would this relieve some of the pressures that presently impinge on the police, but it would also result in better services.[29]

Unfortunately, this view overlooks a centrally important factor. While it is true that policemen often aid sick and troubled people because physicians and social workers are unable or unwilling to take their services where they are needed, this is not the only or even the main reason for police involvement. In fact, physicians and social workers themselves quite often "call the cops." For not unlike the case of the administration of justice, on the periphery of the rationally ordered procedures of medical and social work practice lurk exigencies that call for the exercise of coercion. Since neither physicians nor social workers are authorized or equipped to use force to attain desirable objectives, the total disengagement of the police would mean allowing many a problem to move unhampered in the direction of disaster. But the non-law-enforcement activities of the police are by no means confined to matters that are wholly or even mainly within the purview of some other institutionalized remedial specialty. Many, perhaps most, consist of addressing situations in which people simply do not seem to be able to manage their own lives adequately. Nor is it to be taken for granted that these situations invariably call for the use, or the threat of the use, of force. It is enough if there is need for immediate and unquestioned intervention that must not be allowed to be defeated by possible resistance. And where there is a possibility of great harm, the intervention would appear to be justified even if the risk is, in statistical terms, quite remote. Take, for instance the presence of mentally ill persons in the community. Though it is well known that most live quiet and unobtrusive lives, they are perceived as occasionally constituting a serious hazard to themselves and others. Thus, it is not surprising that the police are always prepared to deal with these persons at the slightest indication of a possible emergency. Similarly, though very few family quarrels lead to serious consequences, the fact that most homicides occur among quarreling kin leads to the preparedness to intervene at the incipient stages of problems.

In sum, the role of the police is to address all sorts of human problems when and insofar as their solutions do or may possibly require the use of force at the point of their occurrence. This lends homogeneity to such diverse procedures as catching a criminal, driving the mayor to the airport, evicting a drunken person from a bar, directing traffic, crowd control, taking care of lost children, administering medical first aid, and separating fighting relatives.

There is no exaggeration in saying that there is topical unity in this very incomplete list of lines of police work. Perhaps it is true that the common practice of assigning policemen to chauffeur mayors is based on the desire to give the appearance of thrift in the urban fisc. But note, if one wanted to make as far as possible certain that nothing would ever impede His Honor's freedom of movement, he would certainly put someone into the driver's seat of the auto who has the authority and the capacity to overcome all unforeseeable human obstacles. Similarly, it is perhaps not too farfetched to assume that desk sergeants feed ice cream to lost children because they like children. But if the treat does not achieve the purpose of keeping the youngster in the station house until his parents arrive to redeem him, the sergeant would have to resort to other means of keeping him there.

We must now attempt to pull together the several parts of the foregoing discussion in order to show how they bring into relief the main problems of adjusting police function to life in modern society, and in order to elaborate constructively certain consequences that result from the assumption of the role definitions we have proposed.

At the beginning we observed that the police appear to be burdened by an opprobrium that did not seem to lessen proportionately to the acknowledged improvements in their practices. To explain this puzzling fact we drew attention to three perceived features of the police that appear to be substantially independent of particular work methods. First, a stigma attaches to police work because of its connection with evil, crime, perversity, and disorder. Though it may not be reasonable, it is common that those who fight the dreadful end up being dreaded themselves. Second, because the police must act quickly and often on mere intuition, their interventions are lacking in those aspects of moral sophistication which only a more extended and more scrupulous consideration can afford. Hence their methods are comparatively crude. Third, because it is commonly assumed that the risks of the kinds of breakdowns that require police action are much more heavily concentrated in the lower classes than in other segments of society, police surveillance is inherently discriminatory. That is, all things being equal, some persons feel the sting of police scrutiny merely because of their station in life. Insofar as this is felt, police work has divisive effects in society.

Next, we argued that one cannot understand how the police "found themselves" in this unenviable position without taking into consideration that one of the cultural trends of roughly the past century-and-a-half was the sustained aspiration to install peace as a stable condition of everyday life. Though no one can fail being impressed by the many ways the attainment of this ideal has been frustrated, it is possible to find some evidence of partially effective efforts. Many aspects of mundane existence in our cities have become more pacific than they have been in past epochs of history. More importantly for our purposes, in the domain of internal statecraft, the distance between those who govern and those who are governed has grown and the gap has been filled with bureaucratically symbolized communication. Where earlier compliance was secured by physical presence and armed might, it now rests mainly on peaceful persuasion and a rational compliance. We found the trend toward the pacification in governing most strongly demonstrated in the administration of justice. The banishment of all forms of violence from the criminal process, as administered by the courts, has as a corollary the legalization of judicial proceedings. The latter reflects a movement away from peremptory and oracular judgment to a method in which all decisions are based on exhaustively rational grounds involving the use of explicit legal norms. Most important among those norms are the ones that limit the powers of authority and specify the rights of defendants. The legalization and pacification of the criminal process was achieved by, among other things, expelling from its purview those processes that set it into motion. Since in the initial steps, where suspicions are formed and arrests are made, force and intuition cannot be eliminated entirely, purity can be maintained by not taking notice of them. This situation is, however, paradoxical if we are to take seriously the idea that the police is a law enforcement agency in the strict sense of legality. The recognition of this paradox became unavoidable as early as in 1914, in the landmark decision of *Weeks v. U.S.* In the following decades the United States Supreme Court issued a series of rulings affecting police procedure which foster the impression that the judiciary exercises control over the police. But this impression is misleading, for the rulings do not set forth binding norms for police work but merely provide that *if* the police propose to set the criminal process into motion, *then* they must proceed in certain legally restricted ways. These restrictions are, therefore, conditional, specifying as it were the terms of delivery and acceptance of a service and nothing more. Outside of this arrangement the judges have no direct concerns with police work and will take notice of its illegality, if it is illegal, only when offended citizens seek civil redress.

Because only a small part of the activity of the police is dedicated to law enforcement and because they deal with the majority of their problems without invoking the law, a broader definition of their role was proposed. After reviewing briefly what the public appears to expect of the police, the range of activities police actually engage in, and the theme that unifies all these activities, it was suggested that *the role of the police is best understood as a mechanism for the distribution of non-negotiably coercive force employed in accordance with the dictates of an intuitive grasp of situational exigencies.*

It is, of course, not surprising that a society committed to the establishment of peace by pacific means and to the abolishment of all forms of violence from the fabric of its social relations, at least as a matter of official morality and policy, would establish a corps of specially deputized officials endowed with the exclusive monopoly of using force contingently where limitations of foresight fail to provide alternatives. That is, given the melancholy appreciation of the fact that the total abolition of force is not attainable, the closest approximation to the ideal is to limit it as a special and exclusive trust. If it is the case, however, that the mandate of the police is organized around their capacity and authority to use force, i.e., if this is what the institution's existence makes available to society, then the evaluation of that institution's performance must focus on it. While it is quite true that policemen will have to be judged on other dimensions of competence, too—for example, the exercise of force against criminal suspects requires some knowledge about crime and criminal law—their methods as society's agents of coercion will have to be considered central to the overall judgment.

The proposed definition of the police role entails a difficult moral problem. How can we arrive at a favorable or even accepting judgment about an activity which is, in its very conception, opposed to the ethos of the polity that authorizes it? Is it not well nigh inevitable that this mandate be concealed in circumlocution? While solving puzzles of moral philosophy is beyond the scope of this analysis, we will have to address this question in a somewhat more mundane formulation: namely, on what terms can a society dedicated to peace institutionalize the exercise of force?

It appears that in our society two answers to this question are acceptable. One defines the targets of legitimate force as enemies and the coercive advance against them as warfare. Those who wage this war are expected to be possessed by the military virtues of valor, obedience and *esprit de corps*. The enterprise as a whole is justified as a sacrificial and glorious mission in which the warrior's duty is "not to reason why." The other answer involves an altogether different imagery. The targets of force are conceived as practical objectives and their attainment a matter of practical expediency. The process involves prudence, economy, and considered judgment, from case to case. The enterprise as a whole is conceived as a public trust, the exercise of which is vested in individual practitioners who are personally responsible for their decisions and actions. Reflection suggests that the two patterns are profoundly incompatible. Remarkably, however, our police departments have not been deterred from attempting the reconciliation of the irreconcilable. Thus, our policemen are exposed to the demand of a conflicting nature in that their actions are supposed to reflect military prowess and professional acumen.

Notes

1. Werner Dankert, *Unehrliche Menschen: Die Verfehmten Berufe*, Bern: Francke Verlag, 1963.
2. G.S. McWatters wrote about the typical policeman, after many years of being one himself, "He is the outgrowth of a diseased and corrupted state of things, and is, consequently, morally diseased himself." Quoted in Lane, *op. cit. supra*, Note 2 at p. 69.

3. Erle Stanley Gardner, the prolific detective story writer, reports being troubled by the apparent need for the "dumb" cop in fiction. When he attempted to remedy this and depicted a policeman in favorable colors in one of his books, bookdealers and readers rose in protest; see his "The Need for New Concepts in the Administration of Criminal Justice," *Journal of Criminal Law, Criminology and Police Science*, 50 (1959) 20-26; see also G.J. Falk, "The Public's Prejudice Against the Police," *American Bar Association Journal*, 50 (1965) 754-757.

4. V.W. Piersante, Chief Detective of the Detroit Police Department, has juxtaposed with remarkable perceptiveness the considerations with remarkable perceptiveness the considerations which, on the one hand, lead to dense and suspicious surveillance of certain groups because of their disproportionate contribution to crime totals, while on the other hand, these tactics expose the preponderant majority of law-abiding members of these groups to offensive scrutiny. He stated, "in Detroit in 1964 a total of 83,135 arrests were made . . . of this 58,389 were Negroes. . . . This means that 89 percent of the Negro population were never involved with the police. . . ." quoted at p. 215 in Harold Norris, "Constitutional Law Enforcement Is Effective Law Enforcement," *University of Detroit Law Journal*, 42 (1965) 203-234.

5. Gilbert Geis, *Juvenile Gangs*, A Report Produced for the President's Committee on Juvenile Delinquency and Youth Crime, Washington, D.C.: U.S. Government Printing Office, June 1965; Carl Werthman and Irving Piliavin, "Gang Membership and the Police," in Bordua (ed.), *op. cit. supra*, Note 3 at pp. 56-98.

6. Allan Silver, "The Demand for Order in Civil Society: A Review of Some Themes in the History of Urban Crime, Police, and Riot," in Bordua (ed.), *op. cit. supra*, Note 3 at pp. 1-24.

7. J.Q. Wilson writes, "The patrolman believes with considerable justification that teenagers, Negroes, and lower-income persons commit a disproportionate share of all reported crimes; being in those population categories at all makes one, statistically, more suspect than other persons; but to be in those categories *and* to behave unconventionally is to make oneself a prime suspect. Patrolmen believe that they would be derelict in their duty if they did not treat such persons with suspicion, routinely question them on the street, and detain them for longer questioning if a crime has occurred in the area. To the objection of some middle-class observers that this is arbitrary and discriminatory, the police are likely to answer: 'Have *you* ever been stopped and searched? Of course not. We can tell the difference; we have to tell the difference in order to do our job. What are you complaining about?'" at pp. 40-41 of his *Varieties of Police Behavior: The Management of Law and Order in Eight Communities*, Cambridge, Mass.: Harvard University Press, 1968.

8. Of primary significance in this respect is that the courts make the same kinds of invidious distinctions even as they follow the law; see J.E. Carlin, Jan Howard, and S.L. Messinger, "Civil Justice and the Poor," *Law and Society*, 1 (1966) 9-89, and Jacobus ten-Broek (ed.), *The Law of the Poor*, San Francisco, California: Chandler Publishing Co., 1966.

9. Reference is made to the evidence that persons of working class origin are more prone than others to harbor attitudes that are favorable to politics of prejudice and authoritarianism; see S.L. Lipset, "Democracy and Working Class Authoritarianism," *American Sociological Review*, 24 (1959) 482-501; "Social Stratification and Right Wing Extremism," *British Journal of Sociology*, 10(1959) 346-382; "Why Cops Hate Liberals—and Vice Versa," *Atlantic Monthly*. (March 1969).

10. Arthur Niederhoffer, a former ranking police official, writes, "The power structure and the ideology of the community, which are supported by the police, at the same time direct and set boundaries to the sphere of police action." at p. 13 of his *Behind the Shield: The Police in Urban Society*, New York: Anchor Books, 1969; Niederhoffer cites an even stronger statement to that effect from Joseph Lohman, a former sheriff of Cook County, Ill. And later Dean of the School of Criminology at the University of California at Berkeley.

11. The normative approach is perhaps best exemplified in Jerome Hall, "Police and Law in a Democratic Society," *Indiana Law Journal*, 2 (1953) 133-177, where it is argued that the structure of police work must be understood as decisively determined by the duty to uphold the law and every police action must be interpreted in relation to this objective. The man on the street, however, approaches police work from a different vantage point. He probably supposes that police work has something to do with law enforcement, but to him this is mainly a figure of speech which

does not limit his freedom to decide what the police are really for from case to case.

12. The leading historian of the police is Charles Reith. See his *A New Study of Police History*, Edinburgh: Oliver & Boyd, 1956. A brief review of American development is contained in S.A. Chapman and T.E. St. Johnston, *The Police Heritage in England and America*, East Lansing, Mich.: Institute for Community Development and Services, Michigan State University, 1962, and in Lane, *op. cit. supra*, Note 2.

13. Ernest Barker, *The Development of Public Services in Western Europe, 1660-1930*, London: Oxford University Press, 1944.

14. J.L. Lyman, "The Metropolitan Police Act of 1829," *Journal of Criminal Law, Criminology and Police Science*, 55 (1964) 141-154.

15. Christopher Hibbert, *The Roots of Evil*, Boston, Mass.: Little, Brown & Co., 1963.

16. Leon Radzinowicz, *A History of English Criminal Law*, New York: Macmillan, 1957.

17. A perhaps overly optimistic review of this trend is contained in Paul Reiwald, *Eroberung des Friedens*, Zurich, Europa Verlag, 1944.

18. The following remarks are not intended as a "well-rounded" picture of the problem of peace and violence during the past 150 years. Instead, they deliberately accent a single trend.

19. Indirect and symbolic forms of authority implementation can be, of course, even more oppressive in their effects than the permanent presence of the fist at the scruff of the neck. But while political power that rests only on means of violence is repugnant on its face, indirect authority contains at least the possibility of consensual governing.

20. Egon Bittner and A.M. Platt, "The Meaning of Punishment," *Issues in Criminology*, 2 (1966) 79-99.

21. W.B. Miller, "Lower-Class Culture as a Generating Milieu of Gang Delinquency," *Journal of Social Issues*, 14 (1958) 5-19; Oscar Lewis, "The Culture of Poverty," *Scientific American*, 215 (October, 1966) 19-25.

22. E.J. Hobsbawm entitled his book dealing with the first one-third of the period, *The Age of Revolution*, London: Weidenfeld & Nicolson, Ltd., 1962. American developments have been superbly reviewed in H.D. Graham and T.R. Gurr (eds.), *Violence in America*, New York: Signet Books, 1969; the preparation of this collection of studies was undertaken for the National Commission on the Causes and Prevention of Violence.

23. For a review of Bentham's teachings concerning penal law and punishment, see James Heath, *Eighteenth Century Penal Philosophy*, London: Oxford University Press, 1963, esp. Pp. 219-220. The sources, mainstream, and influence of Benthamite philosophy are described in Elie Halevy, *The Growth of Philosophical Radicalism*, Boston: Beacon Press, 1955.

24. "Justification for the Use of Force in the Criminal Law," *Stanford Law Review*, 13 (1961) 566-609.

25. "At common law, the rule appears to have been that an officer was entitled to make a reasonable mistake as to whether the victim had committed a felony, but a private person was not so entitled. Thus strict liability was created for the private arrester, and he could not justifiably kill, if the victim had not actually committed a felony. Several modern cases have imposed this standard of strict liability even upon the officer by conditioning justification of deadly force on the victim's actually having committed a felony, and a number of states have enacted statutes which appear to adopt this strict liability. However, many jurisdictions, such as California, have homicide statutes which permit the police officer to use deadly force for the arrest of a person 'charged' with felony. It has been suggested that this requirement only indicates the necessity for reasonable belief by the officer that the victim has committed a felony." *Ibid.*, pp. 599-600.

26. The illustrations are taken from field notes I have collected over the course of fourteen months of intensive field observations of police activity in two large cities. One is located in a Rocky Mountain State, the other on the West Coast. All other case vignettes used in the subsequent text of this report also come from this source.

27. By "non-negotiably coercible" we mean that when a deputized police officer decides that force is necessary, then, within the boundaries of this situation, he is not accountable to anyone, nor is he required to brook the arguments or opposition of anyone who might object to it. We set this forth not as a legal but as a practical rule. The legal question whether citizens may oppose policemen is complicated. Apparently resisting police coercion in situations of emergency is not legitimate; see Hans Kelsen, *General Theory of Law and State*,

New York: Russel & Russel, 1961, pp. 278-279, and H.L.A. Hart, *The Concept of Law*, Oxford: Clarendon Press, 1961, pp. 20-21. Common law doctrine allows that citizens may oppose "unlawful arrest," 6 *Corpus Juris Secundum*, Arrest #13, p. 613; against this, the Uniform Arrest Act, drafted by a committee of the Interstate Commission on Crime in 1939, provides in Section 5, "If a person has reasonable grounds to believe that he is being arrested by a peace officer, it is his duty to refrain from using force or any weapons in resisting arrest regardless of whether or not there is a legal basis for the arrest." S.B. Warner, "Uniform Arrest Act," *Vanderbilt Law Review*, 28 (1942) 315-347. At present, at least twelve states are governed by case law recognizing the validity of the Common Law doctrine, at least five have adopted the rule contained in the Uniform Arrest Act, and at least six have case law or statutes that give effect to the Uniform Arrest Act rule. That the trend is away from the Common Law doctrine and in the direction of the Uniform Arrest Act rule is argued in Max Hochanadel and H.W. Stege, "The Right to Resist an Unlawful Arrest: An Outdated Concept?" *Tulsa Law Journal*, 3 (1968) 40-46. I am grateful for the help I received from 35 of the 50 State Attorney General Offices from whom I sought information concerning this matter.

28. Smith, *op. cit. supra*, Note 1.

29. The authors of the *Task Force Report: Police* note that little has been done to make these alternative resources available as substitutes for police intervention; *op. cit. supra*, Note 56 at p. 14.

Reprinted from Egon Bittner, "The Functions of Police in Modern Society" in *The Functions of the Police in Modern Society* 1980 pp. 6-24, 36-47. ✦

3

Can the Police Be Privatized?

Philip E. Fixler, Jr. and
Robert W. Poole, Jr.

One feature of the police function that people tend to take for granted is that it is a public function, that is, a government service. Understandably, most of us are leery of turning policing over to a private company—can you imagine policing for profit? And yet, (1) so-called private policing played a big role in the historical development of English and American policing, (2) what we call private security today has more employees than the public policing sector, and (3) the general trend over the past decade or two has been to "privatize" more and more government services. In this article, two proponents of privatization explore the possibilities for private policing and some of the practical, legal, and political obstacles to its growth and development. As you read the article, think about the pros and cons of privatizing policing where you live.

One of the most significant developments in state and local government over the past decade has been the privatization revolution. Numerous public services have been shifted, in part or in whole, into the private sector.

Public safety and criminal justice functions have shared in this privatization trend. There are hundreds of for-profit emergency ambulance firms and several dozen private fire protection, jail, and prison operators. There has also been extensive use of private, voluntary alternatives to civil court proceedings, and a growing amount of contracting with private organizations for work-release programs, juvenile rehabilitation, and the like. Policing, however, has generally been considered a service that cannot and should not be privatized.

How coherent is this point of view? Are there characteristics of the police function that render it so inherently governmental that it ought not even be considered for privatization? And if this widespread view is mistaken, how do we account for its persistence among public policy analysts?

Policing as a Public Service

When analysts refer to certain types of services as being inherently governmental, what they generally mean is that the services in question have the characteristics of public goods, as opposed to private goods. In simplest terms, a public good is one that is provided collectively and from whose benefits those not paying for the good cannot be excluded. The classic example of a public good is national defense. If an organization provides defense of a given territory, everyone within that territory receives the benefits, whether or not they pay the costs. Thus clearly identified public goods are generally produced in the public sector and paid for via taxation.

Privatization analyst E. S. Savas has developed a somewhat more sophisticated typology of public and private goods.[1] Savas uses two basic criteria—exclusion and joint consumption—to categorize various services. A good that is consumed privately and available only to those who pay for it is a private good. Savas points out, however, that some goods that are consumed collectively may still be charged for individually in proportion to use—for example, cable television, water and electricity service, and toll roads. Savas terms them "tolled goods." By contrast, a public good is one that is consumed collectively and for which nonpayers cannot be excluded.

How should we categorize police services in this typology? The key to answering that question is to realize that policing is not a single service. Police departments perform a number of functions, some of which have the characteristics of private goods, some of which are toll goods, and some of which are, in varying degrees, collective, or public goods. This being the case, it is clear that there is at least some theoretical scope for privatization in police services.

Some police department functions are essentially of a security guard nature, providing specific protective services to a specific client. Examples include surveillance of a vacant house when the owner is on vacation, police escorts to a funeral, or providing traffic direction at a construction site that blocks a lane of traffic. In Savas's typology, these are basically private goods, which could be provided by a private firm. Some police departments charge for such services.

Other aspects of security-related police work are less private in nature. If a neighborhood, a shopping center, or even a specific block receives regular police patrol, those who live and work there will feel safer than otherwise. In such cases, the consumption of the service is joint, and the key privatization question is whether funding can be provided voluntarily, rather than by taxation. This type of police service falls between a toll good and a collective good.

In addition to understanding the different types of services that police provide, we must also understand the various forms of privatization.[2] To do so, we need to look at two key dimensions of public service delivery: who pays for the service and who delivers it. The traditional form of public service—and the general assumption for all police functions—has the government providing the funding via taxes and directly producing the service using government employees, but private mechanisms may be used in either or both of these areas.

Thus, if government produces the service but charges individual users, in proportion to their use, the funding—but not the delivery—of the service has been privatized via user fees. On the other hand, if government retains the funding responsibility, collecting taxes to provide the funds, but hires the provider in the marketplace, we have the form of privatization known as contracting out. Finally, if both the funding mechanism and the service delivery are shifted into the private sector, we have the most complete form of privatization, referred to as service shedding or load shedding. Government may

retain some degree of control over the terms and conditions of service, as in the case when it issues an exclusive franchise. Alternatively, government may simply bow out, other than for ordinary business licensing, leaving the service to be handled entirely by the marketplace.

Experience With Police Privatization

All three types of privatization have been experienced in the United States with respect to policing: user fees, contracting out, and some degree of service shedding. The following subscriptions provide an overview of these cases.

User-Financed Police Services

While many jurisdictions have traditionally charged special fees for some types of services, such as providing security for parades and special events, one of the most common user fees is a charge for responding to burglar alarms. Oftentimes, these charges are for responding to false alarms, usually after a certain threshold point.

The growing number of home owners who have contracted for alarm services has placed an increasing burden on public police departments, even with the imposition of charges for responding to false burglar alarms. As a result, some police departments have permitted alarm companies to provide response services to answer their subscribers' alarms. When Amarillo, Texas, authorized a local security company to respond to subscribers' alarms, the police department was relieved of the time-consuming responsibility of answering an average of eight alarms per day; it thereby saved approximately 3420 man-hours, or the equivalent of adding one and three fourths people per year. All of this was at no cost to the taxpayer.[3]

Another, more comprehensive, form of user-financed police service is exemplified by the arrangement negotiated between the Montclair Plaza shopping center and the Montclair, California, Police Department. Calls for service from the shopping center became so numerous that the department considered designating the center as a new, separate beat. Because a limited budget precluded establishing such a beat, the department proposed that the shopping center pick up 50 percent of the beat officer's salary and benefits.[4] The arrangement proved to be mutually beneficial. The department was able to accommodate the new service demand, while the shopping center and its security staff achieved greater liaison with the department.

A similar concept was implemented in Oakland, California, where private developers entered into an agreement with the police department to fund special downtown patrol services to attract more shoppers. According to James K. Stewart, director of the National Institute of Justice, "Fear is down in the inner-city areas and development is thriving."[5]

Contracting Out: Private Provision of Police Services

As with a number of other public services, contracting out police services began with support services and later certain auxiliary services. Police departments in many parts of the nation contract out for vehicle maintenance and other support services. In some cities, the towing of illegally parked vehicles is still a police responsibility, but nearly three-fourths of all cities have privatized this function. New York City uses two different methods in privatizing it. First, New York contracts with private firms to tow these vehicles. In addition, the city charges those claiming their towed vehicles a fee to cover the police department's costs.[6]

Among the support services that have been contracted out are communications-system maintenance, police training, and laboratory services;[7] food provision and medical care for jail inmates;[8] and radio dispatching services.[9] Traffic control and parking are other police responsibilities that have been contracted out in some jurisdictions. Several large security companies provide special-event security, and other companies provide such mundane services as guarding school crossings. The city of Los Angeles, for example, has contracted out for school crossing guards. Private firms furnish parking lot enforcement services for the Eastern Idaho Medical Center, the Arizona Department of Transportation, and the University of Hawaii, Hilo.[10]

Contracting out line law enforcement activities is an obvious second level of police services contracting. For example, San Diego, Los Angeles County, and Norwalk, in California, and St. Petersburg, in Florida, have contracted out some public-parks patrol.[11] Private security guards also provide protective services in Candlestick Park in San Francisco and the Giants Stadium in New Jersey.[12] Other jurisdictions—including San Diego; Lexington, Kentucky; and New York City—have contracted for private patrol of crime-ridden housing projects.[13] The Suffolk School District in New York contracts for school security services.[14] In Munich, Germany, private police patrol the subways.[15]

Many state and local governments in this country contract for public buildings and grounds security, among them being Boston; Denver and Fort Collins, Colorado; Houston; Los Angeles County; Pensacola, Florida; New York City; San Francisco; Seattle; and the states of California and Pennsylvania.[16] Many departments of the federal government also contract for private security guards, and U.S. federal courts in many parts of the nation use private court-security officers and bailiffs who are sworn in as U.S. deputy marshals.[17]

Overseas, the British Transport Police stationed at the Port at the Port of Southampton, who had been public employees since 1820, were recently replaced with private security personnel.[18] In several other countries, some licensed security personnel are authorized to exercise police-like powers.[19]

Prisoner custody is also being turned over to contractors by some jurisdictions. For many years, the transportation of prisoners has been contracted out in parts of Maryland and California.[20] Santa Barbara County, California, contracts for some of its prisoner transportation, for example. Private police have also been hired for other specialized custodial services, such as guarding prisoners who are bing transported or who are being treated in public hospitals. For example, New York City and several Alabama prisons, including the West Jefferson, St. Clair, and Hamilton facilities, contract with private firms to guard prisoners receiving hospital treatment.[21]

Choosing to contract out for custodial care has moved beyond these special situations, however. At least six U.S. counties now contract with private organizations to manage local prisons; these countries include Hamilton County, Tennessee; Bay County, Florida; Butler County, Pennsylvania; Hennipin County, Minnesota; Santa Fe County, New Mexico; and Aroostock County, Maine. In 1986, California and Kentucky became the first two states to contract out the management and operation of state prison facilities. California's contract is for a minimum-security, return-to-custody facility for parole violators in Hidden Hills. Kentucky has gone a step further by contracting with a firm that owns its own site.[22]

There is even some precedent for contracting out a basic police service such as investigation. Some federal agencies contracted out for many investigative services up until about 1909.[23] About twenty years ago, the governor of Florida had a short-lived contract for investigative services, to be paid for from private contributions. Some police departments in the Midwest contract out for special narcotics enforcement.[24]

A third level of police privatization is contracting for regular or full police services in a given jurisdiction. The federal government has contracted for full police services at its Mercury test site, operated by the Energy Research and Development Administration in Nevada, and at the National Aeronautics and Space Administration's Kennedy Space Center in Florida.[25]

Perhaps most far reaching, however, are the several examples where local governments have contracted for regular police service and even their entire police force. Apparently the first in modern times to do this was the city of Kalamazoo, Michigan. In the mid-1950s, Kalamazoo contracted for about three and a half years with a local firm for street patrol and apprehension of traffic-law violators.[26] In order to ensure that the contractor's activities were fully in accordance with the law, patrol personnel were sworn in as full deputy sheriffs. A court case—involving a technicality relating to an arrest—led to the demise of the arrangement, even though the decision was in favor of the private firm. One of the dissenting judges made a virulent at-tack on the whole concept of private police, helping to discredit the practice in Kalamazoo.

In 1981, Reminderville, Ohio, contracted out its entire police service. Previously, Reminderville had received policing under contract from Summit County. When the county withdrew its patrol from Reminderville—and unincorporated Twinsburg—for budgetary reasons, Reminderville and Twinsburg first explored the possibility of recontracting with the county at a higher rate. At that point, a private security firm, headed by a former Ohio police chief, submitted a competing bid of $90,000 per year, about half the county's bid. Moreover, the firm agreed to provide two patrol cars rather than one and to reduce emergency response time from 45 to 6 minutes. As part of the arrangement, the firm also agreed to "select trained, state-certified candidates for the police positions, leaving the village to make the final choice. In fact, village officials would have full autonomy in hiring, firing, disciplining, and organizing the police force."[27] The arrangement worked well for two years, surviving threats of a lawsuit by the Ohio Police Chief's Association. Nevertheless, an attack in *Newsweek* and other skeptical publicity disturbed Reminderville officials, and in 1983, they ended the contract and set up their own conventional city police department—at a higher cost.

A similar instance occurred several years earlier in the small town of Oro Valley, Arizona. In 1975, a local company offered the town full police services as part of a comprehensive public safety package including fire protection and ambulance service.[28] The company "agreed to establish a police headquarters and keep all records according to state guidelines for police departments" and to supervise and assume all liability for the conduct of its employees. Oro Valley's town marshal, however, would fully control and have responsibility for the police force and would be able to override the firm's authority at any time. The price for full police service was substantially lower than what it would have cost the town to set up its own public police force.

This time the contracting-out arrangement was undermined when the Arizona Law

Enforcement Advisory Council refused to accept the firm's employees in its training and accreditation program—and the council is the only organization licensed to award accreditation.[29] This development was followed by a state attorney general's opinion that Oro Valley could not commission the firm's employees as police officers. In the face of anticipated high court costs, the company decided to discontinue the arrangement.

Several other small American towns have contracted for private police services for as long as five years, including Buffalo Creek, West Virginia; Indian River, Florida; and several other small Florida[30] and Illinois[31] jurisdictions. Sometimes these contracts were an interim measure until the jurisdiction could form its own police force.

The most recent example of contracting for police services was in connection with the Burbank-Glendale-Pasadena Airport Authority's contract with Lockheed Air Terminal for security services. Unfortunately, a flaw in the 1982 legislation specifically authorizing the hiring of private law enforcement agents with police powers was recently discovered and the arrangement was terminated.[32]

The only other country in which there has been any significant amount of contracting for regular police services is Switzerland. Some thirty Swiss villages and townships contract with a firm called Securitas. According to the Swiss Association of Towns and Townships, contracts offer substantial savings over what it would have cost these small towns to operate their own police forces. The typical contract calls for foot and vehicle patrol, checks on building security, night closing of bars and restaurants, and ticket validation at special events.[33]

Privatizing Finance and Provision: Deputization and Special Powers

The most extensive form of privatization ranges from situations where private security personnel are given arrest powers beyond that of citizen's arrest to be exercised in certain limited areas to situations where private officers have virtually full police powers and jurisdictionwide authority.

A Rand Corporation study for the Department of Justice defined deputization as "the formal method by which federal, state, and city governments grant to specific, named individuals the powers or status of public police [or peace officers]—usually for a limited time and in a limited geographic area."[34]

As one student of the history of private police in the United States observed, "Certain classes of private police such as railroad detectives, campus security guards, and retail security guards may be granted special powers concerning arrest and search."[35]

According to a 1985 study for the Department of Justice, approximately 25 percent of medium-sized and large police departments deputize special officers or give them special police powers, probably more often to proprietary—that is, in-house—than contract—that is, involving an outside firm—security agencies.[36] Of proprietary security managers and contract security managers surveyed in 1984, 29 percent and 14 percent respectively, indicated that their personnel had special police powers.

New York City retail security officers illustrate a limited form of this type of privatization. The police department has authorized retail security officers in some establishments to "provide surveillance, make arrests, transport suspects to police holding facilities, complete records checks, and enter criminal history information."[37] Private security personnel exercising these powers must be trained in the apprehension of suspects and various legal issues. Private security officers in Washington, D.C., may also be awarded certain police powers of arrest. Those licensed to carry weapons are designated as "special police officers."[38] As of the early 1970s, the District had about 2500 such officers. In the 1970s, Boston passed an ordinance to establish training and clothing requirements as well as guidelines for the use of firearms for "special officers" who have the power of arrest on the employer's premises.[39] In Maryland, a law allows the governor to appoint "special policemen" with full police power on the premises of certain private businesses, and North Carolina has a similar law.[40] In Oregon, the governor can appoint "special policemen" in the railroad and steamboat industries. Texas permits its Department of Public Safety to commission "special rangers," who may work for private employers and "who have the full arrest and firearms powers of an official policeman and are empowered to enforce all laws protecting life and property."[41]

Another form of fully privatized police service occurs on the campuses of some private universities and colleges. Seven states have passed legislation giving some degree of police authority to campus securitate universities.[42] In some states, private campus police may receive police powers via deputization by governors, courts, law enforcement agencies, or city governments. Campus police at the University of Southern California have been given certain powers of arrest under California Penal Code §830.7, pursuant to a memorandum of understanding with the Los Angeles Police Department. These powers grant the campus police at that university the same arrest powers as a California peace officer while they are on duty and within their jurisdiction and while responding to calls off-campus in the area surrounding the university.[43]

One of the purest forms of full police privatization is that of railroad police in a number of states. Enabling legislation was originally based on problems of interstate operation and the lack of public police protection in some areas. "In many parts of the country, the railroad police provided the only protective services until government and law enforcement agencies were established."[44] One Pennsylvania study, conducted in the 1930s, cited an 1865 state law that authorized railroad companies to employ security personnel who were also commissioned with full police powers in the county or state. If appointed by the state, railroad officers in Pennsylvania and New York, for example, maintained and exercised full police powers both on and off railroad property.[45] In fact, they were obligated to do so as sworn peace officers. Philadelphia at one time had hundreds of deputized, private security personnel providing police patrol services.

Fully private police services also exist on Paradise Island in the Bahamas. Virtually all island police activities are supplied by a firm employed by the island's hotels and resorts. The firm employs sixty to seventy guards and several vehicles, plus three or four administrative personnel and a captain. The company has responsibility for protecting 25 to 30 firms and the island territory. One analyst concluded that "since [the private security firm took] responsibility for protective services of the island, they have had one of the best records for low incidence of theft, rape, and assault in the area." This is in contrast to major incidences of theft and assault on the main island of New Providence, which has similar tourist attractions.[46]

Perhaps the foremost U.S. example of privately financed and provided police is that of the Patrol Special Police in San Francisco. Patrol specials are private individuals who undergo 440 hours of police academy instruction—the same as for reserve officers—and are sworn in as peace officers, one step below police officers. Once licensed, they are permitted to bid on one or more of some 65 private beats, with their salaries paid by merchants or residents along their beats. On the more lucrative beats, patrol specials hire assistants, who must complete the same training, and in some cases even hire security guards and administrative staff—thus, in effect, becoming mini police departments. They are legally members of the San Francisco Police Department, as reservists are, and are required to respond to police calls in their area.[47] Recently, however, the patrol specials have had to undertake a lawsuit to mandate California's Police Officer's Standards and Training Commission to continue their certification as sworn peace officers.

The Uniqueness of Policing

Why does privatizing the police function seem to be so difficult? It cannot be for lack of traditional roots. In feudal Britain, the nobility hired others to discharge their required protective duties.[48] Some private law enforcement personnel were partially financed from fees for the recovery of stolen goods.[49] In London, some individuals eventually organized private patrols as a deterrent to crime and as a more formal means of pursuing criminals. During the 1700s and early 1800s, the British people were quite skeptical of a tax-supported government police for fear that it would provide political leaders with a means of oppression.[50]

The British system of requisitioning watchmen or using volunteers was transported to America. Gradually, social attitudes and norms accepted the institution of public police forces in major U.S. urban areas, as occurred in London. With the advent of the first public police department in New York in the 1840s, other major cities quickly adopted public police departments. For over 100 years, most police protection in the United States has been publicly provided. Thus it is not surprising that many people now find it difficult to accept the notion of private police, despite their long history.

Another attitudinal factor is that some of the duties and activities undertaken by the police are qualitatively different from most other public services. The police have the right and obligation to use force, even deadly force, in the pursuit of their duties and receive special state authorization to do so.

A further barrier to police privatization is the difficulty of arranging for individuals to finance and consume police services, in contrast to other public services, privately. Moreover, even if a number of individuals in a neighborhood employ a private agency for patrol services, it is difficult to force those who do not wish voluntarily to finance these services to pay for the benefits they receive. One approach to dealing with this public goods problem is the deed-based, or mandatory-membership, home owners' association, in which security services are funded from mandatory membership dues. For example, in Los Angeles neighborhoods such as Bel Air and Beverlywood, a major fraction of the annual association dues goes to pay for the contract services of a private security company. This commercial firm provides 24-hour-a-day armed vehicular patrol by nonsworn security officers.

Another major barrier to police privatization is that of control and accountability. Understandably, people have serious concerns that those who are authorized to use deadly force be held accountable and under the control of the law. It certainly seems reasonable to require that all police personnel be properly trained and certified at the level of responsibility required by their particular duties. Moreover, as with any agency enforcing laws, strict quality-control regulation is appropriate, either through detailed contract provisions or regulatory oversight.

In addition to the public's natural apprehension, perhaps the greatest political barrier to privatizing police services is that of union opposition. As shown in the Reminderville and Oro Valley cases, public-police-officers' associations will strongly react to any local jurisdiction that attempts to privatize police services. But in light of today's budgetary constraints, it is shortsighted to permit special-interest political pressures to override the public's interest in cost-effective public services.

The final barrier to police privatization is legal restrictions. Upon close examination, however, these may not be as much of a problem as one would think. The attorney for Reminderville, Ohio, found that there was no state law preventing the contracting of police services. In the case of Troutman, North Carolina, the state deputy attorney general indicated that it was not technically illegal for the city to contract out its law enforcement, as long as the private police were sworn in as official police officers.[51] Perhaps, as in the Oro Valley case, it is more the political fight or potential legal costs that constitute the barrier.

Conclusion

On the one hand, there has been little progress in privatizing full or regular police services by U.S. local governments. To our knowledge, there is currently no city or county that is contracting for regular police services.

On the other hand, there does seem to be an increasing acceptance of more limited forms of privatization. The concept of special fees to beneficiaries in order to finance specialized police services, such as burglar alarm response, is increasingly accepted as fair and reasonable. Contracting out police support and ancillary services is growing steadily as well.

There are also signs of a gradual load shedding of certain police services to the private security industry, often through deputization or the award of special police powers. Assuming continued fiscal constraints on local governments and continued high levels of crime, it can be expected that police departments will gradually turn over more and more responsibility for law enforcement vis-à-vis private property to security organizations.

Notes

1. E. S. Savas, *Privatizing the Public Sector* (Chatham, NJ: Chatham House, 1982), pp. 29-51.

2. See Charles Feinstein, *Privatization Possibilities among Pacific Island Countries* (Honolulu: East-West Center, 1986), p. 10.

3. Dale Pancake, "Cooperation between Police Department and Private Security," *Police Chief*, June 1983, pp. 34-36.

4. Roger M. Moulton, "Police Contract Service for Shopping Mall Security," *Police Chief*, June 1983, pp. 43-44.

5. James Stewart, "Public Safety and Private Police," *Public Administration Review*, Nov. 1985, pp. 758-65.

6. John Diebold, *Making the Future Work* (New York: Simon & Schuster, 1984), p. 161.

7. Institute for Local Self-Government, *Alternatives to Traditional Public Safety Delivery Systems: Civilians in Public Safety Services* (Berkeley, CA: Institute for Local Self-Government, 1977), p. 14.

8. John J. McCarthy, "Contract Medical Care," *Corrections Magazine*, Apr. 1982, pp. 6-17.

9. Philip E. Fixler, Jr., "Which Police Services Can Be Privatized?" *Fiscal Watchdog*, Jan. 1986, no. 111, p. 3.

10. Ibid.

11. Robert W. Poole, Jr., *Cutting Back City Hall* (New York: Universe Books, 1980), p. 40.

12. Martin Tolchin, "Private Guards Taking the Place of Police," *Rutland Herald*, 29 Nov. 1985.

13. Poole, *Cutting Back City Hall*, p. 40.

14. Institute for Local Self-Government, *Alternatives to Public Safety*, p. 14.

15. Poole, *Cutting Back City Hall*, p. 41.

16. Ibid.; Fixler, "Which Police Services Can Be Privatized?" p. 2.

17. Wackenhut Corp., "Court Officers Now in 21 States," *Wackenhut Pipeline*, Dec. 1984, pp. 1, 4.

18. "Public Police Singing the Blues," *Reason*, Feb. 1985, p. 13.

19. Clifford D. Shearing and Philip C. Stenning, "Modern Private Security: Its Growth and Implications," in *Crime and Justice: An Annual Review of Research*, ed. Michael Tonry and Norval Morris (Chicago: University of Illinois Press, 1981), 3: 193-245.

20. Philip E. Fixler, Jr., "Private Prisons Begin to Establish Track Record," *Fiscal Watchdog*, June 1986, no. 116, pp. 1-4.

21. Steve Joynt, "Private Companies Hired to Guard Hospitalized State Prisoners," *Birmingham Post-Herald*, 22 May 1986; Fixler, "Which Police Services Can Be Privatized?" p. 3.

22. State Government News (Commonwealth of Kentucky), 30 Dec. 1986.

23. George O'Toole, *The Private Sector* (New York: Norton, 1978), p. 28.

24. Ibid.

25. Poole, *Cutting Back City Hall*, pp. 41-42.

26. William Wooldridge, *Uncle Sam, the Monopoly Man* (New Rochelle, NY: Arlington House, 1970), p. 122.

27. Theodore Gage, "Cops, Inc.," *Reason*, Nov. 1982, pp. 23-28.

28. Ibid.

29. "Oro Valley Must Hire Own Police," *Arizona Territory*, 19 Feb. 1976.

30. Poole, *Cutting Back City Hall*.

31. William C. Cunningham and Todd H. Taylor, *Private Security and Police in America (The Hallcrest Report)* (Portland, OR: Chancellor Press, 1985), p. 186.

32. "Private Firms Take Over Public Functions: Germany, Switzerland," *Urban Innovation Abroad*, 4(9): 1 (Sept. 1980).

33. Alan C. Miller, "Law Strips Guard Force at Airport of Authority," *Los Angeles Times*, 26 May 1987.

34. Sorrel Wildhorn and James Kakalik, *The Law and Private Police*, LEAA report R-872-DOJ (Washington, DC: Government Printing Office, 1971), 4: 4.

35. Theodore M. Becker, "The Place of Private Police in Society," *Social Problems*, 21(3): 446 (1974).

36. Cunningham and Taylor, *Private Security and Police in America*, pp. 40, 324.

37. Stewart, "Public Safety and Private Police," p. 761.

38. Athelia Knight, "'Rent-a-Cops' Pose Problems for District," *Washington Post*, 10 Nov. 1980.

39. Toni Schlesinger, "Rent-a-Cops, Inc.," *Student Lawyer*, Dec. 1978, p. 43.

40. O'Toole, *Private Sector*, p. 10.

41. Ibid.

42. Karen Hess and Henry M. Wrobleski, *Introduction to Private Security* (New York: West, 1982), p. 276.

43. Conversation with Lieutenant William Kennedy, University of Southern California, Campus Police, Jan. 1987.

44. Hess and Wrobleski, *Introduction to Private Security*, p. 13.

45. J. P. Shalloo, *Private Police* (Philadelphia: American Academy of Political and Social Science, 1933), pp. 25, 208.

46. James Gallagher, "The Case for Privatizing Protective Services," in *Facets of Liberty*, ed. L. K. Samuels (Santa Ana, CA: Freeland Press, 1985), pp. 93-96.

47. Bill Wallace, "The Patrol Specialists—Salesmen with Badges," *San Francisco Chronicle*, 30 July 1984; idem, "Unique San Francisco Private Cops and How They Operate," ibid.; Christine Dorffi, "San Francisco's Hired Guns," *Reason*, Aug. 1979, pp. 26-29, 33.

48. Becker, "Place of Private Police in Society," p. 444.

49. Hess and Wrobleski, *Introduction to Private Security*, p. 9.

50. T. A. Critchley, *A History of Police in England and Wales* (London: Constable, 1967, 1978), pp. 29, 42.

51. Conversation with Associate Attorney General Eddie Caldwell, Mar. 1984.

4

The County Sheriff as a Distinctive Policing Modality

David N. Falcone and
L. Edward Wells

Most of what we read about policing, and certainly the typical high-profile police story in the national news, focuses on urban police departments—such as Los Angeles's and New York's. In contrast, the county sheriff is often overlooked, by both media and scholars. Sheriff's departments account for about 20 percent of all police agencies and sworn police employees in the United States. They play a major role in providing police services in some states and regions (sometimes the major role, especially in rural areas). In this article, Falcone and Wells discuss the unique role played by sheriffs as well as the historical, legal, and political contexts within which they operate. This article should encourage you to include sheriffs whenever you are thinking about American policing and its issues and problems.

Introduction

In many ways, discussion of policing is generally approached as "all of one cloth," despite significant variations in the types and locations of agencies where it is carried out. Distinctions are sometimes noted between public and private policing, and between federal, state and local policing. However, a general proposition seems to be that:

- at its core, policing is policing, in whatever agency or location it exists; and

- the prototype for this activity is the modern city police department.

James Q. Wilson's (1968) typology of police departments is well known, but deals entirely with variations among urban municipal police agencies. A perusal of contemporary textbooks on policing (e.g. Berg, 1992; Roberg and Kuykendall, 1990; Schultz and Beckman, 1992; Walker, 1992) documents the ubiquitous presence of the urban municipal policing orientation.[1] It seems that little systematic attention, in either scholarly research or textbooks, has been given to the difference between county and municipal modes of policing. Rather, the central tendency is to consider policing types largely as variations on the same basic process (urban municipal policing), only incidentally noting the variations in other settings and contexts.

Purpose

This paper argues that county-level policing, accomplished mainly through the office of the county sheriff, represents an historically different mode of policing that needs to be distinguished more clearly from municipal policing. It has a distinct evolution within American policing that plausibly has led to different community functions and different organizational features, when compared with conventional municipal police departments. This paper examines possible differences between municipal and county-level policing along several analytical dimensions—e.g. historical, political, geographical, functional, organizational and regional variations— and suggests how research might be focused to document and explicate these differences.

To date, surprisingly little empirical research or published documentation exists to describe the specific form of the modern sheriff's office across the US. As with textbooks, the research literature focuses almost entirely on municipal police operations and organizations, with only a few brief references to county-level events. In developing the present discussion, we have relied on several basic sources that are useful but also sketchy and generally out of date, with the exception of Struckoff (1994). These include: a classic essay on the sheriff by Lee Brown

(1978), a mimeographed report issued by the National Sheriffs' Association based on a survey of US sheriffs' offices in the late 1970s (National Sheriffs' Association, 1979), a study of metropolitan police agencies by Ostrom et al. (1978), brief statistical reports on Law Enforcement Management and Administrative Statistics (LEMAS) (1990) from the Bureau of Justice Statistics (Reaves, 1990a, 1990b), and statistical summaries of law enforcement personnel reported in the Uniform Crime Reports (FBI, 1994). In addition, we have drawn on quantitative data from the most recent Directory of Law Enforcement Agencies (Bureau of Justice Statistics, 1987) and qualitative data from almost 200 personal and telephone interviews of sheriffs spread across the United States. The latter were done as part of two recent studies of policing practices in the Midwest (Falcone and Wells, 1993) and in rural and small town areas nationally (Weisheit et al., 1994a). Given the scarcity of systematic research and extensive empirical data on sheriffs, our discussion will yield *empirically derived*, but *not quantitatively verified*, generalizations about patterns, variations and differences among sheriffs' offices and police departments. Empirical testing of these hypotheses will require additional studies and data collections that are not yet available.

Historical Legacy of the Sheriff

The modern-day American sheriff's office traces its historical antecedents to tenth century England and the "shire-reeve", a local political figure, who was appointed to serve and protect the King's interests in the shire. These duties included: maintenance of community order, supervision of local military units (militia), the collection of taxes, and the custody of accused persons (National Sheriffs' Association, 1979; Sattler, 1992). Initially the shire-reeve was chosen from local nobility within the shire; however, after the Norman invasion in 1066 the sheriff was imposed on the local community as an outside administrator.

The office of the sheriff and its attendant functions was transported and extended to the Crown colonies in America. The estimated 3,100 county sheriffs in the United States today (Reaves, 1990b) trace the historical roots of their office in the new world to the mid-1600s, when many of the counties, which later became part of the original colonies, were incorporated under royal imprimatur. In fact, the origins of county-level government in America are linked with the Massachusetts Bay Colony (Lanoie, 1993). Although the functions, responsibilities and mandates associated with the sheriff's office have changed, and substantial regional differences across parts of the US have evolved, many sheriffs' offices today carry out nearly the same range of tasks and services that were required three centuries ago.

Political Dimensions

One very notable feature of the county sheriff in the United States is the basis for political authority and legal powers of this office. Originally set up on the English system where the sheriff's mandate to "maintain the peace" originated with the Crown and not the local community, the sheriff's office in the US was changed during the seventeenth and eighteenth centuries to a directly elective office. Making the sheriff elective rendered the office accountable directly to the local community rather than to a distant executive. Thus, it asserted political autonomy for the colonies. In contrast to its English counterpart, this shift in the political base of authority has ensured the continued importance of the sheriff's office for modern policing in the United States. In England, by virtue of its political ties to the monarchy, the office of the "high sheriff" has devolved into a weak, mostly symbolic position with only ceremonial powers and no real peacekeeping responsibilities (Sattler, 1992).

Because of its distinctive historical evolution, the legal authority of the sheriff diverges both in content and scope from that of local police chiefs. One significant source of difference is the fact that the sheriff, in 35 of the 50 states, is a constitutional office, in contrast to other policing agencies that are statutory or administrative creations (National Sheriffs' Association, 1979:28). As a *constitutional* creation, the sheriff's office is legally stipulated in the charter document for the state, and is authorized at the state level and legally prior to county-level legislation. This means that the form or function of the office may not be changed directly or readily by legislative or executive decisions, but rather only through constitutional amendment. Where the sheriff's office is constitutionally mandated, it cannot simply be abolished, have its powers and responsibilities reduced, or have its personnel decisions made by county boards or commissioners. Although they nominally may control the budget for the sheriff's office, county or state executives cannot dictate sheriff's office policy since they lack direct political authority over the sheriff. A notable (but infrequent) exception to this constitutional mandate occurs in "home-rule" counties. These involve a few highly urbanized counties (usually over one million in population) which are allowed by charter to formulate their own policies and offices that would otherwise be at variance with state statutes or constitutional requirements (Statsky, 1985).

Moreover, the sheriff is described formally as an *office* rather than a department—a commonly blurred distinction that has constitutional and legal dimensions. As J.M. Brown (1993:9) has noted (drawing from *Black's Law Dictionary*), an office involves "a right, and correspondent duty to exercise a public trust. . . . In the constitutional sense, the term implies an authority to exercise some portion of the sovereign power, either in making, executing, or administering the laws." In contrast, a department usually refers to a division within the executive branch of the government—a subordinate agency or branch within governmental administration. As an office, in most states the sheriff is an independent entity within county government, with separately defined responsibilities and powers. As a department, its powers and duties would be determined by the administrative branch under which it is authorized. The former condition provides a measure of administrative and political autonomy from other offices and executives of local government. It also means that oversight of the operations of the sheriff's office must occur through different processes compared with local police departments which are formally

under the executive purview of a city administrator or committee—e.g. a mayor, police commission, or city board. In these terms, the structure of accountability is formally changed by the different bases for legal authority and organizational responsibility.

An additional (and related) source of difference is that the sheriff is an *elective* office, selected by popular election, either partisan or nonpartisan, in all but two states (Rhode Island and Hawaii). On one hand, this expresses the independence of the sheriff from other political offices or executives within local governmental structure. On the other hand, it means that the sheriff is subject directly to the approval of the community and to the power of public opinion. Since terms of office are often fairly short—usually two or four years—the sheriff is dependent on good relationships with voting members of the community who may remove him/her from office at the next available election. In these terms, the sheriff is less insulated from the public than the police chief, lacking the administrative buffer from the general public that most municipal departments have in the mayor, police commission, or city board who oversee them and appoint their chief executive. The ostensible effect of direct election will be that the sheriff's office is more overtly political in a popular sense (i.e. based in popular appeal and voter approval) while being less political in a local governmental sense (i.e. based in local political organizations and influence structures).

Popular election also means that the sheriff might not necessarily be an experienced police professional or executive. According to the NSA survey in the late 1970s (National Sheriffs' Association, 1979), the office of sheriff in most states has no specific requirements regarding training or experience in policing. Many states explicitly exempt county sheriffs from their state-mandated training standards for law enforcement personnel (NSA, 1979:38), even though their deputies are covered, along with municipal police supervisors. Generally, the requirements for sheriff's candidates are comparable to other elective offices within the various states. In some instances of very large, highly urbanized counties, the sheriff may be more of a political figure, with the day-to-day management of office responsibilities (e.g. law enforcement, court services, jail operation) delegated to an appointed "undersheriff" who is an experienced police or correctional administrator. However, we note that for the vast majority of sheriffs' offices in the US, which are located in less urban counties, the sheriff is the actual administrator of the activities of the office. Moreover, a large majority of sheriffs enter the office with substantial backgrounds in law enforcement, jail administration and related fields (NSA, 1979).

Does the popular election of county sheriffs make a real and important difference in how county-level policing is organized and accomplished (in contrast to municipal agencies with appointed police chiefs)? We note that there has been some recent debate about the functional effect (and desirability) of electing police executives. Some proponents of community-oriented policing or problem-oriented policing (e.g. Goldstein, 1990) have argued this would result in stronger police community identifications, reflecting the more direct community influence over police administration. Comparing county sheriffs with police chiefs in the same areas provides a way to test this hypothesis; however, the lack of research on county sheriffs means there are no empirical data from which to make such comparisons systematically. Our interview data from sheriffs and police chiefs in less urbanized areas have been consistent with this hypothesis, but these are nonquantitative, subjective conclusions based on a nonrandom sample of police agencies in the US. Informed debate and policy decisions require a better research database which includes more systematic coverage of county sheriffs' offices and operations.

By virtue of its historical evolution, the legal responsibility and authority of the sheriff are somewhat different from those of local police chiefs, being broader in the range of activities covered and the scope of the legal authority. As the officer charged with maintaining the lawful order and peace of the county, the sheriff is responsible not only for law enforcement (of criminal and traffic laws), but also for providing support services and protection to the county court, for maintaining the county jail and correctional facilities, and (in some states) for collecting many county taxes and fees. By contrast, municipal police departments deal only with the first of these responsibilities. Of special note is that the sheriff also has extensive civil law powers and responsibilities. For instance, the sheriff can make *civil arrests* (with or without warrants) for detaining persons who have not committed any crime but may be a threat to the public order of the community or to themselves—e.g. mentally disordered persons. The sheriff is responsible for enforcement of all civil writs, as well as criminal laws and warrants. The issue of how much of an effect this structural feature of the sheriff's office has on the actual content of county-level policing is again an open concern. While the sheriff's office has formally broader legal powers than the municipal police department, whether these civil powers actually translate into measurable differences in policing behaviors, attitudes, or outcomes, as Goldstein (1990) has suggested in advocating problem-oriented policing, remains a matter of speculation. We lack the empirical studies of policing practices of deputy sheriffs that would allow a systematic comparison and evaluation of such differences.

The legal jurisdiction of the sheriff is also broader geographically than that of the municipal police chief, with several notable implications. For one, the sheriff's jurisdiction is spread out over a larger physical area; thus, the office's resources will be spread thinner across more space and the deputies will be acting over much greater distances. Single-officer patrols operating with no backups nearby will be common, and response times will be much longer (where duty beats are defined in miles rather than city blocks). This is especially true in Western states which contain fewer and much larger county divisions. Indeed, average counties in some Western states (e.g. Arizona) are larger in area than some Eastern states (e.g. most New England states).

A second implication is the redundancy of authority across governmental units. By law, the sheriff's jurisdiction generally includes everything within the county. The overlapping jurisdictions with municipalities within the county have clear potential for political conflicts and legal ambiguities. A few highly urban states have tried to reduce this redundancy by reducing the policing authority and jurisdiction of the county sheriff. However, this is not a common, nor obviously successful, solution given the constitutional basis for the sheriff's office. In actual practice, sheriff's agencies limit ordinary policing services to areas of the county that are outside of incorporated municipalities. Where needed, the sheriff's office may provide some additional police services to municipalities in the county; however, this is accomplished through cooperative agreements, both formal and informal, as well as through contracts. For instance, the sheriff's office may contract out policing services (e.g. patrol, investigation, communications, lockups) to small municipalities that do not have full-function police agencies, or may provide policing part-time to municipalities without full-time departments. This pattern is well documented for metropolitan counties by Ostrom et al. (1978). A recent study of rural policing by Weisheit et al. (1994a) shows that it is even more common (albeit less formalized) in nonmetropolitan counties where personnel and resources are stretched even more by large distances and small budgets.

Funding sources for the sheriff's office represents an additional point of potential difference from municipal police agencies. As a result of historical development, monetary compensation for the sheriff has often come from the collection of fees for services provided—e.g. execution of writs; collection of delinquent taxes and fines; sale of licenses and permits; housing prisoners in the county jail; serving court notices, summons and subpoenas; carrying out foreclosures, seizures and evictions; holding sheriff's auctions of county-seized property. This compensation included both payment of the sheriff's salary as well as funding for operation of the sheriff's office. Reliance on fee compensation has diminished greatly in the past several decades, both in the number of states who retain it in some form, as well as in the degree to which retaining states rely on this funding source for sheriffs' office budgets. However, while we lack current data to document this quantitatively, a few southern states continue to use the fee compensation system substantially for funding county government, including the sheriff's office (National Sheriffs' Association, 1979).

Functional Dimensions

By virtue of its historical role as the chief office charged with "keeping the king's peace", the sheriff traditionally handled a wide array of duties and legally exercised a broad range of powers. Correspondingly, the contemporary sheriff has evolved into a multi-purpose office, characterized by a broader and more diverse assortment of legal responsibilities than those associated with local policing. In most states, the sheriff is responsible for providing any (or all) of the following:

1. criminal law enforcement and other general police services;

2. correctional services, involving the transportation of prisoners and the management of the county jail;

3. the processing of judicial writs and court orders, both criminal and civil;

4. security of the court via bailiffs;

5. miscellaneous services, such as the transportation and commitment of the mentally ill;

6. seizure of property claimed by the county;

7. collection of county fees and taxes; and

8. sale of licenses and permits; plus other services that do not fall neatly under the statutory responsibilities of other law enforcement or social service agencies.[2]

In most states, sheriffs are correctional/custodial officers of the county jail. (Since little or no correctional programs are provided at the county jail level, perhaps custodial is a more descriptive word choice.) In many small rural sheriffs' offices there is no distinction between "road deputies" and "jailers." Both duties are carried out by generalists who are responsible for both functions. In moderately large county sheriffs' offices a more discernable division of duties emerges.

Road deputies (commissioned/sworn officers) provide general police/law enforcement services to the county, while jailers are responsible for the security of county jail inmates. Jailers see to it that prisoners are transported to the trial court (often in the same building) for court appearances, while road deputies transport convicted felony prisoners to state correctional facilities—a duty municipal officers *never* experience.

In relatively small sheriffs' offices, generalist road deputies may find that a large portion of their shifts is taken up with the processing of court writs, either criminal or civil. Since the business of the court involves more civil dealings than criminal, deputies serve more civil than criminal papers, leaving little time for proactive criminal law enforcement that may be favored by their municipal counterparts. In larger, more urbanized sheriffs' offices the processing of civil writs is the sole responsibility of "process servers." These individuals frequently are civilians who are not commissioned/sworn officers or who do not actually function as sworn officers (although they may be commissioned "on paper"). In fact, sheriffs' offices in some urbanized counties formally divide their organizations into separate criminal and civil divisions. This division not only mandates a clear delineation of responsibilities and tasks, but it may also create an anomalous, Siamese twin organizational entity. This distinction releases the road deputy to replicate more closely the duties and tasks of the municipal patrol officer and frequently seems to be a step toward the creation (in home-rule counties) of a semi-autonomous "sheriff's police department," which is administered under but operationally separate from the county sheriff's office.

As an officer of the court, the sheriff's office is the sole policing agency charged with the duty of enforcing the orders of the court and the responsibility of maintaining the security and decorum of the court and courthouse. In small rural sheriffs' agencies this is accomplished by the sheriff him/herself or by a deputy who is assigned that duty when the circuit judge makes his/her monthly appearance. In areas with greater population densities and corresponding court activities, where the court sits every working day, a separate bailiff's division is established. These individuals usually are commissioned officers (deputies) who do not function as road officers; they are considered law enforcement specialists. Still, under other arrangements, they are civilians who function virtually as security officers in the courthouse. In many instances they are not authorized to carry firearms. As is the case in many of the large urbanized counties, this division is managed by a separate administrator, freeing the sheriff from the mechanics of administering this specialized division within the sheriff's office.[3]

What does the presence of such functional diversity mean for the contrast between the county sheriff's office and the local police department? First, it means that the sheriff's attention, time and energies are more divided across multiple and distinct sets of administrative concerns—e.g. law enforcement, court services, jail management and fee collections. These will compete for scarce resources, and the resolution of such goal conflicts will affect how the sheriff sets priorities and policies in ways different from the local police chief. Even though the public image of the sheriff's office may be based mostly on law-enforcement activities, the sheriff cannot afford to concentrate on that task. The funding of the office may depend heavily on doing other tasks that generate important revenues for the county (such as serving court writs and warrants or collecting taxes and license fees) or which involve substantial legal liabilities to the sheriff and the county (such as holding unconvicted defendants in jail pretrial).

A second implication of the diversity of the sheriff's responsibilities is that there may be even greater differentiation in organizational structure between small and large sheriffs' offices than occurs for municipal police departments. The processes will be parallel: officers in small agencies are generalists, while larger organizations have increasingly complex divisions-of-labor and structures. The increased specialization partitions different concerns of policing into separate divisions or bureaus within the agency, where increased segmentation of officers' tasks is accomplished.

At the top end of department size, large police organizations probably have comparable levels of specialization found in sheriffs' offices and local police departments, particularly when very large sheriffs' offices create separate sheriffs' police departments for law enforcement. For small departments, however, the duties of sheriffs' deputies will be much more generalized, being called on to cover the whole gamut of sheriff's office responsibilities, much wider than municipal police officers are expected to do. That is, for small municipal police departments, "generalized duty" means "patrol". For small sheriffs' departments, it means patrol plus jail guard plus process server plus tax collector. Thus, the gap in specialization and segmentation between small and large agencies would seem to be much greater for county sheriffs' offices than for municipal police departments, reflecting a greater functional division and differentiation in professional status within very large sheriffs' offices.

A separate, yet closely related, issue concerns police training requirements and practices. Although sheriffs' deputies provide a much wider range of services than ordinary municipal patrol officers, they are trained under the same state-approved basic curriculum as other officers who function in a much more limited sphere. The sheriff's additional generalist duties (not considered part of the law enforcement mission of police) place the deputy sheriff in a perilous situation, since the state-mandated training does not provide the deputy sheriff with the knowledge necessary either to render needed services or to avoid civil litigation for inadequate performance. For example, available training does not address such issues as the limits regarding the use of force when executing civil writs as opposed to criminal writs (which are explained clearly at the academy). We note that this issue was mentioned repeatedly in our interviews with sheriffs in every state (Weisheit et al., 1994a). While a few states require some additional training for deputies in civil process, the sheriffs in those states indicated that it provides only the barest rudiments for performing such duties.

Geographic Dimensions

While generally associated with county-level government, some sheriffs provide services for independent cities; however, this occurs less than 1 percent of the time (Reaves, 1990b). The geographic area of jurisdiction for most sheriffs is the whole county or parish, but it is the unincorporated areas within those counties/parishes that are of special concern to sheriffs. Unincorporated areas would otherwise be without police coverage if it were not for the sheriff's office, since as a general rule municipal police agencies are responsible for providing police services only within their incorporated municipal limits.[4]

As a county-wide police agency, the sheriff's office/department holds the potential for coordinating police efforts throughout the county. In fact, in rural settings the sheriff's office/department is seen as not only a coordinating agency but as a higher law enforcement authority with better trained criminal investigators and technicians (most of whom are generalist officers) than municipal officers on small rural police agencies. In many cases, the latter are not full time or do not provide 24-hour coverage. Thus, the sheriff's deputies provide services, on request, inside the corporate limits of municipalities who are within the county.

Mutual aid is another area where the jurisdiction of the sheriff comes into play. Thus, no special legal issues arise when the sheriff is called to assist any police agency within the sheriff's home county. When police agencies outside the sheriff's home county request assistance, the jurisdictional issue can be raised. However, like other law enforcement agencies, the sheriff can enter into legal contracts to render aid on request and assume legal jurisdiction, even when outside the county limits. The earlier study by Ostrom et al. (1978) documented the importance of such interagency arrangements and overlapping responsibilities. However, more recent research suggests that a formalized approach to the mutual aid problem is seldom the approach of choice. Sheriffs across the United States commonly assist and supplement one another, even across state lines, without the benefit of contract, under informally understood arrangements (Weisheit et al., 1993). In the last few years, this practice has become even more important for policing in rural areas as state police and highway patrol agencies—who traditionally provided wide-area coverage and coordination, especially of major crime incidents—have been reduced in size and function across many states. Indeed, some states have recently abolished their state bureaus of investigation, merging them into their general service state police agencies, while simultaneously downsizing the general agency.

The possibility of an inverse or "zero sum" relation between the jurisdictions of the county sheriff's office and the state police/highway patrol is a perennial political issue in many states, reflecting an inherent tension between police agencies at these two levels. One plausible hypothesis is that as the jurisdiction of agencies at one level increases, the responsibilities and legal authority of the agencies at the other level will correspondingly diminish. While there are no empirical data to document this hypothesis specifically, our qualitative study of sheriffs' offices across the US (Weisheit et al., 1994a) suggests that where the state police maintain broad jurisdiction over areas traditionally policed by more local agencies, the sheriff's office generally seems to defer and minimizes its coverage to avoid conflict.

Finally, since the county sheriff generally focuses on providing police/law enforcement services to the unincorporated areas of the county, a distinctly rural dimension is associated with his/her work. This is true even in reasonably urbanized counties, since the sheriff has sole responsibility for police services in areas of the county outside the incorporated city limits. In more rural areas, especially the West, counties are mostly unincorporated, and their sheer size compounds the difficulty encountered in delivering, prompt police services often expected, even demanded, in urban areas. As noted earlier, the larger geographic areas and sparser coverages in such rural areas means that response times for deputy sheriffs may necessarily be measurable in hours or quarter hours, rather than in minutes as occurs in municipal departments.

Organizational Dimensions

The preceding sections noted features in the historical and political development of the county sheriff that distinguish it from municipal and local police departments. How much do these features and developments affect the way that policing is done in sheriffs' offices compared with police departments? Several organizational themes stand out as interesting points of comparison and divergence.

One point concerns the *openness* of the policing agency as a social system—i.e. the extent to which information and influence flow across the boundaries between the police organization and its outside social-political environment. Because sheriffs are popularly elected and thus more dependent on maintaining public approval, we expect that the sheriffs' office will constitute substantially more of an "open system" than will traditional police departments with respect to the community in which it serves. This reflects the differing political bases on which the agencies are maintained. Arguably, sheriffs are more directly dependent on maintaining good exchanges and ongoing relationships with members of the community they serve. Sheriffs who seek to insulate their office from public accessibility through bureaucratic or organizational buffers (as routinely occurs for police departments) may not remain in office very long. This condition of political answerability supports open communication between the office and the community, requiring substantial amounts of interaction which goes beyond the occasional public relations campaign. There are no quantitative empirical data to verify this hypothesis, but qualitative interview data seem to strongly confirm it.

We note that sheriffs' offices in a few, very large, metropolitan counties (such as Los Angeles county in California or Cook County in Illinois), which are highly bureaucratized organizations, seem to be distinct (and rare) exceptions to this pattern. Such sheriffs' offices are anomalies in many ways from the traditional picture of the sheriff's office as it commonly exists in most counties. By virtue of their substantial sizes, their location in highly urbanized areas, and their special legal-political status as charter county governments, they have operational procedures and organizational structures more like large urban, paramilitarized police departments. Frequently they are explicitly renamed "county police" departments and have an appointed chief-of-police as their chief administrator, features which highlight their anomalous organizational makeup.

At the same time, employees of the sheriff's office are similarly dependent on the sheriff's reelection, since they "serve at the sheriff's pleasure" in many jurisdictions (as purely appointive—in some cases, patronage—positions, rather than under a civil service or merit arrangement). According to the LEMAS survey (Reaves, 1990), slightly less than half of the large sheriffs' offices in the US (those with over 100 sworn officers) have merit board procedures for personnel decisions; the majority rely on discretionary administrative appointments. This pattern will be even stronger for smaller, less bureaucratized departments (which comprise 90% of sheriffs' offices in the US). Thus, a new person in the sheriff's position often results in a new set of appointed deputies and supervisors in the ranks of the sheriff's office. In these terms, the personnel in a sheriff's office seem to have a more symbiotic relationship with the sheriff than municipal police officers will with their chiefs. Indeed, the bureaucratic paramilitary structure of municipal police organizations often seems to build in a structural antagonism that ensures a natural alienation of officers from administrators.

Another indicator of the openness or accessibility found in the sheriff's office relates to the use of part-time reserve or auxiliary officers. Many urban and suburban municipal police agencies find these adjuncts to be little more than a police headache (Germann, et al., 1982), while sheriffs' offices generally find them to be a valuable asset, as over a quarter-million are used nationally by sheriffs' organizations (Burden, 1993). Unsworn volunteers constitute a conduit for communication and community relations. They are almost always used for non-law enforcement tasks, such as search and rescue or civil defense, where state-mandated certification is not required. Sworn part-time or reserve officers are perceived by sheriffs as more than part-time officers. They function as part of an integral and ongoing community relations program (Francis, 1993). As a general rule, sworn reserve officers are used to augment regular services and perform general patrol tasks. In addition, participation by community members in sheriffs' posses is an historically rooted, but still used, practice in some states to supplement sworn personnel and to maintain organizational involvement of members of the community (Donahue, 1994).

For these reasons, the interest of the sheriff's office in maintaining an open flow of information with the community is fairly strong throughout the entire agency instead of merely in one specialized department charged with handling public relations. This seems to be expressed visibly in the way that the sheriff's office is more accessible to enquiries and calls from the outside community. For example, during the course of two research projects on police practices, we have called hundreds of municipal police departments and county sheriffs' offices. Calls to county sheriffs' offices generally reached the sheriff personally on the first or second call; when they were not available, callbacks usually occurred shortly thereafter. In stark contrast, calls to municipal departments in the same counties have often taken repeated attempts before reaching the police chief, and requests for callbacks were commonly ignored. This generally involved going through several levels of intermediaries and gatekeepers before finally reaching the chief; in some cases final contact was never made. To cite a representative experience: the sheriff of one of the most populous, urbanized counties in the US, Cook County, Illinois, answered our first phone call. The Superintendent of Police for Chicago, the largest city within Cook County, was never reached even after several dozen phone calls and callback messages. This same pattern of accessibility was duplicated in numerous other counties and cities in other states.

A second organizational theme could be adherence to the traditional military model for policing, along with all its symbolic and organizational trappings. The sheriff's office displays considerably less affinity for the strong military model commonly associated with modern policing and derived from the development of the municipal police force for Sir Robert Peel (Walker, 1992). We suggest that the sheriff's office corresponds more closely, both historically and in its modern operation, to a looser militia model that differs in key points from the traditional military (or paramilitary) model. The latter is based on the idea of a professional army, recruited for military ability rather than local residency, trained and organized for warfare, and organized into an impersonal, rule-bound, rank-ordered closed organization. In contrast to a professional, rigidly organized army that is detached from the community it regulates, the idea of a militia represents a group organized out of and by the community for its internal protection. Mahon's (1983) definitive history of the militia and National Guard in the US documents that the militia involved small, locally-based units that were organized effectively around their leaders, who were elected Captains from within their communities. Thus, the militia was strongly rooted in and accountable to the locality (i.e. county or township) being served. Their strong local identifications were often expressed by distinctive, colorful uniforms clearly distinguishing each from the militia for other counties. Mahon also notes that the operation of each militia company was strongly influenced by the abilities and charisma of the elected Captain, who was responsible for maintaining the company's organization and efficacy. Loss of the Captain usually meant dissolution of that company. That description—which parallels our earlier discussion of the county sheriff's office—stands in strong contrast to the professional, detached, bureaucratic "army of occupation" model that characterizes the municipal police departments in many large cities.

As a result of adhering less strictly to the military model, the sheriff's office seems less rigid than the urban municipal police organization in its appearance, procedures and methods of internal operation. This allows for greater flexibility and speed of reaction to local demands. Further, the sheriff's organi-

zation acknowledges overtly the existence of discretion and a greater latitude of discretionary authority of its officers than the municipal model. Low-level discretion and flexibility are inherent in the job of policing, but that is not readily acknowledged in the urban municipal agency (Brown, 1981; Mastrofski et al., 1987). Admission by administrators of endemic low-level discretion would cast doubt on the utility of the professional paramilitary model typified in most large municipal departments.

Readily apparent examples of this less bureaucratized/militarized organizational model include the option of taking the service vehicle home, as well as not being required to appear daily for pre-service roll call and the attendant inspection of uniforms and equipment. None of these latter activities would serve to advance the mission of this more informal organizational entity. And, since the sheriff's office is not bound by either a history or tradition of strict military custom, these activities are not viewed as functional or even ceremonial.

Our interviews affirmed that the sheriff's office is generally more personalistic in the way in which tasks are accomplished and in the way in which the office is organized. For example, the deputies and civilian employees tend to work "for the sheriff" rather than for the organization *per se*. This makes the services that sheriff's employees render less organizational in the sense of functioning within an impersonal, rule bound, hierarchical order. A solid example of this orientation was clear in the way in which the business cards of one sheriff's office which we visited presented its employees. The business card reads: "This card will introduce Deputy _____ representing Sheriff _____ of _____ County".

By virtue of its organizational structure and political context, there is less distance and impersonal separation between the sheriff's office and the community it serves. In most offices, the sheriff's deputies are required to live in the community where they serve. According to the 1990 Law Enforcement Management and Administrative Statistics survey (Reaves, 1990a; 1990b), 87 percent of sheriffs require deputies to be residents of their legal jurisdiction, while just under 50 percent of municipal police make such requirements of their officers. Causing the officers to have roots in the community makes it more difficult for members of the sheriff's office to become an army of occupation, since they function more as a group of defenders selected to serve from within the community. In contrast, municipal police officers (especially in large urban areas) are recruited based on their professional credentials rather than their area of residence. Most will be recruited from outside the municipality being served. Professional chiefs of police are commonly selected through a national search process, while sheriffs are always elected from among local candidates.

Sheriffs' organizations seem to place less emphasis on extensive military symbolism. Consistent with the militia model, these trappings are of far less importance symbolically to the value system of the members and the mission of the organization. Thus, one frequently finds sheriffs' organizations to have a far less formal and military orientation especially in the dress code of its members. Far more employees wear civilian clothing and the uniform does not resemble the military. In fact, military ranks above captain are seldom found; they are given nonmilitary names like chief deputy, undersheriff and assistant sheriff.

Few sheriffs' agencies even have the traditional items associated with warfare, such as the "war room" where strategy and tactics are formulated during times of "combative encounters" with the general public; these are nearly always found in the large municipal departments and state police organizations. Few sheriffs' organizations have a special room designed for the purpose of securing high-tech weaponry. These "arsenals" are found in nearly all but the very smallest municipal departments and state police agencies.

Because of less emphasis on rigid, oppositional hierarchy, we might predict that sheriffs' offices will display less tendency toward both unionization and implementation of formal collective bargaining as an impersonal, rationalized procedure for the management of employees. LEMAS data (Reaves, 1990a; 1990b) show that about 46 percent of the officers in county sheriffs' offices have a

collective bargaining apparatus available; moreover, most of these work for a few large urban county "police departments". In comparison, municipal police officers have collective arrangements available approximately 72 percent of the time. While only 11 percent of all sheriffs' employees are represented by police associations, nearly 36 percent of all municipal employees are affiliated with a police association. These police associations are, generally, police athletic and benevolent associations that function as unions.

Lower adherence of sheriffs' offices to a strong military-like organization may also be demonstrated by a greater tendency toward civilianization of many operations within the organization. For example, according to the Uniform Crime Reports (FBI, 1994), 36 percent of all full-time employees of county-level policing agencies are civilians. In comparison, for municipal police agencies, only 22 percent of full-time employees are civilians. By virtue of being more open to the community and less committed to a strong military model (which is structurally suspicious of outsiders), the sheriff's office seems to display greater willingness and interest in civilianizing non-law enforcement tasks. That is, there seems to be a greater tendency to "farm out" to civilians who serve from "outside the ranks" those tasks not requiring a sworn deputy. Interestingly, the degree of civilianization in rural sheriffs' offices (which have little organizational division of labor) is about the same as in larger urban sheriffs' offices (with much greater differentiation of functions). At the same time, civilian employees are allowed to remain civilians (e.g. to wear ordinary civilian clothing) rather than act as mock officers (e.g. wearing police uniforms without insignia or rank).

Organizational Models of Sheriffs' Offices

According to Lee Brown, four clearly recognizable yet divergent sheriffs' organizational models have emerged throughout the various states. The "full-service model" carries out law enforcement, judicial and correctional duties. The "law enforcement model" (Multnomah County, Oregon) carries out only law enforcement duties, with other duties assumed by separate civil process and correctional agencies. The "civil-judicial model" involves only court-related duties (counties in Connecticut and Rhode Island). Finally, the "correctional-judicial model"(San Francisco County) involves all functions except law enforcement (Brown,1978).

Regional Variations and Local Exceptions

The preceding pages have discussed the office of the sheriff as if it were a single uniform organization. They offer a description of "central tendencies" for policing in counties compared to municipalities, and they ignore local variations in the structure of the office. In fact, the form and content of specific sheriffs' offices vary widely both between states and between counties within the same state. In these terms, it is important to note variations in and exceptions to the ideal-typical description provided above.

First, we suggest that the divergences noted between county-level and municipal-level police agencies will vary according to the sizes of police organizations involved. Specifically, the county-municipal differences will be greatest among mid-sized agencies—e.g. those with 25–100 sworn officers. For very small agencies, the sheriff's office and the local police department will operate similarly, because small police departments must be general purpose agencies and will correspond more closely to the militia model suggested earlier, rather than the paramilitary model of urban policing. By virtue of being mostly in small communities where political structures are informal and personalistic, small police departments are more directly accountable to the public, being less insulated from the community by governmental bureaucracy and layers of executive office. Police in such small departments will be more "sheriff-like." In contrast, very large sheriffs' offices become highly segmented and specialized into separate agencies, with law enforcement split off into separate county police departments headed by appointed police chiefs. In such large organizations, the sheriff's office will become, in effect, more

"police-like." Thus, our hypothesis is that the mid-sized organizations will show the greatest differentiation between county- and municipal-level policing. At present, no empirical data are available that would allow us empirically to test or confirm it.

As mentioned earlier in this paper, sheriffs' offices are generally county-level agencies operating with countywide jurisdiction. However, there are those anomalous political arrangements that require some sheriffs to operate under other than the traditional mode, i.e. the full-service model. A clear example of the independent city arrangement where a city does not lie physically within the confines of a county exists in Saint Louis, Missouri. For numerous reasons, peculiar to the political dynamics of that area and not within the scope of this paper, the city of Saint Louis does not lie within Saint Louis County and does not enjoy the services provided for other cities across the country by county government. For that reason, the City of Saint Louis must replicate all county government services including county courts, the county jail, county tax collection and many others. As a result, the city of Saint Louis must maintain its own jail and the judicial services usually associated with the office of the county sheriff. The sheriff of Saint Louis City provides the services normally provided by the county sheriff in other areas of the state and nation. Note that in this instance, it is a department and not an office and is associated with the executive branch of city government. Here the sheriff functions under what Lee P. Brown has classified as the correctional-judicial model, having no law enforcement powers or responsibilities, as police services are adequately provided by the metropolitan police department.

Beyond unique local variations are some interesting regional variations among sheriffs' offices throughout the various states. Painting with a broad brush, our telephone interviews with sheriffs throughout the US suggested the following generalized patterns by regions across the country (Weisheit et al., 1994a).

Counties located within the South, Southwest, and Midwest states generally have full-service sheriff models. This seems explainable functionally as a result of the original economic structure of these areas with a reliance on agriculture. The tremendous distances involved in these rural areas rendered the paramilitary model, developing in the urban areas of the Northeast, of little use. The full-service sheriff's office as the primary provider of law enforcement and other policing services became the logical choice.

Sheriffs in some Northwestern states have limited civil-judicial models which function in a similar capacity to the city sheriff in Saint Louis. This appears to be a function of the fact that state police units generally provide the services otherwise provided by sheriffs in other areas of the country. In the Northeast, with its highly urbanized character, the sheriff's office appears to be experiencing both some functional shrinking and challenge to its legal authority as a full-service model under judicial interpretation of both state law and state constitutions. Therefore, some Northeastern states, e.g. Connecticut and Rhode Island, employ the limited functions inherent in the civil judicial model. Sheriffs in Pennsylvania recently underwent a legal challenge regarding their criminal arrest powers as fully-commissioned state officers; however, the state's highest court affirmed the sheriffs' law enforcement authority (Policaro, 1993).

Conclusion and Discussion

The office of the county sheriff has shown tremendous adaptability and staying power for more than a millennium. From its early emergence in England under Alfred the Great, to its contemporary form in America, attempts to thwart the power of sheriffs, over the course of history and in the main, have proven ineffective. The office has remained one of the most viable policing institutions in the United States. Despite proclamations that this peculiar Anglo-Saxon office is a twentieth century anomaly and predictions that it is a shrinking institution in urban areas that will eventually be reduced to "paper serving" activities, sheriffs' organizations have demonstrated notable resiliency regarding their political underpinnings, structure, modality, mission, and traditionally mandated responsibilities. For example, attempts to radically alter and "professionalize" this county-based police organization through the creation of sheriffs' police have not proven popular.

Because of its wide-ranging duties and responsibilities, the office of sheriff is a necessary and effective general purpose police agency and will most likely continue to be such as long as county-level government exists. Of central importance to policing is the fact that sheriffs' organizations constitute a distinctive policing modality, devoid of many of the trappings and shortcomings of the traditional paramilitary municipal police model. Therefore, sheriffs' agencies may need to be understood and studied under a considerably different conceptual model than the traditional municipal police agency. Sheriffs' organizations appear to be better described, both conceptually and historically, by a "militia" model than by the traditional (para)military model firmly associated with the municipal police agency.

Analyzing and evaluating all police organizations under one homogenous model, based mainly on large, urban, municipal police departments, can lead to a generalized misunderstanding of the organization being studied. This is particularly true considering that most police agencies in the United States are neither large nor urban. Doing so also ignores the over 3,000 county-level agencies that police the largest portion of America's geography. Given the almost complete absence of research on this latter form of policing, it seems reasonable to propose future research that may be more appropriate for alternative modalities of policing. We have suggested that the militia model is a better description of most county sheriffs' organizations. This is proposed as a tentative guide or template for more detailed analyses of county-level police agencies. Future research is needed to determine its validity and utility in differentiating this form of policing from conventional images.

This overview and analysis of the sheriff has raised as many questions as it has settled, implying a considerable and virtually unaddressed research agenda. If we are to more fully understand, evaluate and explain the variations among police organizations found across the national landscape, these questions will need to be addressed more carefully through systematic empirical research. We suggest the following concerns as a prospectus for this research.

1. What are the various forms and functions that characterize county sheriffs' offices across states and geographic areas? How wide are these variations, and can a broad taxonomy or typology be constructed that adequately covers the important differences and dimensions? This calls for an up-to-date compilation of the types of sheriffs' organizations, their legal mandates, and their functional responsibilities along the lines of the National Sheriffs' Association survey in the late 1970s (NSA, 1979).

2. Is policing by county sheriffs' offices meaningfully different from policing by municipal police departments? What actual differences are there in how the agencies are operated and organized in day-to-day practices? Are there observable differences between deputy sheriffs and municipal officers in how policing is routinely carried out?

3. How significant for policing is the civil law power of the sheriff's office? What is the real (practically usable) extent of their civil law authority, and do county sheriffs' deputies actually exercise the option of police power inherent in that authority (e.g. to gain compliance in conflict resolution situations)? How does this authority influence the form and the practice of policing by county sheriffs' officers?

4. What are the relationships (both formal and informal) between county policing, as carried out by sheriffs' organizations and by policing organizations at other (municipal and state) levels? Are there inherent, or at least common, tensions between sheriffs' organizations and police agencies at other levels, especially state police/highway patrol departments, that influence the content of policing activities or impact on their effec-

tiveness? Is there empirical evidence that a zero-sum division of labor or responsibility occurs in many states; as one grows in coverage or duties, does the other invariably shrink?

5. How do sheriffs' organizations differ between rural and urban settings in their organizational structure and in the content or form of their policing activities? Does the militia model suggested here offer a better description and explanation for less urbanized counties (with urban counties following the traditional paramilitary model more)? Or is it broadly applicable for virtually all county sheriffs' organizations, regardless of their demographic context?

6. What is the actual effect of the elective nature of the sheriff's office on the style, content and accountability of the policing function carried out there? Is there empirical evidence that the sheriff operates in a demonstrably different way because of it?

7. What are the political dynamics and conditions that lead to the development of a separate sheriff's police agency within the county sheriffs' offices? Is this a simple matter of organizational environment of the sheriff's office? Are there substantial differences in orientation and behavior between these sheriffs' police departments and the ordinary county sheriffs' offices?

8. What have been the experiences of municipalities that have opted for contract policing with sheriffs' organizations? That is, where local governments have under contractual agreement provided policing services to their communities through the sheriff's office, instead of directly instituting their own municipal departments, do sheriffs' deputies function differently under such arrangements (in terms of policing behaviors and outcomes) than municipal police officers would in these settings? Are the policing services, under these contractual arrangements, notably different in

terms of content or in public satisfaction?

Notes

1. Of the four policing texts sampled, one was entirely silent on the issue of the sheriff, and none of the others dedicated more than a page to this important and uniquely Anglo-American policing institution. Together, out of more than 1,500 pages of text on policing, the four textbooks included a combined total of less than three pages on the county sheriff.

2. Here "policing" refers to a wide range of governmental activities aimed at maintaining the public order of the polity. It includes law enforcement as one component function, but it also includes a number of other order maintenance activities, many of which are positive in nature and service oriented. Examples of this include: proactive, community-oriented patrolling, order maintenance, rendering aid, giving direction, counseling and advising, expediting vehicular traffic, and many other services and activities. Law enforcement entails a much more restricted task, dealing explicitly with a narrow range of activities involving the enforcement of statutory prohibitions and obligations; at a fundamental level, this can be argued to be an exclusively negative function of government.

3. As a limited variation of county-level policing, a sheriff's police department is a legally recognized organizational unit within a sheriff's office, which has as its sole agenda the responsibilities associated with policing and law enforcement—much like a municipal police agency. Sheriff's police are not involved in civil process and are managed by a chief of police appointed by either the sheriff, a sheriff's commission or the county board. Illinois, for example, allows by statute for the creation of a sheriff's police in counties with a population of 1 million or more (Illinois Revised Statutes: 1991). This organizational form occurs very infrequently, since in the example of Illinois, the sole county required and authorized to establish a sheriff's police department is Cook County with nearly half a million inhabitants. The remaining 101 Illinois counties retain the traditional sheriff's office.

4. Through contractual agreements some states allow municipalities to have jurisdiction outside their corporate limits. Alabama, for example, allows municipal police agencies to extend their jurisdiction (known as a police jurisdiction) several miles beyond the limits of the municipality.

References and Further Reading

Berg, B.L. (1992), *Law Enforcement: An Introduction to Police in Society*, Boston: Allyn and Bacon.

Brown, J.M. (1993, March-April), "Sheriff's department versus office of the sheriff", *Sheriff*, p. 9.

Brown, L.P. (1978), "The role of the sheriff", in Cohen, A.W. (Ed.), *The Future of Policing*, Beverly Hills, CA: Sage. pp. 227-228.

Brown, M.K. (1981), *Working the Streets*, New York, NY: Russell Sage Foundation.

Burden, O.P. (1993), "Reserve and auxiliary law enforcement", *Sheriff*, 45(5), 12.

Bureau of Justice Statistics, US Department of Justice (1987), *Directory of Law Enforcement Agencies, 1986* (Computer File), Ann Arbor, MI: Inter-University Consortium for Political and Social Research (distributor).

"Celebrating 1,000 years of the office of the sheriff" (1992), *Sheriff*, 44(3), 10-13.

Donahue, S. (1994, July 20), "Life imitating art, imitating life: Possemania grips Arizona," *Law Enforcement News*, pp. 3, 10.

Falcone, D.N. and Wells, L.E. (1993), *The County Sheriffs' Office: A Distinctive Policing Modality*, Paper presented to the American Society of Criminology meeting, Phoenix, AZ.

Federal Bureau of Investigation (1994), *Uniform Crime Reports: Crime in the United States, 1993*, Washington, DC: US Department of Justice.

Francis, W.M. (1993), "Personnel and staffing issues for reserve officers", *Sheriff*, 5(5), 13.

Garmire, B.L. (1982), *Local Government Police Management* (2nd ed.), Washington, DC: International City Management Association.

Germann, A.C. et al. (1982), *Introduction to Law Enforcement and Criminal Justice* (29th ed.), Springfield, IL: Charles C. Thomas Publisher.

Goldstein, H. (1990), *Problem-oriented Policing*, New York, NY: McGraw-Hill.

Illinois Revised Statutes (1991), chapter 125, section 51.

Lanoie, D.A. (1993), "Preserve the office of sheriff", *Sheriff* 45(2), 10.

Law Enforcement Management and Administrative Statistics (LEMAS, 1990), Data Set US Department of Justice, Bureau of Justice Statistics: Washington, DC.

Mahon, J.K. (1983), *History of the Militia and the National Guard*, New York, NY: Macmillan.

Mastrofski, S.D., Ritti, R.R. and Hoffmaster, D. (1987), "Organizational determinants of police discretion: the case of drinking-driving", *Journal of Criminal Justice*, 15, 387-402.

NSA (National Sheriffs' Association) (1979), *County Law Enforcement: An Assessment of Capabilities and Needs*, National Sheriffs' Association: Washington, DC.

Ostrom, E., Parks, R.B. and Whitaker, G.P. (1978), *Patterns of Metropolitan Policing*, Cambridge, MA: Ballinger.

Policaro, F. Jr. (1993), "Fighting for the office of sheriff", *Sheriff*, 45(3), 5.

Reaves, B.A. (1990a), "State and local police departments, 1990", *Bureau of Justice Statistics Bulletin*, 1-13.

—— (1990b), "Sheriffs' departments 1990", *Bureau of Justice Statistics Bulletin*, 1-12.

Roberg, R.R. and Kuykendall, J. (1990), *Police Organization and Management: Behavior, Theory, and Processes*, Pacific Grove, CA: Brooks/Cole.

Sattler, T. (1992), "The High Sheriff in England Today: The invisible man?", *Sheriff*, 44(4), 20-23, 48.

Schultz, D.O. and Beckman, E. (1992), *Principles of American Law Enforcement and Criminal Justice* (2nd ed.), Placerville, CA: Custom Publishing.

Statsky, W. (1985), *West's Legal Thesaurus/Dictionary: A Resource for the Writer and Computer Researcher*, St. Paul, MN: West Publishing.

Struckhoff, D.R. (1994), *The American Sheriff*, Chicago: Justice Research Institute.

Walker, S. (1992), *The Police in America: An Introduction* (2nd ed.), New York, NY: McGraw-Hill.

Weisheit, R.A., Falcone, D.N. and Wells, L.E. (1993), "Policing in rural areas", National Institute of Justice, unpublished paper presented at the annual meeting of the National Sheriffs' Association at Salt Lake City, UT.

Weisheit, R.A., Wells, L.E. and Falcone, D.N. (1994a), *Crime and Policing in Rural and Small-town America: An Overview of the Issues* (Issues and Practices Monograph), Washington, DC: National Institute of Justice.

—— (1994b), "Community Policing in Small Town and Rural America", *Crime and Delinquency*, 40(4), 549-567.

Wilson, J.Q. (1968), *Varieties of Police Behavior*, Cambridge, MA: Harvard University.

Part II

History and Context

Introduction

Some version of the police is found in virtually every nation in the world today, suggesting that as an institution the police fulfill an indispensable function. Policing has changed over time in all countries, however, and the forms it takes vary substantially from one country to another. This suggests that cultural and political factors, as well as other variables, influence the shape and direction of these fascinating institutions that represent law and order, come to the aid of citizens in danger, and exercise force on behalf of the state.

In the United States, we tend to take for granted the current and basic structural features of our police system: (1) policing is a government, not a private, activity; (2) it is civilian, that is, nonmilitary; (3) via the doctrine of separation of powers, policing is primarily a function of the executive branch of government and officially separate from the legislative and judicial branches; (4) via the doctrine of federalism, police powers are distributed among the federal, state, and local levels of government, with the authority of the federal government, in particular, quite limited; (5) we do not have a national police force with general jurisdiction (federal law enforcement agencies such as the F.B.I. have authority only over specifically identified

federal statutes); (6) our policing system is extremely fragmented, with over 17,000 police agencies, mostly at the local level; and (7) our policing system is surrounded and infused by the rule of law, including the Bill of Rights and decisions of appeals and supreme courts, such that police use of authority is constrained and regulated. One value of examining our own policing history is to discover how and why these and other characteristics of our system came about. And one value of examining policing in other countries is to discover other ideas, systems, and options that we might want to consider adapting to our own situation.

Historical and comparative analyses are tricky endeavors, however. Unless we are careful, we have a tendency to use them selectively and perhaps nostalgically. As one of the articles in this section argues, it is very tempting in this crazy, fast-paced modern world to yearn for a return to "the good old days." We tend to assume that there was less crime in the past (sometime around the 1950s or earlier), things were more orderly, and the police were more friendly and approachable. In fact, American history is full of crime waves and hysteria about immigrants, foreigners, and other threats to the social fabric. Moreover, policing from 1850 to 1950 was definitely more full of discrimination, brutality, corruption, and general dereliction of duty than almost anything we could expose today. And the historical roles of the police in breaking strikes, returning runaway slaves, enforcing segregation, and the like certainly don't conform with everybody's notions of "good old days."

The first reading in this section traces the development of policing in the U.S. and in several other countries. The next two readings focus on specific aspects of police history—the role of Southern slave patrols in the development of American policing, and the history of that most charismatic and mysterious of police figures, the detective. The final reading introduces us to what is by far and away the most popular theme in modern policing—community policing—and then critiques the revisionist version of police history used by some of its most ardent supporters. This piece directly addresses an important question: whether community policing represents a return to earlier values and practices, or a brand new adventure in the evolution of policing. ✦

5

The Development of Modern Police

David H. Bayley

David Bayley is one of today's most respected police scholars. In this article, he presents a sweeping review of police history that has two particularly intriguing features: (1) instead of dwelling exclusively on policing in the United States and England, he traces developments in several corners of the world; and (2) he focuses on how policing came to be a specialized, professionalized, and public function in the modern world. As you read this article, pay close attention to similarities and differences in the histories of policing in various countries. Try to develop an appreciation for insights and ideas from around the world. This point of view is important because many of us, Americans in particular, tend to ignore experiences from other countries, and thus we miss opportunities to learn from those experiences.

Policing in the world today is dominated by agencies that are public, specialized, and professional. Indeed, as far as most people are concerned, these characteristics partially define police and certainly facilitate recognizing them. Police are thought of as being employees of government selected and trained for a career service, whose responsibility is the forceful enforcement of law. This is a restrictive view. . . . Policing may also be done privately and without particular attention to the rationality of its management.

This chapter will examine the emergence of the combination of public agency, relative specialization, and rational management in world policing. In each case, the chronology of development will be described, and factors that seem to have impelled development will be specified. On the basis of the evidence available, theoretical propositions will be constructed about the evolution of modern police. The propositions are offered to prompt further study and especially testing.

The Nature of Public Police

Communities authorize the use of force in regulating internal affairs and even create formal institutions of government and law without developing public police. Police become "public," as I shall use the term, when they are paid and directed by communities acting collectively. Both payment and direction are necessary to distinguish publicness from privateness. Police have been directed by government but paid privately. Before the nineteenth century, constables in England were directed by magistrates appointed by the crown but were paid privately, usually by persons avoiding the duty of obligatory service (Spitzer and Scull 1977). Members of sheriffs' posses, famous in American cowboy movies, were unpaid volunteers organized by official action. They were privately maintained but directed by a government official. (The posse, by the way, is an ancient invention, the word itself an abbreviation of the Latin phrase *posse comitatus*.) On the other hand, governments sometimes use public funds to maintain services that are privately directed. This is rare in policing, though private security guards for public buildings are an example; it is more common in medical care, street maintenance, and sanitation. Insisting that the public status of policing depends upon the nature of both payment and direction limits the number of instances of it that can be found historically, but it avoids the problem of comparing systems that are public in one respect but not in another. Partially public systems can now be clearly designated.[1]

Remembering that an essential element of the definition of police is authorization in the name of a community, how likely is it that a substantial police system will not be public? Wouldn't it be logical to expect that community authorization would bring with it public direction and support? If this were so, then private policing would turn out to be very rare. This is not in fact the case. Many communities, even many states, have relied exclusively on private policing. Up to the sixth century B.C. in Athens, only wronged persons could institute criminal suits; noninvolved persons, including the state, could not do so. The state prosecuted people by its own agency only for a few subversive and sacrilegious offenses (Bonner and Smith 1928, Vol. 2, chap. 11). Though historical evidence is not entirely clear, the executive administration of justice until Solon appears to have been in private hands. Rome maintained public order in a similar fashion under the *Ius Civile* and the Law of the Twelve Tables until the middle of the third century B. C. (Kunkel 1973). Private individuals brought malefactors to magistrates, usually assisted by friends or relatives. Magistrates decided the guilt of an accused and turned the prisoner back to his captors for administration of whatever punishment was allowed by law— including death, slavery, and monetary payment. Until recently, the *jir* of the Tiv tribe in Africa was the community's only public agency for the administration of justice. Like Roman magistrates, they only adjudicated, leaving executive police action to private persons (Bohannan 1957, chap. 10). In all these cases, policing was performed in the sense of physical constraint legitimately applied in a community's name, but not under public auspices.

Generally in feudalism the lawmaking community and the lawenforcing community were distinct. The development of political sovereignty predicated on territory as well as the sentiment of nationality did not automatically lead to the creation of police capacity by the central government. Indeed, the persistence of decentralized authority to maintain public order was sometimes an explicit condition for the creation of a larger political community. Nor did the development of state adjudicative capacity lead to the development of state police forces. European kingdoms in the Middle Ages became "law states" before they became police states (Strayer 1970, p. 61). The conclusion, then, is that communities can authorize the executive enforcement of law without directing or maintaining a police force.

Enforcement of law in England during the early Middle Ages, for example, was carried out by lords with title to land—"thames" in the reigns of Alfred (871-900) and Edgar (959-975)—or nonlandowning people organized into Tythings (ten households) and Hundreds (ten Tythings) in what was known as the Frankpledge system. Although order was maintained in the king's name, offenses being against the "King's Peace," he did not have officials to enforce his own writ (Bloch 1961, chap. 30; Bopp and Schultz 1972, pp. 9-10; Keeton 1975, chap. I; Lee 1901 [1971], chap. I). A similar arrangement existed in France. For instance, according to the charter granted the people of St. Omer by William Count of Normandy in 1127, the lord of the castle, his wife, or his steward had authority to issue warrants for arrest when a crime had been committed. If the suspects were taken within three days, they were turned over to the lord; after that they could be punished by citizens at large. The citizens were not liable for property damage, bodily injury, or death that resulted (Herlihy 1968, pp. 181-184). Executive as well as judicial authority attaching to title to land granted by sovereigns persisted historically until quite recent times. The right of Prussian landowners (*Junkers*) to administer justice was not abolished until 1872, while that of the Russian squirearchy, though attenuated after the emancipation of serfs in 1864, lasted until the 1918 revolution (Florinsky 1953, p. 572; Holborn 1969, p. 401). In India and China the police power of landowners fluctuated with the strength of empires from time immemorial until well into the nineteenth and twentieth centuries, respectively.

The conclusion, then, is that communities can authorize the executive enforcement of law without directing or maintaining a police force. But this raises a crucial conceptual point. Is it appropriate to call feudal landowners who maintain order *private* as opposed to *public* functionaries? Since membership groups fit within one another, how does one know which auspices are public? If manors are considered the primary effective unit of government during the medieval period in Europe, then retainers like *senchals*, *prevots*, knights, and bailiffs should be considered public police officials, although they certainly did not act in a police capacity all the time.

Publicness is easily determined after the establishment of states. But associating publicness only with state political communities is too restrictive. States are not the only important human communities where a distinction can intelligently be made between collective and noncollective instrumentalities. All sorts of communities, including many that are not defined in terms of territory— like tribes, churches, and castes—can have government in the sense of authority to act for a community. Recognition of the separate roles of rulers and ruled exists in small and large communities, both territorial and nonterritorial. A difference between public and private roles is recognized commonly in human communities; to associate publicness only with states obscures an almost universal distinction.[2] Public agency exists prior to the development of nation-states. And public police agencies may precede the formation of states, just as they may absent from them.

An alternative tack often taken is to broaden the definition of *state*, identifying it with the capacity to govern regardless of the nature of the community. Public auspices remain tied to states, but *statehood* refers to the collective capacity to govern. Since this capacity is almost universal, publicness becomes a common feature of organized social experience. The problem with this formulation is that *state* ceases to delineate a political community organized in a unique way. In my view, it is simpler and closer to usage to associate *state* with sovereign communities that are predicated on control of territory. This is surely the connotation of phrases like *city-state* and *nation-state*. Public and private should be distinguished wherever noncommunity auspices can be distinguished from community ones, regardless of the social basis of the community. In practice, of course, the smaller the community the more difficult it will be to do this: private and public domains become coextensive, community action and individual action are inseparable.

Police are public, then, if they are paid and directed by the community that also authorizes policing. Police are private if the authorizing community neither pays nor directs them. This formulation is compatible with an important reality in governing, namely, delegation of authority to act for the community. The police of Maryland in the United States, Uttar Pradesh in India, and Azerbaijan in the Soviet Union are not private. Why not? Because they are directed by government, by agents of the maximal community. Some subunits of communities are public and others private, depending on whether they are agents of the sovereign power. It follows that medieval manors are public entities, not only because the authority of the king was often minimal but also because they were explicitly derivative units of the kingdom. Vassalage meant sharing with the king, the prerogative to rule. Similarly, geographical subunits of modern nation-states derive their authority from that of the encompassing political community. They are constituent in authority, though unequal in power.

Because communities nest within one another, contending for political preeminence, determination of whether police are public or private depends on judgments about sovereignty. If the Cheyenne Indian nation is considered sovereign during the nineteenth century, then their bands of soldier-police were public; if the United States is considered sovereign, then the Cheyenne soldier-police were private. The police of the East India Trading Company in the eighteenth century were private from the point of view of Englishmen living in England, but public from the point of view of Indians and Englishmen living in India. Application of the dichotomy between public and private agency can only be made intelligently when the relation between the respective communities, especially whether one is superordinate, is specified. Encapsulation of one community by another frequently means competition with respect to autonomy. Unless the units of police predication are specified so that judgments about sovereignty can be made explicitly, changes in the character of policing can be confused with changes in the primacy of political communities. The replacement of the police of a small sovereign unit by a larger sovereign unit is not a change in the character of policing. Both are public. On the other hand, when a political community substitutes police agents paid and directed by it for police agents of constituent groups that are not its creation, like tribes or industrial enterprises, then a change in the character of policing has taken place.

The Development of Public Police

Public policing is an old, not a new, development. It is as old as the existence of sovereign communities that authorize physical constraint and create agents that they direct and maintain. This is borne out by the work of Richard Schwartz and James Miller (1964), which is the only systematic research on police institutions in primitive societies. They found that twenty out of fifty-one primitive societies surveyed had public police, including the Maori, Lapps, Riffians, Thonga, Syrians, Ashanti, Cheyenne, Creek, Cuna, Crow, and Hopi.[3] One of the earliest well-documented cases of the development of public police was in Rome, beginning in 27 B. C., when C. Octavius became *princeps*, taking the name Augustus. One of his first acts was to relieve the Senate of responsibility for civil administration in Rome and assume it himself. Since the fifth century B. C., civil administration had been in the hands of several grades of magistrates appointed by the Senate, some of whom, like the *questor*, had general regulative power for maintaining order in markets and public thoroughfares. These magistrates were not paid, their personal servants being used as professional staff. Augustus realized that a growing, teeming city of almost one million people, divided sharply by class and imbued with habits of violence, needed more efficient policing.[4] He created the post of *preafectus urbi*, filled by appointment from the highest ranks of the Senate, with responsibility for maintaining public order executively and judicially. The staff of the *preafectus irbi*, including the *preafectus vigilium*—chief of police—were paid by Augustus (Kunkel 1973, chaps. 1, 3, and 4). For the first time Rome had a truly public police—executive agents of physical constraint paid and directed by supreme political authority.

For the conceptual reasons already discussed, it is a mistake to regard public police

as having died in Europe during the interregnum between the fall of Rome and the rise of modern nation-states. Policing became exceedingly decentralized, but so too did political sovereignty and the authority to make law. Gradually, new superordinate kingdoms were formed, delegating the power to create police but holding on to the power to make law. Later, public police officials were created who were directly responsible to sovereign power. In England this was the *sheriff*, a term derived from *shire-reeve*, who was made a royal official by the Norman kings in the twelfth century and was granted power to levy fines against criminals as well as the Hundreds for failing to capture criminals (Bopp and Schultz 1972, pp. 9-10; Lee 1901 [1971], chap. I). He was responsible for organizing the Tythings and Hundreds, inspecting their arms, and calling out the *posse comitatus*, which consisted of all able-bodied men over fifteen years old. Complaints about the greed and highhandedness of sheriffs, such as making false charges against Hundreds, were common, as the tale of Robin Hood correctly portrays. As late as the sixteenth century, Hundreds were petitioning the crown for release from these fines (Lee 1901 [1971], chap. I).

English sheriffs were public police officials, but they were not paid in the modern way—a salary for services rendered. Rather, they were allowed to appropriate a portion of money collected in the king's name—thus the temptation to overenforce the law. The money supporting them was nevertheless public, since the sheriff was acting as official collecting agent for the king. The same is true for the celebrated "trading justices" of London during the seventeenth and eighteenth centuries. They, too, should be regarded as public officials. Placing them on a stipendiary footing in 1792 contributed to a higher level of judicial conduct but did not change their status (Keeton 1975, chap. 3).

The constable is another important medieval English invention in law enforcement but cannot be regarded as a public police official. According to the Statute of Winchester, 1285, two constables were to be appointed by every Hundred; their duties were to inspect the arms of the Hundred as prescribed in the Assize of Arms and to act as the sheriff's agents (Lee 1901 [1971], chaps. 2 and 3). As the Frankpledge system decayed, Hundreds could no longer appoint constables, so authority to do so was successively transferred to parish, borough, county, and eventually "police authority." Until the nineteenth century the constable remained an executive agent of law, acting in the king's name but not paid out of public funds. Beginning in London in 1829, constables began to be paid, thus fundamentally transforming their character, although nearly a century passed before the change was implemented throughout the country. The modern English police constable is the medieval Tythingman, still acting under royal authority but now serving at public expense in a chosen career.

Setting aside the conceptual confusion about who were police during feudal times, the only law enforcement agents in England before the eighteenth century who could be regarded as public were the sheriffs and London's "trading justices." Starting in 1735, the first of a series of experiments began that were to nationalize policing. Two London parishes were given authority by statute to pay their watch out of local taxes (Tobias 1972). Later, in the middle of the century, John and Henry Fielding, Bow Street magistrates, began to pay men to serve as constables and to patrol at night (Armitage n.d., p. 123). Though ostensibly paid privately by the Fieldings, the expenses incurred were partially offset by grants from government. In 1792 the new stipendiary magistrates in Middlesex were empowered to pay constables from public funds (Reith 1948, chap. 5). In 1800 the Thames River Police, funded in 1798 by West Indian merchants, became the Thames River Establishment, supported by public revenues (Spitzer and Scull 1977). By 1829 London had become a patchwork of public and private police forces. The City of London had a municipal police force, while police elsewhere were supported by vestries, church wardens, boards of trustees, commissioners, parishes, magistrates, and courtsleet (Hart 1951, pp. 26-27). Because experimentation was so rife and the concept of public police still so unsettled, historians seldom agree about which police agents deserve to be called the first public police. The point I would underscore, however, is that the English developed a specialized police official in the constable seven hundred years before he became a public functionary in the sense of being both directed and maintained out of public funds.

The first public police of the French state may have been the provost of Paris, a post created by St. Louis in the thirteenth century. Headquartered in the Chatelet, which was also the city prison, the provost was assisted by a staff of investigating commissioners and "sergeants" (Stead 1957, chap. I). In addition, the provost commanded a small detachment of mounted military troops and a nightwatch participation in which was obligatory on all male citizens (Tuchman 1979, P. 158). John II (1350- 1364) created a larger military force to patrol the highways and suppress the marauding bands of unemployed knights, foreign mercenaries, and army deserters who pillaged the land (Tuchman 1979, chap. 10). Their responsibilities grew to encompass suppression of crime generally on the king's highway.[5] Three centuries later Cardinal Richelieu (1585-1642) enormously expanded the administrative capacity of the state by creating the *intendant*, an appointed official paid by the king to maintain order, administer justice, and collect taxes in France's thirty-two provinces (*generalité*). In 1667 a specialized deputy for law and order, the lieutenant general of police, was created in Paris (Arnold 1969, pp. 12-13; Stead 1957, chap. I). He commanded the Garde, initially composed of a mounted troop. By 1699 there were lieutenants general in all major cities.

Prussia, the keystone of German unification in 1871, developed a paid bureaucracy very soon after Frederick I, the Great Elector, became *primtis inter pares* among the other *Junkers* in the middle of the seventeenth century. Higher civil servants, like the *Landrat* and *Steurat*, had police powers, though they were simply part of general administrative authority. The first specialized public police official was the police director for Berlin, appointed in 1742 (Emerson 1968, pp. 4-5). As in other continental European countries, a numerous body of public police did not grow until the nineteenth century. At the same time, the *Junkers* were allowed to retain police powers on their estates. Thus, modern state police institutions, largely in towns, coexisted with feudal ones. Since both systems were constituent parts of the sovereign's authority, Prussia should be described as having a dual system of public policing.

Ivan the Terrible created Russia's first state public police, the dreaded Oprichniki, in 1564 (Florinsky 1953, pp. 200-202). Dressed in hooded black cloaks with brooms attached to their horses' heads, its members constituted a mounted military corps that scourged the countryside suppressing Boyar resistance to Ivan's rule. The Oprichniki became the secret police of the Tsar in addition to controlling markets, roads, and other public places. Peter the Great created a specialized public police official in St. Petersberg in 1718. The system was extended to the rest of the country by edicts of Catherine I in 1775 and 1792 (Abbott 1972, sec. I; Monas 1961, pp. 24-29). In cities police rank and file were paid; in rural areas they were not, being lower-class persons who were hired and paid by people who wanted to avoid service, like Englishmen during the same period. As in Prussia, the landed gentry were allowed to maintain their own police system side by side with that of the central state. The landowners remained a law unto themselves even after the emancipation of the serfs in 1864 (Florinsky 1953, p. 101; Monas 1961, p. 274; Seton-Watson 1967, p. 26).

The ebb and flow of public policing in China and India extended over millennia. When powerful dynasties created large empires, paid police officials were invariably established—in towns as the Mauryas and Moguls did, in districts (*hsien*) as the Tangs and Mings did (Basham 1954, pp. 118-121; Starkarum 1963, pp. 91ff; Cox n.d., chaps. 2 and 3). When imperial power declined, nonstate police institutions based on small voluntary communities or the obligations of land settlement reasserted themselves. Flux in the scale of government again confuses judgments about public policing. As in feudal Europe, two systems exist side by side, both with claims to being public, depending on the sovereignty they possessed. Unambiguously public police were not dominant in India until passage of the Indian Police Act in 1862,

and abolition of the princely states in 1948/49, and in China until the Communist Party created a new and effective imperial center in 1949.

Public policing came to the United States with the first settlers. New Amsterdam, later New York, created a burgher watch in 1643, one year after it was founded, but did not pay them until 1712 (Bopp and Schultz 1972, chap. 2). Constables, marshals, and watches were appointed or elected in every settlement, with early recognition that payment was required to ensure effective performance. Compared with the other countries examined, public police became important in the United States about the same time as in England, later than in France, much later than in India or China, and about the same time as in Prussia and Russia. In the American West the unpaid posse remained a mainstay of law enforcement into the twentieth century.

These examples demonstrate how one determines whether public policing exists at a particular time or place. Publicness, a characteristic of forces that dominate policing today, is not a modern invention. Its antiquity is not usually recognized, primarily because of confusion with respect to the concept itself. There is another reason as well. History tends to discount the vigor of failed political systems, systems that gave way to other centers of power, especially if those new centers still exist today. Historical success makes it seem as if Rome had public police but the Duke of Brittany did not, that Emperor Asoka had but zamindars did not, that the state of Colorado had but the Cheyenne nation did not. Because England and France emerged from a welter of estates and manors, the sheriff and the *marechausée* appear to be the first public police. However, if amalgamation had not occurred, then Tythingmen and shire-appointed reeves might be seen as the first public police. In Japan the sovereignty of the emperor was restored in 1868, yet it would certainly be wrong to say that samurai who enforced law and order for the daimyo before that were private police. The samurai were agents of the only effective and legitimate units of government that people acknowledged. They were as public for the Japanese as were King John's sheriffs or Louis XIV's lieutenants general of police. Public policing only looks like a modern development when the vitality of noncontemporary sovereign powers is discounted.

Furthermore, although it is true that police in the world today are for the most part paid and directed by governments of states, it would be a mistake to conclude that privateness in policing is inevitably withering. There is no historical necessity in the movement from private to public police auspices. For example, the collapse of the Roman Empire destroyed state policing, and forced people into desperate reliance on private mechanisms for ensuring security. Neighbors banded together into Tythings and Hundreds in England; clergy proclaimed days of peace and tried to exempt certain places and people from violence; lords formed transitory alliances to subdue rivals who broke the peace; and Peace Leagues took the field against robber barons (Bloch 1961, chap. 30). Today, as well, private policing is growing, enormously, especially in advanced industrial countries. Public forms of policing do not permanently supplant private ones; the process is reversible.

Causes of Public Police Development

Considering the ubiquity of the public form of policing in history, one must strain to argue that particular sets of social or political conditions are required in order to have it. Public policing has existed in societies as different as ancient Syria, classical Rome, absolutist France, industrial Britain, feudal Russia, and contemporary America. Certainly none of the characteristics usually associated with modernity—industrialization, urbanization, technology, literacy, affluence—appear necessary to create public policing. Theoretically it is less interesting that all advanced industrial societies have substantial, indeed dominating, systems of public police than that many societies developed public police long before they became modern.

On the basis of their study of fifty-one primitive societies, Schwartz and Miller (1964) argue that some social complexity is required before public police emerge—specifically, monetization, functional specializa-

tion in some nonpolice sectors, such as religion and education, and creation of government officials not related to the chief. The authors weaken the importance of their discovery when they note that these features often exist without public police being established. Social complexity, then, is only a minimally necessary condition for the creation of public police. The same is true of restitutive sanctions, like mediation and assessment for damages, which, they find, precede establishment of public police. Social complexity and restitutive sanctions are so common in human history that they do not help to explain whether particular societies will or will not rely on the police.

Public police replace private police when the capacity of groups within society to undertake effective enforcement action is no longer sufficient to cope with insecurity. Such a change can occur in societies of very different character. Conversely, urbanization, increased affluence, and industrialization do not inevitably produce public police. They do so only when accompanied by unacceptable insecurity as a perceived result of decay in the vitality of traditional bases of community enforcement. In England, industrialization destroyed the effectiveness of the parish as a unit of community regulation (Silver 1967). In part this may have been the result of changing perceptions of public order needs, reflected especially in a growing concern with immoral pastimes, like drunkenness and animal baiting, as well as decorum, such as vagrancy and brawling (Philips 1977). In any case, by the middle of the nineteenth century the parish no longer commanded the wealth or loyalty necessary to support a reliable constabulary. The same thing happened in Prussia, Russia, and the American South when landowners on large estates discovered they could no longer protect themselves against the disorder generated by their suppressed laborers. In Rome, it was commercial aggrandizement, urban scale, and population heterogeneity that weakened policing based on kin and neighborhood. In short, when traditional private auspices for maintaining order are undermined, either new private groups must become effective centers for regulatory mobilization or the community as a whole will assume responsibility.

The transition from private police auspices to development of police institutions maintained and directed by Government at the most inclusive level of political identification does not occur overnight. Norman kings, Tudor queens, and Whig governments in England tried to breathe new life into local police institutions for centuries. Sheriffs were created initially to supervise the Frankpledge system, fining Hundreds for failing in their duties. Countless directives issued from London for centuries urging justices of the peace to improve the quality of personnel chosen as constables. Private and public police auspices thus sometimes coexist, both in substantial scale. Changes in relative proportions take place slowly and are subject to reverses.

The factor impelling movement from private to public policing is not simply a growth in insecurity but a growth in insecurity traceable to a decline in the efficiency of customary enforcement auspices. A high incidence of crime by itself is not sufficient. To be sure, movement to a public system will be justified in terms of security needs, but this is true as well for the regeneration of private policing. Though crime figures are hopelessly inadequate for the periods discussed here, impressionistic evidence suggests that public police did not supplant private in times of unusual criminality (Lodhi and Tilly 1970). Private policing persisted in England in the eighteenth century despite rampant criminality, while public police were created in Russia and France in the seventeenth and eighteenth centuries without the prompting of ordinary crime. Violence was common in Roman life from at least 131 B.C., most of it inspired by politics. Courts and assemblies were frequently disrupted by mobs, their judgments coerced. Wealthy people hired bands of retainers—slaves and gladiators—to defend themselves and their property. Cicero, for example, is reported to have had three hundred thugs under hire in 61 B.C., mostly to intimidate his political opponents (Lintott 1968, chaps. 5 and 6). Yet Rome did not develop public police, apart from periodic intrusions by the legions, until Augustus. Conversely,

rising crime may actually contribute to the strengthening of private policing if public police are perceived to be ineffective. Vigilantism in the United States in the nineteenth century is a case in point, as is the remarkable increase in private policing throughout the industrial countries since the middle of the 1960s.

A change from private to public police auspices represents an augmentation of the regulative capacity of the maximal community. This being so, it would be logical to expect that the dynamics of political encapsulation—the growth of new political centers—would effect policing in turn. A priori it would seem that the extension of effective political hegemony would be associated with the creation of public police. Surprisingly, this is not the case, for two reasons. First, the units whose capacity for policing is extinguished may have had public policing themselves. British conquest of India did not create public policing; it merely shifted control of it from one place to another. Second, the assertive larger political community has no need to establish public police institutions unless its own interests are threatened. England's Tudor monarchs and Prussia's Frederick the Great created powerful state bureaucracies, but both left traditional police arrangements almost wholly untouched (Rosenberg 1958, pp. 35-38). The preservation of substate enforcement auspices was part of the political settlement underlying the initial growth of both the English and Prussian states. New political centers may assert themselves through taxation, military progress, and the adjudication of disputes without developing marked police capacity (L. Tilly 1971). Public policing is not the taproot of today's nation--states. This point is often not recognized because states have been defined in terms of the capacity to maintain a monopoly of force within the community. The fact is, however, that political communities may have effective and authoritative government without maintaining and directing enforcement agents.

The only time the formation of a new political community brings about a shift from private to public police auspices is when constituent units resist the process by violence.

A section of the French nobility—the Fronde—resisted centralized monarchical rule in 1649, at the cost of their feudal prerogatives and monopolization of policing by the king through the *intendants* and the lieutenants general of police. The English state, on the other hand, developed administratively without resistance from the landed nobility and gentry. The squirearchy shared responsibility with the king for administering the Common Law. They acted as royal agents and justices of the peace, and in exchange the king allowed them to direct the parishes executively. Legislative and judicial centralization was combined with police decentralization under private auspices. Within this political formula, English government steadily grew in power until well into the nineteenth century (Bloch 1961, pp. 425-426). The exception proving the rule is Oliver Cromwell's experiment with a national Military Police from 1655 to 1657. The Military Police was the only attempt by the central Government to create public police, apart from the sheriffs, during the nine hundred years from the Norman conquest to Peel's reform. It came about because the country was polarized on the issue of religion. Protestants and Catholics violently disputed the existing political dispensation, neither side being able to accept a central government ruled by the other. The Military Police, composed of about sixty-four hundred mounted militia, enforced Puritan Rule after the Civil War, their attention extending to lifestyles as well as political reliability. Although religious animosity strained English politics for a long time after Cromwell, the accession of William and Mary in 1688 confirmed Protestant domination and reunited crown and squirearchy, providing again a basis for private, decentralized policing. The system remained unchallenged for another century and a half.

In summary, public policing never permanently replaces private policing. Furthermore, public policing is difficult to explain, because it occurs in all sorts of social circumstances. If public policing were rarer in history or exclusively modern, the search for an explanation would be easier. Two factors appear to be most influential in producing a change from private to public police auspices: social changes that undermine the capacity of private groups to maintain acceptable levels of security, and the formation of superordinate political communities that is met with violent resistance by constituent groups.

Specialized Police

Specialization is a relative term referring to exclusiveness in performing a task. In policing, the defining task is the application of physical force within a community. A specialized police devote all their attention to the application of physical constraint; a nonspecialized police do many other things besides. The seventeenth century *intendant* in France was a nonspecialized police agent; the constable in England was a specialized one. The district magistrate today in Pakistan is nonspecialized, responsible for performing administrative, judicial, and enforcement tasks; the district superintendent of police is specialized. Because police are rarely totally specialized, evaluations of specialization must be made comparatively. That is, they must be made in relation to a standard. Furthermore, having specialized police in a society is not the same as having a single police force. Specialization of function and monopolization of that function are different. Countries can have more than one agency whose primary function is the maintenance of public order. Italy, for example, has three police forces, Spain two, and the United States innumerable. Conversely, a force that monopolizes the application of physical force within the community may not be specialized; it may do other things in addition. . . .

The Development of Specialized Police

The earliest specialized police were watchmen, found almost universally among societies, from village *chowkidars* in South Asia to the nightwatch in medieval Europe. However, although their function was certainly specialized, it is not always clear that it was policing. Very often they acted only as sentinels, responsible for summoning others to apprehend criminals, repel attack, or put out fires. To the extent that watchmen did apply force, they represent specialized police.

Specialized police have usually developed as part of the administrative apparatus of most of the world's great empires. Detectives, spies, and enforcers of public order are found in imperial records of the Mauryas (c. 321–c. 184 B.C.), the Guptas (320–c. 535), and the Moguls (1526–1858) in India, the Mings (1368–1644) in China, and the Heians (794–1185) in Japan.[7] The Romans developed specialized police known as Vigiles in 6 A.D., who by the third century A.D. were deployed in police stations and patrolled the streets both night and day (Reynolds 1926). As far as records are concerned, specialized police personnel seep into the sands of history when imperial vigor declines, going underground to emerge at a later date.

Among the states of Europe that we recognize today, the British were probably the first to develop specialized law and order agents. There were the *posse comitatus* and the constable of the Middle Ages. The French *sergeant*, on the other hand, who appeared about the same time as the constable, was a more multipurpose official who did everything from serving judicial warrants to undertaking military operations (Strayer 1970, p. 78). At the same time Denmark, Norway, and Sweden created the *Lensman*, who enforced laws at local levels and collected taxes for the king. In Norway he was elected by the peasants but served under the direction of the king's territorial representative, known as the *syssler*. *Lensmen* still exist in rural Norway. In Denmark the *Lensman* evolved into a kind of county sheriff, and his privileges became hereditary. From the late twelfth century Scandinavian cities were administered for the king by *gjaldkere*, who collected taxes, enforced law, prosecuted offenders, jailed criminals, and assigned people to the nightwatch (Hjellemo 1979).

Since the Middle Ages, policing on the continent has been less specialized than in England. Certainly this was true for middle level police officials. Continental *intendants, prevots, Landrat, Steurat*, and *Lensmen* did much more than enforce law and maintain public order. They were omnicompetent, serving as the king's representatives in all official matters. The nearest English equivalent is the justice of the peace, developed in the thirteenth century; but he, as the name implies, was more narrowly concerned with matters of public order and justice (Keeton 1975, chap. 3). Continental administrative officials whose abilities included policing may have had more specialized subordinates much like English constables. If this is true, the degree of specialization in Europe was stratified by rank. Policing within the framework of the emerging state was viewed on the continent as an inseparable part of crown administration. The word *police* originally denoted all administrative functions that were not ecclesiastical. In England, contrastingly, the maintenance of the king's peace was a distinct responsibility, antedating the rise of administrative capacity in other areas. Curiously, England appears originally to have been more of a police state in the specialized sense than continental kingdoms. The primacy and early specialization of law enforcement in England within state administration may have acted in fact as a bulwark in tradition against the rise of the continental European *Polizeistaat*.

Another difference between English and continental development was the sequencing of publicness with specialization. Referring to state institutions only, as opposed to feudal ones, English police became specialized before they became public; continental police became public before they became specialized. By roughly the middle of the eighteenth century, specialized royal police officers had been established in larger European cities. Copying the French lieutenant general of police, Tsar Peter I created a police chief in St. Petersburg in 1718, Emperor Frederick II in Berlin in 1742, and Empress Maria Theresa in Vienna in 1751 (Emerson 1968, p. 4-5). Though these officials had wider regulatory responsibilities than the English justice of the peace, they directed personnel who specialized in patrolling, arresting, and spying. In 1760 Paris had a variety of specialized personnel—detectives in each quarter; a patrolling watchguard, both foot and horse; squads of soldiers serving as sentinels; and archers deployed to rid streets of beggars and idlers (Radzinowicz 1957, pp. 540-541). The system had become so elaborate that an English traveler commented wryly that in France, lieutenants general order, inspectors inform, *exempts* apprehend, archers conduct, *commissaires* commit, *chatelets* condemn, and priests grant absolution (Mildmay 1763, p. 6). The other absolutist regimes undoubtedly developed specialized personnel too, but little has been written about them.

American police, like the English, specialized relatively early in national development. Constables and marshals were fixtures of colonial American society from the time of the first settlements. Throughout American history when enforcement was required, government created additional specialized officials. This has been true nationally as well as locally. Specialized federal marshals were created in 1789, one of the first acts of the new national Government. The Federal Bureau of Investigation, established in 1924, continued this tradition, concentrating more exclusively on law enforcement than any other force in the country with the possible exception of some state patrols. Comparing American and British experience with that of continental Europe, it is fair to say that Anglo-Saxon police have tended to be more specialized when the territorial extent of their jurisdiction was larger; European police have tended to be less specialized when the extent of their jurisdiction was larger.

An important part of police specialization has been the removal of the military from the work of maintaining domestic order. Since military units also defend communities externally, their use domestically, which has occurred almost everywhere historically, represents imperfect specialization in policing. This kind of imperfect specialization has been a persistent feature of continental Europe, represented in the *gendarmerie* system. Developed initially in France, *gendarmes* were military personnel assigned responsibility for maintaining law and order in rural areas and along major thoroughfares. *Gendarmerie* was the name given during the French Revolution to the old *marechausée*, which in turn had grown out of the *compagnies d'ordonnance*. *Gendarmerie* became standard in European countries during the first half of the nineteenth century: Prussia in 1812, Piedmont in 1816, the Netherlands in 1814, Spain in 1844, and Austria in 1849 (Bramshill Police College 1974; Carr 1966, pp. 233-234; Cramer 1964, pp. 327-329; Fried 1963, chap. 2; Keppler 1974; Jacob 1963, pp. 11-12). Some contemporary descendants of these *gendarmerie* are the Italian Carabinieri, the Spanish Guardia Civil, the French Gendarmerie, the Netherlands Rijkspolitie, and the West German Landespolizei. Gradually, operational direction was turned over to civilian ministries, but the military often retained control over budget, recruitment, and even training. Links to the military are still strong in Italy and Spain, weak in France and Germany, negligible in the Netherlands. Where they continue to exist, police specialization remains incomplete.

In England and her colonies, military participation in policing was never institutionalized. The army was frequently used to suppress outbreaks of domestic violence, but its intrusion was regarded as abnormal, a breakdown in the proper administration of law and order. The most dramatic exception to this was Cromwell's Military Police, 1655-1657, and in the United States the army's deployment to preserve law and order west of the Mississippi River during the nineteenth century. Regarding the United States Army as a "police" force is an interesting example of a post hoc judgment about sovereignty. From the point of view of American Indians, it was not a police force at all but an army of occupation waging aggressive war. As with Cromwell's Military Police, the American army was quickly supplanted by civilian law enforcement agents such as marshals and sheriffs. Even on the reservations into which the Indians were driven, a specialized nonmilitary force was created. This was the Indian Police, formed by Congress in 1878 and directed by Indian agents acting for the Department of the Interior (Hagan 1966, pp. 2-5).

A major reason everywhere for continued military participation in policing was the need to deal with widespread, prolonged, or severe outbursts of violence by large numbers of people. But specialization eventually prevailed here too, so that by the twentieth century military intervention in aid of civil police had become rare. This final act of exclusion of the military from policing has followed different patterns from place to place. It involved an interplay among three forces: armies, police, and militia.

During the two hundred years bounded by 1650 and 1850, riots, rebellions, and insurrections plagued European countries and were met by military force. The military expedient worked successfully as long as violence was localized and of fairly small scale, involving parochial matters of food supply, prices, and sectorial employment. But vast social changes were afoot that were to change the character of unrest. As a result of the commercialization of agriculture and the destruction of cottage industries, people were forced into cities. The control of landed elites, based on ascriptive deference, was weakened, and in some countries hereditary classes were overthrown. Protest increasingly involved vast numbers of people, often spearheaded by the urban mob, and was directed against general political authority rather than local wrongs (Tilly, Tilly, and Tilly 1975). In these circumstances, introduction of an army became a political act, not simply a technical solution to a law and order problem. Furthermore, military units, often mounted and wielding sabres, were too forceful, killing and wounding indiscriminately. They created martyrs and earned the understandable hatred of the populace. As a result, military leaders became reluctant to act in a police capacity. Their distaste was reinforced by concern for the reliability of the army itself. The loyalties of the rank and file were often with the agitators, as were those of nonaristocratic members of the officer corps. These strains became especially acute in Europe with the rise of large conscripted armies in the early nineteenth century, representing a cross-section of social classes that replaced the mercenary armies raised by kings and landed gentry. Thus demands for increased political participation and greater economic equality threatened armies that were barely coming to grips with their own problems of mass mobilization. Soon neither professional military officers nor civilian politicians were keen to use the army as police—in part out of concern for the integrity of the military machine, in part out of concern for the legitimacy of government.

Another force was commonly used throughout Europe to deal with outbreaks of collective violence. That was the militia—irregular volunteer forces recruited locally that were armed and usually mounted. They were a defensive reaction by elites to violent attacks on the status quo. In England, militia were first created in 1660 following the Civil War; in France, after the Revolution in 1789, although the Garde Bourgeoise of the seventeenth century was a precedent (Bayley 1975). Where feudal institutions were strong, as in Prussia and France, militias were an extension of seignorial power. Militias became more prominent in Europe as demands for increased political participation in the nineteenth century moved like a wave across Europe from the Atlantic coast to the Urals. The problem with militias was that they reflected partisan political interests. They lacked general legitimacy, which explains why revolutionary regimes always reorganized them along more inclusive, democratic lines, while restoration governments reconstructed them from rural landowners and the halite bourgeois (Carr 1966, pp. 233-234, 283; Langer 1969, pp. 332, 391-392). Militias were not an effective substitute for armies in maintaining domestic order. Indeed, their intrusion tended to exacerbate problems, making law enforcement transparently political.

Faced with reluctant but too forceful armies and enthusiastic but unreliable militias, European governments in the nineteenth century withdrew armies from domestic riot duty, abolished militias, and developed a specialized, public police capacity. England was in the vanguard. In 1829 government created a publicly supported civil constabulary in London that was large enough to contain and disperse urban mobs. Instructively, the Duke of Wellington, England's foremost military authority, gave crucial support to Sir Robert Peel in creating the "new police."[8] Substitution of trained civil police for militias and the military spread throughout Europe during the rest of the century, though the military continued to play a more prominent role on the continent than in England due to the existence of substantial forces of *gendarmes*.

By the early twentieth century, however, urban unrest throughout Europe was met for the most part by armed units of civil police specially trained for that purpose. The English and Norwegian police alone disdained the use of arms altogether. The same historical scenario was followed by Japan during the 1870s. The conscript army created in 1872 as an instrument of national revitalization was unsettled by having to suppress violent regional uprisings that were a reaction to the destruction of the decentralized feudal system of the Tokugawas. In 1878 the responsibility for maintaining internal order was formally transferred from the army to the newly created police built along French and Prussian lines (Tsurumi 1970, p. 85).

The United States developed a unique solution to the problem of containing large-scale domestic turmoil. From colonial times, militias—sometimes voluntary, sometimes conscript—had been used to put down rebellion. Indeed, until early in the twentieth century, they were the only substantial armed forces available, apart from the police. The American Civil War was fought essentially by state militias and not by national armies either of the Union or the Confederacy. Militia units were used throughout the nineteenth century to put down popular agitation, much of it associated toward the end of the century with increasingly organized and violent labor disputes (Smith 1925, pp. 29-32). Like other countries, the United States learned the unwieldiness of military units in such situations. It came to rely more and more on specialized police forces, keeping the militia in reserve. In 1903 the militias were nationalized, becoming a volunteer military reserve, and were renamed the National Guard (Hill 1969).

Modern policing is dominated by organizations that have become increasingly specialized during the past two centuries. In Anglo-Saxon countries, specialization involved primarily the substitution of civil for military units in dealing with domestic violence; in continental countries, as well as in Latin America, specialization occurred primarily within the civil administration of the state, involving to a lesser extent formal removal of the military from policing. By and large in modern states, the application of physical forces for the maintenance of domestic order has been entrusted to specialized nonmilitary organizations. This is not to argue that modern police do nothing other than forcefully constrain behavior; but the diversity of tasks performed by police today is . . . more the result of their own adaptation to the requirements of maintaining order and less the result of the directed mixture of police and nonpolice tasks.

Among contemporary countries, the movement from nonspecialized to more specialized policing has so far not been reversed, unlike the situation with respect to private and public agency in policing. On a wider historical stage, there have been returns to unspecialized police, almost always as part of the collapse of political systems and the creation of new police auspices. This was true during imperial interregnums in China and India and after the fall of the Roman Empire.

The Causes of Specialization

A compelling explanation for an increase in police specialization is difficult to construct. It is tempting to argue that increased social complexity in the form of stratification and differentiation brings it about, especially since both are characteristics of contemporary countries that have specialized forces. The problem is that specialization also occurs in the remote past, both in feudal institutions, as in the Frankpledge system, and early in state-building, as with the sheriff and constable. And the English experience is not exceptional. The United States, admittedly following English tradition, had specialized police well before the industrial age. Specialized police officials—the exact degree of specialization being debatable—are also found in empires such as the Mauryian, Heian, and Ming. Day- and nightwatches occur universally in human society and, to the extent that they have enforcement powers, should be regarded as specialized police. The conclusion is, then, that modern social circumstances may facilitate specialization but are not required for it.

It is equally difficult to find an explanation in politics. Certainly regime character is not obviously associated with specialization. In modern times both democratic and autocratic regimes have simplified the focus of their primary police agents. Although state assertiveness and centralization, which are associated with European absolutism, produced "police states," they did not produce specialized police officials as early as in the more decentralized, consensual England. In England, in fact, specialization antedated the rise of the modern bureaucratic state, with the degree of specialization remaining virtually unchanged from the thirteenth to the twentieth centuries. The growth of centralized bureaucratic power, a feature of modern states, may in fact retard police specialization. This seems to have happened at middle levels of administrative responsibility in the absolute monarchies of Europe. Furthermore, when the need for omnicompetent and unified control by government did confront the English in their far-flung colonies, police command became less specialized, not more, and was concentrated in the hands of multipurpose district magistrates and collectors (Bayley 1969, chap. 2). The *Polizeistaat* is not, therefore, a police-specialized state (Raeff 1975). Not only is the growth of centralized state power not required for police specialization, but it does not particularly facilitate it.

Differences in specialization in Europe, clearest at middle levels of state management, are associated with the contrasting traditions of Roman law and common law. A heritage of Roman law retards development of specialized police agents. Even today, as we shall see later, continental European countries tend to assign a wider range of responsibilities to their police than do Anglo-Saxon countries.

The removal of the military from policing is the one aspect of specialization where the historical record does not confound the search for explanation. A military role in policing persists, representing imperfect specialization, when a large standing army is created early in the state experience and when the development of state capacities is met with prolonged or severe civil strife.[9] *Gendarme* police systems developed in France, Prussia, Italy, Spain, and the Netherlands, where these conditions obtained. They

did not develop in Britain, the United States, Japan, or Scandinavia, all of which were spared the need to develop substantial standing armies until late in their national experience. Moreover, in each of these countries national identity was not forged by conquest on the part of one region over the others, nor was the authority of national government contested by force. Though each has known civil strife, such episodes were either brief or occurred after traditions governing the relations between police and military had been set.

The military withdraws from policing in response to two factors: development of mass armies based on conscription, and changes in military technology that make the indiscriminate use of force difficult to avoid. It is important to note that civil strife plays a role both in bringing the military into policing and removing it. What is crucial is not strife itself, but its timing, in relation to other events, notably the existence and nature of a standing army. Domestic violence early in statebuilding creates traditions of military penetration into policing; domestic violence weakens military penetration late in statebuilding when one of the two conditions exists. Violent domestic agitation tends always to bring the military into law enforcement, but the intrusion becomes more episodic as warfare requires mass mobilization and the technologies of massive destruction.

Police specialization cannot be accounted for in terms of social and political change, except in the case of military participation, because specialization, although a characteristic of modern policing, is not peculiar to it. Nor do increased insecurity and a heightened demand for order provide the essential impetus for increased specialization. In part, police specialization appears to have grown because management philosophy in modern nation-states requires it; specialization is assumed to be useful both in terms of ensuring adequate accountability and in enhancing efficiency. The same is true, as we have seen, of the attribute of publicness. The analysis of specialization is hampered particularly by lack of information about the work of police personnel, especially at the lower ranks, in all but the modern period. Often they appear not to exist. My guess is that their absence is more apparent than real. Where detailed historical studies have been done, as in England, specialized police have been found. If future research confirms the supposition that specialized police are often too common to be mentioned by local authorities, then comparisons between England (and its dependencies) and other countries will no longer be anomalous. Instead, the hypothesis will be reinforced that specialization is not uniquely modern.

The Development of Professionalization

Professionalization is a modern attribute of police more clearly than either publicness or specialization. It is also a more complex attribute. Professionalization connotes explicit attention given to the achievement of quality in performance. Minimal indicators of a professional police are recruitment according to specified standards, remuneration sufficiently high to create a career service, formal training, and systematic supervision by superior officers. To some extent the word *professionalization* has become a term of art in police circles today, covering features such as functional specialization of personnel, use of modern technology, neutrality in law enforcement, responsible use of discretion, and a measure of autonomous self-regulation. These elements are controversial, part of the term's honorific baggage, and will be ignored.

Timing the confirmation of professionalization in a police force is problematic for several reasons. First, even in its simpler sense, professionalization has diverse parts. In England, the Bow Street Runners, created by John and Henry Fielding in the middle of the eighteenth century, were selected from among constables with one year's experience, were trained and supervised by the Fieldings, and were paid from public funds, though in the form of rewards out of fines rather than salaries. They could be regarded as primitive professional police (Reith 1948, p. 31; Pringle n.d.). Other partial experiments in professionalization were the Thames River Police, 1798, and the curiously named Unmounted Horse Patrol, 1821 (Critchley 1967, pp. 42-45). The great breakthrough came, of course,

with establishment of the London Metropolitan Police in 1829. Recruitment was made on the basis of sex, height, weight, character, and ability to read and write. Training was mandatory, though it consisted almost exclusively of close-order drill (Gorer 1955).

Second, attempts to establish professionalism may be both fitful and uneven. In Russia during the 1860s great care was given to raising the level of bureaucratic performance, especially the elimination of corruption, sloth, and incompetence. Appraisals made in the mid-1870s, however, indicated that the reforms had largely failed (Abbott 1972, pp. 257-258; Abbott 1973). In the United States, control of police departments by political parties was not eliminated until well into the twentieth century, though some cities successfully professionalized administration in the late nineteenth century. The notorious "spoils system" assured that appointment as a police officer depended on party loyalty. Extreme fragmentation of police authority in the United States compelled the issues of professionalization to be discovered and fought over repeatedly throughout the country. Even today, chief law-enforcement officers, like sheriffs, are chosen by ballot in many rural areas rather than by vetted appointment (Lanc 1979).

A notable exception to the stuttering pattern of professionalization occurred in Japan. Copying boldly from Europe, the Meiji government created a professional national police system in about a decade, beginning with the establishment of the Tokyo Metropolitan Police Department (Keishicho) in 1878. By 1887 personnel throughout the country were rigorously selected, largely from among former samurai, and trained in prefectural police schools (Hackett 1971, pp. 103ff.; Oura 1909). India, too, experienced systematic though penny-pinching professionalization under the British after the shock of the Mutiny (1857) caused responsibility for governing to be transferred from the chartered, private East India Company to the Parliament in London. The Police Act of 1862 created a national police system within which regulations governing recruitment, training, supervision, and discipline for all ranks were gradually introduced. The lesson to be drawn from Japan and India, confirmed in the experience of countries that have become independent after World War II, is that the more recently police reform has been undertaken, the more likely it is to involve professionalization that is national in scope.

Third, professionalization proceeds at varying speeds at different rank levels. France and Prussia began to create a nonamateur bureaucracy at senior administrative levels in the seventeenth century. England allowed public offices, including army commissions, to be bought and sold well into the 1870s (Rosenberg, 1958, pp. 51-52; Webb and Webb 1963, pp. 1-67). On the continent, professionalization percolated downward over almost two hundred years. In England it occurred in a much shorter period and encompassed all rank levels.

Fourth, qualitative judgments must be made to determine whether any facet of professionalization can be said to exist. For example, do standards with respect to height and weight of applicants constitute merit recruitment? India has had these for over a century, but literacy was rare enough that "writer constable" was a meaningful designation through independence. Similarly, there is an enormous difference between a wage that attracts capable personnel and a wage that assures employment of incompetents and misfits. Although constables began to be paid publicly in England in 1829, their wages did not begin to compete with skilled labor until about 1890 (Martin and Wilson 1969, chap. 2). Today Indian constables are paid about as much as government peons, who are the runners and servants of Indian offices.

Recognizing that dating the existence of professional police will be imprecise and judgmental, the great age of professionalization is the nineteenth century. During the hundred years from 1815 to 1915, professionalization was confirmed among major countries in approximately the following order: Japan, France and Germany, Great Britain, India, the United States, and Russia. This does not mean that the quality of performance can be ranked in this order. It only indicates that problems of recruitment, training, pay, and supervision were explicitly addressed and systematically met. Priority is given to Japan because it not only professionalized as the European countries did, but it also pioneered in developing training schools for policemen of all ranks.[10] The tide of professionalization has been at the flood in the twentieth century, but ebbing is possible. Quite obviously it can occur when resources are stretched too thin. It can also occur due to changes in the auspices under which policing is undertaken. Private security forces are generally less professional than their public counterparts. Self-defense policing by voluntary organizations of citizens also inevitably reduces professionalism. This may be seen among neighborhood associations in western Europe, North America, and China and in the "People's Police" of Russia, East Europe, and Cuba. The future of professionalism may be less assured than experience in the past one hundred years would suggest.

The Causes of Professionalization

Perceptible surges in professionalism historically occur after a change from private to public auspices in policing, in most cases after territorial communities have assumed responsibility. Professionalization occurs, therefore, when there is a need for reliable instruments of forceful regulation, either because constituent communities have lost their vitality or because the authority of a new polity is disputed. Perception of this need can occur in communities of varying size, both demographically and territorially. There appears to be no critical threshold.[11] Nor does the taxable wealth available to government affect professionalization. Quite unprepossessing police authorities, like American counties and English boroughs, professionalized in some measure without substantial wealth, though in the English case not until the national government undertook to pay some of the cost. (Philips 1977, chap 2; Tilly et al. 1974). France and Prussia, on the other hand, did not professionalize across all ranks until long after they had developed the capacity to tax, regulate commerce, administer justice, and raise armies. Though resource mobilization is required for professionalization, the amount of wealth available to government, above a small minimum level, is not a determining factor.

In the modern period, professionalization has been accepted as essential to efficient management. It was an axiom of progressive reform. Governments studied innovations made elsewhere and copied them at home. Prussia, Austria, and Russia studied the French experience closely in the eighteenth century. British and Americans knew about continental development and commented critically on the inefficiency of administration in their own countries. Japan borrowed self-consciously from Prussia and France, while European powers exported professionalism to their colonies. Professionalization promised to enhance effectiveness and reliability regardless of the nature of political systems. This explains why professionalization occurred during the nineteenth century in countries radically different both in terms of the character of their regimes and the national organization of the police. The United States, Britain, India, Prussia, Sweden, Japan, and the Netherlands all achieved minimal levels of professionalism at roughly the same time, despite the fact that they had little in common politically apart from a belief that territorial government should be responsible for law and order.

Pressure for enhancement of security under state auspices came from the middle class, as in England, but also from other influential social groups, such as aristocracies, artisans, commercial interests, and armies (Field 1981; Harring, 1983; Lofland 1973, p. 65; Weinberger 1981). Response to this pressure was facilitated by traditions of administrative intervention by government. The French and Prussians were accustomed to professional state administration before they felt obligated to provide it in policing. The English, on the other hand, resisted doing so, because they believed that state intervention was dangerous to liberty (Langrod 1961, pp. 6-7). The administrative state, epitomized in France, was anathema to Englishmen, and they clung to amateurism even at the expense of security.

International learning, then, did not always produce emulation. However, once traditional inhibitions were removed with respect to the role government should play in policing, international learning caused professionalization to adhere to a common form.

Finally, professionalization does not ride on a wave of crime or violence. Although changes in policing of any sort are justified in terms of insecurity and turbulence, a causal link between crime and professionalism is difficult to show. Professionalization is too qualitative as well as too complex to follow directly from critical thresholds of criminality.

Conclusion

Policing in the modern world is dominated by organizations that are public, specialized, and professional. What is new about policing is the combination of these attributes rather than any of the attributes themselves. Public agency and specialization can be found in many places before the modern period; only professionalization is rare earlier, although even it is not unprecedented. Evolution toward this unique combination, which has been confirmed only in the past one hundred years, took place slowly over several centuries. Specialized police developed in England in the Middle Ages, but public agency did not become characteristic of English policing until seven hundred years later. France made policing public in the seventeenth and eighteenth centuries but did not specialize, as England had done, until the nineteenth. The United States had specialized and public police in the seventeenth century but delayed professionalization until the twentieth. Moreover, the order in which the three attributes were assembled varied from country to country, except that professionalization generally came after a shift to public auspices. There is no *a priori* reason why a nationwide system of professional police might not be created under private tutelage, even though historically it has not been done.

Notes

1. Direction of policing and instigation of policing should not be confused. A public system—collectively paid and directed—is not incompatible with private instigation of po-

lice action. Officers in modern systems rarely take action on their own recognizance but wait until contacted by someone needing assistance. It is not the nature of instigation—proactive or reactive—that differentiates public from private policing, but rather the nature of the agencies appealed to. For both private and public forces, the amount of individual as opposed to official instigation must be determined empirically.

2. For an argument on the other side, see Strayer 1970, pp. 7-8.

3. Schwartz and Miller would be surprised at this conclusion, but only on terminological grounds. Their criteria for *specialization* are the ones I have used for *publicness*. Though they define police as "specialized armed forces used partially and wholly for norm enforcement," they continually discuss police as representing a capacity of formal government (1964, p. 161). They confuse *specialization* with *public agency*.

4. Michael G. Mulhall (1903, . 444) gives the population of Rome in 14 A.D. as about 900,000.

5. William Mildmay (1763, p. 23). Twelve articles establishing the *marechausée* were set forth in 1356. For an excellent account of these lawless gangs, see Barbara W. Tuchman, *A Distant Mirror: The Calamitous Fourteenth Century* (London: Penguin Books, 1979, chap. 10).

6. Sybille van der Sprenkel 1977. For a firsthand description of South China during the period of imperial decline, 1908, see René Onraet, *Singapore: A Police Background* (London: Dorothy Crisp and Co. Ltd., 1945, p. 47).

7. In Japan, for example, in the reign of Saga, ca. 820 A.D., a police department was established at Kyoto for the purpose of arresting criminals and bringing them to trial. In 1186 Minamoto-no Yoritomo took the title *sotsuihosi*, or chief superintendent of police (Ogawa and Tomeoka 1909).

8. As first secretary to Ireland, Peel had already experimented with policing when, in 1814, he created the Peace Preservation Forces. They became the Irish Constabulary and later the Royal Irish Constabulary. The "Peelers" were an armed squad, not stationed among the people but moving from one trouble spot to another (Brady 1974, chap. 1).

9. An earlier formulation appears in Bayley 1975.

10. Tokyo had a full-time training program for lower ranks in 1880, Paris not until 1883, and even then it was only on a part-time basis, interspersed with other duties. London's Police Training School was founded in 1907 (Stead 1957, p. 139; Fosdick 1915 [1975], pp. 211 ff.).

11. Professionalization began in London in 1829, when the city had a population of 1.8 million; in Stockholm, 1850, 92,000; in Sydney, 1862, 100,000; and in Calcutta, 1864, 365,000 (Gurr, Grabosky, and Hula 1977, p. 705). At the same time, Erick Monkkonen (1981) argues that American cities developed 100,000 full-time uniformed police after the Civil War as a function of their rank-order in size. I suggest that if there are thresholds of size, as Monkkonen has found, they occur within local climates of opinion about the need to professionalize.

References

Abbott, Robert J. 1972. "Police Reform in Russia." Ph.D. dissertation, Princeton University.

——. 1973. "Police Reform in the Russian Province of Iaroslavl 1856–1876." *Slavic Review* June: 292-302.

Armitage, Gilbert. n.d. *The History of the Bow Street Runners, 1729–1829.* London: Wishart and Co.

Arnold, Eric A., Jr. 1969. "Administrative Leadership in a Dictatorship: The Position of Joseph Fouch in the Napoleonic Police, 1800–1810." Ph.D. dissertation, Columbia University.

Basham, A.L. 1954. *The Wonder That Was India.* London: Sidgwick and Jackson.

Bayley, David H. and Mendelsohn, Harold. 1969. *Minorities and the Police.* New York: Free Press.

Bloch, Marc. 1961. *Feudal Society.* Chicago: University of Chicago Press.

Bohannon, Paul. 1957. *Justice and Judgement Among the Tiv.* New York: Oxford University Press.

Bonner, Robert J. and Smith, Gertrude. 1928. *The Administration of Justice from Homer to Aristotle.* 2 vols. Chicago: University of Chicago Press.

Bopp, William J. and Schultz, Donald D. 1972. *A Short History of American Law Enforcement.* Springfield, Ill: Charles C. Thomas.

Bramshill Police College, Eleventh Senior Command Course. 1974. "A Study of Public Order in Six E.E.C. Countries." June.

Carr, Raymond. 1966. *Spain, 1808–1932.* Oxford: Clarendon Press.

Cox, Sir Edmund C. n.d. *Police and Crime in India.* London: Stanley Paul and Co.

Cramer, James. 1964. *The World's Police.* London: Cassell and Co.

Critchely, T.A. 1967. *A History of Police in England and Wales, 1900–1966.* London: Constable.

Emerson, Donald E. 1968. *Metternich and the Political Police: Security and Subversion in the Hapsburg Monarchy (1815–1830).* The Hague: Martinus Nijhoff.

Field, John. 1981. "Police Power and the Community in a Provincial English Town: Portsmouth, 1815–1875." In *Policing and Punishment in Nineteenth Century Britain*, ed. Victor Bailey, pp. 42–64. New Brunswick, N.J.: Rutgers University Press.

Florinsky, Michael T. 1953. *Russia.* New York: Macmillan Co.

Fried, Robert C. 1963. *The Italian Prefects: A Study in Administrative Politics.* New Haven: Yale University Press.

Gorer, Geoffrey. 1955. "Modification of National Character: The Role of the Police in England." *Journal of Social Issues 11: 25–32.*

Hackett, Roger F. 1971. *Yamagata Aritomo in the Rise of Modern Japan, 1838–1922.* Cambridge, Mass.: Harvard University Press.

Hagan, William T. 1966. *Indian Police and Judges: Experiments in Acculturation and Control.* New Haven: Yale University Press.

Harring, Sidney L. 1983. *Policing a Class Society: The Experience of American Cities, 1865–1915.* New Brunswick, N.J.: Rutgers University Press.

Hart, J.M. 1951. *The British Police.* London: Allen and Unwin.

Herlihy, David, ed. 1968. *Medieval Culture and Society.* New York: Harper Torchbooks.

Hill, Jim D. 1969. "The National Guard in Civil Disorders." In *Bayonets in the Streets: The Uses of Troops in Civil Disturbances*, ed. Robin Higham, pp. 61–84. Lawrence: University of Kansas Press.

Hjellemo, E.O. 1979. "History of the Nordic Police Systems—The Evolution of Policing in Denmark and Norway." In *Police and the Social Order*, report no. 6, eds. Johannes Knutsson, Eckart Kuhlhorn, and Albert Reiss, Jr., pp. 14–31. Stockholm: National Swedish Council for Crime Prevention.

Holborn, Hajo. 1969. *A History of Modern Germany 1840–1945.* New York: Alfred A. Knopf.

Jacob, Herbert. 1963. *German Administration Since Bismarck.* New Haven: Yale University Press.

Keeton, G.W. 1975. *Keeping the Peace.* London: Barry Rose Publishers.

Keppler, Leopold. 1974. "The Gendarmerie in Austria." *Kriminalistic.* Translated in NCJRS 11.

Kunkel, Wolfgang. 1973. *An Introduction to Roman Legal and Constitutional History.* 2nd ed. Oxford: Clarendon Press.

Lane, Roger. 1967. *Policing the City: Boston 1822–1885.* Cambridge, Mass.: Harvard University Press.

Langer, William L. 1969. *Political and Social Upheaval, 1832–1852.* New York: Harper and Row.

Langrod, Georges. 1961. *Some Current Problems of Administration in France Today.* Puerto Rico: University of Puerto Rico.

Lee, W.L. Melville. 1901. *A History of Police in England.* Repr. Ed. 1971. Montclair, N.J.: Patterson Smith.

Lintott, A.W. 1968. *Violence in Republican Rome.* Oxford: Clarendon Press.

Lodhi, Abdul Q. and Tilly, Charles. 1970. "Urbanization, Criminality and Collective Violence in Nineteenth Century France." Paper presented to annual meeting of the American Society of Criminology. Mimeographed.

Lofland, Lyn H. 1973. *A World of Strangers: Order and Action in Urban Public Space.* New York: Basic Books, Inc.

Martin, J.P. and Wilson, Gail. 1969. *The Police: A Study in Manpower: The Evolution of the Service in England and Wales, 1829–1965.* London: Heinemann.

Mildmay, William. 1763. *The Police of France.* London. (Copy found in Rare Book Collection, Princeton University.)

Monas, Sidney. 1961. *The Third Section: Police and Society in Russia Under Nicholas I.* Cambridge, Mass.: Harvard University Press.

Oura, Baron Kanetake. 1909. "The Police in Japan." In *Fifty Years of New Japan*, vol. I, ed. Shiganobu Okuma. London: Smith, Elder and Co.

Philips, David. 1977. *Crime and Authority in Victorian England: The Black Country 1835–1860. London: Croon Helm Ltd.*

Pringle, Patrick. n.d. *Hue and Cry: The Story of Henry and John Fielding and Their Bow Street Runners.* London: William Morrow and Co.

Radzinowicz, Leon. 1957. *A History of English Criminal Law and Its Administration Since 1750*. 4 vols. New York: Macmillan Co.

Raeff, Marc. 1975. "The Well-Ordered Police State and the Development of Modernity in Seventeenth and Eighteenth-Century Europe: A Comparative Approach." *American Historical Review* December: 1221-1243.

Reith, Charles. 1948. *A Short History of the British Police*. London: Oxford University Press.

Reynolds, P.K. Baillie. 1926. *The Vigiles of Imperial Rome*. London: Oxford University Press.

Rosenberg, Hans. 1958. *Bureaucracy, Aristocracy and Autocracy: The Prussian Experience, 1660–1815*. Cambridge, Mass.: Harvard University Press.

Schwartz, Richard D. and Miller, James C. 1964. "Legal Evolution and Societal Complexity." *American Journal of Sociology* September: 159-169.

Seton-Watson, Hugh. 1967. *The Russian Empire, 1801–1917*. Oxford: Clarendon Press.

Smith, Bruce. 1925. *The State Police*. New York: Macmillan Co.

Spitzer, Steven and Scull, Andrew T. 1977. "Social Control in Historical Perspective: From Private to Public Responses to Crime." *Correction and Punishment*, ed. David F. Greenberg, pp. 265-286. Beverly Hills: Sage Publications.

Starkarum, Judanath. 1963. *Mughal Administration*. Calcutta: M.C. Sarkar and Sons, Private Ltd.

Stead, Philip John. 1957. *The Police of Paris*. London: Staples Press.

Strayer, Joseph. 1970. *On the Medieval Origins of the Modern State*. Princeton, N.J.: Princeton University Press.

Tilly, Charles; Levett, Allan; Lodhi, A.Q.; and Munger, Frank C. 1974. "How Policing Affected the Visibility of Crime in Nineteenth-Century Europe and America." Ann Arbor: Center for Research on Social Organization, University of Michigan.

Tilly, Charles; Tilly, Louise; and Tilly, Richard. 1975. *The Rebellious Century, 1830–1930*. Cambridge, Mass.: Harvard University Press.

Tilly, Louise A. 1971. "The Food Riot as a Form of Political Conflict in France." *Journal of Interdisciplinary History* 2: 12.

Tobias, J.J. 1972. "Police and Public in the United Kingdom." *Journal of Contemporary History* January–April: 201-219.

Tsurumi, Kaguko. 1970. *Social Change and the Individual: Japan Before and After Defeat in World War II*. Princeton, N.J.: Princeton University Press.

Tuchman, Barbara. 1979. *A Distant Mirror: The Calamitous Fourteenth Century*. London: Penguin Books.

Webb, Sidney and Webb, Beatrice. 1963. *The Development of English Local Government, 1685–1835*. London: Oxford University Press.

Weinberger, Barbara. 1981. "The Police and the Public in Mid-Nineteenth Century Warwickshire." In *Policing and Punishment in Nineteenth Century Britain*, ed. Victor Bailey, pp. 65-93. New Brunswick, N.J.: Rutgers University Press.

6

Southern Slave Patrols as a Transitional Police Type

Philip L. Reichel

The history of American policing is filled with issues of race. Many contemporary problems also touch on or revolve around race. In this interesting article, Philip Reichel notes that the urban and Northern bias of much of the writing on American police history has caused writers and scholars to overlook an important component of early policing in the United States—slave patrols in the South. He discusses the significance of these slave patrols both in terms of the development of policing structures and techniques and also in terms of their legacy for police-minority relations. The facts in this article raise an important question that you should ponder—given the historical role of the police in enforcing slavery and, later, segregation, how can the problem of strained police-minority relations ever be solved, and how long will a solution take?

Accounts of the developmental history of American policing have tended to concentrate on happenings in the urban North. While the literature is replete with accounts of the growth of law enforcement in places like Boston (Lane, 1967; Savage, l865), Chicago (Flinn, 1975), Detroit (Schneider, 1980) and New York City (Richardson, 1970), there has been minimal attention paid to police development outside the North. It seems unlikely that other regions of the country simply mimicked that development regardless of their own peculiar social, economic, political, and geographical aspects. In fact, Samuel Walker (1980) has briefly noted that eighteenth and nineteenth century Southern cities had developed elaborate police patrol systems in an effort to control the slave population. Walker even suggested these slave patrols were precursors to the police (1980: 59). As a forerunner to the police, it would seem that slave patrols should have become a well researched example in our attempt to better understand the development of American law enforcement. However, the regionalism of many existing histories has meant that criminal justicians and practitioners are often unaware of the existence of, and the role played by, Southern slave patrols. This means our knowledge of the history of policing is incomplete and regionally biased. This article responds to that problem by focusing attention on the development of law enforcement in the Southern slave states (i.e., Alabama, Arkansas, Delaware, Florida, Georgia, Kentucky, Louisiana, Maryland, Mississippi, Missouri, North Carolina, South Carolina, Tennessee, Texas and Virginia) during the colonial and antebellum years. The particular question to be answered is: were Southern slave patrols precursors to modern policing?

Answering the research question requires clarification of the term precursor. The concept of a precursor to police implies there are stages of development preceding the point at which a modern police force is achieved. Several authors have looked at specific factors which influenced the development of police organizations in particular cities. Fewer have tried to make generalizations about police growth across the society. The latter group, which includes Bacon (1939), Lundman (1980) and Monkkonen (1981), draw on case studies of certain cities to hypothesize a developmental sequence explaining modernization of police in America. Lundman (1980), however, presents his ideas with the help of a typology of police systems.[1] The advantage of a historical typology is that it allows conceptualization of a developmental sequence and can therefore be most helpful in determining whether or not slave patrols can be viewed as a part of that sequence.

The Stages of Police Development

Lundman (1980) has suggested three types or systems of policing: informal, transitional, and modern. *Informal policing* is characterized by community members sharing responsibility for maintaining order. Such a system was typical of societies with little division of labor and a great deal of homogeneity. There existed among the people, a "collective conscience" which allowed them willingly to participate in the identification and apprehension of rule violators. As society grew, people had wide-ranging jobs and interests. Agreement as to what was right and wrong became less complete and informal police systems became less effective. Society's response was the development of *transitional policing* which served as a bridge between the informal and modern types. In that capacity, the transitional systems included aspects of the informal networks but also anticipated modern policing in terms of offices and procedures.

Identification of the point at which a police department becomes modern has not been agreed upon. Bacon, for example, cited six factors to be met: 1) citywide jurisdiction; 2) twenty-four-hour responsibility; 3) a single organization in charge of the greater part of formal enforcement; 4) a paid personnel on a salary basis; 5) a personnel occupied solely with police duties, and 6) general rather than specific functions (1939: 6). At the other extreme is Monkkonen's (1981) suggestion that the decisive movement to a modern police department occurs when the police adopt a uniform. Lundman follows Bacon but identifies only four distinctive characteristics of *modern policing* (1980: 17). First, there are persons recognized as having full-time police responsibilities. Also, there is 2) continuity in office as well as 3) continuity in procedure. Finally, for a system to be considered modern it must have 4) accountability to a central governmental authority.

Those four characteristics incorporate most of Bacon's suggestions but ignore Monkkonen's. Walker, however, found the use of uniforms as a starting point for modern policing to be "utter nonsense" (1982: 216), since the development process was not the same in every city and the new agencies varied so much in size and strength.[2] Instead, Lundman's characteristics seem appropriately chosen for present needs to identify the modern police type.

Existing histories of law enforcement provide significant information about informal (e.g. constables, day and night watches) and modern (e.g. London, New York City, Boston) types, but tend to ignore examples of what Lundman might call transitional. The implication is that modern policing was the result of simple formalization of informal systems. This article offers Southern slave patrols as an example of policing which went beyond informal but was not yet modern. Because few people are aware of them, the patrols will be described before being linked to transitional police types.

A Description of Southern Slave Patrols

A number of variables influence the development of formal mechanisms of social control. Lundman's review of the literature (1980: 24) identified four important factors: 1) an actual or perceived increase in crime; 2) public riots; 3) public intoxication; and 4) a need to control the "dangerous classes." Bacon (1939) in a comprehensive yet infrequently cited work, took a somewhat different approach. He identified three factors of social change influencing development of modern police departments: 1) increased economic specialization; 2) formation and increasing stratification of classes; and 3) increase in population size. As a result of these social changes Bacon argues there comes "an increase in fraud, in public disorders, and in legislation limiting personal freedom" which preexisting forms of maintaining order (e.g. family, church, neighborhood) are unable to handle (1939: 782). Variations in enforcement procedures then occur which are "pointed at specific groups, economic specialists, and certain times, places, and objects" until eventually there is a "tendency for specialists to become unified and organized" (Bacon, 1939: 782-783).

Given the scholarly works identifying such numerous and intertwined variables affecting the development of police agencies, it is potentially misleading to concentrate on just one of those factors. However, historical accounts of social control techniques in the South seem to suggest that a concern with class stratification (Lundman's fourth factor and Bacon's second) played a primary role in the development of formal systems of control in that region. Although the conflicts presented by immigrants and the poor have been shown to be important in the development of police in London, New York, and Boston (Lundman, 1980: 29), the conflicts presented by sales have received very little attention. Bacon compared slaves to Southern whites and found the folkways and mores of the two castes were so different that "continual and obvious force was required if society were to be maintained" (1939: 772). The continual and obvious force developed by the South to control its version of the "dangerous classes" was the slave patrol. Before discussing those patrols it is necessary to understand why the slaves constituted a threat.[3]

Slaves as a Dangerous Class

The portrayal of slaves as docile, happy, and generally content with their bondage has been successfully challenged in recent decades. We can today express amazement that slave-owners could have been unaware of their slaves' unhappiness, yet some whites were continually surprised that slaves resisted their status. Such an attitude was not found only among Southern slave-owners. In a 1731 advertisement for a fugitive slave, a New England master was dismayed that this slave had run away "without the least provocation" (quoted in Foner, 1975: 64). Whether provoked in the eyes of slave-holders or not, slaves did resist their bondage. That resistance generally took one of three forms: running away, criminal acts and conspiracies or revolts. Any of those actions constituted a danger to whites.

The number of slaves who ran away is difficult to determine (Foner, 1975: 264). However, it was certainly one of the greatest problems of slave government (Paterson, 1968: 20). Resistance by running away was easier for younger, English-speaking, skilled slaves, but records indicate slaves of all ages and abilities had attempted escape in this manner

(Foner, 1975: 260). Criminal acts by slaves have also been linked to resistance. Foner (1975: 265-268) notes instances of theft, robbery, crop destruction, arson and poison as being typical. Georgia legislation in 1770 which provided the death penalty for slaves found guilty of even attempting to poison whites was said to be necessary because "the detestable crime of poisoning hath frequently been committed by slaves." A 1761 issue of the *Charleston Gazette* complained "Negroes have again begun the hellish practice of poisoning" (both quoted in Foner, 1975: 267).

Possibly the most fear-invoking resistance however, were the slave conspiracies and revolts. Such actions occurred as early as 1657, but the largest slave uprising in colonial America took place on September 9, 1739 near the Steno River several miles from Charleston. Forty Negroes and twenty whites were killed and the resulting uproar had important impact on slave regulations. For example, South Carolina patrol legislation in 1740, noted:

> Forasmuch as many late horrible and barbarous massacres have been actually committed and many more designed, on the white inhabitants of this Province, by negro slaves, who are generally prone to such cruel practices, which makes it highly necessary that constant patrols should be established. (Cooper, b: 568)

Neighboring Georgians were also concerned with the actuality and potential for slave revolts. The preamble of their 1757 law establishing and regulating slave patrols argues:

> it is absolutely necessary for the Security of his Majesty's Subjects in this Province, that Patrols should be established under proper Regulations in the settled parts thereof, for the better keeping of Negroes and other Slaves in Order and prevention of any Cabals, Insurrections or other Irregularities amongst them. (Candler, 1910: 225)

Each of the three areas of resistance aided in slaves being perceived as a dangerous class. There was, however, another variable with overriding influence. Unlike the other three factors, this aspect was less direct and less visible. That latent variable was the num-

Table 6.1
***Colonial Populations by Race, 1680 to 1780*[a]**

	Percentages							
	South Carolina[b]		North Carolina[c]		Virginia[d]		Georgia[e]	
	White	Black	White	Black	White	Black	White	Black
1680	83	17	96	4	96	4	-	-
1700	57	43[f]	94	4	87	13	-	-
1720	30	70	86	14	76	24 (1715)	-	-
1740	33	67	79	21	68	32 (1743)	80	20
1760	36	64 (1763)	79	21 (1764)	50	50 (1763)	63	37
1780	58	42 (1785)	67	3 (1775)	52	48	70	30(1776)

[a]The sources used to gather these data are many and varied. The resulting percentages should be viewed as estimates to indicate trends rather than indication of exact distribution. Slave free blacks and in the early years, Indian slaves, are all included under "black."

[b]1680, 1700, 1720 and 1740 from Simmons (1976: 125); 1763 and 1785 from Greene and Harrington (1966: 172-176).

[c]1680, 1700, 1720 and 174O from Simmons (1976:125); 1764 from Foner (1975: 208); 1775 from Greene and Harrington (1966: 156-160).

[d]1680, 1715, 1743, 1763 and 1780 from Greene and Harrington (1966: 134-143): 1700 from Wells (1975: 161).

[e]Georgia was not settled until 1733 and although they were illegally imported in the mid-1740s, slaves were not legally allowed until 1750. 1750 from Wells (1975: 170); 1760 from Foner (1975: 213); 1776 from Greene and Harrington (1966: 180-182).

[f]Wood (1974: 143) believes black inhabitants exceeded white inhabitants in South Carolina around 1708.

ber of slaves in the total population of several colonies. While an interest in knowing the continuous whereabouts of slaves was present throughout the colonies, slave control by formal means (e.g. specialized legislation and forces) was more often found in those areas where slaves approached, or in fact were, the numerical majority. Table 5.1 provides population percentages for some of the Southern colonies/states. When considering the sheer number of persons to be controlled it is not surprising that whites often felt vulnerable.

The Organization and Operation of Slave Patrols[4]

Consistent with the earliest enforcement techniques identified in English and American history, the first means of controlling slaves was informal in nature. In 1686 a South Carolina statute said anyone could apprehend, chastise and send home any slave found off his/her plantation without authorization. In 1690 such action was made everyone's duty or be fined forty shillings (Henry, 1968: 31). Enforcement of slavery by the average citizen was not to be taken lightly. A 1705 act in Virginia made it legal "for any person or persons whatsoever, to kill or destroy such slaves (i.e. runaways) . . . without accusation or impeachment of any crime for the same" (quoted in Fonor, 1975: 195). Eventually, however, such informal means became inadequate. As the social changes suggested by Bacon (1939) took place and this fear of slaves as a dangerous class heightened, special enforcement officers developed and provided a transition to modern police with general enforcement powers.

In their earliest stages, slave patrols were part of the colonial militias. Royal charters empowered governors to defend colonies and that defense took the form of a militia for coast and frontier defense (Osgood, 1957). All able-bodied males between 16 and 60 were to be enrolled in the militia and had to provide their own weapons and equipment (Osgood, 1957; Shy, 1980; Simmons, 1976). Although the militias were regionally diverse and constantly changing (Shy, 1980), Anderson's (1984) comments about the Massachusetts Bay Colony militia notes an important distinction that was reflected in other colonies. At the beginning of the 18th century, Massachusetts militia was defined not so much as an army but "as an all-purpose military infrastructure" (Anderson, 1984: 27) from which volunteers were drawn for the provincial armies. This concept of the militia as a pool from which persons could be drawn for special duties was the basis for colonial slave patrols.

Militias were active at different levels throughout the colonies. New York and South Carolina militias were required to be particularly active. New York was menaced by the Dutch and French Iroquois conflicts while South Carolina had to be defended against the Indians, Spanish, and pirates. By the middle of the 18th century the colonies were being less threatened by external forces and attention was being turned to internal problems. As early as 1721 South Carolina began shifting militia duty away from external defense to internal security. In that year, the entire militia was made available for the surveillance of slaves (Osgood, 1974). The early South Carolina militia law had enrolled both whites and blacks, and in the Yamassee war of 1715 some four hundred Negroes helped six hundred white men defeat the Indians (Shy, 1980). Eventually, however, South Carolinians did not dare to arm Negroes. With the majority of the population being black (see Table 5.1) and the increasing danger of slave revolts, the South Carolina militia essentially became a "local anti-slave police force and (was) rarely permitted to participate in military operations outside its boundaries" (Simmons, 1976: 127).

Despite their link to militia, slave patrols were a separate entity. Each slave state had codes of laws for the regulation of slavery. These slave codes authorized and outlined the duties of the slave patrols. Some towns had their own patrols, but they were more frequent in the rural areas. The presence of constables and a more equal distribution of whites and blacks made the need for the town patrols less immediate. In the rural areas, however, the slaves were more easily able to participate in "dangerous" acts. It is not surprising that the slave patrols came to be viewed as "rural police" (cf. Henry, 1968: 42). South Carolina Governor Bull described the role of the patrols in 1740 by writing:

The interior quiet of the Province is provided for by small Patrols, drawn every two months from each company, who do duty by riding along the roads and among the Negro Houses in small districts in every Parish once a week, or as occasion requires. (quoted in Wood, 1974: 276 note 23)

Documentation of slave patrols is found for nearly all the Southern colonies and states[5] but South Carolina seems to have been the oldest, most elaborate, and best documented. That is not surprising given the importance of the militia in South Carolina and the presence of large numbers of blacks. Georgia's developed somewhat later and exemplifies patrols in the late 18th and early 19th centuries. The history and development of slave patrol legislation in South Carolina and Georgia provides a historical review from colonial through antebellum times.

In 1704 the colony of Carolina[6] presented what appears to be the South's first patrol act. The patrol was linked to the militia yet separate from it since patrol duty was an excuse from militia duty. Under this act, militia captains were to select ten men from their companies to form these special patrols. The captain was to

muster all the men under his command, and with them ride from plantation to plantation, and into any plantation, within the limits or precincts, as the General shall think fitt, and take up all slaves which they shall meet without their master's plantation which have not a permit or ticket from their masters, and the same punish. (Cooper, 1837: 255)

That initial act seemed particularly concerned with runaway slaves, while an act in 1721 suggests an increased concern with uprisings. The act ordered the patrols to try to "prevent all caballings amongst negroes, by dispersing of them when drumming or playing, and to search all negro houses for arms or other offensive weapons" (McCord, 1841: 640). In addition to that concern the new act also responded to complaints that militia duty was being shirked by the choicest men who were doing patrol duty instead of militia duty (Bacon, 1939; Henry, 1968; McCord, 1841; Wood, 1974). As a result, the separate patrols were merged with the colonial militia and patrol duty was simply rotated among different members of the militia. From 1721 to 1734 there really were no specific slave patrols in South Carolina. The duty of supervising slaves was simply a militia duty.

In 1734 the Provincial Assembly set up a regular patrol once again separate from the militia (Cooper 1838a, p. 395). "Beat companies" of five men (Captain and four regular militia men) received compensation (captains #50 and privates #25 per year) for patrol duty and exemption from other militia duty. There was one patrol for each of 33 districts in the colony. Patrols obeyed orders from and were appointed by district commissioners and were given elaborate search and seizure powers as well as the right to administer up to twenty lashes (Cooper 1838a: 395–397).[7]

Since provincial acts usually expired after three years, South Carolina's 1734 Act was revised in 1737 and again in 1740. Under the 1737 revision, the paid recruits were replaced with volunteers who were encouraged to enlist by being excused from militia and other public duty for one year and were allowed to elect their own captain (Cooper 1838b: 456-458). The number of men on patrol was increased from five to fifteen and they were to make weekly rounds. Henry (1968: 33) believed these changes were an attempt to dissuade irresponsible persons who had been attracted to patrol duty for the pay.

The 1740 revision seems to be the first legislation specifically including women plantation owners as answerable for patrol service (Cooper 1838b: 569-570). The plantation owners (male or female) could, however, procure any white person between 16 and 60 to ride patrol for them. In addition, the 1740 act said patrol duty was not to be required in townships where white inhabitants were in far superior numbers to the Negroes (Cooper 1838b: 571). Such an exemption certainly highlights the role of patrols as being to control what was perceived as a dangerous class.

At this point we turn to the Georgia slave patrols as an example of one that developed after South Carolina set a precedent. Georgia was settled late (1733) compared to the other colonies and despite her proximity to South Carolina she did not make immediate use of slaves. In fact while slaves were illegally imported in the mid 1740s, they were not legally allowed until 1750. Within seven years Georgians felt a need for control of the slaves. Her first patrol act (1757) provided for militia captains to pick up to seven patrollers from a list of all plantation owners (women and men) and all male white persons in the patrol district (Candler 1910: 225-235). The patrollers or their substitutes were to ride patrol at least once every two weeks and examine each plantation in their district at least once every month. The patrols were to seek out potential runaways, weapons, ammunition, or stolen goods.

The 1757 Act was continued in 1760 (Candler 1910: 462) for a period of five years. The 1765 continuation (Cobb 1851: 965) increased the number of patrollers to a maximum of ten, but left the duties and structure of the patrol as it was created in 1757. In the 1765 revision (Candler 1911: 75) the possession and use of weapons by slaves was tightened and a fine was set for selling alcohol to slaves. More interesting was the order relevant to Savannah only which gave patrollers the power to apprehend and take into custody (until the next morning) any disorderly white person (Candler 1911: 81). Should such a person be in a "Tippling House Tavern or Punch House" rather than on the streets the patrol had to call a lawful constable to their assistance before they could enter the "bar." Such power was extended in 1778 when patrols were obliged to "take up all white persons who cannot give a satisfactory account of themselves and carry them before a Justice of the Peace to be dealt with as is directed by the Vagrant Act" (Candler, 1911: 119).

Minor changes occurred between 1778 and 1830 (e.g. females were exempted from patrol duty in 1824) but the first major structural change did not take place until 1830. In that year Georgia patrols finally began moving away from a direct militia link when Justices of the Peace were authorized and required to appoint and organize patrols (Cobb, 1851: 1003). In 1854 Justices of the Inferior Courts were to annually appoint three "patrol commissioners" for each militia district (Rutherford, 1854: 101). Those commissioners were to make up the patrol list and appoint one person at least 25 years old and of good moral character to be Captain.

The absence of significant changes in Georgia patrol legislation over the years suggests the South Carolina experiences had provided an experimental stage for Georgia and possibly other slave states. Differences certainly existed, but Foner's general description of slave patrols seems accurate for the majority of colonies and states: patrols had full power and authority to enter any plantation and break open Negro houses or other places when slaves were suspected of keeping arms; to punish runaways or slaves found outside of their masters' plantations without a pass; to whip any slave who should affront or abuse them in the execution of their duties; and to apprehend and take any slave suspected of stealing or other criminal offense, and bring him to the nearest magistrate (1975: 206).

The Slaves' Response to the Patrols

The slave patrols were both feared and resented by the slaves.[8] Some went so far as to suggest it was "the worse thing yet about slavery" (quoted in Blassingame, 1977: 156). Former slave Lewis Clarke was most eloquent in expressing his distrust:

(The patrols are) the offscouring of all things, the refuse, . . . the ears and tails of slavery; . . . the tooth and tongues of serpents. They are the very fool's cap of baboons, . . . the wallet and satchel of polecats, the scum of stagnant pools, the exuvial, the worn-out skins of slave-holders. (T)hey are the meanest, and lowest, and worst of all creation. Like starved wharf rats, they are out nights, creeping into slave cabins, to see if they have an old bone there; they drive out husbands from their own beds, and then take their places. (Clarke, 1846: 114)

Despite the harshness and immediacy of punishment as well as the likelihood of discovery, slaves continued with the same behavior that brought about slave patrols in the first place. In fact, they added activities of specific irritation to the patrollers (or, as they were variously known, padaroe, padarole, or patteroller). Preventive measures like warning systems, playing ignorant and innocent when caught and learning when to expect a patrol were typically used. More assertive measures included building trap doors for escape from their cabins, tying ropes across roads to trip approaching horses, and fighting their way out of meeting places (Genovese, 1972: 618-619; Rose, 1976: 249-289). As have victims in other terrifying situations, the slaves occasionally resorted to humor as a source of strength. One version of a popular song makes that point:

Run, nigger, run; de patterroller catch you;
Run, nigger, run, its almost day.
Run, nigger, run; de patterroller catch you;
Run, nigger, run, and try to get far away.
De nigger run, he run his best;
Stuck his hand in a hornet's nest.
Jumped de fence and run through de paster;
Marsa run, but nigger run faster.
(Goodman, 1969: 83)

In an ironic sense the resistance by slaves should have been completely understandable to American patriots. Patrols were allowed search powers that the colonists later found so objectionable in the hands of British authorities (Foner, 1975: 221). Add to that the accompanying lack of freedoms to move, assemble, and bear arms, and the slave resistance seems perfectly appropriate.

Problems with the Slave Patrols

In addition to the difficulties presented by the slaves themselves, the patrols throughout the South experienced a variety of other problems. Many of these were similar to problems confronting colonial militia: training was infrequent; the elites often avoided duty; and those that did serve were often irresponsible (Anderson, 1984; Osgood; 1957; Shy, 1980; Simmons, 1976). In addition, the patrols had some unique concerns.

One of the first problems was the presence of free blacks. Understandably, slaves caught by patrollers would try to pass themselves off as free persons. The problem was particularly bad in some of the cities where many free blacks existed. In 1810, for example, the Charleston census showed 1,783 free Negroes (Henry, 1968: 50). Special acts eventually allowed the patrol to whip even free Negroes away from their home or employers business unless they produced "free papers." In all but one of the slave states a black person was presumed to be a slave unless she or he could prove differently. The sole exception to this procedure was Louisiana where "persons of color are presumed to be free" (Louisiana supreme court quoted in Foner, 1983: 106) until proven otherwise.

Other problems centered on the apparently careless enforcement of the patrol laws in some districts. When all was quiet and orderly the patrol seemed to be lulled into inactivity (Henry, 1968: 39). But there seemed always to be individuals having problems with slaves and those persons often complained about the lax enforcement of patrol laws. Flanders (1967: 30) cites several examples from exasperated Georgians who complained that slaves were not being properly controlled. In 1770 South Carolina Governor Bull noted that "though human prudence has provided these Statutory Laws, yet, through human frailty, they are neglected in these times of general tranquility" (quoted in Wood, 1974: 276 note 23). Fifty years later the situation had not improved much as then Governor Geddes suggested in his annual message:

> The patrol duty which is so intimately connected with the good order and police of the state, is still so greatly neglected in several of our parishes and districts, that serious inconveniences have been felt . . . . (quoted in Henry, 1968: 38)

Even when the patrols were active they did not avoid criticism. Genovese (1972: 618) quotes a Georgia planter who complained: "Our patrol laws are seldom enforced, and even where there is mock observance of them, it is by a parcel of boys or idle men, the height of whose ambition is to 'ketch a nigger.'" Earlier it was noted that South Carolina in 1721 modified its patrol law because the "choicest and best men" (planters) were avoiding militia duty doing patrol duty. As Bacon (1939: 581) notes, service by such men was something of a rarity in police work anyway. However, it must have been a rarity in other slave states as well since the more typical opinion of the patrollers was that expressed above by the Georgia planter. As with militia duty in general, the elite members of the districts often were able to avoid patrol

duty by either paying a fine or finding a substitute.

Where the "ketch a nigger" mentality existed, the patrols were often accused of inappropriate behavior. Complaints existed about patrollers drinking too much liquor before or during duty (Bacon, 1939: 587; Rose, 1976: 276; Wood, 1974: 276), and both South Carolina (Cooper, 1838b: 573) and Georgia (Candler, 1910: 233-234) had provisions for fining any person found drunk while on patrol duty. More serious complaints (possibly linked to the drinking) concerned the harshness of punishment administered by some patrols. Ex-slave Ida Henry offered an example:

> De patrollers wouldn't allow de slaves to hold night services, and one night dey caught me mother out praying. Dey stripped her naked and tied her hands together and wid a rope tied to de handcuffs and threw one end of de rope over a limb and tied de other end to de pummel of a saddle on a horse. As me mother weighed 'bout 200, dey pulled her up so dat her toes could barely touch de ground and whipped her. Dat same night she ran away and sta'ed over a day and returned. (quoted in Foner 1983, p. 103)

Masters as well as slaves often protested the actions of the patrol —on which the owners had successfully avoided serving (Genovese, 1972: 618). The slaves were, after all, an expensive piece of property which owners did not want damaged. Attempts to preserve orderly behavior of the patrollers took the form of a fine for misbehavior and occasionally reimbursement for damages (Henry, 1968: 37, 40). However, patrollers were allowed a rather free hand and many unlawful acts were accepted in attempts to uphold the patrol system. Henry saw this as the greatest evil of the system since "it gave unscrupulous persons unfair advantages and appears not to have encouraged the enforcement of the law by the better class" (1968: 40).

This review of the slave patrols shows them to have operated as a specialized enforcement arm. Although often linked to the militia, they had an autonomy and unique function which demands they be viewed as something more than an informal police type yet certainly not an example of a modern police organization. To identify the historical role and place of slave patrols we will turn to the concept of transitional police types.

Discussion

By definition a transitional police type must share characteristics of both informal and modern systems. Drawing from his four characteristics of a modern type, Lundman says transitional systems differ from modern ones by: 1) reliance upon other than full-time police officers; 2) frequent elimination and replacement (i.e. absence of continuity in office and in procedure); and 3) absence of accountability to a central governmental authority (1980: 190). When slave patrols are placed against these criteria they can be shown to have enough in common to warrant consideration as a transitional police type. First, like informal systems, the slave patrols relied on the private citizen to carry out the duties. However, unlike the constable, watchman and sheriff, the patrollers had only policing duties rather than accompanying expectations of fire watch and/or tax collection. The identification of patrollers as "police" was much closer to a social status as we know it today. For example, when South Carolina planter Samuel Porcher was elected a militia captain he described himself as being "a sort of chief of police in the parish" (J.K. Williams, 199: 65). Slave patrols relied upon private citizens for performance of duties, yet those patrollers came closer to being full-time police officers than had citizens under informal systems.

As noted earlier, slave patrols were not always active and even when they were they did not always follow expected procedure. The periodic lapses and frequent replacement of patrols is expected under Lundman's idea of a transitional type. Since the patrols operated under procedures set down in the Slave Codes they did approximate continuity in procedure. However, the South Carolina chronology of patrol legislation suggests those procedures changed as often as every three years.

The final criterion against which slave patrols might be judged is accountability to a central governmental authority. Lundman says such accountability is absent in a transitional system (1980: 20). It is at this point that slave patrols as a transitional police type might be challenged. The consistent link between slave patrols and militia units make it difficult to argue against accountability to a central government authority. Even when the link to militia was not direct, there was a central authority controlling patrols. From 1734 to 1737 South Carolina patrols were appointed by district commissioners and obeyed orders of governor, military commander-in-chief, and district commissioners (Bacon, 1939: 585; Wood, 1974: 275). In 1753, North Carolina justices of county courts could appoint three freeholders as "searchers" who took an oath to disarm slaves[9] (Patterson, 1968: 13). In 1802 the patrols were placed entirely under the jurisdiction of the county courts which in 1837 were authorized to appoint a patrol committee to insure the patrol functioned (Johnson, 1937: 516-517). Tennessee, a part of North Carolina from 1693-1790, also used the "searchers" as authorized by the 1753 act. In 1806, ten years after statehood, Tennessee developed an elaborate patrol system wherein town commissioners appointed patrols for incorporated and unincorporated towns (Patterson, 1968: 38). Louisiana patrols (originally set up in 1807 by Territorial legislation) went through a period of confusion between 1813 and 1821 when both the militia and parish judges had authority over patrols. Finally, in 1821 parish governmental bodies were given complete authority over the slave patrols (J.G. Taylor, 1963: 170; E.R. Williams, 1972: 400). Slave patrols had first been introduced in Arkansas in 1825 and were apparently appointed by the county courts until 1853. After then appointments were made by the justice of the peace (O.W. Taylor, 1958: 31, 209) as was true in Georgia beginning in 1830 (Cobb, 1851: 1003). In 1831 the incorporated towns in Mississippi were authorized to control their own patrol system and in 1833 boards of county police (i.e. county boards of supervisors) could appoint patrol leaders (Sydnor, 1933): 78). The Missouri General Assembly first established patrols in 1825 then in 1837 the county courts were given powers to appoint township patrols to serve for one year (Trexler, 1969: 182-183).

That review of patrol accountability in eight states suggests that slave patrols often came under the same governmental authority as formal police organizations. Or, as Sydnor pointed out in reference to the Mississippi changes: "the system was decentralized and made subject to the local units of civil government" (1933: 78). An argument can be made that the basis for a non-militia government authorized force to undertake police duties was implemented as early as 1734 when South Carolina patrols were appointed by district commissioners or in 1802 when North Carolina placed patrols under the jurisdiction of the county courts. What then does that mean for the placement of slave patrols as an example of a transitional police type? If the various governmental bodies mentioned above are accepted as being examples of "centralized governmental authority," it means two positions are possible. First, slave patrols must not be an example of a transitional type. This position is rejected on the basis of information provided here which shows the patrols to have been a legitimate entity with specialized law enforcement duties and powers.

The other possible position is that "absence of accountability to a centralized governmental authority" is not a necessary feature of transitional policing. This seems more reasonable given the information presented here. Since there has not been any specific example of a transitional police force offered to this point,[10] Lundman's characteristics are only hypothetical. As other examples of transitional police types are put forward we have a firmer base for determining how they differ from modern police.

Conclusion

As early as 1704 and continuing through the antebellum period, Southern slave states used local patrols with specific responsibility for regulating the activity of slaves. Those slave patrols were comprised of citizens who did patrol duty as their civic obligation, for pay, rewards, or for exemption from other duties. The patrollers had a defined area which

they were to ride in attempts to discover runaway slaves, stolen property, weapons, or to forestall insurrections. Unlike the watchmen, constables, and sheriffs who had some non-policing duties, the slave patrols operated solely for the enforcement of colonial and state laws. The existence of these patrols leads to two conclusions about the development of American law enforcement. First, the law enforcement nature of slave patrol activities meant there were important events occurring in the rural South prior to and concurrently with events in the urban North which are more typically cited in examples of the evolution of policing in the United States. Because of that it is undesirable to restrict attention to just the North when turning to understand and appreciate the growth of American law enforcement. Second, rather than simply being a formalization of previously informal activities, modern policing seems to have passed through developmental stages which can be explained by such typologies as that offered by Lundman who described informal, transitional, and modern types of policing.

While those conclusions are important, focusing attention on slave patrols and the South is desirable for reasons which go quite beyond a need to avoid regional bias in historical accounts or to describe a form of policing which is neither informal nor modern. For example, what implication does this analysis have on the usefulness of typologies in historical research? Further, how might typologies and the accompanying description of those types assist in generating a theory to explain the development of law enforcement?

If typologies are helpful as a historiographic technique, is Lundman's the best available or possible? Based on the usefulness of the typology for describing slave patrols and placing them in a specific historical context, it seems to this author that typologies are an excellent way to go beyond descriptive accounts and move toward the development of theoretical explanations. As greater use is made of typologies to conceptualize the development of American law enforcement, it seems likely that existing formulations will be modified. For example, slave patrols seem to exemplify what Lundman called the transitional police type except in terms of Lundman's proposed absence of accountability to a centralized governmental authority. Recall, however, that Bacon also suggested a developmental sequence (without specifying or naming "types") for police which described modern police as having general rather than specific functions (Bacon, 1939: 6). Combining the work of Lundman and Bacon, we might suggest that precursors to modern police are not necessarily without accountability to a centralized governmental authority, but do have specialized rather than general enforcement powers. In this manner, the characteristics of policing which precede the modern stage might be: 1) frequent elimination and replacement of the police type (Lundman); 2) reliance upon persons other than full-time police officers (Lundman); and 3) enforcement powers which are specialized rather than general (Bacon).

In addition to providing organized conceptualization, typologies also provide a basis for theoretical development. For example, there does not as yet appear to be an identifiable Northern precursor, like slave patrols, between the constable/watch and modern stages. Is that because the North skipped that stage, compressed it to such an extent we cannot find an example of its occurrence, or passed through the transitional stage but researchers have not described the activities in terms of a typology? While each of those questions is interesting, the first seems to have particularly intriguing implications for if it is correct it means there may not be a general evolutionary history for policing. For example, are modern police agencies necessarily preceded by a developmental stage comprised of a specialized police force? Is the progression in the developmental history of law enforcement agencies one of generalized structure with general functions, to a specific structure with specific functions, and finally a specific structure with general functions?

As an example of how this type of inquiry can fit with theoretical developments, we should note recent work by Robinson and Scaglion (1987). Those authors present four interdependent propositions which state:

1. The origin of the specialized police function depends upon the division of society into dominant and subordinate classes with antagonistic interests;

2. Specialized police agencies are generally characteristic only of societies politically organized as states;

3. In a period of transition, the crucial factor in delineating the modern specialized police function is an ongoing attempt at conversion of the social control (policing) mechanism from an integral part of the community structure to an agent of an emerging dominant class; and

4. The police institution is created by the emerging dominant class as an instrument for the preservation of its control over restricted access to basic resources, over the political apparatus governing this access, and over the labor force necessary to provide the surplus upon which the dominant class lives. (Robinson and Scaglion, 1987: 109)

The development of law enforcement structures in the antebellum South would seem to support each of the propositions. Slave patrols were created only because of master-slave social structure (proposition 1), existing as colonies became increasingly politically organized as states (proposition 2), and elites were able to convince community members to "police" the slaves (proposition 3), because control of those slaves was necessary to solidify elite positioning (proposition 4).

In order to respond with authority to these questions and implications, it will be necessary to continue research on the history of law enforcement. Detailed study of slave patrols in specific colonies and states is necessary as are research endeavors which assess the applicability of various typologies in different jurisdictions. Hopefully this initial effort will serve to both inform criminal justicians and practitioners about an important but little-known aspect of American police history as well as encourage research on non-Northern developments in the history of law enforcement. It has been argued here that most histories of the development of police have portrayed a regional bias suggesting that evolution was essentially Northern and urban in nature. In addition, existing information has covered the initial organizational stages of policing and the formation of modern police departments, but we are left with the impression that little activity of historical importance occurred between those first developments and the eventually modern department. Lundman has called that middle stage "transitional" policing and it is that concept which has been used here to: 1) debunk the portrayal of American law enforcement history as restricted to the urban North, and 2) provide an example of a form of policing more advanced than the constable/watch type but one which was not modern.

Notes

Author's Note: Historian Gail Rowe and two anonymous American Journal of Police referees provided me with invaluable assistance and suggestions for which I am most grateful. This is an extensively revised version of a paper presented at the 1985 Annual Meeting of the Academy of Criminal Justice Sciences.

1. Lundman's typology of police systems is not to be confused with other typologies (e.g. Wilson's 1968 policing styles) which differentiate contemporary as opposed to the historical types Lundman addresses.

2. Monkkonen's reasons for using uniforms as the starting date can be found in his book (1981: 39-45, 53) and in an article (1982: 577).

3. Some may find the explanation of slaves as a dander to be an exercise in the obvious, but Walker's (1982) comments provide a guiding principle. He suggests that "constructing a thesis around presumed existence of a dangerous class is . . . a sloppy bit of historical writing" unless we are told who composed the group, where they stood in the social structure and in what respect they are a danger (Walker, 1982: 215). While the "who" (slaves) and "where" (at the very bottom) questions have been addressed above and countless other places, the "what" question is less understood.

4. Information about slave patrols is found primarily in the writings of historians as they describe aspects of the slaves life in the South.

Data for this article were gathered from those secondary sources but also, for South Carolina and Georgia, from some primary accounts including colonial records, Eighteenth and Nineteenth century statutes and writings by former slaves.

5. See Rose (1976) for Alabama; O.W. Taylor (1958) for Arkansas; Flanders (1967) for Georgia; Coleman (1940) and McDougle (1970) for Kentucky; Bacon (1939), J.G. Taylor (1963) and Williams (1972) for Louisiana; Sydnor (1933) for Mississippi; Trexler (1969) for Missouri: Johnson (1937) for North Carolina; Patterson (1968) and Mooney(1971) for Tennessee; and Ballagh (1968) and Stewart (1976) for Virginia.

6. In 1712 the northern two-thirds of Carolina was divided into two parts (North Carolina and South Carolina) while the southern one-third remained unsettled until 1733 when Oglethorpe founded Georgia.

7. The right to administer a punishment to slaves was given to patrols in other colonies and states as well. Patrols in North Carolina could administer fifteen lashes (Johnson, 1937: 516) as could those in Tennessee (Patterson, 1968: 39) and Mississippi (Sydnor, 1933: 78) while Georgia (Candler, 1910: 232) and Arkansas (O.W. Taylor, 1958: 210) followed South Carolina in allowing twenty lashes.

8. Rawick (1972: 61-65) provides interesting recollections of patrols by ex-slaves in Alabama, Georgia, Louisiana, North Carolina, Tennessee and Virginia.

9. This oath read: "I, A.B., do swear that I as searcher for guns, swords and other weapons among the slaves of my district, faithfully, and as privately as I can, discharge the trust reposed in me, as the law directs, to the best of my power. So help me God" (Quoted in Patterson, 1968: 13 note 23).

10. Lundman (1980: 20) only notes Fielding's Bow Street Runners, Colquhoun's River Police and mid-Nineteenth century Denver, as possible examples of transitional police.

References

Anderson, F. (1984) *A People's Army: Massachusetts Soldiers and Society in the Seven Years' War*. Chapel Hill, NC: University of North Carolina.

Bacon, S. (1939) *The Early Development of American Municipal Police: A Study of the Evolution of Formal Controls in a Changing*

Society. Unpublished dissertation, Yale University. University Microfilms No. 66-06844.

Ballagh, J. (1968) *A History of Slavery in Virginia*. New York: Johnson Reprint Company.

Blassingame, J.W. (ed.) (1977) *Slave Testimony: Two Centuries of Letters, Speeches, Interviews, and Autobiographies*. Baton Rouge, LA: Louisiana State University Press.

Candler, A. (ed.) (1910) *The Colonial Records of the State of Georgia*, Vol. 18. Atlanta, GA: Chas. P. Byrd, State Printer.

—— (ed.) (1911) *The Colonial Records of the State of Georgia*, Vol. 19, Part 2. Atlanta, GA: Chas. P. Byrd, State Printer.

Clarke, L.G. (1846) *Narratives of Suffering*. Available on Library of American Civilization fiche #12812.

Cobb, T.R. (1851) *A Digest of the Statute Laws of the State of Georgia*, Athens, GA: Christy, Kelsea &, Burke.

Coleman, J.W., Jr., (1940) *Slavery Times in Kentucky*. New York: Johnson Reprint Company.

Cooper, T. (ed.) (1837) *Statutes at Large of South Carolina*, Vol. 2, Part 1. Columbia, SC: A.S. Johnston.

—— (ed.) (1838a) *Statutes at Large of South Carolina*, Vol. 3, Part 1. Columbia, SC: A.S. Johnston.

—— (ed.) (1838b) *Statutes at Large of South Carolina*, Vol. 3, Part 2. Columbia, SC: A.S. Johnston.

Flanders, R.B. (1967) *Plantation Slavery in Georgia*. Cos Cob, CT: John E. Edwards, Publisher.

Flinn, J. (1975) *History of the Chicago Police from the Settlement of the Community to the Present Time*. Mountclair, NJ: Patterson Smith.

Foner, P.S. (1975) *History of Black Americans: From Africa to the Emergence of the Cotton Kingdom*. Westport, CT: Greenwood.

—— (1983) *History of Black Americans: From Africa to the Emergence of the Cotton Kingdom to the Eve of the Compromise of 1850*. Westport, CT: Greenwood.

Genovese, E.D. (1972) *Roll Jordan, Roll: The World the Slaves Made*. New York: Pantheon.

Greene, E. and Harrington, V. (1966) *American Population Before the Federal Census of 1790*. Gloucester, MA: Peter Smith.

Henry, H.M. (1968) *The Police Control of the Slave in South Carolina*. New York: Negro Universities Press.

Johnson, G.G. (1937) *Ante-bellum North Carolina: A Social History*. Chapel Hill, NC: University of North Carolina.

Lane, R. (1967) *Policing the City*: Boston 1822-1885. Cambridge, MA: Harvard University Press.

Lundman, R.J. (1980) *Police and Policing: An Introduction*. New York: Holt, Rinehart and Winston.

McCord, D.J. (ed.) (1841) *Statutes at Large of South Carolina*, Vol. 9, Part 2. Columbia, SC: A.S. Johnston.

McDougle, I.E. (1970) *Slavery in Kentucky 1792-1865* Westport, CT: Negro Universities Press.

Monkkonen, E. (1981.) *Police in Urban America, 1860-1920*. Cambridge, MA: Cambridge University.

—— (1982) "From cop history to social historic: The significance of the police in American history." *Journal of Social History*. 15:575-592.

Mooney, C.C. (1971) *Slavery in Tennessee*. Westport, CT: Negro Universities Press.

Osgood, H.L. (1957) *The American Colonies in the Seventeenth Century*, Vol. 1. Gloucester, MA: Peter Smith.

Patterson, C.P. (1968) *The Negro in Tennessee*, 1790-1865. New York: Negro Universities Press.

Rawick, G.P. (1972) *The American Slave: A Composite Autobiography*. Westport, CT: Greenwood.

Richardson, J. (1970) *The New York Police: Colonial Times to 1901*. New York: Oxford University.

Robinson, C. and Scaglion, R. (1987) "The origin and evolution of the police function in society: Notes toward a theory." *Law and Society Review*. 21:109-153.

Rose, W.L. (ed.) (1976) *A Documentary History of Slavery in North America*. New York: Oxford University.

Rutherford, J. (ed.) (1854) *Acts of the General Assembly of the State of Georgia*. Savannah, GA: Samilel T. Chapman.

Savage, E.A. (1865) *A Chronological History of the Boston Watch and Police, from 1631-1865*. Available on Library of American Civilization fiche #13523.

Schneider, J. (1980) *Detroit and the Problem of Order, 1830-1880: A Geography of Crime, Riot, and Policing*. Lincoln, NE: University of Nebraska.

Shy, J.W. (1980) "A new look at colonial militia." In P. Karsten (ed.). *The Military in America*. New York: Free Press.

Simmons, R.C. (1976) *The American Colonies*. New York: McKay.

Stewart, A. (1976) "Colonel Alexander's Slaves Resist the Patrol." In W.L. Rose (ed.) *A Documentary History of Slavery in North America.* New York: Oxford University.

Sydnor, C.S. (1933) *Slavery in Mississippi.* New York: Appleton-Century Company.

Taylor, J.G. (1963) *Negro Slavery in Louisiana.* New York: Negro Universities Press.

Taylor, O.W. (1958) *Negro Slavery in Arkansas.* Durham, NC: Duke University.

Trexler, H.A. (1969) "Slavery in Missouri: 1804-1865." In H. Trexler, *Slavery in the States: Selected Essays.* New York: Negro Universities Press.

Walker, S. (1980) *Popular Justice* New York: Oxford.

—— (1982) "Counting cops and crime." Book Review, *Reviews in American History.* 10:212.

Wells, R. (1975) *The Population of the British Colonies in America Before 1776: A Survey of Census Data.* Princeton, NJ: Princeton University.

Williams, E.R., Jr. (1972) "Slave patrol ordinances of St. Tammany Parish, Louisiana, 1835-1838." *Louisiana History.* 13:399-411.

Williams, J.K. (1959) *Vogues in Villainy.* Columbia, SC: University of South Carolina.

Wood, P.H. (1974) *Black Majority: Negroes in Colonial South Carolina.* New York: Knopf.

7

The Municipal Police Detective: An Historical Analysis

Jack Kuykendall

Most of the police history that has been published has concentrated on (1) the big picture of evolving strategies and models of policing, (2) cycles of scandal and reform in specific cities, or (3) the day-to-day duties and activities of patrol officers. This article examines a different angle of the developmental life of modern policing—the history of the detective. Jack Kuykendall presents the English and American backgrounds of crime solving and detective work, and then identifies three phases in the evolution of police detectives. You might want to think about both real detectives that you have known and fictional detectives from our popular culture (Sherlock Holmes, Joe Friday, or "Dirty Harry" Callahan, for example) in terms of these three phases or styles of detective work. You should also consider whether or not scientific advancements over the last few decades (such as computerized information systems, automated fingerprint systems, and DNA matching) have changed the nature of detective work, constituting a fourth phase in the historical development of criminal investigation.

The detective, a term first utilized in the 1840s, can be identified by organization position, purpose, and function. Police organizations created the position ostensibly for the purpose of apprehension. Historically, the detection function was associated with practices that made it a troublesome and contro-

versial endeavor. Among those practices were the perceptions that individuals who engaged in detection (1) investigated only either difficult and serious or easily solved crimes; (2) worked primarily for profit and usually only for the middle and upper classes; (3) spied on citizens to acquire information about their actual and possible political and criminal activity; (4) acted as agent provocateurs or thiefmakers to incite crime and entrap citizens; (5) used secrecy, deceit, treachery, coercion, and brutality to acquire information; (6) participated with criminals to both create and cover up illegal behavior; and (7) used and manipulated informers (Wade, 1829; Radzinowicz, 1948-1957; Howson, 1971; Philips, 1977; Miller, 1979; Smith, 1985; Klockars, 1985). In England these characteristics were to become public and political criticisms that had substantial influence on the development of the role of detectives in the 19th century; however, they were less influential in the United States.

English Background

Detection activities were evident in England as early as 1534. Between the 16th century and the early part of the 19th century, detection was the province of citizens and criminals who acted as informers, thieftakers, and constables. The government encouraged both citizens and criminals to provide information about illegal activity. Citizens were either given money or freed from performing obligatory public services. Criminals were provided money, impunity from prosecution, or, in some cases, a pardon (Radzinowicz, 1956: 33-142; Monkkonen, 1981: 35; Klockars, 1985: 64-91).

The emergence of the thieftaker reflected the belief that it "takes a thief to catch a thief." Jonathan Wild's career as the "thieftaker general" provides an example of the public ambivalence concerning this approach to detection. Executed in 1725 for stealing and dealing in stolen property, his death was lamented by some newspapers because of his proven effectiveness in apprehending criminals (Radzinowicz, 1956; Howson, 1971; Klockars, 1974). While there were some notable exceptions, the corruption of thieftakers was apparently commonplace. They were principle actors in "the evil practice by which the legitimate owners of stolen goods should be restored on the understanding that no steps would be taken to prosecute" (Radzinowicz, 1956: 23).

Constables were criticized for being both corrupt and incompetent. Their role was based on the premise that it was not their responsibility to become involved in responding to a crime unless they were requested to do so by victims. Since the monies earned by constables came primarily from victim fees, suspect prosecutions, and association with criminals, they tended to work "by winking at offenses they ought to prevent, by attorneying for parties, by encouraging prosecutions for the sake of obtaining their expenses, (and) by screening the publican, pawnbroker, brothelkeeper and receiver of stolen property" (Wade, 1829: 77-78). When constables were successful in apprehending suspects, it was usually for a theft, assault, or robbery in which the victim could either name the suspect or had a strong suspicion as to the person's identity. When victims could not provide this information, constables were not inclined to provide assistance unless fees and expenses were guaranteed. And even with such guarantees, constables were usually unsuccessful in investigating robberies and burglaries committed by organized gangs (Philips, 1977: 60-61; Tobias, 1972: 103-106).

By 1829, when the Metropolitan Police Act was passed, the English experience with detection had been essentially negative. The problems associated with corruption, secrecy, deceit, and entrapment plus the class-based social and political conflict of the period resulted in the creation of a visible, preventive police (Miller, 1979; Smith, 1985: 61-62). The leaders of the new police, Robert Peel, Charles Rowan, and Richard Mayne acted with caution in their approach to detection. While they were primarily concerned about public acceptance, there was also some question as to how effective the new police would be in apprehending the more skilled criminals (Radzinowicz, 1962: 186; Miller, 1979, Jones, 1982).

However, although a small detective unit was not established until 1842, the London police could not ignore the need for detection activity prior to that time. Plainclothes officers were used to catch pickpockets and to attend union and political meetings. When the detective unit was established, it was justified on the basis of the need to respond to murder, a heinous crime that the police could investigate with the assurance of public support. This established the precedent of the detective as a police officer who responded primarily to the more serious and complicated crimes (Smith, 1985: 61-62; Miller, 1979; Klockars, 1985: 64-91).

While detectives assigned to the new unit were salaried, they were also permitted to investigate crimes for a fee. This was necessary because a proven detective could make more money in the private sector than as a public employee. The gradual transition of detection from a private to public matter began in 1829, but it was not until the 1880s that it was substantially completed. Police leaders attempted to minimize the problems associated with a detective who served two masters, the public and a client, by utilizing only sergeants who were paid more and would have less need to pursue private investigations, by limiting time in the assignment to preclude the development of a reputation that would enhance private opportunities, and by providing close supervision (Klockars, 1985: 70-80).

In the 1850s and 1860s, the detective unit was gradually increased in size while plainclothes officers continued to do the "dirty work" of detection; they were utilized clandestinely to prevent robberies, watch suspected criminals, and attend political demonstrations. However, given the sensitive nature of their duties, they were closely supervised. In 1877, there was a major corruption scandal among detectives in London, and as a result the detective branch was reorganized into the Criminal Investigation Division (CID) in 1878. By the mid-1880s as the CID was expanded, the burden of the thieftaker image was lifted as private ventures were completely abandoned and all serious crimes were investigated at the state's expense. However, detectives were not without their problems; in the same decade there was a widely publicized entrapment case that resulted in public criticism, and the police also failed to apprehend Jack the Ripper. Fortunately, such problems do not appear to have been endemic. Royal Commissions exonerated the police from charges of corruption in 1908 and again in 1929 from allegations of harsh interrogation practices (Klockars, 1985: 74-76; Miller, 1979).

By the 1960s and 1970s, research into detectives' activities began to provide a systematic assessment of their role and effectiveness. It was found that "clear up" rates were relatively low and that crimes were rarely solved except in those cases in which victims could provide information that would lead to suspect identification. In this regard, detectives were not unlike the constables of the 17th and 18th centuries. The classical approach to investigation in which the detective started with the crime and systematically inquired into motive and opportunity was reported to be more myth than reality. Rather, detectives were primarily concerned with "gathering information from the public, locating and interviewing suspects and preparing cases for prosecution" (Reiner, 1985; Morris and Heal, 1981).

United States Development

In the United States, the constable was primarily responsible for detection until the 1830s and 1840s when public concern about crime and disorder resulted in the development of modern, or integrated day-night, police departments to replace the constable-nightwatch system. These new departments were loosely based on the prevention concept of the English police, so detection was initially the responsibility of both the new police and the private sector.[1] In England, constables, who were used until the 1840s, were gradually replaced by uniformed police, plainclothes officers, and detectives. In the United States, constables were gradually replaced by both the new police and by private detectives who tended to function like the English thieftaker (Johnson, 1979; Miller, 1977).

The objective of private detectives was the recovery of stolen property and not apprehension of the criminal. They often had a close association with criminals, were aware in advance of criminal activity, worked for a fee, and would not return stolen property until they were paid (Johnson, 1979: 48-50). Bargaining between detectives and criminals was commonplace (Lane, 1967: 56-67). Crapsey (1872: 54-61) has provided an interesting description of how private detectives collected their fee. If the criminal was not known to the detective, a handbill would be circulated or an advertisement placed in a newspaper, offering a reward for the stolen property. Often the thief returned the property and was paid, thus realizing a profit at no risk. Victims were easily taken advantage of in this system, although it was the concern for the return of the property rather than apprehension that contributed to the development of the detective's methods.

While private detectives continued to play an important role in cities well into the 19th century, and several decades longer at the federal level (Morn, 1982; Kakalik and Wildhorn, 1971: 110; Reppetto, 1978: 256),[2] the transition from private to public detective began in the 1840s (Johnson, 1979: 48-50). There were four major reasons for this transition: (1) in general, it was "a capitulation to the private interests involved in the conflict between the duties of a public employee and . . . a private entrepreneur" (Johnson, 1979: 66); (2) the methods utilized by the "purveyors of hell," as private detectives were called by some critics (McWatters, 1871: 648-660) came increasingly under fire; (3) the prevention concept was increasingly perceived to be inadequate (Johnson, 1979:32-40); and (4) the emergence of insurance companies resulted in property owners becoming less concerned about the return of property and more concerned about prosecution (Monkkonen, 1981: 36). The belief, influential in both England and the United States, that the individual and not the state was responsible for the problems associated with victimization, was gradually abandoned (Radzinowicz, 1948).

Once detection responsibilities became the province of the public detective in municipal police departments, their role and methods changed. However, the evolution of police and the detective in the United States was different from that in England for essentially three reasons: social context, political environment, and variations in law enforcement policies. America was more violent, politicians more meddlesome, and the police were more decentralized and expected to be locally responsive (Johnson, 1981: 17-32). In addition, the American experience with detection was neither as prolonged nor as negative as that of the English. Consequently, there was initially less concern about the more controversial aspects of detection.

Since the emergence of detectives in municipal police departments in the 1840s, both their role and methods have changed. Detectives have evolved through three stages of development: as secretive rogue, inquisitor, and bureaucrat. While these stages cannot be precisely traced chronologically, they can be distinguished by dominant characteristics of the detective's activity. While English detectives have not been without their problems, they appear to have gone through the secretive-rogue stage prior to the advent of the metropolitan police detective and to have substantially avoided the inquisitor stage. However, they are currently not unlike the bureaucrats of American municipal departments. The purpose of this paper is to describe each stage in the development of the detective's role in the United States and to attempt to explain why these chances occurred.

Detective as Secretive Rogue: 1850s–1920s

During the transition from private to public employee, the behavior and methods of detectives were dominant characteristics of their role and were to remain so with gradually decreasing concern well into the 20th century. While some individual detective exploits were romanticized after the emergence of professional thiefs in the middle third of the 19th century,[3] detectives in general were considered to be inefficient and corrupt (Lane, 1967: 65-66). As in England, even the entrepreneurial influence of private detectives diminished slowly. As late as the 1890s some public detectives, even though salaried employees, refused to work cases unless they were promised a fee in the form of a reward (Richardson, 1970: 212).[4]

The corrupting association with criminals was also slow to change. Some corrupt private detectives took jobs in the public sector. Langdon Moore, an infamous criminal in New York City in the 1870s, routinely budgeted a certain amount of money derived from his crimes to pay detectives (Richardson, 1970:208). In the same city but several decades later, two detectives gave a thief $25 to buy tools and $75 to burglarize a building. The detectives waited outside, arrested the burglar, and then went into the building to steal something for themselves. They later asked the owner for a reward for making the arrest. The detectives were discovered because they utilized city vouchers to obtain the $100 to pay the thief (Board of Aldermen, 1913: 16).

The detective-criminal relationship also included the use of "stool pigeons" and "deadlines." "Stool pigeon" crimes were tolerated in exchange for information while a "deadline" established an area in which detectives and criminals agreed there should be a tolerance of criminal activity (Woods, 1914: 687-697). The "dirty business" of detective work of the period had to do with "ways that were dark" both in terms of behavior and an emphasis on secrecy (McWatters, 1871: 652). The police believed that investigative work was a clandestine activity. Detectives were considered to be "members of the secret service" whose identity should remain unknown lest the criminal become wary and flee. Pinkerton (1874, 1884), while critical of the disreputable practices of some detectives, believed that it should be "strongly impressed on detectives that secrecy is the prime condition of success in all their operations. It is the chief strength the detective possesses beyond that of ordinary man" (1874: 243).

Detectives were also called "shadows" to denote the clandestine pursuit, or following, of suspects (McAdoo, 1906: 61). Some detectives did not even want patrol officers to know who they were, and many utilized disguises. The Denver Police Department purchased a trunk of disguises in 1879 from private detectives from Chicago. They were sold because the "crooks" in Chicago were "on to them" (Rider, 1971: 44-45). The concern for secrecy, although abating, was evident even in the second and third decades of the 20th century. In lineup procedures, suspects were asked questions before detectives who were masked so they could not be identified (Dougherty, 1924: 21). Goodwin (1923: 203-205) describes how detectives utilized "black velvet masks" to look at prisoners through "judas windows" in cell doors. Later, bright lights were utilized for the same purpose (Crump and Newton, 1935: 109-111). Some detectives even submitted court testimony in writing to protect their identity.

Many of the detectives of the period tended to function like nonuniformed patrol officers. They were primarily concerned with anticipating criminal acts by looking for suspicious behavior and known criminals (Sprogle, 1887: 117). They were particularly concerned about pickpockets, gamblers, and troublemakers (Ketcham, 1967: 3). Detectives concentrated their efforts where people tended to congregate; they circulated in large crowds, particularly at night, at station house landings, steamboat docks, train stations, streetcars, beer gardens, theaters, and weddings (Savage, 1873: xii; Costello, 1885: 403; Eldridge and Watts, 1897: 312).

Detective as Inquisitor: 1890s–1960s

Police reformers hoped to replace secretive rogues with scientific criminal investigators. This was a reformer's vision that was pervasive in the first few decades of the 20th century. The development and use of the Bertillion system was praised as "unvarying, hence perfect" (Felton, 1888: 305). Detectives in Boston were congratulated for utilizing analytical skills (anonymous, 1910). The importance of physical evidence at crime scenes was stressed (Finney, 1936). "Scientific police" were praised and encouraged to use scientific methods in all phases of their work (Ottolengi, 1913: 876-880). Critics of police believed detectives should be required to become knowledgeable in the taking of Bertillion measurements, fingerprints, and collecting physical evidence (anonymous, 1914: 609-610). Fosdick (1915: 560) called for the development of modus operandi files and the utilization of physical evidence to identify suspects. Vollmer (1922: 251-257) believed that detectives—he called them investigators—needed a systematic approach and a fully equipped scientific laboratory. Smith (1929: 1-27) called for the replacement of "stool pigeons" and the "third degree" with a scientific approach. At both the 1922 and 1926 International Association of Chiefs of Police Convention, an effective summary of an analytical approach to investigation was presented to conference attendees (Matherson, 1922, 1926).

Despite this growing body of opinion, the emerging methods of investigation utilized to "make cases" was not significantly influenced. Crimes that were solved usually had obvious suspects (Smith, 1925: 207). Most suspects were identified by victims or through personal contacts (Henderson, 1924: 366-374). One New York detective discounted what he called the "Sherlock Holmes" approach. "In the . . . story of how the detective gets his man, stool pigeon's the word. Clues, deductions . . . have their place [but] take away information . . . of the stool pigeon and the detection of crime would be paralyzed" (Fiaschetti, 1930: 38).

Detective work was more a haphazard than scientific process (Lavine, 1930: 19-22). The average case did not require any scientific analysis (State of New York, 1935: 471). As one detective who was critical of "self styled scientific detectives" said, "they would have a gullible public believe that the crooks would respond to engraved invitations to visit police headquarters. . . ." (Matherson, 1929: 214-218). Despite attempts to bring the rigor and deductive power of science to the investigation process, detectives still relied on victims, informers, and suspects to solve crimes (Deutsch, 1954). And the methods utilized to obtain that information, particularly in the case of suspects, was to dominate the second phase of the detective's development.

The inquisitorial methods used by detectives to obtain confessions became known as the "third degree." The arrest was the first degree, transportation to the station the second, and interrogation the third. This was also known as "shellacking," "massaging," "breaking the news," and "giving the works" (Lavine, 1930: 3). The typical victim of the third degree was not a suspect in a heinous crime but in a felony case of only medium importance (Hopkins, 1931: 205). While many leaders in law enforcement denied the existence of such methods, there is considerable evidence to the contrary (International Association of Chiefs of Police Proceedings, 1910: 58-78). It was a well-documented police practice into the 1930s and possibly several decades longer. Research in one city found that 289 of 1,235 suspects were physically abused (Hopkins, 1931: 213-215). Undoubtedly, many others confessed in order to avoid such abuse.

The National Commission on Law Observance (1931) reported that many police departments had third degree rooms in which suspects were kept awake, starved, and beaten with fists, clubs, blackjacks, rubber hoses, telephone books, straps and whips. Some suspects were confined to "pitchblack aimless cells" and had tear gas, scopolamine, and chloroform used on them. In Chicago, suspects were taken to a "goldfish room" that was equipped with rubber hoses and blackjacks. Even newspapers provided such rooms to police so their reporters would be first to get the story of a confession (Larson, 1932: 13). Others were made to hold hands with or touch persons they were suspected of murdering. At the extreme, the physical abuse was horrifying. One suspect was forced to lie on the floor and was repeatedly lifted up by his testicles, while another had his tooth ground down to the root.

Apparently the police were supportive of such methods. The research of Beyle and Parratt (1933, 1937) concerning attitudes of the police and public found that almost one half of the police approved of the use of physical violence to obtain confessions. And more than 50% supported such tactics as no sleep, the avoidance of attorneys, and threatening violence. Smith (1941), one of the period's most prominent authorities on police, indicated that in every police department with which he was familiar there was a remote room used by police for interrogation purposes.

The third degree was not limited to physical abuse. Some suspects were put "on the loop" and moved from station to station to frustrate and avoid attorneys. Some were held in "cold storage" and were victims of

"Mutt and Jeff" (one officer is aggressive and threatening, another is supportive and empathetic) interrogation tactics (Hopkins, 1931: 128-226; Willemse, 1931: 344-345). Some suspects were subjected to continuous harassment. In one case, detectives followed a suspect, appeared to be whispering about him on a tramway car, sent him anonymous letters, and even had a theater orchestra stop playing when he and his wife arrived. He confessed that same evening (Larson, 1932: 101).[5]

While the physical abuse of suspects used to obtain confessions may have abated after the 1930s, psychological coercion was still employed. As late as 1964 the Supreme Court in *Escobedo v. Illinois* indicated their belief that such interrogation practices as the "Mutt and Jeff" technique were still in use and were inappropriate. The author's own experience as a police officer in the early 1960s confirms the selective use of physical abuse and extensive use of psychological coercion to obtain confessions.

The Detective as Bureaucrat: 1940s–1980s

Reformers' attempts to change police began to have a substantial impact by the 1930s and 1940s (Kirk, 1954; Fogelson, 1977; Walker, 1977; Bopp, 1977; Johnson, 1981). However, the promise of science continued to be illusive. Physical evidence, while critical in a few crimes, was in general little used and of little value (Greenwood, 1970; Folk, 1971; Parker and Peterson, 1972; Greenberg, Yu, and Lang, 1972; Feeny, 1973; Peterson, Milhajhovie, and Gilliland, 1984). While the roguish and secretive dimensions of the detective's role were present to some degree even into the 1980s, by the 1940s most detectives investigated crimes after they had occurred. By the 1970s, and probably several decades earlier, no more than 10% to 20% of detectives were engaged in clandestine investigations (Heaphy, 1978). The use of "third degree" methods, while not completely abandoned, was probably not as significant a problem as it had been in the 1930s (*Escobedo v. Illinois; Miranda v. Arizona*). To illustrate the changes that took place between the

19th century and mid-20th century, the description of Fuld (1909) can be contrasted with findings of Greenwood and Petersilia (1975) and Greenwood, Chaiken, and Petersilia (1977).

Fuld (1909: 171-172) described detectives of the 19th century as engaging in the activities of a "spy" with a "class of men" one might expect working in the job. Detectives were criminals who considered spying more profitable than committing felonies. Their "chief stock in trade" was knowledge of the criminal classes obtained through association.

Greenwood and Petersilia (1975) and Greenwood et al. (1977) analyzed the detective function in numerous police departments and found that gathering and processing information consumed most of the detective's time. This included reviewing reports, documenting files, and attempting to locate and interview victims. Only about one half of the cases received more than minimal attention. In terms of "solving" cases, the most important information was provided by victims to patrol officers, and detectives displayed little, if any, imaginative skill in identifying suspects on their own. Detectives tended to spend more time in post-clearance processing than in identifying unknown perpetrators.[6] Eck's more recent (1984) research tends to dispute these findings. However, his conclusions are based on an 8% arrest rate for cases investigated by detectives in which there were leads but initially no suspect information.

Both Kenney (1972) and Erickson (1981) have also analyzed how detectives utilize their time. Kenney found that only about 11% of that time was spent in "handling suspects." The rest was invested, in effect, in reconfirming information, processing information already in possession of the organization, interacting with other criminal justice agencies, and in personal matters. Erickson (1981) reported that only about one third of the detectives' time involved case investigation or suspect-accused investigations. "By far the most common activity was to sit at a desk in an open office area to type reports, review films, call citizens . . . and to hold . . . meetings about a variety of matters relating to investigation practices and procedures, and office routine" (Erickson, 1981: 44).

Sanders's (1977) study of one detective unit found the basic detective task to be one of gathering, organizing, and using information. Much of the information was already in possession of the organization. The amount of "paperwork" seemed overwhelming to Sanders and was a source of constant complaint among detectives. He describes the typical duties as "making contacts," "reading reports," "establishing crimes," "catching up on paperwork," "identifying suspects," "making arrests," and "going to court." In the case examples Sanders cites, a suspect was usually obvious and the most important part of the investigation was to ensure that a crime had occurred and could be legally connected to that suspect. The degree of difficulty and complexity associated with making the legal connection varied, but often it was a relatively simple process.

The tendency of detectives to focus on cases with obvious solutions has been an informal practice of long standing (Conklin, 1972; Sanders, 1977). However, it became more formalized under the rubric of "case screening" or "case management" in the 1970s. Research in this area has attempted to identify factors present in the initial or preliminary investigation that would be predictive of making arrests. The results, in general, have been that unless a victim or witness knew the suspect, or could provide an identification and description, a suspect was rarely found. One of these studies found that in the crimes of robbery, rape, auto theft, and assault with a deadly weapon, cases that were solved tended to "solve themselves." These are the types of cases that receive the highest priority (Greenberg et al., 1972; Greenberg, Elliot, Craft, and Procter, 1977; Eck, 1979; Waegel, 1982; Gaines, Lewis, and Swangin, 1983).

There are three exceptions to the tendency of detectives to focus primarily on cases with the most obvious solutions: extremely serious and usually complex crimes; those involving "gang" activity, professional criminals and organized crime; and those requiring clandestine intervention. In the first two exceptions the police organization may decide to invest resources in a "strike force," "task force," or "major crime" or "career criminal" program. In these investigations it is often necessary to focus on individuals as well as cases (Garza, 1976; McGillis, 1977; Reppetto, 1978).

Those investigations requiring a clandestine intervention tend to emphasize individuals suspected of criminal activity. Examples of this type of investigation include "sting" operations and intelligence gathering (Marx, 1983; Klockars, 1983b). Another example of undercover investigative activity is that of narcotics detectives. Manning (1980) found their work to be "boring, unsystematic and catch-as-catch can." And narcotics detectives usually apprehended only the most obvious suspects. While the police officers assigned to such duties usually constitute only a small percentage of personnel utilized as investigators, this percentage is apparently increasing. Between 1965 and 1980 the number of arrests made by narcotics detectives doubled. The 1960s and 1970s were also periods in which systematic crime analysis resulted in the development of more criminally oriented programs (Caiden, 1977; Marx, 1983; Klockars, 1983b).[7]

Role Transition: Secretive Rogue to Bureaucrat

Changes in the activities and methods of detectives are the result of the interactive dynamics of context, problems, and police response. The context is the sociopolitical and legal environment in which police function, the problems are crime and public expectations, and the police response is the organization's attempt both to adjust to and manipulate the environment and the problems. The changes that the police have gone through are part of several "waves of reform" that have had divergent views about the police role, strategic priorities, and stylistic tendencies. However, the integrating theme of all reform movements, at least until the 1960s, was the professional model (Fogelson, 1977; Walker, 1977; Lynch and Diamond, 1983).

The professional model advocated the separation of police from politics; higher salaries, better benefits, and improved working conditions; selection and promotion based on merit; training and education based on knowledge acquired through research; affiliation with higher education to enhance prestige and status; emphasis on science and technology; and the importance of public image and organizational reform. The objective of the professional model was to develop an officer who was rational, technically competent, dedicated, and incorruptible (Carte and Carte, 1975; Fogelson, 1977; Walker, 1977).

To achieve this objective for detectives, the relationship with the criminal had to be changed. Once this was addressed, the organizational mode of response, rationality, and technical competency through bureaucratization would shape and control, even define, the problems confronting detectives. Part of this definition was related to the public image of the police officer as crime fighter. This image was projected by reformers by promising to "wage war" on crime. This crime-fighter image reinforced the values and priorities of the organizational culture and provided peer group support for a working "war theory" of crime control. For police any methods became acceptable to win the war. This image was also reflected in the romanticized, even heroic, presentation of detectives in literature and the media, yet another example of the influence that dramatic events play in determining the actual and perceived role of police (Hopkins, 1931; Fogelson, 1977; Walker, 1977; Manning, 1977; Sherman, 1978; Reuss-Ianni, 1983).

The changing relationship between criminals and detectives and organizational reform was influential in the transition of the detective from secretive rogue to inquisitor. The continuation of the reform emphasis plus the increasingly restrictive due process requirements imposed by the judiciary were influential in the transition from inquisitor to bureaucrat.

Detective-Criminal Relationship

With the change from a private to public detective and a new objective—apprehension rather than bargaining—the "detective criminal partner model" gradually began to break down (Woods, 1914: 681-697). The criminal behavior of "stool pigeons" was still tolerated in exchange for information, but for many criminals the relationship with detectives became more adversarial than collaborative. Avoidance rather than cooperation became the criminal's mode of response. And the time requirements associated with the prosecution of those apprehended were more demanding than for bargaining.

Other factors in the changing relationship were public concern about crime and urbanization. The public apprehension about the impact crime had on quality of life resulted in more problems being reported to police. With the anonymity that came with urbanization, the contextual knowledge police could acquire about people was reduced and investigative effectiveness based on this personal knowledge became problematic. At the same time these trends were occurring, criminals were becoming more skilled and, because of the size and complexity of cities, finding it easier to escape from police (Walling, 1887; Woods, 1914; Lane, 1967; Prassel, 1972; Sherman, 1983).

Technological innovations were also influential. With the development of the telephone and two way radio, police officers could be held more accountable by police administrators and the public could more easily contact officers. Both tended to result in making the police, including detectives, more likely to respond to requests for services than to instigate activities (Sherman, 1983; Walker, 1984).

As detectives became more concerned with investigating crimes after they had occurred, they were more likely to interact with victims and witnesses than with criminals. The former did not usually try to avoid the police, so there was no need for secrecy. Although secrecy was of concern to some detectives even into the 1920s and 1930s, by the 1910s many detectives in New York City no longer objected if their identity was known (Board of Aldermen, 1913: 290). Other factors that contributed to the decline of secrecy were related to the personnel practices of departments. Detectives often remained in an assignment so long they became known. Even the tendency to travel and work in pairs

gave them away (Chamber of Commerce, 1905).

With the decline of the "detective criminal partner model," the "stool pigeon" or informer became the police's primary conduit to the underworld; they, in effect, became the necessary "middle men." The corrupting association with criminals that concerned reformers was replaced by a greater reliance on the manipulation and coercion of informers. However, the informers' utility was limited because they were less effective as cities became larger, and more complex. While they could provide valuable information in some cases, they did so with decreasing frequency and they could not ensure a successful prosecution. Suspect confessions became the most expeditious means of acquiring information to "make cases" and obtain convictions.

Klockars (1985: 80-82) argues that relating detectives to the concept of a case, or investigating a crime after it had occurred and a criminal already existed, was crucial to the acceptance of detectives in England. This not only made it less likely for them to engage in the deceptive practices of their predecessors, it also conferred upon them a professional orientation that provided control over their time and a great deal of personal discretion. While this professional orientation was eventually to become associated with American detectives, the case distinction was more a function of the changing nature of the crime problem and the professional model than it was a direct attempt to obtain public acceptance. Moreover, the American detectives' methods for solving the case were to eventually result in considerable public criticism.

As detectives gradually began to stop functioning as secretive rogues, reformers hoped they would become scientific criminal investigators who would be perceptive and analytical (Leonard, 1943: 85-104; Valentine, 1947: 204). However, this vision was never completely realized. Instead, the detective began to function essentially as an inquisitor.

Administrative Reform

A recurring theme of police reform has been recommendations designed to make police organizations more efficient and accountable. This has resulted in an emphasis on centralization, standardization, specialization, and discipline. The concern for both efficiency and accountability along with the changing crime problem necessitated a greater commitment to gathering, storing, and processing information. The result has been the bureaucratization of municipal police departments (Caiden, 1977).

Specialization began to influence police departments with the establishment of separate detective units. By the 1880s many large cities had such units even though some were separate and independent as late as the 1920s (Felton, 1888: 208; Graper, 1921; Kelling, 1981). Specialization also occurred within detective units (Felton, 1888: 194-221; Crowley, 1894: 170-182). In large cities, there were "plainclothes" officers at district stations with detectives in a centralized bureau. This was partly for political reasons, but it also represented a dividing of labor based on seriousness of crime as plainclothes officers tended to be responsible for trivial cases (Ketcham, 1967: 214). Detectives also became responsible for information about criminals involved in a particular type of crime (for example, that of "sporting fraternities") (Costello, 1885: 402; Flinn and Wilkie, 1887: 372).

The increasing concern for recording and processing information was also evident in the 19th century. New York City had a picture, or rogues', gallery in 1857. St. Louis had a form of modus operandi file called the "record of rascals" in 1868 (Ketcham, 1967: 245-247). Gradually, agencies also adopted the use of assignment books, detailed reports on investigations and their progress, a record of complaints, and books describing stolen property (Costello, 1885:403; Eldridge and Watts, 1897: 333-383; Woods, 1918; Rider, 1971: 348). By 1912 at least 169 police departments had criminal identification systems (anonymous, 1912).

By the first decade of the 20th century, specialized detective units were well established in municipal police departments. In a survey of 75 departments, Graper (1921) found that all cities had detective units. He also identified a number of problems with these units: (1) the low quality and lack of qualifications

of personnel; (2) inadequate supervision; (3) poor record keeping; and (4) in general, inefficient and ineffective performance.

In the first several decades of the 20th century, an increasing number of administrative analyses of police departments were conducted in which detective units were often considered to be the "weak spots" of the organization. The problems identified by Graper were reiterated in these studies and detectives units were criticized for having inadequate record systems, providing inadequate training and supervision, and being excessively decentralized and insufficiently specialized (Civil Service Commission, 1911-1912: 44; Board of Aldermen, 1913: 193; Police Commission, 1914: 31; Woods, 1918; Fosdick, 1921:62-69; Graper, 1921: 181-308; Citizen's Police Committee, 1931: 119-149). The solutions provided by these and other studies were to create entrenched bureaucratic structures (Bellman, 1935; Finney, 1936; Smith, 1941, 1943, 1946; Bureau of Municipal Research, 1943; Wilson, 1950; International City Manager's Association, 1938, 1943, 1950, 1954).[8]

The concern for the development of information or records systems was of particular importance. Since they were established in the 19th century, police departments had served to stabilize fragmented cities. They not only functioned as a focus of public concern about a variety of problems, but also as information centers (Monkkonen, 1981: 147-149). By the 1930s detective bureaus were becoming "a clearing house . . . [for] the matching of information" (Harrison, 1934: 128-135).

As police organizations became more complex and interdependent, the detectives had to spend more time coordinating with people in other specializations and with attorneys. They also became experts in their specialization who possessed knowledge about crimes and criminals not recorded in information systems. As repositors of expertise they began to function as a primary communication link with other organizations.

The bureaucratic structures that emerged in the 20th century required considerable "care and feeding," and became more constraint-oriented than task-oriented. The primary sustenance of bureaucracies is information—information to develop expertise, to validate the need for the organizations' continued existence, to assist in charting a course dedicated to survival, and to address the problems for which the organization was established. Police departments have ambiguous goals, an uncertain technology, and conflicting expectations about their role. This makes them "hard to manage" with the tendency to be primarily concerned about constraining the activities of employees (Wilson, 1978: 204-205). Constraint-oriented organizations tend to be more concerned with accountability and the absence of inappropriate behavior than task-related problem solving.

This tendency did not go unnoticed among critics of police. Beginning in the late 1960s, the professional model of police, particularly the bureaucratic features, were increasingly criticized as being unresponsive to changing problems and public expectations. As a result, many police departments entered into an experimental phase of their development in which innovation was encouraged and rewarded. In the area of detection this resulted in supposedly new tactics and programs that were both crime-specific and criminally oriented. Clandestine intervention, deceit, incitement, and entrapment were characteristics associated with some of these approaches to detection (Caiden, 1977; Marx, 1983; Klockars, 1983b).

Due Process Requirements

While administrative reform of police was significant in the transition of the detective from inquisitor to bureaucrat, it took changes in procedural criminal law to complete the process. What might be called the "due process" revolution began in the 1930s when the United States Supreme Court gradually began to test the suitability of due process and equal protection as it applied to individuals in criminal proceedings. However, it was the "Warren Court" of the 1960s that, from a law enforcement perspective, made the apprehension and prosecution of criminals more difficult. Procedural requirements in the areas of arrest, search and seizure, and right to counsel became more precise and applicable to

municipal police procedures (Novak, 1983). As a result of these changes, one prominent police executive argued that it should be mandatory that detectives have law degrees (Jenkins, 1970: 114). While some of these judicial decisions have been modified in the last decade, the bureaucratic sensitivity to due process requirements has been incorporated into the procedural routine of detectives (Kuykendall, 1982b).

Discussion

A crime is a continuum with three or four phases: a concept or plan, the act itself, escape and fugitive status, and, in some instances, disposal of the fruits of the crime (Kuykendall, 1982a). Municipal police primarily respond to two types of crimes: those involving a victim and a criminal and those with, in effect, two criminals. The latter type of crime usually involves the buying and/or selling of illegal goods or services.

A proactive response to a crime occurs when the police attempt to intervene in the planning phase, during its commission, or even during the disposal phase (for example, a "sting" operation). A reactive intervention occurs after the crime has been committed and the escape and fugitive phase begins. The police response tends to be covert when the intervention is in the planning, act, or disposal phases because the police are required to play the role of a criminal or victim or to observe a specific location or person in anticipation of a crime. Other interventions tend to be overt. When the police respond in a proactive and covert mode, the focus is usually on the criminal. When the response is reactive and overt, the emphasis tends to be on the case or investigation of a crime after the act (Kuykendall, 1982a).

The responsibility of reactive detectives is to establish a case, identify a suspect, locate the suspect, obtain a confession if possible, and dispose of the case (Sanders, 1977). Proactive detectives tend to function in the same way except that instead of obtaining a confession they attempt to clandestinely develop knowledge about and/or a relationship with a criminal. This often involves playing the role of a criminal in the commission of a crime. For both the reactive and proactive detective, the disposal phase of the investigation often includes case development, processing, and coordinating with other criminal justice agencies in order to obtain a prosecution and conviction.

The primary purpose of any investigation is to produce information. Information is most easily obtained from victims and witnesses because of a desire to redress a grievance and/or to meet the civic responsibility of citizenship. Other information-acquiring techniques available to police include bargaining, manipulation or deceit, coercion, and purchase. Some detectives are also capable of deriving information through perceptive observation and analysis (Reppetto, 1978). All of these approaches are utilized to obtain information from informers while all but purchase are employed with suspects.

The types of cases that detectives investigate can be grouped into one of three categories: "walk-throughs," "where are they's," and "whodunit's" (Sanders, 1977; McNerney, 1980). "Walk-throughs" are cases in which a suspect is easily determined and located and detectives must only observe legal guidelines to reach a solution. A substantial majority of all cases "solved" fall into this category. In "where are they" cases a suspect has been tentatively identified but has not been located. These cases may have simple solutions or be complex mysteries. "Whodunit's" are those cases in which there are initially no suspects. A substantial majority of crimes reported to police fall into this category, and they are rarely solved.[9]

Klockars (1985) suggests that detectives can be divided into those who are primarily concerned with either means or ends. Classical detectives or deontologists live by the morality of means; they believe that "the creative, disciplined and determined application of morally exemplary mental means can triumph over even the most skilled and sinister of evils" (Klockars, 1985: 88). While the classical detective tends to be a myth of fiction writers, the character embodies a perspective that has helped to shape public perceptions about the detective.

Consequentialists are the "hard boiled" detectives who are more concerned with ends than means. As fictional characters they are intended to represent the reality of investigative work. For these types of detectives the means used to apprehend suspects can only be judged in terms of consequence. Dirty or immoral means become acceptable, even desirable, if the ends are compelling enough.

To this classification should be added the clerical detective. Detectives of this type spend most of their time coordinating with and providing expertise to criminal justice agencies and recording and processing information that may prove useful to their department, other agencies, and such organizations as insurance companies for which detectives function as external auditors. Only a minimal amount of effort is invested in producing information about the identity or location of suspects. Clerks are "snappy bureaucrats" who do what they are told; bureaucratic performance replaces a concern for either the means or ends of the investigation (Klockars, 1983a: 428-438).

Secretive rogues were consequentialists. They were proactive, covert, and primarily bargained, manipulated, and coerced informers and suspects to produce information. They essentially tried to prevent crimes by focusing on criminals and intervening in the planning phases or during the commission of the crime. In responding to crimes after they occurred they utilized "stool pigeons." Police reformers hoped that the secretive rogue would be replaced by a morally superior scientific criminal investigator, or classicist, who would rely primarily on perceptive observation and analysis. However, this was more the rhetoric of reform than what was to emerge as a reality. Instead, another type of consequentialist, the inquisitor, emerged. This type of detective was essentially reactive and overt but still tended to rely primarily on bargaining, coercion, and manipulation to produce information. They tended to emphasize the most expeditious means of solving cases: obtaining a confession.

With the influence of the bureaucratization of police and the increasingly demanding due process requirements, the role of detective gradually changed to that of clerk. This detective tends to be reactive and overt with the primary responsibility to process "walk-throughs." To the degree that they produce information not already in the possession of the organization, they do so by some bargaining but tend to solicit cooperation by appeals to civic responsibility and through purchase. The detective as clerk is a principal actor in one stage of the complex organization and legal process that has become more concerned with internal requirements than external problems.

While there are some contemporary detectives who tend to be proactive, covert, and more likely to focus on criminals than crimes, they constitute only a small percentage of those engaged in detective duties. These detectives tend to be successful only in the most obvious cases and they must also invest considerable time to satisfy the information requirements of the organization. However, with the emergence of the drug problem and with the innovation emphasis prevalent among some police departments since the 1960s, the detective may be breaking out of the bureaucratic box. Unfortunately, the results of innovation have tended to only revive past practices and probably false hopes. Computerized fingerprint systems and psychological profiles of criminals stress the importance of science, historically of little value in identifying suspects. Sting operations, decoy programs, and other clandestine police pursuits in which officers play the role of criminal or victim, while more structured and closely supervised, are approaches to detection that are controversial and corruption-prone.

From the perspective of apprehension, the detective function has probably never been an efficient or effective activity.[10] Although a speculative observation, it is unlikely that secretive rogues, inquisitors, or clerks are more or less effective, in general, or in solving "whodunit's" or complex "where are they's" (Murphy and Plate, 1977: 183). If secretive rogues had pressed their sources of information too often, the detective-criminal partner model would have dissolved. The decline of inquisitorial methods does not seem to have had any significant impact on the number of persons who plead guilty in criminal cases. Police effectiveness and efficiency is deter-

mined more by the complexity of the problem than the methods, techniques, and skills of those attempting a solution. Police concentrate on the problems with easy solutions because the alternative is problems of such difficulty that only a substantial investment of resources provides a reasonable possibility of success. Since police departments can rarely do this, the range of possible efficiency and effectiveness has been and continues to be constrained.

Are there alternatives to the role presently played by detectives? Since police departments and the court system have become so dependent upon them to process information, changes in the role will be difficult to make. Police organizations are not inclined to ask basic questions about their strategies and organizational design. However, to the degree that they are so inclined, the following questions need to be addressed. Can part or all of detective resources be more productively invested in other strategies like education? Should the persons called detectives concentrate on the easiest crimes to solve or only on the most serious and difficult? When police play the role of criminal or victim, do the costs in the damaged moral capital of society, corruption, human suffering, and mistrust justify the benefits derived? Are crimes in which government uses the deceit and treachery of a few equally as amenable to solution by the skills and tactics of the many?

Notes

1. One reason for this preventive emphasis was the critical public attitude concerning the behavior and methods of private detectives.

2. Private detectives, as they became less corrupt and more professional, tended to be active in cases that transcended the jurisdictions of cities until federal agencies were well established.

3. Clifton Woolridge (1901, 1902) of Chicago is an example of the tendency to romanticize detectives. In two books, he was called the "incorruptible Sherlock Holmes of America." He supposedly made 20,000 arrests in 20 years.

4. One possible reason for this was the practice of using rewards to pay for the expenses as-

sociated with pursuing criminals (Board of Aldermen, 1913: 283).

5. Larson (1925) provides an excellent summary of techniques utilized by police to obtain confessions.

6. Many of these observations have been made before. In 1913 in New York City, it was found that in homicide cases patrol officers usually located suspects at the scene of the crime or suspects were already known (Board of Aldermen, 1913). In Chicago, a Civil Service Commission (1911-1912) investigation resulted in a recommendation that detectives be put back in uniform because they were too costly for the work performed. Smith (1925) found that most solutions to cases were obvious and that 85% were disposed of by patrol officers.

7. The Police Foundation and the Police Executive Research Forum's 1977 survey of police practices identified the number of detectives in general and those in "vice operations," the area in which most undercover detectives would work. Typically, only 10%–20% or less worked in this capacity (Heaphy, 1978).

8. The books of both Wilson and the ICMA have subsequent editions that have continued to reinforce this view of the police role.

9. For example, in California in 1984 there were 800,615 homicides, rapes, robberies, aggravated assaults, burglaries, and auto thefts reported to the police. There were 91,369 arrests (12%) and 52,906 convictions (7%). For all felonies, 19% resulted in an arrest and about 11% in a conviction (Department of Justice, 1985).

10. The position allows the development of specialists in different types of crimes who become repositories of knowledge not available in information systems; it facilitates communication between law enforcement agencies about specific types of crimes and criminals; and detectives provide a vital coordinating function with prosecuting and defense attorneys and, on occasion, with correctional agencies. The position also provides status, task diversity, freedom from shift work and, in many departments, a promotion and higher salary.

References

Anonymous. 1910. "Notes on current events." *Journal of Criminal Law and Criminology* 1: 456-488.

——. 1912. "Notes on current events." *Journal of Criminal Law and Criminology* 3: 93-137.

——. 1914. "Notes on current events." *Journal of Criminal Law and Criminology* 5: 609-610.

Bellman, Arthur. 1935. "A police service rating scale." *Journal of Criminal Law and Criminology* 26: 231-248.

Beyle, Herman and Spencer Parratt. 1933. "Measuring the severity of the third degree." *Journal of Criminal Law and Criminology* 24: 485-503.

——. 1937. "Approval and disapproval of specific third degree practices." *Journal of Criminal Law and Criminology* 28: 526-550.

Board of Aldermen. 1913. *Police in New York City: An Introduction.* New York: Committee to Investigate the Police of New York City. Reprinted by the New York Times and Arno Press, 1971.

Bopp, William. 1977. *O. W. Wilson and a Search for a Police Profession.* Port Washington, NY: Kennikat Press.

Bureau of Municipal Research. 1943. *Police Problems in Newark (New Jersey). New York: Bureau of Municipal Research.* Selected Surveys of Urban Police reprinted by the New York Times and Arno Press, 1971.

Caiden, Gerald. 1977. *Police Revitalization.* Lexington, MA: Lexington.

Carte, Gene and Elaine Carte. 1975. *Police Reform in the United States: The Era of August Vollmer, 1905–1932.* Berkeley: University of California Press.

Chamber of Commerce. 1905. *Papers and Proceedings of the Committee on the Police Problem.* New York: Young. Reprinted by the New York Times and Arno Press, 1971.

Citizen's Police Committee. 1931. *Chicago Police Problems.* Chicago: University of Chicago Press.

Civil Service Commission. 1911–1912. *City of Chicago Police Investigation: Final Report.* Chicago: City of Chicago. Reprinted by the New York Times and Arno Press, 1971.

Conklin, John. 1972. *Robbery and the Criminal Justice System.* Philadelphia: Lippincott.

Costello, Augustine. 1885. *Our Police Protectors.* Published by author. Patterson Smith reprint, 1972.

Crapsey, Edward. 1872. *The Nether Side of New York.* Patterson-Smith reprint, 1972.

Crowley, Patrick. 1894. "Report of the Committee on Police Forces in Cities." In *Proceedings of the Annual Congress of the National Prison Association.* Reprinted by the New York Times and Arno Press, 1971.

Crump, Irving and John Newton. 1935. *Our Police*. New York: Dodd, Mead.

Deutsch, Albert. 1954. *The Trouble With Cops*. New York: Crown.

Dougherty, George. 1924. *The Criminal as a Human Being*. New York: Appleton.

Department of Justice. 1985. *Crime and Delinquency in California, 1984*. Sacramento: State of California.

Eck, John. 1979. *Managing Case Assignments*. Washington, D.C.: Police Executive Research Forum.

——. 1984. *Solving Crimes: The Investigation of Burglary and Robbery*. Washington, D.C.: Police Executive Research Forum.

Eldridge, B. and William Watts. 1897. *Our Rival, the Rascal*. Boston: Pemhamton.

Erickson, Richard. 1981. *Making Crime*. Toronto: Butterworth.

Escobedo v. Illinois. 1964. 378 U.S. 478.

Felton, Charles. 1888. *Police organizations and administration*. Proceedings of the Annual Congress of the National Prison Association. Reprinted by the New York Times and Arno Press, 1971.

Feeny, Fred. 1973. *The Prevention and Control of Robbery* (5 vols.). Davis, CA: University of California Press.

Flaschetti, Michael. 1930. *You Gotta Be Rough*. New York: Burt.

Finney, Don. 1936. "Police duties at crime scenes." *Journal of Criminal Law and Criminology* 27: 231-248.

Flinn, John and John Wilkie. 1887. *History of the Chicago Police*. Chicago: Conkey. Reprinted by the New York Times and Arno Press, 1971.

Fogelson, Robert. 1977. *Big-City Police*. Cambridge: Harvard.

Folk, Joseph. 1971. *Municipal Detective Systems*. Report No. 55. Cambridge: M.I.T. Press.

Fosdick, Raymond. 1915. "The modus operandi system in the detection of criminals." *Journal of Criminal Law and Criminology* 6: 560-570.

——. 1921. *Police Administration: Criminal Justice in Cleveland*. Cleveland: Cleveland Foundation.

Fuld, Felix. 1909. *Police Administration*. New York: Putnam's.

Garza, Michael. 1976. *Multi-Agency Narcotics Manual*. Washington, D.C.: National Institute of Law Enforcement and Criminal Justice.

Gaines, Larry, B. Lewis, and R. Swangin. 1983. "Case screening in criminal investigation." *Police Studies* 6: 22-29.

Goodwin, John. 1923. *Sidelights in Criminal Matters*. New York: Doran.

Graper, Elmer. 1921. *American Police Administration*. New York: MacMillian.

Greenberg, Bernard, Carola Elliot, Lois Craft, and H. Steven Procter. 1977. *Felony Investigation: Decision Model*. Washington, D.C.: National Institute of Law Enforcement and Criminal Justice.

Greenberg, Bernard, Oliver Yu, and Karen Lang. 1972. *Enhancement of the Investigative Function*. Menlo Park: Stanford Research Institute.

Greenwood, Peter, Jan Chalken, and Joan Petersilia. 1977. *The Criminal Investigation Process*. Lexington, MA.: Heath.

Greenwood, Peter and Joan Petersilia. 1975. *The Criminal Investigative Process: Summary and Policy Implication*. Santa Monica: Rand.

Greenwood, Peter. 1970. *An Analysis of the Apprehension Activities of the New York Police Department*. New York City: Rand Institute.

Harrison, Leonard. 1934. *Police Administration in Boston*. Cambridge: Harvard.

Heaphy, John (ed.) 1978. *Police Practices: The General Administrative Survey*. Washington, D.C.: Police Foundation.

Henderson, George. 1924. *Keys to Crookdom*. New York: Appleton.

Hopkins, Earnest. 1931. *Our Lawless Police*. New York: Viking.

Howson, Gerald. 1971. *Thief-taker General*. New York: St. Martin's.

International Association of Chiefs of Police. 1910. *Proceedings of the Annual Conference*. Reprinted by the New York Times and Arno Press, 1971.

International City Manager's Association. 1938–1954. *Municipal Police Administration*, editions 1–4. Chicago: ICMA.

Jenkins, Herbert. 1970. *Keeping the Peace*. New York: Harper and Row.

Johnson, David. 1979. *Policing the Urban Underworld*. Philadelphia: Temple University Press.

——. 1981. *American Law Enforcement: A History*. St. Louis: Forum.

Jones, David. 1982. *Crime, Protest, Community and Police in Nineteenth Century Britain*. London: Rutledge and Keegan Paul.

Kakalik, James and Sorrel Wildhorn. 1971. *The Private Police Industry* (Vol. 11). Santa Monica: Rand.

Kelling, George. 1981. *The History of Detectives.* Unpublished paper.

Kenney, Jack. 1972. *Police Administration.* Springfield, IL: Thomas.

Ketcham, George. 1967. *Municipal Police Reform.* Unpublished doctoral dissertation. Columbia: University of Missouri.

Kirk, Paul. 1954. "Progress in criminal investigation." In Bruce Smith (ed.), *New Goals in Police Management.* The Annals 171: 54-62.

Klockars, Carl. 1974. *The Professional Thief.* New York: Free Press.

——. 1983a. "The Dirty Harry problem." In Carl Klockars (ed.), *Thinking About Police.* New York: McGraw-Hill.

——. 1983b. "The modern sting." In Carl Klockars (ed.), *Thinking About Police.* New York: McGraw-Hill.

——. 1985. *The Idea of Police.* Beverley Hills: Sage.

Kuykendall, Jack. 1982a. "The criminal investigation process: Toward a conceptual framework." *Journal of Criminal Justice* 10: 131-145.

——. 1982b. *Police Use of Deadly Force.* Unpublished paper.

Lane, Roger. 1967. *Policing the City.* Cambridge: Harvard.

Larson, John. 1925. "Present police and legal methods for the determination of the innocence or guilt of the suspect." *Journal of Criminal Law and Criminology* 16: 219-271.

——. 1932. *Lying and Its Deception.* Chicago: University of Chicago.

Lavine, Earnest. 1930. *The Third Degree.* New York: Vanguard.

Leonard, V. A. 1943. "Crime control: A police officer's attempt to state the problem." *Journal of Criminal Law and Criminology* 37: 85-104.

Lynch, Gerald and Edward Diamond. 1983. "Police: Misconduct." In Sanford Kadish (ed.), *Encyclopedia of Criminal Justice.* New York: Free Press.

Manning, Peter. 1977. *Police Work: The Social Organization of Police.* Cambridge: M.I.T. Press.

——. 1980. *The Narcs Game.* Cambridge: M.I.T. Press.

Marx, Gary. 1983. "New undercover policework." In Carl Klockars (ed.), *Thinking about Police.* New York: McGraw-Hill.

Matherson, Duncan. 1922. "Criminal investigation." *In Proceedings of the 29th International Association of Chiefs of Police Convention.* San Francisco: International Association of Chiefs of Police.

——. 1926. "Address." In *Proceedings of the 33rd International Association of Chiefs of Police Convention.* Chicago: International Association of Chiefs of Police.

1929. *The Technique of the American Detective.* The Annals 146: 214-218.

McAdoo, William. 1906. *Guarding a Great City.* New York: Harper and Row.

McGillis, Daniel. 1977. *The Major Offense Bureau.* Washington, D. C.: National Institute of Law Enforcement and Criminal Justice.

McNerney, Tom. 1980. "Interview." Unfinished doctoral dissertation.

McWatters, George. 1871. *Ways and By-Ways in the Hidden Life of American Detectives.* Hanford, CN: Burr and Hyde.

Miller, Wilbur. 1977. *Cops and Bobbies.* Chicago: University of Chicago Press.

——. 1979. "London's police tradition in a changing society." In Simon Holdaway (ed.), *The British Police.* Beverly Hills: Sage.

Miranda v. Arizona. 1966. 384 U.S. 436.

Monkkonen, Eric. 1981. *Police in Urban America: 1860–1920.* Cambridge: Cambridge University Press.

Morn, Frank. 1982. *The Eye That Never Sleeps.* Bloomington, IN: Indiana University Press.

Morris, P. and K. Heal. 1981. *Crime Control and the Public.* London: Home Research Office.

Murphy, Patrick and Thomas Plate. 1977. *Commissioner.* New York: Simon and Schuster.

National Commission on Law Observance. 1931. *Police.* Washington, D. C.: U.S. Government Printing Office.

Novak, John. 1983. "Criminal Procedures." In Sanford Kadish (ed.), *Encyclopedia of Criminal Justice.* New York: The Free Press.

Ottolengi, Salvatore. 1913. "The Scientific Police." *Journal of Criminal Law and Criminology* 3: 876-880.

Parker, Brian and Joseph Peterson. 1972. *Physical Evidence Utilization in the Administration of Criminal Justice.* Berkeley: University of California Press.

Peterson, Joseph, J. Milhajhovie, and S. Gilliland. 1984. *Forensic Evidence and the Police.* Washington, D. C.: National Institute of Justice.

Philips, David. 1977. *Crime and Authority in Victorian England.* London: Rowman and Littlefield.

Pinkerton, Allan. 1874. "The character and duties of a detective force." In *Proceedings of the National Prison Congress.* Reprinted by the New York Times and Arno Press, 1971.

———. 1884. *Thirty Years a Detective.* New York: Carleton.

Police Commission. 1914. *Annual Report, City of Boston.* Reprinted by the New York Times and Arno Press, 1971.

Prassel, Frank. 1972. *The Western Peace Officer.* Norman: University of Oklahoma Press.

Price, Barbara. 1977. *Police Professionalism.* Lexington, MA: Heath.

Radzinowicz, Leon. 1948–1968. *A History of English Criminal Law and Its Administration,* Vols. I-IV. London: Stevens.

Reiner, Robert. 1985. *The Politics of Police.* New York: St. Martin's.

Reppetto, Thomas. 1978. "The detective task: State of the art, science or craft." *Police Studies* 1: 5-10.

Reuss-Ianni, Elizabeth. 1983. *Two Cultures of Policing.* New Brunswick: Transaction Books.

Richardson, James. 1970. *The New York Police.* New York: Oxford University Press.

Rider, Eugene. 1971. *The Denver Police Department, 1858–1905.* Unpublished doctoral dissertation. Denver: University of Denver.

Sanders, William. 1977. *Detective Work.* New York: Free Press.

Savage, Edward. 1873. *Police Records and Recollections.* Reprinted by Patterson-Smith, 1972.

Sherman, Lawrence. 1978. *Scandal and Reform.* Berkeley: University of California Press.

———. 1983. "Patrol strategies for police." In James Wilson (ed.), *Crime and Public Policy.* San Francisco: ICS Press.

Smith, Bruce. 1925. *The State Police.* New York: MacMillan.

———. 1929. *Municipal Police Administration.* The Annals 146: 1-27.

———. 1941. *The Baltimore Police Survey.* New York: Institute of Police Administration.

———. 1943. "The Great Years of American Police Development." *Journal of Criminal Law and Criminology* 34: 127-136.

———. 1946. *New Orleans Police Survey.* New York: Bureau of Government Research. Reprinted by the New York Times and Arno Press.

Smith, Philip. 1985. *Policing Victorian London.* Westport, CN: Greenwood Press.

Sprogle, Howard. 1887. *The Philadelphia Police.* Reprinted by the New York Times and Arno Press, 1971.

State of New York. 1935. *Proceedings of the Governor's Conference on Crime, the Criminal and Society.* Albany, NY.

Tobias, J. 1972. *Nineteenth Century Crime in England: Sources for Social and Economic History.* New York: Barnes and Noble.

Valentine, Lewis. 1947. *Nightstick: An Autobiography.* New York: Dial Press.

Vollmer, August. 1922. "Aims and Ideals of the Police." *Journal of Criminal Law and Criminology* 8: 251-257.

Wade, John. 1829. *A Treatise on the Police and Crimes of the Metropolis.* Montclair, NJ: Patterson-Smith Reprint, 1972.

Waegel, William. 1982. "Patterns of Police Investigation of Crime." *Journal of Police Science and Administration* 10: 452-465.

Walker, Samuel. 1977. *A Critical History of Police Reform.* Lexington, MA: Lexington.

———. 1984. "Broken Windows and Fractured History." *Justice Quarterly* 1: 75-90.

Walling, George. 1887. *Recollections of a New York City Chief of Police.* New York: Claxton Book Concern. Patterson-Smith Reprint, 1972.

Willemse, Cornelius. 1931. *Behind the Greenlights.* New York: Knopf.

Wilson, James Q. 1978. *The Investigators.* New York: Basic Books.

Wilson, Orlando. 1950. *Police Administration.* New York: McGraw-Hill.

Woldridge, Clifton. 1901. *Hands Up! In the World of Crime.* Chicago: Police Publishing.

———. 1902. *Twenty Years a Detective.*

Woods, Arthur. 1914. "The Control of Crime." *Journal of Criminal Law and Criminology* 4: 687-697.

———. 1918. *Crime Prevention.* Princeton, NJ: Princeton University Press.

8

'Broken Windows' and Fractured History

Samuel Walker

In *recent years, nothing has been quite so popular in police and political circles as "community policing," a topic that is addressed later in this anthology. One of several rationales for community policing has been the "broken windows" thesis first proposed by James Q. Wilson and George Kelling in a 1982* Atlantic Monthly *article. In the article you are about to read, historian Sam Walker explains the broken windows thesis and then proceeds to challenge its historical basis. You should follow this debate closely, since community policing has become such a big part of the modern police picture. Also, ask yourself whether Walker is opposed to community policing or simply critical of the historical rationale constructed to support it.*

A fresh burst of creativity marks current thinking about police patrol in the United States. This revival follows a period of doubt and disorientation in the late 1970s when recent research shattered traditional assumptions about patrol strategy. The most notable proposal for a reorientation of police patrol is set forth in "Broken Windows" by James Q. Wilson and George L. Kelling. Drawing partly on recent patrol experiments and partly on a re-thinking of police history, Wilson and Kelling propose a return to what they see as an older "watchman" style of policing (Wilson and Kelling 1982).

This selection examines the use of history by Wilson and Kelling in their proposal for reorienting police patrol. Because the historical analysis is central to their argument, its viability may well depend upon how well they have interpreted police history. Kelling develops his view of police history even more explicitly in a subsequent article co-authored with Mark H. Moore (Moore and Kelling 1983).

We shall argue here that Wilson, Kelling and Moore have misinterpreted police history in several important respects. Their proposal calls for a restoration—a return to a former tradition of police patrol. Joe McNamara, Chief of the San Jose police, has already responded to the "broken windows" thesis by arguing that the good old days weren't all that good (McNamara 1982). This selection elaborates upon that point and argues that the tradition of policing cited by Wilson, Kelling and Moore never existed. This does not necessarily mean that the broken windows thesis is completely invalid. But if there is merit in the style of police patrol Wilson and Kelling propose, that style will have to be created anew. There is no viable older tradition to restore. Obviously, this is a far more difficult and challenging proposition than they have suggested.

Policing and Broken Windows

Broken windows are a metaphor for the deterioration of neighborhoods. A broken window that goes unrepaired is a statement that no one cares enough about the quality of life in the neighborhood to bother fixing the little things that are wrong. While a broken window might be a small thing in and of itself, left unrepaired it becomes an invitation to further neglect. The result is a progressive deterioration of the entire neighborhood. Wilson and Kelling cite research in social psychology where abandoned cars were rapidly vandalized when some sign of prior vandalism invited further destructive acts (Zimbardo 1969).

Policing in America has failed, Wilson, Kelling and Moore argue, because it has neglected "the little things," the law enforcement equivalents of broken windows. This neglect is the product of the development of an efficiency-oriented, crime control-focused style of policing over the past fifty years. Eric Monkkonen argues that the shift toward crime control began even earlier and was substantially complete by 1920 (Monkkonen 1981).

Two developments in the 1930s launched a radical reorientation of police patrol. The first was the greatly increased use of the patrol car, which took the patrol officer off the street and isolated him from the public. The second was the development of the Uniform Crime Reports system which then became the basic measure of police "success." By themselves, these two developments might not have exerted such a profound effect on policing. The crucial difference was the influence of O. W. Wilson who forced a coherent theory of police management in the late 1930s. Wilsonian theory emphasized the suppression of crime as the primary mission of policing. Fulfillment of this mission depended upon maximizing the efficiency of patrol coverage. The automobile allowed a patrol officer to cover his beat more often during one tour of duty, and to do so in a more unpredictable fashion than foot patrol.

Wilson became the leading proponent of one-officer cars, claiming that two single officer patrol cars were twice as efficient as one two-officer car. He recommended that patrol beats should be organized according to a workload formula which distributed the work evenly among patrol officers. Finally, he concluded that rapid response time would increase apprehensions and generally enhance public satisfaction with police service (Walker 1977; Fogelson 1977). Wilson tirelessly propounded his gospel of efficiency from the late 1930s onward. His text *Police Administration* became "the bible" of police management and instructed an entire generation of police executives (Wilson and McLaren 1977). Police departments converted almost entirely from foot to automobile patrol, invested enormous sums of money in sophisticated communications equipment, and encouraged members of the public to avail themselves of their service.

Lost in this process were the personal aspects of routine policing. The car isolated officers from the people in the neighborhoods, which became nothing more than a series of "beat assignments" to the officers. The most professionalized departments, in fact, took extra measures to de-personalize policing. Frequent rotation of beat assignments was adopted as a strategy to combat corruption.

The crime control orientation meanwhile caused the police to concentrate on more serious crimes—primarily, the seven felonies that comprised the Crime Index. Significantly, the police actively adopted the UCR system as the measure of their performance. It was not something imposed on them (Manning 1977). The police lost interest in lesser violations of the law and routine because they just did not count. These nuisances included drunks, loud and intimidating groups of teenagers, public drug dealing, and the like.[1]

According to Wilson, Kelling and Moore, these nuisances are the "broken windows," the little things that convey the message that no one cares about the quality of life in this neighborhood. Wilson, Kelling and Moore base much of their argument on the recent Newark Foot Patrol Experiment (The Police Foundation 1981). The presence of officers on foot patrol did not reduce crime, but did make people feel safer. Officers were able to establish and enforce informal rules of behavior for the neighborhood. It was alright to be intoxicated in public but not to pass out in the gutter, for example. Wilson and Kelling also cite with apparent approval the technique used by some Chicago police officers to maintain order in public housing projects: if groups of teenagers were troublesome, the officers would simply chase them away. "We kick ass," one officer explained (Wilson and Kelling 1982:35).

The "Broken Windows" article argues that policing should be neighborhood-oriented. More officers should be deployed on foot, and those officers should concentrate less on catching criminals and more on enforcing informal neighborhood norms of behavior. To a certain extent it advocates a form of team policing, although with some important differences.

Team policing experiments in the 1970s did not emphasize foot patrol, gave insufficient attention to street-level patrol tactics, and maintained the traditional crime control focus. Indeed, the incompatibility of some elements of team policing with the prevailing organizational structure and management philosophy was one of the factors in the failure of early team policing experiments (Sherman 1973: U.S. Department of Justice 1977; Schwartz and Clarren 1977).

"Broken Windows" offers an alternative model precisely because it focuses on what officers would actually do. It characterizes the recommended style of policing as a return to an earlier (pre-1930s) style of "watchman" or "constabulary" policing. At this point we turn our attention to the historical analysis that underpins this argument.

The Historical Framework

The historical framework presented by Wilson, Kelling and Moore consists of three components: the near-term, which embraces the last fifteen years; the middle-term, which includes the last fifty years; and the long-term, which involves all of police history before the last fifty years.

Their reading of near-term history is excellent. One of the most important developments of the past fifteen years has unquestionably been the enormous expansion of our knowledge about all aspects of policing. We can now discuss in an informed fashion issues that were *terra incognita* to the staff of the President's Crime Commission (Walker 1983). The most important findings constitute a systematic demolition of the assumptions underlying O. W. Wilson's approach to police management. We have learned that adding more police or intensifying patrol coverage will not reduce crime and that neither faster response time nor additional detectives will improve clearance rates. Few authorities on policing today could endorse the basic Wilsonian idea that improved management in the deployment of patrol officers or detectives is likely to reduce the crime rate.

Wilson's, Kelling's and Moore's reading of the last fifty years of police history is mixed. They recognize the most significant developments in the period but misinterpret them in important respects. There are substantial implications of this misinterpretation for their proposed style of policing.

The development of American policing from the 1930s through the 1960s was a far more complex process than historians have lead us to believe. Wilson, Kelling and Moore can be excused in large part because they have simply drawn upon the available historical scholarship. We will focus here on two aspects of police history since the 1930s which have not received sufficient attention. The first involves the impact of the patrol car and the second concerns the crime control orientation of policing.

The Technological Revolution

It is indeed true that American police departments largely converted from foot to automobile patrol between the 1930s and the present. We should, of course, be cognizant of the enormous variations that exist even today. Some departments are almost wholly motorized while others, primarily Eastern cities, still make heavy use of foot patrol (Police Executive Research Forum 1981). And it is also true that car patrols remove officers from the sidewalks, isolate them from casual contacts with ordinary citizens, and damage police-community relations. This analysis is part of the conventional wisdom about policing.

The impact of technology was paradoxical, however. The mid-century revolution in American policing involved not just the patrol car, but the car in conjunction with the telephone and the two-way radio. These served to bring police officers into far more intimate contact with people than ever before. While the patrol car isolated police officers in some respects, the telephone simultaneously increased the degree of contact in other respects. Let us examine this paradox in detail.

In the days of foot patrol, officers had extensive casual contacts with people. But they occurred primarily on the streets or in other public places. The police did not often obtain entry to private residences. The reason for this is obvious: there was no mechanism whereby the ordinary citizen could effectively summon the police. The telephone radically altered that situation with profound ramifications for both policing and public expectations about the quality of life. Stinchcombe (1963) has discussed the impact of privacy considerations on routine police work.

The telephone made it possible for the ordinary citizen to summon the police, and the combination of the two-way radio and the patrol car allowed the police to respond quickly. As we know, the more professional departments acquired a fetish for responding as quickly as possible to all calls. The development of the 911 telephone number was simply the logical conclusion of this effort to advertise and encourage people to use police service. People have in fact availed themselves of this service. The number of calls for service has escalated to the point where serious attention has been given to the idea of restricting or otherwise managing those requests in the last few years (Gay 1977).

Technology radically alters the nature of police-citizen contacts. Most of those contacts now occur in private residences. Albert Reiss reports that 70% of all police-citizen contacts occur in private places, 12% in semi-public, and 18 % in open public places (Reiss 1971:16). The police not only gain access to private places, but observe the most intimate aspects of peoples' lives, and are asked to handle their most personal problems.

Research has confirmed that the bulk of police work involves domestic disputes and other problems arising from alcohol, drugs, mental illness, and poverty. Officers refer to all this as "bullshit" or "social work" because it is unrelated to what they believe to be their crime control mission.

Police-citizen contacts became increasingly skewed. The police lost contact with "ordinary" people and gained a great deal of contact with "problem" people, who included not just criminal offenders but those with multiple social problems. David Bayley and Harold Mendelsohn once observed that police officers had more direct knowledge about minorities than did the members of any other occupation. This knowledge was a direct product of the heavy demands upon police service placed by low-income and racial minorities (Bayley and Mendelsohn 1969:156).

Our understanding of the full impact of the telephone on policing remains problematic. Not all experts on policing accept the argument advanced here. Some argue that the police were indeed intimately involved in people's lives prior to the advent of the telephone.[2] Unfortunately, there is no empirical evidence that would permit the resolution of

this question. Prior to the late 1950s, there were no observational studies of police patrol activities and thus we have no reliable evidence on what American police officers did on patrol in the pre-telephone era.[3]

The Revolution in Public Expectations

One consequence of the technological revolution in policing has been a parallel revolution in public expectations about the quality of life. The availability of police service created and fed a demand for those services. The establishment of the modern police in the early nineteenth century was an initial phase of this process, which created the expectation that a certain level of public order would, or at least should, prevail (Silver 1967).

The technological revolution of the mid-twentieth century generated a quantum leap in those expectations. Because there was now a mechanism for getting someone (the police) to "do something" about minor disorders and nuisances, people came to expect that they should not have to put up with such minor irritations. Thus, the general level of expectations about the quality of life—the amount of noise, the presence of "strange" or "undesirable" people—has undergone an enormous change. Three generations of Americans have learned or at least have come to believe that they should not have to put up with certain problems.

The police are both the source and the victims of this revolution. They have stimulated higher levels of public expectations by their very presence and their policy of more readily available services. At the same time they are the prisoners of their own creation, swamped with an enormous service call workload. The recent effort to restrict or somehow manage this workload faces the problem of a public that expects rapid police response for any and every problem as a matter of right.

Documenting changes in public expectations concerning the police is difficult given the absence of reliable data about public attitudes or police practices prior to the late 1950s and early 1960s. Several indicators do provide evidence of short-term chances in public expectations. The development of three-digit (911) emergency phone numbers for the police increased the number of service calls. In Omaha, Nebraska, for example, the number of patrol car dispatches increased by 36% between 1969 and 1971, presumably as a result of a new 911 phone number (Walker 1983:110). These figures represent the dispatch of a patrol car, not the number of incoming calls. Omaha police officials estimate that about 35% of all calls do not result in a dispatch.

Additional evidence is found in data on the number of civilian complaints about police misconduct. In New York City, for example, the number of complaints filed with the Civilian Complaint Review Board (CCRB) increased from about 200 per year in 1960–62 to just over 2000 per year in 1967–68 and more than 3000 annually in 1971–74. It would be difficult to believe that the conduct of New York City police officers deteriorated by a factor of 10 or 15 during this period. Rather, the increase is probably the result of a lower threshold of tolerance for police misconduct on the part of citizens and the increased availability of an apparent remedy for perceived misconduct.

During the period under discussion, the procedures of the New York CCRB were reorganized several times. Each reorganization facilitated complaint filing and at the same time heightened public awareness of the availability of this particular remedy (Kahn 1975:113). The data on civilian complaints supports the argument made herein concerning police services generally: the availability of a service or remedy stimulates demand for that service, thereby altering basic expectations.

The Mythology of Crime Control

The conventional wisdom states that police organize their efforts around the goal of crime control. Wilson, Kelling and Moore restate this conventional wisdom, but the matter is a bit more complex.

There is an important distinction between the self-image of the police and the day-to-day reality of routine policing (Goldstein 1977). The emphasis on crime control is and has been largely a matter of what the police

say they are doing. Peter Manning argues persuasively that the police consciously created and manipulated this self-image as a way of establishing greater professional and political autonomy (Manning 1977).

As we have seen, however, the day-to-day reality of policing contradicted this self-image. The sharp contrast between the crime-fighting imagery of the police and the peacekeeping reality of police activities was one of the first and most important findings of the flood of police research that began in the 1960s. When Wilson, Kelling and Moore suggest that the police are completely crime control-oriented they seriously misrepresent the nature of contemporary policing.

The discrepancy between crime control imagery and operational reality also becomes evident when we look more closely at how police departments utilize their resources. The most recent Survey of Police Operational and Administrative Practices reveals enormous variations among departments (Police Executive Research Forum 1981). Many still distribute their patrol officers equally among three shifts, ignoring even the most rudimentary workload formulas, which were first developed by O. W. Wilson over forty years ago (Wilson and McLaren 1977: Appendix J). Departments typically do not revise the boundaries of their patrol districts on a regular basis. Districts remain unchanged for ten or twenty years, or longer. Meanwhile, the composition of the urban environment changes radically, as older areas are depopulated, new residential areas created, and so on.

The Question of Legitimacy

The most important long-term development in American policing, according to Wilson, Kelling and Moore, has been the loss of political legitimacy. There can be little doubt that legitimacy, by which we mean acceptance of police authority by the public, is a major problem today.

The interpretation of police history offered by Wilson, Kelling and Moore, which purports to explain how that legitimacy was lost, is seriously flawed. The evidence completely contradicts the thrust of their argument.

The police in the nineteenth century were not merely the "adjuncts" of the machine, as Robert Fogelson (1977) suggests, but were central cogs in it. Wilson, Kelling and Moore maintain that this role offered certain benefits for the police, which reformers and historians alike have overlooked.

As cogs in the machine, the police served the immediate needs of the different neighborhoods. Political control was highly decentralized and local city councilmen or ward bosses exercised effective control over the police. Thus, the police carried out a wide range of services. Historians have rediscovered the social welfare role of the police, providing food and lodging for vagrants (Walker 1977; Monkkonen 1981). The police also performed political errands and were the means by which certain groups and individuals were able to corrupt the political process. These errands included open electioneering, rounding up the loyal voters, and harassing the opponents. Police also enforced the narrow prejudices of their constituents, harassing "undesirables" or discouraging any kind of "unwelcome" behavior.

Wilson, Kelling and Moore concede that there was a lack of concern for due process, but argue there was an important trade-off. By virtue of serving the immediate needs and narrow prejudices of the neighborhoods, the police gained an important degree of political legitimacy. They were perceived as faithful servants and enjoyed the resulting benefits. All of this was destroyed by the reforms of the twentieth century. The patrol car removed officers from the streets, while the new "professional" style dictated an impersonal type of policing. Legal concerns with due process denied officers the ability to use the tactics of rough justice by which they had enforced neighborhood community norms.

This historical analysis is central to the reorientation of policing, presented in the "Broken Windows" article. Wilson, Kelling and Moore propose that the lost political legitimacy could be re-established by what they view as the older "watchman" style of policing. Unfortunately, this historical analysis is pure fantasy.

Historians are unanimous in their conclusion that the police were at the center of urban political conflict in the nineteenth century. In many instances policing was the paramount issue and in some cases the only issue. Historians disagree only on their interpretation of the exact nature of this political conflict. The many experiments with different forms of administrative control over the police (the last of which survives only in Missouri) were but one part of this long and bitter struggle for political control (Walker 1977; Fogelson 1977).

To say that there was political conflict over the police means that the police lacked political legitimacy. Their authority was not accepted by the citizenry. Wilson, Kelling and Moore are seriously in error when they suggest that the police enjoyed substantial legitimacy in the pre-technology era.

The lack of legitimacy is further illustrated by the nature of the conflicts surrounding the police. Non-enforcement of the various laws designed to control drinking was the issue that most often roused the so-called "reformers" to action. Alcohol consumption was a political issue with many dimensions. In some respects it was an expression of ethnic conflict, pitting sobersided Anglo-Saxons against the heavy-drinking Irish and Germans. Drinking was also a class issue. Temperance and, later, prohibition advocates tended either to come from the middle class or at least define themselves in terms of the values of hard work, sobriety, thrift and upward mobility (Gusfield 1963). When nineteenth century Americans fought over the police and the enforcement of the drinking laws, that battle expressed the deepest social conflicts in American society.

In one of the finest pieces of historical scholarship on the American police, Wilbur Miller explores the question of legitimacy from an entirely different angle (Miller 1977). The great difference between the London and New York City police was precisely the extent to which officers in New York were denied the grant of legitimacy enjoyed by their counterparts in London. Miller further argues that the problem of legitimacy was individualized in New York City. Each officer faced challenges to his personal authority and had to assert his authority on a situational level.

Miller does not argue that challenges to police legitimacy were patterned according to class, ethnicity or race. Thus, an Irish-American cop was just as likely to be challenged by a fellow countryman as he was by someone of a different ethnic background. To be sure, the poor, political radicals, blacks, and other people deemed "undesirable" were victimized more often by the police than were other groups, but it does not follow that the police enjoyed unquestioned authority in the eyes of those people who were members of the same class and ethnic groups as police officers.

The Myth of the Watchman

With their argument that the nineteenth century police enjoyed political legitimacy, Wilson, Kelling and Moore have resurrected in slightly different garb the old myth of the friendly cop on the beat. They offer this older "watchman" style of policing as a viable model for contemporary policing. Quite apart from the broader question of political legitimacy, their argument turns on the issue of on-the-street police behavior.

Historians have not yet reconstructed a full picture of police behavior in the nineteenth century. At best, historians can make inferences about this behavior from surviving records. None of the historical accounts published to date presents a picture of policing that could be regarded as a viable model for the present.

What do we know about routine policing in the days before the patrol car? There is general agreement that officers did not necessarily do much work at all. Given the primitive state of communications technology, patrol officers were almost completely on their own and able to avoid effective supervision (Rubinstein 1974). Evidence suggests that evasion of duty was commonplace. We also know that corruption was the norm. Mark Haller (1976) suggests that corruption was possibly the primary objective of all of municipal government, not just the police department.

Wilbur Miller (1977), meanwhile, places the matter of police brutality in a new and convincing light. His argument that brutality was a response to the refusal of citizens to grant the police legitimacy speaks directly to the point raised by Wilson, Kelling and Moore.

Recently some historians have attempted to draw a more systematic picture of police law enforcement activities. The most convincing picture is drawn by Lawrence Friedman and Robert Percival (1981) in their study of the Oakland police between 1870 and 1910. They characterize police arrest patterns as a giant trawling operation. The typical arrestee was a white, working class adult male who was drunk and was arrested for intoxication, disturbing the peace, or some related offense. But there was nothing systematic about police operations. The people swept up into their net were simply unlucky—there was no reason why they should have been arrested rather than others whose behavior was essentially the same. Nor was it apparent, in Friedman's and Percival's view, that the police singled out any particular categories of people for especially systematic harassment.

The argument offered by Wilson, Kelling and Moore turns in part on the question of purpose: what the police saw themselves doing. Historians have established that police officers had a few purposes. The first was to get and hold the job. The second was to exploit the possibilities for graft that the job offered. A third was to do as little actual patrol work as possible. A fourth involved surviving on the street, which meant establishing and maintaining authority in the face of hostility and overt challenges to that authority. Finally, officers apparently felt obliged to go through the motions of "real" police work by arresting occasional miscreants.

We do not find in this picture any conscious purpose of fighting crime or serving neighborhood needs. That is precisely the point made by Progressive era reformers when they indicted the police for inefficiency. Wilson, Kelling and Moore have no grounds for offering this as a viable model for contemporary policing. Chief McNamara is right: the good old days were not that good.

The watchman style of policing described by Wilson, Kelling, and Moore can also be challenged from a completely different perspective. The idea that the police served the needs of local neighborhoods and thereby enjoyed political legitimacy is based on a highly romanticized view of nineteenth century neighborhood life. Urban neighborhoods were not stable and homogeneous little villages nestled in the city. They were heterogeneous, and the rate of geographic mobility was even higher than contemporary rates. Albert Reiss (1971:209-210) in *Police and the Public* critiques recent "community control" proposals on these very grounds: they are based on the erroneous impression that neighborhoods are stable, homogeneous and relatively well-defined.

Summary and Conclusions

In "Broken Windows," James O. Wilson and George Kelling offer a provocative proposal for reorienting police patrol. Their argument is based primarily on an historical analysis of American policing. They propose a return to a watchman style of policing, which they claim existed before the advent of crime control oriented policing in the 1930s. This historical analysis is further developed in a subsequent article by Kelling and Moore (1983).

In this article we have examined the historical analysis used by these three authors. We find it flawed on several fundamental points.

First, the depersonalization of American policing from the 1930s onward has been greatly exaggerated. While the patrol car did isolate the police in some respects, the telephone brought about a more intimate form of contact between police and citizen by allowing the police officer to enter private residences and involving them in private disputes and problems.

Second, the crime control orientation of the police has been greatly exaggerated. Crime control is largely a matter of police rhetoric and self-image. Day-to-day policing is, on the other hand, primarily a matter of peacekeeping.

Third, there is no historical evidence to support the contention that the police formerly enjoyed substantial political legitimacy. To the contrary, all the evidence suggests that the legitimacy of the police was one of the major political controversies through-

out the nineteenth century and well into the twentieth.

Fourth, the watchman style of policing referred to by Wilson, Kelling and Moore is just as inefficient and corrupt as the reformers accuse it of being. It does not involve any conscious purpose to serve neighborhood needs and hardly serves as a model for revitalized contemporary policing.

Where does this leave us? We should not throw the proverbial baby out with the bath water. The fact that Wilson and Kelling construct their "Broken Windows" thesis on a false and heavily romanticized view of the past does not by itself invalidate their concept of a revitalized police patrol. They correctly interpret the lessons of recent police research. Suppression of crime is a will-of-the-wisp which the police should no longer pursue. Enhancement of public feelings of safety, however, does appear to be within the grasp of the police. A new form of policing based on the apparent lessons of the Newark Foot Patrol Experiment, the failures of team policing experiments, and the irrelevance of most official police-community relations programs seems to be a goal that is both worth pursuing and feasible.

Our main point here is simply that such a revitalized form of policing would represent something entirely new in the history of the American police. There is no older tradition worthy of restoration. A revitalized, community-oriented policing would have to be developed slowly and painfully.

There should be no mistake about the difficulty of such a task. Among other things, recent research on the police clearly demonstrates the enormous difficulty in changing either police officer behavior and/or the structure and process of police organization. Yet at the same time, the history reviewed here does suggest that fundamental long-term changes in policing are indeed possible. Change is a constant; shaping that change in a positive way is the challenge.

Notes

1. James Fyfe argues that prosecutorial and judicial indifference to minor "quality of life" offenses is also responsible for neighborhood deterioration and that the police should not

be singled out as the major culprits. By implication, he suggests that reorienting the police role would be futile without simultaneously reorienting the priorities of prosecutors and judges. Personal correspondence, James Fyfe to Walker.

2. Lawrence W. Sherman accepts this view and dissents from the argument advanced in this article. Personal correspondence, Lawrence W. Sherman to Walker.

3. The debate is conducted largely on the basis of circumstantial evidence. Sherman, for example, believes that literary evidence is a reliable guide to past police practices and cites *A Tree Grows in Brooklyn* as one useful example. Personal correspondence, Sherman to Walker.

References

Bayley, D. and Mendelsohn, H. (1969) *Minorities and the Police*. New York: The Free Press.

Fogelson, R. (1977) *Big City Police*. Cambridge: Harvard University Press.

Friedman, L. M. and Percival, R. V. (1981) *The Roots of Justice*. Chapel Hill: University of North Carolina Press.

Gay, W. (1977) *Improving Patrol Productivity*, Volume 1, Routine Patrol. Washington, DC: Government Printing Office.

Goldstein, H. (1977) *Policing a Free Society*. Cambridge: Ballinger.

Gusfield, J. (1963) *Symbolic Crusade: Status Politics and the American Temperance Movement*. Urbana: University of Illinois Press.

Haller, M. (1976) "Historical Roots of Police Behavior: Chicago, 1890-1925." *Law and Society Review*, 10 (Winter):303-324.

Kahn, R. (1975) "Urban Reform and Police Accountability in New York City, 1950-1974." In *Urban Problems and Public Policy*, edited by R. L. Lineberry and L. H. Masotti. Lexington: Lexington Books.

McNamara, J. D. (1982) "Dangerous Nostalgia for the Cop on the Beat." *San Jose Mercury-News*, May 2.

Manning, P. K. (1977) *Police Work*. Cambridge: MIT Press.

Miller, W. (1977) *Cops and Bobbies*. Chicago: University of Chicago Press.

Monkkonen, E. (1981) *Police in Urban America, 1860-1920*. Cambridge: Cambridge University Press.

Moore, M. H. and Kelling, G. L. (1983) "To Serve and Protect: Learning from Police History." *The Public Interest* 70: 49-65.

Police Executive Research Forum (1981) *Survey of Police Operational and Administrative Practices-1981*. Washington, DC: Police Executive Research Forum.

Police Foundation (1981) *The Newark Foot Patrol Experiment*. Washington, DC: The Police Foundation.

Reiss, A. (1971) *The Police and the Public*. New Haven: Yale University Press.

Rubinstein, J. (1974) *City Police*. New York: Ballantine Books.

Schwartz, A. I. and Clarren, S. N. (1977) *The Cincinnati Team Policing Experiment*. Washington, DC: The Police Foundation.

Sherman, L. W. (1973) *Team Policing: Seven Case Studies*. Washington, DC: The Police Foundation.

Silver, A. (1967) "The Demand for Order in Civil Society." In *The Police: Six Sociological Essays*, ed. By David J. Bordua. New York: John Wiley.

Stinchombe, A. (1963) "Institutions of Privacy in the Determination Of Police Administrative Practice." *American Journal Of Sociology* 69 (September): 150-160.

U.S. Department of Justice (1977) *Neighborhood Team Policing*. Washington, DC: Government Printing Office.

Walker, S. (1983) *The Police in America: An Introduction*. New York: McGraw-Hill.

——. (1977) *A Critical History of Police Reform: The Emergence of Professionalization*. Lexington: Lexington Books.

Wilson, J. Q. and Kelling, G. L. (1982) "Broken Windows: Police and Neighborhood Safety." *Atlantic Monthly* 249 (March): 29-38.

Wilson, O. W. and McLaren, R. C. (1977) *Police Administration*. Fourth ed. New York: McGraw-Hill.

Zimbardo, P. G. (1969) "The Human Choice: Individuation, Reason, and Order versus Deindividuation, Impulse, and Chaos." In *Nebraska Symposium on Motivation*, edited by W. J. Arnold and D. Levine. Lincoln: University of Nebraska Press.

Part III

Strategies and Programs

One of the most vibrant areas of police research over the past 25 years, and one that actually seems to have had an impact on police practice, has been evaluation and effectiveness research. Starting with the publication of the celebrated Kansas City Preventive Patrol Experiment in 1974, a succession of studies has examined the merits of a variety of strategies and programs: follow-up criminal investigations, rapid response to reported crimes, field interviews, one-officer versus two-officer patrol cars, directed patrol, foot patrol, crime prevention, police handling of domestic disputes, problem-oriented policing, community policing, and more. Scholars and police have at their disposal today a greater quantity of more reliable information about the relative effectiveness of various police strategies and programs than they had two decades ago. Not all of this information is definitive, of course, and there remain large gaps in the knowledge base, but police are much better armed to make wise strategic decisions than they once were.

Taking a big-picture view of the current situation, we might think of police agencies as having a choice among four overarching strategies. The first, *professional crime fighting*, basically corresponds to policing as practiced since the 1960s: patrol cars are spread throughout the jurisdiction, calls are handled as they come in, all crimes are followed up by detectives, etc. The underlying crime control rationale is general deterrence based on maximum police car visibility and the criminals' perceived risk of getting caught by responding or randomly patrolling officers or, later, by detectives.

The second option for police agencies today is *strategic policing*, essentially a more refined and targeted version of professional crime fighting. This model relies more on directed patrol, proactive tactics, offender-focused investigations, and selected follow-up investigations. Police managers allocate their resources to "hot spots," high-rate offenders, and priority crimes instead of spreading them around uniformly. The crime control approach is based more on specific deterrence and incapacitation than on general deterrence.

The third major strategic alternative is *problem-oriented policing*. This option has some similarities to strategic policing, but it takes a more analytical and multi-faceted approach with less reliance on arrest and enforcement as the sole means of tackling problems of crime, fear, and disorder. The problem-oriented strategy looks for underlying conditions that can be addressed, emphasizes careful analysis before choosing alternatives, and seeks to employ a wide range of social, community, government, and private responses as well as traditional police responses. The basic crime control approach is similar to the public health model (treat the cause rather than just the symptom) and relies more on primary and secondary prevention than on deterrence and incapacitation.

The fourth major option available to police agencies today is *community policing*. This strategy often incorporates problem-oriented policing as a primary tactic, but its most distinctive feature is reliance on the community itself to exert informal social control in order to help reduce crime and disorder. Under community policing, officer assignment patterns are more neighborhood-based, officers work closely and collaborate with community groups, and officers even help organize communities if they are too fragmented to get started on their own. Crime control is expected to be achieved through primary prevention, but also through deterrence and incapacitation as community residents provide officers with more and better information about local crime and suspects.

The selections in this section provide a review of the major effectiveness studies that have led to this current situation, as well as descriptions and evaluations of community policing, problem-oriented policing, and strategic policing. ✦

9

Crime and Policing

Mark H. Moore,
Robert C. Trojanowicz, and
George L. Kelling

This article was one of the first publications in the Perspectives on Policing series begun in 1988 by the National Institute of Justice and Harvard University. The series was very influential in popularizing community policing among police officials and policy makers around the country, partly because of its wide distribution but also because of the talents of its authors and the affiliation with Harvard University. The focus of this article is on police effectiveness in controlling crime. The authors provide an insightful discussion of the narrow conception of serious crime that has traditionally dominated police programming, and then they consider the evidence concerning the effectiveness of both professional-era and community policing strategies. As you read this article, think about how you would like to see your tax dollars spent (and not wasted) on the various police strategies and programs that are in the modern police arsenal today.

The core mission of the police is to control crime. No one disputes this. Indeed, professional crime fighting enjoys wide public support as the basic strategy of policing precisely because it embodies a deep commitment to this objective. In contrast, other proposed strategies such as problem-solving or community policing appear on the surface to blur this focus.[1] If these strategies were to leave the community more vulnerable to criminal victimization, they would be undesirable alternatives. In judging the value of alternative police strategies in controlling crime, how-ever, one should not be misled by rhetoric or mere expressed commitment to the goal; one must keep one's eye on demonstrated effectiveness in achieving the goal.

Professional crime-fighting now relies predominantly on three tactics: (1) motorized patrol; (2) rapid response to calls for service; and (3) retrospective investigation of crimes.[2] Over the past few decades, police responsiveness has been enhanced by connecting police to citizens by telephones, radios, and cars, and by matching police officer schedules and locations to anticipated calls for service.[3] The police focus on serious crime has also been sharpened by screening calls for service, targeting patrol, and developing forensic technology (e.g., automated fingerprint systems, computerized criminal record files, etc.).[4]

Although these tactics have scored their successes, they have been criticized within and outside policing for being reactive rather than proactive. They have also been criticized for failing to prevent crime.[5]

Reactive tactics have some virtues, of course. The police go where crimes have occurred and when citizens have summoned them; otherwise, they do not intrude. The police keep their distance from the community, and thereby retain their impartiality. They do not develop the sorts of relationships with citizens that could bias their responses to crime incidents. These are virtues insofar as they protect citizens from an overly intrusive, too familiar police.

Moreover, the reactive tactics do have preventive effects—at least in theory. The prospect of the police arriving at a crime in progress as a result of a call or a chance observation is thought to deter crimes.[6] The successful prosecution of offenders (made possible by retrospective investigation) is also thought to deter offenders.[7] And even if it does not deter, a successfully prosecuted investigation incapacitates criminals who might otherwise go on to commit other crimes.[8]

Finally, many police forces have developed proactive tactics to deal with crime problems that could not be handled through conventional reactive methods. In drug dealing, organized crime, and vice enforcement, for example, where no immediate victims exist to mobilize the police, the police have developed special units which rely on informants, covert surveillance, and undercover investigations rather than responses to calls for service.[9] In the area of juvenile offenses where society's stake in preventing crimes seems particularly great, the police have created athletic leagues, formed partnerships with schools to deal with drug abuse and truancy, and so on.[10] It is not strictly accurate, then, to characterize modern policing as entirely reactive.

Still, the criticism of the police as being too reactive has some force. It is possible that the police could do more to control serious crime than they now achieve. Perhaps research will yield technological breakthroughs that will dramatically improve the productivity of police investigation. For now, however, the greatest potential for improved crime control may not lie in the continued enhancement of response times, patrol tactics, and investigative techniques. Rather, improved crime control can be achieved by (1) diagnosing and managing problems in the community that produce serious crimes; (2) fostering closer relations with the community to facilitate crime solving; and (3) building self-defense capabilities within the community itself. Among the results may be increased apprehension of criminals. To the extent that problem-solving or community strategies of policing direct attention to and prepare the police to exploit local knowledge and capacity to control crime, they will be useful to the future of policing. To explore these possibilities, this paper examines what is known about serious crime: what it is, where and how it occurs, and natural points of intervention. Current and proposed police tactics are then examined in light of what is known about their effectiveness in fighting serious crime.

Serious Crime

To individual citizens, a serious crime is an offense that happened to *them*. That is why police departments throughout the country are burdened with calls requesting responses to offenses that the police regard as minor. While there are reasons to take such calls seriously, there is also the social and administrative necessity to weigh the relative gravity of the offenses. Otherwise, there is no principle for apportioning society's indignation and determination to punish; nor is there any basis for rationing police responses. The concept of serious crime, then, is necessarily a *social* judgment—not an individual one. Moreover, it is a value judgment—not simply a technical issue. The question of what constitutes serious crime is resolved formally by the criminal code. But the criminal code often fails to give precise guidance to police administrators who must decide which crimes to emphasize. They need some concept that distinguishes the offenses that properly outrage the citizenry and require extended police attention from the many lesser offenses that pose less urgent threats to society.

Like many things that require social value judgments, the issue of what constitutes serious crime is badly neglected.[11] Rather than face a confusing public debate, society relies on convention, or administrative expertise, or some combination of the two, to set standards. Yet, if we are to assess and improve police practice in dealing with serious crime, it is necessary to devote some thought to the question of what constitutes serious crime.

Defining Serious Crime

The usual view of serious crime emphasizes three characteristics of offenses. The most important is physical violence or violation. Death, bloody wounds, crippling injuries, even cuts and bruises increase the severity of a crime.[12] Sexual violation also has a special urgency.[13] Crime victims often suffer property losses as well as pain and violation. Economic losses count in reckoning the seriousness of an offense. Still, society generally considers physical attacks—sexual and nonsexual—as far more serious than attacks on property.[14]

A second feature of serious crime concerns the size of the victim's losses. A robbery resulting in a murder or a permanent, disfiguring injury is considered worse than one that produces only cuts, bruises, and fears. An armored car heist netting millions is considered more serious than a purse snatching yielding the price of a junkie's next fix.

Third, the perceived seriousness of an offense is influenced by the relationship between offenders and victims. Commonly, crimes against strangers are viewed as more serious than crimes committed in the context of ongoing relationships.[15] The reason is partly that the threat to society from indiscriminate predators is more far-reaching than the threat from offenders who limit their targets to spouses, lovers, and friends. Moreover, society judges the evil intent of the offender to be more evident in crimes against strangers. In these crimes, there are no chronic grievances or provocations in the background to raise the issue of who attacked whom first and in what way. The crime is an out-and-out attack, not a mere dispute.[16]

These characteristics—violence, significant losses to victims, predatory strangers—capture much of what is important to societal and police images of serious crime. The intuitive appeal of these criteria is reflected in the categories of the FBI's Uniform Crime Reports. Murder, rape, robbery, burglary, aggravated assault, and auto theft (most presumably committed by strangers) are prominently reported as Part I Offenses. This key national account of crime not only reflects, but anchors society's view of serious crime as predatory street crime.

While this notion has the sanction of intuitive appeal, convention, and measurement, it also contains subtle biases which, once pointed out, might cause society and the police to adjust their traditional views. First, the accepted image of crime seems to downplay the importance of crime committed in the context of ongoing relationships. From the perspective of the general citizenry, such offenses seem less important because they do not pose a *general* threat to society. From the perspective of the police (and other criminal justice officials), such crimes are less clearcut because the existence of the prior relationship muddies the distinction between offender and victim and increases the likelihood that a case will be dropped when the antagonists resolve the dispute that produced the offense.

From the victim's point of view, however, the fact of a relationship to the offender dramatically intensifies the seriousness of the offense. A special terror arises when one is locked into an abusive relationship with a spouse or lover. A date that turns into a rape poisons a victim's psyche much more than an attack by a stranger. And, as Boston Police Commissioner Mickey Roache found when he was heading a unit dealing with interracial violence in Boston, serious interracial intimidation and violence did not appear in crime reports as robberies or burglaries. Rather, the serious crimes appeared as vandalism. What made the vandalism terrifying was that it was directed at the same address night after night.

Second, the view of serious crime as predatory violence tends to obscure the importance of fear as a separate, pernicious aspect of the crime problem. To a degree, the issue of fear is incorporated in the conventional view of serious crime. Indeed, fear is what elevates predatory street crimes above crimes that occur within personal relationships. What the conventional view misses, however, is the empirical fact that minor offenses and incivilities trigger citizens' fears more than actual crime victimization. Rowdy youth, abandoned cars, and graffiti frighten people, force them to restrict their movements, and motivate them to buy guns, locks and dogs. To the extent that the conventional view of serious crime deflects attention from fear and the offenses that stimulate fear, it may obscure an important opportunity for the police to contribute to the solution of the serious crime problem.

Third, defining serious crime in terms of the absolute magnitude of material losses to victims (without reference to the victim's capacity to absorb the loss, or the implications of the losses for people other than the victim) introduces the potential for injustice and ineffectiveness in targeting police attention. In the conventional view, a jewel theft at a swank hotel attracts more attention than the mugging of an elderly woman for her Social Security check. Yet it is clear that the stolen Social Security check represents a larger portion of the elderly woman's wealth than the losses to the hotel's well-insured customers. The robbery of a federally insured bank would attract more attention than the robbery of an inner-city convenience store. But the robbery of the ghetto store could end the entrepreneurial career of the owner, drive the store from the area, and, with the store's departure, deprive the neighborhood of one of its few social underpinnings.

Fourth, to the extent that the conventional view of crime emphasizes the reality of individual criminal victimization, it underplays crimes that have symbolic significance. The current emphasis on child sexual abuse, for example, is important in part because it sustains a broad social commitment to the general care and protection of children. The current emphasis on domestic assault, among other things, helps to sustain a normative movement that is changing the status of women in marriages. The interest in white-collar economic crimes and political corruption can be explained by the desire to set higher standards for the conduct of those in powerful positions. The social response to these offenses is important because it strengthens, or redefines, broad social norms.

In sum, the view of crime as predatory, economically significant violence stresses the substantial losses associated with street offenses. It obscures the losses to society that result from offenses that poison relationships, transform neighborhoods into isolated camps, and undermine important social institutions. It misses the terror of the abused spouse or molested child, the wide social consequences of driving merchants out of business, the rot that drug dealing brings to an urban community, and the polarizing effects of fear. An alternative view of serious crime would be one that acknowledged violence as a key component of serious crime but added the issues of safety within relationships, the importance of fear, and the extent to which offenses collapse individual lives and social institutions as well as inflict individual losses. This enlarged conception rests on the assumption that the police can and should defend more social terrain than the streets. Their challenge is to preserve justice and order within the institutions of the community.

Levels, Trends, and Social Location of Serious Crime

It is no simple matter to represent the current levels, recent trends, and social location of serious crime. Still, several important observations can be made.

First, in any year, a noticeable fraction of American households is touched by serious crime. In 1986, 5 percent of American households experienced the violence associated with a rape, robbery, or assault. Almost 8 percent of households were touched by at least one serious crime: rape, robbery, aggravated assault, or burglary.[17] When considering the likelihood that a household will be victimized sometime in the next 5 years, these figures increase dramatically, for a household faces these risks *each year*. Thus, most American households have first- or second-hand experience with serious crime.

Second, from the mid-1960's to the mid-1970's, the United States experienced a dramatic increase in the level of serious crime. In fact, the level of serious crime reached historic highs. Since the mid-seventies, the level of serious crime has remained approximately constant or declined slightly.[18]

Third, criminal victimization is disproportionately concentrated among minority and poor populations in the United States. Homicide is the leading cause of death for young minority males living in metropolitan areas.[19] Black households are victimized by violent crimes such as robbery, rape, and aggravated assault at one and a half times the frequency of white families. The poor are victimized at one and a half times the rate of the wealthy.[20] These numbers probably underestimate the real differences in the losses—material and psychological—experienced by rich and poor victims, since those who are black and poor have fewer resources to deal with the losses associated with victimization.

Precipitating Causes of Serious Crime

In searching for ways to prevent or control serious crime, the police look for precipitating causes. While it may be useful to examine what some call the root causes of crime (e.g., social injustice, unequal economic opportunity, poor schooling, weak family structures, or mental illness), such things are relatively unimportant from a police perspective since the police exercise little influence over them.[21] The police operate on the surface of social life. They must handle incidents, situations, and people as they are now—not societies or people as they might have been. For these reasons, the immediately precipitating causes of serious crime are far more important to the police than are broader questions about the root causes of crime. Four precipitating causes of crime seem relevant to policing: (1) dangerous people; (2) criminogenic situations; (3) alcohol and drug use; and (4) frustrating relationships.

One way the police view serious crime is to see the precipitating cause in the character of the offender. A crime occurs when a predatory offender finds a victim. One could reduce such events by teaching potential victims to avoid situations that make them vulnerable. And, to some degree, the police do this. But the far more common and attractive path for controlling predatory crime is to identify and apprehend the predators. Thus, dangerous offenders can be seen as a precipitating cause of serious crime and an important focus of police attention.[22]

Recent research on criminal careers provides a firm empirical basis for this view.[23] Interviews with convicted criminals conducted by the Rand Corporation indicate that some criminal offenders committed crimes very frequently and sustained this activity over a long career.[24] Moreover, these violent predators accounted for a substantial amount of the serious crime.[25] Now, an investigation of the root causes of such patterns of offending might disclose strong influences of social disadvantage and psychological maltreatment in shaping the personalities of such offenders. Moreover, the influence of these factors might reasonably mitigate their guilt. One might also hold out some hope for their future rehabilitation (through the natural process of aging if nothing else). So, the criminal proclivities of violent predators need not be viewed as either inevitable or unchangeable. From the vantage point of the police, however, the presence of such offenders in the community can reasonably be viewed as an important precipitating cause of crime. Controlling such offenders through incapacitation or close surveillance thus becomes an important crime control strategy.

Having noted the role of dangerous offenders in producing serious crime, it is worth emphasizing that such offenders account for only a portion of the total amount of serious crime—far more than their share, but still only about half of all serious crime.[26] The necessary conclusion is that a significant portion of the serious crime problem cannot be attributed to determined attacks by career criminals or to predatory offenders. These crimes arise from quite different causes.

Some of these crimes might be produced by situational effects. Darkness and congestion around a subway exit may create an attractive location for muggings. An after-hours bar may host more than its share of fights. A rock house from which crack is being sold may become a magnet for violence. Closing time in a popular disco may produce fights among teenagers leaving the scene. In sum, there are some places, times, and activities that bring people together in ways that increase the likelihood of serious crime.

The fact that this occurs is knowable to police. By analyzing calls for service, they can observe that there are repeated calls made from certain places and at certain times.[27] These "hot spots" become important targets of police attention.[28] For example, patrol units might be dispatched just to sit and observe at the appropriate times. There may also be other solutions including permanent changes in the criminogenic situations. For example, the subway area could be lighted; the attention of a neighborhood watch group could be directed to the troublespot; the after-hours bar could be put out of business; aggressive street-level enforcement could be directed against the rock house; or transportation could be arranged for the kids leaving the disco so the crowd thins out more quickly.[29]

Crimes are also significantly related to alcohol or drug abuse.[30] It is now quite clear that: (1) a surprisingly high percentage of those arrested for serious crimes are drug or alcohol users;[31] (2) many offenders have drunk alcohol or taken drugs prior to committing crimes;[32] and (3) victims as well as offenders are often intoxicated or under the influence of drugs.[33] What is unclear is exactly how alcohol and drugs produce their criminogenic effect. Four hypotheses have been advanced to explain this phenomenon.[34]

The first is that physiological effects stimulate or license the person to commit crimes. The theory of stimulation may be appropriate to methamphetamines or PCP, which sometimes seem to produce violent reactions among consumers. The theory of licensing or disinhibition seems more appropriate in the case of alcohol where the release of inhibitions is arguably the mechanism that permits offenses to occur.[35]

Second, dependence or addiction forces users to spend more money on purchasing drugs, and they turn to crime in a desperate effort to maintain their habits. This is a powerful theory in the case of heroin (under conditions of prohibition), and perhaps for cocaine. It is far less powerful for alcohol or marijuana.

Third, drug use gradually demoralizes people by putting them on the wrong side of the law, bringing them into contact with criminals, and gradually weakening their commitment to the obligations of a civil society. Again, this seems more appropriate for those who become deeply involved with drugs and alcohol over a long period of time, and therefore relies more on the dependence-producing attributes of drugs rather than on the immediate intoxicating effects.

Fourth, intoxicated people make particularly good victims. In some cases, intoxication makes people vulnerable to victimization.[36] In others, it causes victims to provoke their attackers.[37] In either case, a serious crime can result.

Whichever theory, or theories, is correct, the close association among drugs, alcohol, and serious crime suggests that the amount of serious crime might be decreased by reducing levels of alcohol and drug use, or by identifying those offenders who use drugs intensively and reducing their consumption.[38]

Finally, the fact that many serious offenses occur in the context of ongoing relationships suggests that some relationships may be criminogenic. Relationships can cause crime because they create expectations. If the expectations are not met the resulting disappointment produces anger. Anger may lead to vengeance and retaliation. In such cycles, the question of who caused the ultimate crime becomes confused. Usually, the offender is the one least damaged after the fight. A court may conclude that the crime stemmed from the evil intentions of the person identified as the offender. But this may not be the best way to view the problem from the vantage point of crime control or crime prevention.

It might be more suitable to see the crimes as emerging from a set of relationships that are frustrating and provocative. The proper response might be to work on the relationship through mediation, restructuring, or dissolution. Indeed, this is often the challenge confronting the police when they encounter spouse abuse, child abuse, and other sorts of intrafamily violence. In such situations, arrests may be appropriate and effective in deterring future crime and in restructuring the relationship.[39] There are many other crimes which emerge from less obvious relationships: the personal relationships of neighbors and friends; the economic relations of landlord and tenant or employer and employee; or transient relations that last just long enough to provoke a quarrel or a grudge. Seen this way, many serious crimes—including murders, robberies, rapes, and burglaries—are disputes and grievances among people rather than criminal attacks.

Controlling Serious Crime

Currently the police fight serious crime by developing a capacity to intercept it—to be in the right place at the right time so that the crime is thwarted, or to arrive so quickly after the fact that the offender is caught. Reactive crime fighting is intuitively appealing to both the police and those to whom the police are accountable. It is unclear, however, whether the reactive response really works. Over the last two decades, confidence in the reactive approach has been eroded by the accumulation of empirical evidence suggesting that these tactics are of only limited effectiveness. It is not that the approach fails to control crime. (It would be foolish to imagine that levels of serious crime would stay the same if police patrols and investigations were halted.) Rather, the limits of the reactive strategy are now becoming apparent. Further gains in police effectiveness in dealing with serious crime must come from different approaches. Key research findings suggesting the limitations of the reactive approach are these.

First, the Kansas City Preventive Patrol Study found that levels of serious crime were not significantly influenced by doubling the number of cars patrolling the streets.[40] This cast doubt on the potential for reducing serious crime simply by increasing the level of preventive patrol.

Second, a study of the effectiveness of rapid response to calls for service (also in Kansas City) found that the probability of making an arrest for most serious crimes was unaffected by the speed with which the police responded. The crucial factor was not the speed of the police response, but the speed with which citizens raised the alarm. If citizens did not notice the crime, or did not call the police quickly, no amount of speed in the police response helped much.[41]

Third, studies of the investigative process revealed that the key factor in determining whether a crime was solved was the quality of the information contributed to the investigation by victims and witnesses about the iffender.[42] If they could not be helpful, forensic wizardry generally was not up to solving the crime.

It is important to understand that these weaknesses appeared in precisely those areas of crime control where the reactive strategy should have been particularly strong: i.e., in dealing with crimes such as murder, rape, robbery, assault and burglary. These crimes could be expected to produce alarms; they also were interceptable and solvable by a vigilant police force waiting to be mobilized by outraged citizens.

There are, of course, many other kinds of serious crimes for which the reactive police strategy is much more obviously inappropriate.[43] It cannot, for example, deal with consensual crimes such as drug dealing behind closed doors. Nor can it deal with crimes such as extortion and loan sharking where the victims are too afraid to report the crimes. A reactive strategy cannot deal with sophisticated white collar crimes or political corruption where the losses associated with the crimes are so widely distributed that peo-ple do not notice that they have been victimized. Finally, a reactive strategy cannot deal even with traditional street crimes in those parts of cities where confidence in the police has eroded to such a degree that the citizens no longer call when they are victimized.

Although these findings and intrinsic limitations of the reactive strategy have not unseated the intuitive appeal of and wide experience with the reactive crime fighting strategy, they have added to a growing sense of frustration within police departments. Confronted by high levels of crime and limited budgets, the police felt a growing need for initiative and thoughtfulness in tackling serious crime. Working within the logic of their current approaches, but reaching for additional degrees of effectiveness, during the 1970's the police developed new proactive tactics.

Developments in Proactive Crimefighting

To deal with serious street crime, the police developed the tactic of directed patrol. Sometimes these patrols were aimed at locations that seemed particularly vulnerable to crimes, such as branch banks, convenience stores, and crowded bars. Other times, the patrols were focused on individuals who, on the basis of past record or recent information, were thought to be particularly active offenders.[44]

The police sought to attack street robberies and muggings through anticrime squads that sent decoys into the streets to prompt active muggers into committing a crime in the full view of the police. The police also sought to control home robberies and burglaries through sting operations involving undercover officers who operate as fences to identify and gather evidence against the offenders.

Finally, the police sought to enhance the effective impact of their enforcement efforts by increasing the quality of the cases they made. Quality Investigation Programs[45] and Integrated Criminal Apprehension Programs[46] were adopted by many departments to increase the likelihood that arrests would be followed by convictions and long prison sentences.

For the most part, each of these innovations produced its successes. The perpetrator-oriented patrols, sting operations, and quality investigation efforts were a little more successful than the location-oriented directed patrols and the undercover operations directed against street robbery. Nonetheless, the police did demonstrate that concentrated efforts could increase arrests, clearances, and convictions. These efforts did not show that these programs alone—without the support of courts and corrections and the involvement of the community would reduce aggregate levels of serious crime in the cities in which they were tried.

Moreover, insofar as each program took a more aggressive and proactive approach to crime, it also troubled those who were concerned that the police not become too intrusive. Perpetrator-oriented patrols, for example, raised the question of whether it was appropriate to target offenders rather than offenses, and if so, on what evidentiary basis.[47] The use of undercover tactics to deal with both robbery and burglary raised important questions about entrapment.[48] And the emphasis on producing convictions from arrests prompted worries that the police might be motivated to manufacture as well as simply record and preserve evidence. Arguably, these civil liberties concerns were inappropriate at a time when the police seemed unable to deal with high crime rates. The fact that these concerns arose, however, indicated that the police were, in fact, using their authority more intensively than they had when they were relying principally on reactive strategies. Such concerns must be reckoned a cost of the new efforts.

The police also made substantial investments in their ability to deal with those crimes that could not be handled through routine patrol or investigative operations, either because the crimes were too complicated to handle with ordinary arrest and investigative methods, or because the routine operations would not disclose the crime. In terms of dealing with especially demanding crimes, like hostage takings or well-armed offenders, the police developed Special Weapons and Arrest Teams. They also enhanced their capacities to deal with riots and demonstrations. And at the other end of the spectrum, the police developed special procedures for dealing with deranged and disordered offenders who often looked violent (and sometimes were) but mostly were simply mentally disturbed.

To deal with crimes that were not always revealed through the ordinary procedures of complaints by victims and witnesses, the police developed special units skilled in investigating the sensitive areas of child sexual abuse, rape, and domestic assault. They also created special investigative units to deal with high-level drug dealing, organized crime, arson, and sophisticated frauds. These units often relied on special intelligence files as well as special investigative procedures, such as the recruitment of informants, electronic wiretaps, and sustained undercover investigations. These programs also scored their successes and enhanced the ability of the police to deal with serious crime.

Missed Opportunities in Crimefighting?

These innovations demonstrated the resourcefulness and creativity of the police as they faced the challenge of high crime rates with limited financial resources, diminished authority, and constrained managerial prerogatives. With the benefit of hindsight, however, some crucial oversights are apparent.

First, there was little appreciation of the crucial role that better information from the community could play in strengthening police performance.[49] It was not that the police were unaware of their dependency on citizens for information. Long before it was demonstrated that the success of rapid response to crime calls and retrospective investigation depended on the willingness of victims and witnesses to report crimes and aid in their solution, the police had mounted campaigns mobilizing citizens to support their local police.

The real problem was that the police did not adequately consider what was needed to attract that support. They thought that their interest and ready availability would be sufficient. They did not understand that citizens felt vulnerable to retaliation by offenders in the community and needed a closer connection with the police if they were going to help them solve the crime. Nor did the police understand that a partnership with the community could be constructed only from the material of daily encounters with the public; in particular, by taking seriously the public's concern with less serious offenses. In short, while the police knew that they were dependent on the community for information about crime, they never asked the public what was needed to obtain help beyond setting up 911 systems.

Second, the police rarely looked behind an offense to its precipitating causes. Nor did they think about crime prevention in terms of managing the precipitating causes. They knew, of course, that much crime was being produced by dangerous offenders, criminogenic situations, alcohol and drug abuse, and aggravating relationships. But they were ambivalent about acting on that knowledge. They tended to limit their responsibilities to applying the law to incidents to which they were summoned; they did not think in terms of applying instruments of civil law or the capacities of other city agencies to work on the proximate causes of crime. Criminal investigations emphasized legal evidence of guilt or innocence—not the question of precipitating causes.

There were many reasons to maintain this narrow focus on law enforcement. To a degree, it protected police organizations from criticisms that they were lawless and out of control. The police could explain that they merely enforced the laws and that they exercised no discretion beyond this basic function. The narrow focus on law enforcement also protected the organization from failure in its basic crime control mission. If the police role was limited to applying the criminal law to offenses rather than to the more challenging goal of actually preventing and controlling crime, the police could succeed even if crime were not controlled. They could blame the other parts of the criminal justice system for their failures to deter and incapacitate the offenders whom the police had arrested. Finally, the narrow focus was consistent with the training and aspirations of the police themselves. Arresting people and using authority was real police work; mediating disputes, mobilizing communities, and badgering other city agencies for improved services was social work.

Whatever the reasons, the police remained reluctant to develop the internal capabilities needed to make their anecdotal impressions of precipitating causes systematic and powerful. Crime analysis sections merely kept statistics or characterized the location of crime; they did not identify dangerous offenders or trouble spots and avoided examining the role of alcohol and drugs in the serious crime problem. Nor did they propose alternative methods for dealing with crime problems. From the perspective of the police, it was far better to stay at the surface of social life and respond to crimes as they occurred rather than to intervene more widely and actively to manage the immediate conditions that were producing crimes.

Third, the police never fully exploited the self-defense capacities of the community itself. They did offer advice to merchants and citizen groups about how they could protect themselves from criminal victimization. And they helped organize neighborhood watch groups. But the main efforts went into helping the communities become more effective operational auxiliaries to the police departments. Citizens were encouraged to mark their property not only because it helped the police solve the crime, should the item be stolen, but also because it allowed the police to return the property to the owners. Crime watch groups were instructed to call the police rather than to intervene themselves. This was consistent with the desires of the police to maintain their monopoly on both expertise and operational capability in dealing with crime. They did not really want any growth in private security—whether it took the form of volunteer associations such as the Guardian Angels or commercial operations such as Burns Security Guards. Because of that interest, police commitment to building a community's self-defense capacities was always ambivalent. And, because they were ambivalent the police did not think through the question of whether and how such efforts could actually help them control serious crime.

Problem-Solving and Community Approaches to Crime Control

In the 1980's, police departments throughout the country have begun to explore the crime-fighting effectiveness of tactics that build on previous approaches, but seek to extend them by looking behind offenses to the precipitating causes of crimes, building closer relations with the community, and seeking to enhance the self-defense capacities of the communities themselves. These efforts are guided mostly by a theory of what might work and some illustrative examples. The theory is that the effectiveness of existing tactics can be enhanced if the police increase the quantity and quality of their contacts with citizens (both individuals and neighborhood groups), and include in their responses to crime problems thoughtful analyses of the precipitating causes of the offenses. The expectation is that this will both enhance the direct effectiveness of the police department and also enable the police department to leverage the resources of citizen groups and other public agencies to control crime.

Some examples, drawn from recent experiences, suggest the ways in which these new approaches can lead to enhanced crime control.

Enhanced Police Presence. From its inception, patrol has sought to prevent crime through the presence, or potential presence, of a conspicuous officer. Patrolling in cars is only one way to communicate police presence, however. Activities such as foot patrol, visiting citizens in their homes, and attending group meetings also increase the awareness of police to which all citizens respond—those intent on crime as well as those not. This presence both deters potential offenders from committing crimes and affords officers the opportunities to note criminal acts in progress.

Example: A youth walking down a street in a small business section of town sees an unlocked automobile with the key in the ignition. He is tempted to steal it. Glancing around, he notes a police officer a short distance away walking down the street. The youth decides not to enter the car for fear of being caught by the officer.

Example: An officer, through crime analysis, becomes aware of a pattern of burglaries in a neighborhood. Increasing her patrol in alleyways, she notes a youth attempting to enter the back window of a residence. She makes an arrest.

Although the success of foot patrol tactics in controlling crime is counter-intuitive to those accustomed to patrol by automobile, confidence in this approach is common in England. There, when an anticrime unit is sent in to deal with a serious crime problem, as often as not it consists of foot patrol. The approach is successful because foot patrol officers have access to areas unavailable to officers in cars: walkways and areas between houses, for example. Unpublished work by Glenn Pierce suggests that some crimes, such as burglary, tend to be patterned within limited geographical and chronological space. If this is true, when combined with what is known about how burglars enter homes and businesses, properly targeted foot patrol might be the strongest potential anticrime tactic to deal with such crimes.

Better Surveillance and Deterrence of Dangerous Offenders. From the outset, police have sought to control crime through close surveillance of those who have committed crimes in the past. The problem has been to accurately identify those offenders. Police officers who work closely with a neighborhood are in a position to learn who behaves in criminal or delinquent ways within the community. By stationing themselves in particular locations, officers can surveil known troublemakers and forestall criminal behavior.

Example: Police investigation of a rash of robberies committed by juveniles involved house-to-house interviews of the neighborhood. In these interviews, photographs of suspects were shown to residents. While no information about the crimes was produced, the word rapidly spread through the neighborhood that the police were keeping close tabs on specific individuals. The robberies stopped without an arrest.

It is also legally and procedurally possible to consider assigning neighborhood police officers to the surveillance of probationers and parolees. Such surveillance would be more immediate and regular than that now provided by probation or parole officers. Aware that neighborhood police officers had easier access to information about their activities, people who were in the community on a conditional basis might be deterred from committing illegal acts.

Example: Paroled sexual offenders in a conservative state regularly move to a community known for its relatively open values. A plan is worked out between local police and the state correctional agency. Upon parole, all sexual offenders returning to this community are interviewed by the chief of patrol and the neighborhood officer policing the area in which the parolee is to live. An offender known for attacks on teenage girls returns to the community. Regular contacts between the officer and parolee are scheduled to enable the police officer to oversee the parolee's behavior while in the community. The police officer discovers that the parolee is now working in the local fast food restaurants workplace which regularly hires teenage girls. The officer, in conjunction with the parole officer, requires that the parolee find a different job, one in which young girls are not always present.

Increased Access to Information. Community policing emphasizes the development of close communication between citizens and police. This communication helps police gather information for both *preventing* and *solving* crime.

Example: In an area frequented by many street people, a street person approaches a neighborhood police officer to inform him that a stranger from another neighborhood is attempting to recruit assistance to commit a street robbery. The street person describes the newcomer to the police officer. Shortly afterwards while patrolling, the officer notices a person on the street who matches the description. The officer approaches the person, questions him, tells him that he (the officer) is aware of what he is planning, and instructs him to leave the area.

Example: Shortly after leaving her church a woman is mugged on the street. She appears to be seriously injured as a result of being knocked to the ground. Police and medics are called. The neighborhood officer responds by foot. She is approached by several children and their parents. The children were playing in an open space in the public housing project across the street from the church and saw the youth mug the woman. They know the youth and where he lives. Accompanied by a neighborhood entourage, including the parents and children who identified the youth, the officer proceeds to the apartment and makes the arrest.

Familiarity with the social and physical characteristics of their beats also helps neighborhood police officers to understand linkages between various pieces of information gathered from their own observations and from other disparate sources.

Example: Parents have complained to a neighborhood police officer about an increase of drug availability in their neighborhood. Several parents have found drugs in their children's possession. In addition, the officer has noticed many youths congregating around an entrance to a second-story apartment over several stores. The officer contacts the drug unit and informs them of his suspicion that drugs are being sold to children from that apartment. The drug unit arranges an undercover "buy" and then "busts" the dealers.

Work by Pate,[50] Greenwood, Chaiken and Petersilia,[51] Eck,[52] and Skogan and Antunes[53] suggests that use of information gathered by patrol officers is one of the most important ways in which police can improve their ability to apprehend offenders. In 1982, Baltimore County, Maryland initiated a Citizen Oriented Police Enforcement unit (COPE), designed to bring the police into closer contact with the citizens and reduce their fears. A 1985 study showed that not only had COPE reduced fear, but also it had apparently produced a 12 percent reduction in the level of reported crime.[54]

Early Intervention to Prevent the Escalation of Disorder into Crime. In a widely read article, Kelling and Wilson argue that there is an important causal link between minor instances of disorder and the occurrence of serious crime.[55] Disorderly behavior—youths congregating, drunks lying down, prostitutes aggressively soliciting—left untended, can escalate into serious crime. The implication is that intervention by police to stop uncivil behavior keeps it from escalating.

Example: Youths panhandle in a subway station. Citizens give money both out of charitable motives and because they are fearful. Youths, emboldened by citizen fear, intimidate and, finally, threaten and mug subway users. Intervention by police to end panhandling by youths reduces threatening and mugging of citizens.

Although this argument has intuitive appeal, little direct empirical evidence exists about exploiting its anticrime potential.

Crime Prevention Activities. An important part of community policing is providing anticrime consultation to citizens, businesses, and other community institutions. The recommendations range from home target hardening (locks, strengthened doors, etc.) to street and building design.

Example: Residents of a neighborhood have been troubled by daytime burglaries. In addition to planning a police response, police consult with homeowners about ways in which they can make their homes more secure from burglars. Suggestions include moving shrubs away from doorways, strengthening locks, securing windows, and taking other burglary prevention precautions.

A 1973 evaluation of Seattle's Community Crime Prevention Program, which used this approach, found a significant reduction in burglaries.[56]

Shoring up Community Institutions. Institutions of neighborhood social control include families, churches, schools, local businesses, and neighborhood and community organizations.

In many communities, the corrosive effects of social disorganization have seriously weakened such organizations. Police, working with such institutions and organizations, can reinforce their normative strength in a community.

Example: Drug dealing is a serious problem in an inner-city neighborhood. Drug dealers not only have dealt drugs freely, but also have intimidated residents to the extent that they are afraid to complain to police. A local church decides that the problem is so serious that an organized effort must be made to attack the problem. Church officials contact the police and ask them to work closely with the neighborhood group. Citizens demonstrate against drug dealing, getting both police protection and great publicity. Citywide and local political leaders, as well as other public and private agencies, become concerned about the problem and develop a concerted effort to reduce drug dealing and intimidation. Sustained street-level enforcement ends drug dealing in that location.

Example: Using up-to-date technology, police are able to identify the patterns of a burglary ring which is moving through a neighborhood. Police contact the local neighborhood anticrime group and inform its members of the patterns so that they can be alert and watch their own and each others' homes.

Example: A woman who lives in public housing has been troubled by attempts of local gangs to recruit her youngest son. Up to now, his older brother has been able to protect him. Now, however, the older brother is going into the service. Approached by the mother, the neighborhood police officer now keeps an eye out for the youngster on the way to and from school as well as on the playground.

Example: A local school is plagued by dropouts who continually hang around the school intimidating both students and teachers. Crime has increased in and around the school. The principal decides to crack down on the problem. The neighborhood police officer becomes involved in the efforts. He teaches a course in youth and the law, increases his surveillance of the grounds, consults with the teachers about handling problems, and invokes other agencies to become involved with the youths who have dropped out of school.

Although promising, it is unclear what impact the strengthening of community institutions has on serious crime. It is an attractive idea, however.

Problem solving. Police have historically viewed calls for service and criminal events as individual incidents. Many such incidents are part of a chronic problem amenable to diagnosis and preventive intervention by either police or other agencies.

Example: Police and citizens note an increase in daytime burglaries in a particular neighborhood. This neighborhood has been characterized by high rates of truancy. Suspecting that many burglaries are committed by truants, police, citizens, and school officials plan a carefully integrated anti-truancy campaign. Daytime burglaries drop.

Problem solving appears to be a promising approach to deter crime. When, in 1985, the Newport News Police Department turned to problem-oriented policing as an approach to dealing with crime, it was successful in dealing with three stubborn crime problems that had beset the community: a series of prostitution-related robberies; a rash of burglaries in a housing project; and larcenies from vehicles parked in downtown areas. In each case, the problem was solved not simply by solving the crimes and arresting offenders, nor by increasing levels of patrol (though both were done), but also by operating on the immediate conditions that were giving rise to the offenses.[57]

These ideas, examples, and results lend plausibility to the notion that problem-solving or community policing can enhance the crime control capabilities of professional crime fighting. They do not prove the case, however.

A Strategic View of Crime Fighting

While police executives can produce increased levels of arrest and local reductions in crime through the creation of special programs, they are frustrated because they do not know how to produce reductions in city-wide levels of crime. The main reason for this might be that their main force is not engaged in a serious crime-fighting effort even though it seems that it is. After all, it would be unreasonable to imagine that any single small program, typically engaging less than 5 percent of the force, could have much impact on aggregate levels of crime. The important question is what is the remaining 95 percent of the force doing? For the most part, the answer is that they are deployed in patrol cars, responding to calls for service and investigating crimes after they have occurred. These tactics have only limited effectiveness.

What remains unanswered is the consequence of shifting a whole department to a radically different style of policing. Moreover, the answer is hard to determine, since the period of transition would be quite awkward. In the short run, were officers taken from patrol and detective units to do problem-oriented or community policing, it is almost certain that response times would lengthen—at least until the problem-solving efforts reduced the demands for service by eliminating the precipitating problem that was producing the calls for service.[58] And even though an increase in response times does not necessarily indicate a real loss in crime-fighting effectiveness, it would be perceived as such because the public and the police have learned to equate rapid response to crime calls with crime control effectiveness.

What is tempting, of course, is to avoid choosing among these strategies, and to adopt the strengths of these various approaches while avoiding their weaknesses. This would be reflected in decisions to establish special units to do problem-solving or community policing within existing organizations whose traditions and main forces remained committed to reactive patrol and retrospective investigation.

But it may not be this easy. Indeed, experience demonstrates that it is not. Previous initiatives with team policing or split-force policing succeeded in building capacities for both styles of policing within the same department but tended to foster eventual competition and conflict.[59] The problem-solving and community policing aspects have usually eventually yielded to administrative demands to keep response times low, or to officers' desires to avoid the demanding engagement with the community. The reason seems to be partly a matter of resources—there has never been enough manpower to maximize performance in both domains at once. But it also seems to be a matter of administrative style and structure. Problem-solving and community policing both require a greater degree of decentralization than does the current policing strategy. They depend more on the initiative of the officers. And they reach out for a close rather than a distant relationship with the community. These are all quite different than the administrative emphases of the current strategy which prescribe centralization, control, and distance from the community.

So while logic and evidence suggest the crime control potential of adding problem-solving and community policing to the concept of rapid response and retrospective investigation, it is hard to add these functions without increasing the resources and significantly changing the administrative style of a police organization. That is hard for a police chief to decide to do without convincing evidence that it would work. The only things that make such a move easy to contemplate are: (1) a deep sense that the current strategy and tactics have reached their limits; (2) the plausibility of the idea that increased effectiveness lies in working on proximate causes and mobilizing communities; and (3) the little bit of evidence we have that the alternative approach works. A few departments, such as Houston, Newport News, Baltimore County, and Philadelphia, have committed themselves to these alternative approaches. If they succeed over the next 3 to 5 years in reducing serious crime as well as in attracting citizen support, then the field will know that it has a better strategy of policing available than is now being used.

Notes

1. For descriptions of these alternative strategies, see Robert C. Trojanowicz, "Community Policing vs. 'High Tech' Policing: What's in a Name?" (Unpublished paper, Michigan State University, April 1987); Herman Goldstein, *The Urban Police Function* (Cambridge, Massachusetts: Ballinger Publishing, 1977); John Eck and William Spelman, "Solving Problems: Problem-Oriented Policing in Newport News" (Washington, D.C.: Police Executive Research Forum, January 1987).

2. George L. Kelling and Mark H. Moore, "From Political to Reform to Community: The Evolving Strategy of Police" (Program in Criminal Justice Policy and Management, John F. Kennedy School of Government, Harvard University, Cambridge, 1987), Working Paper #87-05-08.

3. President's Commission on Law Enforcement and Administration of Justice, *Task Force Report: Science and Technology* (Washington, D.C.: U.S. Government Printing Office, 1967).

Jan M. Chaiken and Warren Walker, *Patrol Car Allocation Model* (Santa Monica: The Rand Corporation 1985). Richard C. Larson, *Police Deployment From Urban Public Safety Systems*, Vol. I (Lexington, Massachusetts: Lexington Books, 1978). David M. Kennedy, "Patrol Allocation in Portland, OR, Part A: PCAM in the Bureau," Case #C95-88-818.0 and "Patrol Allocation in Portland, OR, Part B: PCAM in the City," Case #C95-88-819.0 (Cambridge: Case Program, John F. Kennedy School of Government, 1988).

4. J. Thomas McEwen, Edward F. Connors III, and Marcia Cohen, *Evaluation of the Differential Police Response Field Test* (Washington, D.C.: U.S. Government Printing Office, 1986). Richard P. Grassie and John A. Hollister, *Integrated Criminal Apprehension Program: A Preliminary Guideline Manual for Patrol Operations Analysis (Washington, D.C.: LEAA, U.S. Department of Justice, 1977)*.

5. James Q. Wilson, "The Police and Crime," in *Thinking About Crime* (New York: Vintage Books, 1975), Chapter 4. Larson, *Police Deployment From Urban Public Safety Systems*.

6. Orlando W. Wilson, *The Distribution of the Police Patrol Force* (Chicago: Public Administration Service, 1941).

7. Alfred Blumstein et al., *Deterrence and Incapacitation: Estimating the Effects of Criminal Sanctions on the Crime Rate* (Washington, D.C.: National Academy of Sciences, 1978).

8. Ibid.

9. Mark H. Moore, *Buy and Bust: The Effective Regulation of an Illicit Market in Heroin* (Lexington, Massachusetts: Lexington Books, 1977). Peter K. Manning, *The Narc's G: Organizational and Informational Limits on Drug Law Enforcement* (Cambridge: MIT Press, 1980). Mark H. Moore, "Invisible Offenses: A Challenge to Minimally Intrusive Law Enforcement," in Gerald M. Caplan, ed., *Abscam Ethics* (Washington, D.C.: Police Foundation, 1983). Gary Marx, "Who Really Gets Stung? Some Issues Raised by the New Police Undercover Work," in Caplan, *Abscam Ethics*.

10. George L. Kelling, "Juveniles and Police: The End of the Nightstick," in Francis X. Hartmann, ed., *From Children to Citizens*, Vol. 2: *The Role of the Juvenile Court* (New York: Springer-Verlag, 1987).

11. The exception is Marvin Wolfgang's work devoted to measuring crime seriousness as perceived by citizens. See Marvin E. Wolfgang and Thorsten Sellin, *The Measurement of Crime Seriousness* (New York: Wiley Publish-

ing, 1964). See also Mark H. Moore et al., *Dangerous Offenders: The Elusive Target of Justice* (Cambridge: Harvard University Press, 1984), Chapter 2.

12. Bureau of Justice Statistics, *The Severity of Crime* (Washington, D.C.: U.S. Department of Justice, January 1984), p. 5.

13. Susan Estrich, *Real Rape* (Cambridge: Harvard University Press, 1987).

14. Bureau of Justice Statistics, *The Severity of Crime*.

15. Ibid.

16. For a view of crime as a dispute rather than an attack, see Donald Black, *The Manners and Customs of the Police* (New York: Academic Press, 1980), Chapter 5. For important empirical evidence, see Vera Institute of Justice, *Felony Arrests: Their Prosecution and Disposition in The New York City Courts* (New York, 1981).

17. Bureau of Justice Statistics, "Households Touched By Crime 1986," *BJS Bulletin* (Washington D.C.: U.S. Department of Justice, June 1987).

18. Bureau of Justice Statistics, *Report to the Nation on Crime and Justice* (Washington, D.C.: U.S. Department of Justice, 1983).

19. Patrick W. O'Carroll and James A. Mercy, "Patterns and Recent Trends in Black Homicide," in Darnell F. Hawkins, ed., *Homicide Among Black Americans* (Lanham, Maryland: University Press of America, 1986).

20. Bureau of Justice Statistics, "Households Touched by Crime."

21. James Q. Wilson, "Criminologists," in *Thinking About Crime* (New York: Vintage Books, 1975), Chapter 3.

22. For a discussion of this concept and its importance to police strategies, see Moore et al., *Dangerous Offenders*, Chapter 7.

23. Alfred Blumstein et al., *Criminal Careers and Career Criminals*, Vol. 1 (Washington, D.C.: National Academy Press, 1986).

24. Jan Chaiken and Marcia Chaiken, *Varieties of Criminal Behavior* (Santa Monica, California: The Rand Corporation, August 1982).

25. Peter W. Greenwood and Sue Turner, *Selective Incapacitation, Revisited for the National Institute of Justice* (Santa Monica, California: The Rand Corporation, 1987).

26. Moore et al., *Dangerous Offenders*.

27. Glenn Pierce et al., "Evaluation of an Experiment in Proactive Police Intervention in the Field of Domestic Violence Using Repeat Call Analysis" (Boston, Massachusetts: The Boston Fenway Program, Inc., May 13, 1987).

28. Lawrence W. Sherman, "Repeat Calls to Police in Minneapolis" (College Park, Maryland: University of Maryland, 1987).

29. This example of youth transportation comes from Christine Nixon's experience in New South Wales, Australia. For other examples, see John Eck and William Spelman, "Solving Problems: Problem-Oriented Policing."

30. Mark H. Moore, "Controlling Criminogenic Commodities: Drugs, Guns, and Alcohol," in James Q. Wilson, ed., *Crime and Public Policy* (San Francisco: Institute for Contemporary Studies Press, 1983).

31. Eric Wish, "Drug Use Forecasting System" (Unpublished working paper at the National Institute of Justice, Washington, D.C., January 1988).

32. Ibid.

33. Marvin E. Wolfgang, *Patterns in Criminal Homicide* (Montclair, New Jersey: Patterson Smith Publishing, 1975). James Collins, *Alcohol Use and Criminal Behavior: An Executive Study* (Washington, D.C.: U.S. Department of Justice, 1981).

34. Mark H. Moore, "Drugs and Crime: A Policy Analytic Approach," Appendix to Report of the Panel on Drug Use and Criminal Behavior, *Drug Use and Crime* (Washington, D.C.: The National Institute on Drug Abuse and Research Triangle Institute, 1976).

35. David Hanson, "Alcohol Use and Aggression in American Subcultures," in Robin Room and Gary Collins, eds., *Alcohol and Disinhibition: Nature and Meaning of the Link* (Washington, D.C.: U.S. Department of Health and Human Services, 1983).

36. Moore, "Controlling Criminogenic Commodities."

37. Wolfgang, *Patterns in Criminal Homicide*.

38. M. Douglas Anglin and Yih-Ing Hser, "Treatment of Drug Abuse," manuscript to be published in Michael Tonry and James Q. Wilson, eds., *Drugs and Crime*, a special volume of *Crime and Justice: A Review of Research* (Chicago: University of Chicago Press, forthcoming).

39. Sherman, "Repeat Calls to Police in Minneapolis."

40. George L. Kelling, *Kansas City Preventive Patrol Experiment: A Summary Report* (Washington, D.C.: Police Foundation, 1974).

41. Response Time Analysis (Kansas City, Missouri: Kansas City Police Department 1977).

42. Peter W. Greenwood, Jan M. Chaiken, and Joan Petersilia, *The Criminal Investigation Process* (Lexington, Massachusetts: D.C. Heath, 1977). John Eck, *Managing Case Assignments: Burglary Investigation Decision Model Replication* (Washington, D.C.: Police Executive Research Forum, 1979).

43. Moore, "Invisible Offenses."

44. Antony Pate, Robert Bowers, and Ron Parks, *Three Approaches to Criminal Apprehension in Kansas City: An Evaluation Report* (Washington, D.C.: Police Foundation, 1976).

45. Jerome E. McElroy, Colleen Cosgrove, and Michael Farren, *Felony Case Preparation: Quality Counts*, Interim Report of the New York City Police Department Felony Case Separation Project (New York: Vera Institute of Justice, 1981).

46. Grassie and Hollister, *Integrated Criminal Apprehension Program*.

47. Moore et al., *Dangerous Offenders*, Chapter 7.

48. Marx, "Who Really Gets Stung?"

49. Wesley G. Skogan and George E. Antunes, "Information, Apprehension, and Deterrence: Exploring the Limits of Police Productivity," *Journal of Criminal Justice*, 1979, No. 7, pp. 217-242.

50. Pate et al., *Three Approaches to Criminal Apprehension*.

51. Greenwood et al., *The Criminal Investigation Process*.

52. Eck, *Managing Case Assignments*.

53. Skogan and Antunes, "Information, Apprehension, and Deterrence."

54. Philip B. Taft, Jr., "Fighting Fear: The Baltimore County COPE Project" (Washington, D.C.: Police Executive Research Forum, February 1986), p. 20.

55. James Q. Wilson and George L. Kelling, "Broken Windows," *Atlantic Monthly*, March 1982, pp. 29-38.

56. Betsy Lindsay and Daniel McGillis, "Citywide Community Crime Prevention: An Assessment of the Seattle Program," in Dennis P. Rosenbaum, ed., *Community Crime Prevention: Does It Work?* (Beverly Hills, California: Sage Publications, 1986).

57. Eck and Spelman, "Solving Problems: Problem-Oriented Policing."

58. Calls for service declined in Flint, Michigan, after foot patrol was established and officers were handling less serious complaints informally. Robert Trojanowicz, *An Evaluation of the Neighborhood Foot Patrol Program in Flint, Michigan* (East Lansing: Michigan State University, 1982), pp. 29-30.

59. George L. Kelling and Mary Ann Wycoff, *The Dallas Experience: Human Resource Development* (Washington, D.C.: Police Foundation, 1978). James Tien et al., *An Alternative Approach in Police Patrol: The Wilmington Split-Force Experiment* (Cambridge, Massachusetts: Public Systems Evaluation Inc., 1977).

Reprinted from Mark H. Moore, Robert C. Trojanowicz, and George L. Kelling, "Crime and Policing," in *Perspective on Policing*, No.2. U.S. Department of Justice, June 1988. ✦

10

Elements of Community Policing

Gary W. Cordner

Community policing has been around, as both a label and a specific police strategy, for about twenty years. It started out as a fuzzy notion about increasing police-citizen contact and reducing fear of crime, then settled into a period during which it was seen as having two primary components—problem solving and community engagement. This article presents a more elaborate framework of 12 community policing elements, providing examples of each and some evidence of their effectiveness. As you read the article, be thinking about community policing as you have seen it practiced where you live and work—are all 12 of these elements in place? If not, which ones are being used and which ones are not? Differential use of these elements helps account for the huge variation in community policing as actually practiced around the country (and around the world).

In less than two decades, community policing has evolved from a few small foot patrol studies to the pre-eminent reform agenda of modern policing. With roots in such earlier developments as police-community relations, team policing, crime prevention, and the rediscovery of foot patrol, community policing has become, in the 1990s, the dominant strategy of policing—so much so that the 100,000 new police officers funded by the 1994 Crime Bill must be engaged, by law, in community policing.

Despite all this activity, four complicating factors have made it extremely difficult to determine the effectiveness of community policing:

- **Programmatic complexity**—There exists no single definition of community policing nor any universal set of program elements. Police agencies around the country (and around the world) have implemented a wide array of organizational and operational innovations under the label "community policing." Because community policing is not one consistent "thing," it is difficult to say whether "it" works.

- **Multiple effects**—The number of intended and unintended effects that might accrue to community policing is considerable. Community policing might affect crime, fear of crime, disorder, community relations, and/or police officer attitudes, to mention just a few plausible impacts. The reality of these multiple effects, as opposed to a single bottom-line criterion, severely reduces the likelihood of a simple yes or no answer to the question "Does community policing work?"

- **Variation in program scope**—The scope of community policing projects has varied from single-officer assignments to department-wide efforts. Some of the most positive results have come from projects that involved only a few specialist officers, small special units, or narrowly defined target areas. The generalizability of these positive results to full-scale department-wide implementation is problematic.

- **Research design limitations**—Despite heroic efforts by police officials and researchers, most community policing studies have had serious research design limitations. These include lack of control groups, failure to randomize treatments, and a tendency to measure only short-term effects. Consequently, the findings of many community policing studies do not have as much credibility as we might hope.

These complicating factors are offered not as excuses but rather to sensitize us to the very real difficulty of producing reliable knowledge about the effects of community policing. Additionally, they identify priority issues that need to be addressed in order to substantially improve what we know about the effectiveness of community policing.

What is Community Policing?

Community policing remains many things to many people. A common refrain among proponents is "Community policing is a philosophy, not a program." An equally common refrain among police officers is "Just tell me exactly what you want me to do differently." Some critics, echoing concerns similar to those expressed by police officers, argue that if community policing is nothing more than a philosophy, it is merely an empty shell (Goldstein 1987).

It would be easy to list dozens of common characteristics of community policing, starting with foot patrol and mountain bikes and ending with the police as organizers of, and advocates for, the poor and dispossessed. Instead, it may be more helpful to identify four major dimensions of community policing and some of the most common elements within each. These four dimensions of community policing are:

- The Philosophical Dimension
- The Strategic Dimension
- The Tactical Dimension
- The Organizational Dimension

The Philosophical Dimension

Many of its most thoughtful and forceful advocates emphasize that community policing is a new philosophy of policing, perhaps constituting even a paradigm shift away from professional-model policing. The philosophical dimension includes the central ideas and beliefs underlying community policing. Three of the most important of these are citizen input, broad function, and personalized service.

Citizen Input

Community policing takes the view that, in a free society, citizens should have open access to police organizations and input to police policies and decisions. Access and in-put through elected officials is considered necessary but not sufficient. Individual neighborhoods and communities should have the opportunity to influence how they are policed and legitimate interest groups in the community should be able to discuss their views and concerns directly with police officials. Police departments, like other agencies of government, should be responsive and accountable.

Mechanisms for achieving greater citizen input are varied. Some police agencies use systematic and periodic community surveys to elicit citizen input (Bureau of Justice Assistance 1994a). Others rely on open forums, town meetings, radio and television call-in programs, and similar methods open to all residents. Some police officials meet regularly with citizen advisory boards, ministry alliances, minority group representatives, business leaders, and other formal groups. These techniques have been used by police chief executives, district commanders, and ordinary patrol officers; they can be focused as widely as the entire jurisdiction or as narrowly as a beat or a single neighborhood.

The techniques used to achieve citizen input should be less important than the end result. Community policing emphasizes that police departments should seek and carefully consider citizen input when making policies and decisions that affect the community. Any other alternative would be unthinkable in an agency that is part of a government "of the people, for the people, and by the people."

Broad Police Function

Community policing embraces a broad view of the police function rather than a narrow focus on crime fighting or law enforcement (Kelling and Moore 1988). Historical evidence is often cited to show that the police function was originally quite broad and varied and that it only narrowed in recent decades, perhaps due to the influence of the professional model and popular media representations of police work. Social science data is also frequently cited to show that police officers actually spend relatively little of their time dealing with serious offenders or investigating violent crimes.

This broader view of the police function recognizes the kinds of non-enforcement tasks that police already perform and seeks to give them greater status and legitimacy. These include order maintenance, social service, and general assistance duties. They may also include greater responsibilities in protecting and enhancing "the lives of those who are most vulnerable—juveniles, the elderly, minorities, the poor, the disabled, the homeless" (Trojanowicz and Bucqueroux 1990: xiv). In the bigger picture, the police mission is seen to include resolving conflict, helping victims, preventing accidents, solving problems, and reducing fear as well as reducing crime through apprehension and enforcement.

Personal Service

Community policing supports tailored policing based on local norms and values and individual needs. An argument is made that the criminal law is a very blunt instrument and that police officers inevitably exercise wide discretion when making decisions. Presently, individual officers make arrests and other decisions based on a combination of legal, bureaucratic, and idiosyncratic criteria, while the police department maintains the myth of full or at least uniform enforcement (Goldstein 1977). Under community policing, officers are asked to consider the "will of the community" when deciding which laws to enforce under what circumstances, and police executives are asked to tolerate and even encourage such differential and personalized policing.

Such differential or tailored policing primarily affects police handling of minor criminal offenses, local ordinance violations, public disorder, and service issues. Some kinds of behavior proscribed by state and local law, and some levels of noise and disorder, may be seen as less bothersome in some neighborhoods than in others. Similarly, some police methods, including such aggressive tactics as roadblocks as well as more prevention-oriented programs such as landlord training, may coincide with norms and values in some neighborhoods but not others.

Even the strongest advocates of community policing recognize that a balance must be reached between differential neighborhood-level policing and uniform jurisdiction-wide policing. Striking a healthy and satisfactory balance between competing interests has always been one of the central concerns of policing and police administration. Community policing simply argues that neighborhood-level norms and values should be added to the mix of legal, professional, and organizational considerations that influences decision-making about policies, programs, and resources at the executive level as well as enforcement-level decisions on the street.

This characteristic of community policing is also aimed at overcoming one of the most common complaints that the public has about government employees in general, including police officers—that they do not seem to care and that they are more interested in "going by the book" than in providing quality, personalized service. Many citizens seem to resent being subjected to "stranger policing" and would rather deal with officers who know them, and whom they know. Of course, not every police-citizen encounter can be amicable and friendly. But officers who generally deal with citizens in a friendly, open, and personal manner may be more likely to generate trust and confidence than officers who operate in a narrow, aloof, and/or bureaucratic manner.

The Strategic Dimension

The strategic dimension of community policing includes the key operational concepts that translate philosophy into action. These strategic concepts are the links between the broad ideas and beliefs that underlie community policing and the specific programs and practices by which it is implemented. They assure that agency policies, priorities, and resource allocation are consistent with a community-oriented philosophy. Three strategic elements of community policing are reoriented operations, geographic focus, and prevention emphasis.

Reoriented Operations

Community policing recommends less reliance on the patrol car and more emphasis on face-to-face interactions. One objective is to replace ineffective or isolating operational practices (e.g., motorized patrol and rapid response to low priority calls) with more effective and more interactive practices. A related objective is to find ways of performing necessary traditional functions (e.g., handling emergency calls and conducting follow-up investigations) more efficiently, in order to save time and resources that can then be devoted to more community-oriented activities.

Many police departments today have increased their use of foot patrol, directed patrol, door-to-door policing, and other alternatives to traditional motorized patrol (Cordner and Trojanowicz 1992). Generally, these alternatives seek more targeted tactical effectiveness, more attention to minor offenses and "incivilities," a greater "felt presence" of police, and/or more police-citizen contact. Other police departments have simply reduced their commitment to any form of continuous patrolling, preferring instead to have their patrol officers engage in problem solving, crime prevention, and similar activities when not handling calls and emergencies.

Many police agencies have also adopted differential responses to calls for service (McEwen, Connors, and Cohen 1986). Rather than attempting to immediately dispatch a sworn officer in response to each and every notification of a crime, disturbance, or other situation, these departments vary their responses depending upon the circumstances. Some crime reports may be taken over the telephone, some service requests may be referred to other government agencies, and some sworn officer responses may be delayed. A particularly interesting alternative is to ask complainants to go in person to a nearby police mini-station or storefront office, where an officer, a civilian employee, or even a volunteer takes a report or provides other in-person assistance. Use of differential responses helps departments cope with the sometimes overwhelming burden of 9-1-1 calls and frees up patrol officer time for other activities, such as patrolling, problem solving, and crime prevention.

Traditional criminal investigation has also been reexamined in recent years (Eck 1992). Some departments have de-specialized the activity, reducing the size of the detective unit

and making patrol officers more responsible for follow-up investigations. Many have also eliminated the practice of conducting an extensive follow-up investigation of every reported crime, focusing instead on the more serious offenses and on more "solvable" cases. Investigative attention has also been expanded to include a focus on offenders as well as on offenses, especially in the form of repeat offender units that target high-frequency serious offenders. A few departments have taken the additional step of trying to get detectives to expand their case-by-case orientation to include problem solving and crime prevention. In this approach, a burglary detective would be as concerned with reducing burglaries through problem solving and crime prevention as s/he was with solving particular burglary cases.

Not all contemporary alternatives to motorized patrol, rapid response, and criminal investigation are closely allied with community policing. Those specific operational alternatives, and those uses of the freed-up time of patrol officers and detectives, that are consistent with the philosophical and strategic foundations of community policing can be distinguished from those that conform to other philosophies and strategies of policing (Moore and Trojanowicz 1988).

Geographic Focus

Community policing strategy emphasizes the geographic basis of assignment and responsibility by shifting the fundamental unit of patrol accountability from time of day to place. That is, rather than holding patrol officers, supervisors, and shift commanders responsible for wide areas but only during their eight or ten hour shifts, community policing seeks to establish 24-hour responsibility for smaller areas.

Of course, no single officer works 24 hours a day, seven days a week, week in and week out. Community policing usually deals with this limitation in one or a combination of three ways: (1) community police officers assigned to neighborhoods may be specialists, with most call-handling relegated to a more traditional patrol unit; (2) each individual patrol officer may be held responsible for long-term problem solving in an assigned neighborhood, even though s/he handles calls in a much larger area and, of necessity, many of the calls in the assigned area are handled by other officers; or (3) small teams of officers share both call-handling and problem solving responsibility in a beat-sized area.

A key ingredient of this geographic focus, however it is implemented, is permanency of assignment. Community policing recommends that patrol officers be assigned to the same areas for extended periods of time, to increase their familiarity with the community and the community's familiarity with them. Ideally, this familiarity will build trust, confidence, and cooperation on both sides of the police-citizen interaction. Also, officers will simply become more knowledgeable about the community and its residents, aiding early intervention and timely problem identification and avoiding conflict based on misperception or misunderstanding.

It is important to recognize that most police departments have long used geography as the basis for daily patrol assignment. Many of these departments, however, assign patrol officers to different beats from one day to the next, creating little continuity or permanency. Moreover, even in police agencies with fairly steady beat assignments, patrol officers are only held accountable for handling their calls and maintaining order (keeping things quiet) *during their shift*. The citizen's question, "Who in the police department is responsible for *my area*, my neighborhood?" can then only truthfully be answered "the chief" or, in large departments, "the precinct commander." Neither patrol officers nor the two or three levels of management above them can be held accountable for dealing with long-term problems in specific locations anywhere in the entire community. Thus, a crucial component of community policing strategy is to create some degree of geographic accountability at all levels in the police organization, but particularly at the level of the patrol officer who delivers basic police services and is in a position to identify and solve neighborhood problems.

Prevention Emphasis

Community policing strategy also emphasizes a more proactive and preventive orientation, in contrast to the reactive focus that has characterized much of policing under the professional model. This proactive, preventive orientation takes several forms. One is simply to encourage better use of police officers' time. In many police departments, patrol officers' time not committed to handling calls is either spent simply waiting for the next call or randomly driving around. Under community policing, this substantial resource of free patrol time is devoted to directed enforcement activities, specific crime prevention efforts, problem solving, community engagement, citizen interaction, or similar kinds of activities.

Another aspect of the preventive focus overlaps with the substantive orientation of community policing and problem-oriented operations. Officers are encouraged to look beyond the individual incidents that they encounter as calls for service and reported crimes in order to discover underlying problems and conditions (Eck and Spelman 1987). If they can discover such underlying conditions and do something to improve them, officers can prevent the future recurrence of incidents and calls. While immediate response to in-progress emergencies and after-the-fact investigation of crimes will always remain important functions of policing, community policing seeks to elevate before-the-fact prevention and problem-solving to comparable status.

Closely related to this line of thinking, but deserving of specific mention, is the desire to enhance the status of crime prevention within police organizations. Most police departments devote the vast majority of their personnel to patrol and investigations, primarily for the purposes of rapid response and follow-up investigation *after* something has happened. Granted, some prevention of crime through the visibility, omnipresence, and deterrence created by patrolling, rapid response, and investigating is expected, but the weight of research over the past two decades has greatly diminished these expectations (Kelling, Pate, Dieckman, and Brown 1974; Greenwood and Petersilia 1975; Spelman and Brown 1982). Despite these lowered expectations, however, police departments still typically devote only a few officers specifically to crime prevention programming, and do little to encourage patrol officers to engage in any kinds of crime prevention activity beyond routine riding around.

Moreover, within both informal and formal police cultures, crime solving and criminal apprehension are usually more highly valued than crime prevention. An individual officer is more likely to be commended for arresting a bank robber than for initiating actions that prevent such robberies. Detectives usually enjoy higher status than uniformed officers (especially in the eyes of the public), whereas, within many police agencies, crime prevention officers are seen as public relations functionaries, kiddie cops, or worse. To many police officers, crime prevention work is simply not real police work.

The preeminence of reactive crime fighting within police and popular cultures is understandable, given the dramatic nature of emergencies, crimes, and investigations. Much of police work is about responding to trouble and fixing it, about the contest between good and evil. Responding to emergencies and fighting crime have heroic elements that naturally appeal to both police officers and citizens. Given the choice, though, almost all citizens would prefer not being victimized in the first place to being dramatically rescued, to having the police successfully track down their assailant, or to having the police recover their stolen property. Most citizens would agree that "an ounce of prevention is worth a pound of cure." This is not to suggest that police should turn their backs on reactive handling of crimes and emergencies, but only that before-the-fact prevention should be given greater consideration.

A final element of community policing's preventive focus takes more of a social welfare orientation, particularly toward juveniles. An argument is made that police officers, by serving as mentors and role models, and by providing educational, recreational, and even counseling services, can affect peoples' behavior in positive ways that ultimately lead to reductions in crime and disorder. In essence, police are asked to support and augment the efforts of families, churches, schools, and other social service agencies. This kind of police activity is seen as particularly neces-sary by some in order to offset the deficiencies and correct the failures of these other social institutions in modern America.

The Tactical Dimension

The tactical dimension of community policing ultimately translates ideas, philosophies, and strategies into concrete programs, practices, and behaviors. Even those who insist that "community policing is a philosophy, not a program" must concede that unless community policing eventually leads to some action, some new or different behavior, it is all rhetoric and no reality (Greene and Mastrofski 1988). Indeed, many commentators have taken the view that community policing is little more than a new police marketing strategy that has left the core elements of the police role untouched (see, e.g., Klockars 1988; Manning 1988; Weatheritt 1988). Three of the most important tactical elements of community policing are positive interaction, partnerships, and problem solving.

Positive Interaction

Policing inevitably involves some negative contacts between officers and citizens—arrests, tickets, stops for suspicion, orders to desist in disruptive behavior, inability to make things much better for victims, etc. Community policing recognizes this fact and recommends that officers offset it as much as they can by engaging in positive interactions whenever possible. Positive interactions have further benefits as well, of course: they generally build familiarity, trust, and confidence on both sides; they remind officers that most citizens respect and support them; they make the officer more knowledgeable about people and conditions in the beat; they provide specific information for criminal investigations and problem solving; and they break up the monotony of motorized patrol.

Many opportunities for positive interaction arise in the course of call handling. Too many officers rush to clear from their calls, however, often in response to workload concerns and pressure from their superiors, their peers, and dispatchers. As a result, they typically do a mediocre job of handling the immediate incident and make little or no attempt to identify underlying conditions, secure additional information, or create satisfied customers. The prime directive seems to be to do as little as possible, in order to clear the call quickly and get back in the car and on the radio, ready to go and do little or nothing at the next call. Getting there rapidly and then clearing promptly take precedence over actually delivering much service or accomplishing anything. Community policing suggests, instead, that officers should look at calls as opportunities for positive interaction, quality service, and problem identification.

Even more opportunities for positive interaction can be seized during routine patrol, if officers are willing to exit their vehicles and take some initiative. Officers can go in and out of stores, in and out of schools, talk to people on the street, knock on doors, etc. They can take the initiative to talk not only with shopkeepers and their customers but also with teenagers, apartment dwellers, tavern patrons, and anybody else they run across in public spaces or who are approachable in private places. Police should insert themselves wherever people are and should talk to those people, not just watch them.

Partnerships

Participation of the community in its own protection is one of the central elements of community policing (Bureau of Justice Assistance 1994c). This participation can run the gamut from watching neighbors' homes to reporting drug dealers to patrolling the streets. It can involve participation in problem identification and problem solving efforts, in crime prevention programs, in neighborhood revitalization, and in youth-oriented educational and recreational programs. Citizens may act individually or in groups, they may collaborate with the police, and they may even join the police department by donating their time as police department volunteers, reserves, or auxiliaries.

Under community policing, police agencies are expected not only to cooperate with citizens and communities but to actively solicit input and participation (Bureau of Justice Assistance 1994b). The exact nature of this participation can and should vary from community to community and from situation to situation, in keeping with the problem-oriented approach. As a general rule, though, police should avoid claiming that they alone can handle crime, drug, or disorder problems, and they should encourage individual citizens and community groups to shoulder some responsibility for dealing with such problems.

Police have sometimes found it necessary to engage in community organizing as a means of accomplishing any degree of citizen participation in problem solving or crime prevention. In disorganized and transient neighborhoods, residents are often so distressed, fearful, and suspicious of each other (or just so unfamiliar with their neighbors) that police have literally had to set about creating a sense of community where none previously existed. As difficult as this kind of community organizing can be, and as far from the conventional police role as this may seem, these are often the very communities that most need both enhanced police protection and a greater degree of citizen involvement in crime prevention, order maintenance, and general watchfulness over public spaces.

One vexing aspect of community organizing and community engagement results from the pluralistic nature of our society. Differing and often conflicting interests are found in many communities, and they are sometimes represented by competing interest groups. Thus, the elders in a community may want the police to crack down on juveniles, while the youths themselves complain of few opportunities for recreation or entertainment. Tenants may seek police help in organizing a rent strike, while landlords want police assistance in screening or managing the same tenants. Finding common interests around which to rally entire communities, or just identifying common interests on which to base police practices, can be very challenging and, at times, impossible.

It is important to recognize that this inherent feature of pluralistic communities does not arise because of community policing. Police have long been caught in the middle between the interests of adults and juveniles, landlords and tenants, and similar groups. Sometimes the law has provided a convenient reference point for handling such conflicts, but just as often police have had to mediate, arbitrate, or just take the side of the party with the best case. Moreover, when the law has offered a solution, it has frequently been a temporary or unpopular one, and one that still resulted in the police taking sides, protestations of "we're just enforcing the law" notwithstanding.

Fortunately, nearly all citizens want to be safe from violence, want their property protected, and want some level of orderliness in their neighborhoods. Officers can usually find enough consensus in communities upon which to base cooperative efforts aimed at improving safety and public order. Sometimes, apparently deep conflicts between individuals or groups recede when attention is focused on how best to solve specific neighborhood problems. It would be naive to expect overwhelming community consensus in every situation, but it is equally mistaken to think that conflict is so endemic that widespread community support and participation cannot be achieved in many circumstances.

Problem Solving

Supporters of community policing are convinced that the very nature of police work must be altered from its present incident-by-incident, case-by-case orientation to one that is more problem-oriented (Goldstein 1990). Certainly, incidents must still be handled and cases must still be investigated. Whenever possible, however, attention should be directed toward underlying problems and conditions. Following the medical analogy, policing should address causes as well as symptoms, and should adopt the epidemiological public health approach as much as the individual doctor's clinical approach.

This problem solving approach should be characterized by several important features: (1) it should be the standard operating method of policing, not an occasional special project; (2) it should be practiced by personnel throughout the ranks, not just by specialists or managers; (3) it should be empirical, in the sense that decisions are made on the basis of information that is gathered systematically; (4) it should involve, whenever possible, collaboration between police and other agencies and institutions; and (5) it should incorporate, whenever possible, community input and participation, so that it is the community's problems that are addressed (not just the police department's) and so that the community shares in the responsibility for its own protection.

The problem solving process consists of four steps: (1) careful identification of the problem; (2) careful analysis of the problem; (3) a search for alternative solutions to the problem; and (4) implementation and assessment of a response to the problem. Community input can be incorporated within any or all of the steps in the process. Identification, analysis, and assessment should rely on information from multiple sources. A variety of alternative solutions should be considered, including, but not limited to, traditional enforcement methods. Typically, the most effective solutions are those that combine several different responses, including some that draw on more than just the police department's authority and resources.

A crucial characteristic of the problem-oriented approach is that it seeks tailored solutions to specific community problems. Arrests and law enforcement are *not* abandoned—rather, an effort is made in each situation to determine which alternative responses best fit the problem. Use of the criminal law is always considered, as are civil law enforcement, mediation, community mobilization, referral, collaboration, alteration of the physical environment, public education, and a host of other possibilities. The common sense notion of choosing the tool that best fits the problem, instead of simply grabbing the most convenient or familiar tool in the tool box, lies close to the heart of the problem solving method.

The Organizational Dimension

It is important to recognize an organizational dimension that surrounds community policing and greatly affects its implementation. In order to support and facilitate community policing, police departments often consider a variety of changes in organization, administration, management, and supervision. The elements of the organizational dimension are not really part of community policing *per se*, but they are frequently crucial to its successful implementation. Three important organizational elements of COP are structure, management, and information.

Structure

Advocates of community policing often look at various ways of restructuring police agencies in order to facilitate and support implementation of the philosophical, strategic, and tactical elements described above. Any organization's structure should correspond with its mission and the nature of the work performed by its members. Some aspects of traditional police organization structure seem more suited to routine, bureaucratic work than to the discretion and creativity required for COP.

The types of restructuring often associated with community policing include:

- **Decentralization**—authority and responsibility can sometimes be delegated more widely so that commanders, supervisors, and officers can act more independently and be more responsive.

- **Flattening**—the number of layers of hierarchy in the police organization can sometimes be reduced in order to improve communications and reduce waste, rigidity and bureaucracy.

- **De-specialization**—the number of specialized units and personnel can sometimes be reduced, with more resources devoted to the direct delivery of police services (including COP) to the general public.

- **Teams**—efficiency and effectiveness can sometimes be improved by getting employees working together as teams to perform work, solve problems, or look for ways of improving quality.

- **Civilianization**—positions currently held by sworn personnel can sometimes be reclassified or redesigned for non-sworn personnel, allowing both cost savings and better utilization of sworn personnel.

Management

Community policing is often associated with styles of leadership, management, and supervision that give more emphasis to organizational culture and values and less emphasis to written rules and formal discipline. The general argument is that when employees are guided by a set of officially sanctioned values they will usually make good decisions and take appropriate actions. Although many formal rules will still probably be necessary, managers will need to resort to them much less often in order to maintain control over subordinates.

Management practices consistent with this emphasis on organizational culture and values include:

- **Mission**—agencies should develop concise statements of their mission and values and use them consistently in making decisions, guiding employees, and training new recruits.

- **Strategic Planning**—agencies should engage in continuous strategic planning aimed at ensuring that resources and energy are focused on mission accomplishment and adherence to core values; otherwise, organizations tend to get off track, confused about their mission and about what really matters.

- **Coaching**—supervisors should coach and guide their subordinates more, instead of restricting their roles to review of paperwork and enforcement of rules and regulations.

- **Mentoring**—young employees need mentoring from managers, supervisors, and/or peers—not just to learn how to do the job right but also to learn what constitutes the right job; in other words, to learn about ethics and values and what it means to be a good police officer.

- **Empowerment**—under COP, employees are encouraged to be risk-takers who demonstrate imagination and creativity in their work—this kind of empowerment can only succeed, however, when employees are thoroughly familiar with the organization's core values and firmly committed to them.

- **Selective Discipline**—in their disciplinary processes, agencies should make distinctions between intentional and unintentional errors made by employees and between employee actions that violate core values versus those that merely violate technical rules.

Information

Doing community policing and managing it effectively require certain types of information that have not traditionally been available in all police departments. In the never-ending quality vs. quantity debate, for example, community policing tends to emphasize quality. This emphasis on quality shows up in many areas: avoidance of traditional bean-counting (arrests, tickets) to measure success, more concern for how well calls are handled than merely for how quickly they are handled, etc. Also, the geographic focus of community policing increases the need for detailed information based on neighborhoods as the unit of analysis. The emphasis on problem solving highlights the need for information systems that aid in identifying and analyzing community-level problems. And so on.

Several aspects of police administration under community policing that have implications for information are:

- **Performance Appraisal**—individual officers can be evaluated on the quality of their community policing and problem solving activities, and perhaps on results achieved, instead of on traditional performance indicators (tickets, arrests, calls handled, etc.).

- **Program Evaluation**—police programs and strategies can be evaluated more on the basis of their effectiveness (outcomes, results, quality) than just on their efficiency (effort, outputs, quantity).

- **Departmental Assessment**—the police agency's overall performance can be measured and assessed on the basis of a wide variety of indicators (including customer satisfaction, fear levels, problem solving, etc.) instead of a narrow band of traditional indicators (reported crime, response time, etc.).

- **Information Systems**—an agency's information systems need to collect and produce information on the whole range of the police function, not just on enforcement and call-handling activities, in order to support more quality-oriented appraisal, evaluation, and assessment efforts.

- **Crime Analysis**—individual officers need more timely and complete crime analysis information pertaining to their specific geographic areas of responsibility to facilitate problem identification, analysis, fear reduction, etc.

- **Geographic Information Systems (GIS)**—sophisticated and user-friendly computerized mapping software available today makes it possible for officers and citizens to obtain customized maps that graphically identify "hot spots" and help them picture the geographic locations and distribution of crime and related problems.

What Do We Know?

Despite the programmatic and evaluation complexities discussed earlier, we do have a substantial amount of information from empirical studies of community policing. This study summarized the "preponderance of the evidence" on the effects of community policing based on a review of over 60 such studies (recent reviews have also been completed by Normandeau 1993; Bennett 1994; Leighton 1994; and Skogan 1994).[1]

Nearly all of the evaluations conducted to date have focused on the tactical dimension of community policing, leaving us with little or no information on the effects of philosophical, strategic, and organizational changes. This gap in community policing research is undoubtedly caused by a combination of two factors: (1) most community policing efforts, at least until recently, have been limited programmatic and street-level initiatives rather than large-scale strategic or organizational-change initiatives; and (2) evaluation of narrowly-focused programmatic initiatives is much easier and more feasible than evaluation of philosophical and organization-wide change.

Crime

The evidence is mixed. Only a few studies have used experimental designs and victimization surveys to test the effects of community policing on crime; many others have relied on simple before-after comparisons of reported crime or single-item victimization questions drawn from community surveys. Overall, a slight majority of the studies have detected crime decreases, giving reason for optimism, but evaluation design limitations prevent us from drawing any authoritative conclusions.

Fear of Crime

Again the evidence is mixed, but it leans more heavily in the positive direction. A number of studies have employed community surveys to make before-after comparisons of fear and related perceptions, some with experimental designs. Fear has typically been measured using a variety of survey items, lending the studies more credibility. The now widely-accepted view that community policing helps reduce levels of fear of crime and increases perceptions of safety seems reasonably well-founded, although some efforts have failed to accomplish fear reductions.

Disorder

The impact of community policing on disorder, minor crime, incivilities, and signs of crime has not been subjected to careful testing as frequently as its impact on crime and fear. The available evidence suggests, though, that community policing, and especially foot patrol and problem solving, helps reduce levels of disorder, lending partial support to the "broken windows" thesis (Wilson and Kelling 1982).

Calls for Service

Community policing might reduce calls for service in several ways: problem solving might address underlying issues that generate calls; collaboration might increase call referrals to other government agencies; foot patrols and mini-stations might receive citizen requests directly, thus heading off calls to central dispatch; and workload management might find alternative responses for some types of calls. Although the ability of the last approach (workload management) to reduce the volume of calls dispatched to sworn units for immediate response has clearly been demonstrated (McEwen et al. 1986), the rest of the evidence on the effects of community policing on calls for service is mixed. Several studies have found positive effects but several others have not.

Community Relations

The vast majority of the studies that have looked at the impact of community policing on citizens' attitudes toward the police have uncovered positive effects. Clearly, citizens generally appreciate mini-stations in their neighborhoods, foot patrols, problem-solving efforts, and other forms of community policing. These very consistent findings are all the more remarkable because baseline measures of citizen satisfaction with, and support for, their police are frequently quite positive to begin with, thus offering relatively little room for improvement.

Police Officer Attitudes

A clear majority of the studies that have investigated the effects of community policing on officers' job satisfaction, perceptions of the community, and other related attitudes have discovered beneficial effects. Officers involved in community policing, especially if they are volunteers or members of special units, typically thrive on their new duties and responsibilities. Also, there is some evidence that organizing and managing officers differently (the so-called "inside-out" approach) can have positive effects on their morale and related attitudes (Wycoff and Skogan 1993).

What is somewhat less certain, however, is (1) whether the positive effects of community policing on officers will survive the long term and (2) whether these benefits are as universal when all officers are required to engage in community policing. Whenever community policing is practiced only by specialists, as has generally been the case until recently in most departments, one condition that is nearly universal is conflict between the specialists and other members of the agency, frequently reflected in derogatory remarks about "the grin and wave squad."

Police Officer Behavior

Significant anecdotal evidence suggests that foot patrol, problem solving, permanent assignment, mini-stations, and other features of community policing lead to changes in some police officers' behavior, but these behavioral effects have only been lightly documented thus far (Mastrofski, Worden, and Snipes 1995). Evidence also suggests that many officers resist changing their behavior, out of opposition to the philosophical underpinnings of community policing, doubts that community policing really works, or just plain habit.

Conclusion

A great deal of energy has been invested since 1980 in determining the nature of community policing and its effects. These efforts have paid off to the extent that the scope and variation of community policing is much better understood today and some of its effects have been fairly well documented. Since community policing has evolved significantly during this period, however, some of its elements have been more carefully evaluated than others. In addition, programmatic complexity, multiple effects, variations in scope, and research design limitations have hampered many of the community policing evaluations conducted thus far. Nevertheless, the tactical elements of community policing do seem to produce several beneficial outcomes for citizens and officers, and have the potential to impact crime and disorder. Whether the more philosophical, strategic, and organizational elements of community policing will become firmly rooted, and whether they will ultimately have beneficial effects, is yet to be seen.

Note

1. Preparation of this chapter was supported, in part, under award # 94-IJ-CX-0006 from the National Institute of Justice, U.S. Department of Justice. Points of view in this document are those of the author and do not necessarily represent the official position of the U.S. Department of Justice. This chapter is a substantial revision of an earlier article in Police Forum (July 1995).

References

Bennett, Trevor. 1994. "Community Policing on the Ground: Developments in Britain." In Dennis P. Rosenbaum, ed., *The Challenge of Community Policing: Testing the Promises.* Thousand Oaks, CA: Sage, pp. 224-246.

Bureau of Justice Assistance. 1994a. *A Police Guide to Surveying Citizens and Their Environment.* Washington, DC: author.

——. 1994b. *Neighborhood-Oriented Policing in Rural Communities: A Program Planning Guide.* Washington, DC: author.

——. 1994c. *Understanding Community Policing: A Framework for Action.* Washington, DC: author.

Cordner, Gary W. and Robert C. Trojanowicz. 1992. "Patrol," in Gary W. Cordner and Donna C. Hale, eds., *What Works in Policing? Operations and Administration Examined.* Cincinnati, OH: Anderson, pp. 3-18.

Eck, John E. 1992. "Criminal Investigation," in Gary W. Cordner and Donna C. Hale, eds., *What Works in Policing? Operations and Administration Examined.* Cincinnati, OH: Anderson, pp. 19-34.

—— and William Spelman. 1987. *Problem Solving: Problem-Oriented Policing in Newport News.* Washington, DC: Police Executive Research Forum.

Goldstein, Herman. 1977. *Policing A Free Society.* Cambridge, MA: Ballinger.

——. 1987. "Toward Community-Oriented Policing: Potential, Basic Requirements, and Threshold Questions," *Crime & Delinquency* 25: 236-258.

——. 1990. Problem-Oriented Policing. New York: McGraw-Hill.

Greene, Jack R. and Stephen D. Mastrofski, eds. 1988. *Community Policing: Rhetoric or Reality?* New York: Praeger.

Greenwood, Peter W. and Joan Petersilia. 1975. *The Criminal Investigation Process, Volume I: Summary and Implications.* Santa Monica, CA: Rand Corporation.

Kelling, George L., Tony Pate, Duane Dieckman, and Charles E. Brown. 1974. The *Kansas City Preventive Patrol Experiment: A Summary Report.* Washington, DC: Police Foundation.

Kelling, George L. and Mark H. Moore. 1988. "The Evolving Strategy of Policing." *Perspectives on Policing* No. 4. Washington, DC: National Institute of Justice.

Klockars, Carl B. 1988. "The Rhetoric of Community Policing." In Jack R. Greene and

Stephen D. Mastrofski, eds., *Community Policing: Rhetoric or Reality?* New York: Praeger, pp. 239-258.

Leighton, Barry N. 1994. "Community Policing in Canada: An Overview of Experience and Evaluations." In Dennis P. Rosenbaum, ed., *The Challenge of Community Policing: Testing the Promises.* Thousand Oaks, CA: Sage, pp. 209-223.

Manning, Peter K. 1988. "Community Policing as a Drama of Control." In Jack R. Greene and Stephen D. Mastrofski, eds., *Community Policing: Rhetoric or Reality?* New York: Praeger, pp. 27-46.

Mastrofski, Stephen D., Robert E. Worden, and Jeffrey B. Snipes. 1995. "Law Enforcement in a Time of Community Policing." *Criminology* 33, 4: 539-563.

McEwen, J. Thomas, Edward F. Connors III, and Marcia I. Cohen. 1986. *Evaluation of the Differential Police Responses Field Test.* Washington, DC: National Institute of Justice.

Moore, Mark H. and Robert C. Trojanowicz. 1988. "Corporate Strategies for Policing." *Perspectives on Policing* No. 6. Washington, DC: National Institute of Justice.

Normandeau, Andre. 1993. "Community Policing in Canada: A Review of Some Recent Studies," *American Journal of Police* 12, 1: 57-73.

Skogan, Wesley G. 1994. "The Impact of Community Policing on Neighborhood Residents: A Cross-Site Analysis." In Dennis P. Rosenbaum, ed., *The Challenge of Community Policing: Testing the Promises.* Thousand Oaks, CA: Sage, pp. 167-181.

Spelman, William and Dale K. Brown. 1982. *Calling the Police: Citizen Reporting of Serious Crime.* Washington, DC: Police Executive Research Forum.

Trojanowicz, Robert and Bonnie Bucqueroux. 1990. *Community Policing: A Contemporary Perspective.* Cincinnati, OH: Anderson.

Weatheritt, Mollie. 1988. "Community Policing: Rhetoric or Reality?" In Jack R. Greene and Stephen D. Mastrofski, eds., *Community Policing: Rhetoric or Reality?* New York: Praeger, pp. 153-176.

Wilson, James Q. and George L. Kelling. 1982. "Police and Neighborhood Safety: Broken Windows," *The Atlantic Monthly* (March): 29-38.

Wycoff, Mary Ann and Wesley K. Skogan. 1993. *Community Policing in Madison: Quality From the Inside Out.* Washington, DC: National Institute of Justice.

11

The Problems of Problem-Solving

Michael E. Buerger

Perhaps the single most powerful tool of community policing is problem solving. Developed in 1979 by Herman Goldstein, problem-oriented policing encourages police agencies to (1) focus the bulk of their attention on substantive problems in the community rather than on internal administrative issues, (2) take a more analytical and empirical approach to their own functions, (3) focus on underlying problems instead of merely on individual incidents, and (4) employ a wider range of problem solutions instead of relying so exclusively on the criminal law and its actual or threatened enforcement. In this article, Michael Buerger explores the realities of problem solving as experienced in Minneapolis during its repeat complaint, or "hot spots," initiative in the 1980s. He demonstrates that full-fledged problem-oriented policing may be easier to talk about than to implement.

Fifteen years after it was first proposed, the concept of problem-oriented policing has a well-established foundation in the police practice of problem solving.[1] Herman Goldstein first proposed problem-oriented policing (now known more familiarly as POP) as an alternative to the means-over-ends orientation of traditional reactive policing. To measure police performance in terms of outcomes rather than activities, Goldstein proposed the police abandon both their reliance on broad, legalistic categories that are essentially catchalls, and their tendency to look at calls as episodic, unconnected events (Goldstein, 1979). He argued that the police need to go beyond the immediate dimensions of incidents in order to properly identify the real problems, and devise realistic, workable solutions.

Goldstein and Susmilch (1981; 1982a; 1982b; 1982c) went on to explore the possibilities of POP with the Madison (WI) Police Department in two studies of the drunk driver and the repeat sex offender. While the police provided valuable information, data collection and analysis were produced by the researchers, not by police officers (as true POP envisions). In Maryland in 1983, Goldstein helped Baltimore County's COPE (Citizen Oriented Police Enforcement) Team integrate problem-solving into its fear-of-crime mandate (Cordner, 1985). The Newport News (VA) Police Department engaged in a series of problem-solving initiatives in conjunction with PERF, the Police Executive Research Forum (Eck & Spelman, 1987). Functional problem solving was an essential element of the Community Patrol Officer Program (CPOP) begun in New York City in 1984, even though CPOP is now promoted as "community policing" rather than problem-oriented (McElroy, Cosgove, & Sadd, 1993). Many departments across the country now use problem-solving (even when it is not so identified by title, such as in the "Beat Health" program in Oakland, California [Green, 1993]), and major projects are underway elsewhere.

Methodology

This article is a qualitative analysis, drawing upon the author's participant observation of the Minneapolis RECAP Experiment (from May 1987 through the end of the Experiment in December 1987, and continued during the next two years), and a content analysis of the original RECAP case files. Those files contained the officers' own written notes and analyses of their work at their assigned addresses, but like many police reports, omitted many pertinent details. However, in early 1988, the RECAP officers wrote up their experiences for a casebook edited by the author (Buerger, 1992), an interactive process which allowed for greater examination of the issues involved and the development of details not contained in the text files.

A Summary of the RECAP Experiment

In December of 1986, the Minneapolis (MN) Police Department inaugurated Repeat Call Address Policing, known more familiarly as RECAP. Devised by Lawrence Shennan (1987), the RECAP Unit was a small team charged with developing problem-solving techniques that could be transferred to other elements of the department. It was both an experimental Unit and a developmental process. Four hand-picked patrol officers and a sergeant were detached from 911 response to work at reducing calls for police service at 250 of the most active addresses in Minneapolis.[2] They were to devise and implement strategies to resolve the underlying problems that produced repeat calls for police service at their addresses. They had the latitude (informally granted by then Chief of Police Anthony V. Bouza) to "do anything they wanted to solve the problems at their addresses, as long as it was legal, Constitutional, and ethical" (Sherman, Buerger, & Gartin, 1988:6).

Theoretically, the basis for the RECAP strategy lies in Cohen and Felson's Routine Activities Theory (1979), which proposes that crime occurs during the intersection, in time and space, of motivated offenders and suitable victims (or targets), under circumstances of absent or inadequate guardianship: a Crime Triangle similar to the fire triangle of fuel, heat, and oxygen. Crime was presumed amenable to suppression if any of the three legs of the triangle was removed, or neutralized. If RECAP officers could influence one or more human actors in the Crime Triangle to change their behavior—which for guardians might involve making changes in the physical environment—it could reduce the need for continued police intervention.

Operationally, RECAP sprang from the growing awareness that police administrators had all but surrendered the control and direction of patrol forces to the telephone. Through attrition and layoffs, the great hiring balloon of the late 1960s and early 1970s slowly shrank (Goldstein & Susmilch, 1981:24-25), forcing police to devote much more of their time to reactively answering calls, and much less to proactive law enforcement strategies (though Reiss [1971] and others have correctly noted that unassigned time and proactive law enforcement activities are not synonymous). Police continued to devote the major portion of their resources responding to mobilizations by citizens, dealing with incidents deemed serious by the citizenry. With their time dominated by the uncritical, egocentric demands of "an oligarchy of chronic users" (Sherman, 1987), the police could not work proactively on crime problems or those related to fear of crime (Wilson & Kelling, 1982).

The RECAP Target Identification Process

Target identification for prior experiments in problem-oriented policing was done on relatively subjective bases: the collective insight of a departmental task force in Madison; the input of citizens solicited for their concerns about crime in their Baltimore County neighborhoods; and a combination of a police task force and official crime statistics in Newport News. RECAP substituted an objective measure of problem seriousness: any address that generated a high level of police responses was deemed to be a "problem" for the purposes of the experiment, regardless of factors such as population density or number of daily users.[3] Excessive demand for police resources at a single address, rather than public perceptions of crime or deteriorating civility, became the standard by which "problems" were measured. RECAP thus preserved the Newport News definition of problem—"[a] group of incidents occurring in a community, that are similar in one or more ways, and that are of concern to the police and the public" (Eck & Spelman, 1987)—but imposed geographical commonality instead of similarity of type of incident. Single addresses were to be the focus of the officers' attentions, to the exclusion of larger spatial units, such as neighborhoods or even blocks.[4]

RECAP began by identifying the chronic users of police services, by addresses. A database of all known calls for police service for a 12-month period was compiled from archived 911 tapes of the Minneapolis Emergency Communications Center (MECC). Addresses were divided into separate commercial and residential lists (because commercial addresses dominated the top end of the list in terms of numbers of calls), and rank-ordered according to the number of calls in the baseline year. The top 250 addresses on each list were randomly assigned to either the experimental or the control group, each of which was divided equally into 125 commercial and 125 residential addresses.[5] The addresses in the experimental group were then divided among the four officers, who carried individual caseloads of approximately 60 addresses through the Experiment.

The program sought to identify as many types of problems, and generate as many innovative police responses to them, as possible. Because the only criterion for selection of an address was the number of calls for police service it generated during the baseline year, RECAP "featured a heterogeneous mix of the nature of the problems, of tactics employed, and the level of effort applied across experimental addresses" (Sherman, Buerger, & Gartin, 1989: abstract). RECAP target identification gave up the narrow range of police preferences in defining problems for a definition which embraced the full range of citizen definitions of problems. Instead of the glory assignments of "real police work"—visible and highly symbolic law enforcement targets like robberies and drug houses—the process embraced the broader spectrum of conditions which demanded (and got) police resources of time and attention. This widening of the net had the effect of identifying chronic problems instead of flare-ups (though the boundary between those two conditions often is difficult to distinguish at any given moment), and established a substantive base distinct from those employed elsewhere. Quantitative analysis of call data also provided a means to measure objectively the effectiveness of the Unit's work across the wide range of problem types. Call data represented a wider range of public concerns, with a lower level of police gatekeeping, than official crime reports.

Statistical Results of the Experiment

Analysis of the calls to both groups during the experimental year indicated that the RECAP Unit failed to achieve its target goal, to "prevent" as many calls as the officers would likely have answered had they remained on active patrol service. That number was estimated at 1,000 calls per officer, based on the number of calls and the number of officers assigned to patrol duties during that year. "Rather than preventing 4,000 calls, [RECAP] was only able to prevent 475 within the experimental design" while analysis of the prevalence of call reductions rather than frequency of calls showed "no statistically significant differences using a six-celled chi-square test" (Sherman, Buerger, & Gartin, 1989:21).

In short, based on the criteria for statistical success established before the development of the strategies, RECAP was a failure in experimental terms. But even before the statistical results were known, the Minneapolis Police Department established RECAP as a permanent Unit. Though the Unit's successes were statistically overwhelmed by the effects of the case load (including addresses which became "turned around" late in the year, after early accumulation of large numbers of calls), the localized effects of the successes were obvious to observers. Though they could not "prevent their weight in calls," the RECAP officers paid for themselves in a different coin. In addition to some dramatically successful interventions at pernicious addresses (e.g., Buerger, 1992: 1-6; 133-139; 327-331), the Unit helped streamline ineffective police responses like the shoplifting program (Buerger, 1992: 308-318) and helped develop several plans for solutions to city-wide problems.

Specific findings included the following, quoted verbatim (though presented in different form) from the RECAP Final Report:

- the residential locations, relative to the control group, showed a 21 percent reduction in assault, a 12 percent reduction in disturbances, and a 15 percent reduction in calls related to drunkenness;

- commercial targets showed a nine percent reduction in theft calls, and a 21 percent reduction in shoplifting calls at seven stores participating in a special program;

- residential burglaries were up 27 percent compared to controls;

- calls for commercial predatory crime (criminal sexual conduct, robbery and kidnapping combined) were up 28 percent at the experimental addresses relative to controls (Sherman, Buerger, & Gartin, 1989:23).

Overall, the experimenters concluded that these "mixed results . . . suggest that merely focusing police attention on chronic problems cannot guarantee their solution . . . the results of a test with objective target selection seem far more modest than results of quasi-experimentals using subjective target selection (e.g., Lindsay & McGillis, 1986; Schneider, 1986). When the most troublesome addresses in a city are intentionally selected as targets, perhaps a more appropriate goal would be 'managing' rather than 'solving' (Eck & Spelman, 1987) problems" (Sherman, Buerger, & Gartin, 1989:24).

The modest statistical outcomes were the result of the case assignments outstripping the resources which the Unit could bring to bear on them, resulting in a large number of addresses remaining essentially static from the Time 1 to Time 2 measurement (Buerger, 1993). The cases upon which this analysis draws represent a smaller group of addresses, those "most troublesome" locations actively worked by RECAP, with persistent problems that defied easy solutions.

RECAP Tactics and Operations

The wide range of RECAP problems and tactics have been recorded elsewhere (Sherman, 1987; Buerger, 1992; Buerger, 1993a). The officers received weekly printouts of the calls to each RECAP address during the previous week. They worked with the persons involved in the calls, or with the guardians of the address, as appropriate. The solutions which they devised included referrals to social services; law enforcement actions; changes in the physical environment; informal counseling and cautioning in the traditional police manner; and occasionally more innovative responses, such as trying to arrange for a management takeover of a failing boarding house run by deeply religious but incapable guardians (Buerger, 1992: 103-109).

The first commander of the Unit, Sgt. (now Lt.) Bud Emerson, analyzed RECAP's work as having three phases: cooperative, insistent, and coercive. Working from a non-traditional justification for target selection ("high demands for police service" rather than a recognizable illegal activity) made "cooperation" a necessary first step for two reasons. First, the underlying problems were not always discernible from the call data alone, and the officers were to some decree dependent upon the formal guardians for information about the activity at the address (history, tenancy, external conditions which imposed on the address, etc.). Second, without a clear-cut criminal violation, there were few coercive tools available to the officers in most cases.

This, plus the fact that they were an experimental unit testing uncharted waters, led to a tactical decision with both positive and negative consequences. The cooperative approach was more likely to secure compliance where the guardians or participants were genuinely interested in being good citizens, but it left the officers vulnerable to manipulations of the truth (lies, half-truths, lip service, and "redefinition," as below) where the primary motivations were otherwise. The case loads were so great that considerable time could elapse before the officers learned that supposedly cooperative guardians were just paying lip service to RECAP requests (particularly in terms of long-term solutions, such as the use of tenant screening, and the enforcement of "house rules"). Several addresses accumulated high numbers of calls before the officers shifted from cooperation and insistence to a more coercive aspect.

RECAP was an interactive process, one in which other actors had power equal to and sometimes exceeding that of the officers. This article addresses the actions (and omissions) of the other players, including problem-causing people, formal guardians, intermediaries, and nominal allies of the RECAP officers. The three main sub-sections examine the methods of resistance employed by address guardians and others; the problems RECAP faced in being dependent upon others to implement their problem-solving ideas; and competing interests, chief among which was the Capitalist Imperative, which demands profits ahead of all other concerns. The latter was the most important element of resistance, and has the greatest implications for problem-solving and problem-oriented policing.

Conflicting Interests

One of the curious aspects of the RECAP cases was the degree to which a spirit of voluntarism pervaded the early efforts. Without stooping to the buzzwords of "co-production" or "partnership" that infest policing publications today, RECAP nevertheless appealed to a presumed altruism on the part of the people with whom they interacted. Rational self-interest was not stinted, by any means, but the phrase "you can help" is a constant theme in the RECAP cases, so well-rehearsed that there is little doubt but that it was the approach the officers took. Exchanges observed directly, during the persuasion phase and during attempts at coercion, all stressed the notion of individual and corporate responsibility to the larger units: the block, the neighborhood, the city. For example, fliers distributed by the team in the high-rises in August carried the banner headline, "The Minneapolis Police need your help!"

In some cases, the officers' definition of altruism ran contrary to different visions of altruism, primarily in the social services areas. The manager of the downtown YMCA refused to cooperate with the RECAP officer's suggestion that a security system be installed to restrict access to the YMCA to residents after a certain hour (after analysis showed a concentration of late-night calls to remove drunk and disorderly "street people" from the lobby). The manager defined himself as "an ultra-liberal," furthering the YMCA's mission of being available to the street people, not restricting them (Buerger, 1992: 78-83). The staff at the women's shelter were far more concerned with the well-being of their clients than with the small demands the shelter made on a public system that had otherwise failed their clients. Though profit was an issue in all of the RECAP dealings with the lodging/shelter facility below, there was no doubt that the owner was sincerely dedicated to the welfare of his clients, however naive his management may have been in some particulars.

Across the wider spectrum of resistant addresses, however, the appeal to altruism ran hard aground on the Capitalist Imperative: the desire to make the maximum profit from minimal expenditures. In one way or another, most of the resistance to RECAP interventions centered on financial matters, and RECAP had to find ways to make public safety and order competitive with the profit motive. Generally, among residential addresses their success was greater with the smaller landholders, for whom the two conditions were more closely linked, than with those with larger holdings and greater experience (who had developed effective means of insulating themselves from the direct impact of their business practices). The unit's success with commercial properties was more mixed, as the corporate responses were not correlated with any known measure of corporate resources except possibly that of local ties.

Commercial Addresses

Shoplifting dominated the calls to the larger commercial addresses, and was a significant problem in many of the smaller ones. RECAP began with the assumption that the stores would have a desire to curb their shoplifting losses, only to find that corporate hierarchies were much more concerned with the financial losses to lawsuits. A second theme, which runs through the officers' records of their initial contacts at various stores, is the stores' desire for help with employee pilferage, which was the cause of much greater losses than shoplifting. RECAP was most ill-equipped to work on that type of problem, since it has traditionally been considered out of the realm of public crime and was not represented in the calls for police assistance that were their mandate and evaluation. In only one case, a downtown hotel, did RECAP deal with an internal matter, using a standard police technology of bait money soaked with dye to apprehend a housekeeping employee who was stealing from guests' rooms (Buerger, 1992: 66-68).

Corporate Liability. An employee of one of the chain convenience stores put the matter in perspective when he observed, as quoted by the case officer, "When you're making sixty thousand dollars a month in profits, who cares if you lose three thousand to shoplifting?" Because awards in lawsuits could run into the millions, the shoplifting losses were essentially written off as an acceptable cost of doing business.

RECAP's interest in the shoplifting activities were more localized, and incidentally shared by the employees of the stores, who were frustrated at not being able to take action against the predators. An "easy mark" such as a SuperAmerica convenience store, where corporate directives (since changed) allowed the criminally inclined to pilfer cigarettes and beer without challenge, bordered on being an attractive nuisance. Though the link between the uncontested crimes allowed by corporate policy (for all intents and purposes) and other criminal conduct in the area is only speculative, RECAP officers were inclined to see the disorder attracted by the stores as spilling over into the neighborhood, a "Broken Windows" type of situation (Wilson & Kelling, 1982).

The Capitalist Imperative worked both ways in the case of the SuperAmerica stores: an employee (described by the regional officers as "disgruntled") filed a Workman's Compensation disability suit for stress related to the job. As a result of the case officer's work at the address, the employee had been aware of the RECAP statistics, and the case officer was deposed in the lawsuit on behalf of the plaintiff. Despite that, however, local franchise managers and the regional representatives refused to accept RECAP suggestions (and offers of free help) to restore a climate of order at the stores. They appealed to the higher authority of the parent company's Security Manual, which forbade employees to interfere with shoplifters because the law supposedly gave them no authority to do so (Minnesota law did, in fact, contain a Shopkeeper's Statute which permitted them to do so, but the financial ties of franchise management were stronger than RECAP's invocation of the law).

The turning point came with a shooting incident at the gas pumps of one of the inner-city SuperAmerica stores. The Unit's commander sent to the regional manager a registered letter describing the store as a nuisance property, and threatening to have the store's license revoked unless the company took more responsive action to deal with the disorder at their addresses. It is uncertain whether the connection could be sustained in court between the shoplifting and disorderly customers problems, and an essentially random event like the shooting, but the letter restarted negotiations at a different level.

The SuperAmerica case was a difficult one for RECAP, as the regional representatives of the company resisted all of RECAP's initiatives. A direct appeal to the parent company, Ashland Oil, eventually broke the deadlock over the shoplifting policies, but the real gains that resulted may have been only peripherally the result of RECAP's actions. Over the summer, a series of early-morning armed robberies of SuperAmericas on the south side of Minneapolis may have provided the spur. An employee at one store advised the case officer that the company responded to the robberies by placing closed-circuit monitors at the counter: all customers entering the store could see themselves on the monitor, with the quiet but clear message that their features were now recorded somewhere on videotape. The employee observed that there seemed to be fewer problems at the store since that device was installed. At RECAP's urging, SuperAmerica did hire security guards at night, rotating guards among the stores in the inner core to deal with disorder problems, but the practice was instituted late in the year, and probably had little impact on the call loads.

Occasionally, the Imperative worked in more subtle ways. When the Unit first proposed to enforce the juvenile curfew, the officers worked to enlist the assistance of the 24-hour convenience stores. The 7-Eleven stores balked at the proposal to exclude juveniles from the premises after curfew hours. Southland Corporation (the parent company of 7-Eleven) had tied the 7-Eleven stores to the national McGruff House child safety/crime prevention campaign, and the policy proposed by RECAP was in direct conflict with that initiative. This particular conflict was not resolved: the 7-Eleven stores were in the first commander's caseload, and the issue died quietly when he left for a year at Harvard's Kennedy School.

Impact on Good Customers. The case files for both SuperAmerica and a large independent grocery on the near north side contain notes indicating that the owners or managers claimed that a police presence on the premises—to deal with disorder and curb thievery at the former; to curb shoplifting and bar juveniles after hours at the latter—would offend their good customers. In both cases, the RECAP plan was put in force against the protests of the ownership—the parent company authorized the hiring of security guards in the SuperAmerica stores (under an existing contract with a national security company), and the RECAP case officer patrolled the grocery store aisles in uniform during peak shoplifting periods (to prove his point to the owner that it was better to deter than to catch). The case notes for both files contain notes that customers and employees made a point of thanking the officers, saying that they felt safer, and expressing hope that the change would be permanent.

Interference by Police Officers. The Capitalist Imperative extended beyond those with proprietary interests, to those who derived secondary benefits from employment at the stores. While regular employees of the establishments were appreciative of the Unit's efforts, police officers who were part-time employees by virtue of their off-duty security jobs felt threatened by the shoplifting program. It was stridently opposed by several officers who feared it would lead to the termination of the off-duty jobs (though why it should have done so was not clear, since the officers did not process shoplifters, and only stood near the front entrance like greeters; and in fact, the institution of the shoplifting program did not lead to their termination). One officer, assigned to another specialty unit, reportedly was actively working against the case officer's plan for the northside independent grocery, for reasons which were never fully determined. And one officer in the Fourth Precinct went beyond his brief in opposing the hiring of a private security service

at a large low-income housing complex,[6] apparently because he had hoped to secure the security contract for off-duty Minneapolis officers. While these situations were more irritants than obstacles, they demonstrate the complexity that problem-solving can encounter in police agencies.

Residential Addresses

A renters' market that prevailed in Minneapolis in 1987 was a driving force behind the Capitalist Imperative at residential addresses. Homeowners were moving or threatening to move to the suburbs,[7] many rental units were vacant, and landlords struggled to get and keep paying tenants in order to meet mortgage or contract for deed payments. A bumper crop of abandoned properties was scattered throughout the city, providing squats for homeless men who declined to accept the regulations of shelters, and abandoned properties were part of the growing crack cocaine trade. It fell to the City to take the properties through legal action.

A change in the tax laws had encouraged the purchase of rental properties as investments, which brought new, inexperienced landlords into the business. Many would-be entrepreneurs, lacking sufficient capital to purchase buildings outright, negotiated "Contract For Deed" agreements with the titled owners of properties. The building's formal owner held the deed, and essentially acted as the financing agent. In return for privately-negotiated downpayments, the deed-holder wold turn the property over to the new "owner" who ran it, put whatever investments into it he or she wanted or could afford (which for the RECAP addresses often seemed to be "nothing"), and collected all the rental income from the property. The difference between the rents collected and the contract-for-deed payment was profit for the new owner, but the legal deed remained in the possession of the titled owner until the contract payments were all made—if they ever were.

Since most of the new generation "investors" were looking for little more than ready cash income, improvements to the housing stock were rarely made and little attention was given to management practices, especially to tenant screening. If income dropped to an unacceptable level, or the hassles of landlording became too great, the owner-of-the-moment had two choices: pass the property on to another investor through a second "balloon" contract for deed, or default on the contract, walking away from the property and letting it lapse back to the original owner. Both entailed potential costs, either continued expenditures or the loss of investment capital.

The practical consequence was that many landlords accepted any tenant who had the next month's rent in hand: empty apartments meant either no profit that month, or perhaps a shortfall which took money out of the owner's pocket to make the mortgage or contract-for-deed payment. Some landlords accepted Section 8 tenants because it meant an automatic vendored rent payment each month, direct from the Welfare Department, without the usual hassles of collecting the rent moneys.

Because most landlords were absentee owners, they were insulated from the behavioral problems that their tenants brought with them. Newer, smaller landlords tended to be "on the line" more, both in collecting the rent, making repairs, and dealing with various complaints that more experienced property owners delegated to on-site caretakers or management companies. Many residential operations (both new and experienced) had neither leases nor "house rules," and thus effectively had no means of imposing control over their tenants' behavior when the need arose. For the slumlords who basically used the properties to warehouse people, behavioral problems were irrelevant unless and until they extended to physical damages which cut into the profit margin—at which point the tenant would be evicted.

When RECAP officers intruded, essentially demanding that house rules be instituted, or prospective tenants screened for references, the financial house of cards was threatened. In the case of one medium-sized apartment building, the property manager was dismayed to learn that the person he considered the best tenant in the building was a major drug dealer who the police wanted evicted. From the property manager's perspective, the low profile that the dealer used

to protect his operation (never making demands, always paying the rent on time, and in cash) made him an ideal, no-problem tenant. The eviction took place, but was rendered moot by the revocation of the dealer's parole (Buerger, 1992: 275-278).

Addresses in transition felt the Capitalist Imperative even more keenly: buildings with vacant apartments did not sell quickly, or as well, as those that were full. A property manager who could show a potential buyer a full, occupied building was peddling a commodity that was a "proven" maximum-income generator: the buyer could take ownership by paper or electronic transfer and immediately reap the benefits of ownership both making the payments and making a profit. A buyer who took control of a partially-empty building faced the necessity of filling it, which meant lower income, more work, and certainly more hassles.

The Capitalist Imperative very simply dictated the maximum profit for the minimum expenditure of capital, whether that capital be financial or the "sweat equity" variety. RECAP's requests and demands threatened the elegant simplicity of the equation for those who looked at their investments as short-term, though the suggestions and assistance RECAP offered was frequently of great use to those whose generally more modest investments were directed toward the long term.

Forms and Tactics of Resistance

Broadly, resistance to RECAP initiatives fell into three distinct categories, each specific to a target group. *Owners and managers of commercial addresses* felt the problems could be controlled if the patrol officers came around more often. *Owners and managers of residential addresses* claimed that problems at their building were a product of the surrounding neighborhood, both directly and indirectly (the former attributing the calls to neighborhood characters coming to the address, the latter taking the form of a claim that because of the neighborhood the building was in, the owner could not get any good tenants). *Persons involved in disputes* in the residential addresses either denied there was any problem at all, or asserted that it was a private matter and so denied the legitimacy of RECAP intervention (despite the clear, printed evidence that the dispute was in fact not private, but repeatedly required public resources in the form of police assistance).

The simplest way for an owner or manager to thwart RECAP was to stonewall, either by lying or by doing nothing at all. The caseload and time factors worked to their advantage. One store owner cloaked himself as a community activist dedicated to maintaining the neighborhood, until citizen protests and further investigation revealed that he was using the store as a front for an extensive drug distribution business (Buerger, 1992: 5-52; 332-333). The owner of one of the worst residential properties on the RECAP list promised to institute all the recommendations of the case officer. As soon as the officer left, however, the owner instructed his on-site manager to ignore all the promises and to continue the prior business practices, renting to anyone with the rent money in hand (Buerger, 1992: 143-149).

In some cases, an ambiguous or inconclusive diagnosis led to the creation of an exhortational Action Plan that was a "plan" only by courtesy of the title. In such instances, there was little that even a cooperative guardian could do, and resistant guardians were facile in finding excuses in imprecise recommendations, or those that used supportive rather than directive language. That was due in part to the role that owners and managers played in the diagnosis itself, through which the RECAP officers were initially dependent upon them for preliminary information about the address. If given false or misleading information, the officers at first had no empirical or intuitive alternatives for the "information" provided by a resistant owner (below).

The same was true for participants in the 911 events. The process that turned 911 data into RECAP printouts took several days, and it was not unusual for the officers to learn of an event a week to ten days after it occurred. The resulting delay in their follow-up forfeited many advantages of timely intervention in interpersonal disputes, though it occasionally yielded new information which was not reflected in the call data. The time factor forced RECAP to depend upon patrol

officers for either supportive action on calls at the RECAP addresses, or timely notification of new events. Assistance of both types was rendered only sporadically.

Another tactic common to both commercial and residential owners was to insulate themselves from the RECAP officers by using intermediaries. It is essentially a "due process" dodge: if the owner is never informed about the problems, the owner incurs no obligation to do anything about them. Several of the residential case files contain stories about owners who were dedicated to not hearing about the problems at their addresses. RECAP officers overcame the difficulties of tracking down owners by a variety of tactics, including registered letters (e.g., Buerger, 1992: 196-200) and in at least one case, driving out to the owner's rural home to leave a written message. Employing incompetent intermediaries (chemically dependent, mentally slow, or mentally ill) accomplished the same end, while giving the appearance of responsiveness. For commercial properties, the corporate structure provided a similar form of insulation. Refusals to return phone calls or keep appointments also served to keep RECAP officers at arm's length, at least temporarily.

Commercial Addresses

In all phases, the officers' first tool was information: the call data, supplemented at times by information from Offense or Arrest reports. Use of that type of information prompted a comparable tactic in rebuttal. Incriminating information supplied by the officers was countered with exculpatory information which supported the business perspective, though such "information" was often naked opinion unsupported by any empirical evidence or data. Within the "information" category were three primary countermeasures: (1) crying poverty, (2) attempting to redefine the problem, and (3) appealing to an alternate authority.

Crying Poverty. During the first year, the owner of a lodging facility (which served a mix of long-term residents and emergency shelter clients) consistently rejected the case officer's demands for better security and greater control over residents' behavior. The owner claimed that his business was operating so close to the margin that he could not afford to make the improvements being demanded, or hire security guards or off-duty police officers recommended by the officer. He claimed that if Hennepin County (the statutory provider of social services, and thus his funding source) upgraded its rating of his facility so that the facility was eligible for a higher per diem rate, he would be able to do so.[8] The original case officer was stymied by the owner's refusal to show him the books to substantiate these claims (the officer suspected he was lying), and a year-long stalemate developed (Buerger, 1992:110-115).

In the Unit's second year, another officer with better contacts in the Welfare Office took the case over, and confirmed that the owner was trying to play RECAP off against the Welfare agency. The facility's operations were nowhere near to meeting the requirements for the higher rating, and the owner was attempting to manipulate the police definition of the problem in such a way that RECAP would broker his suit to the County. Once equipped with reliable information,[9] the RECAP Unit was able to move their tactics to the next level, at the threshold between persuasion[10] and threat, which was moving to have the facility's contract with the County Welfare Office terminated (Buerger, 1992: 334-335).

The boarding house/shelter was a special case. Because the establishment was a recipient of public funds, there existed an alternate source of information about its financial health that was not available for privately-held properties or corporations. The larger stores and national chains clearly had no cause to resort to this particular defense, but still balked at the expensive solutions proposed by RECAP (security cameras at a luxury hotel, security guards or off-duty police officers in convenience stores, etc. [Buerger, 1992: 13-15; 18-20; 44-471).

Redefining the Problem. Redefining the problem meant one of three things at the commercial properties. By far the most common response to RECAP's initial proposals were variations of, "This is what we pay so much in taxes for, to have you cops take care of the problem."[11] It was fairly easy for RE-CAP officers to sweep aside the objection by pointing out that the address in question was using a disproportionate amount of resources compared to other addresses in the city. The second response was to attribute the high call levels to the failure of another entity or agency: scapegoating. The third was to acknowledge the problem, but to minimize it by asserting that other considerations were more worthy of the organization's resources.

Scapegoating. Frequently, the tax argument was intertwined with an indictment of the police department's operations though this usually came from the smaller business owners. The most vivid example was the owner of a small corner grocery store, who had a history of adversarial contacts with the police (Buerger, 1992: 16-17). In addition to several outstanding lawsuits against patrol officers over their handling of problems at his store (which included arresting him for brandishing a pistol on the sidewalk as part of his "Informal social control" measures against shoplifting), he had issued an edict to the Precinct Captain that no black officers were allowed to respond to calls at his store. Officers of larger corporations were sophisticated enough to understand the nature of the problems,[12] and in any case the nature of their resources placed their dealings with RECAP on a much different footing than those of the smaller entrepreneur.

Almost everyone tried the gambit that the police weren't doing their job: the excuse took on the aspect of a general, prophylactic, knee-jerk reaction to the news that an address was on RECAP's list. However, a few addresses had a well-developed list of particulars in that record, and chief among them were the social service agencies. One of the case officer's greatest frustrations at a woman's shelter was their single-minded insistence on talking about the poor attitudes and non-responsiveness of patrol officers who came to take domestic violence reports. The RECAP officer wanted to talk to them about their false alarms, and all the staff wanted to do was to lambaste the performance of his friends and former patrol colleagues (Buerger, 1992: 86-88). The staff and people associated with a church-run shelter had similar complaints, though their relationship with another RE-

CAP officer was more positive, based in part on the officer's better reaction to the criticism (Buerger, 1992: 91-94).

Minimizing. Public agencies were the most likely to try to trivialize the problem, placing it lower in their list of priorities than the officers tried to make it. A senior corporate executive of the Minneapolis Public Library bluntly stated to the Unit commander and the case officer assigned to a branch library address that the Library Board had to be concerned with personnel costs, long-term financing, and brick-and-mortar issues. While the fact that the librarians called upon the services of the Minneapolis Police Department some thirty-three times in 1986 was unfortunate, it was not important enough for the Library Board to divert resources away from other more pressing needs.[13] (Buerger, 1992: 53-58).

Appeal to an Alternate Authority. The Minneapolis Community Development Authority (MCDA) administered the public housing addresses, including the several high-rise apartment buildings in the Experiment. The middle and upper management levels of the NICDA simply appealed to higher authorities: those of HUD, which dictated that the vacancy rate be reduced, and of the courts, where recent case decisions had held that maintaining buildings exclusively for senior citizens was a discriminatory practice which denied equal access to public facilities. The MCDA's resort to HUD (which, like the corporate headquarters of SuperAmerica, was physically removed from the officers' jurisdiction) was the most obvious case of this tactic[14] (Buerger, 1992: 281-301).

Another example was provided by the branch library case: after the meeting with the senior Library officials, RECAP received a follow-up note from them. The Library Board had contacted the Captain in charge of the precinct, and had arranged to have a beat officer stop in periodically. The letter stated that they preferred that option rather than to implement RECAP's managerial suggestions, and basically told RECAP to stay out of their hair (Buerger, 1992: 53-58).

When RECAP floated trial balloons about instituting an ordinance to require licenses for rental properties, one or more of the landlords with whom they were dealing called in a powerful ally: the Minnesota Multiple Housing Association (MMHA) called for a meeting with the Unit commander. Although the meeting was entirely cordial and full of the language of mutual cooperation, the underlying message was clear: any attempt to institute license provisions for rental housing would be met with well-organized, well-financed political opposition from the MMHA. While RECAP secured a promise of cooperation from MMHA, to put "peer pressure" on resistant landlords and slumlords, it was clear that MMHA represented its members, and was unlikely to put any pressure whatsoever on any member who the police might consider to be a slumlord.

The most obvious appeal to higher authority, going directly to the City Council Member responsible for the ward, did not materialize during the Experiment. RECAP officers anticipated it in dealing with the bar cases, particularly with Moby Dick's Bar, whose owners were reported to be well-connected politically by virtue of heavy campaign contributions to City Council members (Buerger, 1992: 133-140). They prepared for such an eventuality, but did not encounter the problem.

Residential Addresses

Crying Poverty. Despite being an even more frequent reaction than at the commercial properties, the "crying poverty" reaction was not always illegitimate at residential addresses (e.g., Buerger, 1992: 232-236). Some landowners reacquired responsibility for an address they had once but sold, after the buyer(s) defaulted on the contract-for-deed payment. In order to protect their investment (because as deed-holders they were still obligated to make their own mortgage payments), the once-and-present owners had to resume management of the property, often inheriting a vastly different clientele and a neglected physical plant. These owners, however, were the most amenable to RECAP's suggestions, since the direct benefits of cooperating with RECAP were obvious, and since compliance brought with it some minimal police presence that could be inflated into a tacit threat when dealing with potential problems at the address.

"Poverty" was not a problem for slumlords who could easily make the physical changes mandated by the Housing Inspectors. "Profitability" was a greater concern for them, but their resistance to spending money that they had was as great an obstacle as the smaller holder's reluctance to incur debt spending money they did not have.

Redefining the Problem. The case files record very little use of the minimizing tactic at residential addresses—outright denial was more the rule, and it was easily defeated by the call printouts—but initial attempts to redefine the problems by scapegoating was close to universal. The neighborhood influence was a reasonable defense, since RECAP and Control addresses were close to each other in many areas, especially in the neighborhoods with concentrations of social problems. However, in all instances, there was evidence both of lackadaisical management practices particular to the address, and of buildings in the same area which did not generate large numbers of calls for police assistance. The officers could reject that defense with relative ease.

A second type of scapegoating was to blame what was known locally as "the Gary Syndrome," claiming that an influx of welfare-seekers from other states was making it impossible for the owners to get good tenants (Leinfelder 1988).[15] The technique itself—trying to distract the officers from a specific problem by declaiming about a general one—failed, primarily because RECAP officers insisted on keeping the focus on the management of the buildings. However, in private statements the officers sometimes indicated that they were sympathetic to that analysis.

Appeal to an Alternate Authority. The invocation of the political power of the MMHA, discussed above, also constitutes one appeal to a higher political power. Aware of the City Council's concern for both suburban flight and the number of abandoned properties in the City, some landlords attempted to ward off RECAP attention with another, a threat to "walk away from" the address. The officers basically just ignored such threats, in part because, as one observed, an abandoned building couldn't be any worse for the neighborhood than it was in its current status. RECAP

officers were aware of the larger problem, and were concerned that their efforts not have a backfire effect in that way. Nevertheless, they counted on the Capitalist Imperative to minimize the amount of investment loss the owner would be willing to accept (in essence, reading the statement as a bluff, and calling it), and the non-response proved correct. No owner that RECAP dealt with just "walked away"; all found someone else to take over the property. Even when the formal guardianship changed hands properly, though, the instability of ownership required the officer to "go back to Square One," in many cases forfeiting even the marginal gains that the officer had wrung from the resistant owner.

Interdependencies and the Struggle for Legitimacy

As the several references above indicate, RECAP's ability to identify the problems, and devise appropriate plans to ameliorate them, did not guarantee that the plans would be implemented. Some of their interventions were appropriate to, and effective because of, the one-on-one relationships that the officers established and maintained with the individuals involved. Some, particularly the handful where CPTED tactics were appropriate, produced a long-term passive benefit once the initial plan was executed.

A few singular addresses required that the officers interact with specialty groups who held power that the Unit did not have: the Mental Health Roundtable in the case of a halfway house in a suburban-character neighborhood (Buerger, 1992: 75-77) and the anonymous Welfare Department sources of information about the financial situations of the boarding/shelter facility discussed above are examples.

For residential addresses, the Unit's work was in part hampered by the workload of the Hennepin County Sheriff's Office. By law, only the Sheriff could effect forcible evictions from a premises, even after the landlord properly obtained an Unlawful Detainer (eviction) notice from the courts. In several cases, landlords and the RECAP officers had to fight a holding action against tenants who had received an eviction order from the court—and therefore had nothing to lose by being destructive and belligerent—but refused to move until forcibly evicted. The Sheriff's Office was at one point backlogged a full month with eviction orders, and would not change its schedule to accommodate the Minneapolis Police (Sheriff is an elected office in Minnesota; jumping a RECAP case to the head of the list would benefit one voting landowner—if the landlord lived in the County—but might offend many more.)

For the most part, though, when individual persuasion failed to achieve the desired results, and coercion was needed, the RECAP strategy depended on the assistance of four main groups: the City Attorney's office, the Housing Inspectors, police officers assigned to patrol duties, and the police administration.

The City Attorney's Office. The City Attorney's Office was specifically needed for the shoplifting program, but deliberate inaction by that office ultimately eviscerated what might have been a promising solution to a widespread (if not overly serious) problem. Despite some reasonably good working relationships between RECAP officers and individual attorneys, all of the policies of the City Attorney's Office were gatekeeping devices, and two practices were particularly galling. The Office refused to prosecute any shoplifting case under a certain dollar amount, and changed that amount internally several times without any notice to RECAP (their suggested alternative was that shopkeepers use a civil recovery process, which often cost more in filing fees than the original loss, and in any case was an unrealistic resort against welfare and poverty-level suspects who were impervious to civil judgment out of simple inability to pay). Second, when RECAP arranged an alternative sanction, a non-punitive decision-making course similar to the DWI schools used in some jurisdictions, the Office refused to cooperate in sending a letter to the apprehended suspects telling them that attendance at the school was an alternative to prosecution. The Office maintained that it was an extortionate threat: since they had made an internal decision not to prosecute cases under a certain amount, there was no prosecution for the school to be an alterna-

tive to, even if the statute defined the offense as prosecutable under criminal law (Buerger, 1992: 308-318).

Similarly, the officers had difficulty getting cooperation with any issues relating to the domestic assaults that were so frequent at RECAP residential addresses. Citing the overwhelming problem of lack of commitment on the part of domestic violence victims, the City Attorney's Office refused to commit resources to that area, even for the cases that RECAP officers were trying to shepherd through the system. Requiring victims to come to the City Attorney's offices in the Hennepin County Government Center downtown, in order to give a statement about the assault and to swear out a complaint, was perceived by RECAP as a significant factor in victim reluctance (Buerger, 1992: 174-176).

The conflicts with the City Attorney's Office represented an interesting case of dueling managerial dictates. The City Attorney's Office correctly decided that it could not deal on an individual level with every officer or unit of the Minneapolis Police Department who might have some new idea on how cases could be better handled. The police administration, in turn, was promoting bottom-up innovation, delegating a significant amount of authority to lower-level workers. (As frequently happens in such instances, conflicts became personalized: RECAP officers saw themselves working past the old litany of "we can't" excuses in order to improve the quality of life in the city, and they could find no justification for the intransigence of the City Attorney's Office.) The impasse over the handling of domestic violence cases was temporarily broken when the Hennepin County Criminal Justice Coordinating Committee selected the domestic violence issue as its first major project: RECAP was selected by the police administration to represent the Department on the Domestic Violence Task Force. The addition of other players with political power forced the representatives of the City Attorney's Office into a more cooperative stance, at least temporarily (Buerger, 1992: 319-314). Ultimately, the Task Force proved to be a classic case of suppressing action while appearing to take action: to the author's knowledge, nothing substantive was accomplished during the RECAP Experiment, or in subsequent years, and the issue soon disappeared from the headlines.

Housing Inspectors. The Housing Inspectors were vital to the attempt to "get the attention" of certain stonewalling landlords, and the natural affinity of street-level workers provided for a solid alliance. Reliance on the Housing Inspectors ultimately ran afoul of the Inspections Office's own bureaucratic mandates, however: at least one officer came to rely exclusively on the Inspectors as a way to punish uncooperative landlords. He lost sight of the fact that the Inspections Office was limited by its own procedural safeguards against abuses, and was subject to political control which the experienced slumlords had learned to manipulate. (In the most resistant cases, the slumlords were as impervious to the relatively weak sanctions available to the Housing Inspectors as they were to the empty threats of the officer.)

The Patrol Force. The patrol force was needed to put teeth into both the juvenile sweeps and the domestic violence policy. The job of enforcing threats to arrest for domestic assault at 125 residential addresses was beyond the capacity of the Unit, even if there had been a way around the four-hour limit for misdemeanor assault arrests. To have any deterrent effect at all, the domestic violence policy had to be consistently applied, a job that had to be shouldered by the patrol force.

In order to quell the wide range of problems caused by unsupervised juveniles abroad at night, the Unit needed to be able to transfer the responsibility for curfew enforcement to the patrol units. RECAP officers could not work both daytime hours to make their commercial contacts, and nighttime hours to conduct juvenile sweeps. Even when they changed their work schedules in order to do sweeps, five officers in three cars were not enough to have a significant impact on a city-wide problem. To be effective, juvenile curfew enforcement had to be done consistently, by all patrol officers in all areas.

The patrol force—already critical of RECAP as a specialty unit, and more critical after a late August meeting in which the domestic violence policy was reasserted—supported neither initiative (several individual

exceptions to this only served to prove the rule). The case notes from the startup phase mirror the RECAP officers' confidence that they could obtain the assistance they needed by prevailing upon their former mates to help them on an individual basis. By late May, that confidence had begun to erode, and soon turned to frustration and resentment as officers who had agreed to follow RECAP's wishes continued to do nothing when they answered domestics at RECAP addresses.

In part, the resistance of the patrol force to RECAP initiatives was directly related to the amount and direction of change it meant for the officers' daily work life. The shoplifting program produced a positive change in an activity that patrol officers were already doing. Despite the usual "Yeah, but . . ." objections that were dredged up at the beginning of the program (while the details and unanticipated problems were being worked out of the system), patrol officers quickly recognized the change as an improvement in their work life. Most officers hated the toothless taxi service that the universal arrest policy had become. As soon as it became obvious that the squads were not being called to the stores as much, appreciation for the new procedures grew rapidly, and RECAP's stock with the patrol force rose a bit.

By contrast, the RECAP initiative for juvenile curfew enforcement was essentially a new activity for the patrol force, which had already convinced itself that it was overworked and understaffed. Though the curfew law had been on the books for years, it was a long-ignored regulation, and even the RECAP officers could not recall a time when it had been vigorously enforced. The domestic violence policy was already despised, since its obligations ran counter to the local police culture's conclusion that "nothing could be done" about domestic violence. Being called upon to do more work, or to take more seriously an activity that they wished they could shed outright, did not improve the patrol officers' work lives, and they resisted.

Patrol officers had the power to avoid the domestic violence policy in most cases by redefining the event: recoding it as an UNWANT (Unwanted Person); handling the event as they saw fit and radioing that the abuser was **GOA** (Gone On Arrival) even when he was not; or simply clearing with a statement that the event did not meet the guidelines for invoking the department's pre-ferred-arrest policy. Since officers worked in a low-visibility environment, and many supervisors were more sympathetic to their platoons than to RECAP or the department's policy changes, there was little the Unit could do to except to appeal up the chain of com-mand for assistance.

The Police Administration. The police administration was needed to gain even the grudging cooperation of the patrol force, as well as that of external entities unused to dealing with requests from line police offi-cers, such as the City Attorney's Office, the YMCA board, or the higher echelons of the MCDA. The intercession of the administra-tion was more effective with the independent entities than with the subordinate units nominally under its command.

RECAP was a bottom-up form of problem-solving, and the unit frequently had to fight internal and inter-agency battles that do not seem to have been obstacles to the Newport News officers. RECAP was a small experi-mental project, given a free hand but mini-mal resources, and introduced by an outsider (Sherman) through personal lines of commu-nication with the Chief of Police. The influ-ence of the Chief of Police was used with out-side interests, but sparingly, as the officers wanted to push the limits of what they (and other line officers) could accomplish by themselves. Within the department itself, the Chief's backing could be as much a liability as an asset: the Minneapolis department was still fighting the last rear-guard battles of a nine-year internal struggle for reform, in which Chief Bouza was seen almost from the first as "The Enemy" by the unionized rank-and-file officers.

Chief Bouza was a reform chief, brought in by Mayor Don Frazer to stabilize and trim a politicized department that had grown top-heavy with rank. His primary adversaries at the time of the RECAP Experiment were the civil-service Captains, who commanded the four precincts and the various divisions within the investigative division. The em-bodiment of the conservative, thin-blue-line status quo, they commanded the allegiance of the line officers and supervisors who had come into the department with those expec-tations, and they vehemently opposed inno-vations (including RECAP) which stemmed from the Chief's office. Essentially, the Cap-tains were the vestigial remains of the old politicized system, and they held the power of "No": they could not be removed from of-fice because of Civil Service rules. They pro-vided both a rationale for continued resis-tance and buffer against sanctions for non-performance, which encouraged patrol offi-cers to resist. At the same time, they ob-structed as much as possible the administra-tion's attempts to shine a brighter light on the patrol force's activities, effectively undermin-ing discipline. To bypass the logjam, Chief Bouza had appointed the first untenured (non-Civil Service) Inspector to command a precinct, a move which had been challenged by the Captains through a civil suit, and was pending in the courts during the entire Ex-periment.[16]

With the resolution of the power struggle between the Chief's office and the Captains pending in the courts, change in the depart-ment was essentially in abeyance, as every-one waited to see in which direction the fu-ture would be. The more progressive officers might be able to see a different future if the Chief's Inspectors plan prevailed, but those officers were for the time being under the command (and arguably at the mercy) of the Captains.

RECAP officers worked hard to overcome the patrol force's disdain of special units, a particularly difficult undertaking at a time when department staff levels were under authorized strength, and the patrol force saw itself as being bled dry by transfers to new specialty units, "taking bodies out of the pre-cincts." In a corporate climate where "special unit" was synonymous with working day shift Monday to Friday, RECAP won a meas-ure of respect for working during the eve-nings and on weekends, doing juvenile sweeps and other enforcement actions. Whenever they were on the air, they were available to assist patrol units as backup, and occasionally they took radio calls at their ad-dresses, freeing patrol units for other work.

And they worked hard to incorporate their work into that of the patrol force, sharing the lessons of problem-solving in training sessions and providing 911 call information on troublesome buildings identified by district squads. (In the latter case, they were constrained by the scientific requirements of the Experiment: they could not work on buildings outside of their assigned caseload, which occasionally generated some resentment.) Ultimately, their gains in this regard were modest, sufficient to retain their individual integrity but not enough to move the corporate mindset of the patrol division in a direction favorable to problem-solving.

Discussion

The issue of generalizability of results is important when evaluating the RECAP experience. At first glance, it would appear that the problems encountered by the Unit were the particular product of the Experiment, and of the unusual method of determining "problems" to work on. The modest gains of RECAP seem dim against the firmament of published accounts of the successes of other programs with more traditionally "logical" targeting. Nevertheless, the lessons of the RECAP Experiment may have greater utility for the field than first glance would indicate.

First, as police administrators have known for years, "every new program is successful." The professional magazines of police practitioners and the scholarly journals of their academic partners are filled with success stories, almost all of which have been told in the first flush of victory. Few recount the problems encountered along the way, except to triumphantly report that they were overcome, and few have the perspective of the year-long RECAP project. The programs that do take a longer view report a decline in a variety of areas: officer satisfaction, citizen satisfaction, displacement of crime, or the return of crime to the "reclaimed" area (e.g., Schwartz & McClarren, 1977: Wyckoff, 1988; for a review, see Buerger, 1993b).

Second, although it is a minor footnote to the main point, the *statistical* failure of RECAP initiatives occurred within an experimental framework that included both the learning curve of the first half of the year and the more mature problem-solving efforts of the later months. The latter were frustrated by a lack of coercive tools and supportive resources, which contributed to the difficulties of doing realistic problem-solving. The RECAP experiences highlighted to the civil authorities the need for more resources, and since the end of the experiment some have come into being and are facilitating current problem-solving efforts. RECAP officers lobbied long and hard for a City ordinance to license rental properties, and for a "wethouse" facility to take inebriated persons who were not in need of medical detoxification for alcohol (the only resource available during the Experiment was a medical facility run by the county). Both have since come into being, in part because of the documentation and groundwork provided by the Unit.

Third, as the community policing movement becomes more and more divined operationally as problem-solving (regardless of the deployment scheme used), and police departments open up more of their prioritization to citizen input, they may well end up with problem addresses similar to those worked on by RECAP. The recent past has been dominated by the impact of the drug trade on city neighborhoods, particularly crack houses. As a "problem," crack houses are amenable to resolution at the immediate local level by traditional law enforcement tactics (though the issue of displacement continues to be a thorny one). However, a growing body of literature is beginning to document—almost haphazardly, in footnotes and academic asides—that the citizenry bring other types of problems to the police which are not so easily resolved (e.g., Guyot, 1990).

The techniques of problem-solving are not yet adequate to all the tasks brought to it, and the rhetoric of both the problem-solving advocates and the community policing movement frequently oversells the possible gains to be had. Because both approaches require that the officers involved "buy in" to the premise, there is a strong emphasis on "celebrating the small successes" as a way of stimulating additional participation. Possible outcomes are promoted as if they were automatic, painless, and inevitable, when in fact they are not.

That is a double-edged sword: while the marketing of success may bring in new participants, it also sets them up for the failure of unfulfilled expectations. The unrealistic exhortations do not just fail to convince the "I'll just wait and see before I buy in" officers in a department. More dangerously, they can lead to the burnout and bail-out of formerly committed officers whose enthusiasm is a critical element of the successes, small or otherwise (most recently, see the final report on the eight LNOP projects sponsored by the Bureau of Justice Assistance [Sadd & Grink, 1993]).

Naturally, not every department now faces the same combination of political and economic factors that attended the RECAP Experiment, but many may conceivably face similar circumstances in the future. The lessons of the RECAP experience can help temper the unrealistic enthusiasm of the promotional industries which attend community- and problem-oriented policing (enthusiasm which is more or less falling on intentionally deaf ears anyway, at least in some quarters). Their inclusion in a training regimen, for instance, can help stimulate more realistic discussions of available resources, particularly those of information and political support. The prime benefit to others of the RECAP experience may well be to make the exercise of problem-solving more real, and to more fully engage the participation of police officers who are grounded in what *is*, not what ought to be.

Notes

Research for this article was supported in part by Grant #86-IJ-CX-0037 and a Graduate Research Fellowship, Grant #91-IJ-CX-0029, from the National Institute of Justice, whose support is gratefully acknowledged. The views expressed herein are those of the author alone, and neither represent nor purport to represent the official views of the United States Department of Justice, the Office of Justice Programs, the National Institute of Justice, the Crime Control Institute, the City of Minneapolis, or the Minneapolis Police Department. The access and encouragement provided by Lawrence W. Sherman is also greatly appreciated, as are the helpful comments of the anonymous reviewer.

1. As Eck and Spelman (1987) note, problem-*oriented* policing is a department-level commitment that involves all members of the department. Problem-solving can be done at an individual or precinct level without the full commitment of the department. As a practical matter, since development and dissemination of the techniques of problem-solving have evolved fairly slowly—resting primarily on the SARA (Search, Analysis, Response, Assessment) method developed from the Newport News experience (Eck & Spelman, 1987)—most police departments are not problem-*oriented*, though many now use problem-*solving* as a tactical tool.

2. "Experimental" in the police sense of "a trial, a try-out," as opposed to the researchers' definition of experimental though the evaluation of the Unit's work was indeed a randomized field experiment as below.

3. Sherman had eschewed subjective target identification for three reasons: (1) the potential criticism as discriminatory law enforcement; (2) its susceptibility to police officers' "pet peeves," to the exclusion of "major consumers of police resources or major sources of bloodshed"; and (3) the potential for selection bias in evaluations, resulting from "the picking of easier to solve problems" (Sherman, Buerger, & Gartin, 1989: 4-5). "Easier to solve" is perhaps a trifle harsh. "Easier to identify" might be a more accurate description of the efforts of officers in the other cities, which were either identified by traditional crime analysis methods or were highly localized geographically. For a more in-depth analysis, see Buerger 1993a: 69-71, note 3.

4. Several areas had numerous RECAP and control addresses cheek-by-jowl, even those independent of common ownership or management; to have selected RECAP targets on any basis other than that of individual buildings, e.g. by block or block-face, would have required far more extensive and time-consuming analysis. "Addresses" in this context were widely variable—including bridges; intersections; single-family homes; multi-story office complexes that occupied a full city block; and city parks as large as four square blocks—but each was thought to correspond generally to one identifiable place.

For the experiment, however, addresses that were bridges, intersections, parks, police stations, and hospitals were to be eliminated from consideration. Since the Crime Triangle hinges upon the *routine* intersection of offenders and targets of guardianship, the experimenters and the officers themselves all felt that a stable user population was essential to testing the officers' problem-solving skills. The user groups of parks, bridges, and intersections were believed to be too irregular, too diffuse for interaction to take place over time, and there were unresolved issues of guardianship that attend what was essentially open, public space. Other locations, including addresses in the notorious vice-ridden "E Block," and the 3-story indoor mall of City Center, were disqualified because they were already the focus of additional police attention. In addition, intersections create special problems concerning boundary definition (Buerger, Cohn, and Petrosino, 1988), and the widely variable size of parks was thought to be as problematic as their continuously-changing, sporadic user groups. Both police stations and hospitals were known as locations to which people went (or were taken) from locations at which crimes occurred, rather than criminogenic locations in their own right.

Although the original plan for residential addresses had been to identify chronic apartments, the computer consultants who worked on the project advised that such analysis would far outstrip the computer resources available, and the plan was amended to the level of street addresses rather than apartments.

5. The Crime Control Institute compiled and analyzed records of all police calls for service for the period December 15, 1985, through December 14, 1986, and found that approximately three percent of all addresses in the city had produced 50 percent of all calls for police service.

6. The four buildings of this complex were two active RECAP addresses, including one high-rise tower which was the second worst residential address in the entire city in terms of calls for police service, and two more in the Control group.

7. An earlier City Council survey which solicited homeowners about their concerns revealed that many of the City's middle-class homeowners were considering moving to the suburbs within the next five years. One of the main reasons given for their consideration of this option was the crime/disorder situation in the center city. One direct consequence of the survey was the creation by the Mayor of the joint police-and community organizers S.A.F.E. teams.

8. The County's response was that the facility first had to provide the programs, and then would receive the additional money; the per diem was money paid for contracted service, not seed money to develop those services.

9. The information was nominally protected, and came to RECAP through private, covert connections within the county agency. A variety of people at many levels were equally displeased with the situation at the facility, but they were stymied by internal Welfare regulations, and in any case were unable to take an advocate's role. They were, however, more than glad to be able to assist anyone who seemed to be in a position to make some changes.

It is perhaps a commentary on the general state of protected information that the owner accepted without a murmur the fact that the police had access to such data. While it may reflect on the owner's personal capacities, it is probably more an indication of his ignorance of the law. The ethical dilemma here is similar to the "Dirty Harry Problem" (Klockars, 1980): the law's primary purpose is sound, but in this case it stood in opposition to the primary purpose of the agency, to provide decent shelter and care for disadvantaged persons. In this case, protection of the data was integrally linked to a prolonged failure to deliver services to those clients.

10. The initial suggestions were couched in positive terms, such as "If you do X and Y, which you can do without additional cost by changing your practices, you'll be closer to eligibility."

11. Though it was usually couched in more careful and sometimes legalistic language, one of the managers of a national chain store had put the issue that bluntly to RECAP early in the negotiations over implementing the shoplifting program. The commander responded by obtaining the public records of the store's taxes paid on the south-side store, then dividing it proportionally according to the general disbursements in the City budget. The result was a minuscule amount earmarked for police services, and by the time the shoplifting conference was held to launch the experimental shoplifting program, that particular objection was moot.

12. When RECAP officers began working with the Downtown Security Council, a private con-

sortium of retail stores' security officers, in the wake of the shoplifting conference, they were impressed with the extensive database that already existed on known professional shoplifters. Although it was proprietary information, and all involved knew that the private and public sectors could not legally trade information, it was clear that their informational network was for more sophisticated than the RECAP shoplifting database that had been proposed. Although RECAP's had a specific jurisdictional and legal focus and purpose, the private one had a greater wealth of detail over space and time.

13. The case is curious in two respects. For all their denial that the drunks and street people were a problem worth taking any preventive measures about, the librarians called frequently about the drunks in the neighborhood. An abandoned house at the rear of the branch library was used by the locals as an informal "liquid picnic" grounds, and that house was also a RECAP address . . . primarily on the strength of complaints called in by the librarians.

14. It did not stop the officers from trying, however. When several of the team members went to an associate's wedding in Maryland, they took the opportunity to go to the Washington offices of the Housing and Urban Development department to make their case. The officers described getting the run-around, and the visit ultimately produced no tangible effects at the MCDA addresses (it was a change in MCDA management rather than a change of heart or mind at HUD that brought new directions), but the officers did try.

15. A recent Hennepin County study both challenges this viewpoint, and partially explains and validates it. Analysis of 1990 Census data revealed that "Recent migrants to Hennepin County are more likely to be poor and to wind up in jail and homeless shelters than those who have lived in the county for more than five years . . . But it also showed they are no more likely than long-term residents to be on welfare . . . The study made no racial comparisons" though it noted that 80 percent of the migrants from 1985 to 1990 were white, and "drew no conclusions as to how many migrants move to the county to take advantage of public assistance programs" (Draper 1993).

16. The courts ruled in favor of the police administration, and all four precincts and the investigative bureaus are now commanded by Inspectors who serve at the discretion of the Chief of Police. All but two of the old Captains had resigned at the time of this writing, and though the rank remains because of Civil Service, it is considerably reduced in both numbers and stature.

References

Buerger, M. (ed.). *The Crime Prevention Casebook: Securing High Crime Locations*. Washington, DC: Crime Control Institute.

—— (1993a). *Convincing the Recalcitrant: Reexamining the Minneapolis RECAP Experiment*. Unpublished dissertation. Ann Arbor, MI: University Microfilms, Inc.

—— (1993b). "The Challenge of Reinventing Police and Community." In D. Weisburd and C. Uchida (eds.), *Police Innovation and Control of the Police: Problems of Law, Order, and Community*. (pp. 103-124). New York, NY: Springer-Verlag.

Buerger, M., E. Cohn, and A. Petrosino (1988). "Defining the Hot Spots of Crime: Minneapolis." Crime Control Institute, internal memo. Accepted for a forthcoming book edited by D. Weisburd and J. Eck, in preparation.

Cohen, L. and M. Felson (1979). "Social Change and Crime Rate Trends: A Routine Activity Approach." *American Sociological Review*, 44: 588-608.

Cordner, G. (1985). "The Baltimore County Citizen Oriented Police Enforcement (COPE) Project: Final Evaluation." Paper presented to the American Society of Criminology, San Diego, CA (November).

Draper, N. (1993). "'Welfare Magnet' Theory is Disputed. New Hennepin Arrivals Studied." *Minneapolis Star Tribune*. Minneapolis, MN. December 21.

Eck, J. and W. Spelman (1987). *Problem Solving: Problem-Oriented Policing in Newport News*. Police Executive Forum. Washington, DC: National Institute of Justice.

Gainesville (FL) Police Department (1986). *The Convenience Store Robberies in Gainesville, Florida; An Intervention Strategy by the Gainesville Police Department*. Gainesville, FL: Author.

Gilsinan, J. (1989). "They Is Clowning Tough: 911 and the Social Construction of Reality." *Criminology*, 27: 329-344.

Goldstein, H. (1979). "Improving Policing: A Problem-Oriented Approach." *Crime and Delinquency*, 25: 236-258.

—— (1990). *Problem-Oriented Policing*. Philadelphia, PA: Temple University Press.

Goldstein, H. and C. Susmilch (1981). *The Problem-Oriented Approach To Improving Police Service: A Description of the Project and an Elaboration of the Concept*. Madison, WI.

—— (1982a). *The Drinking-Driver in Madison: A Study of the Problem and the Community's Response*. Madison, WI.

—— (1982b). *The Repeat Sexual Offender in Madison: A Memorandum on the Problem and the Community's Response*. Madison, WI.

—— (1982c). *The Problem-Oriented Approach To Improving Police Service: A Report and Some Reflections on Two Case Studies*. Madison, WI.

Green, L. (1993). *Treating Deviant Places: A Case Study Examination of the Beat Health Program in Oakland, California*. Unpublished dissertation. Ann Arbor, MI: University Microfilms, Inc.

Greenwood, P., J. Petersilia and J. Chaiken (1977). *The Criminal Investigation Process*. Lexington, MA: Heath.

Guyot, D. (1991). *Policing As Though People Matter*. Philadelphia, PA: Temple University Press.

Hennessey, M., and D. Foster. (1990). *Minneapolis SAFE Program: Final Evaluation Report*. (Budget and Finance Department, Minneapolis Finance Department.) Minneapolis, MN: City of Minneapolis.

Klockars, C. (1980). "The Dirty Harry Problem." *The Annals*, 452 (November 1980): 33-47. In C. Klockars and S. Mastrofski (eds.), *Thinking About Police: Contemporary Readings*, Second edition. (pp. 413-423). New York, NY: McGraw-Hill, 1991.

Klockars, C. and S. Mastrofski (eds.). (1991). *Thinking About Police: Contemporary Readings*, Second edition. New York, NY: McGraw-Hill.

Leinfelder, J. (1988) "The Gary Syndrome." *Twin Cities Reader*. January 27. Minneapolis. pp. 10-12.

McElroy, J, C. Cosgrove, and S. Sadd (1993). *Community Policing: The CPOP in New York*. Newbury Park, CA: Sage Publications.

Percy, S., and E. Scott (1985). *Demand Processing and Performance in Public Service Agencies*. University, AL: University of Alabama Press.

Petersilia, J. (1989) "Implementing Randomized Experiments: Lessons From BJA's Intensive Supervision Project." *Evaluation Review*, 13: 435-458.

Pierce, G. S. Spaar, and L. Briggs, IV (1984). *The Character of Police Work*.

Sadd, S. and R. Grink (1993). *Issues in Community Policing: An Evaluation of Eight Innovative Neighborhood-Oriented Policing Projects*. Report submitted to the National Institute of Justice. Volume 1. New York, NY: Vera Institute of Justice.

Schwartz, A. and S. Clarren (1977). *The Cincinnati Team Policing Experiment: A Summary Report*. Washington, DC: Police Foundation.

Sherman, L. (1987). *Repeat Calls to Police in Minneapolis*. Washington, DC: Crime Control Institute.

Sherman, L. et al. (1988). *Policing Repeat Calls: The Minneapolis RECAP Experiment*. Preliminary Report to the National Institute of Justice. Washington, DC: Crime Control Institute.

—— (1989). *Repeat Call Address Policing: The Minneapolis RECAP Experiment*. Final report to the National Institute of Justice. Washington, DC: Crime Control Institute.

Spelman, W. (1992) *Criminal Careers of Public Places*. Final Report to the National Institute of Justice. Executive Summary. Washington, DC: NIJ.

Wilson, J. and G. Kelling (1982). "Broken Windows: The Police and Neighborhood Safety." *The Atlantic Monthly* (March): 29-38.

Wycoff, M. (1988). "The Benefits of Community Policing: Evidence and Conjecture." In J. Greene and S. Mastrofski (eds.), *Community Policing: Rhetoric or Reality* (pp. 103-120). New York, NY: Praeger.

Implications for Service Delivery. Boston, MA: Center for Applied Social Research, Northeastern University.

Reiss, A., Jr. (1971). *The Police and the Public*. New Haven, CT: Yale University Press.

Reuss-Ianni, E. (1983). *Two Cultures of Policing: Street Cops and Management Cops*. New Brunswick, NJ: Transaction Books.

Rosenbaum, D. (ed.). (1986). *Community Crime Prevention: Does It Work?* Sage Criminal Justice System Annuals, Vol. 22. Beverly Hills, CA: Sage Publications.

Reprinted from Michael Buerger, "The Problems of Problem-Solving" in *American Journal of Police* 13(3): 1-36. Copyright © 1994 by *American Journal of Police*. Reprinted by permission. ✦

12

The Kansas City Gun Experiment

Lawrence W. Sherman,
James W. Shaw, and
Dennis P. Rogan

This article focuses on a tactical and enforcement-oriented approach to policing, often called directed patrol. In this case, directed, or targeted, patrols were deployed experimentally in Kansas City to see whether gun seizures could be increased and whether gun-related crimes could be reduced. These kinds of directed patrols, focused either on specific types of incidents such as gun crimes or on geographic "hot spots," are used frequently today. They are also sometimes associated with the "zero tolerance" and "quality of life" forms of policing popularized recently by New York City. See what you think of the results of this Kansas City study, including whether it passes the cost-benefit test. More generally, what do you see as the pros and cons of directed patrol versus community policing?

Handgun crime is increasing rapidly throughout the nation,[1] especially in inner-city areas where youth homicide rates have skyrocketed.[2] While some scholars argue that more gun carrying by law-abiding citizens may be the best deterrent to gun violence,[3] others find little evidence to support that view[4] but much more evidence that increases in gun availability produce increases in gun homicides.[5] Still others argue that it is not the total number of guns in circulation that increases gun violence, but the carrying of guns in high-risk places at high-risk times.[6] This argument suggests the hypothesis that greater enforcement of existing laws against carrying concealed weapons could reduce gun crime. But this hypothesis had never been tested until the Kansas City gun experiment.

The experiment developed out of the first Federal grant awarded under the Bureau of Justice Assistance (BJA) "Weed and Seed" program in 1991. The Kansas City (Missouri) Police Department (KCPD) was given wide latitude in planning its Weed and Seed strategy. Shortly after the BJA award to the KCPD, the National Institute of Justice (NIJ) awarded the University of Maryland a grant to evaluate the Kansas City effort. This timing allowed the police and the researchers to collaborate in planning a focused program with a strong research design.

This Research in Brief explains the study's methodology and key findings, analyzes the reasons for the findings, and concludes with a discussion of policy implications.

Study Design

The program was based on the theory that additional patrols would increase gun seizures, which, in turn, would reduce gun crime. Two possible mechanisms were suggested: deterrence and incapacitation. The deterrence theory assumed that if police took guns away, illegal gun carriers would become less likely to carry them in the area. The incapacitation theory assumed that if enough potential gun criminals in the area had their guns seized, they would be unable to commit gun crimes—at least for as long as it took them to acquire a new gun.

Neither of these theories could be directly examined within the limits of the study. Rather, the evaluation study focused on the basic hypothesis that gun seizures and gun crime would be inversely related. From the outset, the project team recognized that confirmation of the hypothesis would not *prove* that more gun seizures result in reduced gun crime. The design could not eliminate all competing explanations that could be suggested for the results. But if an inverse correlation between gun seizures and gun crime were found, it could suggest the value of further research and development. It could also support a policy of extending the patrols, regardless of the exact reason for their effectiveness.

Since the target area, patrol beat 144, already selected for the "Weed and Seed" grant had the second highest number of driveby shootings of any patrol beat in 1991, the police and academic team designing the experiment chose the reduction of gun crime as the principle objective of the program. The program budget for police overtime and extra patrol cars was then dedicated to getting guns off the street as cost-effectively as possible.

While the evaluation concentrated primarily on this first phase of the Weed and Seed grant, additional findings from the evaluation show what happened when the initial funding of patrols stopped (first half of 1993) and continuation funding allowed resumption of the patrols (second half of 1993).[7]

Target Area

The target beat is an 80-by-10 block area with a 1991 homicide rate of 177 per 100,000 persons, or about 20 times the national average.[8] In addition to its 8 homicides in 1991, there were 14 rapes, 72 armed robberies, 222 aggravated assaults (142 with firearms), and a total of 349 violent felonies—close to one a day. Exhibit 2 shows that the beat's population is almost entirely nonwhite, with very low property values for the predominantly single-family detached homes. Home-ownership rates are very high; more than two-thirds of all occupants own their homes.

Exhibit 1
Firearm Offenses/Guns Siezed per 1,000 Persons

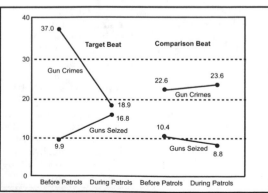

Exhibit 2
1991 Characteristics of Target and Comparison Beats

Characteristic	Target Beat (144)	Comparison Beat (242)
Population	4,528	8,142
% Female	53 %	56 %
% Under 25	38 %	41 %
Median Age	32	31
% Nonwhite	92 %	85 %
% Age 25+ and High School Graduates	53 %	73 %
Residential Square Blocks	80	150
Population Density Per Mile	7,075	4,308
% Single Family Housing	84 %	93 %
% Land Parcels Vacant	34 %	14 %
% Houses Owner-Occupied	63 %	71 %
Median Years Owned	12	10
Median Parcel Value	$14,181	$23,953
1991 Firearms-Related Crimes	183	252
(Rate Per 1,000)	40	31
1991 Shots Fired Incidents	86	120
(Rate Per 1,000)	19	15
1991 Drive by Shootings	24	25
(Rate Per 1,000)	5	3
1991 Homicides	8	11
(Rate Per 1,000)	1.77	1.35

Exhibit 3
Kansas City, Police Reporting Areas

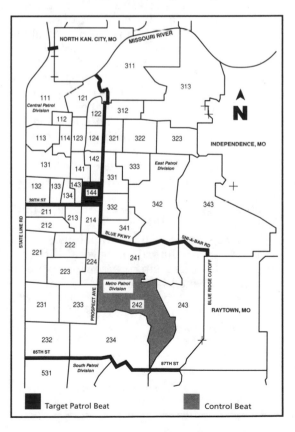

Because the program was restricted to one target patrol beat—see exhibit 3—the planning team selected a before-after comparison design. The primary basis for selecting patrol beat 242 in the Metro Patrol District was its almost identical number of driveby shootings[9] in 1991; 25 driveby shootings in the control beat compared to 24 in beat 144.

Exhibit 2 also shows that the comparison beat, beat 242, is similar to the target beat in many ways. The major difference is that beat 242 has almost twice the population and three times the land area, including a park. The comparison beat also has slightly higher housing prices. Both beats have substantial volumes of violent crime, which provided reliable statistics for assessing trends over time.

Patrol Operations

For 29 weeks, from July 7, 1992, to January 27, 1993, the Kansas City Police Department focused extra patrol attention on gun crime "hot spots"[10] in the target area. The hot spot locations were identified by a University of Maryland computer analysis of all gun crimes in the area. The extra patrol was provided in rotation by officers from Central Patrol in a pair of two-officer cars working on overtime under the BJA-funded Weed and Seed program. Four officers thus worked 6 hours of overtime each night from 7 p.m. to 1 a.m., 7 days a week, for a total of 176 nights, with two officers working an additional 24 nights, for a total of 200 nights, 4,512 officer-hours, and 2,256 patrol car-hours. They focused exclusively on gun detection through proactive patrol and did not respond to calls for service.

While no special efforts were made to limit police activities in the comparison area, beat 242, there were no funds available for extra patrol time in that area. Several different strategies for increasing gun seizures were attempted in beat 144 (see "Trial and Error in Gun Detection"), but Federal funds for extra police patrol were expended entirely upon the overtime patrols.

Trial and Error in Gun Detection

In early 1992, the success of directed patrols in Kansas City gun crime hot spots was preceded by two apparently unsuccessful attempts to detect guns. These programs are described below.

Door-to-door gun patrol. The first attempt was a comprehensive program of door-to-door visits to all 1,259 residences in the 80-block target beat 144, informing residents about a new crackdown on gun carrying and asking them to call an anonymous gun tip "hotline" if they knew of anyone carrying a gun illegally. The officers knocked on 1,410 doors in 173 hours of regular patrol time from March to May 1992, speaking with an adult at 72 percent of the occupied residences[11]—one of the highest success rates in any door-to-door policing program.[12] Of the 786 adult residents to whom the police explained the "gun tips" program, 96 percent (756) said they would be willing to call the hotline, and many were extremely enthusiastic. Unfortunately, only two calls were received. The door-to-door gun tip results reveal an important limitation on the police-citizen "partnership" concept of community-based policing. The fact that the officers were white and the area was predominantly black may have made a difference. But the fact that two-thirds of the persons later found carrying guns in the beat reside outside the area may have been more important.[13] Residents of high crime areas may simply not have all the information police need to deal with many crime problems. However, the door-to-door program may have produced beneficial results. Exhibit 5 (see page 7) shows that the number of gun crimes in the target beat began to fall sharply in June 1992, the month after the 10-week program of door-to-door visits was completed. Gun crimes continued to decrease up to and after the start of the hot spots patrols. The fact that the number of guns seized in beat 144 declined in the second quarter of 1992[14] eliminates the high-risk gun seizure theory as an explanation of the June decrease in gun crime. The principal remaining explanations are either the deterrent effect of making all the door-to-door visits (with word of mouth spreading about a police crackdown on gun carrying), or simply random fluctuation that is evident elsewhere in the time series for the target beat—such as in the August to October 1991 period (see exhibit 5). Moreover, the second author found a drop in total serious crimes in the target beat that also began in June 1992, a finding consistent with other door-to-door patrol experiments.[15] Thus, even if door-to-door visits failed to increase gun seizures, they may still have been useful for preventing gun crime and other serious crime.

Body language training. A second unsuccessful attempt to detect guns in Kansas ☞

☞ City was a method that had worked well in New York City. Detective Robert Gallagher (retired) of the New York City Police Department trained a group of Central Patrol Division police officers in the body language "cues" he used to recognize when someone was carrying a concealed weapon. These indicators, such as frequent touching of the waist to ensure that a gun stuffed in a belt will not fall down a pants leg, helped Gallagher make more than 1,000 arrests for carrying concealed weapons. But using the same methods, Gallagher was unable to spot any gun carriers during several nights on patrol in the most violent areas of Kansas City in June 1992.

This difference may reflect the enormous difference in density between the two cities: New York has 30 times as many people in about the same amount of land. Therefore, in New York most people walk and use public transit; in Kansas City, most people travel by car. The Kansas City officers trained to use these methods did report a few cases in which the techniques led to detection of a concealed weapon, but only 9 percent of guns were found in pedestrian checks.[16]

Despite these results in Kansas City, both gun tips hotlines and body language cues may still work well in other cities. The social and physical characteristics of cities vary widely, and these methods may work better in different kinds of communities. Most important, the Kansas City experience demonstrates the importance of trial and error in any city's efforts to get guns off the streets. Given the complexity of the problem, it is unrealistic to expect the first method tried to be an automatic success. ✦

Measures Used

Because the extra patrol hours were federally funded, separate bookkeeping was required to document the time. In addition, an onsite University of Maryland evaluator accompanied the officers on 300 hours of hot spots patrol and coded every shift activity narrative for patrol time and enforcement in and out of the area. Property room data on guns seized, computerized crime reports, calls for service data, and arrest records were analyzed for both areas under the study. No attempt was made to conduct victimization surveys, although a before and after survey of the target and comparison beats was conducted to measure citizen perceptions of the program.[17]

Traffic Stops and Reasonable Suspicion

Many lay people—and even some police—underestimate police powers to search for guns. When a police officer can articulate a reason for believing that a gun crime may be about to occur, the U.S. Supreme Court has ruled that the officer may pad down the outside of the suspect's clothing to check for guns (Terry v. Ohio, 392 U.S. 1, 1968). This ruling does not give police the right to stop cars or persons in an arbitrary manner. But it does imply that when police stop people for other legally sound reasons, they may find further evidence that justifies proceeding to frisk a suspect and to search the passenger compartment of the car.[18] When one considers that traffic stops are the leading cause of police murders in the line of duty, the logic of this policy may be clearer, as the following true case study from Indianapolis implies:

> An officer stopped a car in a high crime neighborhood for running a stop sign. As the officer approached the driver, he saw the driver reaching into a belt pack. He then directed the driver to get out of the car so he could pat down the belt pack. Feeling hard metal inside, the officer opened the pack and found a small revolver.

The evidentiary standard of reasonable suspicion is necessarily lower than the standard of probable cause, which is the level of evidence required to justify an arrest. In the case study, the driver could not have been arrested for reaching into his belt pack. But the behavior did provide a basis for articulating why the officer thought the driver might have had a gun. Only after the gun was actually found was there sufficient evidence to make an arrest for carrying a concealed weapon without a permit. But the articulable suspicion allowed the officer to detect the hidden evidence in a lawful and constitutional manner.

Other methods used in Kansas City included looking into the car for guns in plain view on the seat or the floor and looking for body language of pedestrians for telltale signs of a gun stuffed inside a suspect's clothing. Consent searches of glove compartments or car trunks are also legal, as long as the consent is truly voluntary. ✦

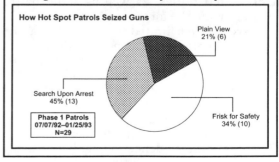

How Hot Spot Patrols Seized Guns

Plain View 21% (6)

Search Upon Arrest 45% (13)

Frisk for Safety 34% (10)

Phase 1 Patrols 07/07/92–01/25/93 N=29

Data Analyses

The data were examined several different ways. The primary analyses compared all 29 weeks of the phase 1 patrol program (July 7, 1992, through January 25, 1993, when the phase 1 funding for the special patrols expired) to the 29 weeks preceding phase 1, using difference of means tests. Other analyses added all of 1991 and 1993. The 1993 data included 6 months with no overtime patrols and phase 2 overtime patrols for 6 months in the second half of 1993. These analyses thus covered six-month periods, two of which had the program and four of which did not. The citizen survey analysis compared the amount and direction of before-after differences in attitudes within beats.

Both shorter and longer periods around the program were also examined for overall impact. Autoregressive moving averages (ARIMA) models were used to compare gun crime in the 52 weeks before and after the patrols in both the target and comparison beats. Standard chi-square tests were used to compare 1991 versus 1992 differences in gun crimes for all four quarters, as well as both half-years, in both target and comparison beats. No matter how the data were examined, the results were similar.

The Program in Action

Patrol Activity

Officers reported spending 3.27 car-hours of the 12 car-hours per night actually patrolling the target area (27 percent), for a total of 1,218 officer-hours of potential gun detection and visible patrol presence in the area. The officers thus spent 70 percent of their time processing arrests and performing other patrol-related duties, as well as some patrol work outside the target area.

Despite their limited time in the area, the officers generated a lot of activity. Both in and out of target beat 144, the directed patrols issued 1,090 traffic citations, conducted 948 car checks and 532 pedestrian checks, and made 170 State or Federal arrests and 446 city arrests, for an average of 1 police intervention for every 40 minutes per patrol car. There is some evidence that activity usually

does at the onset of colder weather.[19] The average number of car checks made per day, for example, began at a high of 6.5 in July, and dropped to a low of 3.2 in November, but time in the target area, miles driven, and traffic citations issued did not change substantially during the first 6-month period.

The actual techniques the officers used to find guns varied, from frisks and searches incident to arrest on other charges to safety frisks associated with car stops for traffic violations (see exhibit 3).[20] Every arrest for carrying concealed weapons had to be approved for adequate articulable suspicion with a supervisory detective's signature.

Results of Increased Patrol

Gun Seizures

The federally funded hot spots patrol officers found 29 guns in addition to the 47 guns seized in the target beat by other police units during phase 1 (second half of 1992), increasing total guns found in the beat by 65 percent over the previous 6-month period and almost tripling the number of guns found during car checks. The ratio of guns seized to directed patrol time in the target area was 1 gun per 156 hours, but the ratio to time actually spent in the area (and not processing arrests) was 1 gun per 84 hours and 1 gun per 28 traffic stops. Overall, there was an increase from 46 guns seized in beat 144 in the first half of 1992 to 76 seized in the last half.

Once the guns were seized, most of them were then permanently removed from the streets. Not all of the guns were carried illegally; about one-fifth (14) of the total 76 guns seized in the target area during phase 1, and 4 of the 29 guns seized by the extra hot spot patrols were confiscated by police for "safekeeping," a practice followed by many police agencies when officers have reason to believe gun violence may otherwise occur. While guns taken for this reason are usually returned to their registered owners upon application at the property room, the process can take several days to several weeks to complete. Illegally carried guns, on the other hand, are destroyed by Kansas City police and not returned to circulation.

Gun Crime

There were 169 gun crimes in the target area in the 29 weeks prior to the hot spot patrols, but only 86 gun crimes in the 29 weeks during the phase 1 patrols—a 49 percent decrease, with 83 fewer gun crimes (see exhibit 4). This change was statistically significant in both a test of differences of means (t-test) for that period, and in an ARIMA model covering an even longer before and after period.[21]

Exhibit 4
*Gun Crimes Before and During
Phase 1 by Beat*

Beat	Before 12/17/91-7/6/92	During 7/7/92-1/25/93	% Change
Target (144)	169	86	- 49% *
Comparison (242)	184	192	+ 4%
Adjoining Target			
141	76	57	- 25%
142	106	84	- 21%
143	39	44	+13%
213	143	158	+10%
214	104	138	+33%
331	143	175	+22%
332	153	160	+5%
All Kansas City	4,359	4,287	- 2%

* Statistically significant "t" value p < .05. Before and during weekly gun crime means were tested for significant differences in all areas displayed. Only the target area showed enough change for it to be unlikely a result of chance or random fluctuation.

The comparison beat 242 showed a slight drop in guns seized, from 85 in the first half to 72 in the second half of 1992. It also showed a slight increase in gun crimes, from 184 in the 29 weeks before the program to 192 gun crimes in the 29 weeks during the program (see exhibit 5). Neither change was statistically significant.[22]

In addition, while gun crime dropped in beat 144, none of the seven contiguous beats showed any significant change in gun crime, as exhibit 5 shows for the 29 weeks before and after tests. Both the increases and decreases in gun crime found across the contiguous beats were small enough to have occurred by chance. The 52 weeks before and after special tests (ARIMA models) showed significant reductions in gun crimes in beats 141 and 143.

Exhibit 5
*Total Offenses With Firearms by Month in
Target and Comparison Beats*

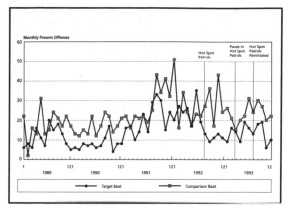

Driveby Shootings

Driveby shootings in beat 144 dropped significantly during both 6-month periods of hot spots patrols (second halves of 1992 and 1993) compared to the 6-month periods without them. The same analysis showed no differences in the beats surrounding 144 and an increase in the comparison beat 242.[23]

Homicides

Homicides were also significantly lower in beat 144 during the two 6-month program periods than in other 6-month periods, from 1991 through 1993, while there were no significant differences in homicides across those periods in comparison beat 242.

Other Crimes

Neither total calls for police service, calls about violence, property or disorder crimes, total offense reports, nor property or violent offenses showed any effect of the increased patrol. There were no changes in these measures in either the target or comparison area. The target area hot spots patrols focused specifically on guns, and their effects were limited to gun crimes.

Community Perceptions

Community surveys before and after the intensive patrols showed that respondents in the target area, beat 144, became less fearful of crime and more satisfied with their neighborhood than respondents in the comparison beat 242. Target area respondents also perceived less physical and social disorder after phase 1. While target beat respondents were marginally more likely to say that the shooting problem had gotten better and no more likely to say that overall crime problems had improved, they were significantly more likely than comparison area respondents to say that neighborhood drug problems had gotten better.

When the experimental period was over, crimes involving firearms gradually increased again for 5 months in the first half of 1993, consistent with the typical police crackdowns pattern.[24] When the phase 2 patrols began in the second half of 1993, gun crimes dropped again, although not as consistently as phase 1.

Analysis of the Gun Crime Reduction

Assuming that there are 100,000 handguns in Kansas City,[25] the seizure of 29 handguns may be considered a drop in the bucket, an implausible reason for any significant reduction in gun crime (Exhibit 6 indicates how gun crime was defined and recorded). But there are at least three plausible theories for how the patrols may have caused a reduction in gun crime: high-risk places, high-risk offenders, and deterrence.

Exhibit 6
Gun Crimes

"Gun crimes" are defined as any offense report in which the use of a gun by an offender is reported. The data presented in this report include the following offense types reported as gun crimes on one or more occasions in either the target or comparison area during the year before and after the initiation of the hot spot patrols (July 7, 1991, to July 6, 1993):

Offense Type	Beat 144 (Target Area)	Beat 242 (Comparison Area)
Criminal Homicide	10	30
Rape	6	5
Armed Robbery and Attempts	124	222
Aggravated Assault	293	409
Aggravated Assault on Police	3	1
Burglary	0	1
Simple Assault (gun pointed)	1	0
Destruction of Property	18	38
Kidnapping	0	1
Casualty injury (firearm)	2	4
Suicide and Attempts	1	1
Totals	468	712

High-Risk Places

One scholar has argued that most guns are not at immediate risk of being used in crime.[26] Guns seized by police in high gun crime areas at high crime times may be far more at risk of imminent use in crimes than the average handgun. Another researcher estimated that for each new cohort of 100 guns, 33 uses of those guns in crime are reported.[27] Those uses could be heavily concentrated among the small fraction of that cohort that are carried in gun crime hot spots.

Still, criminals may easily replace guns seized by police. Connecting the 29 guns seized to the 83 gun crimes prevented may thus require a further assumption that gun crime is more likely to be a spontaneous incident of opportunity than a planned event and is relatively infrequent in the career of any criminal. The contrary assumption—that criminals with guns commit many gun offenses in a 6-month period in the same small area—may be harder to defend. Even if the suspects who lose their guns to police quickly replace them, the opportune circumstances for the crimes prevented by the guns being seized might not recur as quickly.

High-Risk Offenders

Some gun carriers, of course, may be far more frequent gun users than others. If 10 percent of the 170 State and Federal arrests by directed patrols captured high frequency gun users and if the arrestees spent the next 6 months in jail on serious charges from outstanding warrants, then the program's incapacitation of those 17 offenders alone may have prevented 83 gun crimes—a not implausible average of 5 gun offenses each or less than 1 per month.

Deterrence of gun carrying may be an even more plausible cause of reduced gun crime. The 29 extra gun seizures, 1,434 traffic and pedestrian stops, or the total of 3,186 arrests, traffic citations, and other police encounters, could have specifically deterred potential gun criminals who encountered police. Visibility of police encounters in the hot spots may have also created a general deterrent effect among those who were not checked by police. This argument appears plausible enough to conclude that directed patrols can reduce gun crime, regardless of the theoretical rationale.

Conclusion

The most important conclusion from this evaluation is that police can increase the number of guns seized in high gun crime areas at relatively modest cost. Directed patrol around gun crime hot spots is about three times more cost-effective than normal uniformed police activity citywide, on average, in getting guns off the street.[28] The raw numbers of guns seized in each beat may not be impressively large, but the impact of even small increases in guns seized in decreasing the percentage of gun crimes can be substantial. If a city wants to adopt this policy in a high gun crime area, this experiment proves that it can be successfully implemented.

There is still much more to be learned, however, about the entire process of gun detection and seizure by police. Until recently, it has not been a priority of either police administrators or researchers to understand or encourage the factors leading to gun seizures. Little is known about differences across police agencies or police officers in their respective rates of gun detection, and it is not even known how many more guns could be detected if patrol officers generally were given more direction and training in how to locate guns in the course of their routine activities. What is clear from the Kansas City gun experiment is that a focus on gun detection, with freedom from answering calls for service, can make regular beat officers working on overtime very productive.

Officer Safety

A related conclusion is that gun detection does not require large tactical operations. Some police agencies require three to five patrol cars to be present at gun patrol car stops in high gun crime areas, primarily for reasons of officer safety. Yet in the Kansas City experiment, with 20 times the national homicide rate, a pair of two-officer cars working independently was able to increase gun seizures by 65 percent. No gun attacks on officers were reported in the course of these patrols, and no one was injured. Rather than assigning three to five cars to one traffic stop, police agencies could disperse those cars over a wider area to obtain even greater numbers of guns seized from the same investment in police patrols. Whether that will increase the risk of officer injury in the long run is impossible to say. But whatever the level of that risk, the Kansas City officers were willing to assume it without hesitation.

Cautions

Now that police know how to increase gun seizures in target areas, the key question is whether that policy will reduce gun crime without total displacement. The Kansas City evidence suggests that the policy can reduce gun crime without local displacement. Only repeated tests of the hypothesis, however, will show whether the policy can predictably produce that result. Previous NIJ research has also reported unreplicated findings,[29] only to have replications show more mixed results.[30] The need for replications is a major caution for interpreting any research results.

Intensified gun patrols also need other cautions. They could conceivably have negative effects on police-community relations or be a waste of time and money. They could also pose great risks to officer safety. They could even provoke more crime by making youths subjected to traffic stops more defiant of conventional society.[31]

All of these hazards are possible but unknown. The tradeoff is the well-known risk of gun violence, which is extremely high in many inner cities and still rising. Firearm crimes in Indianapolis, for example, have risen by 220 percent since 1988. In October 1994, the Indianapolis Police Department implemented a citywide policy implied by the Kansas City results in gun crime hot spots. Whether a citywide program can succeed in doing what Kansas City did in a small area is an important next question for both research and policy.

Notes

1. Rand, Michael, *Guns and Crime*, Washington, D.C.: Bureau of Justice Statistics, 1994.

2. Reiss, Albert J., Jr., and Jeffrey A. Roth, eds., *Understanding and Preventing Violence*,

Washington, D.C.: National Academy of Sciences, 1993.

3. Kleck, Gary, *Point Blank: Guns and Violence in America*, New York: Aldine de Gruyter, 1991.

4. Cook, Phillip, "The Technology of Personal Violence," In M. Tonry, ed., *Crime and Justice: A Review of Research*, Chicago: University Press, 1991.

5. McDowall, David, "Firearm Availability and Homicide Rates in Detroit, 1951-1986," *Social Forces*, (69)(1991): 1085-1101.

6. Wilson, James Q., "Just Take Away Their Guns: Forget Gun Control," *New York Times*, March 20, 1994:46-47.

7. Data on guns seized by beat, however, are only available for the first phase.

8. Shaw, James W., "Community Policing Against Crime: Violence and Firearms," Ph.D. dissertation, Department of Criminal Justice and Criminology, University of Maryland at College Park, 1994.

9. As defined by the KCPD Perpetrator Information Center, which classifies driveby shootings from an ongoing review of incident reports and produces monthly statistics by beat that are employed in all analyses of those events discussed in this report.

10. Sherman, Lawrence W., Patrick R. Gartin, and Michael E. Buerger, "Hot Spots of Predatory Crime: Routine Activities and the Criminology of Place," *Criminology*, (27) (1989): 27-55.

11. See Shaw, 240.

12. See Shaw, 239.

13. See Shaw, 260.

14. See Shaw, table 9.

15. See Shaw, figure 14.

16. See Shaw, 107 and 263.

17. See Shaw, chapter 7.

18. See Pennsylvania v. Mimms, 434. U.S. 106 (1977); Michigan v. Long, 436 U.S. 1032 (1983).

19. See Shaw, 243.

20. See Terry v. Ohio in 392 U.S. 1 (1968)

21. There were two reasons for extending the ARIMA model to cover 52 weeks before and 52 weeks after the phase 1 startup date of July 7, 1992. One is that ARIMA models generally require more data points than the 29 actual program weeks for more reliable estimates and the elimination of such factors as seasonality. This is true even though there is no specific minimum requirement. The other reason is that under police crackdown theory (see Sherman, 1990), it was predicted that the effects of the hot spots patrols would linger as a form of residual deterrence even after cessation.

22. No difference was found either in a 29-week before/after t-test or a 52-week before/after ARIMA model.

23. KCPD data on driveby shootings in beats contiguous to the target beat are not displayed but are available from the authors upon request.

24. Sherman, Lawrence, "Police Crackdowns: Initial and Residual Deterrence," In M. Tonry and N. Morris, eds., *Crime and Justice: A Review of Research*, Chicago; University of Chicago Press, 1990.

25. See Kleck, 18. There are estimates of at least 65 million handguns in the United States, with a population of more than 250 million people. A rough application of this same ratio to the Kansas City population of some 400,000 people suggests at least 100,000 handguns in Kansas City.

26. See Wilson, 46-47.

27. See Reiss and Roth, 282.

28. See Shaw, 288.

29. Sherman, Lawrence W., and R.A. Berk, "The Specific Deterrent Effects of Arrest for Domestic Assault," *American Sociological Review*, (49)(1984):261-272.

30. Sherman, Lawrence W., *Policing Domestic Violence: Experiments and Dilemmas*, New York: Free Press, 1992.

31. Sherman, Lawrence W., "Defiance, Deterrence and Irrelevance," *Journal of Research in Crime and Delinquency*, (30)(1993):445-473.

Reprinted from Lawrence W. Sherman, James W. Shaw, and Dennis P. Rogan, "The Kansas City Gun Experiment" in *National Institute of Justice: Research in Brief,* January 1995. ✦

Part IV

The Nature of Police Work

Introduction

In the preceding sections we have explored policing primarily at the organizational and institutional level—the overall role and function of the police, contemporary issues such as privatization and interesting structures such as the sheriff, the history and development of policing in the United States and elsewhere, and such organizational strate gies as problem-oriented policing and community policing. In this section we shift more toward the individual level of analysis—what do patrol officers and detectives really do, how do they learn to do it, and how do young officers adapt to the unusual features of the police role?

Police work is a substantially different type of work than what most people do for a living. Police officers are granted the authority to restrict our freedom and to use force against us, and they are even given discretion in using these powers. Also, they face challenging conditions, including uncertainty, unpredictability, stress, and danger. They are expected to display courage and fortitude. Police are popular in some quarters but very unpopular in others—and it is often in the latter that they are required to carry out their most difficult assignments. Officers see some of the most gruesome and hateful things that people do to each other, but are expected to

maintain a balanced, reasonable, and healthy outlook toward people and society. To many, policing is a tainted and stigmatized business, one result of which is that officers often bond closely together, form their own distinctive groups and culture, minimize their interactions with "civilians," and end up feeling like a threatened and discriminated-against minority group.

Police officers are not all the same, however, nor are all aspects of police work the same. Different officers react to the job and to their experiences differently, so that there is no monolithic "police personality" or "police culture." As the first reading in this section demonstrates, individuals bring to the police role different experiences and personalities, and then they adapt to the demands of the role based on these pre-existing characteristics and on the guidance they get from senior officers and supervisors. Consequently, we tend to identify particular types or styles of police officers, although in truth each officer's adaptation to the job is unique.

The middle two articles in this section focus, respectively, on patrol work and detective work. They provide real insight into what police really do in two important aspects of policing—patrol officer encounters with citizens and detective handling of criminal investigation cases. These articles dig below the surface and pull away the veneer of drama and mystery in order to illuminate the real craft of basic police work.

The final article in this section is similarly interested in the craft of policing, but from a different perspective—how do police officers learn the craft? Certainly, society and the policing "industry" have made a huge investment over the past 20-30 years in police training. Police officers today are generally required to complete extensive recruit training before they are certified as officers, additional field training immediately after finishing the academy, periodic refresher or "in-service" training, and occasional specialized training. Despite all this training, however,

many in the police business have lingering doubts about whether young officers are really well prepared when they complete their training, and whether veteran officers really engage in the kind of continuous, "life-long" learning that is expected today in most professions. Moreover, for all the training, some question whether the craft of policing, by which they mean the accumulated wisdom of how best to handle different sorts of problems, is very effectively communicated from one generation of officers to another. In some ways it seems that police training concentrates on everything *but* how to really do the job effectively. ✦

13

Four Policemen

William Ker Muir, Jr.

This article is drawn from William Ker Muir's book Police: Streetcorner Politicians. *In the book, Muir explores the ways in which individual police officers adapt intellectually and morally to the central feature of their role—the use of coercive authority against other people. To gather the information he needed, Muir interviewed and observed twenty-eight officers from a West Coast police department over an extended period of time. This selection from the book focuses on four officers who best exemplify different ways of adapting to the use of force. Think about which of the four types would make the most well-adjusted and effective police officer. What would be the best way to help all officers develop most effectively? Which type would you likely become if you were a police officer?*

I

To introduce ourselves to these twenty-eight young policemen, let us talk about four of them in particular—Jay Justice, John Russo, Bob Ingersoll, and Bill Tubman.[1]

Each of the four was a young man. They were in their twenties at the time of the first interview. None had been a Laconia policeman for longer than three years. Each had undergone the same departmental training program. All were married; all were white; and all described themselves as "average middle class." All were breadwinners, bringing home the same pay. All worked under the same laws and were formally obliged to do the same work. Each was a Laconia policeman, patrolling the same flatlands in 1971.

Historically, none had fathers who had gone to college. None had been the oldest child in the family he grew up in. None had completed a year of college except Jay Jus-

tice, who had completed two. All were intelligent; each scored well on standard intelligence tests except Bob Ingersoll, whose test-taking skills had rusted a bit in the nine years between high school graduation and appointment to the police department.[2] Each said he had become a policeman out of a desire to help "others."[3]

But in philosophy they differed. They differed in their vision of reality and, more particularly, in their views of human nature. To the great questions, What is man? and, What is society?, they supplied different answers. Moreover, they were dissimilar in their feelings about the propriety of power. Some accepted the use of coercion in human affairs; others felt extremely uncomfortable about the employment of threats and reacted to power as a bad and unfortunate phenomenon.

The products of these two factors, one intellectual and the other moral, were differing standards of personal success. These four men had dissimilar notions of "the police role," of what they expected of themselves in doing their police work. Some had exalted and perfectionist standards of accomplishment; some developed less exacting definitions of success.

These three elements—their intellectual outlooks on the world, their emotional feelings about power, and their self-imposed moral definitions of success—were systematically interrelated. The character of any one element—circumstances, means, or ends—had implications for the other two, just as, when one corner of a polygon is moved, the other corners must rearrange themselves.

In "general," these men were all policemen, but seen up close and more completely, they were very unlike one another.

II

Officer Jay Justice was the oldest of the four (twenty-nine), had been longest on the department (thirty-three months), and was the only one with prior police experience. He was a powerful man. With his police hat on, he seemed taller than his six foot three; and in his down-filled police jacket he looked even more massive than his 235 pounds.

Justice's brief life story was the stuff from which Hollywood scripts were made. His father, a Texan, a truck driver, and "a straight shooter," raised him in a Gulf Coast city, in "a pretty tough neighborhood" of navy men and longshoremen. Justice did a hitch in the army, won the service's boxing championship, and then went back home, where he joined the local police department on a "whim" while going to junior college. He remained on the department for two years before he was fired "for conduct unbecoming an officer while off duty." Justice was a man who liked his drinks, and he was dismissed for being involved in a barroom brawl. He went to Alaska and got a job as a heavy-equipment operator, but quit soon after to join a police department in a nearby town. He quickly was promoted to sergeant, but after two years gave up his seniority there to enter the Laconia Police Department. As a policeman, he was imperturbable and superior: "a great officer, one of the best there is," as one proud old-timer put it.[4]

Justice was an attentive observer of human nature, and what he looked for were the pressures which people were under, their suffering from the conflict between those pressures, and the efforts they made to cope with their internal torment.

To him all human nature was one: he looked on humankind at a sufficiently abstract level that he could see uniformities and discover what the psychiatrist Erikson once called "the simple truths of existence hidden behind the complexity of daily 'necessities.' "[5] Sensing what was common "behind the complexity," he developed a reflexive quality of mind. He applied knowledge about himself to infer the problems of others and in turn used what he learned about others to increase his own self-knowledge.

An illustration will make the discussion clearer. I asked him to tell me about "one of the more difficult spots" he had been in as a police officer.

Here is his description:

We had a warrant—a felony warrant—to make an arrest out of a family situation. We reasonably felt he was there, in a big Victorian house. I went to the front door; my partner went to the back, and my partner heard him scrambling around. About twenty people, relatives and in-laws, were living in the house. They denied he was there. We decided to go in and get him. The whole family offered resistance. Most of the people were arrested—12 or 13 arrests, including a pregnant mother, who stood blocking the doorway. She was also the mother of the person we were looking for. To me, that's the worst scene. She's involved in her family, emotionally involved.

We ended up giving a call for assistance. That ended up in Internal Affairs. In that situation we pleaded for ten minutes. It was impossible to handle that well. By "well" I mean without a big hoorah. We could have backed off.

Now, my guess is that would not have happened ten years ago. The mother would have turned her boy in. Like I said before, we are in the middle of a social revolution. No one's sure. People are rights-conscious. They think they don't have to be pushed around, and there have been groups telling them about rights. People are real confused. The police represent, so to speak, the Establishment, and this may be the one chance they think they have to get back. They get their kicks defying us.

Notice the unitary quality of his conception of human nature. First, individuals were essentially social. They were always getting "involved" in the lives of one another, complicating their own sense of self-interest with a concern for others. As a result of empathy and interdependence, their inner feelings became identified with the well-being of others. In this particular incident, for example, all the "relatives and in-laws" developed such a sense of mutual responsibility that they all "offered resistance" to save one member of the family. They sacrificed their own security to secure someone else.

Second, this sense of social responsibility created complications. These self-inflicted pressures to respond in terms of what was good for others inevitably conflicted with one another. People were always getting caught between incompatible responsibilities. As a result, they became "real confused," often bothered by feelings of inadequacy, and sometimes they responded erratically to the qualms of conscience. In this incident, the decision to defy the police was made in confusion, executed with misgiving, and justified in the name of equivocal principles.

Third, moral confusion was more likely to occur in some periods than in others. Historical cycles occurred; standards of right and wrong fell into dispute from time to time, challenging personal solutions to the problem of moral confusion and undermining established codes of self-restraint. The older rules by which the mother had governed herself were being undone "in the middle of a social revolution," when arguments against self-control and in favor of kicking back at "the Establishment" were current.

Fourth, Justice applied the same analysis to policemen as to citizens. In other comments Justice noted the social nature of policemen, the moral complexity of their lives, and the unsettling influence of events on their old certitudes. For one thing, policemen had a reciprocal concern for one another: they got "involved"—his word for that involvement was "camaraderie" ("After all we're dependent on each other"). Moreover, policemen also got "real confused" about the many "responsibilities" they felt, and consequently some behaved unpredictably (they began "using their job to work out their own hang-ups, . . . using people as scapegoats more or less"). Furthermore, young policemen went into and out of periods of uncertainty; they sometimes got told "about their rights" by malcontent policemen, unsettling their self-restraint and sense of responsibility.

It was man's fate to suffer doubt and to shape his answers to these conflicting pressures in anguish about what was right and wrong. The only certainty was that individuals suffered doubt and confusion. This understanding of mankind's uniform lot permitted Justice to respond to others intuitively. By force of habit, he resorted to a natural reservoir of information in order to size up others-his own self-understanding. He told me how he handled ticklish situations:

> I'll tell you what I do generally: I always try to preserve the guy's dignity. I leave him an out. I make it so that it's his idea

to sign the ticket. Especially in a crowd situation, I leave him his dignity. My philosophy in the thing is a combination of, the fact I like to think that I thought of it myself, plus over the years I've watched . . . . Everything I do falls within that category of saving his dignity.

He would do what he would have others do unto him. He did not have to learn about others who were unlike him. On the contrary, he was one of them. His substance and theirs was the same. He had "a common sense."

That a man needed to preserve his "dignity," his sense of ethical fulfillment, was the "simple truth of existence," the "category" into which"everything . . . falls." All men came from the same mold. He had verified that truth over the years by all that "I've watched"—from the perch of triumph in the army, from the depths of disgrace in his first police job, from the second chance provided by the Laconia department.

Related to Justice's outlook on the human condition was his sense of limited purpose. His own ethical accounting system was satisfied short of perfection. He felt no responsibility for improving things totally. He held no utopian or perfectionist standards. Limited help was all that he required himself to give. In his view a degree of human suffering was inevitable, ineradicable, and perhaps necessary. The thought that a policeman could single-handedly save a neighborhood or regenerate another individual was pretentious and romantic.

Justice provided a simple example. I asked him why delinquents sometimes straightened out? "I've seen a few get turned around," he said, "but not necessarily through my efforts. I can think of a guy who began assuming responsibilities, maybe like a family. He did it more on his own." There was nothing heroic that Justice could have done to turn the "guy" around. Justice was without the means by which he could salvage a man's destiny and felt no qualms about his inability to do so. There were proper limits to his responsibility to release fellow mortals from their suffering. Perfection was not for this world.

Justice saw two reasons for being content with imperfect situations: the interest of the long run, and the complexity of right and wrong.

The long-run question, What will the day after tomorrow be like?, crimped any heroic pretensions. Even if the world could be made perfect for a day, unless it could take care of itself after its rescuer had departed, the extreme effort would have really been wasted. History extended beyond the lifetime of its putative saviors. The conflicts and infirmities of life recurred. Justice discussed the outlook of policemen he admired who

see the overall picture. . . . To consider one big picture and you are just a part of it. How does this affect the social trend? Not, "I'm making 15 arrests by the end of the day." He questions the system as a whole. What good does this do to pick up a drunk? Foremost in his mind is the problem on hand, but he keeps the overall picture in mind. How does it—whatever he does—fit in? You've got a family beef, and the wife asks you to arrest the husband. But he thinks, Who's going to pay to put the food on the table? You have to keep a lot of things in mind.

The husband and the wife have to suffer out a solution to their own problems. A policeman could stop the beef, but he could not cure its causes. Justice's goal was not to bring a generation of peace to a family; it was sufficient to preserve the moment from irremediable deterioration so that each party could have a second chance to make amends. Keeping the social enterprise going so that accident, a sober second thought, or new information could have their play was not heroic. In Justice's mind, it was just wise.

Thus, one limit of responsibility stemmed from Justice's knowledge that eternity was a long time. Another limit derived from a complex system of moral considerations. Justice kept his mind on the fact that his job was an "overall" one, consisting of many parts: a law enforcer, a welfare worker, a psychiatrist, a peace-keeper, an executor of the laws, a member of a police team, a private family man, and a part of a generation. He did not confine himself to one role, but compromised all the roles, rationalizing shortcomings along any one dimension by denying he was a one-dimensional man. Moderation, he might have

said with Aristotle, was all; compromise was optimal. In a world of multiple obligations, the pure pursuit of a single responsibility caused injustice. The conscientious policeman, Officer Justice would say, "is aware he has more responsibilities than throwing people in the bucket or interpreting the penal code."

Then Justice continued his thoughts about the ways he worked through his own moral ambiguities:

Let me think about it. Right now, we're peace officers. We're trying to preserve the peace. That's how I extend myself. Our job is to protect the Establishment, which is being pressured to make changes faster than it is prepared to cope with them. We're in an area that has not changed much for ever so long. The sciences have changed a lot, but the social sciences have lagged behind. There are going to be a lot of changes, though there are not many so far. So I see our job as protecting the Establishment, which is under a lot of pressure right now.

Let me paraphrase Justice's interesting commentary.

"The sciences" and technology have changed the world. Along with the good consequences, they have brought some secondary harmful effects, disrupting people's lives and magnifying their problems. Furthermore, science and technology have given people the illusion that misfortunes which had been deemed inevitable could now be remedied. These rising expectations have intensified the pressures on government and leadership ("the Establishment") to cure problems for which they have neither the social technology nor the "social sciences." Moreover, the misleading implication of this illusion is that if the problems persist, they do so because the Establishment is cold-hearted and malicious. "The sciences," then, have intensified suffering and at the same time have created the impression that suffering is both easily preventable and also the responsibility of the government.

"Our job" as policemen is not to "cope with" and solve these problems. Rather it is to help individuals survive for the time being, to buy time "right now," to offset the despair of the moment, and to "protect the Establishment" until the people soberly reconsider and recognize the falsity of their expectations. In these desperate times—right now—Justice was choosing to make his first duty that of calming people. Other obligations had momentarily lesser priority. Calming people was a big enough job to occupy a mortal. It meant he had to be a jack-of-all-trades, a Johnny-on-the-spot. It meant, for example, that he had better learn a little insurance law to help families recover indemnity for malicious damage done to their houses. It meant he had better apply a little knowledge of psychology so that he could get an old man hospitalized before the neighborhood kids taunted and drove him into desperate and destructive actions. In short, his job was "to work his beat."

But he could not take care of everything. He had no illusions that, were he to extend himself, all would be secure and well. Hence, he had no feelings of guilt or regret about what he had not accomplished. On the contrary, problems would always be with us, and it was incorrect to "carry about these guilt feelings. . . . You did the best you were able to at the time." In short, Justice tried always "to consider one big picture and you are just part of it." In the phrase of E. B. White's Charlotte, the word for Justice's conception of the police role was "humble." As Justice put it, outstanding policemen "did not hog the show." It was the bad policemen who thought police "alone are waging their crusade."

If Justice's ends were humble, what means did he contemplate as necessary to fulfill them? He always tried to talk: "You try to get the respect of people." He recognized that service to others often got cooperation in return: "You spend the time with people in trouble spots." But he also was comfortable about exercising force. We turn to Justice's understanding of coercion.

Throughout the interview Justice returned frequently to the efficacy of "fear." Of certain youths he would say, "You can't do much when they don't fear the law, . . . when they are not afraid of anything." Coercion was essential to gaining control of individuals who were otherwise ungovernable. Active men, men who wished to lead events rather than be led by them, had to master the techniques of evoking fear in others. Justice had learned that lesson a long time ago, "in the pretty tough neighborhood" in which he grew up. He had learned that making others fearful required action, frequently painful, difficult action. As a child, "you learn—you fight back because you do find—. . . you let 'em push you today, they'll push you more tomorrow. They pick on you less, the more you fight back and make them sorry." Fear implied harsh examples sometimes, making bullies "sorry."

To Justice, a policeman could not be "afraid" to fulfill his threats. "If the situation warrants it, you can take whatever action you deem necessary"—necessary to make others regret their bullying ways. Justice was aware that a policeman was set apart from his wife, his friends, his fellow citizens, by his authority to hurt others. The license to use force imposed responsibilities on the policeman which no other men had: to act "aggressively," not passively, not avoiding the pitfalls of power, not being personally prudent.

The word for Justice's understanding of the police job was boldness. Boldness amounted to an unwillingness to remain passive in the face of what was wrongful, no matter what the risks involved. To be bold was to overcome the fears ordinary men submitted to. Boldness was "sticking your neck out in any situation."[6] It was the audacity to try to dominate events when events were out of control.

Justice perceived a relationship between the limited ends he pursued and the extortionate means he used in that pursuit. He had defined for the policeman a modest responsibility. The goals were limited, the aspirations modest, the claims unpretentious. On the other hand, he seemed to have no qualms about using the extreme means of coercion to bring about results in accord with those limited aims. He felt no guilt for making the bully "sorry" or acting without charity to achieve these modest goals. He enjoyed seeing force used well when it was "proportionate"—in keeping with the limited purposes policemen fulfilled. He had no fear that he might be tempted to use extreme force, because he had no taste for extreme objectives.

In Justice's mind, the best guard against mis-using coercive means was to limit himself to human—sized ends.[7]

III

Now contrast John Russo at the time I first met him, two years after he had joined the department. He was a compact, agile, twenty-three-year-old man, who spoke and thought quickly. He knew judo, had studied karate, and rode his own motorcycle to and from work. He was the child of a broken marriage: "My parents separated, and I went to a lot of new schools, and I had to fight at each one." Russo had a stepmother who was an alco-holic, and a tempestuous one by his account. His father was a carpenter and a small-time building contractor, who praised his son for his toughness and manhood, "even at age eleven." Russo's father "thought there was nothing better than a workingman," and he employed his son on construction jobs and encouraged the boy to earn money in what-ever other employment he could get. Russo wanted the dignity his father heaped on him; he even gave up high school sports so he could work after school, hauling in "working-man's wages" and his father's "respect." Russo apparently hated school, and when-ever he had time between jobs, the local po-lice were likely to pick him up, suspecting that he had perpetrated some prank against the school or respectable society. Russo never went to college. He married young, had chil-dren, worked hard on riverboats on the Mis-sissippi for several years after high school, and at twenty-one joined the department. The older officer who called Justice "a great officer" characterized Russo as "an eager beaver," "a hot dog," and "a young kid."

Russo's outlook on the world was ex-pressed in a carpenter's metaphor: "Being a policeman is like building a house. You frame it, then during the night someone comes along and tears it all down." It was a rough-hewn image, but it revealed much about Russo's roughhewn vision. The world was di-vided into two camps, the builders, who "like to see progress," and the "night people," the predators, the destroyers. On the "good" side were the "family men," who "hustled," were ambitious, had "pride," got the "job done," could handle ruffians, kept their defenses up and their powder dry. They were pure of heart, heroic, "adult." They were working-men. They were "We."

On the other side was the enemy: the "run-ners," the "fighters," the "big-mouthers," the "crowd-gatherers," the "rats," the "SOBs" the "jailbirds," the "felons," "the guys who get my goat," the "bad asses," the "pretty bad charac-ters," the guys who "by all rights . . . should be in jail," the "dirty." They were "conwise," villainous. Their only "handiwork" was crime. They were "They."

The events of life were explicable in terms of the war between "Them" and "Us." The house that was vandalized, the city that dete-riorated, the chief's regulations that re-stricted effective police work, the anger which the citizenry directed at the depart-ment, the mellowness which the older cops developed, the "weak decisions" which the judges made—all had implications within this outlook. "Smart-ass little punks" undid the "progress" the city would otherwise have been making. The chief had bowed to "agita-tors." A lenient cop "did not carry his own load." The judges encouraged the enemy by "teaching" the "punks" they had nothing to fear: "it's continued probation every time."

The police job was to win the war—to eradicate the impure of heart, to take back "our streets" from the barbarians and return them to the workingman citizenry. It was a series of fights to the finish, and "I've never lost one." "My dad didn't ever want a son of his to lose one. He read me his plaque he hung over his desk: 'Don't ever let anyone bully you, or they will keep right on bullying you.'"

Russo's explanation of the world was shaped not by insight but by indignation. It was part of the paraphernalia of battle. Russo was no more ready to give up this vision than he was to surrender his .38. Any educational effort or training program which would chal-lenge his dualistic perspective was a "bunch of huckledy-buck," "public relations," a "waste of time."

The war outlook which Russo had, how-ever, was not so firmly in place as one might have expected. Perhaps it was because Russo was only twenty-three. For whatever reasons, he did not have his world view completed. There were gaps. The structure of the jigsaw puzzle was not firm and resistant to hard knocks—yet. He was surprised by people. He was "confused" by human motives, particularly in "routine matters," between battles, when the "shit was not hitting the fan." Listen to the bafflement of his description of his beat: "The children in an apartment building, they welcome you by singing Old MacDonald, only except they only know one verse: Old MacDonald had a pig. And there's no reason for it to occur. You have not done anything to them." Nor was he able to understand his own department. The surprise, the inability to predict accurately, overwhelmed him from the first day he was interviewed for the job: "The oral board is a good idea except you don't know what they want. It's a wonder anybody gets by." He was in the dark about why police officers had so many family problems, why so many citizens in Laconia had family problems, why people were on welfare, why kids didn't go straight after they were given a break, what caused crimes of violence, why commanding officers would "whittle down" their men. The dualistic vision pitting the good against the bad could explain some, but not all, the "great, blooming, buzzing confusion" of city life.[8]

Russo described his puzzlement about a routine family disturbance.

> You know, the parents call and say their kid is out of control, and all they want you to do is come and get him out of there. So you go in, and they tell you Junior is in the back room. Go get him. You go in, and Junior swings at you, and suddenly it is on the ground. Then suddenly it's no longer you and the parents against Junior. Now it's you against the world. If a guy swings at you, you should swing back, the way I see it. You can't let him swing at you, or let him hit you, yet the parents say, you can't use force. They'll say, take him to jail, but don't hurt him.

Russo's description of this family with the one Justice gave of the household which had defied him. It is easier to see Russo's confu-

sion in the perspective of Justice's intellectual certainty.

Never once did Russo draw upon his personal experience for insight about what was going on. The omission was even more remarkable because Russo's own parents had so many disruptive and violent encounters with one another. Where Justice would incorporate the learning from his private life into the problems of the beat, Russo separated the two, drew on neither to illuminate the other.

Quite the contrary, Russo maintained independent explanatory systems for himself and for others. He originally placed the family encounter into his dualistic categories. The hero-rescuer came aboard to save the victimized parents from their uncontrollable predatory son, Junior. But instead of the knight errant's getting his due appreciation, the parents jumped all over him. His expectation proved dead wrong. The results disconfirmed his theories. He suffered disillusion. Russo made no attempt to explain the erratic behavior of the parents in terms of their "involvement" with others, the central insight feeding Justice's outlook. The relationship of the family members was insignificant. Russo was unaware of its implication. Nor did Russo put the event in historical perspective. He was ignorant of what had caused the child to be "out of control," and he was not much interested in what would happen once he had got the son "out of there." There was no sense of context, no time frame in which events were bunched and related—no mention of the civil rights movement, to which Justice referred, for example. Russo closed his eyes to the circumstances of the situation.

Acting within his dualistic world view of Us against Them, Russo wanted to help. To him, police work was a simple job: "to put a lot of bad asses in jail," thereby cutting "down on crimes of violence." To him, that was "all they wanted you to do": Junior was to go to jail, for he was a malefactor.

Notable were the concerns left out of "the job," that did not have to be done: concern for the personal consequences for the malefactor or for anyone to whom he may have been attached, concern for the victims of the crime or for innocent bystanders, concern for ameliorating the overall problem, concern for the example of law-abiding behavior he was setting, concern for equal treatment, concern for securing future public cooperation with the police. His simple goal was to quarantine the bad characters.

The single task assigned to him was unquestionably morally gratifying. Russo was called a "hot dog" by his fellow officers and took it as a compliment. By doing "a lot of work" he derived satisfaction—he was saving lives, aborting burglaries, preventing families from being "cleaned out," and protecting human enterprise. He was confident he was helping this family and the rest of his beat in the only ways he felt appropriate—pacifying it, forcing the rats out of it, doing sentry work on its perimeters.

Preoccupied with his simple task, Russo came to feel that every crime committed within his beat was a personal shortcoming of sorts. A burglary meant that he had failed to scare off a suspicious person; he had ignored his "sixth sense"; he had left unmade a possible car stop. A burglary was a blot on his record. Perhaps, thought Russo, he could have prevented it if he had only worked harder.

Another consequence arose. Since crimefighting was the only job which was morally legitimate under his one-dimensional scale of values, whenever Russo acted in other capacities, he felt he was wasting his time. Talking with victimized families was "public relations; it couldn't be a bigger waste of time." Resolving family beefs happily through patient talk was "bullshit" or dishonesty. Writing a good report for police or social services was "secretarial work." Each of these achievements counted for nothing; worse, they diverted him from cutting down crime, thus increasing his sense of inadequacy and frustration in the face of continued crime.

Still another consequence of focusing on one criterion of success was to heighten the threshold of achievement which satisfied him. Where Justice was content to protect his beat from criminals as well as he could within the limits imposed by the multiplicity of duties, Russo had no countervailing, legitimate obligations to justify his falling short of perfection. The simpler the morality, the more

obsessive became its demands. Keeping the beat as clean as possible transformed itself into keeping the beat perfectly clean. If Justice was concerned about reaching some kind of optimal compromise, Russo was driven by an assertive maximization principle. Justice had human limits imposed on him by the obvious incompatibility of his tasks; Russo set himself a superhuman job to perform: perfection along a one-dimensional moral scale.

There was a similarity between Justice and Russo. They both were "unafraid" of using force. Manipulating people by making threats was not incomprehensible, immoral, or difficult for either of them. Russo had a sophisticated understanding of deterrence theory, learned in the two "toughest" high schools in town and at his father's knee: "Don't ever let anyone bully you, or they will keep right on bullying you." He understood the value of a harsh example: "a show of force is a deterrent," he would insist. He appreciated the value of a nasty reputation: "Being a good guy does not work in Laconia." In short, Russo had worked through a great deal of the intellectual meaning of coercion.

Likewise, he found force a moral means. Resort to threats was proper. With pride, he talked of his detached technique of calming a family dispute: "I say to her, 'There's no need for you to be screaming in front of us. We've got better things to do': That's what I tell them. That kind of upsets them. But I've had luck with it. I've had very few return calls. Usually I threaten people. With a firm tone I say, 'I don't want to take you to jail. If I have to come back, someone's gotta go to jail.'"

Finally, Russo was, by his own lights, skillful in coercion. "I've had luck with it." As we shall see, other policemen differed from Justice and Russo; for them, coercive means were distasteful, wrong, and full of pitfalls.

Russo sounded a theme absent in Justice's discussion of force. Russo felt morally compelled to use force when laws and departmental regulations forbade it. As a result he "was getting in the shit six times a year." Worse, when he behaved according to the officially approved code, he had a vague sense of double-crossing himself: "You can't treat anyone out there as you know they should be treated—as a jailbird. You have got to treat them as an average person." He found himself "pushing aside the rules a little bit"; he bent the truth on occasion ("What I do is lie"); he was flirting with the idea of "padding" reports "like a lot of policemen do," to cover up the discrepancy between what he knew was legal and what he felt was morally justified.

Why? I suggest it was the compulsion of the ends he felt obliged to achieve. Russo's moral philosophy, his stringent standard of success and failure, was so one-dimensional, so uncomplicated by contradictory purpose, that it made imperative the use of the policeman's fullest capability. The urgency of the job undercut any excuse for moderation in the employment of force. There was no moral excuse for restraint. The law may have forbidden maximum force, but Russo perceived it to be an act of betrayal and cowardice to knuckle under to the law. His need for moral worth, his "pride," would eventually overcome his timidity; defiance of the laws and the regulations would be the hallmark of good police conduct. "I worked dredges before I came on the department, and one supervisor would say, 'If you don't fall overboard six times a year, you're not doing the job.' It's the same way here. If you're not getting in the shit six times a year, you're not doing the job."

IV

Bob Ingersoll was a big man; he weighed 220 pounds and he was six feet four inches tall. His voice tended to break in the treble register, yet his size and calmness overcame any implication of anxiety or weakness. His father had been murdered by a strong-arm robber when Ingersoll was one year old. His mother had raised him and an older brother, who later became a professor of engineering.

The family was very poor: "I guess my childhood ambition was to be rich; not rich, but wealthy." Ingersoll had had polio, and he still limped discernibly when he was tired. Ingersoll had become a handyman and worked steadily and responsibly for seven years before becoming a policeman at age twenty-six. With only a high school diploma,

and several years removed from the classroom to boot, he had difficulty with the department's intense training program. Despite his poor academic rating, however, officers who evaluated his field performance came away impressed. For his own part, Ingersoll was modest: "I don't really know much. I've only worked a year."

Ingersoll was intensely interested in the problem of human motivation. "On a family call you try to understand what caused the people to get to the point where they had to call you in the first place, to get the big picture, I guess." Note the detail of the "picture" of human behavior Ingersoll could recall:

A fight between the husband and wife. The guy had come unglued. There was no way to reason with him in the field. That's what bothered me. Usually you can make heads and tails of what is happening and why it's happening. His wife spent all the month's welfare money. He was trying to make good, trying to toe the mark. He had been laid off, and he was in Sparta [a public housing project] and giving his welfare check to an organization to pay off all his bills and rent and what not. He was trying to keep his head above water, and he had come home and his wife had spent the check. There was no way to calm him down. Alcohol, maybe drugs had played a part. We're out there to preserve the peace, and the fact that we were no way near doing that really bothered me. When we arrived, it was not a criminal matter yet, although the pots and pans were really flying. We were not being able to relieve the situation at all, being there. We just had to take him in. As I said, drugs and alcohol maybe had played a part. I kind of understood the guy's problems. He had made an honest effort to make good. He had two children and he had come home and the money's not there. I understood, but I couldn't solve the problem. He was sure tearing up the place, which was sad because they were nice furnishings. I've come across three or four situations like this, where the guy—it's always the male—where there's no way to get to him. . . . The problems are so immense. The guy can't get a job. He doesn't have a high school diploma or he has a record. He has no money. He lives in a crummy house. It's dirty. His kids are real unfortunate. It's not gratifying, these family beefs.

He took in "the whole situation"; he bothered about causes, the underlying "problems" which would compel a man to become other than his usual "decent" self. Drugs, alcohol, difficulties, even a youthful lark, could cause people to act up. However, if a police officer could "slow down the pace of things," decency could reassert itself. With a second chance, the experience of the earlier debacle would teach the man something. All mankind profited from its mistakes: "We all make mistakes. When I was young, I swiped a couple of candy bars. I was taken downtown once and put into jail for putting soap into the water fountain on Broadway." With a second chance, persons cooled off, calmed down, slept on it, solved the problem, got things straight.

There was no separation between Us and Them, no dualism. Policemen and citizens alike were put in the same bag: "All put on their pants in the same way," he said of his fellow officers, but he meant it to apply to all mankind.

This monistic, reflexive view of human nature as born good, bolted down as it was in the "ten years of life before I came to the department," bore a resemblance to Justice's, except in one respect. There was no accounting for the differences in human nature across space or over time. Justice saw human beings as being "involved" in codes of moral responsibility, but the substance of these codes was constantly changing and could be altered by culture, the nature of the crowd, the family setting, changing relationships to persons and things. Ingersoll's picture of human nature was more fixed and less dynamic. Mankind was basically decent, had been, and always would be, whatever the setting. Aberrations might occur in individual cases, depending on the extent and severity of the problems which eroded that decency. But the historical setting made no great difference. Hence, Ingersoll made no allusions to history, to the "overall picture," things which concerned Justice.

Ingersoll's vision was in no way like Russo's. He did not lump people into legal categories, as "felons" or burglars or car thieves, or their colloquial equivalents. On the contrary, the Laconia citizen was like Rousseau's noble savage or the Hebrew Poet's Job, sorely tried, clinging to life, capable of rallying from self-pity, rekindling his energies, and thrusting his decency into the face of terrible oppression.

In a world full of such tragic figures, Ingersoll's moral duty was clear: to assist them in coping with their individual oppressions. It made no difference that they were malefactors or victims. Relieving problems—getting an ambulance, giving consolation, getting a workman his payment, finding a shelter for a drunk, calling an expert in—was the police equivalent of the handyman's fixing a leaky roof. His standard of success was his client's happiness. "I don't know whether being a police officer differs from any other line of work. What makes him liked in any line of work makes him liked in police work." Ingersoll had a talent for helping and consoling, and he dispensed his services for "gratifying" consideration: thanks, recognition, cooperation, inner pleasure. He sought out ways to provide these services. "It's gratifying to me to talk with business establishments and stores to let them know you are out there and to assure them that they should call you, not their cousin or their bosses." He was the true servant of the people.

But by no means was he a compulsive rescuer. If his offer to help was turned down, or if his compassionate, consoling, empathetic approach was insufficient to rekindle the strength to set things straight; if "all I can do" failed to relieve the difficulty, it was not a personal failure on his part. As he liked to repeat, he did "not take the tragedies of others home with me." Ultimately, it was the individual citizen's responsibility to "forget it," to rally around, and to make an accommodation with his own problems. Ingersoll was content to assist only those who wanted his assistance. It was enough to lend a hand to those who wished to save themselves in a trying world.

What Ingersoll did "take . . . home with me," what really bothered him, was not his inability to rescue everybody, but the problems of force. He was truly relieved to find that older policemen regarded him as a good cop, because the assurance permitted him the luxury of "being too easy." For his part, he wanted to "reason" with the citizenry; he was bothered when reason failed to calm a situation and could not understand the justification for wielding authority against the people rather than helping them.

> So many people are low income. They can't get jobs. There's a big circle there. They drive old, beat-up cars. And you issue citations. Their headlight is out, their taillights don't work. He's emitting excess smoke. He can't afford to fix it. But if he gets a warrant, he'll have to go to jail. And there's a tremendous lot of bail. It's a vicious circle. . . . We give him a mechanical citation, and it costs to get it fixed. And if he doesn't it's a $44 traffic warrant. So you take him to jail.

Threats were "a strange way to operate"; they led to paradoxical results, putting decent people into jail, "locked up, confined."[9] Coercion was an intellectual enigma and a moral evil.

Several consequences flowed from his remedial outlook and emotional aversion to force. One was his joy in coming on a citizen who aroused his indignation, who deserved to be coerced, who was a moral arrest, like a dangerous man performing a "hot activity." Interestingly enough, included in this category of moral arrests, against whom threat and force might be used legitimately, were citizens who tried to deceive. In Ingersoll's mind the ultimate sin was personal dishonesty. "I really get mad. I don't know why I do." Ingersoll expected others to avoid fraud. The obligation not to cheat was the key clause in the social contract. In this suffering world, one might do violence, be careless, lapse into self-pity, but one lived up to one's word. If a suspect betrayed his trust, Ingersoll's indignation overrode any misgivings he had about making the arrest, about jailing people in "a little room, by yourself, with no way out."

Another consequence was frequent personal discomfort on the job. Presupposing that the best in people would ultimately surface gave Ingersoll a frame of reference in which to preserve a great many memories of citizens who eventually redeemed themselves: the irate woman who turned contrite, the juvenile motorcyclist "you . . . got through to," the husband and wife who saw the light after "sleeping on the situation." The presupposition that "people are decent" sifted out disappointing memories and stored corroborating ones. Yet some surprises occurred: truthful-appearing people gulled Ingersoll into errors. If outsiders, particularly fellow officers, were present, and if they thereafter reminded him of his false prediction through their silent or explicit criticism, it nettled him. He was especially vulnerable because he did not enjoy justifying his outlook. He was a man of action, and he was content to let his overall results speak for themselves. He was not willing to create a time and place to explain a prediction which had gone awry. A more eloquent officer might have said to his partner, "Let's go for coffee" and then explained, as Justice did, "It's more important not to lose the chance than that I'm right. I believe in people more than some of the other guys do." Ingersoll would not. Rather he would just fall back within himself. Often criticism got under his skin, however, and his resentment would burst out in the next incident on some surprised or rebuffed citizen. Despite his considerable confidence in the way he saw life, disappointments were a source of considerable discomfiture, the more so because he lacked the extraordinary verbal skills which could have persuaded his fellow officers to see the world his way.

Ingersoll's philosophy contrasted with Justice's in another respect. Both described the good policeman as one who saw a larger picture. Despite the similarity of language, they actually were speaking of different things. For Justice, the "overall picture" consisted of social repercussions: the implications of police action for the city, the society, the general welfare, the future, the "Establishment," the institutions of leadership and education and finance, the foundations of law and morality on which confidence, reliance, and hope depended. For Ingersoll, however, "the full picture" consisted of the immediate causes of what he could see was happening. What was meaningful to him was the individual and his problem—its causes, its consequences, and its remedy. "Society" was an abstraction that meant little to him.

In fact, in Ingersoll's view of human nature as decency beset by corrupting impersonal forces, society was not worth much. Rather it had to be defended against, beaten back, throttled to preserve the individual. On the contrary, Justice's view of human nature made the "Establishment" essential, for the individual was enlarged by human association, enriched by civilized culture, and ennobled by the higher responsibilities society imposed on him. "Society" had meaning for Justice; it determined human behavior for good or ill.

With such different understandings of the consequences of society, Justice and Ingersoll approached the concept of coercion with contrary emotions. Ingersoll thought the policeman was obliged to help the individual, to cure him, to treat him solely as an end, never as a means. His job was clinical in nature, between cop and client. To make an example of the malefactor, to hurt him as a way to convince others to live up to their social responsibilities, made no sense to Ingersoll. It was an unjustifiable use of people as means. For Justice, however, the short-run well-being of an individual might properly be sacrificed to preserve the going concern, the "society," the long run. Ingersoll's concept of the beneficent individual made it much more problematic to justify deterrent coercion than did Justice's concept of the "civilized man," according to which civilization had a value apart from any one individual.

V

Bill Tubman was five feet nine inches tall and weighed 160 pounds, but he looked thinner. He was twenty-three. He had been raised in a peaceful town in rural Kansas, where his father had owned a service station and his entire family busied themselves making ends meet. Hard work and family unity were the values of the Tubman family; the intellectual bounds were confined: "My dad and mom didn't talk to us much about public service

and all that. His service station usually kept him busy."

Halfway through his first year in college, Tubman quit and came to Laconia to join the police department. Upon completing his training, he began to go to college again. He therefore obtained a permanent assignment to the third watch (3-11 pm). As a result, whenever the regular squads rotated every six weeks to a different watch, he began working with a new group of men. Always working third watch was an unsettling and rootless experience. For a diffident and somewhat frightened young man like Tubman, it compounded his isolation from the department. It meant that he had no ready access to the locker room bull sessions among friends; he could not participate in those recurring conversations which would help develop a gift of gab, permit the airing of experiences, and sharpen the eye for detail.

Bill Tubman was intelligent. He had one of the highest scores on the melange of vocabulary, math, and spatial perception questions which the department used to evaluate police candidates, and in his training class he ranked at the midpoint. The world, however, especially the big-city world of Laconia, was hard for him to understand. Although he had been a policeman for two years when I first met him (the same length of time as Russo and a year longer than Ingersoll), he still got "lost up there" on his beat. He recalled seeing the city on his first visit there: "We looked at Laconia, and it seemed so big, so overwhelming."

His incomprehension was even greater at the human level. He had little intuitive understanding about people; he had nurtured no presuppositions about what made society tick; he made frequent wrong guesses about what was going to happen.

Unlike Ingersoll, who inquired about the personal details of his citizenry, Tubman never hankered for that kind of information. He had no concept of human nature into which he could organize his experience. As a result, the human aspect of events dribbled right out of his mind.

To be sure, he did sort policemen into two types: those whose daring "panicked" him and those officers who were "cautious." Moreover, he had begun to notice interesting "similarities in the job," which made things "easier . . . the next time around." Yet he could not put words to the kinds of similarities he was seeing; he could not create pigeonholes into which he could file human events and history. He labored under a learning incapacity, and he never recognized that his problems in understanding existed and could be worked on. Because of his timidity and his organizational isolation on a permanent third watch, and because no one was formally obligated to talk within the department, no one engaged him in dialogue to hammer out the meaning of his experiences.

Nor did he have a historical perspective, of how things changed and why they developed as they did. In the entire eleven hours I was with him (three hours of interviewing and eight hours of field observation), he made not one allusion either to the past or the future, with the single exception of this bit of baseless optimism: "Maybe people are getting wise, and the use of narcotics will go down." He was at sea in speculating on the causes of crime: "Burglaries and robberies are going up, and that's due to narcotics, but rape is going up too. I don't know, what explains the rising crime rate."

His inability to anticipate events caused him to be surprised and often humiliated. Here is his own description of how he handled one family row:

It was a day watch, and I got a 975, stand by and preserve the peace. It was on the third floor of this big apartment building. I was alone and had no transceiver. I went in, and things had quieted down. She wanted to get her stuff. So anyway in the course of the deal, I found a marijuana joint. I found a little more grass around. Anyway I found it. It was the man's anyway. He was there, and she was there. I saw it, and she had showed it to me and wanted him to go to jail. I was alone and had no transceiver. He was a real big guy, and he had some friends around the apartment. I didn't arrest him. I was just out of recruit school. I might have done the same thing now. I would have tried to get a cover unit, and if I had waited for it, he might have still been around. I just let it slide. She took off with all her clothes. The decision was whether to arrest him

or not. He got a little upset about it. I told her to hurry and get her stuff out. I didn't want to make anything of it.

There was a bumbling quality about this piece of police work. No transceiver (a portable two-way radio), no cover, no anticipation of what was likely to happen. It was not as if Tubman had just happened on an incident to which he had to adapt quickly. The activity stemmed from a radio call.

What really happened is not clear from his description. But it says all that Tubman knew. He had almost no perception of who the girl was, who the guy was, why they were fighting. All he saw was that the guy was "real big" and "got a little upset" about the prospect of being arrested for having marijuana. The girl was small and friendless and wanted to make "something of it"; so Tubman became gruff with her. Might was right, and weakness was wrong.

This humiliation occurred in his first year on the department. Yet after another year of police experience, he still "might have done the same thing now": failed to get cover and to carry a transceiver, let things "slide," lack control, be gruff with her, be abjectly humiliated in front of that "real big guy" and his friends. In that story one can see why an older officer could say of Tubman, "He sometimes comes on too hard with suspects, and other times too easy with the wrong ones." Under the pressures of his daily encounters with the public, Tubman began to develop a dualistic view of human nature. The similarity to Russo's vision of mankind ended there. The categories were not Us and Them, the builders and the wreckers, but the "nonintimidating" and "the intimidating." His antennae were out, picking up cues by which he could make the necessary identifications in each case. He did not ask himself why some individuals fell in one category and some in the other. The terrors of police work gave him little time for such detached reflection. He had enough on his mind just to survive.

Tubman liked the idea of being a policeman because he had "always wanted to help people," and he found that being a policeman had its satisfying moments. He liked being on the scene of automobile accidents, helping the injured. He liked doing investigations after a crime. He liked testifying in court. He liked the pleasure of being useful to others, of having "a part in the overall picture." He enjoyed bringing to the nonintimidating segment of the public the experience of security which the unintimidating citizens of his Kansas town had shared. When the opportunity arose to re-create rural Kansas in Laconia, no task was too time-consuming, no detail too small, no job too unusual. He wanted to help—and to receive the gratitude due the full-spirited public servant.

However, in the presence of the intimidating, he was intimidated. He lacked the skill and the knowledge to use coercion successfully. I asked him how he handled young juveniles on his beat. "If you mean the teen-age burglar, a young criminal, a guy who breaks the law, then you say, 'This is my beat, man; keep it clean.'" The way he said it convinced me that he had rehearsed that remark many times in his fantasies but never delivered it on the street. He had not thought through what could happen when his bluff was called and when his motivation to follow through on his threat was challenged. His interview was laced with memories of when he "backed down," "let things slide," did "not follow through," "did not want to make anything of it," "had not been involved enough," "accomplished nothing." He was not competent in governing others who initially resisted him. He was not bold.

Nor did he understand the psychology and the ethics of force. In his prosaic and busy peaceful childhood, people were hardworking and Godfearing. There was no need for force, and his parents had never talked about its utility. I asked him if his parents had ever advised him about bullies, and he responded, "If they did, I don't remember, but they probably said, 'Just ignore them.'" Tubman had taken this advice to heart and had proceeded to ignore situations where skillful use of force might be necessary.

The personal necessity to ignore danger, however, eventually eroded his desire to help. His fears began to preoccupy his sense of responsibility. Success in police work became the job of staying alive, of keeping aware of possible dangers, of finding ways to fill time with uneventful safe activities, of justifying staying out of harm's way.

Thus, despite the fact he "always wanted to help people," he developed distinctions which justified his avoidance of danger. For one thing, he began to define police work as dealing only with matters defined as criminal by the penal code. "Civil" matters were not his business (despite the fact that accident investigation was archetypically civil): "A lot of calls don't belong to us. A lot of civil problems. Landlord-tenant problems and the like, which are civil problems. They don't even belong to us. They could be channeled elsewhere. Maybe they could be taken care of over the phone." Many officers made a distinction between civil and criminal matters, but for them it had a meaning different from the implication it had for Tubman. For officers like Russo, the distinction permitted them to economize on time, to give them more minutes and hours each day to put the bad guys into jail. Justice, and others like him, appreciated the distinction but accepted both spheres as their job, seeing the connection between the two. Arbitrating disputes between citizens and helping them settle disputes produced information about the people of Justice's beat, permitted him to set a good example, earned him friends. In short, civil problems were his opportunity to work his beat. Tubman, on the other hand, found the distinction a handy way to avoid a vast assortment of potential entanglements which he could not govern. "Policing," to Tubman, "was often a matter of knowing how many ways tell them, 'We can't help you.'" With "civil" matters defined as out-of-bounds and "criminal" matters defined as too dangerous for the "cautious" policeman, one might wonder whether Tubman would ever have involved himself in police work were there no activity sheet requiring him to account for his time. He wanted to act only where his safety and self-esteem were out of danger. To avoid a sense of falling short, he cut his sense of public responsibility down to size, whittling away at the part of the population to whom he had to respond. Lacking the skills, the motives, the courage of public life, he pulled back within himself, avoiding power, hating, much of his work, despising the diversity and the challenge of the world, fleeing from the confusions to which much of his work exposed him, and suppressing the memory of obligations unmet. He could get away with it by changing squads every six weeks, working a one-man patrol, keeping a sharp eye out for safe jobs, and maintaining a low profile. He was, as a professional put it, one of "those fellows who got their fingers burnt" and thought that the best way was to avoid risky situations altogether.

VI

These four men differed from each other intellectually and morally.

Intellectually, Justice and Ingersoll both looked at human nature as one: they had "a common sense," a unitary conception of mankind, in which the uniformities between individuals permitted one person to walk in the shoes of another. Russo and Tubman, on the other hand, each held dualistic conceptions, divided people into categories essentially and ultimately different from one another.

Morally, the four had opposed conceptions about the means of coercion. Justice and Russo alike were comfortable using coercive means to manipulate others. Each had an understanding of the utility of force in society; each felt that threats were a proper means to bring about worthwhile ends; each felt he was competent in using force to govern others. In contrast, Ingersoll and Tubman were uncomfortable with coercion. They knew of few, if any, circumstances under which force could produce good results. They would rather deal with people than dominate them.

As a consequence of these intellectual and moral differences, the men differed in what gave them satisfaction. They disagreed about the proper goals of police work. Justice and Ingersoll, with their unitary visions of mankind, set limits on the policeman's responsibility for rescuing his fellow man. But Ingersoll's distaste for coercion led him to isolate a set of enjoyable responsibilities different from the limited social obligations Justice as-

sumed. In Russo's and Tubman's cases, the responsibilities they owed to individuals were more total—to rescue a certain segment of the populace from the sources of their unhappiness. But they had different feelings about coercion, Russo wanted to stand up and fight the victimizers; Tubman wanted to give succor to the victims.

The moral and intellectual diversity of these four policemen was representative of the diversity among the men in the ranks, as we shall see. The causes of the philosophical and emotional variation among them undoubtedly flowed from many sources. Long before they became policemen, they had been shaped by influences of every kind. Yet the effect of their police work on their most deeply held attitudes was undoubted. One could see that, but for their police experiences, they would not have laced their discussion of the basic intellectual questions about man's nature and society's function with the same richly textured illustrations. Had they not become policemen, they would not have responded so feelingly to the big moral questions of guilt and courage, honesty and loyalty. And but for the fact that the tools of their occupation included that ultimate weapon of coercive power, the gun, they would not have been so bothered by, or thought so deeply about, the problem of force—of the relationship between cruel means and worthwhile ends.

Notes

1. These sketches are based exclusively on my first interview with each of them. The reader should bear in mind that policemen, particularly young ones like these, were likely to change their philosophies over time. Indeed, the significant point of this book is to define the dynamics of the intellectual and moral changes policemen undergo as a result of their police experience. Nevertheless, by seizing a moment, by limiting our focus to a single snapshot of the past, we can capture the range of outlooks within a police department at aorical time.

2. Each had taken the Otis Self-Administered Intelligence Test and the Army General Classification Test upon applying to the department. Their scores were: Justice, 62 and 113; Ingersoll, 45 and 98; Russo, 55 and 113; and

Tubman, 54 and 131. For what it is worth, each also submitted at the time of appointment to an ersatz 21-question F-scale measure of Authoritarianism. Their raw scores on this methodologically problematic but intellectually provocative test were: Justice, 2; Ingersoll, 2; Russo, 10; and Tubman, 6. The higher the score, the more "authoritarian" the personality. See T. W. Adorno, Else Frenkel—Brunswick, Daniel J. Levinson. and R. Nevitt Sanford,*The Authoritarian Personality*, (York: Harper & Brothers, 1950), chap. 7. For examples of the criticism to which this measure has been subjected, see Richard Christie and Marie Jahoda, eds., *Studies in the Scope and Method of "The Authoritarian Personality"* (Glencoe, Ill.: The Free Press, 1954).

3. Throughout the interviews with each of the twenty-eight young policemen, I was reminded of one of Ross Macdonald's law enforcement protagonists when asked, "What sort of a man are you": "I feel more strongly for other people than I do for myself. For one thing my parents had a bad marriage. It seems to me I spent a lot of time when I was a kid trying to head off quarrels, or dampen down quarrels that had already started. Then I started college in the depths of the Depression. I majored in Sociology. I wanted to help people. Helpfulness was like a religion with a lot of us in those days. It's only in the last few years, since the war, that I've started to see around it. I see that helping other people can be an evasion of oneself, and the source of a good deal of smug self-satisfaction. But it takes the emotions a long time to catch up. I'm emotionally rather backward" (Ross Macdonald, *Meet Me at the Morgue* (1953; New York: Bantam, 19721, p. 130). The chronology did not apply, the family background often was extremely different, but "helpfulness *was* like a religion" for many of the young Laconia policemen.

4. If the reader feels a sense of skepticism, of deja vu—if this portrait of the swashbuckling, hard-drinking, misunderstood, gentle giant, who embraced the good and kayoed the bad,

sounds like a stereotype—it may be some consolation to know I shared those same reactions. Indeed, I worried lest certain artistic preconceptions born of seeing too many Clark Gable and Pat O'Brien movies in a misspent youth simply blinded me to life. As Jonathan Rubinstein has pointed out, however, mystery writers long have drawn on the real exploits of policemen. Art has been more influenced by life than the other way around. Jonathan Rubinstein, *City Police* (New York: Farrar, Straus & Giroux, 1973),p. ix.

5. The phrase is Erik Erikson's. See his *Identity: Youth and Crisis* (NewYork:Norton,1968), p. 32.

6. One eloquent Laconia officer described the boldness of two policemen he admired:"They both will step out into the bright lights. 'Here I am,' they'll say; 'You know who I am.' They'll step into a situation and announce their presence, as opposed to not wanting to get involved. You have to be willing to expose yourself. You personify the law, and if you identify yourself and stand out, then people can react to you. They can run away from you or they can run to you, but there is no mistake that you represent the law."

7. Cf. Robert F. Kennedy, *Thirteen Days* (New York: Norton, 1969), p. 104: "President Kennedy dedicated himself to making it clear to Khrushchev by word and deed—for both are important—that the U.S. had limited objectives and that we had no interest in accomplishing these objectives by adversely affecting the national security of the Soviet Union or by humiliating her."

8. The phrase is William James's, quoted in Walter Lippmann, *Public Opinion* (1922; New York: Macmillan, 1961), p. 80.

9. On a grander scale, Ingersoll talked of war and how he hated it: "If I were president, I would get rid of all weapons."

14

Patterns of Police Investigation of Urban Crimes

William B. Waegel

What do detectives really do? How do they decide which cases are worthy of serious attention and which ones are not? These and related questions are addressed in William Waegel's article, in which he examines investigative practices employed in the handling of burglary, robbery, assault, rape, and homicide cases in an urban police department. As you read the article, pay close attention to what distinguishes routine from nonroutine cases for each crime type, and how the routine/nonroutine interpretation affects case handling. As a member of the public and a potential crime victim, do you approve of this differential handling of serious cases? As a detective, would you do anything differently?

The response of police investigators to citizen complaints of serious crimes constitutes a neglected area in the sociological literature of the police. Yet these activities are crucial to an understanding of the operation of the criminal justice system, for in most jurisdictions it is the exclusive task of detectives to investigate serious crimes. An examination of the interaction between police investigators, crime victims, witnesses, and perpetrators can enhance our understanding of the administration of justice and the functioning of the social control system.

Studies of uniformed police through participant observation are central among the works which have contributed to an understanding of day-to-day police activities. Skolnick (1967), Bittner (1967), Reiss (1971), Rubinstein (1973), Lundman (1974, 1979), Sykes and Clark (1975), Van Maanen (1978), and Manning (1978) have produced field studies which have examined and clarified the social world of the police, police-citizen encounters, and routine police practices.

However, few participant observation studies have focused on the critical area of detective work. Skolnick (1967) does devote some attention to specialized divisions, such as vice and detective bureaus, but much of his attention centers around police relationships with informers. This article utilized data obtained through participant observation to examine the patterned activities involved in police investigations of urban crimes.[1]

Case Handling Orientation

The organizational context in which detective work is carried out places significant constraints on investigative activities. In the department studies, the salient constraints are not rooted in supervisory surveillance, which generally is minimal, but rather in the bureaucratic requirements of producing completed investigative reports for each case within a rigid time frame while also producing an expected number and type of arrests.

For every case assigned, the detective must produce a completed investigative report within 14 days. In this report, there must be a description of the relevant information about the incident, the investigative activities undertaken, and a classification of the status of the investigation. Three classifications are available: (1) *closed*, which indicates that an arrest has been made and no further activity will be devoted to the case; (2) *suspended*, where the available information is such that further investigation is not warranted; and (3) *open*, which indicates that a continued investigation beyond the 14-day period holds some promise of resulting in an arrest. However, generally only "major cases" may remain classified as open, and special justification is always required. Supervisors seldom challenge the content of these reports, but compliance with time deadlines is closely monitored and used as a basis for evaluating individual performance. Detectives experience paperwork deadlines as a central source of pressure in their work, and view these deadlines as a fundamental constraint on how thoroughly any case can be investigated.

Detectives must also produce arrests, especially in burglary cases which comprise the majority of cases handled. While there is no formal arrest quota in the detective division, an informal understanding exists that one should produce at least two arrests per week if one desires to remain a detective and avoid transfer "back to the pit" (that is, back into uniform in the patrol division). Assignment to the detective division is the most prestigious position in the department, and it entails the additional benefit of rotating between only two, rather than three, work shifts. Although salary scales of patrol officers and detectives are the same for each rank, the latter have the luxury of wearing plain clothes and are free from the requirement of being available to handle radio calls. There is additionally the sense that detectives are engaged primarily in the "real police work" (that is, crime control as opposed to peacekeeping). The novitiate detective soon learns that he must produce an acceptable number and type of arrests, while at the same time comply with paperwork deadlines, if he is to remain a member of the detective division.

These features of the work setting generate an orientation to case handling which detectives refer to as "skimming." Skimming refers to selecting out for vigorous investigative effort those cases from one's workload which appear likely to result in an arrest, while summarily suspending or performing only a cursory investigation in the remainder of one's ordinary cases. Supervisors are certainly aware of this practice and of the fact that it ensures that the majority of ordinary cases receive a thorough investigation. However, supervisors themselves find their performance assessed in crude quantitative terms and are likely to be questioned by superiors if arrest levels drop from previous norms.

Within this context, understanding detective work thus requires an examination of the processes by which cases are attended to and assessed with regard to their likelihood of producing an arrest. Case-handling decisions are not guided by formal procedures for allocating time and effort to cases having different configurations of information. Rather, a set of informal interpretive schemes are used by detectives to manage the twin practical problems of paperwork deadlines and producing arrests. Through experience in working cases and through interaction with other members, detectives employ an instrumental short-hand for recognizing potentially productive cases which warrant vigorous investigative effort, and unproductive cases which are viewed as consuming time but having no tangible rewards. Because all the detectives experience similar problems in managing their caseloads, and because of the recognized utility of this case assessment shorthand, the interpretation and handling of cases by different detectives tend to be quite similar.

Burglary and robbery cases which are viewed as having little likelihood of producing an arrest are termed "routine cases" and receive minimal investigative effort. Assault, rape, and homicide cases generally receive a somewhat higher level of investigative effort. However, these latter offenses frequently involve acquainted parties,[2] and information is readily available to the investigator identifying the perpetrator. Such straightforward personal offense cases are also referred to as routine cases, for little effort is required to close the case. However, since no great investigative acumen is involved, less credit is accorded arrests in this type of case. Assault, rape and homicide cases involving nonacquainted parties ordinarily are designated major cases by supervisors, and methodical investigative work is called for. In general, the police are rather unsuccessful in solving this latter type of case.[3]

Case Interpretation Schemes

The preceding has suggested that detectives are constrained in their conception and handling of cases, not by the formal organization of their work or by supervisory surveillance, but rather by the bureaucratic pressure of writing reports and producing the proper number and quality of arrests. Given the case-working orientation previously described, an understanding of detective work requires an examination of the shorthand

Table 14.1
Incident Features and Investigative Patterns

Crime	Readily Available Information	Case Interpretation	Case Handling
Burglary	Identifies suspected perpetrator	Nonroutine	Vigorous effort, arrest anticipated
	No concrete identifying information	Routine, "pork chop" burglary	Case suspended; level of effort varies according to victim characteristics
Robbery	Potentially identifying	Nonroutine	Vigorous effort
	Does not identify	Routine robbery	Case suspended; level of effort varies according to victim characteristics and whether weapon used
Assault	Identifies perpetrator	Routine "Mom and Pop," "barroom" assault	Arrest made; minimal investigative effort
	Does not identify	Nonroutine	Level of effort varies depending on severity of injury and victim characteristics; may be major case
Rape	Acquaintance of victim identified as perpetrator and victim seen as having certain characteristics	"Suspect," "morning after" rape	Vigorous effort to test veracity of victim's account
	Unknown perpetrator	Nonroutine	Major case
Homicide	Identifies perpetrator acquainted with victim	"Killing"	Perfunctory investigation
	Does not identify perpetrator	"Murder"	Major case

schemes which link typical case patterns with specific investigative activities.[4]

Observation of detective-victim interviews and examination of written case reports provide the data for specifying the content of the interpretive schemes used by detectives. In the victim interview, the kinds of questions asked and the pieces of information sought are revealing of the case patterns recognized as typical for different offenses. However, in attempting to make sense of the incident at hand, the detective attends to much more than is revealed in his explicit communication with the victim. His interpretation of the case is also based upon his understanding of the victim's lifestyle, racial or ethnic group, class position, and possible clout or connections, as these factors bear upon such con-cerns as the likelihood of the victim inquiring into the progress of the investigation, the victim's intentions regarding prosecution, and the victim's competence and quality as a source of information.

The interpretive schemes employed also receive partial expression in the written investigative reports which must be produced for each case. These reports contain a selective accounting of the meaning assigned to a case, the information and understandings upon which this interpretation is based, and the nature of the investigative activities undertaken.[5]

The following sections examine typical case patterns and associated investigative activities for the five offenses commonly dealt with by detectives: burglary, robbery, aggravated assault, rape, and homicide. Table 14.1 provides a summary of case-handling patterns.

"Pork Chop" Burglaries

Routine burglary incidents which are seen as warranting only low-effort treatment are commonly referred to as "pork chop" burglaries. Where an instant case displays sufficient correspondence with this general category, detectives understand that appropriate ways of handling the case are to summarily suspend it, suspend it after a brief victim interview or perfunctory investigation, or reclassify it to a lesser offense.

Since burglary cases constitute roughly two-thirds of all cases handled the interpretive schemes for these cases tend to be the most crystalized and non-problematic. A burglary victim's ability or inability to provide information identifying the perpetrator or a probable perpetrator constitutes the single feature of burglary cases which is given greatest interpretive significance. In those few cases where the victim provides the name of a suspected perpetrator (often an ex-boyfriend, a relative, or a neighboring resident),[6] the case is a nonroutine one. When burglary cases are distributed at the beginning of each work shift, detectives quickly scan the original report prepared by a patrol officer and select out any cases having named suspects for immediate attention.

However, less than 10 percent of the patrol reports list a suspect by name. For the remaining cases, the initial inclination is to treat them as routine burglaries deserving of only minimal investigative effort.[7] In these cases, the social characteristics of the victim, particularly the victim's class position and race, have a decisive impact on the particular handling strategy adopted.

For example, where the victim is a low-status individual, detectives generally feel that it is safe and appropriate to summarily suspend the case or suspend it after briefly contacting the victim by telephone. A personal visit to the crime scene and a neighborhood canvass seldom are undertaken. Detectives assume that the patrol officer probably got all the information that was available from "the kind of people in that area."

When the victim is middle-class or when the burglary occurred in a "respectable" commercial establishment, detectives will commonly inspect the crime scene in person, interview the victim at some length, inquire of neighboring residents if they witnessed anything unusual, and, in general, sponsor the appearance of a reasonably thorough investigation. A more detailed investigative report is prepared explaining and justifying why the case has been suspended. This higher-effort handling strategy is employed largely because of a belief that this latter type of victim is more likely to inquire as to the progress of the investigation or complain to superiors about the detective's lack of success in solving the case. Detectives speak of cases "coming back on them" when they have not taken sufficient steps to impress victims that the case is being thoroughly investigated.

The Victim Interview

The detective's fundamental concern upon receiving burglary cases centers around an effort to assess the typicality of the incident. This assessment is made on the basis of information contained in the original patrol report and/or information obtained during an interview with the victim.

Two contrasting types of victim interviews for routine burglary cases will be examined. In cases 1 and 2, the incidents are initially interpreted as routine and the detectives structure interviews with the victims accordingly. In case 3, the available information generates an understanding that appropriate handling of the case must include a rather lengthy victim interview and an attempt to sponsor the impression that the incident is being investigated thoroughly.

Case 1

A burglary had occurred at a disreputable bar located in a low-income area of the city. A few bottles of liquor were the only items taken. The fingerprint report from the evidence detection unit had not been received, so the detective introduced himself to the proprietor of the bar and asked to see the point of entry. He examined the area around the door which had been dusted for fingerprints and concluded that no useful prints had been obtained. Turning to the proprietor, the detective asked three questions: Do you have any idea who broke into your place? Do you think any of the neighbors around here might have seen anything when occurred? Have you seen or heard about anyone suspicious hanging around here? After receiving negative replies to all three questions, the detective informed the proprietor that he would be contacted if anything came up and left the bar. Approximately 6 to 8 minutes were spent with the victim. As we got back into the car the detective told me he was suspending the case and remarked, "This (referring to the victim interview) is basically public relations work."

Case 2

A detective drove to the scene of a residential burglary in the same area of the city. The stolen items were noted, the victim stated that she had no idea who was responsible, and we left the victim's residence less than 4 minutes after we had arrived. "Kids," the detective remarked as he made some notes for future use in writing the investigative report. "I'll break it down to a criminal mischief." In the investigative report, the case was reclassified from burglary (a felony) to a misdemeanor and suspended. This handling strategy is encouraged by superiors, for it deletes both the incident and the fact that an arrest was never made from Part 1 crime statistics and the felony clearance rate.

Some burglary cases, in spite of the fact that the detective has interpreted the incident pattern as routine and unproductive, nevertheless are seen as requiring a different kind of victim interview and handling strategy.

Case 3

A detective was assigned a residential burglary in a transitional area of the city. He stopped in front of the address, read the original patrol report, and mentioned that this was the only white family on the block and that the row houses on either side of the victim's were vacant. An evidence detection report showed that four cards of fingerprints had been obtained from the scene. The detective asked the victim to show him the point of entry, and we were led through comfortably furnished rooms to the basement, where a large hole had been made in the brick wall separating her basement from the basement of the vacant house next door. The victim, a middle-aged woman who had lived in the house for over 20 years, stated that the loss was substantial and consisted mostly of jewelry, coin collections, camera equipment, and cash.

After returning upstairs, the detective pulled out his notebook and explained that he wished to record as much information about the incident as the victim could provide. She replied that an older group of males had come into the area recently, and she thought they were an organized group of house burglars. "I see them every morning when I leave for work. There's one guy who stands on either corner, and they're the lookouts. Apparently, they work with whoever is doing these burglaries, and they sit there and watch to see who works during the day, what time they leave, and what time they come back. Then they have all day to break into a place and rob it blind." The detective asked if she knew the names, or even nick-names, of any of these persons. She replied that she didn't and that she would have trouble pointing out specific persons because the group was new in the area. The detective listened to her extended response to his original question, but did not record any of it.

A complete listing and description of all items taken in the burglary was then compiled. The detective took voluminous notes, paying particular attention to items with recorded serial numbers and to pieces of jewelry which had identifying engraving. He assured the victim that this information would be followed up, and that she would be contacted if any of the articles were recovered or there were any other developments. The interview lasted 1 hour and 40 minutes.

Once outside, I asked the detective what he thought of the case. He replied by asking whether I had noticed that the burglars ignored two color television sets which were sitting out in plain view. He remarked, "The guys who did this weren't kids. They knew what they were doing."[8]

The detective's superficial handling of this case differed considerably from the handling strategies employed in cases 1 and 2. However, the minor nature of the subsequent investigative activities undertaken by the detective indicate that his interpretation of the case was that it was routine and unproductive. He entered serial numbers and other identifying information regarding the stolen articles into the computerized stolen property file "to cover myself, just in case." Later in the week he asked another detective assigned to the same sector if he had heard anything from his informants about anyone involved in daytime burglaries in that particular area of the city. The other detective replied that he had not, and at the end of the second week the investigator suspended the case and concluded his investigative report by stating that "all avenues of investigation have been exhausted."

The above discussion has presented contrasting examples of the handling of routine burglary cases. Handling strategies for such cases range from essentially no investigative effort, where a detective simply contacts the victim and inquires if the person has any idea who committed the burglary, to a perfunctory investigation in which weak information or minimal leads are pursued in a casual manner. The latter handling strategy usually involves an effort to convince the victim that "something is being done" about the incident in question. These different methods of handling routine burglary cases stem largely from differences in the characteristics of, and assumptions made about, the victims.

The Investigative Report

Further clarification of the relationship between typical case patterns and associated handling strategies may be gained by examining the content of the formal investigative reports produced by detectives. This section will also serve to highlight the general nature of the organizational constraints and demands which form the context in which case assessments are made.

The case reports presented here are reproduced verbatim.[9]

Case 4

Correct Offense: Burglary. Total value stolen: $280.

Investigative Procedure: At [time, date] this investigator spoke with the victim in this complaint, at her residence. [She] gave this investigator the same basic information as is stated in the original report. Also, adding that she does not have any serial numbers on the stolen items, and that she has a few suspects from the neighborhood, some boys that live in the east 10th Street area, between Poplar and Wilson Streets. The victim does not know the names of these individuals, but stated that they frequent the area of the 900 block of Wilson Street.

Conclusion: This complaint is to be *suspended* at this time, N.I.L.

N.I.L. is an acronym for "no investigative leads" that is often used regarding routine burglary cases. The detective suspended this case after simply contacting the victim by telephone. Less than 2 minutes were spent speaking with the victim, and another 3 to 4 minutes dictating the report.

Case 5

Correct Offense: Burglary, 2nd degree. Total value stolen: $110.

Summary: This is a burglary that occurred between [date, time] at [address in a public housing project] where unknown person(s) entered that location by removing a board from the rear door, and once inside, removed the below described article.

Property Stolen: One (1) Sharp 19-inch portable color TV in a brown and black cabinet. The television had a dial broken from off the side. [Victim] said value was $100. Miscellaneous frozen meats at $10.

Physical Evidence: No physical evidence was obtained at this time.

Victim Interview: [Name], black female, [address]. On [date, time] this investigator spoke with the victim who informed me that between the above dates, some unknown person(s) entered her house by knocking a board from the rear door and once inside removed the above TV and frozen meats. [Victim] had no serial or model numbers on the TV and has no suspects in this investigation. The victim stated she did not wish any prosecution in this case. She is only concerned about recovering her TV.

On [date, time] the investigator made a canvass of the neighborhood for possible witness, but met with negative results.

A check of pawn sheets has been made with negative results.

Conclusion: Due to the fact that all avenues of investigation have been exhausted, and the victim does not want to prosecute, this case is suspended.

The detective who wrote the report fabricated both the neighborhood canvass and check of the pawn sheets to impress his supervisor that he had done as much as possible in a case where only meager information was available. For all practical purposes, the decision to suspend the case was made at the conclusion of the victim interview. The detective took for granted that in this neighborhood no one would volunteer that they witnessed the incident and that a search through the pawn sheets would be fruitless.

Cases 1 through 5 highlight the basic features of routine burglary cases and the associated patterns of investigative activity. The feature of burglary cases which is accorded primary interpretive significance is the availability of information which identifies a suspected perpetrator. Any case having an identified suspect is selected out for vigorous effort. Since there are no named suspects in the great majority of burglaries, most are interpreted and treated as routine. The amount of effort devoted to such cases is most directly linked to the victim's social status. Additional interpretive features include: (1) the victim's expressed or presumed attitude toward prosecution; (2) whether the offense was committed in such a way that physical evidence is available which could conclusively link a suspect to the crime; and (3) the area in which the incident occurred, particularly as this bears on the detective's beliefs about the inclinations of potential witnesses in that area.

The discussion of routine burglary cases and their handling illustrates the content of the shorthand schemes used by detectives in working burglary cases. Discussion of the remaining four types of routine offense patterns is based on the same kind of observa-

tion and documents, although space considerations will not permit the same volume of illustrative material to be presented.

Routine Robberies

The majority of persons who are apprehended for robbery are caught within 10 to 15 minutes after the commission of the crime. Those cases in which a suspect is not apprehended shortly after the incident are assigned to detectives for investigation. Detectives have less latitude in the handling strategies they may employ when a firearm is used in a robbery and the victim is a business establishment or a middle-class individual. Where a robbery incident has these features, the detective must conduct at least a perfunctory investigation and produce a very detailed investigative report. There is an assumption of offense repetition in armed robberies, and detectives anticipate that information in the report may have future value if a person is apprehended for a similar robbery incident.

Greater latitude exists in the handling of strong-arm robberies or muggings. Routine purse-snatching incidents usually receive either a perfunctory investigation or are suspended after an unproductive victim interview; the former strategy tends to be employed when the victim is middle-class and the latter when the victim is a poor person. When the victim of a strong-arm robbery is seen as a thoroughly "disreputable type" (such as a skid-row resident who has been "rolled"), the incident may be reclassified to a simple theft and suspended.

The feature accorded primary interpretive significance in assessing the routine or nonroutine nature of robbery incidents is the ability of the victim or witnesses to provide potentially identifying information regarding the perpetrator. Robbery occurs in a face-to-face setting, although masks are occasionally worn and perpetrators sometimes strike quickly from behind the victim. Victims and witnesses are often stunned by the speed and shock of the incident and, accordingly, the nature of the information they are able to provide varies widely. When this information takes the form of a simple clothing description, the incident is likely to be treated as a routine one. Regardless of the victim's characteristics, where potentially identifying information is provided which holds out the possibility of making an arrest, the case is defined as nonroutine, and a vigorous investigation is conducted. The crucial question asked during the victim or witness interview is "Would you recognize the guy if you saw him again?" or "Would you recognize the guy if you saw a picture of him?"

The interpretation of robbery incidents is also based on the manner in which the offense was committed. The typical armed robbery is seen as involving one or two young males wearing nondistinctive clothing and masks who enter a small business establishment (generally a corner grocery store, liquor store, or convenience store) for less than 2 minutes and do not leave fingerprints or other physical evidence behind. The typical mugging incident is seen as involving a middle-aged or elderly female victim and one or more teenage males who approach the victim from behind and then quickly move to a place where they are out of view of searching police. Further, detectives take into consideration the area of the city in which the incident occurred and, as in burglary cases, make assumptions about residents with regard to their cooperation with the police and the likelihood of a neighborhood canvass.

Cases 6 and 7 are illustrative of the interpretation and handling of routine and nonroutine robbery incidents.

Case 6

A young cab driver who was new to the job had been robbed by two males who hailed the cab and then displayed a gun and ordered the driver to take them to a street bordering the city reservoir. They took the cash box and the driver's wallet, pulled out the cab's microphone cord, and ordered the driver to lay down in the seat as they fled.

In the detective hall, the victim was questioned at length regarding a description of the two males. He could only provide a general clothing description since they had been in the back seat. It was noted that they had worn gloves during the incident. The driver was shown "hot" mugshots of persons recently involved in armed robberies, but none of these was identified as the perpetrator. Still visibly shaken by the incident, the driver was unclear about where he had picked the two up and the precise location where they had exited the cab. The driver stated that he thought he would be able to identify the male with the gun, and he was asked to come back the next day to look through additional mugbooks.

After the driver had left, and approximately 2 ½ hours after the robbery had occurred, the detective remarked: "That kid doesn't know what he's doing. And what kind of witness would he make. I'm ready to suspend the case right now."

Arrangements were never made for the victim to return to look through mugbooks because it was assumed that this would be fruitless (mugshots are very small (2" x 3") and are commonly several years old; identification through mugshots is rare). Nor was a neighborhood canvass for witnesses conducted, for it was assumed that residents in that area would be unlikely to volunteer information. The case was suspended 3 days later.

Robbery cases in which an arrest is not made shortly after the incidents are solved either through luck or gross incompetence on the part of the perpetrator, or through a major and time-consuming investigation involving informants and stakeouts. The latter situation occurs when an individual or group of persons is believed responsible for a series of robberies. The former situation is more common than one might suspect, as illustrated in the following case:

Case 7

An armed robbery had occurred at a small cleaning establishment when only one female clerk was present. Two males entered, placed a jacket on the counter, and asked to have it cleaned. As the clerk was filling out the slip, one male displayed a gun, ordered the clerk into a backroom, emptied the cash register and fled.

Two detectives responded and one began questioning the clerk. As she was describing the incident, she pointed to the jacket on the counter which the perpetrators had not taken with them when they fled. The second detective casually picked up the jacket and began looking through the pockets. In a small inside pocket was a document from the public defender's office containing a person's name. The case was solved simply by obtaining a photograph of this person and showing it to the clerk.

In summary, case features which constitute the basic interpretive framework for robbery incidents include:

1. The availability of information potentially identifying a suspect from the victim or witnesses

2. The social characteristics of the victim and witnesses which, within the interpretive schemes employed by detectives, make different categories of people more or less consequential as victims and more or less reliable sources of information

3. The victim's actual or presumed attitude toward spending the time and effort necessary in prosecuting the case

4. Whether the incident was carried out in such a way that physical evidence is obtainable

5. The area in which the incident occurred and the perceived likelihood of obtaining useful information from residents of that area through such procedures as a neighborhood canvass.

Routine Assaults

The majority of aggravated assault incidents observed occurred between persons who knew one another. Detectives use the term "Mom and Pop assault" or "barroom assault" to refer to incidents which involve acquainted parties. Unlike burglary and robbery cases, in assault incidents the victim frequently is able to provide the name of the perpetrator to responding police. Therefore, routine assault cases—those which are dealt with by means of low-effort handling strategies—generally result in an arrest. Where the victim and assailant were not previously acquainted in an assault incident, the case generally is defined as a nonroutine one requiring vigorous investigative effort.

There are no formal guidelines for handling assault incidents having different statutorily defined degrees of severity. Thus, an attempted murder incident involving a husband and wife in which the victim tells police that she was shot by her spouse is commonly handled in a purely routine manner. The detective takes written statements from both parties and any witnesses, attempts to locate and confiscate the weapon if one was used, orders photographs taken of the crime scene, and collects any relevant physical evidence. However, these tasks are performed in a casual, almost mechanical way, for the detective does not feel that he is actively seeking information about what happened, but merely collecting information and evidence which is largely superfluous. This casual investigative approach is partly traceable to a belief among detectives that their investigative methods will seldom come under court scrutiny in routine assault cases because most cases of this type will be resolved through a negotiated plea of guilty.

Since the time lag between the occurrence of the offense and the police response is seen as critical, detectives usually respond directly to the scene of felony assaults. Thus, within a short period of time detectives are able to ask the questions and seek out the basic information enabling them to make sense of the event and assess its routine or nonroutine nature.

The feature of assault cases having primary interpretive significance is the existence and nature of a prior social relationship between the involved parties. Detectives obtain a sense of what happened and what needs to be done in an assault incident when they learn that it involved a man and woman who have been living together, acquaintances who got into an argument outside a bar, or strangers.

The following incident, although involving an assault with a deadly weapon, was understood by the detective as requiring essentially no investigative effort.

Case 8

During the early morning hours, a man had assaulted his common-law wife with a knife, inflicting a laceration which required hospital treatment. During the drive to the public housing project where the parties lived, the detective remarked, "the drunks over here are always fightin' and cuttin' one another." It was noted from the patrol report that uniformed officers had advised the woman to sign a warrant and she had done so. The detective found the man standing in front of his residence and called out, "C'mon John, come with me. I gotta lock you up." No questions were asked about the incident during the drive to the station or during the handling of the arrest paperwork. No attempt was made to obtain a statement from the man for use in prosecuting the case. I later expressed surprise that the man had been released on his own recognizance for a felony assault, but the detective matter-of-factly replied, "Why not? She'll never show up in court and prosecute it anyhow. Why waste my time and everybody else's on it?"

No investigation was conducted. In assault cases of this type, detectives ordinarily write a brief report detailing the victim's account of the incident and "let the courts sort it out."

Detectives also attend to whether the precipitating circumstances were normal for the parties involved. Domestic assaults are seen as typically growing out of a heated, verbal argument over any number of personal issues. With regard to barroom-type assaults between males, one detective expressed the opinion that "money, booze, and women are the main reasons the natives go at it." If the precipitating circumstances are not seen as corresponding to such normal motives, but are found to lie in a dispute over stolen goods or a drug deal, a more vigorous investigation may be undertaken.

Detectives also base their interpretation on the life-styles and social characteristics of the involved parties. A shared belief exists among detectives that physical violence is a normal aspect of the lifestyles of lower-class persons and especially members of minority groups. As one detective remarked during the early stage of my field work, "There's one thing you've got to understand. These people are savages, and we're here to keep peace among the savages." On the other hand, where physical confrontation is not seen as a normal aspect of the lifestyle of the parties

involved, a detective is likely to interview the parties at greater length in an effort to determine why the assault occurred. Photographs of the victim's injuries may be ordered and an interview with the attending physician conducted, for parties having different social characteristics and lifestyles are seen as having different likelihoods of resolving the matter through plea bargaining or through formal judicial procedures.

Routine assault cases are constructed from the following elements. The existence and nature of a prior social relationship between the involved parties constitutes the feature of assault incidents which is accorded primary interpretive significance. The interpretation and handling of assault incidents is also contingent upon:

1. Understanding of the lifestyles and social characteristics of the parties involved

2. The victim's attitude toward prosecution, which may derive from explicit statements made by the victim or which may be assumed on the basis of understandings about the relationship between, and the lifestyle of, the involved parties

3. Whether the precipitating circumstances are seen as normal for the type of incident in question.

The seriousness of the injury to the victim has little bearing on the assessment of the incident as routine or nonroutine, but it has substantial impact on whether the case will be summarily suspended or whether some investigative activities will be performed.

'Morning After' Rapes

Rape generally is viewed as so serious an offense that it warrants an intensive investigation. If the victim is attacked by an unknown assailant, supervisors almost invariably impose a major case definition on the incident, assign several detectives to the case full time and sometimes play an active role in the investigation themselves. Where the victim is a poor person or a member of a minority group, the police response is typically of a lesser magnitude, although initially one or two detectives are likely to be assigned to the case full time. In other words, rape complaints generally receive a vigorous investigative effort.

However, there is one commonly recognized pattern of features regarding rape complaints which elicits a qualitatively different police response. When this configuration of features exists in a specific allegation of rape, detectives refer to the incident as a "morning after" or "suspect" rape, their initial reaction to the complaint is one of suspicion. Initial police efforts are concerned with and concentrate on attempting to establish the legitimacy of the complainant's allegations. Among detectives, it is viewed as a mark of investigative competence and acumen to "see through" a suspect rape complaint. This status dimension is sustained by frequent recounting of past cases in which a female did in fact falsely allege rape, in combination with the oft-repeated caution that "rape is the only crime where a person's word can send a guy to jail for life."[10]

The following case displays typical features of incidents categorized as "morning after" rapes.

Case 9

Two detectives were assigned to investigate a rape complaint which had been reported at approximately 3:00 A.M. After notifying police, the victim was immediately taken to a hospital for a medical examination. The physician indicated that the test for ejaculate was negative, but the victim had noticeable bruises on her vulva and inner thighs. The complainant was returned to the detective hall and questioned for over 4 hours. She stated that she had been alone walking to her residence at about 11:30 P.M. when a car pulled up to the curb beside her. She recognized the driver as a person she had known in high school and, after some discussion, agreed to ride around with him as he attempted to buy some marijuana. Some time later, she indicated that she needed to use a bathroom and asked to be taken home. The driver replied that she could use the one in his apartment. The complainant stated that when she arrived, she was sexually assaulted by the driver and three other males already in the apartment. She had difficulty expressing exactly what had happened, stating simply that they had "attacked her." One detective remarked that the victim appeared to be mentally retarded.

At 8:00 A.M., I asked a supervising detective what he thought of the case. He replied, "It stinks. She keeps changing her story. She knows the guys who were supposed to have done it plus no sperm showed up in the test at the hospital. There is one guy locked up downstairs on a 2-hour detention, but it looks right now like there probably won't be any arrests made."

The case was eventually handled as an unfounded complaint, meaning that the investigators believed there was not sufficient evidence to warrant a criminal charge.

There is a shared belief among detectives that young, lower-class females are the most likely persons to falsely allege rape. Any indication of mental or emotional disturbance on the part of the victim heightens the detective's suspicion regarding the legitimacy of her allegation. Where a victim having these characteristics alleges that she has been raped by someone with whom she is acquainted, the initial orientation of detectives is to seek out information to categorize the event as a suspect or legitimate rape. It is standard procedure in rape investigations to transport the victim to a hospital immediately for a medical examination to test for the presence of ejaculate. Although there is an awareness that ejaculation within the victim does not occur in all rapes and that penetration and ejaculation are not statutorily required elements of the crime of rape, detectives nonetheless assign considerable interpretive significance to whether or not the rape has been "confirmed" by medical examination.

Additional information enabling detectives to categorize an incident as suspect or legitimate is sought out during the victim interviews. Where the victim possesses social characteristics believed to be typically associated with false allegations of rape, the questioning tends to take on a predictable form. Do you know the guy? How long have you known him? Have you ever had sexual relations with him before? Did he use a weapon or other means of force? Did you report this to the police as soon as you were able to? How did you come in contact with him prior to the incident? Did you voluntarily get into his car or accompany him home? Did you resist?

Where the victim provides the name of her alleged assailant, this person is brought in for questioning. The primary issue of interest is whether or not he indicates that the victim consented. At this point, sufficient information has usually been obtained to categorize the incident as suspect or legitimate. Investigative strategies differ radically depending on this assessment. Suspect rape incidents typically are unfounded or reduced to a lesser charge such as sexual assault or sexual misconduct.

"Morning after" rape cases consist of some combination of the features presented below. The feature assigned primary interpretive significance is whether a victim having specific social characteristics believed to be typical of females who falsely allege rape knew her assailant prior to the incident. An interpretation of a rape complaint as suspect is likely to be made when this feature exists in combination with some or all of the following elements:

1. Certain conduct by the victim prior to and during the incident may be construed as cooperative or consenting behavior. Voluntarily accompanying the alleged perpetrator to the place where the incident occurred, or voluntarily entering his vehicle, may be taken as indications of willingness on the part of the victim. The victim's failure to fight back to attempt to resist the assault may be seen as an indication that "she really didn't mind." Consumption of alcohol or other drugs by the two parties together prior to the incident is seen as cooperative and contributing behavior on the part of the victim.

2. Any delay in reporting the incident to police is seen as entailing the possibility that the victim has some ulterior motive in making the complaint. Revenge against the person named by the victim is seen as the most common motive for false allegations of rape.

3. An emotional state and attitude displayed toward the incident by the victim which are viewed as inappropriate for a female who has just been sexually abused raises suspicion. After listening to a rape complainant calmly and matter-of-factly describe the details of an incident, one detective expressed doubt regarding the victim's account, noting, "She should be more upset than this." Another detective stormed out of an interview with a 15-year-old resident of a juvenile group home who alleged that she had been raped by three other residents of the home and stated, "If she doesn't give a shit about what happened then why should I?"

4. Any contradictions or inconsistencies in the victim's account of the incident during extended questioning by different detectives are seen as indicative of a false complaint. One older, experienced detective expressed the opinion to the researcher that many investigators expect a clear, coherent, and consistent account of the incident in spite of the fact that the interview is being conducted within hours after the assault and in spite of the likelihood that many victims are embarrassed by, and are trying to forget, what has just happened to them. If the victim is asked to take a polygraph examination and declines for any reason, detectives are likely to conclude that a legitimate rape did not occur. If the victim consents to a polygraph examination and the results are termed "inconclusive" (a rather frequent outcome), the same inference is likely to be drawn.

5. A medical examination which does not confirm the presence of ejaculate within the victim is seen as reason for suspicion regarding the validity of the complaint.

6. The person named as the perpetrator provides an account of the incident in which the female consented to sexual relations.

Killings

Detectives distinguish two types of homicides: killings and murders. In the former, the information and evidence available at the crime scene rather easily leads to the identification of the perpetrator. Commonly, such information is available from: (1) the perpetrator who remains at the scene of the crime when police arrive (such as the remorseful spouse); (2) persons who either witnessed the crime or have knowledge of a person who had threatened the victim, had been arguing with the victim, or had reason to assault the victim; or (3) a "dying declaration" provided by the victim.[11] Detectives recognize that most homicides occur between persons who know one another, and that often in such cases the perpetrator makes no serious attempt to conceal his or her deed. Where a particular case is seen as corresponding to the general category of routine killings, detectives view their task as a reasonably straightforward one involving apprehending the perpetrator, gathering any potential evidence, taking statements from any relevant parses, and writing a detailed report for use by the prosecutor.

In contrast, an incident is defined as a murder when available information does not readily identify the perpetrator. Different motives or precipitating circumstances are believed to be associated with this type of homicide, and methodical investigative work is deemed necessary.

The following case is typical of the interpretation and handling of routine killing incidents:

Case 10

Two detectives were assigned to a homicide case which had originally been handled by patrol officers as a routine assault case. The incident involved a lover's triangle between two males and a female who lived in the same block in one of the most deteriorated, skid-row type areas of the city. All three persons were described as long-term alcoholics. Patrol officers originally responded to the scene following a report of an assault in progress. Apparently the younger of the two males had argued with the female about her relationship with the other male. The female had been struck on the forehead during this argument and had suffered a serious scalp laceration. The older male was found lying in his apartment with a head laceration and was taken to a hospital where he was treated and kept for observation. He informed patrol officers that he had been beaten by the younger man, but he was highly intoxicated during this interview. Patrol officers arrested the younger man for assault on the female, and he was released on an unsecured bond. Three days later the older man died in the hospital.

The case was assigned to two detectives the following morning as a possible homicide. The detectives discussed possible classification of the incident: death from natural causes, homicide, or self-defense. It was decided that nothing further would be done until the medical examiner's office classified the death in the afternoon. When it was learned that the cause of death was a fractured skull, the detectives cursed and discussed what would have to be done "to cover ourselves." They obtained the victim's bloodstained clothing as possible evidence. An attempt was made to locate the suspect in the immediate area of his residence, but he was not found. After a brief inspection of the room where the victim was found, photographs were taken, and it was decided that a slipcover and a chair showing what appeared to be blood should be tagged as evidence. Both detectives repeatedly expressed their revulsion over the condition of the residence and the tasks they were performing. It was decided to make no further attempt to locate the suspect that day, but rather to wait and see whether he would show up for a scheduled court appearance the next day pertaining to the assailant charge. "I could care less about this case, I'd be just as happy if drunks like these were left to kill each other off."

The following morning the suspect came into the detective hall to turn himself in. He was advised of his rights and told that he had an opportunity to make a statement about what happened. He stated that he had been extremely intoxicated that night, had passed out, and doesn't remember anything that happened. No further attempt was made to interrogate the suspect, and the interview lasted less than 30 minutes.

Obtaining a formal statement from the female assault victim about the incident and preparing a four-page investigation report concluded the detectives' work on the case. The total time and effort devoted to this investigation was comparable to that for a minor burglary case having a named suspect.

In homicide cases, primary interpretive significance is accorded a combination of two case features: (1) whether information available at the scene or in initial interviews identifies and links a person to the crime, and (2) whether there was a prior relationship between that person and the victim. Where both of these features are present in an instant case, the event ordinarily is interpreted as a killing and handled routinely.

The assessment of the routine or non-routine nature of homicide incidents is also based on the social characteristics and lifestyles of the parties involved. In part, this assignment of identities to the principals in the case is made on the basis of territorial knowledge which includes assumptions and understandings about the typical inhabitants of an area and their likely patterns of behavior.

Detectives also attend to whether the motive and the circumstances precipitating the incident were normal for the parties involved. If the apparent motive and precipitating circumstances in a case map onto a common and understandable pattern for domestic killings or barroom-type killings, the incident tends to be readily categorized and treated as routine. In domestic killings, a heated argument regarding one party's sexual fidelity is seen as an ordinary precipitating circumstance. Similarly, for barroom-type killings involving two males, a verbal argument or challenge concerning a woman, money, or a number of other normal bases for heated arguments are seen as ordinary motives and precipitating circumstances. Further investigative effort is seen as necessary when such a common and readily understandable pattern is not evident in a case.

Summary and Conclusions

Police handling of criminal investigations is guided by a set of interpretive schemes through which cases having different configurations of information are seen as warranting different levels and methods of investigation. Organizational demands and constraints generate a distinctive work orientation for the frequently handled crimes of burglary and robbery. Detectives select out for vigorous effort readily solvable cases while devoting only cursory effort to the remaining cases. Case stereotypes also function to provide standard recipes for the handling of assault, rape, and homicide incidents which display typical features.

Investigative work in the department studied was vigorous and methodical in only a small percentage of the cases handled. Indeed an image of detective work as involving a special arsenal of sophisticated techniques is substantially misleading for most ordinary criminal investigations. If the victim or witnesses are able to provide potentially identifying information in burglary and robbery incidents, the case will be vigorously pursued. In the great majority of cases, such information is not available, and minimal effort is devoted to the case. The work orientation referred to as "skimming" enhances our understanding of the low clearance rates for burglary and robbery. The relatively small portion of incidents categorized as major cases receive a higher level of investigative effort and a wider variety of investigative techniques are used.

Case-handling methods also vary according to the victim's social status. The differential treatment of crime victims flows in part from a set of stereotypic assumptions about the detectives' concern with potential solvability. Thus, in certain neighborhoods methodical investigative procedures, such as an area canvass seldom are undertaken because of a belief that they would prove fruitless. A work orientation emphasizing practicality and productivity serves to encourage this substitution of assumptions for information gathering.

Notes

1. The description and analysis presented here are based on 9 months of participant observation field work in a city police detective division. At the conclusion of the field work, the

formulations contained in this article were discussed with various detectives in the context of "how the work is actually done." The patterned activities described here were recognized by experienced detectives as standard features of everyday practices. Further information about departmental characteristics, access problems, daily routines, and the field role adopted during the research is available from the author.

2. Statistics on the offender and victim relationship for personal offenses are broken down into categories for primary relationship, nonprimary (such as acquaintance, neighbor, sex rival, or enemy), stranger, other, and unknown. For homicide the respective figures are 33.7 percent, 28.1 percent, and 38.2 percent; for aggravated assault, 20.6 percent, 25.3 percent, and 55 percent; and for rape, 10.2 percent, 32.6.percent, and 57.2 percent (Dunn 1976:11).

3. This finding is also documented in survey research on police investigations. A recent study found that substantially more than half of all serious reported crimes receive no more than superficial attention from investigators. Further, if information identifying the perpetrator is not available at the time the crime is reported, the perpetrator generally will not be subsequently identified. See Greenwood et al. (1975).

4. A theoretical interpretation of the centrality of typificatory schemes in decision making by police and other legal agents is provided in Waegel (1981).

5. Garfinkel (1967:186-207) argues that organizational records are not to be treated as accurate or mirror reflections of the actual handling of a client or case by organizational members. However, these records can be employed to examine how members go about constructing a meaningful conception of a client or case and use it for their own practical purposes. Any valid sociological use of such records requires detailed knowledge on the part of the researcher regarding the context in which the records are produced, background understandings of members, and organizationally relevant purposes and routines.

6. Although "named suspects" (persons named in the original patrol report) are most commonly obtained from victims, other sources occasionally provide this information. A neighbor may come forward and volunteer that he or she witnessed the incident or has heard that a certain person or persons have been committing burglaries in the vicinity. Informants sometimes provide similar information.

7. There is a formal constraint on the detective's discretion regarding how much effort to devote to a burglary case. If the loss is in excess of $2,000, a lieutenant may impose a major case definition on the incident. The vast bulk of the city burglaries I observed involved much smaller losses.

8. There is a widespread misunderstanding concerning the utility of fingerprints obtained from a crime scene. Prior to my research, I had believed that a fingerprint obtained from a crime scene could automatically be used to identify the perpetrator. Unknown latent fingerprints from a crime scene cannot be identified from fingerprint files. The FBI fingerprint laboratory will only compare unknown latent prints with the file prints of identified suspects. Unknown prints from a crime scene and file prints of a suspect or suspects must be packaged together and sent to the FBI lab where technicians simply make comparisons. There are presently no automated procedures for comparing an unknown fingerprint against the millions of file prints.

9. The detectives dictate investigative reports through the desk telephones in the large detective room. The fact that this room is often crowded and noisy accounts for much of the fractured grammar in these reports. Identifying information has been deleted.

10. This statement means that rape cases are sometimes prosecuted successfully without corroboration of the victim's testimony and without direct evidence, such as fiber intermingling on clothing.

11. A surprising number of homicide victims do not expire immediately after receiving mortal injuries. Detectives immediately respond to any call involving a serious assault and, if the victim is conscious, ask two questions: Do you know who did this to you, and do you know why? If a dying declaration is obtained under the proper legal circumstances, the victim's statement will be admissible in court as an exception to the hearsay rule.

References

Bittner, Egon. 1967. The police on skid row: A study of peace keeping. *Am. Social. Rev.* 32:699-715.

Dunn, Christopher S. 1976. *The patterns and distribution of assault incident characteristics*. Albany, NY: Criminal Justice Research Center.

Garfinkel, Harold. 1967. *Studies in ethnomethodology*. Englewood Cliffs: Prentice-Hall.

Greenwood, P; Chalken, J.; Petersilia, J.; and Prusoff, L. 1975. *The criminal investigation process: Volume III*. Santa Monica, CA: Rand Corporation.

Lundman, Richard J. 1974. Routine arrest practices: A commonwealth perspective. *Social Problems* 22: 127-141.

——. 1979. Organizational norms and police discretion: An observational study of police work with traffic law violators. *Criminology* 17:159-171.

Manning, Peter K. 1974. Police lying. *Urban Life* 3: 283-306.

Reiss, Albert. 1971. *Police and the public*. New Haven: Yale Univ. Press.

Rubinstein, Jonathan. 1973. *City police*. New York: Ballantine.

Skolnick, Jerome. 1967. *Justice without trial*. New York: Wiley.

Sykes, Richard and Clark, John P. 1975. A theory of deference exchange in police-civilian encounters. *Am. J. Sociol.* 81: 584-600.

Van Maanen, John. 1978. The asshole. In *Policing: A view from the street*, edited by Peter K. Manning and John Van Maanen. Santa Monica, CA: Goodyear.

Waegel, William B. 1981. Case routinization in investigative police work. *Social Problems* 28: 263-275.

15

What Is Patrol Work?

Gordon P. Whitaker

This article presents data and findings from the Police Services Study, by far the most comprehensive attempt to discover first-hand, through the use of ride-along observers, what police patrol officers really do with their time and what types of encounters they have with the public. As you read the article, pay particular attention to the distribution of encounters among the categories of crime, disorder, service, and traffic, and also to the specific actions taken by officers in encounters with citizens. How does this picture of patrol work square with your own view of what patrol officers do? What common theme runs through patrol officers' most frequent actions in encounters? Do you think this study's findings, generated in the late 1970s, apply equally well today, or do you think that patrol work has changed? If the latter, what changes do you suspect have occurred?

As Goldstein notes, most police departments themselves have little systematic information about how their officers spend their time or the range and frequency of actions they take toward citizens. Even for patrol, which constitutes the largest part of almost all police departments' operations, there is little systematic data available about what officers do. Research on police patrol activities has begun to shed additional light on what goes on in some departments, but these studies are reported in scattered places. The most comprehensive review is by Cordner (1979). That review does not include some of the most detailed, more recent studies of patrol work. This paper reviews a number of the more detailed recent studies and

contrasts their findings with those from observations of patrol operations in 24 other departments, which have not been previously reported.

This overview of patrol work is organized in three sections: how officers spend their time on patrol; what problems patrol officers deal with in their encounters with citizens and what actions officers on patrol take to control some citizens and help others. Throughout, the categories used by each of the different research teams have shaped the sorts of data that are available from their studies. Because they used different categories and definitions, it is often difficult to make exact comparisons of patrol work in the various departments. Despite this limitation it is possible to compare and contrast these studies to expand our understanding of the content of police patrol operations. In addition to previously reported data, this paper also makes use of data from the Police Services Study.[1] These data on patrol operations in 60 neighborhoods served by 24 departments were collected using a standard set of categories and definitions and consistent observation and recording procedures. The departments studied were in the Rochester, New York; St. Louis, Missouri; and Tampa-St. Petersburg, Florida, metropolitan areas. The study was conducted during the summer of 1977. These data increase considerably the confidence we can place in the general picture of patrol work which emerges from this review.

How Officers Spend Their Time

Answering assigned calls and conducting general surveillance by "patrolling" are the two most time-consuming sorts of patrol activity. There is great variation in the amount of time officers on patrol spend answering assigned calls. In most places, however, assigned calls take considerably less than half of officers' work time. Patrolling the beat usually occupies a higher proportion of officers' time. However, "patrolling" also typically takes less than half of the time of officer assigned to patrol.

Most studies of how officers spend their time are based on calls for service (or dispatch) records and consequently focus primarily on time answering calls for service. Dispatch records from Wilmington, Delaware, for example, indicate that patrol officers in that city spent almost three hours (174 minutes) of every eight-hour shift answering calls for service (Tien *et al.*, 1978:4-l5). In contrast to average time on calls for service in four other departments, the Wilmington figures seemed rather high to Tien and his colleagues. They calculated that average time on calls for service per eight-hour shift was 134 minutes in Worcester, Massachusetts; 96 minutes in St. Louis, Missouri; 89 minutes in Kansas City, Missouri; and only 72 minutes in Arlington, Massachusetts (pp. 4-19). They concluded that:

> Wilmington has the highest known unit utilization factor ["fraction of time a patrol unit is responding to calls for service during an eight-hour tour"]. The paucity of available workload or productivity-related data suggests that an intensive national effort should be undertaken to fill this important gap. (pp. 4-20)

In fact, however, the range of time on assigned calls is even greater than Tien *et al.* described. Another study which appeared about the same time indicates a substantially higher percentage of patrol officer time spent on calls for service. In their study of patrol staffing in San Diego, Boydstun and colleagues (1977:53) found that officers averaged more than 270 minutes (four and a half hours) on calls for service per eight-hour shift. These figures were obtained from dispatch records for San Diego's Central Division where the staffing study was conducted.[2] Although over half of each eight-hour shift in San Diego's Central Division was, on the average, devoted to calls for service, this high average was not characteristic of the city as a whole. Boydstun and Sherry (1975:60), in their study of the Community Profile Project, report that only about 120 minutes (2 hours) of each eight-hour shift were spent answering calls for service in San Diego's North Division. The Community Profile Project was conducted two years before the patrol staffing study, but it is unlikely that the average time spent on calls for service more than dou-

bled in that period. It is more probable that differences between the areas being policed account for the differences in how officers spent their time.

Calls for service or dispatch records usually do not provide a complete account of the time officers on patrol spend on encounters with citizens. Calls records are maintained by the dispatcher, who does not know about (or knows about, but does not record) many encounters which are initiated by officers or citizens "in the field." Field interrogations, for example, are often excluded from calls for service records. Traffic stops are also frequently not recorded by the dispatcher unless a citation is issued. On the other hand, dispatch records may include meal breaks, errands, maintenance stops, and dispatched runs in which no police encounter with a citizen resulted. Thus the total time accounted for on these records may miss some encounter time and include some non-encounter time. Practices vary from department to department.

Another source of inaccuracy in dispatch records of officers' use of time arises from self-reporting of the time spent on each call. Because the officer's report that an encounter is ended indicates that the officer is free for reassignment, an incentive exists for officers to delay such reports. This management use of the report that an encounter is ended conflicts with its use as a source of data about time devoted to encounters.

Two other sources of data on patrol officers' use of time are available: officer logs and observer reports. Both may be freer of bias than dispatch records because they are less likely to be used for management of individual officers. Officer logs from Wilmington, Delaware, indicate that officers there spent an average of 166 minutes (two and three-quarter hours) per eight-hour shift on both field-initiated and dispatched encounters with citizens in 1976 (Tien *et al.*, 1978:4-18). This is quite similar to the average of 174 minutes per shift calculated from Wilmington calls for service records, suggesting that in Wilmington officers either tend to report all field-initiated encounters to the dispatcher or else fail to record on their own logs encounters which they do not report to the dispatcher. Another piece of information from officer logs is the amount of time spent on administrative and personal activities (and thus not spent patrolling). Officers in Wilmington reported an average of about 90 minutes per eight-hour shift on meals, breaks, car checkups, arrest processing, phone calls, and so forth (Tien *et al.*, 1978:4-18).

Observer reports are a more expensive form of data collection, but they can also give a fuller picture of police activities They remove the bias often present in officer self-reporting, yet, if carefully conducted, avoid interfering with officer activities. Observers in the Kansas City Preventive Patrol Experiment indicate that almost 40 percent of each shift was spent on encounters with citizens (both dispatched and field-initiated) (Kelling *et al.*, 1974:500). Thus about 190 minutes (just over three hours) of every eight-hour shift were, on the average, spent on citizen-police encounters. Another 75 minutes per shift were devoted to report writing and other administrative tasks. An average of 73 minutes per eight-hour shift were spent on personal breaks and errands (see pp. 504-509). This is considerably more time on administrative and personal activities reported for Kansas City than for Wilmington, but it is important to remember that the Kansas City estimates are from observer records while the Wilmington estimates are from officer logs. Some difference is probably due to variation in police practices between the two cities, but some of the difference is also likely to result from officers' tendency to be quite conservative in reporting how much shift time they spend on personal errands.

Observers using consistent coding rules and observation techniques in several different departments can provide data which permit a better estimate of the extent to which the activities of officers in different departments differ. In the Police Services Study (PSS), observers recorded how officers spent their time and what they and citizens did in encounters for approximately 120 hours in each of 60 residential neighborhoods. Officers from 24 departments were observed. In each case, observations were made for 15 shifts at the same time of day and day of the week in each neighborhood.[3] With these data it is possible to compare officer activities across neighborhoods within the same department's jurisdiction as well as to compare officer activities across departments. It is important to note that these data relate to patrol in residential areas where commercial activity varied from moderate to nil.

Officers in all 60 PSS neighborhoods devoted considerably less than half their time to assigned calls and field-initiated encounters. The average for all neighborhoods was 128 minutes (just over 2 hours) per shift. On the average there were 6 encounters per shift, for an average encounter length of just over 20 minutes. The most time spent on encounters was an average of 217 minutes (over three and a half hours) per eight-hour shift. The least time spent on encounters was an average of 53 minutes per eight-hour shift. In half of the neighborhoods officers averaged less than 130 minutes (two hours and ten minutes) per eight hours on encounters with citizens. There was also considerable variation within departments in officers' use of time. In the city with the highest overall average, time on encounters ranged from 217 minutes to 103 minutes per shift for the neighborhoods studied.

It is useful to divide time on encounters according to whether the encounter was assigned or officer initiated. On average, 96 minutes per eight-hour shift were spent on encounters resulting from assigned calls. These findings suggest that Tien and colleagues were correct in asserting that Wilmington's average time on assigned calls is high. The national norm is likely to be between an hour and a half and two hours per eight-hour shift on encounters resulting from assigned runs.

Administrative activities report writing, and police assignments other than calls for service took an average of 68 minutes per eight-hour shift in the 60 PSS neighborhoods. This compares with an average of 75 minutes on such activities in Kansas City during the Preventive Patrol Experiment. Again, there is considerable difference among the 60 neighborhoods in the Police Service Study. In one lower income neighborhood of a large city, an average of 153 minutes per eight-hour shift was devoted to report writing, administration, and other assignments besides calls for service. This was the highest average PSS observed. In a middle-class neighborhood in another large city, officers averaged only 34 minutes per eight-hour shift on these kinds of activities. This was the lowest average observed.

The amount of time officers have available for "proactive" police work also varies considerably from place to place. If we combine the time officers spend answering assigned dispatches and the time they spend on reporting and other administrative duties, we get the total "assigned time" they have. For the 60 PSS neighborhoods, assigned time averaged 167 minutes per eight-hour shift. This left an average of 313 minutes per eight hours (or two thirds of a shift, on the average) "unassigned." It is this unassigned time which officers use for initiating encounters in the field, for conducting general surveillance "patrolling"), and for meals and other personal activities. The least unassigned time for the 60 neighborhoods was an average of 202 minutes less than three and a half hours) per eight-hour shift. The most was 398 minutes more than six and a half hours) per eight-hour shift. The average of 67 percent unassigned time found in the PSS study is considerably higher than the 55 percent "uncommitted" time reported by Cordner for a Midwestern city and also higher than the 60 percent reported by Kelling *et al.* for Kansas City.

About 10 percent of officers' *unassigned* time was spent on officer-initiated encounters with citizens in the 60 neighborhoods observed by PSS. An average of 29 minutes per eight-hour shift was allocated to encounters which officers themselves initiated. Most of these were traffic stops. Overall, PSS observers reported an average of one traffic stop per shift. In five neighborhoods, officers averaged more than two traffic stops per shift, while in two other neighborhoods PSS observers noted only a single traffic stop in the 15 shifts studied. Officers in the 60 neighborhoods were less likely to stop people for reasons other than traffic or vehicle violations. PSS observers recorded non-traffic stops in an average of two out of three shifts. In one neighborhood there were nearly two such

stops per shift; in another neighborhood there was only one in the 15 observed shifts. An average of once every two shifts, patrol officers observed by PSS themselves initiated a follow-up investigation of a problem or case they had dealt with before. In four neighborhoods there was an average of at least one such encounter per shift, while in another neighborhood no officer-initiated follow-up investigations were observed. Officers provided unassigned assistance to fellow officers an average of about once every five shifts. In only one neighborhood was there an average of one such encounter per shift. In seven neighborhoods no officer-initiated backup was observed.

Much less unassigned time is used by officers in response to requests they receive directly from citizens: an average of only five minutes per eight hour shift. Overall, PSS observers noted one encounter of this type for every two observed shifts. In three neighborhoods there was an average of more than one encounter of this kind per shift, but in another there was none. In general, about one encounter in six is initiated by an officer or citizen (on the street). Five in six are dispatched.

Making security checks and issuing parking tickets are two other activities officers may perform during unassigned time. Officers conducted security checks of commercial buildings in all of the 60 PSS neighborhoods, but at substantially different rates. In only three neighborhoods did officers average one commercial security check per hour of unassigned time. In 15 of the neighborhoods officers averaged fewer than one commercial security check in every 10 hours of unassigned time. The PSS neighborhoods were primarily residential and varied in the extent to which they included commercial areas. Some of the difference in frequency of commercial security checks is therefore due to less opportunity for these activities in neighborhoods with very few commercial structures. But while all 60 neighborhoods afforded ample opportunity for residential security checks, these were much less frequent than commercial checks. No residential security checks at all were observed in 10 of the 60 neighborhoods. In only three neighborhoods was there more than one residential security check per two hours of unassigned time. Officers issued parking tickets even less frequently. Obviously, residential security checks and parking control in residential areas are not high priorities in most of these areas.

The major part of *unassigned* time is spent patrolling. This consists of driving about the beat, looking for problems which may require police action and demonstrating the presence and ready availability of police. These activities are usually not directed either by supervisory personnel or by conscious planning of the patrol officers themselves. In some neighborhoods as few as two hours per eight-hour shift were spent patrolling, but the average for the 60 PSS neighborhoods was 214 minutes (about three and a half hours) per shift. In one neighborhood an average of more than five hours in eight were spent this way. Thus, undirected patrol takes more time than any other activity in most departments, although often less than half of a patrol officer's time is spent this way.

In the 60 neighborhoods observed by PSS, patrol officers spent an average of 65 minutes per eight-hour shift on meals and other personal activities. This is about 8 minutes less per shift than Kelling *et al.* (1974) report for Kansas City and about the same as Cordner reports for an anonymous midwestern city. There was considerable variation both among and within the 24 PSS departments. In three neighborhoods officers averaged more than 100 minutes per eight-hour shift on meals and personal activities. In two neighborhoods officers averaged less than 30 minutes per shift on these activities. The highest average time (109 minutes per eight hours) was recorded in a middle-income neighborhood of a large city. In another neighborhood of that same city, officers averaged only 43 minutes of meal and personal activity time per eight-hour shift. The lowest average time (19 minutes per eight-hour shift) was recorded in an inner city neighborhood in another large city. In that city the highest average time on these same activities was recorded at 54 minutes per eight hours.

Overall, officers assigned to patrol spend about one third of their time on specific assignments responding to dispatches and carrying out administrative duties. The remaining two-thirds of their time is spent on patrolling the beat, officer-initiated encounters with citizens (mostly traffic stops), citizen-initiated encounters (begun directly on the street), and personal business of the officer. Patrolling accounts for most of this unassigned time. These overall averages conceal a wide variation, however. Not only do individual shifts vary greatly from each other, but the pattern of officers' use of time varies by beat and by jurisdiction. Data from one department, or even averages from a number of departments, can not be used to estimate how officers do or should spend their time in another department. The kinds of problems areas present vary so greatly that wide variation in officers' use of time is to be expected.

The Kinds of Problems Officers Deal With in Encounters

In general, crime is involved in a minority of the calls police are assigned to handle. Webster (1970:95) reports that fewer than 17 percent of the "dispatches" in "Baywood" involved crime. This contrasts with almost 40 percent of all "dispatches" which were for "administration."

Another 17 percent were for "social services," 7 percent for "traffic," and 20 percent "on view." This is a striking statement of the extent to which police patrol involves work on non-crime matters. It is an overstatement. Webster's classification of all incidents in which the officer took a report of a crime under the heading "administration" reduces the percentage of calls classified as dealing with crime. Moreover, Webster includes in "administration" (and hence in the total number of "dispatches" on which all the percentages are based) officers' meals, errands, and court time. Bearing those classifications in mind, Webster's report for types of calls in Baywood does not differ greatly from that of Boydstun *et al.* (1977) for the Central Division of San Diego. They suggest that while only about 20 percent of all calls assigned involved "current" Part I and Part II crimes, another 15 percent involved taking reports of crimes which had already occurred and 8 percent in-

Table 15.1
Average Daily Calls for Service Dispatched in Wilmington, Delaware

Types of Calls Assigned to Primary Patrol Units	1974-75		1976	
	Daily Average	Percentage	Daily Average	Percentage
Part I crime	24.4	16.3	25.8	16.7
Part II crime	70.0	46.9	62.2	40.2
Traffic	28.7	19.2	21.0	13.6
Medical	3.1	2.1	5.2	3.4
Alarm	12.9	8.6	12.2	7.9
Miscellaneous	10.4	7.0	28.1	18.2
Total per day	149.4		154.6	

Source: Adapted from James M. Tien *et al., An Alternative Approach in Police Patrol: The Wilmington Split-Force Experiment* (Washington, DC: U.S. Government Printing Office), 1978.

volved checking on suspicious persons or circumstances (pp. 22, 28). Thus, a total of about 43 percent of the calls for service answered by San Diego's Central Division patrol officers involved crime. About 30 percent of the San Diego Central Division calls were related to peace-keeping, 10 percent to traffic, 10 percent to medical emergencies, and 7 percent to other miscellaneous problems. Officers' meals, breaks, and errands are not included in these figures.

Wilmington, Delaware, appears to be an exception. Records show the majority of calls there concerned crime. Tien and colleagues (1978:44) use a somewhat different classification in reporting types of problems dealt with by Wilmington patrol officers. Table 15.1 presents the breakdown they report. Note that they show 63 percent of all calls involved crime in 1974-75, and 57 percent in 1976. These percentages exceed those reported for both Baywood and San Diego. The coding rules are different, but there may also be real differences among the cities. Certainly there appears to have been a decrease in Part II crimes dealt with by patrol officers in Wilmington in 1976. This may be partly due to a change in classification. Note that traffic calls became less numerous, while miscellaneous calls increased substantially. It seems possible that at least some of the kinds of calls which were classified as Part II crimes and traffic in 1974-75 were included in the miscellaneous category in 1976.

We have seen that from 43 to 63 percent of the calls police handled in Wilmington and

Central Division San Diego were related to crime. These estimates are based on dispatch records. Difference in coding from one city to another may account for much of the apparent difference in the kinds of problems their patrol officers deal with, but it is also possible that differences in coding rules make an apparent difference less than it actually is. Without data collected in some standard way, we do not know. Patrol observer reports using a standard set of categories shed some light on the range of problems patrol officers actually work on. PSS researchers observed a total of 5,688 encounters between citizens and officers in the 60 neighborhoods they studied. Each encounter concerned one or more "problems" which occasioned police action.

Crime was the primary problem in only 38 percent of the encounters observed by PSS. This is considerably less than the proportion reported for Wilmington and also less than the proportion reported for San Diego. Comparisons of the kinds of problems officers deal with on patrol are difficult to make when they must rely on reports from different sources. In general, however, it appears that patrol observers record more traffic-related encounters than are found in dispatch records. Thus, the total number of encounters includes more traffic encounters and this reduces the proportion of all encounters which concern crime. As Table 15.2 shows, one fourth of all encounters observed by PSS involved traffic accidents or violations. (For 22 percent of all encounters, traffic was the primary problem in the encounter.) Observers record more traffic encounters because these are officer-initiated and not reported to dispatchers. Only 20 percent of these traffic encounters were dispatched runs: 77 percent were officer-initiated, and the rest were initiated by citizens in the field.

Another source of the difference may be the information requests. Citizens' requests for information from officers were the sole basis for six percent of the PSS encounters. Eighty percent of these requests were initiated by citizens in the field. Such encounters were probably rarely if ever included in the San Diego or Wilmington data. It is also possible that some of the incidents Tien and his colleagues classified as Part II Crime in Wilmington would be classified as interpersonal disputes or nuisances in PSS categories.

The lower proportion of crime-related encounters in the PSS study may thus be due in part to including more traffic and information encounters in the total number of encounters on which the percentages are based, as well as to differences in categories. But there are also differences in the kinds of problems officers confront in different places.

A clearer picture of the extent to which police patrolling different areas deal with different types of problems can be gained by closer examination of the PSS data. Table 15.3 presents the median and range for types of problems in the 60 neighborhoods. In two of the 60 neighborhoods, over half of all encounters between patrol officers and citizens involved crime. In one neighborhood about 54 percent of the encounters concerned crime as defined by the PSS typology; in another, 51 percent concerned crime. The lowest percentage of encounters concerning crime was recorded in a middle-income suburb. There were also considerable differences within Jurisdictions. In the city where 54 percent of the encounters dealt with crime in one neighborhood, only 27 of the encounters in another neighborhood dealt with crime.

In one of the 60 neighborhoods PSS studied, 46 percent of all encounters dealt primarily with traffic. Officers assigned to patrol in that city devote a substantial part of their efforts to traffic. (In the two other neighborhoods which PSS observed in that same city, 31 percent and 37 percent of all encounters involved traffic problems.) In contrast, 9 of

---

Table 15.2
Kinds of Problems Dealt With by Police in Their Encounters With Citizens
(Police Services Study)

Problem Category	Percentages of All Encounters With Any Problem of This Type		Percentages of All Encounters With This Primary Type of Problem
Crime	39%		38%
Violent crime		4%	
Non-violent crime		18	
Morals offense		2	
Suspicious person/ circumstances		11	
Other (warrants, assist officers, etc.)		4	
Disorder	23		22
Interpersonal dispute		10	
Nuisance		13	
Service	26		18
Medical		4	
Dependent persons		6	
Information request only		6	
Other assistance		10	
Traffic	26		22
Total	114%		100%
Total Number of Encounters	5,688		5,688

*Does not sum to 100% because some encounters involved two or three types of problems.

Table 15.3

*Kinds of Problems Dealt With by Police in Their Encounters With Citizens: Differences
Among Residential Neighborhoods*

	Percentage of Encounters With This as Primary Problem		
Problem Category	*Minimum Neighborhood*	*Median Neighborhood*	*Maximum Neighborhood*
Crime	22%	38%	54%
Disorder	8	20	43
Service	8	18	33
Traffic	5	23	46

the 60 neighborhoods had fewer than 10 percent of all encounters in which traffic was the primary problem. In two of the study neighborhoods in a large city, only 5 percent of the encounters dealt with traffic problems. There was considerable variation within that city, however, since in another of its neighborhoods, PSS observers found that 28 percent of the encounters concerned traffic.

The percentage of encounters where officers dealt with disorders ranged from 43 percent in one PSS neighborhood to 8 percent in another. Encounters dealing primarily with services other than those concerning crime, traffic, and disorder accounted for a high of 33 percent of all encounters in one neighborhood and a low of 8 percent in another. Clearly, police officers assigned to patrol deal with a great variety of problems, and in only a few areas is crime their most common problem.

Officer Actions to Control and Help Citizens

Officers' actions during encounters with citizens are an important aspect of their work. A wide variety of actions are involved in dealing with suspects, and with witnesses, victims, and others who need police assistance. Table 15.4 presents the percentages of encounters observed by PSS in which officers took some common actions.

Information gathering was the most frequent officer activity. Both those who were to be helped and to be controlled were the subject of police inquiry. Officers interviewed witnesses or persons requesting services in about two-thirds of all encounters involving crime, disorder, or service. In almost three-quarters of all traffic-related encounters but in less than half of the crimes and disorders officers interrogated suspects. The high percentage of interrogations for traffic encounters reflects the circumstances of these encounters. Most of these involve stopping drivers suspected of traffic violations. The others are investigations of traffic accidents where one or more of the drivers present was suspected of violations. Searches and visual inspections were less common, but occurred in over 40 percent of all encounters dealing with crime.

Police use several techniques to control citizens' behavior. Officers threatened or used force in about 14 percent of all encounters PSS observed. The threat of force is much more common than its use, however. Force was used in only about 5 percent of all encounters. Most of this was an officer handcuffing or taking a suspect by the arm. Most of the encounters where force was used concerned crime or disorder.

More often than threatening or using force, police lectured people whose behavior they wanted to change. In over 40 percent of the disorder and traffic encounters observed by PSS, police lectured or threatened legal sanctions. Persuasion is another technique officers use in attempting to change citizens' behavior. Officers used persuasion in about 23 percent of all disorders observed by PSS.

Arrests were observed in about 5 percent of the PSS encounters, including over 4 percent of all traffic and disorder incidents, as well as about 7 percent of all encounters dealing with crimes. The most common instigation of legal proceedings observed by PSS was not arrests, but the issuance of tickets. Tickets were issued in more than one-third of all traffic encounters. On the average, one

Table 15.4

Officer Actions Taken in Encounters Involving Each Type of Problem
(Police Services Study)

Type of Problem Dealt With in Encounter	Interviewed a Witness or Person Requesting Service	Interrogated a Suspect	Conducted a Search or Inspection	Used Force or Threat of Force	Lectured or Threatened (other than threat of force)	Used Persuasion	Made an Arrest	Gave a Ticket	Gave Reassurance	Gave Information	Gave Assistance	Gave Medical Help
						Percentages of Encounters in Which an Officer Took This Action						
Any Crime	64%	34%	43%	17%	19%	7%	7%	1%	28%	24%	8%	1%
Disorder	68	45	15	15	41	23	5	1	30	26	11	2
Service	66	6	18	2	7	2	*	2	22	39	20	5
Traffic	26	74	28	16	48	2	4	35	9	24	8	*
All Encounters	57	40	29	14	28	8	5	9	23	27	11	2

*Less than .5%.

traffic ticket was issued for every two eight-hour shifts observed. The number of tickets over the 15 observed shifts ranged from one (in one large city neighborhood) to 22 (in another large city neighborhood). A few tickets of various kinds were issued to participants in other kinds of encounters as well. These were misdemeanor tickets for offenses against municipal ordinances.

Overall, officers in the 60 PSS neighborhoods made arrests in somewhat fewer encounters and gave tickets in somewhat more encounters than did the officers observed in the Kansas City Patrol Study. There, officers made arrests in 6.8 percent of all encounters and issued tickets in 6.8 percent of all encounters (Kelling *et al.*, 1974:466). Boydstun *et al.* (1977) report San Diego arrests in about 5.6 percent of incidents for which there were dispatch records (pp. 29-30). This is quite close to the PSS average.

Arrests are relatively infrequent occurrences for patrol officers. On the average about one encounter in 20 observed by PSS involved an arrest. Officers observed by PSS averaged a little over six encounters per eight-hour shift. On the average, then, each patrol officer in the 60 neighborhoods was involved in one encounter where an arrest was made once every three working days. Arrests are considerably more frequent in some areas than in others, however. [In] two of the 60 PSS neighborhoods, 13 arrests were observed in the 15 shifts studied. In contrast, six of the 60 neighborhoods had only one arrest during the 15 observed shifts. Many police officers (especially those working "quiet" neighborhoods) may go for months without making an arrest. Forst *et al.* 1978:48) report that 46 percent of all sworn officers in the Washington, D.C. department, made no arrests in 1974. Most of these were patrol officers.

Officers do not use legal sanctions at every opportunity, of course. In 10 percent of all encounters, officers remarked to PSS observers that they could have instigated legal action against a participant, but did not do so.

Officers also provide comfort and assistance to those who are distraught or without other sources of help. In almost one-fourth of all encounters PSS observed, an officer reassured someone. This sort of police activity was most common in encounters dealing with disorder. It was observed least often in encounters involving traffic problems. Police gave information in more than one-fourth of the encounters PSS observed. They rendered some sort of physical assistance other than medical help in more than 10 percent of the encounters and gave medical assistance in about 2 percent of all encounters.

We have seen that in most neighborhoods police patrol officers are assigned to spend substantial portions of their time in encounters dealing with situations that do not involve crime. Often a majority of their encounters involve non-crime matters. Moreover, in most places police institute formal legal proceedings in only a fraction of the encounters they have with citizens. Many of the encounters in which legal proceedings are begun concern traffic problems or disorders rather than crime. But what police routinely do in one locality is frequently quite different from what they do elsewhere. Both the mixture of problems which confront police and the kinds of police actions taken to deal with those problems vary considerably from neighborhood to neighborhood, even within a single department's Jurisdiction.

Learning More About Activities of Officers on Patrol

How an officer assigned to patrol uses the work time of any given shift depends on department and personal priorities and on the kinds of public problems that come to police attention during that shift. The particular actions an officer takes in dealing with citizens depend on the same sort of personal, departmental, and public factors. We have not attempted here to isolate the contributions each of these factors make to the activities of officers on patrol. Rather, our purpose was to describe the range of patrol officer activities.

Despite their importance for performance measurement and planning, many police activities receive little attention and are not known in any systematic way by public officials, the courtroom workgroup, or the public at large. Indeed, most police departments themselves have no standard reporting procedures or other means for systematically describing what their own officers do. Thus, all too often police themselves, as well as the various other constituents of police performance, have an inaccurate picture of officers' activities.

The few systematic studies which have been reported suggest that police deal regularly with many kinds of problems other than crime. These problems need to be acknowledged in assessing what police accomplish. Police officers also conduct a variety of activities which are neither highly visible nor the subject of much police training. Whether they should continue to do these things (and if so whether they can be helped to do them better) are questions that can only be answered after further careful study of what police do now and how it affects those to whom it is done.

While it is clear that the content of patrol work varies from beat to beat, department to department, and by shift and day, it is also possible to offer some generalizations about its central tendencies. On the average, about five hours of an officer's eight-hour shift are allocated at the officer's discretion, while three hours are spent on assigned tasks. An average of over three hours in eight are spent by officers driving around "on patrol." About an hour is spent on personal business. Half an hour is spent on officer-initiated contacts with citizens. An hour and a half more are spent on contacts with citizens which originated as dispatched to the officer. Almost an hour and a half are also spent on administrative matters.

The problems police deal with on patrol are often complex and difficult to neatly categorize. Moreover, they also differ from place to place and time to time. In general, however, it appears that only about 40 percent clearly involve a response to some reported or suspected crime. The other 60 percent of the problems police deal with are roughly equally divided among disorders, traffic problems, and requests for various other sorts of assistance not relating to crimes.

Police assigned to patrol take a wide variety of actions with the citizens they encounter. Asking questions is perhaps their most common activity. Threats of force are considerably more common than the use of force or the exercise of arrest powers. More commonly, however, officers lecture or seek to persuade those whose behavior they seek to chance. Officers also commonly provide reassurance, information, or some form of physical assistance. A patrol officer needs to have a wide repertoire of actions available to deal with the diverse situations he or she is asked to handle.

Notes

1. The Police Services Study was conducted by Elinor Ostrom and Roger B. Parks of Indiana University in Bloomington and Gordon P. Whitaker of the University of North Carolina at Chapel Hill under funding provided by the National Science Foundation, Grant No. 43949.
2. Boydstun *et al.* (1977:47) report the mean number of calls and minutes per call for one officer and two-officer units. The figure of 270 minutes per shift was calculated using these data and the total number of calls for each type of unit.
3. Gay *et al.* (1977) document the patterns of peaks and valleys in calls for service which recur over a week's time. Spreading observations over various shifts and days of the week is necessary to obtain a balanced view of patrol work.

References

Boydstun, John E.; and Michael E. Sherry. *San Diego Community Profile. Final Report*. Washington, D.C.: Police Foundation, 1975, 39-66.

Boydstun, John E.; Michael Sherry; and Nicholas P. Moelter. *Patrol Staffing in San Diego*. Washington, D.C.: Police Foundation, 1977.

Cordner, Gary W. "Police Patrol Work Load Studies: A Review and Critique." *Police Studies* (Summer 1979), 50-60.

Forst, Brian; Judith Lucianovic; and Sarah J. Cox. *What Happens After Arrest?* Washington, D.C.: U.S. Government Printing Office, 1978.

Gay, William G.; Theodore H. Schell; and Stephen Schack. *Improving Patrol Productivity, Volume 1: Routine Patrol*. Washington, D.C.: U.S. Government Printing Office, 1977.

Goldstein, Herman. *Policing a Free Society*. Cambridge, Massachusetts. Ballinger, 1977.

Kelling, George L.; Tony Pate; Duane Dieckman; and Charles E. Brown. *The Kansas City Preventive Patrol Experiment: A Technical Report*. Washington, D.C, Police Foundation, 1974.

Tien, James M.; James W. Simon; and Richard C. Larson. *An Alternative Approach in Police Patrol: The Wilmington Split Force Experiment*. Washington, D.C.: U.S. Government Printing Office, 1978.

Webster, John A. "Police Task and Time Study." *The Journal of Criminal Law, Criminology and Police Science* LXI, 1970, 94-100.

16

Learning the Skills of Policing

David H. Bayley, and
Egon Bittner

Two of the most respected scholars of policing here tackle the questions of how police officers really learn to do their jobs, and whether the learning process could be improved. Of course, the oldest cliché in the police culture is "forget what you learned in the academy; we'll teach you what you need to know and how to do your job out here on the street." In recent years, police agencies have attempted to turn this cliché to their advantage by creating FTO (Field Training Officer) programs, in which they carefully choose and train the veteran officers who ultimately "break in" rookies and teach them "the ropes." Still, as Bayley and Bittner point out, police departments spend most of their training time presenting specific types of information (e.g., the law) and teaching specific skills (e.g., driving), and very little time actually teaching new officers how to do their jobs effectively. What do you think of their critique? How should police training be revised to overcome these limitations?

I

Introduction

How important is experience in learning to become an effective police officer? Police officers say vehemently that there is no substitute. The training given in police academies is universally regarded as irrelevant to "real" police work. Policing, it is argued, cannot be learned scientifically, in the sense that if A is done in Y situation and B is done in X situation, then Z will result. The life police officers confront is too diverse and complicated to be reduced to simple principles. As police officers continually say, every situation is different. What is needed, then, is not learning in the book sense but skills derived from handling a multitude of what seem like unique situations over and over again.

If this view of policing is correct, then it follows that the best officers are likely to be the most experienced, those who are older and have been in service longer. By extension, the only people fit to judge police activity in encounters with the public are other experienced officers. Certainly civilians could not make fair judgments, but neither could supervisors who had not experienced the peculiarities of a specific situation. In effect, the mysteries of the occupation are so profound that one not immersed repeatedly in police operations could not possibly understand the constraints as well as the possibilities of particular circumstances. Few officers would state the case as baldly as this, but these implications are fairly plain.

That this view of policing is self-serving is obvious. More troubling, however, is that it suggests that policing is not amenable to rational analysis and, by extension, to formal learning. Contrary to the pretensions of police "professionalism," officers commonly portray policing as being essentially a craft in which learning comes exclusively through experience intuitively processed by individual officers. Admittedly, policing is not yet a science in the sense that a body of principles has been generated that officers may follow with a reasonable probability of achieving successful outcomes. Officers correctly perceive that there is a gap between the operational world and the classroom, between the lore of policing as it is practiced and principles of human behavior discovered by social scientists. It should not be forgotten that people who teach, such as the many academic observers of policing, have as large a vested interest in portraying policing as amenable to science and classroom learning as police officers do in rejecting it.

The purpose of this article is to show that the antinomy between policing as a craft and policing as a science is false. What police say about how policing is learned is not incompatible with attempts to make instruction in the skills of policing more self-critical and systematic. Progress in police training will come by focusing on the particularities of police work as it is experienced by serving officers and by analyzing that experience and making it available to future police officers. In order to achieve this, this article examines the work that patrol officers do, recognizing that while skills are required to carry out more specialized police duties such as criminal investigation, patrol work is the centerpiece of policing, occupying the majority of all police personnel, accounting for most of the contacts with the public, and generally initiating the mobilization of police resources.

II

The Need for Learning

If patrolmen acted like automats most of the time, then there would be little scope for learning. This, of course, is far from the case. A vast amount of research has shown that patrol work is fraught with decision: patrol officers exercise choice constantly.[1] It should be noted in passing, however, that the importance of choice in patrol work is a variable, especially when viewed on a worldwide basis. In the United States, Britain, and Canada, responsibility for tactical decisionmaking is delegated to the lowest ranks. But in many countries of Africa, Asia, and Latin America, regulations expressly prohibit lower-ranking officers from making particular decisions. In such systems, patrolmen and constables are hardly more than spear-carriers in the police drama, mechanically patrolling according to fixed schedules and calling superior officers to handle almost any interaction with the public beyond detaining suspects in crimes personally witnessed.[2] Even in countries where legal authorization is not truncated, organizational practice may require higher-ranking officers to be summoned in specific circumstances.

In addition to command direction, the scope for learning in patrol work varies with the nature of situations encountered. Situations can be ranked along a continuum from the cut-and-dried to the problematic. For example, American officers have few doubts about what to do when a man is found drunk lying on the ground in the winter. He must be picked up and taken to a shelter. The choices are also fairly limited in serious traffic accidents, alleged housebreaking, and assault with a deadly weapon witnessed by an officer. This is not to argue that some choices are not involved in such cases—officers can turn a blind eye or overreact—but rather that the appropriate responses are clearly recognized by everyone involved—patrolman, public, and command officers. The appropriate action may not be easy to take, but it is obvious. A robbery in progress is dangerous, but the patrolman's appropriate response is straightforward. Investigating a young person on the street late at night after curfew is rarely dangerous, but the decision as to what corrective action should be taken is often perplexing.

American patrol officers recognize these variable features of the work they do and can talk about them with discernment. They have an acute sense of where danger lies and what kinds of situations cause them the greatest difficulty in deciding what to do. In fact, they are so accustomed to thinking about the place of discretion in policing that a favorite in-house joke is that their most problematic situation during each shift is deciding where to go for lunch. In our experience, patrol officers single out disturbances as the most problematic calls they receive, especially domestic disputes, meaning quarrels among people who are living in the same household. These include wife beatings, child abuse, fights between gay roommates, disputes over property by people living in a common-law relationship, violations of restraining orders, and unruly children. The next most problematic activities that police officers mention are proactive traffic stops, in which they choose to stop a moving vehicle for some reason, and maintaining order among teenagers congregating in public places. Observers of police work have also chosen these situations when illustrating the complexity of police work.[3]

Survey data supports these impressionistic conclusions. Domestic disputes were by far the situation most commonly cited in 1966-67 by Denver police officers as requiring street decisionmaking, followed somewhat distantly by traffic violations.[4] In 1981, police officers in Battle Creek, Michigan also mentioned domestic disputes most frequently as their most problematic encounter.[5] Traffic violations were largely ignored. It seems likely that perceptions of the problematic nature of situations are related to the frequency of their occurrence in the working life of police officers. That is, if a particular kind of situation is rarely encountered, officers may not be sensitized to its complexity. Proactive traffic stops, for example, allow considerable scope for choice, but officers may not know this unless departmental policy encourages such activity.

Although some work that patrolmen do is clearly discretionary, it is uncertain precisely how much of it is. If situations calling for the use of discretion occur frequently, then the ability to make decisions becomes central to patrol work. On the other hand, if they occur infrequently, then the kinds of skills that experience teaches are less helpful. The uncomfortable fact is that despite the enormous attention given to studying patrol work, especially to charting the nature of calls for service, little is known about the degree to which police exercise is discretion. Information has not been collected about how problematical the different kinds of encounters are.[6] Specifying the scope for decision is not a necessary part of a description of situations. It is a conclusion requiring information about what officers *could*. Nor can inferences about the scope for choice be drawn from typical outcomes that situations generate. "Service" situations, occasions in which law enforcement action is unlikely or inappropriate, are not necessarily less complex than "enforcement" situations.[7] The designation "order-maintenance" covers situations in which enforcement is appropriate but not automatically utilized. Although the decision is implied by definition, the choice may not be particularly difficult.

Unless studies are undertaken of the problematical nature of particular situations, even data from very detailed studies of the composition of police work will not reveal how much police work actually involves decision. However, information is available about the relative frequency of domestic disputes, which have been identified by patrolmen as being especially problematic. Eric Scott, for example, reported a breakdown of 26,000 calls for service in twenty-four metropolitan police forces in 1977 according to seventy-two categories.[8] He found that domestic conflict accounted for 2.7% of calls for service. Moving violations accounted for 1%, but this statistic is not informative because the study was of citizen calls for service, not of all observed policy mobilizations.[9] In another study, "domestic trouble" also accounted for 2.7% of all calls for service.[10]

These fragments of information suggest that the situations police consider most problematic are not encountered often. If these are the best examples police have of heavily discretionary situations, then making choices may not be the quintessence of patrol work, apart from the need to decide whether to act at all. Police officers may be exaggerating the proportion of problematic work, in part perhaps to enhance their own self-esteem and in part because such situations are especially disconcerting to officers. What is needed before firm conclusions can be drawn about how important experience might be in policing is a systematic mapping of the range of responses actually employed by patrol officers in the situations that occur most frequently.

Interestingly, the situations officers believe provide the greatest scope for decision are among the most dangerous police face. Federal Bureau of Investigation statistics show that, between 1975 and 1979, disturbances (including family fights, quarrels, and "man-with-a-gun") accounted for the largest proportion of police officers killed (17%). Robberies in progress, which are not particularly problematic, were next (16%), and traffic stops and pursuit were third (12%).[11] Although dangerousness and "problematicalness" are conceptually distinct, they appear to be associated to some extent. Because officers know these figures, it may be that their evaluations of the problematical nature of situations reflect their fears.

III

What Experience Teaches Patrol Officers

Recognizing that focusing on domestic disputes and proactive traffic stops may overemphasize the problematic character of police work, we find that experience on the job contributes to learning about (1) goals, (2) tactics, and (3) presence. That is, when officers talk about what is informative in practical experience, these are the matters most frequently mentioned.

A. Goals

Decisions about goals are antecedent to choices about tactics, which is not to imply that officers are always purposive. Some officers are essentially aimless, in that they do not try to align tactics and objectives. Any attempt to do so occurs after the fact, involving the false attribution of a rational purpose. Nonetheless, in explaining what they seek to achieve, whether truly or spuriously, patrol officers describe their operating goals as (a) meeting departmental norms, (b) containing violence and controlling disorder, (c) preventing crime, (d) avoiding physical injury to themselves, and (e) avoiding provoking the public into angry retaliation that threatens their careers. No priority can be given to these items; they are simply objectives that patrol officers try to achieve in varying combinations from situation to situation as they work. Each will now be explored in turn.

Departmental norms about what actions are to be undertaken are conveyed in many ways. Officers complain most about the "numbers game," numerical quotas that must be met by each officer. For example, commanders sometimes unfavorably compare the number of felony arrests made by one shift with those made by another, or the number of traffic tickets issued, or the amount of time spend "out of service" as opposed to patrolling. If the quotas are not met, officers are told to "earn their pay." Generally announced policies also constrain tactics, for example, with respect to using firearms against fleeing felons, arresting for minor offenses, or arresting without signed complaints in domestic disputes. The problem is that departmental policy is often not clearly expressed or understood. Supervisors indicate—sometimes subtly, sometimes directly—what they prefer by way of action. Officers are aware that what they normally do is not what "the sergeant" or "the lieutenant" would do. Officers cynically remark that calling a supervisor for assistance in a domestic fight usually produces "two domestics," one among civilians, another among police. Finally, tactical decisions are powerfully shaped by departmental procedures for reporting action. Many contacts with the public require filling out forms that are filed with the department. Often these forms present blocks to check, enumerating the actions taken. These forms structure choice, because officers know that if they take an action not specified, they will be required to provide an explanation. Explicit and detailed forms not only simplify reporting, they raise the cost of exercising initiative. They may also encourage specious reporting.

All of these cues as to what departments consider to be acceptable action are noticed by patrol officers, even when they are not followed. The expectations of departments are so constraining that officers, like youths walking through a graveyard at night, frequently strike brave postures privately about what is required. An officer may say proudly that, "When I'm on patrol I forget about all the higher-ups, I'm on my own little police force." He may be, but the department has made him anxious nonetheless.

One of the great imperatives of a patrolman's life is the need to "reproduce order," in Richard Ericson's apt phrase.[12] It has been observed that police characteristically are called to deal with "something-that-ought-not-be-happening-and-about-which-someone-had-better-do-something-now."[13] An essential part of police work is taking charge. The means used to accomplish this end depend on the circumstances. They can involve hitting, shooting, referring, rescuing, tending, separating, handcuffing, humoring, threatening, placating, and discussing. The objective is to minimize the disruptions of normal life. As one officer said, "We keep the peace, we don't settle problems." Police recognize the superficiality of what they do, often blaming this on the pressure of work. The fact is that the police frequently seem to have too much time on their hands and they are forever apologizing for how slow a particular tour of duty is. Actually, officers may be right: they *are* too busy to give the kind of attention that would make any permanent difference to the circumstances encountered. The requirements for dealing with deeper levels of problems are too exorbitant for police to meet. Doing whatever is necessary to restore order is all that can reasonably be expected of the police.

Not only do police want to restore order, they want to lower the likelihood that future disorder, particularly crime, will occur. Thought they tend to deny it, police officers are future oriented. The test of success in domestic fights, for example, is "no call-backs." Even while they deprecate the effect that their actions can have on the root causes of problems, they accept uncritically that they should work to deter future criminality. They do not view law enforcement as an end in itself but as a tool for convincing people not to do wrong.[14] Faced with the threat of disorder, officers use laws to get leverage over people, to threaten that if police orders are not followed, the police will go to jail.[15] This is one reason police condemn the decriminalization of nonconforming behavior in public places, such as drinking alcoholic beverages, being drunk, and loitering, that has taken place over the last generation. Such laws are needed, the police argue, to help them gain control before more serious incidents occur. But the police employ even longer time perspectives. This perspective shows up when they explain why they do not enforce the law in certain situations. Time and again they argue that an arrest or a citation would do more harm than good. Why give a traffic ticket, for instance, to an elderly woman who has run a red light and whose hands are shaking with fear as the officer comes up to the car window? A ticket is gratuitous in such circumstances. Why encourage a woman to sign a complaint against the drunken husband who has just blackened her eye when she admits she does not want a divorce, it is apparent the

family cannot make bail, and even a short detention in jail may jeapordize the family's income? Whether the public approves or not, patrol officers continually make judicial types of decisions, deciding whether the imposition of the law will achieve what the spirit of the law seems to call for. Police officers are convinced that they know more about the deterrent utility of law than does anyone else. This attitude probably explains why they become so angry at prosecutors and courts that are more lenient than the police expected. They view prosecutors and courts as second-guessing the evaluations made by officers who are more immediately in touch with the practical reality of the situation.[16]

Patrol officers are continually alert to the danger of physical injury to themselves. They take great care with protective equipment such as guns, nightsticks, and sturdy multi-celled flashlights. Many officers now routinely wear light-weight protective vests under their uniform shirts. Sometimes vests are provided by police departments, but they are often purchased out of the officer's own pocket. Police conversation is thick with stratagems for avoiding injury, an urgency stressed from their earliest days in training: when knocking at residences where violence is suspected, do not stand in front of doors; when making traffic stops at night, blind the eyes of the driver with cruiser spotlights or a flashlight; when approaching a vehicle, one officer should linger slightly behind the vehicle on the right side, hand on weapon, while the other interrogates the driver; when questioning a driver, do not stand in front of the door so that its sudden opening could harm you; carry a small blackjack in the rear pocket in order to provide protection less provocatively than with a nightstick; unbutton holsters when responding to calls in particular areas; always keep your head covered in certain tenement neighborhoods; and never turn your back on particular types of people. Police work, according to officers, is fraught with unpredictable and frequently deadly violence. Getting home safely is a primary concern.

Police concern with deadly force is to some extent exaggerated. The death rate for police is well below that of several other occupations. In 1980, for example, the death rate per 100,000 police officers was 32.4, while it was 61 per 100,000 workers in agriculture, 50 per 100,000 workers in mining and quarrying, and 43 per 100,000 construction workers.[17] Police deaths, however, unlike those in other occupations, are not acts of God; they are generally the result of willful, deliberate attacks. They are personal, human-to-human, and imbued with malice in the same way that crime is generally. Just as the public funds small comfort in statistics showing that they are safer on the streets than in their bathtubs, police are more anxious in their work than construction workers are in theirs.

There is another aspect to policing, however, that accounts for officers' pervasive concern with personal injury. Police continually deal with situations in which physical constraint may have to be applied against people who are willing to fight, struggle, hit, stab, spit, bite, tear, hurl, hide, and run. People continually use their bodies against the police, forcing the police to deal with them in a physical way. While police seem to be preoccupied with deadly force, the more common reality in their lives is the possibility of a broken nose, lost teeth, black eyes, broken ribs, and twisted arms. Few officers are ever shot or even shot at, but all except the rawest rookie can show scars on their bodies from continual encounters with low-level violence.

As a result, officers develop an instinctive wariness, what one officer called "well-planned lay-back." While they never want to give the impression of being afraid, especially to their peers, they try to avoid having to struggle with people. Since they are obliged at the same time to establish control, they feel justified in acting with preemptive force. In effect, they learn to act with a margin of force just beyond what their would-be opponents might use. One officer likened it to taking a five-foot jump over a four-foot ditch. Never cut things too closely; if personal injury is likely, strike first with just enough force to nullify the threat. When guns are believed to be present, this margin can be deadly. Sometimes police concern with avoiding injury comes across as a peculiar fastidiousness, not simply anxiety, but distaste for having to soil themselves. Officers complain continu-

ally about having gotten blood on their shirts, rips in their down jackets, dirt on their trousers, and vomit in their cars. Many officers carry soft leather gloves for manhandling dirty people. In many residences officers will not sit down for fear of bugs. Police officers often act like people who have gotten dressed up to go to a party only to be confronted with having to wipe up spilled food or change a tire. The point is that police life is rough-and-tumble. Through preemption, overreaction, and simple avoidance, officers try to minimize the unpleasant, sometimes deadly, physical contact that is part of their job.

According to patrol officers, experience sharpens the ability to read potential violence in an encounter. The experienced officer avoids the use of unnecessary physical force, as the "hot dog" does not, but at the same time he is fully prepared to meet such force when necessary, especially by preempting it. The experienced officer has learned when to relax and when to attack. Competence involves the ability to do both and get away with it.

Finally, police worry a lot about repercussions from the actions they take that may affect their careers. They have in mind, in particular, complaints and civil suits. Police, unlike workers in most other jobs, are constantly being reminded of the fatefulness of their actions to themselves as well as to the public. They believe their jobs are on the line daily. So for police to avoid what would be viewed as a mistake by the department or the courts is an imperative.[18] One aspect of what police learn on the job, then, is what *not* to do. As an officer remarked, "In policing, don'ts are often more important than do's."[19]

In sum, experience has a great deal to teach police about goals. Essentially, it teaches an instinct for priorities. What kind of goals can reasonably be achieved at the least cost to the officer? In Peter Manning's words:

> The central problem of [policing], from the agent's perspective, is not moral but distinctly practical. The aim is to define the work in ways that will allow the occupational members involved to manage it, to make reasonable decisions, control it, parcel it out into meaningful, solvable,

and understandable units and episodes, and make this accomplishment somewhat satisfying day after day.[20]

This task involves juggling disparate goals that operate in varying time frames. By and large, police goals are short-range in that their achievement can be determined almost immediately. This observation is true with respect to departmental expectations, the establishment of control, the avoidance of injury, and the protection of the officer's career. The only exception is the objective of preventing future crime and disorder. It seems reasonable to suppose that short-run imperatives prevail in most cases because the information needed to judge whether preventive actions have worked are beyond the ken of the serving police officer. Learning to subordinate long-range to short-range goals makes police officers appear uncaring and hard-bitten. Their own awareness that they are dominated by short-run concerns tends to make them cynical. But this deprecation of their own efforts is not unique to police officers: it is an attitude developed by people in many occupations who learn to substitute practical, instrumental goals for larger visions of social effectiveness. It is found among teachers, doctors, lawyers, social workers, and businessmen. To some extent, then, what experience teaches the police is an acceptance of social impotency.

If experience teaches policemen how to juggle complex priorities in action, one can understand why civilian review is so threatening to them. Police officers say civilian review is unfair because outsiders do not have the experience to judge which actions are required in real-life situations. This view is plausible, but it ignores the fact that choices among tactics are only one part of the problem. Indeed, impressionistic evidence suggests that civilian review boards are frequently willing to accept police expertise. A greater danger, from the police point of view, is that civilian reviewers will insist on a different ordering of objectives, especially ones that ignore altogether the policeman and his career. This concern explains, perhaps, why hostility to civilian review seems to go with the job. It follows naturally from learning

that goals have to be set in chaotic moments of action.

B. Tactics

Tactical choices are the second area in which the police claim that experience is essential to learning. It is no longer informative to point out that patrol officers do much more than enforce the law. This fact has been thoroughly established by research. But the range of options employed by patrol officers is much greater than this observation conveys. Patrol officers can discern as well as discuss an array of tactical alternatives. Moreover, they can distinguish actions that are appropriate at different stages of an intervention. What patrol officers do has commonly been described according to their culminating actions—arrest, referral, friendly advice, threats, and so forth.[21] But officers have done many things already before they decide how they will leave an encounter. Adequate description of police tactics requires paying attention to different stages in the evolution of police-public interactions.[22] An exploration of the tactics police use must distinguish at least three different stages: contact, processing, and exit. Each stage offers distinctly different choices to patrol officers. These choices will be explored in the cases of domestic disputes and proactive traffic stops, recognizing that these may be the most problematic situations for police officers.

At contact in domestic disputes, police may choose from at least nine different courses of action. As one would expect, these serve by and large to establish immediate control over events, to shift the axis of interaction from the disputants to the officers. The possible courses of action are: to listen passively to disputant(s), verbally restrain disputant(s), threaten physical restraint, apply physical restraint, request separation of disputants, impose separation on disputants, physically force separation, divert attention of disputants, or question to elicit the nature of the problem.

As officers settle into an encounter, having established control on their own terms, they may choose from among eleven tactics: let each disputant have his say in turn, listen in a nondirective way, actively seek to uncover the nature of the problem, accept the situation as defined by the complainant, reject the view of the complainant, follow the request made by the complainant, physically restrain someone, urge someone to sign a complaint, talk someone out of signing a complaint, investigate the incident further without indicating likely action, and indicate that there is nothing the police can do.

Finally, police need to terminate the encounter and make themselves available for other business. Their exiting actions may again be substantially different from anything done before; they may fail to find the other disputant, find the other disputant and warn or advise, arrest someone, separate disputants temporarily by observing one of the premises, by transporting one from the scene or by arranging a pickup by someone else, exsputants about the consequences of future trouble, give friendly advice about how to avoid a repetition, provide pointed advice to disputant(s) about how to resolve the issue, suggest referral to third parties, promise future police assistance, transport injured persons to a medical facility, issue a notice of police contact, or simply leave.[23]

Even if these lists of tactics are not exhaustive, the number of alternatives open to officers is already formidable—nine at contact, eleven at processing, and eleven at exit. Experienced patrol officers have strong opinions about which of these courses of action to pursue under different circumstances. Moreover, they criticize one another for choosing the wrong one. For example, police academies often teach that officers should separate disputants immediately and never let them continue to argue. Officers say, however, that the ventilation of grievances is sometimes all that both parties want. The best defusing tactic, therefore, is to let them get things off their chests, with police playing the role of friendly referee. For wives, particularly, calling the police is an act of assertion in itself and they are satisfied when they have made their point. Rather than arresting the husband, police are better advised to provide her with a safe opportunity to make a statement. When neighbors dispute, arrival of the police may actually exacerbate the argument as both parties feel they need not

worry about things getting out of hand. So some officers covertly restrain the growing altercation by turning their backs or pulling away, indicating that they really do not care what happens. Frequently this action causes the dispute to lose some of its steam.

Officers are especially sensitive to actions they take that may make situations more explosive. They are particularly careful, for example, to avoid laying hands on people unless they absolutely must. Touching connotes restraint and it is apt to be resented. Officers say that people of a minority group are especially quick to anger when police touch them. So police learn to move people about verbally or by imposing their bodies without actually reaching out. This tactic is related to the need to save "face," something most officers recognize as being important. Police must be careful not to inflict humiliation gratuitously. For this reason, patrol officers think twice before writing out traffic tickets to fathers in front of their children, unless the violation is serious or the man uncivil.[24] Officers believe that older people get angry at traffic stops because they are accustomed to disciplining rather than being disciplined. They feel belittled. Thus, officers tread warily so as not to make acquiescence difficult. Similarly, many officers testify to thanks earned by not handcuffing men in front of their children but doing so outside the residence or in the patrol car. It also seems that men submit to handcuffs more tractably than do women, who frequently become hysterical and sometimes violent.

Demonstrating the importance of obtaining control without physical injury in the hierarchy of operating values, patrol officers have a great fund of stories about how violent situations were defused through cunning verbal plots. For example, an officer who was a born-again Christian spotted religious decor in the home of a couple who had had a violent argument. He asked them what they thought the Lord would want them to do and ten minutes later they were reconciled. One tactic is to divert the attention of disputants, thus allowing emotions to cool. Noting what appears to be handmade furniture, an officer may say, "Do you make furniture? So do I." Others ask if they may use the bathroom, obliging the residents to point it out, or inquire what the score is of the baseball game on TV, or request a cup of coffee or a soft drink. One officer gained control in a domestic dispute by sitting down indifferently in front of the television set and calmly taking off his hat. The husband and wife were so nonplussed at this lack of concern for their fight that shortly they, too, lost interest. Stories like these are so common among officers that they should probably be taken with a grain of salt. The same stories crop up too often, suggesting that they have become part of the mythology of policing, passed on uncritically from officer to officer. Told always with pride, they are used to illustrate the subtlety of police officers. Most of the ploys so lovingly described are also clearly not in general use,[25] as most officers admit that while they try to defuse violence without using physical restraint, their own stratagems are more direct.

Officers also tend to agree on what actions are to be avoided, such as failing to gain control quickly enough when injury is likely, making threats that cause people to lose face, taking sides in an argument, leaving a dispute with a threat about what the police will do when they return, and making take-it-or-leave-it statements that the police cannot honor. These are the mistakes rookies make. Only experienced officers are presumed to have the diagnostic skills to know when these tactics can be used safely.

It is precisely with respect to the choice of tactics that the separation between the craft of policing and the science of policing is most destructive. Officers say experience teaches them what works. But does it? They manage to get along, which means avoiding affronting the department or getting seriously hurt or sued, but are they intelligently discriminating in their tactical choices so that they are raising the probability of achieving stated goals? Perhaps almost anything "works" most of the time, largely because the police are so authoritative in relation to the people with whom they have to deal. The questions that need to be answered scientifically are: (1) can the tactics and the circumstances of encounters be better matched so that patrol officers can more certainly avoid failures according to their own criteria; (2) are the long-run, post-encounter effects that officers want to accomplish truly achieved through the actions they choose; and (3) do the tactics they choose produce unintended consequences that deserve to be considered? At the moment, this kind of factual knowledge is not being provided to officers. The fault is not that of the serving police officer. By necessity, he must fall back on the lore that experience venerates. The problem is that science has not illuminated the operational imperatives of the work that patrol officers do. Nor have police departments acknowledged that guidance could be useful. Crouched behind the statement that "every situation is different," they have failed to pay attention to what their own rank and file are telling them: namely, that learning about what "works" is possible and that it is taking place already through the haphazard mechanism of individual experience. While the partisans of science have failed to focus on the tactical world of the serving officer, police officers have not seen that it is contradictory to say that, although every situation is different, experience is crucial.

Turning to traffic stops, we have identified ten actions considered appropriate at contact, seven at processing, and eleven at exit. At contact, officers may leave the driver in the car, order him out, leave passengers in the car, order passengers out, ask the driver for documents, ask passengers for documents, order the driver to remain in the car, order passengers to remain in the car, point out the violation that prompted the stop, and ask the driver if he knew why the stop was made. At processing, officers may check whether the car and the driver are "clear," give a roadside sobriety test, make a body search of the driver, make a body search of the passengers, search the vehicle from outside, search the vehicle from inside, and discuss the alleged traffic violation. At exit, officers may release the car and the driver, release with a warning, release with a traffic citation, release with both a citation and an admonishment, arrest the driver for a prior offense, arrest for being drunk, arrest for crimes associated with evidence found during the stop, arrest for actions during the encounter, impound the car, insist that the driver proceed on foot, help the driver to arrange for other transportation, arrest the passengers for the same reasons as the driver, transport the driver someplace without making an arrest, and admonish the passengers.

Officers have different opinions about what tactics to apply at each stage, recognizing, of course, that some situations permit little latitude. On initial contact, for example, officers favor different gambits. Some tell the driver why he was stopped before asking for his license and registration. This settles the driver's natural curiosity and puts him on the defensive. Others first ask for documents, thus ensuring that the driver will not escape and demonstrating that information will be given only when the officer chooses. Still others like to begin with the question "Do you know why I stopped you?" hoping that the drivers, most of whom drive on the edge of the law, will admit an infraction even more serious than the one that led to the stop. The officer can then be magnanimous, agreeing to forgive the more serious offense in favor of the lesser that the officer was going to ticket anyhow. Not all these gambits can, of course, be tried in every situation; they depend on particular circumstances. But it is easy to see that each gives a distinctive impetus to the police-citizen interaction. At least police believe so, making choice of action on their part a test of professional savvy.

The crucial stage, from the public's point of view, is exit, where there are eleven different possibilities that are used singly or in combination. Most officers disagree strongly with the teaching that they should make to issue a ticket before approaching a stopped vehicle. Although some officers will ticket anyone—even their grandmothers, as other officers contemptuously say—most believe that individuation is essential to justice. It is unnecessary, for example, to give tickets for driving without a license to responsible people who admit their offense but can't produce their licenses. Officers, too, have left their wallets at home while running to do an errand or have forgotten to take their licenses out of their checkbooks after going to the bank. Drivers have been "cleared" on the ba-

sis of all sorts of identification, including credit cards and fishing licenses.

The key ingredient in exit decisions, apart from the seriousness of the offense, is the attitude of the driver. If the violation is minor, drivers who admit error and do not challenge the authority of the officer are likely to be treated leniently, unless departmental policy decrees otherwise. On the other hand, drivers who dispute the offense, question the value of what the officer is doing, use disrespectful language, and threaten to complain will virtually write themselves a citation. Officers are especially resentful of well-to-do people driving expensive late-model cars who threaten to complain to "the chief" or "the mayor." Officers are proud of their one-line put-downs of such people, such as, "Do you know the chief too? When you see him tell him Officer Jones gave you a ticket today." While much of this bravado is probably indulged only off the street, it accurately reflects what officers may consider in making exit choices. At the same time, officers often take amazing amounts of verbal abuse from people for whom profanity is as natural as breathing. The same is true for racial put-downs by blacks of white officers, such as studied, face-saving condescension and mutterings about "honky cops." Officers also know the importance that their own demeanor has in shaping the results of a stop. If they do decide to give a ticket, they try to be matter-of-fact, unless provoked, and to avoid verbal humiliation. The choice is between ticketing or lecturing and releasing. In the words of one officer, "chew or cite, but not both."

It would appear that the tactical choices patrol officers make, at least for domestic disputes and traffic stops, are much more extensive than is generally recognized. They have to learn what "works" in terms of objectives that they can reasonably judge in circumstances that vary enormously. They are anxious about the fatefulness of their actions for themselves as well as for others, fearful that the instant diagnoses they make will be incorrect. This is undoubtedly what prompts the often repeated assertion that every situation is different, which according to the officers' own testimony about the utility of experience, is not true. Donald Black has shown that tactical choices with respect to exiting actions in domestic disputes are affected by a small number of structural features in each encounter—race, class, age, status of complainant in the household, intimacy between the people involved, institutional affiliation of complainants, and attacks on police legitimacy.[26] However, the effect of these factors does not appear large, accounting for between ten and twenty-five percent of the variance.[27] As has been noted, officers want to emphasize the difficulty of their work. Confronted by social scientists probing to uncover choices, they may even exaggerate small differences in procedural detail, falsely attributing forethought to automatic decisions. None of this, however, contradicts the fact that choices are made, sometimes among a bewildering number of alternatives, and that officers cannot readily state the principles that they use to simplify the situational complexities faced. The best they can do is to tell anecdotes. That they do simplify, as Black points out, in no way diminishes the uncertainty they feel in making tactical choices. Having implicit operating principles does not lessen anxiety. Nor does it follow that experience is not important in learning to apply them. Moreover, officers are often genuinely trying to forecast the effects of their actions on a recurrence of the situation. Unfortunately, they have only rough-and-ready rules for doing so, probably involving the factors Black has noted. Here is where the lore of policing with respect to tactics is probably the least well informed and the chances for bias to intrude the greatest.

What officers need, of course, is information that shows what the likely results will be from the use of tactics of different sorts in various situations. As Herman Goldstein has said:

> [S]ystematic analysis and planning have rarely been applied to specific behavior and social problems that constitute the agency's routine business. The situation is somewhat analogous to a private industry that studies the speed of its assembly line, the productivity of its employees, and the nature of its public relations program, but does not examine the quality of the product being produced.[28]

Such testing will not be easy to carry out, although the principles for doing so are clear.[29] This is scant comfort to patrolmen. In the absence of tested knowledge about what works, patrol officers have no resource to call on except their own collective experience. From their perspective, choice is an operational necessity, and they see trial and error as the only way to learn about it.[30]

C. Presence

The third important feature that experience teaches is "presence." Effective policing is more than simply doing things, it involves being something. The key elements of effective presence are external calm and internal alertness. Police say repeatedly that it is essential to be nonprovocative in contacts with the public—to adopt a demeanor that pacifies, placates, and mollifies. "Always act," said an experienced officer, "as if you were on vacation." In effect, be careful not to heighten the tension already present. At the same time, officers must never relax. They must be constantly watchful and alert because danger can arise in an instant. Danger, however, is not the only threat. All officers with any seniority speak bitterly of the times they were "conned," accepting uncritically a story told to them on which they then acted. Police learn quickly that appearance and reality are often sharply different. People will use the police for their own purposes if they can, even if it means telling elaborate lies. Some people, police know, really are evil. As a result, police officers often appear indifferent, cynical, and unsympathetic in the most heartrending situations. The presence that police officers cultivate is much like that of professional athletes, who talk, too, about the importance of balancing concentration and relaxation. One must be keyed up but not "choke." In policing, this means that officers must protect without provoking. The inward equanimity that leads to outward poise is not something people are born with, nor can it be taught. As in sports, it is learned through practice.

In summary, then, from the point of view of the patrol officer, policing is more like a craft than a science, in that officers believe that they have important lessons to learn that are not reducible to principle and are not being taught through formal education. These lessons concern goals—which ones are reasonable; tactics—which ones ensure achievement of different goals in varying circumstances; and presence—how to cultivate a career-sustaining personality. "Experience-tested good sense," as one officer said, is what police must learn over the years.

What has not been grasped, however, is that even as policing at the present time is more craft than science, learning *can* take place, skills *can* be increased, and levels of expertise *can* be discerned. Officers themselves recognize this point when they talk about how they "learned" to become effective. They also continually complain that standards of performance should distinguish degrees of coping ability, not mechanical conformity to specific do's and don'ts—excluding horrendous errors, of course.

Although seldom admitted, learning in policing involves discovering how each officer can achieve stated goals within his own personal limitations. If tactics are as varied as has been shown, then different styles may be equally effective. Some officers have a gift of gab, others do not. Some officers are so physically imposing they can reduce violence simply by "blotting out the sun"; others have to raise their voices, threaten retaliation, or spin a yarn. Being skilled in policing, as in carpentry, is a matter of learning to be effective with the materials and tools at hand.

The police community is very judgmental about skills displayed on the job, quite apart from formal systems of performance appraisal. Policemen judge the work of colleagues all the time. To begin with, patrol work is often performed before an audience of other officers. In domestic disputes, for example, several cars frequently respond when violence has been reported. As the premises suddenly fill up with large men in blue uniforms, the first officer on the scene has to give a lead as to how the situation will be handled. Whether comfortable or not, he dare not back away. He has to perform on-view. Rookies particularly feel the presence of this attentive audience. Remembering his own days as a

rookie, one officer said, "It's like your ears are on stalks." Rookies cannot help notice when an experienced officer gives a snort of laughter or contemptuously turns his back.

And well they should be concerned, because police officers make judgments about the strengths and weaknesses of colleagues all the time which they do not hesitate to express. Reputations are made in a twinkling, especially for recruits or newly transferred personnel. Every unit has its known hotheads, deadbeats, unreliables, and head-knockers. They also have respected master craftsmen, although this designation is not used. These officers are cool, poised, inventive, careful, active, and nonviolent—officers who can cope without jeopardizing themselves or others. Appraisals of colleagues are a staple of police conversation, often taking place between partners in patrol cars and prompted only by hearing an officer speak over the radio: "Go get 'em, hot dog"; "Surprised he's not taking his fifth coffee break"; "Uh, oh, we'll have to cover that screw-up for sure"; and "Smith has got a rookie tonight." Judgments are also conveyed through preferences officers express for partners. Some are shunned, others are sought out. Occasionally, doubts about performance will be so serious that officers will indicate privately to supervisors that they will not work with a particular officer. Only the most insensitive policeman could fail to appreciate that if people are talking about others as openly as they do, they must be talking about him too. Officers know that reputations are on the line whenever they work. Among their own kind, they want to be known as master craftsmen, hoping to escape from the stigma of apprentice as soon as possible.

In policing, then, it is legitimate to talk about skills and to make judgments about performance. The critical question is whether there is a consensus about craftsmanship. That is, although officers recognize differences in performance, do they agree on what constitutes better as opposed to worse activity? Police officers could be in the tragic situation of wanting desperately to learn from experience yet receiving conflicting signals from their peers. Approval of skills may be given for nothing more profound than doing things "my way." In these circumstances, learning would consist of developing a mode of operation that bore little relation either to objective measures of effectiveness or approval by peers. The situation may not, however, be so dismal. Like teaching, good policing may be easier to recognize in practice than to define abstractly. Perhaps officers really do agree on who is especially skilled, raising the possibility that learning through emulation is possible. The truth of this matter would be important to test. It would also be easy to do. Officers would be asked to identify by name others whom they consider to be particularly skilled. If there was reasonable agreement, observers would then determine whether these individuals acted in terms of similar goals, chose similar tactics,he same presence. Observation would be better than asking officers about the qualities that caused them to identify others as being skilled, because officers might simply project onto others what they thought should be valued in themselves. Since patrol officers believe, almost as an article of faith, that supervisors evaluate performance superficially, ignoring displays of skill that do not show up in numbers, it would be important to solicit opinions about skilled officers from all ranks. Supervisors may not be quite as out of touch as they are portrayed to be. Alternatively, they may be emphasizing norms that increase the uncertainty patrol officers feel as they go about their daily work.

The final and indispensable step would be to determine whether the tactics chosen by master craftsmen really worked as intended. As in medicine, a proper bedside manner does not guarantee correct diagnosis or treatment. Only rigorous testing of the efficacy of tactical choices can at last transform police lore into the wisdom its practitioners think it to be.

IV

Can the Craft Be Taught?

If learning to make correct choices takes place by and large in the crucible of experience, rather than through formal training, then the development of occupational skills is likely to be a lengthy process whose outcome is far from certain. It does not follow, however, that learning could not be accelerated and made more systematic. We would like to make four suggestions for making the transition from apprentice to master craftsman both faster and more assured.[31]

First, formal training programs must give more attention to the problematic nature of police work. Oddly, police keep talking as if policing were a craft, but recruits are instructed as if it were a science. As Manning remarked, "The striking thing about order-maintenance methods is how little they are taught, how cynically they are viewed, and how irrelevant they are thought to be in most police departments."[32] The reason is probably that training staffs do not know how to instruct in craftsmanship. As in colleges, teaching mainly consists of lecturing and listening. What is needed in police training, instead, is frank discussion, with case studies of the realities of field decision. Training in police academies is too much like introductory courses on anatomy in medical schools and not enough like internships. The problem, however, is that this kind of training would require admitting what command staffs would rather hide, namely, that in many situations no one is really quite sure what is the best thing to do.

Training must focus on the need for choice in specific, clearly delineated situations. The reality of police work must be brought into the classroom so that students and staff can discuss appropriate goals and tactics. They should also be encouraged to think reflectively about the cues that should be used to shape decisions and those that should not. These training objectives can be accomplished in several ways. Students and staff can simulate "street" encounters, taking the roles of citizens and police. Students can be asked to discuss how they would respond to a variety of written scenarios. Discrepancies among students should be highlighted, with an analysis made of what the likely results of responding in each way would be. Films and videotapes, now being developed fairly widely, could be used to portray the hurly-burly of real life. In all of these cases, master craftsmen, if they can be identified, should be used to help train recruits. This does not mean that they should have classes turned over to them, since they are generally not trained in instruction, nor should they be brought in primarily to excite the recruits with "war stories."[33] Rather, they should be used as authentic exhibits to help instructors explore the uncertainties of choice that police face on the street. It is their experience that should be deliberately and systematically tapped. Finally, academic discussion must alternate with discussion observation of patrol operations. This practice is followed now in many departments. Unfortunately, debriefing is rarely systematic; field experiences are not used to prompt discussion about the range of goals and the probable effectiveness of various tactics.

Second, master craftsmen should be used as field instructors for rookies. This is the rationale behind programs in many departments in which probationary officers are assigned to experienced patrolmen for periods of time. Though field instruction programs are a considerable advance over training wholly in classroom settings, the full potential for uncovering significant craft skills is not being developed. Too often, appointment as a field instructor is a reward for having an unblemished record, not for recognition of superior skills, or it is a reward for meeting departmental criteria of performance, which are not necessarily those of craft operatives. The importance of discovering whether this gap in performance norms really exists has already been explored. Furthermore, field instructors are rarely trained to draw lessons from their own experience. They have no more insight into what they are doing than do other officers. In particular, they may be totally blind to alternative ways of accomplishing the same objective. They may be especially confident, which makes their advice particularly persuasive, but they are not nesessarily more informed. Finally, because field instructors are often responsible for evaluating the performance of trainees, they are viewed as judges rather than as mentors. They intimidate the recruit rather than draw out his perplexity about police work. Training and evaluation should be more carefully separated, even though that may lengthen the probationary period.

Third, if policing does encompass varying levels of skill related to experience, it follows that learning can be continual and cumulative. The shape of the learning curve would need to be determined through research. It may be found that diminished returns set in relatively soon after an officer leaves the academy, or that learning continues fairly steadily throughout most of an officer's career. If learning tapered off rapidly, it would be necessary to find out whether this was due to the unexpected simplicity of the work or to the lack of encouragement for continued growth in skills. On the testimony of police themselves, learning should not be viewed as a short-run matter. It needs to be built into policing throughout an officer's career. This need is generally recognized under the rubric of in-service training. Unfortunately, in-service training relies primarily on sending people back to classrooms for traditional lectures and note-taking. If skills are to be further developed, what is needed are seminars among patrol personnel in which they share their understanding of appropriate goals and useful tactics. Officers must be helped to learn from one another less haphazardly than they do in the front seats of patrol cars. Such seminars should not be bull sessions, where people talk in a nondirective way. Seminars must be carefully led by people who are trained in maintaining focus, imposing discipline, and drawing out participants. In our own seminars with officers, we found that patrolmen frequently disagree about elementary facts concerning law, departmental policy, and the functioning of the criminal justice system. Opportunities for relevant instruction emerge out of the perplexity of officers themselves. Furthermore, although officers recognize that there are different ways for handling situations, they have never had an opportunity to share insights about the relative utility of these approaches. They do what comes naturally, which may be good or may be bad. The final benefit from forthright discussion is that it may resensitize jaded officers to the problems and potentialities of the job. Experience may teach, but it also rigidifies. Being comfortable in one's work is not the same as being effective in it.

In-service seminars may contribute to raising performance levels even though immediate skill development does not occur. Because they are a visible sign that departments take seriously the complexity of patrol work and value the learning that experience engenders, in-service seminars may raise the standing of patrol work. Officers are proud of what they have learned, not always with reason, and interested in demonstrating their skill. As in the famous Hawthorne study of industrial productivity, institutional attention to their workday life may rekindle the enthusiasm of officers for their work.

Fourth, assuming that experience is valuable in learning about police work, departments should regard advancement in skill development. Presently, police departments regard superior achievement by promoting people into supervisory positions or transferring them to non-patrol duties. Thus, they lose skills in patrol without assuredly gaining talent for other pursuits. Good patrolmen are not necessarily good supervisors, any more than they are good detectives, planners, or juvenile counselors. Police departments must find ways to encourage continued growth in patrol skills among the people who remain in patrol work.

Identifying and using master craftsmen in departmental training is an important first step. It demonstrates to the rank and file that skills are recognized, that what is learned on the street is valued. But there are other possibilities that should be explored as well. Pay raises might be given to people recognized by their peers as master craftsmen. Departments might also establish a special title, rank, or insignia for officers who are especially skilled in patrol work. The point is to convince patrol officers that the creative use of experience in learning to perform more effectively is appreciated.

V

The Bottom Line

Experience teaches lessons to patrol officers that they consider crucial to effective performance and career longevity. Complicated decisions are being made on the street about circumstances. This being the case, obvious benefits would result from ensuring that what is being learned bears a close relation to approved goals that correct tactical lessons are being reinforced, and that learning takes place as quickly as possible. In order to accomplish this, it is important to study the coherence among what pass as craft skills in departments and the connection between tactics and both short-range and long-range outcomes. Most important of all, police departments must face up to the implications for training or their own argument that policing is learned by experience.

The benefits of doing all this are obvious. First, giving institutional attention to the skills that experience teaches will raise morale and self-esteem among the most numerous police rank, the patrolmen, who bear the major responsibility for police performance. Emphasizing the subtlety of patrol work also redresses the overemphasis on criminal investigation, so often deplored by policemen and observers alike.[34] Patrol work would begin to be perceived as a disciplined activity, no less demanding than the work of detectives.

Second, police departments would be forced to develop techniques for measuring degrees of skill. It is a matter for fierce debate in police circles whether existing measures do so. Most patrolmen think they do not, arguing that evaluation is based on quantitative indicators which measure activity rather than effectiveness. As we have suggested, a careful study of the performance traits of officers recognized by their peers as being especially good at patrol work would help to clarify this matter. It does not follow, of course, that patrolmen are right. If a discrepancy exists between what officers and the organization think is good patrol work, it should be eliminated. If, on the other hand, the discrepancy exists only in the minds of the rank and file, steps should be taken to correct this impression.

Third, only by developing canons for better/worse, proper/improper, more/less useful patrol action can policing become truly professional. Professionalism—meaning the development and imposition of operating principles out of an ongoing cooperative analysis—is essential in both scientific and craft domains of work. Indeed, it is precisely when operating principles are unclear that responsible learning requires the systematic and sensitive pooling of experience. Paradoxically, policing has not developed the self-consciousness that claims about the craft nature of policing would entail. For all the talk, the police community has not acted as if it really believes that there is utility in studying experience. Policemen have wanted the autonomy of professionals without accepting the counterbalancing responsibility for regulating the work of practitioners in operational terms. It is not being argued that policemen are more duplicitous than other claimants to professional status, but police have not successfully convinced either themselves or the public that their work is highly skilled. Until they do, their talk about professionalism will seem presumptuous.

Here is the rub: Substantial risks are involved for the police in openly admitting that goals are not fixed, that law enforcement is often uncertain, and that tactical choices are matters of opinion. They become politically more vulnerable if they say outright that patrol work requires the development of skills over time, for it implies that the great mass of police officers are flying by the seat of their pants. Police officers may chafe at the fact that their work is undervalued because its subtlety is not understood, but the fiction of automatic decisionmaking protects them from being second-guessed.

Little imagination is required to foresee what would happen to public confidence in the police if they admitted that age, education, class, race, and sex were considered when they decide what to do. These factors *are* considered, however, and the police believe, on the basis of hard-won experience, that they must be considered. Here are some examples. A white man and a black man, each well-dressed, each carrying a television set from a retail store to the trunk of a car at 5:30 p.m., will probably be treated differently by the police. Officers will not only be more suspicious of the black man and more likely to stop and question him, they will also be more circumspect in their approach if they

decide to confront him. They know that black men have had a belly full of "hassling" and are much more likely than white men to get angry. Another example deals with spouse assault reports made by Hispanic, as opposed to black, women. Because Hispanic women have been found to be less willing than black women to file complaints against husbands who beat them, police officers have to work harder to provide equal protection. Their approach to marital discord has to follow different lines from the beginning. Antagonism toward the police is often more intense in some places in a community than in others. Officers, therefore, take more precautions in those areas. From their point of view, this behavior is reasonable; from the public's, it is hostile, provocative, and demeaning. On a warm Friday night, shortly after dark, cruising patrol officers saw a small car pull away from the side door of a public school. As the car went past them, they saw that the driver was a white middle-aged man who hardly gave the police a passing glance. "Your basic pillar?" said one officer. "Yep," replied the other, "your basic pillar." The car was not stopped for investigation. Can such a decision be explained to the public without controversy?

A real distinction does exist between useful operational intelligence and prejudice, but because both utilize the same cues, they are difficult to separate in practice.[35] It would certainly be unrealistic, as well as unreasonable, to expect patrolmen not to make decisions about goals and tactics on the basis of situational circumstances such as the visible appearance of the people involved. Unless choice is precluded altogether in police work, officers cannot avoid developing stereotypes. To achieve the goals of control, crime prevention, personal safety, and career protection, patrol officers must adapt what they do to what they see.[36] In order to protect such decisions from prejudice, however, more examination of the link between visible cues and the results of particular tactics must be made. In particular, research must be undertaken to determine what really does work both tactically and strategically. Is it true, for example, that disproportionate attention to black teenager activity on the streets produces more criminal arrests than arrests of teenagers indiscriminately; that a criminal complaint pressed by the police with a wife's approval is not as effective in providing protection for the battered spouse who is Hispanic, even if the complaint is eventually withdrawn, as for the spouse who is black and prosecutes to the end; or that preemptive force against strapping black males controls violence and avoids injuries to police more surely than less provocative tactics? Addressing such questions is essential if prejudice and operational intelligence are to be distinguished. However, the point remains that if different approaches are found efficacious based on ascriptive stereotypes, as police officers certainly believe, imparting these lessons will look very much to nonpolice observers like legitimating discrimination.

In point of fact, the public may not disagree with police decisions as much as the police fear it does. John Clark compared what the police and public respectively thought were appropriate police actions in six hypothetical situations.[37] He found that the police tended to recommend arrest more and that they thought the public wanted more arrests than they really did. This evidence would suggest that the public would welcome more individuation, but that it is the police who are reluctant. In an international testing of what the public would approve in four criminal situations, the public agreed that police decisions should be affected both by the nature of the crime and the class of the perpetrator.[38] The public appeared to believe, as the police do, that actions should be bent to considerations of natural justice.

Undoubtedly, there are serious potential costs to the police in responding to the challenge of improving skills by forthrightly addressing how policing is learned. This is not the last word, however, about the public's likely reaction. Failure to confront the learning requirements of patrol work not only affects police performance and morale, but also does not solve the problem of public perception. Police are fooling themselves if they think so. If choice is unavoidable in police work, because goals and tactics must be determined situationally, pretending otherwise becomes a living lie that the public soon de-

tects. Although facing the training implications of patrol work will be controversial, not doing so is also controversial. The police lose the opportunity for developing public acceptance of their professional status that would not only be gratifying but that they believe would enhance effectiveness. Part of the reason the public questions the use of discretion is that the police have always tried to appear exclusively as technical agents of law rather than instruments of public morality. A vicious circle has arisen. If police improved performance by testing the "lessons of experience" for efficacy, both through controlled observation and the sharing of collective police experience, and then imparted those lessons more systematically to police officers, the public might have more confidence in the police as moral arbiters. Unfortunately, at the present, the public's distrust of the police impels officers to hide the problematic nature of their work, causing departments to undervalue what the rank and file believe is critical to their work, to neglect intelligent appraisal of collective experience, and to pass up the opportunity to regard those who do patrol work particularly well.

Notes

1. See *generally* D. Black, The Manners and Customs of the Police (1980); K. Davis, Discretionary Justice (1969); W. LaFave, Arrest (1965); P. Manning, Police Work (1977); W. Muir, Police—Street Corner Politicians (1977); A. Reiss, Police and the Public (1971); J. Rubinstein, City Police (1973); B. Smith, Police Systems in the United States (1940); J. Wilson, Varieties of Police Behavior (1968).

2. D. Bayley, The Police and Political Development in India (1969); D. Bayley, Patterns of Policing (forthcoming).

3. *See* D. Black, *supra* note 1, at 188-89; W. Muir, *supra* note 1, ch. 6; J. Rubinstein, *supra* note 1, at 153.

4. D. Bayley & H. Mendelsohn, Minorities and the Police 72 (1969). The authors cite figures of 38% and 14%, respectively.

5. Domestic disputes were mentioned by 29.3% of the officers surveyed. D. Bayley, Police and Community Attitudes in Battle Creek, Michigan: An Interim Report on the Evaluation of the Police Improvement Project (September,

1981) (unpublished report by the Police Foundation).

6. M. Farmer & M. Furstenberg, Alternative Strategies for Responding to Police Calls for Service 2 (1979).

7. M. Banton, The Policeman in the Community (1964); W. LaFave, *supra* note 1; P. Shane, Police and People (1980); J. Wilson, *supra* note 1; LaFave, *The Police and Nonenforcement of the Law*, 1962 Wis. L. Rev. 104.

8. E. Scott, Calls for Service: Citizen Demand and Initial Response, 28-30 (1980) (Bloomington, Indiana: Workshop in Political Theory and Policy Analysis, University of Indiana) (unpublished paper).

9. J. McIver & R. Parks, Identification of Effective and Ineffective Police Actions 13 (March 1982) (paper for the annual meeting of the Academy of Criminal Justice Sciences). Five percent of all calls for police service involved domestic and nondomestic conflict.

10. Lilly, *What Are the Police Now Doing?* 6 J. Police Sci. & Ad. 51, 56 (1978).

11. U.S. Department of Justice, Sourcebook on Criminal Justice Statistics 326, table 3.81 (1981).

12. R. Ericson, Reproducing Order: A Study of Police Patrol Work 4 (1982).

13. Bittner, *Florence Nightingale in Pursuit of Willie Sutton: A Theory of the Police*, in The Potential for Reform in the Criminal Justice System 30 (1974).

14. A. Reiss, *supra* note 1, at 134-38.

15. Bittner, *supra* note 13, at 22-29; W. LaFave, *supra* note 1, at 138; C. Silberman, Criminal Violence, Criminal Justice 136 (1978).

16. Reiss argues that anger against the courts also arises from the fact that police arrest only when they feel it is morally justified. When courts are lenient, the policeman's sense of justice is affronted. A. Reiss, *supra* note 1, at 134-38.

17. Bureau of the Census, U.S. Department of Commerce, Statistical Abstract of the U.S. 179, 403, 415 (1981).

18. F. Ianni & Reuss-Ianni, Street Cops vs. Management Cops: The Two Cultures of Policing 24-28 (December 1980) (paper prepared for the seminar on policing at Nijenrode, The Netherlands).

19. This remark fits the dominant management strategy of police departments, which James Q. Wilson characterizes as constraint-ori-

ented rather than task-oriented. J. Wilson, The Investigators 197-98 (1978).

20. P. Manning, The Narcs' Game 17 (1980).

21. Black uses categories of this kind: penal, compensatory, therapeutic, and conciliatory. D. Black, The Behavior of Law 6 (1976); Black *supra* note 1, ch. 5.

22. R. Sykes & E. Brent, Policing: A Social Behaviorist Perspective (1984). This sophisticated work tried to determine how antecedent stages shaped later ones.

23. Parnas, *The Police Response to the Domestic Disturbance*, 1967 Wis. L. Rev. 914-60; M. Haist & R. Daniel, Draft of a Report on Structure and Process of Disturbance Transactions (January, 1975) (unpublished draft at the Police Foundation), and J. McIver & R. Parks, *supra* note 9, are the only attempts to map tactics in domestic disputes known to the authors.

24. See also D. Black, *supra* note 1, at 34.

25. M. Brown, Working the Street ch. 9 (1981), found significant differences in the tactics officers said they would use in four scenarios presented to them. The scenarios involved drunken driving, quarreling neighbors, assault between husband and wife, and disorderly juveniles in a public place.

26. D. Black, *supra* note 1, at 75-80. Black's analysis applies to his four categories of action, which are termed exit actions in this article. He does not try to explain the structural determinants of the tactics police use at earlier stages of disputes.

27. R. Friedrich, The Impact of Organization, Individual, and Situational Factors on Police Behavior (1977) (unpublished Ph.D. dissertation, available at University of Michigan, Ann Arbor, Dept. Of Political Science).

28. Goldstein, *Improving Policing: A Problem-Oriented Approach*, 25 J. Crime & Delinq. 236, 243 (1979).

29. The authors will explore this problem and suggest specific research projects in a forthcoming paper.

30. On the absence of research on this topic, see M. Wycoff, Reconceptualizing the Police Role (November 1980) (draft report from the Police Foundation for the National Institute of Justice). The Police Division of the National Institute of Justice has recognized the importance of this problem; their grant supported the work that let to this article.

31. In putting forward these four recommendations, this article does not mean to imply that

all police departments in the United States are remiss in these respects. There are departments in which these proposals have already been substantially incorporated. Nonetheless, many departments have not done so and should give these ideas serious consideration.

32. P. Manning, Police Work 289 (1977).

33. Van Maanen, *Working the Street: A Developmental View of Police Behavior*, in The Potential for Reform in Criminal Justice 88-91 (H. Jacob ed. 1974).

34. P. Manning, *supra* note 32, at 372.

35. M. Puch, Policing the Inner City 124 (1979), and C. Shearing, Cops Don't Always See It That Way (1977) (unpublished paper), show how police distinguish good people from bad people on the basis of ostensible features.

36. Clark & Sykes, *Some Determinants of Police Organization and Practice in a Modern Industrial Democracy*, in Handbook of Criminology 467 (D. Glazer ed. 1974).

37. Clark, *Isolation of the Police: A Comparison of the British and American Situations*, 56 J. Crim. L. Criminology & Police Sci. 327 (1965).

38. Criminal Education and Research Center, Perception of Police Power: A Study in Four Cities 63-64 (1973).

Part V

Doing Police Work

Those who study police work frequently draw a distinction between proactive policing and reactive policing. The former generally includes activity in which the police must go out and discover crimes or other problems themselves—i.e., events not likely to be reported, at least not through the 911 system. The main reason they are not reported is that they involve so-called victimless crimes. Participants in these kinds of crimes are usually consenting parties, so that there is no obvious outraged victim likely to pick up a telephone and report the crime to the police. Reactive policing, on the other hand, usually does begin with a call from a citizen. Calls involving crimes, disorder, and other matters are received by the police routinely, and the police then "react," usually by sending a patrol officer to the scene.

Studies have consistently shown that most police work involving crime and disorder is reactive. Police do not become aware of most crimes until after they occur and the victim makes a report. With respect to disorder (drunkenness, noise, loitering, etc.), police have more opportunity to discover this kind of behavior themselves but still often wait for a citizen complaint before taking action. One major aspect of modern policing that is primarily proactive, however, is traffic enforcement. While police certainly do respond to traffic accidents and occasionally receive reports of speeders or drunk drivers, their primary strategy is to discover traffic law violations "in progress" and then to take enforcement action.

One of the most common and most controversial types of reactive police work is the domestic dispute. These disputes are sometimes reported by neighbors but most often by victims. Police have traditionally dreaded such domestic calls, claiming that they were very dangerous (research has shown that this is not true), that victims often changed their minds about pressing charges (true), that repeat calls to the same households were common (true), and that such calls were frustrating to handle. Overlooked for many years were two important underlying conditions: (1) domestic assaults are crimes, and probably the most common of all violent crimes; and (2) most police officers, being male, probably had a tendency to identify with husbands rather than wives, or at least to fail to fully empathize with the victims of these crimes. In the first article in this section, these and other characteristics of police handling of domestic disputes are discussed.

The middle two articles in this section address proactive policing. The first examines the consequences of a police tactic frequently used in proactive policing—undercover work. The second looks at a variety of operational and policy issues surrounding one of the biggest and most problematic targets of proactive policing today—drugs. These two issues, undercover work and drug enforcement, have serious ramifications for police officers, police organizations, and society, as discussed in the two articles.

Another type of problem that police find troublesome and are frequently asked to handle involves people with mental illness, the topic of the fourth article in this section. Disturbed people sometimes act in a disruptive, alarming, or even violent manner, but in an important sense it is not "their fault," and they are usually not held criminally liable. Mental illness afflicts a substantial portion of the population, regardless of race, gender, or social class. So police officers are expected to handle the mental illness with a great deal of restraint and understanding, and generally are asked to process them informally or else through the medical system, instead of taking them to jail. This might work reasonably well, except that in most jurisdictions the medical system is reluctant to get involved, and officers are often left with no good alternatives, especially in the middle of the night, during the weekend, or out in the country far away from the nearest hospital offering emergency mental health services. These problems have been exacerbated by the policy of deinstitutionalization—as a society we have opted to confine fewer people in mental institutions, but we have failed to create sufficient community-based and out-patient services to compensate for the closing of larger institutions. Consequently, police have increasingly been asked to handle people with mental illnesses, but generally they have not been provided with appropriate response alternatives. ✦

17

The Law Enforcement Response to Spouse Abuse

*J. David Hirschel,
Ira W. Hutchison,
Charles W. Dean, and
Anne-Marie Mills*

Probably no other specific type of problem or crime has received more attention in police circles over the past 15 years than domestic violence. Over a relatively short period of time, the conventional wisdom about how best to handle "domestics" changed from (1) do nothing to (2) mediate the conflict to (3) arrest; the typical organizational response changed from one of giving officers complete discretion to one of adopting restrictive policies and procedures. The evolution of police practices and policies regarding spousal abuse is discussed in this article, as well as the evidence pertaining to the relative effectiveness of different practices. Once you have digested all this information, ask yourself which policies and practices you would prefer if you were a victim of domestic violence. If you were a police officer? If you were a police chief?

For many centuries husbands had the right to use force to coerce their wives to conform to their expectations. Until very recently, spouse abuse has been considered more a problem of public order than a criminal matter.

Societal acceptance of spouse abuse as criminal has been slow and inconsistent, and attitudes favoring nonintervention have been slow to change. Competition for resources occurs when the criminal justice system is asked to assign higher priority to this problem. On the felony level the battle has been won; there is no dispute that felonious spouse abuse is considered a matter for the criminal justice system. This is not the case, however, on the misdemeanor level. Because domestic violence accounts for a significant proportion of all calls for police service, assigning a higher priority to such calls requires a major reallocation of police resources. Although many people do not question the morality of arresting a man for assaulting his wife or partner, the real question is whether to arrest and prosecute those who commit this crime at the expense of other governmental responsibilities or of law enforcement and judicial responses to other crimes.

This article examines the historical treatment of wives and the evolution of the law enforcement response to spouse abuse. We first address the issue of definition: some confusion exists between the generic concept of spouse abuse and other types of family disturbance that may or may not be similar. Both conceptual and practical problems are present in defining abuse. The definitional problem is particularly noteworthy in view of the fact that most domestic calls for police service involve situations which are either shouting matches or in which there are no victims with apparent injuries. Verbal abuse seldom qualifies as criminal behavior, so police can do little in this respect.

It is important to address current social attitudes towards spouse abuse and to discuss how we reached this point. An examination of the historical treatment of wives helps us to understand why hostile behavior, now viewed as spouse abuse, was acceptable for so long, why it is currently an unresolved public policy issue, and why both the public and the legal system resist in treating all spouse abusers as criminals.

In this article we also address different estimates of the prevalence of spouse abuse, and then focus on that segment of spouse abuse which is reported to police. We examine problems of definition, different data sources, and varying probabilities of calling the police in order to explain the difficulties in measuring the extent to which spouse abuse actually constitutes a law enforcement problem.

The basic question at the center of the current public debate is the proper role of law enforcement in spouse abuse. Significant research now has been conducted on the police response to spouse abuse, but the findings are not entirely consistent with each other or with the position of advocacy groups. Nationwide there has been considerable momentum toward the adoption of pro-arrest policies. We explore the rationale for such policies and examine the empirical studies that test the effectiveness of arrest in reducing subsequent recidivism by spouse abusers. We conclude by discussing the multiple issues involved in achieving a more comprehensive understanding of the place of law enforcement as only one possible societal response to spouse abuse.

Definitions

A preliminary issue involves an understanding of the key concepts that are the focus of this article: *spouse* and *abuse*. Although these words have apparent common sense meanings, each may be used in a variety of ways which makes effective comparisons more difficult.

The common, popular understanding of *spouse* is congruent with dictionary definitions, and focuses on married couples. The more common definition of spouse in research literature, however, pertains to persons in conjugal or conjugal-like relationships, including married, separated, and cohabiting couples (Berk and Loseke 1981; Buzawa and Buzawa 1990; Ford and Regoli forthcoming; Goolkasian 1986; Williams and Hawkins 1989). This difference is relatively important because a large proportion of abusive incidents reported to police involve cohabiting couples, an issue that we will examine later in greater detail.

The term *spouse* is gender-free and may erroneously imply a parity between men and women. As we will discuss later, husbands often are the targets of abuse, but their probability of being injured is much lower than that of wives. Morley and Mullender (1991)

note that the gender-specific term *woman-battering* has given way to the androgynous terms *domestic*, *spouse*, *marital*, and *family* violence. It is unclear whether the broadening of this concept has had a positive or a harmful effect on family violence studies. The variation both in concepts and in their references (i.e., who is included) creates some confusion.

A second major issue is whether to define *abuse* as measured by aggressive actions or as measured by the outcome of such acts (i.e., injuries; Straus 1990). According to Berk et al. (1983), there is little consensus on the kinds of behavior to which the term *abuse* refers. Feld and Straus (1989:143) define violence as "an act carried out with the intention or perceived intention of causing physical pain or injury to another person." Schulman (1979), Straus (1979), and Straus, Gelles, and Steinmetz (1980) also use acts as a definition of abuse. On the other hand, Berk et al. (1983) emphasize the severity of injuries as the focus of their study.

This article defines spouse abuse to include married, separated, divorced, cohabiting, and formerly cohabiting couples, and focuses primarily on female victims unless noted otherwise. The literature we include here encompasses abuse as defined either by act or by outcome. In general we concentrate on physical aggression because of the paucity of data on verbal aggression such as threats. Although we recognize both the frequency and the seriousness of threats, this type of abuse is less likely to produce a law enforcement response.

Evolving Attitudes Toward Spouse Abuse

Historical Overview

Wife abuse appears to be a cultural universal that has been approved implicitly or explicitly until very recently. From an anthropological perspective it may be observed that a large proportion of societies have given adult males authority to coerce the behavior of dependent females. This authority appears to be an integral part of a monogamous marriage relationship, which involves differential power between the partners in a setting culturally defined as private. When formal governments emerged and legal codes developed, the wife consistently was treated as legally subordinate to the husband; wife beating either was not considered criminal or was formally approved.

Roman law, which has been served as a basis for many legal systems in the Western world, originally gave a husband sovereign authority over his wife, who acquired the status of daughter at marriage. This authority, known as *patria potestas*, included the power of life and death and the right to unrestrained physical chastisement of the wife and other family members (Hecker 1914:13; Pleck 1987:9).

A modified form of *patria potestas* was incorporated into English common law (Oppenlander 1981:386) under the guise of family protection (Gamache, Edleson, and Schock 1988:194; Sigler 1989:2; Walker 1990:48). Although the male's authority in this system did not include the power of life and death, physical chastisement was both accepted and expected (Dobash and Dobash 1978: Hecker 1914:124-27; Smith 1989:3). In 1768 Blackstone described the husband's right to chastise his wife moderately in order to enforce obedience (1897:147). The criterion for "moderate" was the "rule of thumb," which allowed a husband to use any reasonable instrument, including a rod no thicker than his thumb, to correct his "wayward" wife.

The English heritage was brought to the American colonies; husbands in America, as in England, retained the power to chastise their wives. Although the Puritans enacted the first laws against wife beating in 1641 with the passage of the Massachusetts *Body of Laws and Liberties*, the integrity and privacy of the family still were considered more important that the protection of victims. This orientation contributed greatly to tolerance and indifference toward wife beating (Pleck 1987:21-2; 1989). Between 1633 and 1802, for example, only 12 cases involving wife beating are to be found in the court records of Plymouth Colony (Pleck 1989:25).

Although it is debatable how accurately these cases represent the law in the United States in general (Pleck 1989:32-33), a number of appellate court decisions in this period upheld a husband's right to chastise his wife physically. In 1824 the Mississippi State Supreme Court declared in *Bradley v. State* that "the husband be permitted to exercise the right of moderate chastisement." The Court emphasized that "family broils and dissentions" were not proper matters to bring before a court of law, but were best left inside the walls of the home (158).

Other cases reinforced this position, holding that a wife was incompetent to testify against her husband in a case where "a lasting injury or great bodily harm" was not inflicted or threatened (*State v. Hussey* 1852:128); that "the law gives the husband power to use such a degree of force as is necessary to make the wife behave herself and know her place," and that bruises left by a horsewhip or switch may be justified by the circumstances so as not to give a wife a right to abandon her husband and "claim to be divorced" (*Joyner v. Joyner* 1862:202-53); that the effect, not the instrument, was the standard to be used in determining whether the husband had exceeded his authority (*State v. Black* 1864; *State v. Rhodes* 1865); and that a husband was permitted to use the force necessary to control an unruly wife, even if they were living apart by agreement. The court would "not invade the domestic forum unless some permanent injury be inflicted" except in cases of excessive violence to "gratify . . . bad passions" (*State v. Black* 1864:163).

The Puritan attitude of indifference or outright approval was maintained until the late 1830s (Pleck 1989). Working initially through churches and later through the temperance societies, the women's rights movements gained momentum during the nineteenth century. Whereas the Puritans placed family preservation ahead of women's rights, the temperance movement reversed the order (Pleck 1989).

Women's growing activism evolved in the 1850s into a push for women's rights which helped to sponsor legislation regarding married women's property, conventions on women's rights, and recommendations on divorce (Pleck 1989). The interest in women's rights, however, did not peak until the 1870s. After the Civil War, state [intervention] in the family was viewed as more acceptable than in the past because of the broader governmental control allowed by the war (Pleck 1987:89). As a consequence, state legislatures began to pass Married Women's Acts, which allowed married women to enter contracts, sue, and own property in their own right, and liberalized the divorce laws, thus eroding men's absolute dominance over women.

A focus on law and order and a humanitarian concern for the victims of spouse abuse led to attempts to enact legislation that expressed a more serious view of this problem (Pleck 1989:35). Between 1876 and 1906 bills were introduced in 12 states, and were passed in three, to punish wife beaters with a whipping (Pleck 1989:40). Passing a statute and enforcing it, however, are not the same. After Maryland enacted a law in 1882 to punish wife beaters with either a whip or a year in jail, no one was prosecuted under that statutory provision for a year and only two convictions occurred in three years. Although unused, the provision remained on the books until 1948 (Pleck 1989:41).

During this period dicta and holdings in court cases likewise became less supportive of a husband's right to exercise physical control over his wife. In the Alabama case of *Fulgham v. State* (1871) the court denied the right, declaring that wife whipping was "at best, but a low and barbarous custom" (147). Three years later, in *State v. Oliver* (1874), a lower court found guilty a husband who had whipped his wife with two thin switches, leaving bruises. The North Carolina Supreme Court affirmed this judgment, stating that the old "rule of thumb" no longer was the law in North Carolina. Yet despite the legal rejection of the right to chastise, the belief that spouse abuse belonged within the privacy of the home continued to be very much a part of American culture. Physical cruelty was disapproved, but it was not grounds for a woman to obtain a divorce especially because nagging women were regarded as having provoked their husbands (Pleck 1987:25).

The de facto decriminalization of spouse abuse was reinforced by the emergence of family courts in the second decade of the twentieth century. These courts tended to view family violence as a domestic problem rather than as a crime, and urged reconciliation whenever possible (Pleck 1987:136-37). From 1920 until the late 1970s, relatively little occurred, legislatively or judicially in the area of spouse abuse.

Because law both reflects and shapes societal values, we can expect its development and enforcement to be inconsistent over time among jurisdictions and among agencies within a given jurisdiction. The legislation and court rulings discussed above trace the uneven evolution of law regarding spouse abuse. Generally the changes in legislation and in enforcement were roughly parallel. Yet in spousal relationships, moderate force that otherwise would be treated as criminal often went unpunished.

Past and Current Attitudes

A certain ambivalence toward spouse abuse always has existed and still persists today. A number of reasons are advanced for this attitude: the privacy of the home, the social approval of violence, the inequality of women in society, and noninvolvement by criminal justice officials (Gelles and Straus 1988:25; Oppenlander 1981:385; Pleck 1989: 20-21).

Spouse abuse has been viewed differently from "ordinary" assault between other principals because spouse abuse has been regarded as less serious on the grounds that the wife belongs to the husband and the home is his castle; therefore what happens in the castle is not a concern for his neighbors or the criminal justice system (Belknap 1990:248; Dobash and Dobash 1991; Fyfe and Flavin 1991; Pleck 1989:21). Although the state can punish violators, it continues to give family members special immunity to protect family life and the marriage (Oppenlander 1981:385; Pleck 1989:20). Senator Jesse Helms argued against federal funding of domestic violence shelters because they constituted "social engineering," removing the husband as the "head of the family" (126 Cong. Rec. 24, 12058, 1980).

The cultural belief in the sanctity of family privacy prevents societal, legal, or personal intervention (Balos and Trotzky 1988:83; Berk and Loseke 1981:319; Buda and Butler 1984:366; Gelles and Straus 1988:27; Roy

1977:138; Sigler 1989:2; Waits 1985:299). Modern industrial societies—characterized by urbanization, anonymity, high residential mobility, neolocal monogamous family patterns, and religiously reinforced family privacy—seem to have difficulty in developing and enforcing effective community standards that would limit wife abuse.

Because "violence is as American as apple pie" (Gelles and Straus 1988:26), some researchers suggest that abuse in the family is a result of the approval given to other forms of violence (Breslin 1978:298; Gelles and Straus 1988:26; Oppenlander 1981:394; Sigler 1989:98). The family is less authoritarian and more egalitarian than in the past; spouse abuse continues, however (Pleck 1989).

Men receive implicit social permission to beat their wives when nothing is done to stop abuse (Buzawa and Buzawa 1985:143; Roy 1977:138, Walker 1990:48). The problem is convincing the police to arrest, the prosecutors to prosecute vigorously, and the court system to sanction (Balos and Trotzky 1988:106; Goolkasian 1986:3). The criminal justice system is reluctant to punish batterers (Waits 1985:271), thus giving the impression that the abuser faces very little risk (Gelles and Straus 1988:24). Although spouse abuse is condemned in theory, the law still allows it to continue (Waits 1985:299).

The Extent of the Problem

The empirical study of family violence is relatively recent; only since the 1970s has it been studied in depth and extensively. Accurate prevalence and incidence data remain beyond reach, however. Both official records, such as those based on calls to police, and self-report data are best regarded as rough estimates of the extent of actual abuse.

Scope and Probability of Abuse

Despite 20 years of empirical research, estimates of the number of women abused by their partners each year vary greatly, ranging from 2.1 million (Langan and Innes 1986) to more than 8 million (Straus 1989). It has been estimated that violence occurs each year in approximately one relationship in six (Straus et al. 1980). The probability estimate

is that between 25 and 30 percent of couples will experience a violent incident in their lifetime (Gelles and Straus 1988; Nisonoff and Bitman 1979; Straus et al. 1980).

The widespread variation in numerical estimates is due to four factors. First, definitional differences are great; they range from any threat of unwanted touching to the infliction of serious injuries. Straus and Gelles (1990:96) estimate rates of *any* husband-to-wife violence at 116 per 1,000 couples per year (6,250,000 women), whereas they estimate any *severe* husband-to-wife violence at 34 per 1,000 couples per year (1,800,000 women). Second, estimates are based on different data sources: police data, shelter intakes, injuries reported to police or hospitals, and extrapolations from surveys. Even if there were no definitional differences, the different sources of data would produce widely varying parameters because they capture different segments of the abused population. Third, the time factor varies: published reports do not always make clear whether authors are using a data base to project estimates for a given year or for a lifetime probability of ever-abuse. In a given year, an estimate for that year will include those who entered the pool of abused women in a previous year, as well as those who are "new" to the pool. Fourth, although everyone agrees that abuse is underreported, nobody agrees about the extent of underreporting; this issue is discussed in greater detail below.

Predictors Associated With Spouse Abuse. In review of characteristics associated with spouse abuse, Hotaling and Sugarman (1986) investigated more than 400 empirical studies of husband-to-wife violence. Their review produced a total of 97 potential risk markers; a risk marker is defined as "an attribute or characteristic that is associated with an increased probability to either the use of husband-to-wife violence, or the risk of being victimized by husband-to-wife violence" (1986:102). Because this review unquestionably is the most comprehensive available, we rely on it for our overview.

Of the 97 characteristics investigated, Hotaling and Sugarman found very few to be consistent risk markers. In particular, attributes of women associated with being abused by men were rare. Of the 42 female-related characteristics investigated, only one appeared as a consistent risk marker: witnessing violence between parents while growing up. All of the other female characteristics investigated were determined to be inconsistent or nonrisk markers: for example, experiencing violence as a child (although this trait almost qualified), age, race, educational level, income, traditional sex role expectations, alcohol use, and self-esteem.

Far more predictive of spouse abuse in Hotaling and Sugarman's (1986) review were the characteristics associated with men. Of the 38 potential risk markers attributed to men, nine appeared as consistent predictors of abuse: being sexually aggressive toward their wives, violence toward their children, witnessing violence as a child, witnessing violence as an adolescent, occupational status, alcohol use, income, assertiveness, and educational level. Hotaling and Sugarman (1986) also investigated risk markers associated with the couple, and found five variables associated with higher levels of spouse abuse: frequency of verbal arguments, religious incompatibility, family income/social class (primarily through the husband's income), marital adjustment, and marital status. In sum, it is far more difficult to predict victimization of women in spouse abuse situations on the basis of any characteristic of the woman than on the basis of her male partner's attributes. Hotaling and Sugarman (1986) conclude that the psychiatric model of spouse abuse receives strong support from their review.

As new research is conducted, other factors may emerge as consistent risk markers; perhaps some of those now identified as increasing the probability of abuse will emerge as less accurate predictors. One dilemma is that comparisons (both within and across studies) include men who have abused a woman only once as well as those who are chronic batterers. We should not expect to find a consistent set of predictors when the entire range of wife abuse is reduced to the threshold requirement of a single incident. Greater progress on the question of prediction would be made if more attention were given to developing typologies of abusers,

victims, and relationships and then to determining predictor variables associated with particular types. For example, it may be that chronic abusers (of one or more female partners) are differentiated from occasional abusers by particular characteristics associated with both personality and situational variables.

Social Class Characteristics. As documented by both police reports and numerous researchers, marital violence exists in every class and income group, regardless of race and social class (Finesmith 1983; Lockhart 1987; Schulman 1979; Straus et al. 1980). Years of research, however, have failed to produce clear-cut and convincing documentation on the degree to which spouse abuse is distributed *equally* across various demographic groups. The most accurate current conclusion is that spouse abuse is comparable across social class variables; that is, more similarity than difference exists between groups. Yet although intragroup differences are greater than intergroup differences, we simply cannot conclude that demographic differences are absent. Some studies have discovered an inverse relationship between income and violence: as income increases, violence decreases (Finesmith 1983; Yllo and Straus 1981).

Schulman (1979) found, however, that although abusive families tend to be urban, young, and nonwhite, these violent families are not differentiated easily from similar nonabusive families. In a study of 307 black and white women from various social classes, Lockhart (1987) found no significant intergroup difference in victimization by domestic violence.

We speculate that researchers and the interpreters of research sometimes may bend over backward in their efforts to avoid any bias, and thus may distort results unwittingly by down playing any intergroup differences. It is clear that spouse abuse is not characteristic of any particular group. It is less clear whether all groups are truly equal in both prevalence and incidence of abusive behavior.

Abusive Incidents Reported to the Police. The proportion of spouse assaults reported to the police differs widely, depending on how the study was conducted (Bowker 1984). According to estimates, from one-tenth to two-thirds of abused women call the police to report an incident. In a survey of 1,793 Kentucky women, Schulman (1979) found that women called police in only 9 percent of the incidents. Compared to findings from other studies, this figure implies an extremely high proportion of unreported incidents. The generally accepted estimate (based in particular on national samples) is that approximately one-half of all incidents are reported to the police. Analysis of 1973-1976 National Crime Panel Survey data revealed that approximately 55 of every 100 incidents of intimate violence went unreported to law enforcement (U.S. Department of Justice 1980). Analysis of 1978-1982 data showed that 48 percent of the incidents were not reported to the police (Langan and Innes 1986). In a study of 420 women who sought treatment in a domestic abuse program in Washington State, Kuhl (1982) discovered that 66 percent of the women had not filed a report.

Characteristics of Persons Calling Police. Much of the dilemma in understanding demographic material in abuse rates is due again to data sources; there is no way to reconcile somewhat disparate information. As in some other areas of the criminal justice system, citizens who call the police to report a particular criminal action are not representative of all who experience that particular crime. An inherent self-selection process is present in the use of police services. Thus no one concludes that abused women who call the police are a representative demographic sample of all women who experience abuse.

Although domestic disturbances cut across all demographic boundaries, police are involved most often in domestic disturbances among the poor and uneducated (Hamberger and Hastings 1988; Moore 1979; Parnas 1967). Bowker (1982, 1984) reports that the police are more likely to come into contact with couples of relatively low socioeconomic status, with low-quality marital relationships, and suffering or inflicting severe violence. Nonwhite and lower-income women (under $7,500) are more than twice as likely to report an incident to the police as

are white, high-income women (over $15,000) (Schulman 1979). Underreporting occurs at all socioeconomic levels but is particularly likely among middle-and upper-income persons.

Reasons for Underreporting. A clear relationship between selective perception and underreporting has emerged in various studies. An unknown number of victims do not consider their assault to be a crime, or, if they do so, they do not report the incident or disclose to any official how they received their injuries (Breslin 1978). Because spouse abuse is so common in society, many victims do not view it as a crime and therefore do not report it to the police. As Langley and Levy (1978:5) note, these are the missing persons of official statistics.

Some women do not perceive a slap in the face as abuse, and so do not report it; others perceive such an action as abusive, but only a fraction of those women report it. The more severe the behavior, the more likely it is to be both perceived as abusive and reported often; often, however, even very severe abuse is never reported to the police. Langan and Innes (1986) found that the primary reason offered by women for not reporting an abusive incident to the police was that they considered it a private or personal matter (49 percent of respondents). A further 12 percent of the victims did not report because they feared reprisal. Similar proportions failed to report because they thought the crime was not important enough, or because they believed the police could not or would not do anything.

Some women report most incidents of abuse, some report some incidents, and some never report any incident that takes place. Unfortunately, the accumulation of studies does not tell us how many of each type are found in the reported and in the unreported incidents.

Abuse Reported in Surveys. Other than police reports, surveys provide the most comprehensive data on spouse abuse. Yet these, too, must be interpreted with some caution for a number of reasons. First, the perception of what constitutes abuse remains a problem. As Straus (1989:27) points out, victims and suspects may not view abuse as a crime and therefore may not report it in a crime survey.

National Crime Surveys (NCS) estimates of the crime of woman battering are one-fiftieth of the rate revealed in a national survey produced by Straus (1990). Second, national surveys face the problem of distilling spouse abuse from other forms of domestic violence as well as from nonfamily violence. National crime surveys find family offenses a difficult subject to quantify: neither the Uniform Crime Reports (UCR) nor the NCS are designed to measure family violence specifically (Rose and Goss 1989). As a result, an assault on a spouse is counted among the other nondomestic assaults (Miller 1979). Third, surveys such as the NCS can be problematic because interviews may be conducted with both the victim and the offender present. It is reasonable to assume that many victims would not report violence because of fear of reprisal by the offender (Straus 1989).

Nonwife Abuse. The common perception of spouse abuse involves a husband and a wife, with the latter as the victim. Although wife abuse is the modal adult domestic violence, there is a growing recognition of the abuse of husbands, cohabitants, and—to a lesser extent—gay or lesbian partners. Offenders are not always men, nor are victims always women; instead the problem is one of "spouse" abuse because men also are victims (Dobash and Dobash 1991:350).

The same elements in society that explain violence against wives cause women's violence towards men (Straus 1980). Violence against men, however, was and still is perceived as unusual in patriarchal societies, where men are expected to dominate and control the female (Dobash and Dobash 1991). Many women hit and beat their husbands, but the data have been "misreported, misinterpreted, and misunderstood" (Gelles and Straus 1988:90).

Steinmetz (1977) estimated that of 47 million married couples, more than a quarter-million husbands experience several beatings from their spouses. In Straus, Gelles, and Steinmetz's 1975 study (Gelles and Straus 1988), 2 million men were victims of violence inflicted by their wives. Straus and Gelles (1986, 1990) showed that the rate of wife-to-husband assault is slightly higher than that of husband-to-wife assault, but an attack by a woman is less severe and less likely to cause injury. In addition, men are much less likely to report an attack by a women (Dutton, 1988; Edleson and Brygger 1986; Jouriles and O'Leary 1985; Stets and Straus 1989; Straus 1989; Szinovacz 1983).

Gelles and Straus (1988) concluded that violence against women has received more publicity because men's greater strength causes more damage and because the women are acting in self-defense in about three-quarters of the cases. Some feminists, however, have tried to maintain a low profile on battered husbands so that battered women would receive funding (Gelles and Straus 1988:188).

Any discussion of spouse abuse must also include some attention to cohabitants. The number of cohabitants has increased almost fourfold in the past 20 years, and such individuals are primarily young: two-thirds of males and three-fourths of females are less than 35 years old (Spanier 1983). There is increasing evidence that cohabitants are particularly prone to abusive relationships. In their comparison of married, dating, and cohabiting couples, Stets and Straus (1989) report that the highest rates of assault and the most severe assaults are found among cohabiting couples. Hutchison, Hirschel, and Pesackis (1988) found that the number of calls for abusive situations to police by cohabitants equaled the number of similar calls by married couples, although the latter group made up a far greater proportion of the population. Stets concluded that cohabitants experience more aggression than married couples because of a combination of factors: youth, minority status, problems including depression and alcohol use, and the lack of "social control associated with participation in organizations and being tied to their relationships" (1991:678).

Family and Spouse Homicides

Murder data are more systematic, more extensive, and more reliable than abuse data. Because such data have been collected nationally for many years, it is possible to determine both patterns and changes with some degree of precision. Nonetheless, distilling spouse abuse data from national data sources, such as the Uniform Crime Reports, presents possibilities of misinterpretation and confusion.

In 1984 the Attorney General's Task Force on Family Violence found that almost 20 percent of murders involve family members and that nearly one-third of female homicide victims are murdered by their husbands or boyfriends (U.S. Department of Justice 1984:11). A review of FBI Uniform Crime Reports data (1985-1990) shows that the percentage of all murder victims who were killed by a spouse or boyfriend/girlfriend has remained relatively constant over the past few years. In the five-year period 1986-1990, 28 to 30 percent of all female murder victims were killed by husbands or boyfriends; in the same period, 4 to 6 percent of all male victims were killed by wives or girlfriends. Despite the escalation of homicide rates, some consistency remains in homicide rates of offenders and victims. In the past few years, 75 percent of the murder victims have been male. In addition, just as males are killed primarily by other males, females also are killed by males: approximately 90 percent of female victims are murdered by men (U.S. Department of Justice 1986-1991).

FBI homicide data disclose that women make up only 14 percent of the homicide offenders; the relationship between offender and victim varies, however (Straus 1989). In contrast to women's low representation as offenders in stranger homicide, Straus (1989) found a much higher proportion in family homicide: women murder male partners 56 to 62 percent as often as men murder female partners. It appears that men kill "across the board," but women are more likely to kill husbands or boyfriends. Zahn and Sagi (1987:394-95) found that although males were the predominant offenders in family homicides, a much higher proportion of family homicides than of any other homicide type involved a female offender. Males were almost equally likely to offend against males and against females in the family. In contrast, female offenders' victims were almost exclusively male.

These data do not suggest any kind of murder "parity" between husbands and wives; the cold facts disguise the family dynamics. Wives are seven times more likely than hus-

bands to have killed in self-defense (Jolin 1983) or in response to an assault initiated by the male partner (Straus 1989). In a study of 144 women who killed a mate in a domestic incident, Mann (1986:10) found that 58.6 percent stated self-defense as a reason for the killing. Recognition of the family dynamics involved in these killings is evidenced by the growing use of the "battered women's syndrome" defense by wives on trial for killing their husbands.

The Role of Law Enforcement

Historical Background

In the past, domestic violence calls often were assigned low priority (Fleming 1979; Parnas 1971; U.S. Commission on Civil Rights 1982). Police responded reluctantly to abuse calls, attempted to restore peace and order between the disputants, and typically left without taking more formal action.

Explanations for the long-term avoidance of formal action are manifold. First, violence within the family had been considered to be essentially a private matter; this view allowed adults to use force to solve personal disputes (Breslin 1978; Martin 1976). Second, female victims had been perceived as uncooperative; this situation, it was claimed, made arresting and prosecuting abusers a waste of time (Parnas 1967:931; U.S. Commission on Civil Rights 1982). Third was a concern that taking action against abusers hurt their families, especially members financially dependent on the offenders (Parnas 1967:931; U.S. Department of Justice 1984). Fourth, intervening in family disputes was not regarded as "real police work" (Buzawa and Buzawa 1990:29; Fyfe and Flavin 1991:4; Parnas 1971:54-2). Finally, Martin (1976) and others argued that responding officers, who usually were male, typically sided with offenders. This taking of sides reinforced a cultural norm stressing male superiority; this norm was exemplified, as discussed in an earlier section, by laws in colonial and later times that allowed a man to chastise his wife.

The police response to spouse abuse changed little until the 1960s. Under the influence of social scientists, psychologists, and a developing women's movement, the order maintenance approach received a professional twist. Mediation and crisis intervention were promoted as the appropriate tools for dealing with family violence. This development led to police training in crisis intervention techniques (Bard 1970, 1973, 1975; Spitzner and McGee 1975), the establishment of police family crisis intervention units (Bard 1970, 1975), and mixed police crisis teams composed of police officers and social workers (Burnett et al. 1976).

Despite the added training and the use of specialized units, there is little evidence that crisis intervention and mediation have had much success in reducing abuse. Oppenlander (1982), for example, reported that police tended to make more arrests in abusive situations than in other cases, even though crisis intervention approaches often took precedence over arrest. Relatively few evaluations were made, however (see, e.g., Pearce and Snortum 1983; Wylie et al. 1976), to assess the effects of these changes; most of the innovations occurred before controlled experimental research on the effects of police policy was conducted.

In addition, many police officers did not welcome these changes. Mediation seemed more like social work than police work. Moreover, some commentators (e.g., Langley and Levy 1978) thought that the police were inadequately prepared to perform family crisis intervention. Others were concerned about applying crisis intervention techniques and mediation to abuse situations. Loving (1980), for example, wrote that techniques designed for situations involving verbal abuse were being applied inappropriately to situations involving physical assaults.

The Attorney General's Task Force on Family Violence (U.S. Department of Justice 1984) identified what may well be a fundamental flaw in the mediation approach. The process of mediation assumes some equality of culpability between the parties to a dispute. The assumption of equal culpability and the failure to hold the offender accountable for his actions give him no incentive to reform. Thus, "rather than stopping the violence and providing protection for the victim, mediation may inadvertently contribute to a dangerous escalation of violence" (U.S. Department of Justice 1984:23).

These concerns about crisis intervention and mediation, coupled with arguments that female victims' rights were violated by the failure of police enforcement, produced demands for the arrest of abusers as the appropriate police response (Langley and Levy 1978; U.S. Commission on Civil Rights 1982). In some jurisdictions, women's groups filed suits to effect this change in policy (see, e.g., *Bruno v. Codd* 1977; *Scott v. Hart* 1976; *Thurman v. City of Torrington* 1984). The rationale for advocating arrest was clear. As the Attorney General's Task Force on Family Violence stated unequivocally, "*The legal response to family violence must be guided primarily by the nature of the abusive act, not the relationship between the victim and the abuser*" (U.S. Department of Justice 1984:4).

Contemporary Preferred Arrest Policies

Many vexing issues are raised by the meaning, implementation, and effects of the preferred arrest movement, but the current trend toward preferred arrest policies is indisputable. In recent years we have seen a major increase in the number of police departments that apply such policies. It is uncertain to what extent this increase is attributable to changes that have taken place in state statutes. Lerman, Landis, and Goldzweig observed in 1983 that "twenty-seven of the recent state laws on domestic violence expand(ed) police power to arrest in domestic abuse cases" (1983:44). Ferraro notes that as of 1986, six states had passed laws requiring arrest with a positive determination of probable cause and the presence of the offender on the scene (1989:61). By 1988, 10 states had enacted such laws (Victim Services Agency 1988:3).

Often, however, the potential of such statutory provisions is limited by the existence of requirements that must be satisfied before the laws can be invoked. Some state laws, for example, require the existence of a visible injury and/or the elapsing of only a short time between the commission of the offense and the arrival of the police. In their survey of police departments with preferred arrest policies, Hirschel and Hutchison (1991) reported that although all of the departments applied such a policy in cases of visible injury or a threat with a deadly weapon, only in a minority of the departments was such a policy in effect for situations involving verbal threats or property damage. Moreover, there is evidence that (subject to jurisdictional variation) about half of all offenders leave the scene before the police arrive (Hirschel and Hutchison 1987:11), and thus would not be arrested unless the victims swore out arrest warrants. Finally, policy trends favoring either preferred or mandatory arrest decisions do not necessarily include all abuse victims. It is known, for example, that cohabiting women call police disproportionately more than married women for domestic assault (Hutchison et al. 1988:14). Nonetheless, in at least some states nonmarried couples are not included in preferred arrest policies (Ferraro 1989).

The police also are asked to take action against abusers who have violated provisions of protective orders granted to abused women by the courts. Such orders currently are available in 48 states and in Washington, DC (Finn and Colson 1990:1). Suspected violation of the provisions of these orders may (and in 10 states must; Victim Services Agency 1988:4) result in arrest of the offender.

Preferred arrest (also called pro-arrest or presumptive) policies are far more common than mandatory policies. A 1986 study by the Crime Control Institute ("Roughening Up" 1987; Sherman and Cohn 1989) investigated arrest policies and found that the number of departments with such policies had increased fourfold, since 1984. The study, however, did not include police departments in cities with populations of less than 100,000, so we cannot determine the extent to which the trend in large cities is being replicated elsewhere.

In general, the literature does not examine whether police departments adopted these arrest policies on their own initiative or as a result of changes in state law. It is clear that a number of factors have prompted police departments to change their policies. The same forces that operated on state legislatures also have influenced police departments. Foremost among these are various women's

groups, including the National Coalition Against Domestic Violence, state chapters of this organization, and local coalitions that formed to alter existing policy and practice.

Although it is difficult to unravel the various factors that have motivated police departments to move toward preferred arrest policies, it is important to gauge the extent to which departments have adopted these policies willingly. This point is important because the orientation of top administrators influences rank-and-file enforcement of the policies. Available information suggests that police departments generally have not played a leading role in adopting arrest policies, and occasionally have been very reluctant to do so. In 1980, for example, Arizona's legislature passed a law that expanded police arrest powers. The chief of the Phoenix Police Department, however, adopted a presumptive arrest policy for his department only when faced with the possibility of legislation *mandating* arrest (Ferraro 1989:63). Miller (1979:16) in Oregon, Bell (1985:532) in Ohio and Buzawa (1988:174-75) in New Hampshire have noted a similar reluctance on the part of police departments to change their policies to conform with new statutory provisions.

The success of formal policies depends upon the support of both command and line personnel. The impact of negative attitudes among chiefs of police regarding the use of arrest in abuse cases is demonstrated clearly by Buzawa's (1988) research in New Hampshire. She found that a lack of support by chiefs was associated with low enrollments in the voluntary state-administered training program, the absence of written departmental policies, low or nonexistent arrest rates for domestic violence incidents, and a feeling among officers that responding to abuse calls was usually a waste of time (Buzawa 1988:175-78). In one jurisdiction the chief even said that "he could not recall a 'genuine' call for domestic violence in his numerous years as an administrator," and consequently "did not highly value" (undoubtedly an understatement) "the role of police intervention in this area" (Buzawa 1988:175).

Whatever policy might be, police officers are accustomed to making their own decisions on the street and traditionally are antagonistic to policies that limit their discretion. In his survey of Minneapolis officers, conducted after the Sherman and Berk experiment, Steinman found a strong indication of independence: 99 percent of respondents voiced the belief that they "should make their own decisions about problems that arise on duty," 77 percent reported that they "usually do what they think necessary even if they expect supervisors to disagree," and 43 percent declared that "they should use their own standards of police work even when department procedures prohibit them from doing so" (1988:2).

In the only available in-depth study of police response to a new presumptive arrest policy, Ferraro (1989) provides a fascinating study of the Phoenix Police Department. Even though the State of Arizona passed such legislation in 1980, little actual change occurred until 1984, when the Phoenix Police Department finally adopted a presumptive arrest policy. On the basis of ride-along observational data, Ferraro reports that in spite of this policy, arrests were made in only 18 percent of the battering incidents to which her research team responded. One problem was that in interpreting probable cause, officers were employing "a level of evidence high enough for felony arrests" (1989:64). In the face of opportunity and discretion to interpret both policy and circumstance, there is no reason to expect that police in general suddenly will reverse their traditional reluctance to arrest.

Research shows that certain factors are associated with positive attitudes toward preferred arrest policies. Not surprisingly, an officer's general orientation toward domestic violence is likely to affect his or her attitude (Berk and Loseke 1981:320-21; Ferraro 1989:66-67; Homant and Kennedy 1985; Walter 1981). Female police officers tend to be more supportive of arrest policies than male police officers (see, e.g., Ferraro 1989; Homant and Kennedy 1985). Training also influences police attitudes; studies have found that training is associated positively with both officers' perception and citizens' evaluation of officers' handling of disturbance calls (Pearce and Snortum 1983), with improvement in officers' attitudes toward domestic situations (Buchanon

and Perry 1985), and with officers' willingness to arrest domestic violence offenders (Buzawa 10.82:421-22).

Two final issues that affect police officers' attitudes toward domestic violence calls arise from their perceptions of the danger posed by such calls and from their fear of being sued at civil law for false arrest of an alleged offender. First, there persists a common perception that domestic disturbances are unusually dangerous for police in regard to frequencies of both assaults and homicides (Buzawa and Buzawa 1990:29). This perception has been "transmitted largely through police folklore" (Konstantin 1984:32). Such a perception has been supported by the interpretation of FBI "disturbance calls" data. These data grouped family quarrels with other types of disturbances, such as bar fights and "man with gun" calls, and were easily misinterpreted by some individuals, who took all of the disturbance calls to be domestic disturbance calls (see, e.g., Bard 1974: foreword; Stephens 1977:164). In addition, it has been suggested that crisis intervention trainers projected this perception of danger deliberately to attract the attention of antagonistic recruits (Fyfe and Flavin 1991:8). It is clear, however, that only a small percentage of police officers killed in the line of duty died while responding to abuse calls (see, e.g., Konstantin 1984; Margarita 1980a). An in-depth analysis by Garner and Clemmer (1986) concluded that domestic disturbances are one of the least frequent contributors to police homicide. The danger of assault and injury likewise has been exaggerated (see, e.g., Geller and Karales 1981; Margarita 1980b). Recent studies, however, suggest that in some locations, domestic calls still may constitute the most dangerous category both in assault (see, e.g., Uchida, Brooks, and Koppers 1987) and in injury (see, e.g., Stanford and Mowry 1990; Uchida et al. 1987).

In addition, the fear of being sued (at least successfully) in civil court for wrongful arrest of an alleged offender has been exaggerated greatly. Although this concern is raised frequently by officers in police departments that adopt preferred arrest policies, in reality this is a rare occurrence. It is possible that officers and police departments in fact are as likely to be sued successfully for failure to arrest an alleged offender (see, e.g., *Nearing v. Weaver* 1983; *Thurman v. City of Torrington* 1984) as for wrongful arrest of an alleged offender. Such suits for failure to arrest have been based on allegations of denial of due process or equal protection of the law (see, e.g., *Balistreri v. Pacifica Police Department* 1990; *Dudosh v. City of Allentown* 1987; *Thurman v. City of Torrington* 1984) or infringement of rights granted victims by state statutes (see, e.g., *Nearing v. Weaver* 1983; *Turner v. City of North Charleston* 1987). Yet despite some large awards (e.g. $2.3 million in *Thurman*), not many suits have been successful. It has been suggested that recent Supreme Court case law (*Deshaney v. Winnebago County Department of Social Services* 1989) will make it more difficult for abused women to win civil suits in federal court against police departments that failed to protect them (Zalman forthcoming).

Deterrence and Preferred Arrest Policies

An argument that has been raised both for and against arresting spouse abusers arises from the findings of research studies designed to test the deterrent effect of arrest in such cases. Although the deterrence argument generally is not considered necessary to justify the arrest of the alleged perpetrators of other criminal offense, such as rape, robbery, burglary, and auto theft, it has played a central part in the debate about the role of arrest in the social measures adopted to combat spouse abuse.

The Minneapolis Study. The formulation of social policy involves at best an amalgam of competing interests, viewpoints, and resources. Maintenance of the status quo is likely except in the face of compelling evidence that seems to justify a change. Extant procedures are likely to remain in effect unless policy makers are convinced that an alternative is either essential or better. Experimental research offers both the scientific community and policy makers a plausible basis for policy recommendations. Experimental methodology, in brief, is the most convincing of methodologies. Perhaps the major contribution of the Minneapolis experiment lies not in its substantive findings but in its recep-

tion by those involved in spouse abuse policies. We speculate that neither police departments nor advocates of change would have paid so much attention if the Minneapolis study had not been a controlled scientific experiment.

The Minneapolis experiment, conducted by Sherman and Berk in 1981-1982, was the first study to test the deterrent effect of arrest in spouse abuse cases—more accurately domestic violence cases, because the research design also included same-sex and other familial relationships (Sherman and Berk 1984a, 1984b). In that study certain predefined misdemeanor domestic assault cases, in which both the offender and the victim were present when the police arrived on the scene, were assigned randomly to one of three treatment responses: 1) advising the couple (including informal mediation in some cases); 2) separating the couple by ordering the offender to leave for eight hours; and 3) arresting the offender, which meant that he stayed overnight in jail. The selected cases then were tracked for six months: official record checks were made on offenders, and interviews were conducted with victims every two weeks to determine whether subsequent abuse occurred. A "police recorded failure" occurred when the offender generated a written offense or arrest report for domestic violence. A "victim reported failure" occurred when a victim reported "a repeat incident with the same suspect, broadly defined to include an actual assault, threatened assault or property damage" (Sherman and Berk 1984b:266).

During the course of the study, the participating officers (about 52 in number) produced a total of 330 eligible cases; three officers turned in 28 percent of the cases (Sherman and Berk 1984b:263-64). Sixteen cases were excluded from analyses because no treatment was applied or because reports had been generated on cases with victim-offender relationships that were outside the ambit of the study.[1] Whereas 99 percent of the cases targeted for arrest received the "arrest" treatment, only 78 percent of the "advise" cases and 73 percent of the "separate" cases were treated as assigned. All 12 follow-up interviews were obtained from 161 victims, for an interview completion rate of 49 percent (Sherman and Berk 1984b).

Analysis of the data showed that arrest was more effective than the other two responses in deterring subsequent abuse. According to police data, the overall failure rate was 18.2 percent; the arrest treatment returned the lowest failure rate (13%), and the separate treatment the highest (26%; Sherman and Berk 1984b).[2] Only the difference between the arrest and the separate treatments, however, was significant at the .05 level. The victim data showed a failure rate of 19 percent for those assigned the arrest treatment, as compared to 33 percent for those assigned the separate treatment and 37 percent for those assigned the advise treatment. Here the only significant difference was between the advise and the arrest treatments (Sherman and Berk 1984a, 1984b).

Both the researchers themselves (e.g., Sherman and Berk 1984b:263-66, 269) and others (e.g., Binder and Meeker 1988; Elliot 1989:453-54; Lempert 1989:152-54) have pointed out problems with the study. These problems include inadequate sample size; the submission of a disproportionate number of cases by a few officers; inadequate controls over the treatments actually delivered; the possibility of surveillance effects caused by multiple follow-up interviews; and lack of generalizability of the findings due to attributes of the city in which the sample was obtained, and of the sample itself.

Despite these methodological problems, the Minneapolis study received unprecedented national attention and is credited with helping to promote the nationwide movement toward arrest as the preferred response in abuse cases ("Roughening Up" 1987; Sherman and Cohn 1989). Yet if fundamental policy changes were to be undertaken with a clear (i.e., generalizable) basis for estimating the effects of an arrest policy, additional field experiments based on random assignment were needed. Accordingly, in order to test the validity of the results obtained in the Minneapolis experiment, the National Institute of Justice funded additional experiments in Omaha, Atlanta, Colorado Springs, Dade County (Florida), Milwaukee, and Charlotte (North Carolina).

Subsequent Studies. Like the Minneapolis study, the six later studies examined whether arrest is the most effective law enforcement response for deterring spouse abusers from committing subsequent acts of abuse. Certain elements were common to the six projects: all employed an experimental design in which cases that met predefined eligibility requirements were assigned randomly to treatment responses; all used arrest as one of the treatment responses; all focused on the misdemeanor range of cases, in which the police were empowered but not required to make an arrest; and a six-month follow-up was conducted on all eligible cases through use of police records and interviews with victims.

The Omaha study, which was funded about two years before the others, employed a two-part research design that focused on whether the offender was present when the officers arrived on the scene. If the offender was present, the case was assigned randomly to one of the treatments employed in the Minneapolis study; arrest, separate, or mediate. If the offender had gone when the police arrived, the case was assigned randomly either to receive or not to receive a warrant for the offender's arrest. Like the Minneapolis and the Milwaukee studies (but not the other four), the Omaha study extended beyond heterosexual couples who were or had been married or cohabiting. It also included same-sex couples as well as victims and offenders in other familial relationships.

Analysis of the 330 eligible cases in which the offender was present revealed no significant differences between the failure rates of the three treatments, whether official measures or victim-reported measures of recidivism were employed (Dunford, Huizinga, and Elliot 1990). Analysis of the 247 cases in the offender-absent part of the experiment, however, showed that cases in which warrants were issued were both less likely and slower to result in further abuse than cases in which no warrant was issued (Dunford et al. 1989; Dunford 1990).

The Charlotte Project was the only one to employ the entire patrol division in round-the-clock and citywide sampling for the full duration of the project. It used three treatment responses: 1) advising and possibly separating the couple; 2) arresting the offender; and 3) issuing a citation to the offender (an order requiring the offender to appear in court to answer specific charges). Analysis of the 650 eligible cases obtained by the project produced only two significant findings: the differences between the effects of the advise/separate and the citation treatments and between the effects of the informal (advise/separate) and the formal (arrest and citation) treatments on the official incidence (but not the prevalence) measures of arrest recidivism. In no case, whether official- or victim-reported measures of recidivism were employed, did the failure rate of the arrest treatment differ significantly from those of the other two treatments (Hirschel et al. 1991; Hirschel, Hutchison and Dean, 1992).

The Milwaukee Project also employed three treatment responses: 1) full arrest accompanied by a relatively long period of detention in jail (a mean of 11.1 hours); 2) short arrest, which resulted in the release of the offender within a few hours (a mean of 2.8 hours); and 3) no arrest (warning only). Analysis of the 1,200 eligible cases revealed, in general, no significant differences between the treatments. However, according to interviews and one official measure (the commission of subsequent violence against *any* victim), short arrest had a substantial initial (30-day) deterrent effect in relation to warning only, although this deterrent effect dissipated over a longer follow-up period. These data highlight the importance of both multiple measures of recidivism and an adequate follow-up period to determine treatment effects. On the basis of the official measure that the authors consider to be their most comprehensive indicator of official recidivism (police reports to the local shelter's hotline concerning all probable-cause domestic violence cases), the short-arrest group consistently showed significantly higher rates of long-term recidivism than the warning-only group (Sherman et al. 1991).

Comments. The results of these three studies (Omaha, Charlotte, and Milwaukee) present an unambiguous picture: arrest of misdemeanor spouse abusers is no more or less effective in preventing recurrence of abuse than the other responses examined. These re-

sults, coupled with the concerns that have been raised about the validity of the Minneapolis findings (e.g., Binder and Meeker 1988), suggest a lack of adequate support for a mandatory or presumptive arrest policy based on specific deterrence. Possibly this picture will be modified when the three other sites present their findings. At this point, the hope that arrest alone could contribute significantly to solving the problem of spouse abuse is unfulfilled.

We offer several possible explanations why arrest has not been found to deter subsequent abuse. First, the majority of offenders in these studies have previous criminal histories: 59 percent in Minneapolis (Sherman and Berk 1984b:266), 65 percent in Omaha (Dunford et al. 1990:194), 69 percent in Charlotte (Hirschel et al. 1991:37), and 50 percent in Milwaukee (Sherman et al. 1991:827). Thus in many cases, arrest is neither a new nor an unusual experience.

Second, for many of the couples in these studies, abuse is a common rather than an occasional occurrence. Indeed, for some, abuse is chronic. For offenders who have criminal histories or who have been offenders in chronically abusive relationships, it is unrealistic to imagine that arrest will have much impact.

Third, arrest alone, which was a focal point of the research projects, may not constitute as strong a societal response as commonly perceived. The popular conception is that the arrested person is put in jail and that that punitive action is sufficient to change behavior. The fact is that "time in jail" is often minimal beyond the booking time required: it is estimated to have averaged about 16 hours in Omaha (Dunford et al. 1990:191), nine hours in Charlotte (Hirschel et al. 1991:151), and three hours for short and 11 hours for long arrest in Milwaukee (Sherman et al. 1991). Thus arrest with immediate release simply may not mean much, particularly when the offenders have been arrested before.

Fourth, although not technically within the scope of the project, some information was gathered on the processing of offenders through the criminal justice system. The data support the conclusion that a spouse very rarely is found guilty and ordered to spend any significant time in jail. In Minneapolis "only 3 (2%) of the 136 arrested offenders were formally punished by fines or subsequent incarceration" (Sherman and Berk 1984b:270). In Charlotte only four (1%) of all the men who had been issued a citation or arrested spent time in jail beyond the initial arrest; another eight (2%) received credit for time served before going to trial (Hirschel et al. 1991:147). In Milwaukee initial charges were filed in 37 (5%) of the 802 arrest cases, and only 11 (1%) resulted in convictions (Sherman et al. 1991). In Omaha, however, 64 percent of those arrested were sentenced to jail, probation or fine (Dunford, Huizinga and Elliot 1989:31).

Fifth, these studies focus on whether arrest constitutes a deterrent for spouse abusers as a whole. For the most part they do not examine whether there is any particular subgroup of spouse abusers for whom arrest may serve as a deterrent. In a study in southern California, Berk and Newton (1985) generally confirm the deterrent value of arrest (on the basis of an ex post facto analysis of 783 wife-battering incidents) but argue carefully that a conditional effect is present. They note in particular, that arrest is most effective for batterers whom police ordinarily would be inclined to arrest. In subsequent analyses of the Milwaukee data, Sherman et al. (1992) found, however, that arrest exerted a deterrent effect on those with high stakes in social conformity (the employed, married, high school graduates and whites), but an escalation effect on those with the opposite attributes (the unemployed, etc.) as measured by reports of subsequent abuse to the domestic violence hotline.

Preferred Arrest Policies as Part of a Coordinated Community Response

In some jurisdictions, police departments have moved to a preferred arrest policy without the involvement of other agencies. In other jurisdictions the movement to such a policy has been part of a new, coordinated, community response to the problem of abuse. In general it is the latter departments that have reported positive results with their new policies. Gamache et al. (1988) report

that after the introduction of community intervention projects in three Minnesota communities, rates of both arrests and successful prosecutions increased; similar results are recorded by Steinman (1988:2) in Lincoln, Nebraska, by Ferguson (1987:9) and Goolkasian (1986:37-38) in Seattle, by Pence (1983:257-58) in Duluth, and by Burris and Jaffe (1983:312) in London, Ontario. After noting that police policies in Lincoln, Seattle, Duluth, and London are coordinated with community wide support, Steinman suggests that "this is probably not the case in most communities where departments have adopted arrest policies" (1988:2).

In addition, with the exception of Seattle, the cities that have been studied most closely are small, with relatively modest crime and domestic violence rates. In the three Minnesota communities studied by Gamache et al., the populations range from 15,000 to 36,000 inhabitants and recorded five or fewer domestic violence arrests a month per community during the research period (1988:195,201). Duluth has received considerable national attention for its Domestic Abuse Intervention Project, which coordinates the efforts of nine law enforcement, criminal justice, and human service agencies; this city has a population under 100,000 and recorded only some 10 arrests a month during the research period reported by Pence (1983:258-59). These observations suggest that postarrest coordination can be achieved more easily in smaller communities with relatively modest crime and domestic violence rates. Yet even this type of coordinated community response, however commendable for other purposes, provides no evidence that abuse rates are affected.

Summary and Discussion

Describing the law enforcement response to spouse abuse requires some understanding of the social and legal foundations. In this article we have presented a brief review of the historical attitudes toward wife abuse, the evolution of the response by the legal system to such abuse, the contemporary scope of the problem, the traditional law enforcement role of the past, and the current and sometimes controversial movement toward the arrest of spouse abusers. We have focused primarily on the abuse of women who are in marital or spouselike (e.g., cohabitant) relationships. Although we recognize that the abuse of men in both marital and cohabitant relationships falls clearly within the parameters of spouse abuse, both the research literature and social concern regarding abused men are quite limited.

As we have shown in this article, the United States has a long and inglorious tradition, inherited from our English origins, of ignoring and minimizing spouse abuse. Indeed, only recently has our society begun to consider such behavior as "abuse," much less as a social "problem." Males' rights to chastise and abuse females are rooted deeply in our social and legal traditions.

Although protective laws had been passed as long ago as the latter part of the seventeenth century, they hardly were enforced. The predominant patterns, lodged in the perceived rights of male power and primacy, reflected highly permissive attitudes toward spouse abusers. Legal intervention was minimal, at least as may be determined through extant court records; serious laws, with serious enforcement, were not initiated until the latter part of the twentieth century. We have identified some of the reasons for the traditional police reluctance to intervene in family disputes. As described above, we have traced such reluctance to a combination of factors including traditional values of family privacy, the perception that family disputes are inappropriate as police work, and the perception of danger in responding to domestic violence calls. In addition, many police simply do not believe that intervening in spouse abuse does much to address the problem—either for a particular couple or for the larger social issue. In this regard, such sentiments may be typical of much work that police do for a variety of criminal offenses.

Our review concludes with a significant focus on the current scene: perhaps it can be summarized adequately as a gradual strengthening of spouse abuse laws by state legislatures, but it is marked by a continued and pervasive reluctance of police to do more than is absolutely required by law. We also review the original movement toward pro-arrest policies, and discuss the nearly conclusive current evidence that arrest for misdemeanor spouse abuse has little unique deterrent effect in reducing further abuse.

A number of issues remain to be addressed, ranging from the interpretation of data to the design and implementation of effective social policies.

First, as made clear by this review and by comprehensive assessments of the scope of spouse abuse, there is much room for misinterpretation, distortion, and manipulation of data. Because spouse abuse itself (finally) raises social concern, if not anger, it almost begs for exaggeration. Estimates both of the number of people affected and of probabilities of abuse vary widely, depending on definitions, data sources, and the quality of work performed by the researchers, interpreters, and disseminators of results. One cannot dispute that spouse abuse is an immense social problem; the scope needs no exaggeration in order to warrant concerted, unrelenting action in search of solutions. We believe that carelessness or exaggeration in reporting estimates actually may contribute to less rather than more concern for the problem. There is no reason to expect policy makers, often already jaded by causes, to believe exaggerated claims or to act on them.

Second, some confusion exists about the true extent of popular support for taking significant action to combat spouse abuse. Like any cause for any social problem, this cause has ardent supporters who are in the forefront of change. Most communities know by now that spouse abuse is a major problem and that there is a great need for social support services such as shelters, victims' assistance agencies, treatment programs for men, and employment and relocation services for abused women. It is beyond the scope of this article to determine whether the generally inadequate level of social services represents weariness of community support or reflects the reality that limited resources must be allocated to multiple and therefore competing programs.

Third, the law enforcement role in spouse abuse is hinged inevitably to both state law and community pressures. In this review we have documented the gradual change in state laws, which have moved toward giving police more authority and more responsibility for intervening in abusive situations. Police authority always is defined and limited by state law; the fact is that such law, although stronger than 50 or even 20 years ago, still leaves much to be desired. Law is influenced in turn by pressure brought to bear on lawmakers; such pressure often has developed from women's groups within communities, with varying degrees of success at the state level. Thus, what police ultimately are empowered to do (or are prohibited from doing) derives from state laws, most of which were enacted originally by men and now are under attack primarily by women. It is an unequal battle, and real successes in changing state laws typically come only after much pressure. Ironically although not surprisingly, in this situation (as in others) it is primarily women who are battling for the rights of other women, to protect them against a social and personal problem inflicted largely by men (at least in cases of serious injury).

Fourth, one can make a case that the recent movement toward pro-arrest policies for police, although motivated nobly by the sincere (but perhaps futile) hope that arrest will make a difference, also reflects a "quick fix" mentality by both activists and sympathizers. Placing hopes on the success of arrest as a deterrent to spouse abuse removes pressure from other possible responses, such as the social support services mentioned above. It would be satisfying and simple if the fact of arrest had made a difference in the Minneapolis replication studies, but unfortunately, the hoped-for results have not yet materialized.

Fifth, study of the role of arrest of spouse abusers has been limited. All of the experiments funded by the National Institute of Justice focused on the misdemeanor range of spouse abuse, in which police are empowered, but not required, to make warrantless arrests on the scene. Only the Omaha study examined situations in which police obtained warrants, located offenders, and made arrests off-scene. A significant issue is the degree to which police officers may interpret the facts of a situation (upon their arrival at the scene of a reported incident) so as to find

that it does not meet the criteria for an on-the-scene arrest for an offense committed in their absence. State law stipulates the general conditions for a finding of the legal authority to make such an arrest, but interpretation always depends on the responding officers. When the threshold requirements are high, it is virtually guaranteed that the great majority of reported incidents will not be subject to official police action beyond a simple response to the incident because many police officers will decide subjectively that the minimum requirements have not been met.

If state laws were to cast a wider net so as to encompass a broader range of abusive behavior, and if local police departments stood solidly behind pro-arrest policies, far more abusers would be arrested. In the Charlotte study, for example, only a minority (approximately 18%) of domestic calls to which police responded were classified as misdemeanors and hence as subject to the discretionary power of police to make an arrest. A very small minority were felony-type cases, in which police almost always make an arrest. Thus in the great majority of calls to which police responded, the incident was evaluated by responding officers as not meeting the legal criteria for either a felony or a misdemeanor. Very simply, officers decided that no crime had been committed.

Sixth, spouse abuse is probably the only area of criminal behavior in which it has been considered necessary to justify the arrest of offenders on the grounds that such arrests will serve as a deterrent. To our knowledge, it has never been suggested that drug dealers, thieves, or rapists not be arrested because arrest had failed to reduce subsequent recidivism for these crimes. Ironically, the great hope placed in the arrest of spouse abusers as a deterrent ultimately may be counterproductive if either police or lawmakers react to the replication experiments with diminished concern for making such arrests. As we argue elsewhere (Hirschel et al. 1991), one can make a strong case that spouse abusers should be arrested for a variety of other reasons beyond any deterrent value of arrest. Even if arrest may not have much punitive value, it still may constitute a more conscionable choice than nonarrest. Not to arrest may communicate to men the message that abuse is not serious and to women the message that they are on their own. It may communicate to children, who very often witness abuse of their mothers, that the abuse of women is tolerated, if not legitimated. It may communicate to the public at large that a level of violence which is unacceptable when inflicted by a stranger is acceptable when inflicted by an intimate.

Seventh, the law enforcement role, on which this article has focused, inevitably is shaped by the response of the judicial system. It is a reasonably human response of police to question the efficacy of arresting spouse abusers when they already are reluctant to do so because of traditional beliefs, and when they know that little will happen to such abusers as they enter the judicial system. As we stated earlier, the popular perception is that arrest means time in jail, in this case time in jail for spouse abusers. In fact, as we pointed out, actual time in jail (beyond booking time) is extremely rare. For the many men who already have been in jail for other offenses, such nonaction hardly can be expected to be punitive. Indeed, the impotence of the criminal justice system in sentencing abusers to active time could even have a reinforcing effect on the norm held by some males, that abusing one's partner simply does not matter very much. We have received the impression, although it is well beyond the scope of this article, that creative sentencing for spouse abusers is an option used infrequently by the courts. Thus neither police nor offenders have reason to believe in either the deterrent or the punitive powers of arrest.

Finally, as jail space becomes even more crowded and as communities are hard pressed to confine offenders for other crimes viewed as more "serious," some hard decisions must be made and alternatives to jail (e.g., mandated treatment for offenders) must be imposed.

What, then might realistically be the most suitable law enforcement role in dealing with spouse abuse? A number of avenues seem both plausible and appropriate. The law enforcement role must be integrated more carefully with the social support systems within communities. Although we do not believe that

such coordination provides a measurable deterrent to further abuse, it creates both real and symbolic support for abuse victims.

Although we do not suggest a return to the now-discarded crisis mediation approach, there is some evidence that police characteristics and the manner in which police manage incidents influence women's perceptions of the adequacy of the police response. In those departments which can afford to assign specialized teams to respond to abuse calls, it is likely that women will feel more strongly supported (even if they are not, in fact, protected any better) by the existence of such teams. There is some evidence that simply calling the police to report an abusive incident is an advantage in reducing subsequent incidents (Langan and Innes 1986). We speculate that if women felt that they were supported more strongly when reporting incidents to police, some change might occur in the long run for some couples. The problem of spouse abuse is so intractable that no single approach will have a major impact; the accumulation of small successes is the most that can be anticipated.

In addition, it is both incredible and quite baffling that neither social science researchers nor the police have developed more sophisticated ways of profiling and responding to spouse abusers. To our knowledge, the ordinary police policy in responding to a reported incident is to treat it as a new event and to respond (except for information that the responding officer may possess) only on the basis of that event. For many couples, such a response is perfectly appropriate. For many other couples, however, abuse is both serious and chronic. There is no logical reason why these couples should be treated as one would treat a new couple in the initial stages of abusiveness. It would seem that researchers and police could cooperate to identify "high-risk" couples, if for no other reason than that police receive the most virulent criticism when often-reported abuse terminates in a murder.

Finally, we are left with the question "What should be the law enforcement response to spouse abuse?" The only answer is quite simple, if unsatisfactory: to enforce the law. Police deserve some criticism for their laxity in enforcing the existing laws, but much of the criticism is undeserved because it disregards the reality that police are limited severely in what they can and cannot do. Responsible communities will look as critically at strengthening the prosecutorial, judicial, and social support systems as they have viewed the police for their apparent inability to solve this problem; it is a police problem only insofar as it is a law enforcement problem. Police do not possess the legal mandate, the credentials, or the resources to solve the problem by themselves. They have the responsibility to enforce the law, however. Beyond that, it is the responsibility of concerned citizens and lawmakers to address the multiple legal and social service issues encompassed by the problem of spouse abuse.

Notes

1. Later changed to 17 (see Berk, Smyth, and Sherman 1988; Berk and Sherman 1988:71).
2. The failure rate for the advise treatment is not reported here, but is reported elsewhere as 19 percent (Sherman and Berk 1984a). This figure is slightly high in view of the overall failure rate reported in the publication cited in the text (Sherman and Berk 1984b). Furthermore, discrepancies exist between the failure rates reported in different publications. For example, Sherman and Berk (1984a) report official failure rates of 10 percent for cases in the arrest treatment, 19 percent for cases in the advise treatment, and 24 percent for cases in the separate treatment.

References

Balos, Beverly and Katie Trotzky (1988) "Enforcement of the Domestic Abuse Act in Minnesota: A Preliminary Study." *Law & Inequality* 6:38-125.

Bard, Morton (1970) *Training Crisis Intervention: From Concept to Implementation*. Washington, DC: U.S. Department of Justice.

—— (1973) *Family Crisis Intervention: From Concept to Implementation*. Washington, DC: U.S. Government Printing Office.

—— (1975) "Role of Law Enforcement in the Helping System." In Alan R. Coffey and Vernon E. Renner (eds.) *Criminal Justice as a System: Readings* pp. 56-66. Englewood Cliffs, NJ: Prentice-Hall.

Belknap, Joanne (1990) "Police Training in Domestic Violence: Perceptions of Training and Knowledge of the Law." *American Criminal Justice Society* 14 (2):248-67.

Bell, Daniel (1985) "Domestic Violence: Victimization, Police Intervention, and Disposition." *Journal of Criminal Justice* 13:525-34.

Berk, Richard A., Sarah F. Berk, Donileen R. Loseke, and David Raume (1983) "Mutual Combat and Other Family Violence Myths." In David Finkelhor, Richard J. Gelles, Gerald Hotaling, and Murray V. Straus (eds.), *The Dark Side of Families: Current Family Violence Research* pp. 197-212. Beverly Hills: Sage.

Berk, Sarah and Donileen R. Loseke (1981) "Handling Family Violence: Situational Determinants of Police Arrest in Domestic Disturbances." *Law and Society Review* 15:317-46.

Berk, Richard and Phyllis Newton (1985) "Does Arrest Really Deter Wife Battery? An Effort to Replicate the Findings of the Minneapolis Spouse Abuse Experiment." *American Sociological Review* 50:253-62.

Berk, Richard A., and Lawrence W. Sherman (1988) "Police Responses to Family Violence Incidents: An analysis of an Experimental Design with Incomplete Randomization." *Journal of the American Statistical Association* 83:70-76.

Berk, Richard, Gordon Smyth, and Lawrence Sherman (1988) "When Random Assignment Fails: Some Lessons from the Minneapolis Spouse Abuse Experiment." *Journal of Quantitative Criminology* 43:209-23.

Binder, Arnold and James W. Meeker (1988) "Experiments as Reforms." *Journal of Criminal Justice* 16:347-58.

Blackstone, William (1987) *Commentaries on the Laws of England*, edited by W. Hardcastle Browne. St. Paul: West.

Bowker, Lee (1982) "Police Services to Battered Women: Bad or Not So Bad?" *Criminal Justice and Behavior* 9:476-94.

—— (1984) "Battered Wives and the Police: A National Study of Usage and Effectiveness." *Police Studies* 7:84-93.

Breslin, Warren J. (1978) "Police Intervention in Domestic Confrontations." *Journal of Police Science and Administration* 6:293-302.

Buchanon, Dale R. and Patricia A. Perry (1985) "Attitudes of Police Recruits towards Domestic Disturbances: An Evaluation of Family Crisis Intervention Training." *Journal of Criminal Justice* 13:561-72.

Buda, Michael A. and Teresa L. Butler (1984) "The Battered Wife Syndrome: A Backdoor Assault on Domestic Violence." *Journal of Family Law* 23:359-90.

Burnett, Bruce B., John J. Carr, John Sinapi, and Roy Taylor (1976) "Police and Social Workers in a Community Outreach Program." *Social Casework* 57:41-49.

Burris, Carole A. and Peter Jaffe (1983) "Wife Abuse as a Crime: The Impact of Police Laying Charges." *Canadian Journal of Criminology* 25:309-18.

Buzawa, Eve S. (1982) "Police Officer Response to Domestic Violence Legislation in Michigan." *Journal of Police Science and Administration* _-:415-24.

—— (1988) "Explaining Variations in Police Response to Domestic Violence: A Case Study in Detroit and New England." In Gerald T. Hotaling, David Finkelhor, John T. Kirkpatrick, and Murray A. Straus (eds.), *Coping with Family Violence* pp. 169-82. Beverly Hills: Sage.

Buzawa, Eve S. and Carl. G. Buzawa (1985) "Legislative Trends in the Criminal Justice Response to Domestic Violence." In Alan J. Lincoln and Murray A. Straus (eds.), *Crime and the Family* pp. 134-47. Springfield, IL: Thomas.

—— (1990) *Domestic Violence: The Criminal Justice Response*. Newbury Park, CA: Sage.

Dobash, Russell P. and R. Emerson Dobash (1978) "Wives: The 'Appropriate' Victims of Marital Violence." *Victimology* 3-4:426-42.

—— (1991) "Gender, Methodology, and Methods in Criminological Research: The Case of Spousal Violence." Paper presented at the British Criminology Conference, York.

Dunford, Franklyn W. (1990). "System Initiated Warrants for Suspects of Misdemeanor Domestic Assault: A Pilot Study." *Justice Quarterly* 7:631-53.

Dunford, Franklyn W., David Huizinga and Delbert S. Elliot (1989). *The Omaha Domestic Violence Police Experiment: Final Report*, Washington DC: National Institute of Justice.

—— (1990) "The Role of Arrest in Domestic Assault: The Omaha Police Experiment." *Criminology* 28:183-206.

Dutton, Donald G. (1988) *The Domestic Assault of Women: The Psychological and Criminal Justice Perspectives*. Boston: Allyn & Bacon.

Edleson, Jeffrey L. and Mary P. Brygger (1986) "Gender Differences in Reporting of Battering Incidences." *Family Relations* 35:377-82.

Elliot, Delbert S. (1989) "Criminal Justice Procedures in Family Violence Crimes." In Lloyd Ohlin and Michael Tonry (eds.), *Family Violence* pp. 427-80. Chicago: University of Chicago Press.

Feld, Scott L. and Murray A. Straus (1989) "Escalation and Desistance of Wife Assault in Marriage." *Criminology* 27:141-61.

Ferguson, Harv (1987) "Mandating Arrests for Domestic Violence." *FBI Law Enforcement Bulletin* 56:6-11.

Ferraro, Kathleen J. (1989) "Policing Woman Battering." *Social Problems* 36:61-74.

Finesmith, Barbara K. (1983) "Police Response to Battered Women: A Critique and Proposals for Reform." *Seton Hall Law Review* 14:74-109.

Finn, Peter and Sarah Colson (1990) *Civil Protection Orders: Legislation, Current Court Practice, and Enforcement*. Washington, DC: U.S. Department of Justice.

Fleming, Jennifer B. (1979) *Stopping Wife Abuse: A Guide to the Psychological and Legal Implications for the Abused Woman and Those Helping Her*. Garden City, NY: Anchor.

Ford, David A. and Mary J. Regoli (forthcoming) "The Preventive Impacts of Policies for Prosecuting Wife Batterers." In Eve S. Buzawa and Carl G. Buzawa (eds.), *Domestic Violence: The Changing Criminal Justice Response to Domestic Violence*. Westport, CT: Greenwood.

Fyfe, James J. and Jeanne Flavin (1991) "Differential Police Processing of Domestic Assault Complaints." Paper presented at the annual meeting of the Academy of Criminal Justice Sciences, Nashville.

Gamache, Denise J., Jeffrey L. Edleson, and Michael D. Schock (1988) "Coordinated Police, Judicial, and Social Service Response to Woman Battering: A Multiple-Baseline Evaluation across Three Communities." In Gerald T. Hotaling, David Finkelhor, John T. Kirkpatrick, and Murray A. Straus (eds.), *Coping with Family Violence* pp. 193-209. Beverly Hills: Sage.

Garner, Joel and Elizabeth Clemmer (1986) *Danger to Police in Domestic Disturbances: A New Look*. Washington, DC: U.S. Department of Justice.

Geller, William A. and Kevin J. Karales (1981) *Split-Second Decisions: Shoots of and by Chicago Police*. Chicago: Chicago Law Enforcement.

Gelles, Richard J. and Murray A. Straus (1988) *Intimate Violence*. New York: Simon and Schuster.

Goolkasian, Gail A. (1986) *Confronting Domestic Violence: A Guide for Criminal Justice Agencies.* Washington, DC: U.S. Department of Justice.

Hamberger, L. Kevin and James Hastings (1988) "Characteristics of Male Spouse Abusers Consistent with Personality Disorders." *Hospital and Community Psychiatry* 39:763-70.

Hecker, Eugene A. (1914) *A Short History of Women's Rights.* Westport, CT: Greenwood.

Hirschel, J. David, Ira W. Hutchison, Charles W. Dean, Joseph J. Kelley and Carolyn E. Pesackis (1991) *Charlotte Spouse Assault Replication Project: Final Report.* Washington, DC: National Institute of Justice.

Hirschel, J. David and Ira W. Hutchison (1991) "Police-Preferred Arrest Policies." In Michael Steinman (ed.), *Wife Battering: Policy Responses* pp. 49-72. Cincinnati: Anderson.

Hirschel, J. David, Ira W. Hutchison and Charles W. Dean (1992). "The Failure of Arrest to Deter Spouse Abuse" (1992) *Journal of Research in Crime and Delinquency* 29:7-33.

Homant, Robert J. and Daniel B. Kennedy (1985) "Police Perceptions of Spouse Abuse: A Comparison of Male and Female Officers." *Journal of Criminal Justice* 13:29-47.

Hotaling, Gerald T. and David B. Sugarman (1986) "An Analysis of Risk Markers in Husband to Wife Violence: The Current State of Knowledge." *Violence and Victims* 1:101-24.

Hutchison, Ira W., J. David Hirschel, and Carolyn E. Pesackis (1988) "Domestic Variations in Domestic Violence Calls to Police." Paper presented at the annual meeting of the Southern Sociological Association, Nashville.

Jolin, Annette (1983) "Domestic Violence Legislation: An Impact Assessment." *Journal of Police Science and Administration* 11:451-56.

Jouriles, Ernest N. and K. Daniel O'Leary (1985) "Interspousal Reliability of Reports of Marital Violence." *Journal of Consulting and Clinical Psychology* 53:419-21.

Konstantin, David N. (1984) "Homicides of American Law Enforcement Officers 1978-1980." *Justice Quarterly* 1:29-45.

Kuhl, Anna F. (1982) "Community Responses to Battered Women." *Victimology* 7:49-59.

Langan, Patrick and Christopher Innes (1986) *Preventing Domestic Violence Against Women.* Washington, DC: U.S. Department of Justice.

Langley, Roger and Richard G. Levy (1978) "Wife Abuse and the Police Response." *FBI Law Enforcement Bulletin* 47:4-9.

Lempert, Richard (1989) "Humility Is a Virtue: On the Publicization of Policy Relevant Research." *Law and Society Review* 23:145-61.

Lerman, Lisa G., Leslie Landis, and Sharon Goldzweig (1983) "State Legislation on Domestic Violence." In J. J. Costa (ed.), *Abuse of Women: Legislation, Reporting and Prevention* pp. 39-75. Lexington, MA: Heath.

Lockhart, Lettie L. (1987) "A Reexamination of the Effects of Race and Social Class on the Incidence of Marital Violence: A Search for Reliable Differences." *Journal of Marriage and the Family* 49:603-10.

Loving, N. (1980) *Responding to Spouse Abuse and Wife Beating.* Washington, DC: Police Executive Research Forum.

Mann, Coramae R. (1986). "Getting Even: Women Who Kill in Domestic Encounters." Paper presented at the Annual Meeting of the American Society of Criminology, Atlanta.

Margarita, Mona (1980a) "Killing the Police: Myths and Motives." *Annals of the American Association of Political and Social Science* 452:63-71.

——(1980b) "Criminal Violence against Police." Doctoral dissertation, University of New York at Albany.

Martin, Del. (1976) *Battered Wives.* San Francisco: Glide.

Miller, Marilyn G. (1979) *Domestic Violence in Oregon.* Salem: Governor's Commission for Women, State of Oregon Executive Department.

Moore, Donna M. (1979) *Battered Women.* Beverly Hills: Sage.

Morley, Rebecca and Audrey Mullender (1991) "Preventing Violence against Women in the Home: Feminist Dilemmas Concerning Recent British Developments." Paper presented at the British Criminology Conference, York.

Nisonoff, Linda and Irving Bitman (1979) "Spouse Abuse: Incidence and Relationship to Selected Demographic Variables." *Victimology* 4:131-40.

Oppenlander, Nan (1981) "The Evolution of Law and Wife Abuse." *Law and Police Quarterly* 3:382-405.

—— (1982) "Coping or Copping Out: Police Service Delivery in Domestic Disputes." *Criminology* 20:449-65.

Parnas, Raymond I. (1967) "The Police Response to the Domestic Disturbance." *Wisconsin Law Review* (Fall):914-60.

—— (1971) "Police Discretion and Diversion of Incidents of Intra-Family Violence." *Law and Contemporary Problems* 36:539-65.

Pearce, Jack B. and John R. Snortum (1983) "Police Effectiveness in Handling Disturbance Calls: An Evaluation of Crisis Intervention Training." *Criminal Justice and Behavior* 10:71-92.

Pence, Ellen (1983) "The Duluth Domestic Abuse Intervention Project." *Hamline Law Review* 6:247-75.

Pleck, Elizabeth (1987) *Domestic Tyranny: The Making of Social Policy against Family Violence from Colonial Times to the Present.* New York: Oxford University Press.

—— (1989) "Criminal Approaches to Family Violence 1640-1980." In Lloyd Ohlin and Michael Tonry (eds.), *Crime and Justice: A Review of Research* pp. 19-58. Chicago: University of Chicago Press.

Rose, Kristina and Janet Goss (1989) *Domestic Violence Statistics.* Rockville, MD: Justice Statistics Clearinghouse.

"Roughening Up: Spouse Abuse Arrests Grow" (1987) *Law Enforcement News* 13:1-13.

Roy, Maria (1977) "Some Thoughts Regarding the Criminal Justice System and Wife-Beating." In Maria Roy (ed.), *Battered Women: A Psychosoc-iological Study of Domestic Violence* pp. 138-39. New York: Van Nostrand Reinhold.

Schulman, Mark A. (1979) *A Survey of Spousal Violence against Women in Kentucky.* Washington, DC: U.S. Department of Justice.

Sherman, Lawrence W. and Richard A. Berk (1984a) *The Minneapolis Domestic Violence Experiment.* Washington, DC: Police Foundation.

—— (1984b) "The Specific Deterrent Effects of Arrest for Domestic Assault." *American Sociological Review* 49:261-72.

Sherman, Lawrence W. and Ellen G. Cohn (1989) "The Impact of Research on Legal Policy: The Minneapolis Domestic Violence Experiment." *Law and Society Review* 23:117-44.

Sherman, Lawrence W., Janell D. Schmidt, Dennis P. Rogan, Patrick R. Gartin, Ellen G. Cohn, Dean Collins, and Anthony R. Bacich (1991) "From Initial Deterrence to Long Term Escalation: Short Custody Arrest for Poverty Ghetto Domestic Violence." *Criminology* 29:821-50.

Sherman, Lawrence W. Janell D. Schmidt, Dennis P. Rogan, Douglas A. Smith, Patrick R. Gartin, Ellen G. Cohn, Dean J. Collins and Anthony R. Bacich (1992) "The Variable Effects of Arrest on Criminal Careers: The Milwaukee Domestic Violence Experiment." *The Journal of Criminal Law and Criminology* 83: forthcoming.

Sherman, Lawrence W., Douglas A. Smith, Janell D. Schmidt, and Dennis P. Rogan (1991) *Ghetto Poverty, Crime and Punishment: Legal and Informal Control of Domestic Violence.* Washington, DC: Crime Control Institute.

Sigler, Robert T. (1989) *Domestic Violence in Context: An Assessment of Community Attitudes.* Lexington, MA: Heath.

Smith, Lorna J. F. (1989) *Domestic Violence: An Overview of the Literature.* London: Her Majesty's Stationery Office.

Spanier, Graham B. (1983) "Married and Unmarried Cohabitation in the United States: 1980." *Journal of Marriage and the Family* 45:277-88.

Spitzner, Joseph H. and Donald H. McGee (1975) "Family Crisis Intervention Training, Diversion, and the Prevention of Crimes of Violence." *Police Chief* 42:252-53.

Stanford, Rose M. and Bonney L. Mowry (1990) "Domestic Disturbance Danger Rate." *Journal of Police Science and Administration* 17(4):244-49.

Steinman, Michael (1988) "Anticipating Rank and File Police Reactions to Arrest Policies Regarding Spouse Abuse." *Criminal Justice Research Bulletin* 4:1-5.

Steinmetz, Suzanne K. (1977) *The Cycle of Violence: Assertive and Abusive Family Interaction.* New York: Praeger.

Stephens, Darrell V. (1977) "Domestic Assault: The Police Response." In Maria Roy (ed.), *Battered Women: A Psychosociological Study of Domestic Violence* pp. 164-72. New York: Van Nostrand Reinhold.

Stets, Jan E. (1991) "Cohabiting and Marital Aggression: The Role of Social Isolation." *Journal of Marriage and the Family* 53:669-80.

Stets, Jan E. and Murray A. Straus (1989) "The Marriage License as a Hitting License: A Comparison of Assaults in Dating, Cohabiting and Married Couples." *Journal of Family Violence* 41:33-52.

Straus, Murray A. (1979) "Measuring Intrafamily Conflict and Violence: The Conflict Tactics (CT) Scales." *Journal of Marriage and the Family* 41:75-88.

—— (1980) "Victims and Aggressors in Marital Violence." *American Behavioral Scientist* 23:681-704.

—— (1989) "Assaults by Wives on Husbands: Implications for Primary Prevention of Marital Violence." Paper presented at annual meetings of the American Society of Criminology, Reno.

—— (1990) "Conceptualization and Measurement of Battering: Implications for Public Policy." In Michael Steinman (ed.), *Woman Battering: Policy Responses* pp. 19-47. Cincinnati: Anderson.

Straus, Murray A. and Richard J. Gelles (1986) "Societal Change and Change in Family Violence from 1975 to 1985 as Revealed in Two National Surveys." *Journal of Marriage and the Family* 48:465-79.

—— (1990) *Physical Violence in American Families.* New Brunswick, NJ: Transaction Books.

Straus, Murray, Richard Gelles, and Suzanne Steinmetz (1980) *Behind Closed Doors: Violence in the American Family.* Garden City, NY: Anchor.

Szinovacz, Maximiliane (1983) "Using Couple Data as a Methodological Tool: The Case of Marital Violence." *Journal of Marriage and the Family* 45:633-44.

Uchida, Craig D., Laure W. Brooks, and Christopher S. Kopers (1987) "Danger to Police during Domestic Encounters: Assaults on Baltimore County Police, 1984-1986." *Criminal Justice Policy Review* 2:357-71.

U.S. Commission on Civil Rights (1982) *Under the Rule of Thumb: Battered Women and the Administration of Justice.* Washington, DC: U.S. Government Printing Office.

U.S. Department of Justice (1980) *Intimate Victims: A Study of Violence among Friends and Relatives.* Washington, DC: U.S. Government Printing Office.

—— (1984) *Attorney General's Task Force on Family Violence: Final Report.* Washington, DC: Author.

—— (1986-1991) *Crime in the United States: 1985-1990.* Washington, DC: U.S. Government Printing Office.

Victim Services Agency (1988) *The Law Enforcement Response to Family Violence: A State by State Guide to Family Violence Legislation.* New York: Author.

Waits, Kathleen (1985) "The Criminal Justice System's Response to Battering: Understanding the Problem, Forging the Solutions." *Washington Law Review* 60:267-329.

Walker, Gillian A. (1990) *Family Violence and the Women's Movement: A Conceptual Politics of Struggle.* Toronto: University of Toronto Press.

Walter, James D. (1981) "Police in the Middle: A Study of Small City Police Intervention in Domestic Disputes." *Journal of Police Science Administration* 9:243-60.

Williams, Kirk R. and Richard Hawkins (1989) "The Meaning of Arrest for Wife Assault." *Criminology* 27:163-81

Wylie, Peter B., Louis F. Basinger, Charlotte L. Heinecke and Jean A. Rueckert (1976) *An Approach to Evaluating a Police Program of Family Crisis Intervention in Six Demonstration Cities: Final Report.* Washington, DC: U.S. Government Printing Office.

Yllo, Kersti and Murray A. Straus (1981) "Interpersonal Violence among Married and Cohabiting Couples." *Family Relations* 30:339-47.

Zahn, Margaret A. and Philip C. Sagi (1987) "Stranger Homicides in Nine American Cities." *Journal of Criminal Law and Criminology* 78(2):377-97.

Zalman, Marvin (forthcoming) "The Court's Response to Police Intervention in Domestic Violence." In Eve S. Buzawa and Carl G. Buzawa (eds.), *Domestic Violence:The Changing Criminal Justice Response.* Westport, CT: Greenwood.

Cases Cited

Balistreri v. Pacifica Police Department 901 F.2d 696, 9th Cir. (1990)

Bradley v. State 2 Miss. 156 (1824)

Bruno v. Codd 396 N.Y.S. 974 (1977)

Deshaney v. Winnebago County Department of Social Services 489 U.S. 189 (1989)

Dudosh v. City of Allentown 665 F. Supp. 381, E.D. Pa. (1987)

Fulgham v. State 46 Ala. 143 (1871)

Joyner v. Joyner 59 N.C. 322 (1862)

Nearing v. Weaver 295 Or. 702 (1983)

Scott v. Hart No. 6-76-2395, N.D. Cal. (1976)

State v. Black 60 N.C. 262 (1864)

State v. Hussey 44 N.C. 124 (1852)

State v. Oliver 70 N.C. 44 (1874)

State v. Rhodes 61 N.C. 452 (1865)

Thurman v. City of Torrington 595 F. Supp. 1521, D. Conn. (1984)

Turner v. City of Charleston 675 F. Supp. 314, D.S.C. (1987)

18

Attempting Gang Control by Suppression: The Misuse of Deterrence Principles

Malcolm W. Klein

What are gangs, why do people, especially youths, join them, and what should the police do to control them? These questions have been on the minds of the public quite a lot lately, and are important concerns for the police. Perhaps the two most common strategies for gang control in local communities have been (1) to ignore gangs and deny they exist or (2) to employ severe crackdowns in order to discourage gang-related activity. The latter tendency is addressed by Malcolm Klein in this chapter, and he argues that it may be counter-productive. See if you agree with him and ask yourself what other strategies might be adopted by the police if crackdowns really are not very effective in suppressing gangs.

Introduction

A famous American athlete once offered this advice: Don't look back, someone may be gaining on you. The street gang is still largely an American product—and a rapidly proliferating one within the U.S. borders—but its counterparts in other nations are becoming more visible. Gang-like structures are reported in Stockholm, Berlin, Frankfurt, London, Manchester, Zurich, Madrid, and half a

dozen cities in Russia among other western cities. Melbourne, Papua-New Guinea, Beijing, Tokyo, and Hong Kong are among Eastern cities from which gang reports are emerging. South America and Canada provide additional nominations.

It behooves us then, not to dismiss street gangs as "just an American problem," but to learn from the American experience and the failures there to control gang crime and promote pro-social life styles for potential gang members. In particular, the current U.S. reliance on gang suppression programs calls for special attention, especially as an exercise in deterrence principles at work. Over the past decade, the U.S. has all but given up on gang prevention programs.

The Context of Anti-Gang Enforcement Efforts

Defining as ambiguous a phenomenon as street gangs is a somewhat arbitrary process, but for purposes of this discussion the following depiction may suffice:

A street gang is a collectivity of youth (adolescent and adult), primarily male, who see themselves as a distinct entity (usually with a group name) with an anti-social orientation. It is generally perceived in its neighborhood as both distinct and anti-social, and has been involved in enough criminal activity to call forth a consistent negative response from community residents and enforcement officials. The street gang is generally but not always territorial and generally but not always composed of ethnic or racial minorities. Its crime pattern is versatile.

Drug distribution gangs often appear to be a variant of street gangs, developing independently or as offshoots of established street gangs. They are far more focussed on drug sales and associated criminal activities than are traditional street gangs, and less likely to be territorially oriented.

Excluded from this depiction are terrorist groups, motorcycle gangs, car clubs, "stoner" groups, normal peer networks, and organized adult criminal groups.

An assessment of current law enforcement approaches to gang activity makes most sense when placed in the context of enforcement efforts over the past several decades. The current emphasis on gang suppression has emerged from at least four developments which can be seen as both shaping and justifying its status. The four developments are:

1. A growing acknowledgement that treatment/rehabilitation approaches have been unsuccessful;

2. The growth in gang intelligence sophistication and technologies;

3. Pressures from the emergence of various gang forms in several hundred American cities, and their expansion in size and violence in such gang hubs as Los Angeles and Chicago;

4. Pressures generated by real and purported involvements of urban gangs in drug distribution, most notably in crack distribution.

Deterrence

In this section, I cover four background issues: The components of deterrence theory, pertinent portions of the deterrence literature, deterrence and drugs, and then deterrence and gangs.[1] As we discuss the elements of deterrence theory and their limitations, the reader may be aided by having in mind some of the gang suppression programs to which the deterrence principles will be applied. Included, and described more fully in a later section are the following:

- *Street sweeps*, in which hundreds of police officers—usually with public forewarning—crack down on high-intensity gang and drug distribution neighborhoods, round up hundreds of suspects, and subject them to an accelerated booking and disposition process.

- *Special gang probation and parole caseloads*, in which officers deal with gang members only, employ high surveillance techniques and revoke probation and parole status for any violation noted, returning the suspects to detention.

- *Prosecution programs* that target gang leaders and serious gang offenders for intensive vertical prosecution and special court handling to increase successful prosecution rates to 95% or more.

- *Various civil procedures*—use of civil abatement laws, using gang membership to define arrest for conspiracy or unlawful association—in order to emphasize the special nature of gang membership and the special enforcement activities to which gang members may be subjected.

- *School programs*, including overt surveillance and covert buy-bust operations.

These are examples of suppression programs that exemplify various deterrence principles. Obviously, it is not the case that enforcement officials or city councils have undertaken careful analyses of deterrence theory and then designed intervention programs based upon the theory. But in explaining the rationale and value of such programs, officials *do* explicitly make reference to propositions that are immediately recognizable as articulating deterrence theory. Public statements—even promises—have been made about "obliterating" gangs. Programs are described as "sending a message" to drug dealers in gangs. Speed of enforcement (celerity) and certainty of punishment are stressed; severity of sanctions is promised, and laws promulgated to increase it; targeting for sanctions is both broadened by increasing gang intelligence and pinpointed by the concentration of enforcement efforts and development of special control units in the various agencies. Gang leaders are selected for special attention to spread the effect, while known gang symbols such as graffiti and "colors" are singled out for special attention. Yet, what is missing in all this is any considered attention to the gap between message delivered and message received. This gap, in a broad sense, should be the eventual target of suppression program evaluations.

Theoretical Components

Deterrence theory comes not so much in many forms as in many emphases. The watershed in illuminating the theory came in the mid-1970s with the publication of Zimring and Hawkins' *Deterrence: The Legal*

Threat in Crime Control (1973) and Gibbs' *Crime, Punishment, and Deterrence* (1975).

Suppression approaches are loosely based on a deterrence perspective, especially among justice officials (Zimring and Hawkins). Gibbs and others make it clear that deterrence is a component of "preventive consequences of punishment." This is especially true with respect to general deterrence. Thus one can turn to deterrence theory to sharpen the operations encompassed under the suppression rubric, thereby increasing the chances for useful prevention. Two of the properties of deterrence are celerity and severity of applied punishment. The use of aperiodic massive police sweeps in high drug and gang neighborhoods is said to serve as a general deterrent for actual and potential gang members and crack sellers. Sweeps, it is claimed, send an unmistakable message about the punitive consequences of drug distribution by gang members.

But what takes place in such a sweep? On a typical weekend in Los Angeles, it may yield four hundred arrests, half gang, many mere traffic violations, other warrants already outstanding; quick booking and release; prior warning (sometimes first night, always subsequent nights). The general impression is one of a police gnat attack—we know it's coming, its targets are diffuse, it leads for some persons to minor sanctions quickly abated by quick release. Sherman's (1990) review of police crackdowns, including those aimed at drug sales, defines them as increases in *either* certainty or severity of sanctions. But, *celerity* is achieved at the expense of *certainty* and *severity*—two of the three major properties of deterrence theory. This contradictory implication involving different deterrence properties is foreshadowed by Nagel's (1982) suggestions about the interaction between certainty and severity and is in accord as well with data reported by Tittle (1980).

The police say they are sending a message (presumably of certainty and celerity). But, especially given the group processes in the gang world, one might guess that the messages *received*—interpreted, reinterpreted, cognitively altered to serve the purposes of the gang audience—may well be: "the police

are incompetent," "I can beat the rap," "They're just getting minor offenders," "Only fools get caught, or guys who want some excitement." The *objective* (Gibbs' "presumptive") properties here are questionable. The subjective or *perceived* properties may actually work *against* the desired deterrent effect; their preventive value may be essentially nil. Gang group process can turn a street sweep into a source of gang bravado and cohesiveness.

Each of various suppression operations described in this paper involves the potential application of deterrence propositions, but also carries the potential for a boomerang effect. The failure to achieve prevention via suppression operations can be due to poorly operationalized deterrence properties, or to the failure to consider the perceptual or broader cognitive counterpart to the objective or presumptive property.

To set the stage for this enterprise, I need to offer a brief review of the state of deterrence theory and its principal propositions. Among many writers, there has been a good deal of pessimism about constructing a comprehensive theory of deterrence. As Zimring and Hawkins put it in 1973, ". . . the net effect of increasing attention and study is something less than a knowledge explosion" (1973:3). But this kind of pessimism is sometimes hard to discern among public officials or the general public who, to quote Zimring and Hawkins again, ". . . seem to think in a straight line about the deterrent effect of sanctions; if penalties have a deterrent effect in one situation, they will have a deterrent effect in all; if some people are deterred by threats, then all will be deterred; if doubling a penalty produces an extra measure of deterrence, then trebling the penalty will do still better. . . . This style of thinking imagines a world in which armed robbery is in the same category as illegal parking, burglars think like district attorneys. . . ." (1973:19).

Part of the problem in this "straight line" thinking is one of distinguishing between *specific deterrence* and *general deterrence*. Another is a blurring of *severity*, *certainty*, and *celerity* of sanctions. Yet another is the distinction between *objective* (or "presumptive") and *perceived* properties of deterrence. Then there is the place of deterrence among *other processes* related to crime levels, and the relation of deterrence to the broader notion of prevention. These issues were succinctly covered in Gibbs (1975), and little improved upon since, so we rely rather heavily on that volume to lay out for the reader some basic components of deterrence theory.

Specific deterrence has to do "with the impact of legal punishment on those who have suffered it."[2]

General deterrence pertains "to the impact of legal punishment on the public at large."

It is worth noting at this point that specific deterrence is loosely based on behavioristic learning theories for individuals while general deterrence applies these mechanistic principles to non-involved populations with little attention to intervening processes. This is mirrored in gang suppression programs.

Severity is generally described as an observable, measurable characteristic of sanctions in terms of the punitive consequences of the sanctions on the offender. Greater severity should lead to greater deterrence. Zimring and Hawkins cite an earlier practice in Beijing of displaying, next to the 15 mph speed signs, the severed heads of those caught exceeding the limit. In 1982, we found that practice supplanted by the use of photographs of the executed. No comparative impact statement is available.

Certainty represents the probability that a sanction will be applied to an offender as a consequence of a particular offense or pattern of offenses out of many. Higher certainty should lead to greater deterrence.

Celerity refers to the speed with which a sanction is applied, i.e., how close in time to the offense; the closer in time, the greater the deterrence.

These are objective properties of sanctions, but are not related to their effect in a simple linear fashion. For instance, low levels of severity may be relatively indistinguishable in effect, while above a reasonably high level, any additional quantum of severity may be superfluous. Or consider the problem with certainty, given the fact that juvenile offenses in general and many minor offenses may have a commission-to-detection ratio of 20 to 1. Increasing such a low level to ratios of 20

to 2 or 20 to 5 may well be inconsequential, even unnoticeable. As to celerity, any student of American enforcement and judicial processes can recite the delays which normally occur between the commission of a criminal act and subsequent official detection, apprehension, and court sanction.

Applicability was offered by Zimring and Hawkins as the degree to which a sanction is believed to apply personally to the offender. Higher applicability yields greater deterrence—specific deterrence in particular.

Credibility, also added by Zimring and Hawkins, refers to the belief that the sanctioning agency can indeed deliver on its threat. Higher credibility leads to greater deterrence, in part, we assume, through higher levels of certainty.

The reader may discern in these latter two propositions a shift away from the objective level to the perceived level. While economists and other rational choice theorists prefer to eschew the perceptual level, much deterrence theory and research pertains directly to the objective/perceptual distinction and the capacity of measures of the *perceived* properties to predict deterrent efforts at higher levels of impact.

Perceived severity, certainty, and celerity (and other properties such as applicability and credibility) are the processual translations between general deterrence and specific deterrence, such that higher perceived levels should produce greater deterrence. However, from our point of view in translating deterrence into prevention among the non-sanctioned, these *perceived properties* become paramount as well. It helps in the translation to turn again to Gibbs who notes several levels of importance to us:

- Some people never *contemplate* committing the acts in question. They are beyond the concern of deterrence, and beyond our concern in this paper.

- "Absolute deterrence" refers to those who never commit criminal acts because of a general risk assessment. This is clearly in the arena of primary prevention, and of interest to us.

- "Restrictive deterrence" is defined in terms of the perceived odds for a given individual to be punished. This seems to combine the notions of applicability and credibility above, and also relates directly to our interests.

Thus *absolute and restrictive deterrence* are also relevant properties, with higher levels of each yielding greater deterrent impact. This proposition, along with that on perceived properties, leads us on the path of equating deterrent and preventive effects. Lest the reader underestimate the complexity of the propositional status of deterrence theory, consider that Logan (1982) developed a set of 26 interrelated hypotheses. This path from deterrence to prevention is far from simple.

Deterrence, Gangs, and Group Process

Our own research consistently has revealed gangs as qualitatively different from other delinquent or criminal collectivities (Klein, 1971; Maxson, Gordon, and Klein, 1985; also see Short and Strodtbeck, 1965). Gangs are not merely located toward the end of some criminal continuum; internal group processes and the mutual interactions between such groups and their communities— schools, playgrounds, police, store owners, etc.—set the gangs apart qualitatively. Street gangs, by self and other definition, become set apart so as to be distinctive from other peer groups in which some criminal involvement is evidenced. Gang suppression takes on a different character (as will be seen from our description of gang suppression programs) but also must be studied in some special ways because of the influence of group process on the way program components are received and interpreted.

Deterrence in the gang setting is difficult. Consider, for example, the non-gang findings of Erickson and Gibbs (1978) that the positive correlation between perceived certainty and crime rate disappears when one controls on the social condemnation of crime; Alcorn's (1978) finding that while deterrent properties had no effect, delinquent peers and values did, and Meier, Burkett, and Hickman's (1984) confirmation that sanction threats had no effect but peer influences did.

The gang/drug connection over the years has been more assumed than demonstrated. What the literature suggests about the gangs and drugs connection would seem to be confusing. Many people *assume* the connection, but to judge from the literature, the potential for the gang/drug connection has not to date been fulfilled.

Chein's (1964) report on 18 New York City gangs found very low drug usage and absolutely no organized sale procedures. Short and Strodtbeck (1965) found marijuana use and sales to rank 48th in a list of 69 gang activities, while narcotics use and sales ranked 59th (in contrast to alcohol at the 22nd position). Retreatist gangs were almost non-existent in this Chicago research. Carney, Mattick, and Calloway (1969), also in Chicago, found hard drug use very uncommon in gangs: "The drug user was held in contempt." In Philadelphia, Robin (1967) found gang member drug offenses too few to register in his offense categories. Neither the incisive account by Cohen (1955) nor by Suttles (1968) mentions the problem. The report of the New York City Youth Board (1960) acknowledges drugs among its gangs only briefly as part of the "full gamut of juvenile offenses." Los Angeles gangs described by Klein (1971) had drug *and* alcohol offenses comprising from three to eleven percent of recorded offenses prior to intervention efforts. In later reports from Chicago, Cartwright, Tompson, and Schwartz (1975) suggest the place of drug involvement in gangs by reference to the gang leader who "belt-whipped a member of his gang suspected of using drugs." Short (1968), while describing minor use to be common in groups, found that hard drugs were unusual except in one gang, and that "addiction was virtually unknown." Blum's (1972) extensive study in the Bay Area yielded 350 pages on dealers with not one mention of street gangs.

In sum, with almost unbroken consistency the earlier literature yielded the counter-intuitive conclusion that gang involvement in the drug world had been relatively minor, and had emphasized "soft" rather than "hard" drugs. Moore's (1978) research with ex-convict, older gang members in East Los Angeles offers the only principal exception.

The situation of drug distribution is no better: experience with and observation of drug sales systems has not been well captured in the empirical literature. For instance, major reviews such as those by Ray (1983), Gottschalk, McGuire, Heiser, Dinovo, and Birch (1979), Gandossy, Williams, Cohen, and Harwood (1980), and O'Donnell, Voss, Clayton, Slatin, and Room (1976) cover drug use and users extensively, but not distributors (beyond their role as users). Chin and Fagan's 1990 analysis of violence among users and user/sellers of crack shows little increment over prior violence levels, and *no* consideration of gang involvement.

Typically, older studies of drug distribution have described systems principally involving white, middle-class actors (Adler and Adler, 1983; Blum, 1972; Atkyns and Hanneman, 1974; Langer, 1977; Mouledoux, 1972; Lieb and Olsen, 1976). Descriptions by Hughes, Crawford, Barker, Schumann, and Jaffe (1971), Preble and Casey (1969), Blum (1972), and Goldstein (1981) deal with various distribution roles among heroin users. Cocaine distribution is almost untouched in this literature.

One exception to some of the above is Ianni's (1974) article on black and Hispanic intrusion into Mafia-controlled rackets, including drug trafficking. Another is the Goldstein, Brownstein, Ryan, and Bellucci (1989) graphic and disheartening descriptions of violence and death related to what he calls the "systemic" aspect of drugs, referring to the interaction between use and distribution systems.

However, research during the past few years has suggested a trend toward stronger and more direct connections between gangs and both drug use and drug sales. Our own gang/crack research in Los Angeles (Maxson and Klein, 1990) revealed gang members involved in up to 25% of all crack sales arrests, most of these being at the street level. Hagedorn (1988) reports similar levels of general drug sales and high levels of use as well. Skolnick, Correl, Navarro, and Rabb (1988) have reported even closer relations at the middle levels of crack distribution. Taylor (1989) describes an almost complete involvement of gangs and drugs in the deteriorating heart of Detroit. Hayeslip concludes that "In many cities, gangs control street sales" (1989:3).

But the picture is mixed. In Los Angeles, the police department and the Sheriff's department differ considerably in imputing gang involvement to drug sales and violence. A. Goldstein (1990) cites a recent New York Task Force report as concluding that gang involvement in the drug business is very low. In Washington, D.C., now famous for its high levels of crack, little evidence exists of gang involvement. Washington has in fact never been among the major gang cities.

Fagan (1989) probably has drawn the most accurate picture: gangs, drugs, and violence are often found together, and yet there are many instances of gangs without much drug involvement, drugs sales groups that are not gangs, and both gangs and drug systems with and without violence. The connections are probably both spurious and causal, and the former can become the latter. Thus, Spergel concludes that "effective but exclusive suppression of gang activity may also be associated with conversion of the gang to more criminal gain-oriented activity such as drug trafficking" (1990:3), and Clayton (1986:13) cites the conclusion of the Select Committee on Narcotics Abuse and Control that the federal Office of Juvenile Justice and Delinquency Prevention ". . . should consider the problem of gangs and gang violence in relation to drug abuse both in its research and programmatic endeavors."

Gang suppression efforts have received scant attention in the research literature. Hayeslip (1989), writing for the National Institute of Justice, makes the gang/drug equation and then gives brief attention to street enforcement techniques, including police sweeps, and to civil abatement procedures. But Stapleton and Needle noted in one of the very first descriptions of gang enforcement procedures that:

Contemporary gang prevention and control practices are in an early developmental stage, not primitive, but certainly not approaching maturity. The state-of-the-art barely approaches that found in newer police program areas, such as community crime prevention or riot control, let alone the more fundamental areas such as patrol and investigations. Basic collective technology—proven practices, standard training curriculum, job specifications, evaluations, evaluation methodologies, and even a body of literature—has not yet emerged in this area of police concern. (1982:xiii)

In a following section of this paper I will provide brief sketches of the various suppression programs to be found specifically in selected American cities such as Los Angeles, but following the description by Stapleton and Needle above, only one significant effort has been undertaken to describe *generic* suppression approaches to gang activity (with or without connections to drug use and sales). This is the national assessment recently completed at the University of Chicago under the direction of Irving Spergel. Spergel and his co-authors state about police suppression programs, "A principal assumption is that gangs and gang members should not be tolerated or even helped" (1989:171). This police strategy, they say

> . . . is clear and simple. It is to arrest, prosecute, and sentence gang members, especially hard-core or leaders, quickly, effectively and to keep them in jail as long as possible. The strategy is achieved through such tactics as surveillance, stake-out, aggressive patrol and enforcement, follow-up investigation, the development of extensive intelligence, and infiltration of gangs in contexts in which gangs are found, e.g. schools. Gangs are to be broken up and harassed. Saturation patrol and sweeps are periodically employed. The aim often is to acquire improved fire power to deal with "drug gangs". . . .

Spergel also describes suppressive approaches to probation and parole gang caseloads, based in large part on the Los Angeles approach. The "primary emphasis is strict supervision, search of the homes of youths, with police protection." The trend has been away from younger members "to target more 'hard-core youth' similar to those served by the Los Angeles Police and Sheriff's gang units." There is also a Gang Drug Pushers and Sellers Program using heavier sanctions and electronic surveillance of gang drug

sellers, and daily assignment of probation officers to a school Crime Suppression Program to deal with gang activities on school campuses.

Other school based components have been described by the National School Safety Center, including dress codes, graffiti removal, crisis management, and so on. The Center, we might add, has adopted and widely disseminated an image of youth gangs that perpetuates a violence orientation far beyond reality; the image may well justify extreme suppression and surveillance, but it is a false image.

Finally, although in less detail, the Spergel group has described gang suppression programs run by prosecutor's offices. With an emphasis on obtaining high conviction rates and maximum sentences, these programs try to avoid plea bargaining, and put some of their best efforts into gathering intelligence through special warrant and search training for investigators, concentration on gang leaders and the most serious gang offenders, and the use of vertical prosecution. Whether this translates into any form of deterrence other than that of specific offender incapacitation is the kind of question requiring our attention.

Let me be clear about the foregoing: the message is not so much that suppression does or does not "work:" evidence one way or the other is sorely lacking. *There are logical, as well as experiential, reasons to believe that suppression programs can have deterrent effects and thus, by our reasoning, can contribute substantially to gang and drug activity prevention.* But there is also evidence to the contrary from the continued rise in gang violence in Chicago and Los Angeles, cities with suppression emphases. The issue for us is finding ways that such programs may be effectively sharpened so that they do not shoot themselves in the foot, as experience and our understanding of group process suggest they do.

The Gang Suppression Programs

Gibbs reminds us "that individuals cannot be deterred from an act unless they regard it as criminal and therefore subject to some kind of punishment" (1975:227). There needs to be, he notes, a "cognitive consensus" in the relevant populations. Zimring and Hawkins move us further: "It follows that communication can be of decisive importance in the process. For the effective operation of deterrence as a means of social control must depend, among other things, on the effective communication of threats of punishment and their concrete exemplifications to the public." And again, "The deterrence threat may perhaps be best viewed as a form of advertising" (1973:141). And yet again: "If the first task of a threatening agency is the communication of information, its second task is persuasion" (1973:149).

Communication and persuasion are social psychological processes. They take place most effectively with group support (see any standard text). They also are blocked or reinterpreted most effectively by group processes. The group—in our case, the street and drug gangs—becomes, therefore, a strong actor in turning suppression programs into justifications of gang offending, *or* into the prevention of the same. How well, then, do the various gang and drug suppression programs seem formulated to do the one or the other? Here I will illustrate the question by reference to the cafeteria of gang suppression programs in my own city of Los Angeles:

CRASH and OSS

CRASH (Community Resources Against Street Hoodlums) is the Los Angeles Police Department's special gang control operation, with 235 officers in gang patrol units in each of the department's geographic bureaus. OSS is the Sheriff's Department counterpart of about 110 officers, with units located in each of the individual stations with gang problems. There is also a central OSS command group which coordinates and collects gang intelligence, whereas in the Los Angeles Police Department the centralized gang intelligence unit is divorced from CRASH.

CRASH is a high profile gang control operation, carried out by uniformed patrol officers, stressing high visibility, street surveillance, pro-active suppression activities, and investigative follow-through on arrests. As is typical of Los Angeles Police Department operations, officer transfer and turnover is relatively rapid as new officers replace CRASH operatives after, typically, a two-year period.

In deterrence terms, the emphasis is on specific deterrence through implied certainty and severity of sanctions. Applicability and credibility may be weak.

OSS is a less high profile operation. It concentrates on targeted gangs (an approach recently favored more by Los Angeles Police Department as well), and places more emphasis on the intelligence function in proportion to control. OSS officers often stay with their assignment over many years, becoming experts on the local community and surprisingly close to traditional gangs in that community. The central OSS unit maintains an updated gang roster not only for its jurisdiction but for the county as a whole (including Los Angeles Police Department gangs). Because of the roster system and the greater emphasis on gang intelligence, LASD has emerged with a wider image for its gang expertise, while Los Angeles Police Department has emerged with more of a street control and suppression image. Compared to CRASH, the OSS operation lays less stress on severity and, by reputation at least, has higher credibility.

Operation Hammer

This is the aperiodic street sweep program operated by Los Angeles Police Department, primarily in South Bureau, which encompasses the largest portions of Los Angeles Police Department's gang areas. Over a two-day period, typically, Operation Hammer sends a coordinated force of between 200 and a thousand officers into a predesignated area to react to every legal violation and suspicious setting possible. Armed as well with prior warrants, the officers crack down on the area with high visibility, often announced beforehand and with heavy media coverage. A typical sweep will net several hundred arrests, primarily for misdemeanors including traffic violations, about half of which are gang-related in some way.

Because of the massive arrests, Hammer also consists of an expedited booking and release system in a mobile command post, thus maximizing officers' time in the sweep rather than its resulting paperwork.

The stated purposes of Operation Hammer are to crack down on gang and street dealing (specific deterrence) and to "send a message" to the local community (general deterrence). After several years of operations, it has been noted that gang violence has declined in South Bureau, with the implication that the message has been received. Skeptics, on the other hand, point to other activities in the community and question the direct ties between the times and locations of Operation Hammer and those of the reported decline. Even Hammer officials belatedly are acknowledging the need for community involvement.

More pertinent to our purposes are the questions raised about the suppressive or deterrent character of the operation. For example:

a. The medium proportion of *gang* arrests may weaken the gang-specificity of the message;

b. The high proportion of arrests for minor incidents and hence low sanction severity may weaken the image of the suppression of serious gang and drug offenses;

c. The timing and media coverage may decrease the deterrent effects—Hammer comes as little surprise to the community;

d. The quick booking and release may mitigate the perceived severity of sanctions, as well as allow gang members to return to their group claiming victory over a low-credibility police operation.

Other jurisdictions have eschewed following the Los Angeles Police Department example for some of the reasons noted above.

Operation Cul de Sac

Particular blocks and neighborhoods that have become open drug markets are targeted for traffic barricades to stop all vehicular traffic, concurrently with intensive police surveillance and crackdown and the encouraging of resident mobilization against street dealers. Program audiences are primarily the local dealers and secondarily local residents. Issues of displacement (of dealing) or expansion (of community-level control) have not been confronted.

Operation Hardcore

This is the vertical prosecution program in the District Attorney's office. Originally aimed at gang leaders and serious gang offenders it now must concentrate on gang-related homicide cases because of their increasing prevalence (771 gang-related homicides in the county in 1991). Working closely with police agencies on gang intelligence, warrant procedures, and witness protection, Hardcore deputy District Attorneys seek high conviction rates and full sentences (incapacitation), with the further general deterrence *intention* of having these gang convictions provide examples of the consequences of serious gang involvement. So far as we can determine, however, no serious attempt is made to follow through on this message; its successful dissemination is assumed.

Specialized Gang Supervision Program

This is a project in the Los Angeles County Probation Department. Carefully selected probation officers are given greatly reduced caseloads consisting of gang members only, juvenile and adult. The emphasis is on those convicted of violent offenses; there is close liaison with enforcement agencies; operations stress close surveillance of gang probationers and, in the case of detected probation violations, returning cases to court for recommitment to secure institutions. Program objectives are stated in specific deterrence terms only with no attention to the broader implications of the program. Certainty of sanctions is emphasized in a specific deterrence context. This stands in stark contrast to the handling of drug offenders, now so overloading the system that many convicted offenders receive no or minimal jail time, while many of their companions are simply released without being charged. The deterrence *context* is weak.

Parole Gang Program

This is the parole counterpart to the above, run by the California Youth Authority for its wards following their release from secure placement.

Street Terrorism Enforcement Program (STEP)

This is a new approach enabled by the state legislature. STEP operates on the legal finding that gang membership is based on knowledge of the criminal involvement of the group. But in order to be on safe constitutional grounds, the legislation provides that gang members be given formal notice of their suspected affiliation. Then charges of complicity and conspiracy can be lodged against them in connection with offenses charged against the group. Deputy city or district attorneys or police officers typically move into a targeted gang area with their gang rosters to deliver notices to individual members. Thereafter, arrest can lead to convictions with more severe sentencing. The STEP approach translates general deterrence messages into individual specific messages and comes close to a direct primary prevention mechanism by emphasizing certainty and applicability properties. But it is in conflict with the realities of an overloaded system that sends back a message of minimum sanctions.

Civil Abatement

Especially in connection with drug distribution, the city attorney's office has turned to a number of statutes which can be used to harass and discourage those who facilitate gang and drug activities operating out of homes, apartments, or business settings. These statutes include plumbing and electrical inspections; zoning rule adherence; unlawful gatherings; graffiti removal; and occupancy and use limitations. Because drug trafficking tends to become concentrated in areas of tolerance, especially if accompanied by intimidation related to gang presence, these civil abatement procedures are designed less to prevent illicit operations as much as to keep them disorganized, on the move, and ineffective as market systems. We see low credibility and applicability as limiting the value of this program as currently constituted.

School Programs

These come in a number of forms, including closed campuses, increased use of armed and uniformed security personnel, undercover drug buys followed by mass arrests at the end of each semester (Los Angeles Police Department and Los Angeles city schools), and placement of police and probation units on campus. One may reasonably expect these approaches, and variations on the theme, to proliferate in the context of the increasing gang and drug problems in Los Angeles. They tend to be school-specific and thus need to be monitored at the individual school level. Relationship to DARE and SANE drug and gang prevention/education programs should also be carefully noted—prevention from opposite ends of the continuum. However, in the concentrated peer group atmosphere of the school campus, one can speculate that the DARE and SANE programs may have more long-term effect because they deliberately *employ* aspects of group process while the suppression programs may well be *subverted* by group process.

Group Process and Prevention Directions

I have made the point, and need not dwell on it long, that the straightforward intentions of gang suppression programs may backfire. Their implicit deterrent properties and messages may be altered by the receiving gang members. This is less likely to be the case with nongang audiences, although drug dealing cliques may evidence the same character as traditional street gangs. We must, in due time, survey the effects of suppression programs on both grouped and non-grouped audiences but for the moment I am concerned specifically with the group setting. In interstitial and inner city areas where formal social controls are weak, group processes more easily emerge to direct youthful behaviors.

This gang setting, it should be added, has derived increasing importance in recent years because of the impact of more sophisticated theoretical *and* methodological advances in understanding developmental phases for delinquency and drug use. Longitudinal research outcomes reveal, with great consistency, peer relations as becoming the most important, proximal contributor to drug and delinquency involvement (e.g., Elliott, Huizinga, and Menard, 1989; Thornberry, 1990; Farrington et al., 1990).

Moore and Vigil suggest quite properly that "gangs maintain an oppositional, rather than a deviant subculture," and thus represent "an institutionalized rejection of the values of adult authority—especially as exhibited in the Anglo-dominated schools and the police department" (1989:31). In a context in which a major law enforcement official declares that his department will "obliterate" gangs and that "casual drug users should be shot," the oppositional value system makes sense. War mentalities distort the communications between the antagonists.

The gang literature—that portion of it that derives directly from researchers' field time spent with gang members—is replete with descriptions of the oppositional, reinterpreting pattern of gang members (Short and Strodtbeck, 1965; Klein, 1971; Horowitz, 1983; Hagedorn, 1988). It is effectively restated in deterrence terms by Zimring and Hawkins:

- "It seems possible that threats of punishment, so far from being disincentives to crime, may in these [gang] circumstances even function as incentives to it" (1973:216).

- "The operation of deterrence is greatly complicated when group pressures may not only inhibit the expression of the fear of sanctions but also in some instances convert stigmata into status symbols" (1973:317).

The gang setting discourages the acceptance or assignment of legitimacy to police, prosecution, and court accounts of acceptable behaviors. It denies the wrongfulness of many offense incidents (though not of all offenses *per se*). It encourages the bravado that accompanies anti-social deeds and utterances. It legitimates violence in the setting of gang rivalry and protection of drug dealing; it accepts the gang's moral superiority in unequal battles and its predicates against both the weak and those in authority. In the drug arena in particular, where personal indulgence and profits are immediate and personalized, the credibility of anti-drug messages is seriously endangered. And in the context of a neighborhood that tolerates trafficking, straightforward deterrence messages fall on

deaf ears. The differences in effect between such programs as Operation Hammer and STEP may provide considerable illumination on how to use suppressive deterrence programming for prevention purposes.

These are very practical issues in prevention. There are two principal ways in which *successful specific deterrence* can be preventive. First, in the tertiary prevention sense, it will reduce the sanctioned activity—e.g., drug use or dealing, gang recruiting, and various related criminal offenses. Secondly, one can fairly assume that such success can have primary or secondary preventive success with those at-risk youth (gang sibs, elementary and junior high school students) in the inner city who model, imitate or otherwise are influenced by their directly sanctioned peers and elders. Here, group process both by itself and as affected by deliberate interventions can be used for preventive ends. Thus a *successful* Operation Hammer or STEP or Probation Gang Caseload, guided by well-articulated deterrence principles and deliberate follow-up interventions with at-risk youth, could greatly expand their targeted populations.

Similarly, *successful general deterrence*, using messages with appropriate content for appropriate audiences, can have a direct primary prevention effect on at-risk youth. Here one would most certainly want to enlist the collaboration of the schools, the media, and a number of community youth-serving organizations to pass on and train in the program messages. Where prevention/education programs are already in place, the collaboration could be particularly effective.

But—in order to facilitate these preventive procedures and help shape their form and substance, we must learn more about the processes taking place via the available suppression programs. For illustration, let us take just a few examples out of the many possible.

- Suppose the Operation Hammer message is interpreted to be that sanctioning is over rapidly and is mild. One might advise the police to give up the mobile booking operation as part of Hammer, thus forcing the swept-up arrestees into the normal, longer, less clearly manage-

able arrest and arraignment procedures. Both severity and credibility are
increased.

- Suppose that STEP properly notifies
known gang members of their liability
for arrest and conviction, but would-be
gang members are untouched (properly) by this legal process. There are
other avenues—the media, the schools—
by which they could be made clearly
aware of the legal risks associated with
membership. Certainty and applicability are increased.

- Suppose that Operation Hardcore, being limited to the most serious gang offenders, successfully incapacitates most
of its "clients," but because these are
strictly individual convictions they remain relatively unknown to others. One
can imagine various procedures whereby
drug dealers and others willing to commit violence to protect their trade can
be alerted to Hardcore results—not only
the severity of the sanctions, but the
truly high rate of conviction, i.e., certainty. An experiment using posters with
name and picture of convicted violent
offenders is currently underway.

- Suppose that drug offenders subjected
to electronic surveillance and intensive
supervision are so successfully deterred
that, from the point of view of their peers
or former criminal colleagues, they all
but disappear from the scene: out of
sight, out of mind. Their plight will not
affect other offenders on the street. It
seems clear that probation, school, and
other officials could easily heighten the
awareness of these restricted lives among
the at-risk populations. We then get at
least some increment in certainty and
credibility.

Of course, we cannot know in the absence
of careful research whether such examples
are realistic but they do illustrate the kinds of
connections that can be made between successful or improvable suppression programs
and the targets for rationally planned prevention intervention. What I think we *do* know
about street gangs is that, once formed, they
have a life of their own that feeds off their sur-

roundings. The urban setting of their development serves to maintain them. Gang rival-
ries serve to strengthen them. And little that
we have devised by way of intervention seems
to weaken them. My informed hunch is that
suppression programs, left to their own devices, may deter a few members but also increase the internal cohesiveness of the group.

By focussing on the gang *per se*, calling
special attention to it, calling out its leaders,
derogating its members, these programs will
provide the very status and identity that
youths join gangs to receive in the first place.
The logic of deterrence fails in suppression
programs because the programs assume, erroneously, a rational gang world. The gang
world is not a rational choice model, but a
social psychological one. Deterrence principles will act through group-determined perceptual processes. The critical task then is to
understand these processes so that deterrence principles do not boomerang, thus creating more of the monster they are designed
to modify.

Notes

1. [Editors' note: extended reviews of the scholarly literature on deterrence theory are included in the original article, but excluded
here for the sake of brevity.]
2. Gibbs' preference for limiting deterrence to
legal punishment is not necessary, and not followed in most literature or this paper.

References

Adler, P.A. & Adler, P. (1983). Shifts and oscilla-
tions in deviant careers: The case of Upper-
level drug dealers and smugglers. *Social
Problems* 31:195-207.

Alcorn, D.S. (1978). *A social psychological perspective of deterrence: Development and test of
a causal model.* Ann Arbor: University Microfilms.

Atkyns, R.L. & Hanneman, G.J. (1974). Illicit
drug distribution and dealer communication
behavior. *Journal of Health and Social Behavior* 15:36-43.

Blum, R.H. (1972). *The dream sellers*. San Francisco: Jossey-Bass.

Carney, F.J., Mattick, H.W., and Callaway, J.D.
(1969). Action in the streets: A handbook for

inner city youth work. New York: Association Press.

Cartwright, D.S., Tomson, B., & Schwartz, H., eds., (1975). *Gang delinquency*. Monterey, CA: Brooks/Cole.

Chein, I. (1964). Narcotics use among juveniles. In Cavan, R., ed., *Readings in Juvenile Delinquency*. New York: J.P. Lippincott.

Chin, K. & Fagan, J. (1990). The impact of crack on drug and crime involvement. Paper read at the meeting of the American Society of Criminology.

Clayton, R.R. (1986). Drug use among children and adolescents. Paper prepared for the OJJDP Workshop, Annapolis, MD. Lexington, KY: University of Kentucky.

Cohen, A.K. (1955). *Delinquent boys: The culture of the gang*. New York: Free Press.

Elliott, D.S., Huizinga, D. & Menard, S. (1989). *Multiple problem youth: Delinquency, substance use, and mental health problems*. New York: Springer-Verlag.

Erickson, M.L. & Gibbs, J.P. (1978). Objective and perceptual properties of legal punishment and the deterrence doctrine. *Social Problems*. 25:253-64.

Fagan, J. (1989). The social organization of drug use and drug dealing among urban gangs. *Criminology*, 27(4):633-669.

Farrington, D.P., Loeber, R., Elliott, D.S., Hawkins, J.D., Kandel, D.B., Klein, M.W., McCord, J., Rowe, D.C., & Tremblay, R.E. (1990). Advancing knowledge about the onset of delinquency and crime. In Lahey, B.J., & Kazdin, A.D., eds., *Advances in Clinical Child Psychology*. New York: Plenum.

Gandossy, R.P., Williams, J.R., Cohen, J., & Harwood, H.J. (1980). *Drugs and crime: A survey and analysis of the literature*. Washington, D.C.: National Institute of Justice.

Gibbs, J.P. (1975). *Crime, punishment, and deterrence*. New York: Elsevier.

Goldstein, A. (1990). *Delinquent gangs: A psychological perspective*. A pre-publication manuscript. Syracuse University.

Goldstein, P.J. (1981). Getting over economic alternatives to predatory crime among street users. In Inciardi, J.A., ed., *The Drugs-Crime Connection*. Beverly Hills, CA: Sage Publications.

Goldstein, P.G., Brownstein, H.H., Ryan, P.J., & Bellucci, P.A. (1989). Crack and homicide in New York City, 1988. *Contemporary drug problems*, 16(4):651-87.

Gottschalk, L.A., McGuire, F.L., Heiser, J.F., Dinovo, E.C., & Birch, H. (1979). *Drug Abuse deaths in nine cities: A survey report*. Washington, D.C.: National Institute of Drug Abuse.

Hagedorn, J.M. (1988). *People and folks: Gangs, crime and the underclass in a Rustbelt city*. Chicago: Lake View Press.

Hayeslip, D.W.,Jr. (1989). Local-level drug enforcement: New strategies. *Research in Action #213*. Washington, D.C.: National Institute of Justice.

Horowitz, R. (1983). *Honor and the American dream*. New Brunswick: Rutgers University Press.

Hughes, P.H., Crawford, G.A., Barker, N.W., Schumann, S., & Jaffe, J.H. (1971). The social structure of a heroin copping community. *American Journal of Psychiatry* 128:551-8.

Ianni, F.A. (1974). New mafia: black, Hispanic, and Italian styles. *Society* 2.

Klein, M.W., ed., (1971). *Street gangs and street workers*. Englewood Cliffs: Prentice-Hall.

Klein, M.W., Maxson, C.L. (1989). Street gang violence. In: Weiner, N. & Wolfgang, M. E., eds. *Violent crimes, violent criminals*. Newbury Park: Sage Publications.

Langer, J. (1977). Drug entrepreneurs and dealing culture. *Social Problems* 24:377-86.

Lieb, J. & Olsen, S. (1976). Prestige, paranoia, and profit: On becoming a dealer of illicit drugs in a university community. *Journal of Drug Issues* 6:356-67.

Logan, C.H. (1982). Propositions for deterrence theory at [the] aggregate level. Presentation to the Panel on Deterrence, meetings of the American Society of Criminology.

Maxson, C.L., Gordon, M.A. & Klein, M.W. (1985). Differences between gang and non-gang homicides. *Criminology* 23:209-22.

Maxson, C.L. & Klein, M.W. (1990). Street gang violence: Twice as great or half as great? In Huff, R., ed., *Gangs in America: Diffusion, diversity, and public policy*. Newbury Park: Sage Publications.

Meier, R.F., Burkett, S.R. & Hickman, C.A. (1984). Sanctions, peers, and deviance: preliminary models of a social control process. *Sociological Quarterly* 25:67-82.

Moore, J.W. (1978). *Homeboys: Gangs, drugs, and prison in the barrios of Los Angeles*. Philadelphia: Temple University Press.

Moore, J.W. & Vigil, D. (1989). Chicano gangs: Group norms and individual factors related to adult criminality. *Aztlan* 18:27-44.

Mouledoux, J. (1972). Ideological aspects of drug dealership. In Westhues, K., ed., *Society's Shadow: Studies in the Sociology of Countercultures*. Toronto: McGraw-Hill.

Nagel, S.S. (1982). Tradeoffs in crime reduction among certainty, severity, and crime benefits. *Rutgers Law Review* 35:100-32.

New York City Youth Board. (1960). *Reaching the fighting gangs*. New York: New York City Youth Board.

O'Donnell, J.A., Voss, H.L., Clayton, R.R., Slatin, G.T., Room, R.G.W. (1976). *Young men and drugs—A nationwide survey*. Rockville, MD: National Institute of Drug Awareness.

Preble, E.A. & Casey, J.J., Jr. (1969). Taking care of business—the heroin user's life on the street. *International Journal of the Addictions* 4:1-24.

Ray, O. (1983). *Drugs, Society and Human Behavior*. St. Louis: C.V. Mosby.

Robin, G.D. (1967). Gang member delinquency in Philadelphia. In Klein, M.W., ed., *Juvenile Gangs in Context: Theory, Research, and Action*. Englewood Cliffs: Prentice-Hall.

Sherman, L.W. (1990). Police crackdowns. *NIJ Reports*, 219 (March/April):2-6.

Short, J.F., Jr., ed., (1968). *Gang delinquency and delinquent subcultures*. New York: Harper and Row.

Short, J.F., Jr. & Strodtbeck, F.L. (1965). *Group process and gang delinquency*. Chicago: University of Chicago Press.

Skolnick, J.H., Correl, T., Navarro, E., and Rabb, R. (1988). The social structure of street drug dealing. Sacramento: Office of the Attorney General of the State of California.

Spergel, I.A. (1990). Youth gangs: Continuity and change. In Tonry, M. & Norris, N., eds., *Crime and Justice, Vol. 12*. Chicago: University of Chicago Press.

Spergel, I.A., Curry, G.D., Kane, C., Chance, R., Ross, R., Alexander, A., Rodriquez, P., Seed, D., and Simmons, E. (1989a). Youth Gangs: Problem and Response. A Review of the Literature. A draft report of the National Gang Suppression and Intervention Project. Chicago: University of Chicago, School of Social Service Administration.

Stapleton, W.V., and Needle, J.A. (1982). Police handling of youth gangs. Sacramento: American Justice Institute.

Suttles, G.D. (1968). *The social order of the slum: Ethnicity and territory in the inner city*. Chicago: University of Chicago Press.

Taylor, C.S. (1989). *Dangerous society*. East Lansing: Michigan State University Press.

Thornberry, T.P. (1990). Empirical support for interactional theory: A review of the literature. Working paper #5, Rochester Youth Development Study. Albany: The University at Albany.

Tittle, C.R. (1980). *Sanctions and social deviance: The question of deterrence*. New York: Praeger.

Zimring, F.E. (1978). Policy experiments in general deterrence: 1970-1975. In Blumstein, A., Cohen, J, & Nagin, D., eds., *Deterrence and Incapacitation: Estimating the Effects of Criminal Sanctions on Crime Rates*. Washington D.C.: National Academy of Sciences.

Zimring, F.E. & Hawkins G.J. (1973). *Deterrence: The legal threat in crime control*. Chicago: University of Chicago Press.

19

Local-Level Drug Enforcement: New Strategies

David W. Hayeslip, Jr.

As a society we have been wrestling with the problem of drug abuse for decades. In recent years, overall usage patterns have gone up and down, as has the popularity of different drugs. The only constant has been public concern, translated through the political arena into one "War Against Drugs" after another. In this article, David Hayeslip describes several drug enforcement tactics that have been developed or refined during the last decade. These include improvements on some traditional techniques as well as new methods such as asset forfeiture, problem solving, and community policing. As you read this chapter, think seriously about both the effectiveness of these different tactics and the "bigger picture" of how best to police such an enormous and chronic social problem. If you were a police chief or sheriff with limited resources, what drug control strategy would you adopt? How high on your department's overall list of priorities would you put drug enforcement?

Faced with growing drug-related violence, crime, and mounting public concern, police departments across the country are devising new approaches for combating drug dealing. The strategies include enlisting the support of community groups, seizing assets of both sellers and users, and cracking down on street sales.

The National Institute of Justice has begun to take a look at some of these new strategies. This article shares some preliminary information gathered in discussions with metropolitan police departments, and it concludes with questions that need to be answered concerning the impact of these approaches.

Public Concern Mounts

The magnitude of drug dealing activity has increased public pressure for police to take stronger action. A May 1988 *New York Times*—CBS News Survey found that 16 percent of respondents considered drugs to be the Nation's number one problem.[1] That is in sharp contrast to a 1985 Gallup Poll in which only 2 percent said drug abuse was number one.[2]

Police share the public's concern. They are especially worried about the rise in cocaine use, particularly in its most potent form known as "crack" or "rock." In many jurisdictions police report that crack has become the street drug of choice.

Crack's popularity is relatively new but has been building for several years. NIJ Drug Use Forecasting (DUF) tests have shown significant increases in cocaine use among arrestees in a number of major cities over a 3-year period.[3] In Washington, D.C., cocaine use more than tripled.[4]

Crack is considered highly addictive. It is also readily available, trafficked in the open, of high quality (not significantly cut), and cheap. Crack users come from all social strata, and many turn to both property and street crime to finance their habits.

Police and other experts think that rising crime is linked to crack sales. Indeed, threatened and actual violence by drug dealers is a growing concern. Homicides associated with the control of drug markets are up in many cities, with residents of high-crime drug-sales areas living in constant fear. In some places, community residents are afraid to call the police because of threatened retaliation by drug dealers. Some drug dealers are reported to have forced public housing residents out of their homes so they could use the vacated apartments for temporary drug distribution or consumption.

The importation and distribution of illegal drugs appear to be well organized and to follow a basic four-step process. Producers of illegal drugs, or "kingpins," funnel narcotics to midlevel distributors. These in turn pass the drugs to lower level distributors who control street sellers.

Actually, the entire importation and distribution process is far more complex. Many individuals are involved as drugs move from stage to stage in a series of complicated relationships that vary according to geographical location and type of drug distributed. In many cities, gangs control street sales, like the "Bloods" and the "Crips" of the West Coast, or Jamaican "posses" and other ethnic minority gangs in other areas.

Street sales of powdered cocaine and crack follow several patterns. One of the most common means of distribution is through "crack houses." Typically, these are abandoned houses, some highly fortified against police intrusion and easily identified by both police and local citizens. In "open" crack houses, users can purchase and consume crack or other drugs on the premises. Hotels, motels, and apartments in rental buildings or public housing projects form yet another distribution avenue. On-the-corner street sales are also commonplace.

Because of the high volume and high visibility of illegal drug sales, police in many jurisdictions have been besieged with complaints from residents of neighborhoods where drug dealers and "dope houses" operate. In addition, there has been significant political and media pressure for metropolitan police departments and Federal law enforcement agencies to "do something" about drug sales in U.S. cities.

In response, Congress has recently stiffened the penalties for those who traffic in or use drugs, and it has committed greater resources to aid the war against drugs. The 1988 Anti-Drug Bill signed into law on November 18, 1988, provides Federal assistance to communities for treatment, prevention, education, and drug enforcement programs.

Law Enforcement Responds

At all levels, law enforcement agencies are stepping up their activities. They are joining hands with schools to help children resist drugs in prevention efforts such as Project DARE. Local law enforcement agencies are cooperating with each other in the fight. The International Association of Chiefs of Police recently reported, for example, that approximately 72 percent of the departments they surveyed participated in multijurisdictional drug enforcement task forces.[5]

A number of police departments, particularly in large metropolitan areas, are using new approaches in conjunction with more traditional ones. They are targeting alternative strategies against street sales and users and retaining traditional strategies for enforcement efforts against the kingpins and producers.

Control of drug supplies is generally a Federal responsibility, but Federal law enforcement agencies regularly receive help from State and local personnel through regional, statewide, or citywide task forces. Supply control efforts at the Federal level include source crop eradication, shipment interdiction, asset seizure and forfeiture, and investigations into organized crime and money laundering. These strategies are often interrelated.

In dealing with midlevel distribution, local law enforcement agencies use some of these same traditional approaches. They form task forces and employ interdiction strategies. They also use the traditional undercover and surveillance techniques that lead to search and arrest warrants against midlevel distributors. Where midlevel distribution is controlled by gangs, police emphasize gang enforcement investigations.

Street sales enforcement is almost exclusively a local responsibility. Among such traditional tactics are undercover surveillance and "buy busts," in which undercover officers buy drugs on the street and then arrest the sellers. Arresting drug dealers for possession and for possession with intent to distribute is another strategy traditionally employed at this stage.

Finally, at the end of the distribution chain, police arrest individual users for possession.

New Strategies Join the Old

A number of new approaches are being tried against street sales and users, primarily by larger metropolitan police departments under funding from the Bureau of Justice Assistance and the National Institute of Justice. The newer approaches are not necessarily discrete; some departments combine several to mount a comprehensive attack on drug sales.

Figure 19-1
Local Law Enforcement Strategies Against Drugs

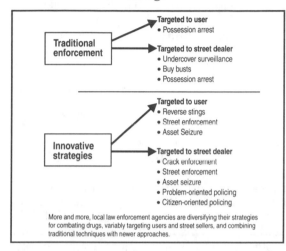

More and more, local law enforcement agencies are diversifying their strategies for combating drugs, variably targeting users and street sellers, and combining traditional techniques with newer approaches.

Nor are all of the "new" techniques entirely new. Some, like crackdowns and civil abatement procedures, are refinements of techniques police have long been using to deal with prostitution, for instance. The innovation is their application to combating drug sales. The new approaches, like the old ones, are designed to disrupt drug distribution through incapacitation and deterrence, with the ultimate goal of reducing drug consumption, street and property crime, and violence.

At the street-sales level, the new efforts can be roughly categorized as street enforcement, crack enforcement, problem-oriented policing, and citizen-oriented enforcement. Asset seizure and forfeiture also play a role, most often as integral parts of these other strategies. Figure 19.1 presents a summary of both traditional and innovative strategies for local enforcement of drug laws.

Street and Crack Enforcement

Both street enforcement and crack enforcement are street-sales oriented; street programs deal with all types of drug sales, and crack programs focus on sales of this increasingly popular drug. These programs target drug sales locations and the street distributors themselves. Police use surveillance, informants, and information from drug hotlines to locate street sales and identify sellers.

Undertaking street enforcement and crack enforcement programs means increasing police personnel hours for narcotics control. Narcotics staff or tactical squads may work overtime, or patrol officers may be assigned to street-sales enforcement duty.

Specific police strategies depend on the nature of the drug problem. In cities where distribution takes place primarily through fortified crack houses, tactical or narcotics squads use search and arrest warrants, sometimes gaining entry by using heavy construction equipment. Where street sales are commonplace, the police may conduct saturation patrols or periodic large-scale arrests of suspected dealers in drug hot spots. These are frequently referred to as "sweeps" or "round-ups."

Civil enforcement procedures are gaining acceptance as well, and police are relying more and more on asset seizure at this distribution level. For example, if a house is being used as a crack house, the police typically notify the owner—through the public works department or the city attorney's office that the property is being used for illegal drug sales. If the owner fails to take action, civil seizure of the property takes place and the house may be forfeited or even destroyed.

Street and crack enforcement strategies make use of building and fire code enforcement, along with tenant eviction if the property is rented. In jurisdictions where public housing projects are the center of drug sales, the police and public housing authorities cooperate in securing tenant evictions and enforcing lease conditions.

Many innovative street enforcement programs focus on the purchaser and user of illegal narcotics. Police keep drug sales hotspots under surveillance and arrest both purchasers and sellers. Where it is permitted, police seize user assets, such as automobiles.

Another innovative approach is the "reverse sting," in which undercover police pose as drug dealers and arrest users who ask to buy narcotics or actually engage in what they assume is a drug transaction. User arrests may take place at the time of the sale or later in large-scale roundups of suspects, depending on the users' transience. This strategy is not as common as some of the others because of legal and operational concerns about police posing as dealers and engaging in what look like actual drug sales.

Some 17 cities across the United States are using street and crack enforcement programs administered by the Institute for Law and Justice and funded by the Bureau of Justice Assistance through its Narcotics Control Technical Assistance Program.

Problem-Oriented Policing

Problem-oriented approaches apply the model successfully developed in Newport News, Virginia.[6] Under this approach, police collect and analyze data on individuals, incidents, and police responses to crimes as the first step in developing particular prevention or enforcement strategies. The Police Executive Research Forum is currently managing the implementation of this approach in five cities with funds from the Bureau of Justice Assistance.

Instead of relying on subjective or anecdotal assessments of their local drug problem, police departments employing problem-oriented policing techniques collect and analyze objective data like crime statistics and citizen surveys. By looking at drug-arrest data, police in some cities have found that young adults are the group most actively involved in the drug trade; in other cities they have found juveniles to be the more heavily involved group.

Problem analysis often shows that many conditions that are not the responsibility of the police—such as the presence of abandoned buildings and the lack of recreational facilities—contribute to a city's drug problem.[7]

Citizen-Oriented Policing

The premise of the citizen-oriented model of policing is that the police cannot solve the drug problem alone but must join with the community in controlling crime and ensuring public safety. The National Institute of Justice is evaluating implementation of the citizen-oriented approach to fighting drugs in several jurisdictions.

Local citizens establish community groups to eliminate the conditions that contribute to neighborhood drug sales. In Seattle, for example, citizens have set up their own drug hotline, pressured the legislature for new abatement laws and jail space, and conducted neighborhood cleanup projects.[8] The distinctive feature of this approach is that a major responsibility for breaking the drug distribution chain rests not just with the police but also with neighborhood groups who work hand in hand with the police.

Evaluating the Strategies

While research in the 1970's examined conventional narcotics enforcement in selected jurisdictions,[9] little is known about the effect of more recent police innovations. A number of primarily descriptive assessments of the evolution or implementation of particular programs exist,[10] but scientific and professional law enforcement literature contains only limited quantitative evidence on program effects.

Reports of program outputs (actions of police) rather than program outcomes (reduction in crime) have been published. Some authors report that local enforcement efforts have resulted in more drug confiscation, seizures, and arrests.[11] These findings are not surprising. When greater resources are focused on a problem, higher program output can be expected.

Yet recent evaluations of some specific programs in several cities indicate that innovative law enforcement may indeed be affecting drug distribution. In Lynn, Massachusetts, a vigorous street-level enforcement program attacked an open, active heroin trade in the city.

Six State troopers and a detective from the Lynn Police Department were assigned to a drug task force to crack down on street sales by making such transactions more difficult. By using undercover operations, surveillance, and information gathered from a drug hotline, police made more arrests and executed more search warrants in the targeted area. Following this crackdown, heroin consumption appeared to decline, robberies and burglaries decreased sharply, and the very visible street sales traffic disappeared with no evidence of displacement into substitute markets in the city.[12]

New York City implemented Operation Pressure Point a vigorous street-level enforcement program in Manhattan.[13] During the operation's initial phase, narcotics enforcement was strengthened and a highly visible saturation patrol was initiated, leading to a substantial increase in narcotics and misdemeanor arrests. Traffic and parking enforcement efforts in the area were also stepped up. The results resembled Lynn's: many open markets were closed and crime was reduced. It was unclear, however, if displacement of the markets occurred.[14]

Evaluations of other street-level efforts, however, showed different outcomes. In Lawrence, Massachusetts, for example, a program similar to Lynn's did not seem to affect robbery and burglary rates, and alternative street markets in neighboring jurisdictions appeared to draw purchasers away from Lawrence so that the trade did not decline in real terms.[15]

While the research conducted thus far is limited and the findings mixed, evaluations currently under way hold promise of useful findings. The Police Foundation, under a National Institute of Justice grant, is assessing the effects of community-oriented street-level enforcement in Birmingham, Alabama, and Oakland, California.[16]

In both these cities, research is measuring the effects of street enforcement and police-community contact on crime, on citizens' perceptions and fears of crime, and on other attitudes. In one area of Oakland, police implemented a door-to-door campaign to stimulate police-citizen interaction. In a second area they implemented a rapid undercover response to drug hotline calls, and in a third they used both strategies. The effects in these areas are being compared to those in a control area.

In Seattle, a study is evaluating the implementation of the citizen-oriented policing strategy. The research will examine the problems incurred and the reactions of the public, the police, and other agencies.

Questions for Future Study

Upcoming research must address a number of issues so that sound conclusions can be drawn about the utility of the innovative approaches discussed in this article. Answers to the following questions will aid informed policy choices:

- What is the exact nature and extent of the drug problem in our cities? Many departments implementing new strategies lack baseline data or the analysis capability to assess the problem.

- What is the link between drug use and crime and what is meant by drug-related crime?

- To what extent is implementation of innovative strategies coopted in favor of "tried and true" traditional methods'?

- Some of the new approaches call for quite different police responses from the reactive ones developed over the past few decades. Are there particular organizational or management factors that contribute to the potential success or failure of these new approaches?

- What are the long-term consequences, if any, of these new programs?

- How do these programs compare in cost and effectiveness with other approaches, such as education, interdiction, and traditional narcotics investigation techniques?

- Do the programs reduce drug sales? Or do they just disperse them to other locations?

Notes

1. *Time*, May 30, 1988. "Thinking the Unthinkable," p. 14.
2. George Gallup, Jr., 1995. *The Gallup Report*, Report No. 235. Princeton, New Jersey, The Gallup Poll, pp. 20-21.
3. National Institute of Justice, 1988. "Attorney General Announces NIJ Drug Use Forecasting System," *NIJ Reports*, No. 208, March/April 1988. Washington, D.C., NIJ, p. 8.

4. Ibid.

5. International Association of Chiefs of Police, June 1988. *Reducing Crime by Reducing Drug Abuse: A Manual for Police Chiefs and Sheriffs.* Gaithersburg, Maryland, IACP, p. 65.

6. William Spelman and John E. Eck, 1987. "Newport News Tests Problem-Oriented Policing," *NIJ Reports,* No. 201, January/February 1987. Washington, D.C., NIJ, p. 2.

7. Tia Clark, 1988. "Cuyler: A Joint Effort," *Problem Solving Quarterly,* Vol. 1, No. 3, p. 4.

8. For additional information concerning the South Seattle Crime Reduction Project, contact George D. Shollenberger, Program Manager, Public Safety and Security, National Institute of Justice, 1-202-724-2596.

9. See for example: L. B. DeFleur. 1975, "Biasing Influences on Drug Arrest Records: Implications for Deviance Research," *American Sociological Review,* 40, pp. 88-103; P. Manning, 1980, *The Narc's Game: Organizational and Informational Limits on Drug Law Enforcement,* Cambridge, Massachusetts, MIT Press; W.F. McDonald, 1973, "Administratively Choosing the Drug Criminal: Police Discretion in the Enforcement of Drug Laws," *Journal of Drug Issues,* Spring, pp. 123-124; M. Moore, 1977, *Buy and Bust: The Effective Regulation of an Illicit Market in Heroin,* Lexington, Massachusetts, D.C. Heath; J. Skolnick, 1975, *Justice Without Trial,* New York, John Wiley and Sons:

and J. Williams et al., 1979, *Police Narcotics Control: Patterns and Strategies,* Washington, D.C., U.S. Government Printing Office.

10. For example, Jack Crowley, 1986. "A Community Helps Put a 'CAP' on Drug Pushers," *Law and Order,* December, pp. 136-139.

11. For example, Institute for Law and Justice, 1988, "Crack Enforcement Program: Minneapolis," *Narcotics Control Technical Assistance Program Newsletter,* Vol. 2, No. 3, p. 1.

12. Mark Kleiman, *Bringing Back Street-Level Heroin Enforcement, summarized in NIJ Reports,* No. 202, March/April 1987, Washington, D.C. NIJ, p. 5.

13. Bocklet, Richard, 1987. "Operation Pressure Point," *Law and Order,* February, pp. 48-52.

14. Mark Kleiman, 1988. "Crackdowns: The Effects of Intensive Enforcement on Retail Heroin Dealing" in *Street Level Drug Enforcement: Examining the Issues,* Marcia Chaiken (ed.), Washington, NIJ.

15. Ibid.

16. For additional information, contact Dr. Craig Uchida, National Institute of Justice, 1-202-724-2959.

20

Police Handling of People With Mental Illness

Elizabeth B. Perkins,
Gary W. Cordner, and
Kathryn E. Scarborough

One longstanding feature of the police function is that society asks the police to deal with certain kinds of chronic problems that "nice, upstanding citizens" would rather not be bothered with—skid row drunks, panhandlers, homeless people, illegal aliens, and other such social outcasts. One interesting variation on this aspect of policing concerns people with mental illness, who are less likely to be confined in this era of deinstitutionalization, and more likely to be out in society and on the streets. We often treat such people as outcasts too, and mental illness can sometimes cause disturbing and even violent behavior, inevitably bringing such matters to the attention of the police, with the expectation that order will be restored so that good citizens are not offended or alarmed. On the other hand, mental illness can strike the rich as well as the poor, so society has more of an ambivalent view, and police tend to act with more circumspection than when handling, say, a homeless person. Do you think the police are the best agency to handle these types of problems? What other alternatives are there?

Police handling of people with mental illness has been a topic of great debate ever since the 1960s and 1970s, when deinstitutionalization policies went into effect (see, for example, Bittner, 1967 and Matthews, 1970). Laws have been enacted that make it hard to have people with mental illnesses involuntarily committed to hospitals for treatment (Finn, 1989). These laws emphasize that it is not a crime to have a mental illness. Now that a person who has a mental illness must be "dangerous to themselves or others" in order to be committed, it is often difficult to get help for those who seem to need it (Pogrebin, 1986).

At the present time, there are no cures for mental illness, only treatments that can alleviate some of the symptoms and help control behavior. Because (1) there is no cure for mental illness, (2) many times a person with mental illness is not aware of their illness, and (3) there is no way to force people with mental illness into treatment unless they are considered dangerous to themselves or others, a large portion of the mentally ill population is left "on the street." This poses problems for police officers. Most of the time the problem is not people with mental illness as serious offenders; usually crimes committed by such offenders are misdemeanors (Janik, 1992). More often, the problem lies in police officers being called to handle a person with mental illness "whose public behavior warranted some form of social intervention" (Finn and Sullivan, 1988: 1). Many times persons with mental illness come to the attention of the police because they are causing a disturbance by trespassing or loitering, or they call the police themselves for help with "imaginary" problems that are brought on by their illness. Although such problems may not seem particularly serious, they can be some of the most time-consuming matters that police are asked to handle.

A majority of any police department's man-hours are spent handling minor crimes, disorder, and providing services (Hanewicz, Fransway, and O'Neill, 1982; Pogrebin, 1986); as much as 10% of police officers' "encounters" in such situations may involve people with mental illness (Janik, 1992: 23). Even this statistic may underestimate the true amount of man-hours spent dealing with people with mental illness, though, because these encounters tend to use a disproportionate amount of officers' total time. Pogrebin (1986: 69) found that the average length of time an officer spent on mental health calls was 74 minutes, remarkably long for non-criminal cases.

Deinstitutionalization

In the mid-1960s, deinstitutionalization policies went into effect, and the country moved toward what is referred to as "community-based treatment." Deinstitutionalization and community-based treatment were made possible by "the development of psychotropic medications, research that identified the benefits of community care, patients' rights litigation, and cost-saving incentives" (Murphy, 1986: 12).

It was hoped that psychotropic medications could effectively control the dangerous and destructive impulses of persons with mental illness. The idea was that, with their erratic behavior under control, persons with mental illness would be able to function in the community. These new medications made the hospital environment unnecessary for the majority of people with mental illness (PERF, 1997). Patients' rights litigation also persuaded states to begin passing legislation with strict criteria that a person must meet before being committed to a mental health facility involuntarily.

In 1961, research revealed that mental institutions were not treating people with mental illnesses effectively and that, since people with mental illnesses were not receiving the care necessary to reintegrate to their respective communities, they should be released into the community so that they could learn necessary skills with the help of a support system (PERF, 1997). Consequently, federal programs were established to assist in building and operating community mental health centers which provided mental health treatment, education, and job training to people with mental illness.

The philosophy of community mental health is based on the postulate that a person with mental illness should not be isolated from the community because of their mental illness. The most important aspect of the community-based treatment movement was to establish networks within communities that would enable people with mental illness to live freely in the community, rather than being locked away in a mental ward. These networks were to consist of public and private agencies that would help people with mental illness adapt to living in the community, and to service them with mental health care (Murphy, 1986). Unfortunately, these networks never reached their potential because of financial problems and unanticipated resistance from persons with mental illnesses (Wachholz and Mullaly, 1993).

The Police Role

Across the country, cooperative law enforcement/social service networks have been formed with the hopes of easing tensions, relieving police officers from having to deal with people with mental illness who have not committed crimes, and providing proper care for people with mental illness (Gillig, Dumaine, Widish Stammer, Hillard and Grubb, 1990). Though such networks do not solve all of the problems that communities face in dealing with people with mental illness, many police departments are beginning to see the benefits of working with social service workers, and vice-versa. One of the most important aspects of these networks is opening the lines of communication. This enables agencies to educate one another, gain a better understanding of what the other does, and build a working relationship that not only benefits the police department and mental health workers, but also those with mental illness.

These networks include a variety of arrangements, ranging from committees of law enforcement and mental health workers that meet to discuss problems on a regular basis, to mental health workers providing 24-hour on-scene emergency assistance. Early results have shown that everyone benefits. For example, in communities that have networks, the time police officers spend dealing with people with mental illness has dropped, there is less danger involved, and greater job satisfaction is experienced by police officers (Finn, 1989). Mental health workers in communities with networks also benefit because they spend less time evaluating unnecessary police referrals, and people with mental illness are handled by those better equipped to deal with their needs.

Some police officers appreciate the greater involvement of mental health workers in the field, while others take a dim view of this practice. The officers who are critical of the mental health profession feel that the mental health system should be doing even more than it does. For example, Perkins (1996) found that officers felt that many of the problems they had in dealing with mental illness situations were caused by failures of other agencies, rather than their own lack of skill or knowledge. Police officers often feel that the mental health system is responsible for the majority of problems they have in dealing with people with mental illness. Their rationale for this is that "the mental health field owns the responsibility for the breakdown in treatment for the insane—not the police. You guys broke it—you fix it" (Gillig et al., 1990: 665). One likely reason for this sentiment is that the police were excluded from the policy decisions that led to deinstitutionalization, and were never fully prepared for the impact that persons with mental illness would have on their communities (Goldstein, 1990).

Information sharing between law enforcement and mental health agencies is also pertinent. Some police officers complain that they do not receive enough information, especially case specific data, from mental health workers. Most mental health workers do not give away information on patients because of confidentiality requirements. Much of the tension that exists between mental health workers and police officers centers around "the issue of confidentiality of patient information versus the needs of officers on the beat" (Gillig et al., 1990: 665). While it is obvious that mental health workers must respect the privacy of their patients, we might also examine the situation from the police officers' point of view. Officers are expected to assess the mental well-being of a person on the street without the benefit of much training or any kind of background information on the person. Lack of specific information on mentally ill persons has been found to be a primary concern of police officers (Perkins, 1996). She found that officers' views about the adequacy of their training were mixed,

however. Interestingly, younger officers felt more adequately trained than their older and more experienced colleagues.

Police officer reaction to people with mental illness depends on several different things, including department policy, training, and officer personality (Ruiz, 1993; Territo, 1983). The majority of police departments include a section of training in their academies on how to handle people with mental illness, and some also address the issue during in-service training. However, training related to dealing with people with mental illness averages less than four hours for police academies, and considerably less than that during in-service training (Ruiz, 1993). This is not nearly enough time for officers to become educated about an area as complex as mental illness. Of course, police officers are not expected to become experts on mental illness. But considering the percentage of calls that departments respond to involving individuals who are suffering from mental illness, it makes sense, at the very least, to familiarize officers with the different aspects of mental illness (Ruiz, 1993; Janik, 1992). Reflecting the pragmatic orientations of most police, though, Perkins (1996) found that patrol officers emphasized the need for more training in effectively *handling* people with mental illness, as opposed to training to distinguish different *types* of mental illness.

Ruiz (1993) conducted research on interactions between police and persons with mental illness, and discovered that one main problem police departments have with people with mental illness is that they lack clear policies and procedures for dealing with such persons (see also Hanewicz et al., 1982). He found that some departments have very detailed policies and procedures for officers to follow when dealing with people with mental illness. However, other departments have policies that have not been updated since deinstitutionalization policies took effect, and many departments lack formal policies and procedures altogether.

Ruiz (1993) found that when a police department lacks specific policies and procedures on how best to deal with persons with mental illness, it leaves the decision making up to the individual police officer, who probably has little or no understanding of mental illness. For some officers, this can be intimidating and frustrating, leading to a large number of arrests of people with mental illness on misdemeanor offenses (Hanewicz et al., 1982). This is an unfortunate practice since individuals with mental illness will not usually receive any psychiatric treatment while in jail (Gillig et al., 1990).

People with mental illness are often fearful when confronted by police officers. This fear may stem from the officer's uniform, or because of an officer's intimidating attitude. This fear may cause the person with mental illness to become aggressive, or may simply make it more difficult for the person to comply with the requests and/or orders of the officer. Moreover, if an officer feels awkward dealing with a person with mental illness, he or she may try to force the person to comply with requests and commands before the person is completely aware of what is occurring. This tactic is an attempt by the officer to hurry the situation, so that he may be finished with this person who makes him uncomfortable (Ruiz, 1993).

Police officers should be aware that all people with mental illness are not violent, though recent studies show that people with mental illness do have a slightly higher rate of violence when being arrested than the general population. This is especially true when mental illness is mixed with substance abuse (Mulvey, 1994). But this does not mean that all people with mental illness are violent, and in fact many have the ability to reason (Ruiz, 1993). Often, the misconceptions that police officers have about mental illness come from a lack of information about the subject.

Another problem area is the frequent lack of specific contextual information in dealing with people with mental illness. When officers are dispatched, they are usually given limited information. For example, a call to handle a person with a mental illness will show up as an individual "disturbing the peace" or some other type of "disorder" call, or the individual may be calling to complain about a "suspicious" person or harassing communication, and sometimes no further information is given (Ruiz, 1993). Perkins (1996) found that newer officers felt that

their lack of familiarity with previously identified mentally ill individuals was especially problematic, both for officer safety and for efficient handling of calls and incidents. On the other hand, if a person is pre-identified as having a mental illness, this may create problems if the officer is inadequately trained in how to respond to the mentally ill. Unfortunately, officers may approach these situations expecting to deal with an aggressive person and the situation often escalates.

If we want to destroy the myths surrounding mental illness, we would do well to educate and train police officers more effectively (Hanewicz et al., 1982). This would enable police officers to handle calls involving people with mental illness in a safer and more competent manner (Territo, 1983). Considering that the average citizen does not understand mental illness and all of its nuances, police officers cannot be expected to adequately understand the nature of mental illness without proper training. This will hopefully erase any personal biases that an officer has about those with mental illness (see Lester and Pickett, 1978). It should also raise their level of tolerance in dealing with "strange" behavior that may be caused by mental illness. This in turn may increase their sensitivity and ability to interact with people with mental illnesses in a more patient and effective manner (Murphy, 1986).

Another objective should be to educate officers as to why they are called upon by citizens to deal with persons with mental illness. This is important, since a call for service involving a person with mental illness is not regarded as a "choice" call (Gillig et al., 1990; Wachholz and Mullaly, 1993). In fact, most officers consider calls dealing with people with mental illness to be nuisances, or even frightening because of the risk involved in dealing with people who may behave in an unpredictable manner. Therefore, it would be beneficial if officers understood that citizens in the community have fears and prejudices about people with mental illness just as they have. Further, the general public is not known for its tolerance of "bizarre" behavior by people they fear might be dangerous (Murphy, 1986).

Since the police are easy to reach, and available 24-hours a day, they are the logical choice when a citizen feels threatened by a person with an apparent mental disorder. Also, police officers have the authority to detain, arrest, and use force if necessary, and they have a legal obligation to respond to calls (Finn and Sullivan, 1988). Mental health agencies may also call upon the police for assistance in dealing with people with mental illness. For example, if mental health officials have a patient who is violent or disruptive, or if the patient needs to be transported, the police may be called upon for help. People with mental illness also call the police themselves for help with "incidents" that are a result of their illness (PERF, 1997).

Critics of the way police handle persons with mental illness feel that the problem extends far beyond deinstitutionalization, stricter commitment guidelines, and a fragmented mental health system. Wachholz and Mullaly (1993: 291), for example, contend that because of our "incomplete and underdeveloped welfare state," the police are forced to deal with people with mental illness when they are brought to their attention. This puts the police in the role of "agents of social control, and associates the mentally ill and the poor as classes of people who need to be controlled."

Community Policing

One way to reconceptualize the whole issue of police handling of people with mental illness is to consider it within the context of community policing (Cordner, 1997). At least six of the elements of community policing (COP) presented in Chapter 10 of this anthology seem to be pertinent to this topic—broad police function, citizen input, prevention focus, geographic emphasis, community partnerships, and problem solving—as described below (adapted from PERF, 1997: 61-63).

Under a broad view of the police function, responding to people with mental illnesses might be seen as just as much a part of "real police work" as other, more directly crime-related activities. In fact, this aspect of police work corresponds closely with five traditional objectives of policing, as follows:

- *Crime Control*–People with mental illness may be victims, witnesses, or perpetrators of crime. Dealing with these people well, whether as victims, witnesses, or perpetrators, is obviously important.

- *Order Maintenance*–Police often encounter people with mental illness when other citizens call to report disorderly or disturbing behavior. In these situations, officers need to restore order—doing so is greatly aided by information and training about mental illness.

- *Fear Reduction*–Citizens often have unnecessary or uninformed fears about people with mental illnesses. Police officers can help reduce these fears by their own actions and by educating neighbors and complainants about mental illness.

- *Aiding Those in Danger*–Persons with mental illness are sometimes taken advantage of or threatened by others out of ignorance or avarice. Police officers have a responsibility to protect all people in danger of harm, including people with mental illness.

- *Helping Those in Need*–Persons with mental illness sometimes simply need help—they may have been abandoned by friends and family, they may have "fallen through the cracks" of society, and/or they may not be taking proper care of themselves. Police officers have a responsibility to provide help to all kinds of people who cannot help themselves, including persons with mental illness.

Citizen input, another element of COP, could assist the police greatly in determining how best to respond to people with mental illness in their jurisdictions. Most citizens probably do not have strong views on this subject or even care very much. But some citizens and some professional groups have particular viewpoints and interests and should have input to a police department's policies and programs for dealing with people with mental illness. These might include (1) individual people with mental illness, (2) family members of people with mental illness, (3) coalitions and groups of people with mental illness, such as local chapters of the National Alliance for the Mentally Ill, (4) mental health service providers, (5) related social service providers, and (6) medical service providers.

Police departments could also adopt, as much as possible, a preventive approach to handling people with mental illness. They could try to prevent crimes involving such people (whether as victims or perpetrators), prevent disorder caused by people with mental illness, prevent fear of such individuals, and so on, rather than merely waiting for such conditions to occur and then applying a reactive response. Preventing such problems from occurring in the first place benefits everyone—people with mental illness, other citizens, the community in general, and the police department.

Officers with geographically-based assignments, an element of COP, would be familiar with any chronic problems in their areas, including those related to persons with mental illness. They would know the people and the conditions involved better than officers whose assignments are less permanent. People in the community, with or without mental illness, would then recognize the officers who work in their neighborhoods and trust them to deal with problems fairly and effectively. While it is true that the overall problem of dealing with people with mental illness is a community-wide issue, problems created by specific individuals and facilities are usually neighborhood-based and best dealt with by officers who are intimately familiar with the neighborhood and its residents.

Police officers could also develop partnerships with citizens, community groups, government agencies, and private organizations to help deal with problems related to persons with mental illness. This could be as simple and locally-based as organizing neighborhood residents to help watch out for the interests of a specific Alzheimer's patient, or as extensive as networking with mental health providers and others to improve the overall system in the jurisdiction for handling persons with mental illness. The key point is that, by developing and using such partnerships, police officers increase their chances of dealing effectively with problems surrounding people with mental illness, *and* they relieve themselves of shouldering the entire burden of handling such problems. While handling people with mental illness often is a police responsibility, it is not solely a police responsibility. Sometimes police need to remind other individuals and institutions of their responsibilities and then work with them to effect more viable solutions.

Finally, police officers could do more than just handle calls and incidents involving people with mental illness—whenever possible, they could try to identify underlying conditions that, if improved, might help avoid future calls and incidents. This might involve referring individuals to service providers, looking for repeat-call locations and individuals, taking the time to educate neighbors, bringing legal pressure upon family members, or a host of other possible actions. In each situation, the best actions depend on the circumstances—sometimes, the officer has to do some digging for information in order to understand the dynamics and underlying conditions of the situation. This problem-oriented approach is discussed further in the next section.

Problem-Oriented Policing

The first thing that needs to be understood is that police cannot solve the problem of mental illness—they are not neurologists, psychiatrists or pharmacists. The kinds of problems that police *may* be able to solve are crime, disorder, and service problems in the community that involve people with mental illness as victims, offenders, or otherwise interested parties. For example, in Madison, Wisconsin, several years ago, the bizarre and sometimes offensive conduct of people with mental illness on the streets led to city-wide concern about the problem of deinstitutionalization. The number of persons with mental illness on the streets of the city was repeatedly estimated in news accounts as being in excess of 1,000. When the problem was studied, however, it was determined that no more than 20 individuals accounted for most of the incidents, and that their behavior often resulted from failure to take prescribed medications. The local mental health service then established a program of special, intensive care for these individuals, monitoring them through a variety of arrangements including, when deemed necessary, obtaining court approval for a limited guardianship. The program has continued since then, with newly identified patients being added to the monitored group. The original problem—both the fear and the actual incidents—has been greatly reduced, and it appears that the people with mental illness in the program have also benefitted.

Problem solving, or problem-oriented policing (POP), is a method of policing in which officers search for the underlying causes and conditions that give rise to crimes, calls for service, and other incidents. When such underlying causes and conditions are identified, and once they are analyzed, officers then search for alternative solutions. A wide range of both enforcement-oriented and non-enforcement alternatives is considered, with the objective of making a long-term impact on the problem.

The traditional approach to patrol often leads to rather superficial police work—officers race from call to call, not doing very much at each one other than writing a report or demanding that people cease their disruptive behavior. Then officers jump back into their cars to wait for the next call at which they will not do very much either. After doing this kind of reactive work for a few years, many officers find it rather frustrating and not very satisfying.

The problem solving approach offers the opportunity to have a more significant and lasting impact. When underlying problems are identified, officers take the time to create and implement solutions that are not as superficial as just writing a report or demanding that people straighten up. Sometimes these solutions lead to real and lasting improvements that give officers a sense of accomplishment and satisfaction.

It is important to explain what POP means (and does not mean) by underlying problems, causes, or conditions. For the most part, police officers cannot hope to correct the real root causes of crime and disorder—things like poverty, racism, adolescence, and mental illness. But there may be mid-range causes

and conditions that can be dealt with—things like abandoned houses, poor street lighting, badly positioned bus stops, negligent landlords, unresponsive city agencies, lax procedures at halfway houses, and so forth. These kinds of conditions are "incubators" or "generators" of crime, disorder, and calls for service. Doing something about such conditions can prevent future crimes, disorder, and calls from occurring.

People with mental illness may be involved in virtually any kind of problem in the community—just like any other citizen. However, there are several ways in which problems might arise that have specific connections to people with mental illness:

- *Chronic calls involving the same individual*: as a criminal offender, a crime victim, a disorderly subject, a missing subject, etc.

- *Repeat calls to the same location*: a residence, a public place, a group home or shelter, a treatment facility, etc.

- *Community-wide issues*: how best to respond to the needs of Alzheimer patients, for example.

- *Breakdowns in the system*: poor coordination between police and mental health service providers, unnecessary jailing of persons with mental illness, conflict over judicial treatment of people with mental illness, etc.

- *Internal police department problems*: inadequate training, failure of dispatchers to fully notify officers about calls involving people with mental illness, information systems that fail to identify chronic individuals and locations, etc.

In each of these types of situations, a problem-solving approach has the potential to significantly reduce the scope and impact of the problem. If all that officers do is to respond to calls, write reports, and scold people, however, (1) problems will not be solved, (2) underlying conditions will not be improved, (3) neither the community in general nor people with mental illness in particular will be well served, and (4) the 911 phones will just keep on ringing.

As one illustration of the potential benefits of taking a **POP** approach, Perkins (1996) analyzed all calls for service in one year in Lexington, Kentucky, that were issued a primary or secondary code for mental illness. Out of 609 such calls, 201 emanated from just 17 addresses (two hospitals, two social service centers, three boarding homes, and ten apartment buildings) that were responsible for three or more calls each, and 54 calls came from just five addresses. Clearly, there existed a relatively small number of "hot spots" (Sherman, 1989; Sherman, Gartin, and Buerger, 1989) responsible for a disproportionate share of calls involving people with mental illnesses.

Additional analysis revealed two other interesting situations. First, these 17 addresses were found to generate a large number of other types of calls as well, ranging from disorder and noise to personal and property crimes. The total annual number of all types of calls at these repeat addresses ranged from 20 to 577. Secondly, the suspicion that the city-wide total of 609 mental illness calls for one year was a gross underestimate was confirmed in at least one case. At an apartment building officially logged for six such calls, a total of 33 calls were discovered to have been made by one chronic complainant known to suffer from mental illness. This strongly suggested that the problem is much more extensive than indicated by the call for service data, and verified that chronic mental illness-related repeat call locations could be identified and then made the focus of sustained attention.

Conclusion

Thirty years after the onset of deinstitutionalization, police handling of people with mental illnesses remains a major concern for both the police and the community. At the level of individual incident-handling, five sets of issues seem to be most problematic and worthy of addressing:

- *Attitudes*–Many police officers and citizens continue to have misconceptions about, and irrational fears of, people with mental illness.

- *Training*–The extent of training provided to police officers is often inadequate, and the proper mix and focus of training (understanding vs. diagnosis vs. street-level handling) continues to be debated.

- *Policies*–Many police agencies do not have precise, clear, and well-understood policies and procedures to guide their officers in their responses to mental illness-related situations.

- *Communication*–Frequently, communication within police departments, as well as among the police, the medical community, and social service providers about the handling of people with mental illnesses is inadequate.

- *Systems*–Often, systems for obtaining involuntary commitment decisions are unnecessarily slow and cumbersome, as are processes for actual commitment after decisions are made.

Improvements in any of these areas would likely lead to improved police handling of cases involving people with mental illness. Further progress might be possible if police agencies utilize the community policing and problem-oriented policing approaches described above. These methods attempt to rectify chronic conditions, rather than merely respond better to repeated individual incidents, and they try to engage more community resources in addressing the problem. While it would be foolish to expect any miracle cures for such an endemic issue, it does seem feasible that real gains could be made, so that individuals are handled more humanely, problems are dealt with more efficiently, professional frustrations are reduced, and the community experiences less fear, less disorder, and more confidence in both the police and the mental health system.

Note

Preparation of this chapter was supported, in part, under award # 94-IJ-EX-KOOG from the National Institute of Justice, U.S. Department of Justice. Points of view in this document are those of the authors and do not necessarily represent the official position of the U.S. Department of Justice.

References

Bittner, E. (1967) "Police Discretion in Emergency Apprehension of Mentally Ill Persons." *Social Problems* 15: 278-292.

Cordner, G.W. (1997) "Community Policing: Elements and Effects," in R.G. Dunham and G.P. Alpert, eds., *Critical Issues in Policing: Contemporary Readings*, 3rd ed. Prospect Heights, IL: Waveland, pp. 451-468.

Finn, P. (1989) "Coordinating Services for the Mentally Ill Misdemeanor Offender." *Social Service Review* 63,1: 127-141.

—— and M. Sullivan (1988) "Police Response to Special Populations." *Research in Action*. Washington, DC: National Institute of Justice.

Gillig, P.M., M. Dumaine, J. Widish Stammer, J.R. Hillard and P. Grubb (1990) "What Do Police Officers Really Want From the Mental Health System?" *Hospital and Community Psychiatry* 41(6): 663-665.

Goldstein, H. (1990) *Problem-Oriented Policing*. New York: McGraw-Hill.

Hanewicz, W.B., L.M. Fransway and M.W. O'Neill (1982) "Improving the Linkages Between Community Mental Health and the Police." *Journal of Police Science and Administration* 10(2): 218-223.

Janik, J. (1992) "Dealing with Mentally Ill Offenders." *FBI Law Enforcement Bulletin* (July): 22-26.

Lester, D. and C. Pickett (1978) "Attitudes Toward Mental Illness in Police Officers." *Psychological Reports* 42: 888.

Matthews, A.R. (1970) "Observations on Police Policy and Procedures for Emergency Detention of the Mentally Ill." *Journal of Criminal Law, Criminology and Police Science* 61,2: 283-295.

Mulvey, E.P. (1994) "Assessing the Evidence of a Link Between Mental Illness and Violence." *Hospital and Community Psychiatry* 45(7): 663-668.

Murphy, G.R. (1986) *Improving the Police Response to the Mentally Disabled*. Washington, DC: Police Executive Research Forum.

PERF (1997) *The Police Response to People with Mental Illnesses*. Washington, DC: Police Executive Research Forum.

Perkins, E.B. (1996) "Police Handling of People With Mental Illness: Feasibility and Ramifications of a Problem-Oriented Approach." Master's thesis, Eastern Kentucky University.

Pogrebin, M.R. (1986-1987) "Police Responses for Mental Health Assistance." *Psychiatric Quarterly* 58(1): 66-73.

Ruiz, J. (1993) "An Interactive Analysis Between Uniformed Law Enforcement Officers and the Mentally Ill." *American Journal of Police* 12(4): 149-177.

Sherman, L.W. (1989) "Repeat Calls for Service: Policing the 'Hot Spots'," in D.J. Kenney, ed., *Police and Policing: Contemporary Issues*. New York: Praeger, pp. 150-165.

Sherman, L.W., P.R. Gartin and M.E. Buerger (1989) "Hot Spots of Predatory Crime: Routine Activities and the Criminology of Place." *Criminology* 27,1: 27-55.

Territo, L. (1983) "Assessing Police Procedures in Handling Mentally Disturbed Persons." *Trial* 19: 74-79.

Wachholz, S. and R. Mullaly (1993) "Policing the Deinstitutionalized Mentally Ill: Toward An Understanding of its Function." *Crime, Law, and Social Change* 19: 281-300.

Part VI

Ethics and Deviance

Because police officers are granted substantial authority plus wide discretion in use of that authority, ethical issues and dilemmas arise in the course of police work. Sometimes the issues concern personal gain—should an officer accept free coffee? What about free clothes or liquor or a deeply discounted car? What about Christmas gifts from grateful citizens and business owners? How about keeping found property that will probably never be claimed versus just turning it in to the property room? What about stealing a few items at a burglary scene, knowing the owner will be reimbursed by the insurance company? Or how about stealing drug dealers' money—surely they don't deserve it, do they? And how about the motorists who would really rather not receive another speeding ticket—why not let them give you their fine?

Some of these ethical situations are more clear-cut, with clearer right and wrong choices, than others. There are, of course, even more flagrant forms of graft, bribery, and corruption that could be cited, from police testimony that is "bought and paid for" to vice protection arrangements or out-and-out police extortion. But just where to draw the line between ethical and unethical behavior has long been a divisive issue in policing, with idealists insisting that anything free taints the officer and realists arguing that

some coffee and meals here and there really do little harm. Besides where to draw the line, the other key question is how to make police behavior as ethical as possible—how to eliminate bribery and corruption and minimize acceptance of petty handouts. Police reformers and police administrators have wrestled with this question for years without much success.

Other ethical issues have less to do with personal gain and more to do with the means and ends of policing. Some officers are tempted to rely on their own views of the proper objectives of policing instead of their departments' official goals—for example, they may want to use police authority to keep minorities out of certain neighborhoods or to enforce a dress code on skateboarding youngsters. Similarly, some officers are tempted to bend the rules and use "dirty" means in order to accomplish what they think are good ends. This might include lying in court to obtain a conviction, creating a nonexistent informant in order to obtain a search warrant, or using physical coercion to encourage a suspect to confess. Sometimes these kinds of ethical issues can take the form of real dilemmas, in which the officer is "damned if he does and damned if he doesn't."

The first article in this section covers the whole territory of police ethics, sketching out the terrain and suggesting ways of encouraging more ethical behavior by officers. The other three articles describe and analyze particular types of ethical violations, from lying and drug-related corruption to a particularly deviant type of action, police sexual violence against women. The latter form of police deviance is one that stands well outside any reasoned discussion of ethics and ethical dilemmas. Instead, it represents the more abusive forms of police misconduct in which officers use their authority to personally harm other people—not financially, but physically and psychologically. Moreover, police sexual violence goes beyond the more typical forms of police brutality, as it involves victims who are usually not resisting arrest, or sometimes not even subject to arrest at all, but who are simply the object of desire, humiliation or domination by an officer. This type of behavior is perplexing as well as abhorrent. Although officially condemned everywhere, it seems to persist, perhaps because the police culture remains so male-dominated. ✦

21

Learning Police Ethics

Lawrence Sherman

Open and frank discussion of police ethics is a relatively new phenomenon. Previously, it was not uncommon to discuss specific police problems—corruption or brutality, for example—although even these topics were rarely introduced during police recruit training, when they might seem most effective. Also, it was not unusual for police to talk about their discretion, but such conversations typically focused either on legal constraints or simply on the effectiveness of different alternatives. But what rarely received any serious attention, in practical or academic settings, were the issues surrounding right and wrong—i.e., which police practices were moral and which immoral, which discretionary alternatives were more ethical and which less ethical, how to create more ethical police officers, etc. As you read this article, take note of all the ethical issues and dilemmas involved in police work, and think about how to make policing in the future more ethical.

There are two ways to learn police ethics. One way is to learn on the job, to make your moral decisions in haste under the time pressures of police work. This is by far the most common method of learning police ethics, the way virtually all of the half million police officers in the United States decide what ethical principles they will follow in their work. These decisions are strongly influenced by peer group pressures, by personal self-interest, by passions and emotions in the heat of difficult situations.

There is another way. It may even be a better way. You can learn police ethics in a setting removed from the heat of battle, from the opinions of co-workers, and from the pressures of supervisors. You can think things through with a more objective perspective on the issues. You should be able to make up your mind about many difficult choices before you actually have to make them. And you can take the time to weigh all sides of an issue carefully, rather than making a snap judgment.

The purpose of this article is to provide a basis for this other, less common way of learning police ethics by making the alternative—the usual way of learning police ethics—as clear as possible. This portrait of the on-the-job method is not attractive, but it would be no more attractive if we were to paint the same picture for doctors, lawyers, judges, or college professors. The generalizations we make are not true of all police officers, but they do reflect a common pattern, just as similar patterns are found in all occupations.

Learning New Jobs

Every occupation has a learning process (usually called "socialization") to which its new members are subjected. The socialization process functions to make most "rookies" in the occupation adopt the prevailing rules, values, and attitudes of their senior colleagues in the occupation. Very often, some of the existing informal rules and attitudes are at odds with the formal rules and attitudes society as a whole expects members of the occupation to follows. This puts rookies in a moral dilemma: should the rookies follow the formal rules of society, or the informal rules of their senior colleagues?

These dilemmas vary in their seriousness from one occupation and one organization to the next. Young college professors may find that older professors expect them to devote most of their time to research and writing, while the general public (and their students) expects them to devote most of their time to teaching. With some luck, and a lot of work, they can do both.

Police officers usually face much tougher dilemmas. Like waiters, longshoremen, and retail clerks, they may be taught very early how to steal—at the scene of a burglary, from the body of a dead person, or in other opportunities police confront. They may be taught how to commit perjury in court to insure that their arrests lead to conviction, or how to lie in disciplinary investigations to protect their colleagues. They may be taught how to shake people down, or how to beat people up. Or they may be fortunate enough to go to work in an agency or with a group of older officers, in which none of these violations of official rules is ever suggested to them.

Whether or not rookie police officers decide to act in ways the wider society might view as unethical, they are all subjected to a similar process of being taught certain standards of behavior. Their reactions to that learning as the years pass by can be described as their *moral careers*: the changes in the morality and ethics of their behavior. But the moral career is closely connected to the *occupational career*: the stages of growth and development in becoming a police officer.

This article examines the process of learning a new job as the context for learning police ethics. It then describes the content of the ethical and moral values in many police department "cultures" that are conveyed to new police officers, as well as the rising conflict within police agencies over what those values should be. Finally, it describes the moral career of police officers, including many of the major ethical choices officers make.

Becoming a Police Officer

There are four major stages in the career of anyone joining a new occupation:[1]

- the *choice* of occupation
- the *introduction* to the occupation
- the first *encounter* with doing the occupation's work
- the *metamorphosis* into a full-fledged member of the occupation

Police officers go through these stages, just as doctors and bankers do. But the transformation of the police officer's identity and self-image may be more radical than in many other fields. The process can be overwhelming, changing even the strongest of personalities.

Choice

There are three aspects of the choice to become a police officer. One is the *kind of person* who makes that choice. Another is the *reason* the choice is made, the motivations for doing police work. The third is the *methods* people must use as police officers. None of these aspects of choice appears to predispose police officers to be more or less likely to perform their work ethically.

Many people toy with the idea of doing police work, and in the past decade the applicants for policing have become increasingly diverse. Once a predominately white male occupation, policing has accepted many more minority group members and attracted many more women. More college-educated people have sought out police work, but this may just reflect the higher rate of college graduates in the total population.

What has not changed, apparently, is the socioeconomic background of people who become police. The limited evidence suggests police work attracts the sons and daughters of successful tradespeople, foremen, and civil servants—especially police. For many of them, the good salary (relative to the educational requirements), job security, and prestige of police work represent a good step up in the world, an improvement on their parents' position in life.

The motivation to become a police officer flows naturally from the social position of the people who choose policing. People do not seem to choose policing out of an irrational lust for power or because they have an "authoritarian personality"; the best study on this question showed that New York City police recruits even had a *lower* level of authoritarian attitudes than the general public (although their attitudes become more authoritarian as they become adapted to police work, rising to the general public's level of authoritarian attitudes).[2] Police applicants tend to see police work as an adventure, as a chance to do work out of doors without being cooped up in an office, as a chance to do work that is important for the good of society, and not as a chance to be the "toughest guy on the block." Nothing in a police position seems to predispose police officers towards unethical behavior.

Nor do the methods of selecting police officers seem to affect their long-term moral careers. There was a time when getting on the force was a matter of bribery or political favors for local politicians, or at least a matter of knowing the right people involved in grading the entrance examinations and sitting on the selection committees. But in the 1980s the selection process appears to be highly bureaucratic, with impersonal multiple-choice tests scored by computers playing the most important role in the process.

To be sure, there are still subjective background investigations, personal interviews, and other methods that allow biases to intrude upon the selection process. But these biases, if anything, work in the direction of selecting people who have backgrounds of unquestioned integrity. Combined with the high failure rate among all applicants—sometimes less than one in twenty is hired, which makes some police departments more selective in quantitative terms than the Harvard Law School—the selection process probably makes successful applicants feel that they have been welcomed into an elite group of highly qualified people of very high integrity.

Introduction

But this sense of high ideals about police work may not last for long. The introduction to policing provided by most police academies begins to convey folklore that shows the impossibility of doing things "by the book and the frequent necessity of "bending the rules."

Police recruit training has changed substantially over the past thirty years. Once highly militaristic, it has recently taken on more of the atmosphere of the college classroom. The endurance test-stress environment approach which trainees may be punished for yawning or looking out the window, may still be found in some cities, but it seems to be dying out. Dull lectures on the technical aspects of police work (such as how to fill out arrest reports) and the rates and regulations of the department are now often supplemented by guest lectures on theories of crime and the cultures of various ethnic groups.

But the central method of *moral* instruction does not appear to have changed. The "war story" still remains the most effective device for communicating the history and values of the department. When the instructor tells a "war story," or an anecdote about police work, the class discipline is relaxed somewhat, the interest and attention of the class increase, and an atmosphere of camaraderie between the class and their instructor is established. The content of the war story makes a deep impression on the trainees.

The war stories not only introduce police work as it is experienced by police officers—rather than as an abstract ideal—they also introduce the ethics of police work as something different from what the public, or at least the law and the press, might expect. Van Maanen recounts one excerpt from a police academy criminal law lecture that, while not a "story," indicates the way in which the hidden values of police work are conveyed:

> I suppose you guys have heard of Lucky Baldwin? If not, you sure will when you hit the street. Baldwin happens to be the biggest burglar still operating in this town. Every guy in this department from patrolman to chief would love to get him and make it stick. We've busted him about ten times so far, but he's got an asshole lawyer and money so he always beats the rap. . . . If I ever get a chance to pinch the SOB, I'll do it my way, with my thirty-eight and spare the city the cost of a trial.[3]

Whether the instructor would actually shoot the burglary suspect is open to question, although he could do so legally in most states if the suspect attempted to flee from being arrested. More important is the fact that the rookies spend many hours outside the classroom debating and analyzing the implications of the war stories. These discussions do help them decide how they would act in similar circumstances. But the decisions they reach in these informal bull sessions are probably more attributable to peer pressure and the desire to "fit in" to the culture of the department than to careful reflection on moral principle.

Encounter

After they leave the academy, the rookies are usually handed over to Field Training Officers (FTOs). In the classic version of the first day on patrol with the rookie, the FTO says, "Forget everything they taught you in the academy, kid; I'll show you how police work is really done." And show they do. The rookie becomes an observer of the FTO as he or she actually does police work. Suddenly, the war stories come alive, and all the questions about how to handle tough situations get answered very quickly and clearly, as one police veteran recalls:

> On this job, your first partner is everything. He tells you how to survive on the job . . . how to walk, how to stand, and how to speak and how to think and what to say and see.[4]

The encounter with the FTO is only part of the rookie's "reality shock" about police work. Perhaps the rookie's encounters with the public. By putting on the uniform, the rookie becomes part of a visible minority group. The self-consciousness about the new appearance is heightened by the nasty taunts and comments the uniform attracts from teenagers and others.[5] The uniform and gun, as symbols of power, attract challenges to that power simply because they are there.[6] Other people seek out the uniform to manipulate the rookie to use the power on behalf of their personal interests. Caught frequently in the cross fire of equally unreasonable citizen demands, the rookie naturally reacts by blaming the public. The spontaneous reaction is reinforced by one of the central values of the police culture: the public as enemy.[7]

This is no different from the way many doctors view their patients, particularly patients with a penchant for malpractice suits. Nor is it different from the view many professors have of their students as unreasonable and thickheaded, particularly those who argue about grades. Like police officers, doctors and professors wield power that affects other people's lives, and that power is always subject to counterattack. Once again, Van Maanen captures the experience of the rookie:

> [My FTO] was always telling me to be forceful, to not back down and to never try to explain the law or what we are doing to a civilian. I really didn't know what he was talking about until I tried to tell some kid why we have laws about speeding. Well, the more I tried to tell him about traffic safety, the angrier he got. I was lucky just to get his John Hancock on the citation. When I came back to the pa-

trol car, [the FTO] explains to me just where I'd gone wrong. You really can't talk to those people out there, they just won't listen to reason.[8]

It is the public that transforms the rookie's self-conception, teaching him or her the pains of exercising power. The FTO then helps to interpret the encounters with the public in the light of the values of the police culture, perhaps leading the rookie even further away from the values of family or friends about how police should act.

The FTO often gives "tests" as he or she teaches. In many departments, the tests are as minor as seeing if the rookie will wait patiently outside while the FTO visits a friend. In other departments, the test may include getting the rookie involved in drinking or having sex on duty, a seriously brutal slugfest against an arrestee, or taking bribes for nonenforcement. The seriousness of the violations may vary, but the central purpose of the test does not: seeing if the rookie can keep his or her mouth shut and not report the violations to the supervisors. A rookie who is found to be untrustworthy can be, literally, hounded and harassed from the department.

Finally, in the encounter stage, the rookie gets the major reality shock in the entire process of becoming a police officer. The rookie discovers that police work is more social work than crime fighting, more arbitration of minor disputes than investigations of major crimes, more patching of holes in the social fabric than weaving of webs to catch the big-time crooks. The rookie's usual response is to define most of the assignments received as "garbage calls," not *real* police work. Not quite sure whom to blame for the fact that he or she was hired to do police work but was assigned everything else, the rookie blames the police executive, the mayor and city council, and even previous U.S. presidents (for raising public expectations). But most of all the rookie blames the public, especially the poor, for being so stupid as to have all these problems, or so smart as to take advantage of welfare and other social programs.

Metamorphosis

The result of those encounters is usually a complete change, a total adaptation of the new role and self-conception as a "cop." And with that transformation comes a stark awareness of the interdependence cops share with all other cops. For all the independence police have in making decisions about how to deal with citizens, they are totally and utterly dependent on other police to save their lives, to respond to a call of an officer in trouble or need of assistance, and to lie on their behalf to supervisors to cover up minor infractions of the many rules the department has. This total change in perspective usually means that police accept several new assumptions about the nature of the world:

- loyalty to colleagues is essential for survival
- the public, or most of it, is the enemy
- police administrators are also the enemy
- any discrepancy between these views and the views of family and friends is due simply to the ignorance of those who have not actually done police work themselves

These are their new assumptions about the *facts* of life in police work, the realities which limit their options for many things, including the kinds of moral principles they can afford to have and still "survive," to keep the job, pay the mortgage, raise the kids, and vest the pension. This conception of the facts opens new police officers to learning and accepting what may be a new set of values and ethical principles. By the time the metamorphosis has been accomplished, in fact, most of these new values have been learned.

Content of Police Values Teaching

Through the war stories of the academy instructor, the actions and stories of the FTO, the bull sessions with other rookies and veterans, and the new officer's encounters with the public, a fairly consistent set of values emerges. Whether the officer accepts these values is another question. Most students of police work seem to agree that these are the values (or some of them) that are taught:

1. Discretion A: *Decisions about whether to enforce the law, in any but the most seri-*

ous cases, should be guided by both what the law says and who the suspect is. Attitude, demeanor, cooperativeness, and even race, age, and social class are all important considerations in deciding how to treat people generally, and whether or not to arrest suspects in particular.

2. Discretion B: *Disrespect for police authority is a serious offense that should always be punished with an arrest or the use of force.* The "offense" known as "contempt of cop" or P.O.P.O. (pissing off a police officer) cannot be ignored. Even when the party has committed no violation of the law, a police officer should find a safe way to impose punishment, including an arrest on fake charges.

3. Force: *Police officers should never hesitate to use physical or deadly force against people who "deserve it," or where it can be an effective way of solving a crime.* Only the potential punishments by superior officers, civil litigation, citizen complaints, and so forth should limit the use of force when the situation calls for it. When you can get away with it, use all the force that society should use on people like that—force and punishment which bleeding-heart judges are too soft to impose.

4. Due Process: *Due process is only a means of protecting criminals at the expense of law-abiding citizens and should be ignored whenever it is safe to do so.* Illegal searches and wiretaps, interrogation without advising suspects of their Miranda rights, and if need be (as in the much admired movie, *Dirty Harry*), even physical pain to coerce a confession are all acceptable methods for accomplishing the goal the public wants the police to accomplish: fighting crime. The rules against doing those things merely handcuff the police, making it more difficult for them to do their job.

5. Truth: *Lying and deception are an essential part of the police job, and even perjury should be used if it is necessary to protect yourself or get a conviction on a "bad guy."* Violations of due process cannot be

admitted to prosecutors or in court, so perjury (in the serious five per cent of cases that even go to trial) is necessary and therefore proper. Lying to drug pushers about wanting to buy drugs, to prostitutes about wanting to buy sex, or to congressmen about wanting to buy influence is the only way, and therefore a proper way, to investigate these crimes without victims. Deceiving muggers into thinking about you are an easy mark and deceiving burglars into thinking you are a fence are proper because there are not many other ways of catching predatory criminals in the act.

6. Time: *You cannot go fast enough to chase a car thief or traffic violator, nor slow enough to get to a "garbage" call; and when there are no calls for service, your time is your own.* Hot pursuits are necessary because anyone who tries to escape from the police is challenging police authority, no matter how trivial the initial offense. But calls to nonserious or social work problems like domestic disputes or kids making noise are unimportant, so you can stop to get coffee on the way or even stop at the cleaner's if you like. And when there are no calls, you can sleep, visit friends, study, or do anything else you can get away with, especially on the midnight shift when you can get away with a lot.

7. Rewards: *Police do very dangerous work for low wages, so it is proper to take any extra rewards the public wants to give them, like free meals, Christmas gifts, or even regular monthly payments (in some cities) for special treatment.* The general rule is: take any reward that doesn't change what you would do anyway, such as eating a meal, but don't take money that would affect your job, like not giving traffic tickets. In many cities, however, especially in the recent past, the rule has been to take even those rewards that do affect your decisions, as long as they are related only to minor offenses—traffic, gambling, prostitution, but not murder.

8. Loyalty: *The paramount duty is to protect your fellow officers at all costs, as they would protect you, even though you may have to risk your own career or your own life to do it.* If your colleagues make a mistake, take a bribe, seriously hurt somebody illegally, or get into other kinds of trouble, you should do everything you can to protect them in the ensuing investigation. If your colleagues are routinely breaking the rules, you should never tell supervisors, reporters, or outside investigators about it. If you don't like it, quit—or get transferred to the police academy. But never, ever, blow the whistle.

The Rising Value Conflicts

None of these values is as strongly or widely held as in the past. Several factors may account for the breakdown in traditional police values that has paralleled the break-down of traditional values in the wider society. One is the increasing diversity of the kinds of people who join police departments: more women, minorities, and college graduates. Another is the rising power of the police unions which defend individual officers who get into trouble—sometimes even those who challenge the traditional values. A third factor is the rise of investigative journalism and the romantic aura given to "bucking the system" by such movies as *Serpico*. Watergate and other recent exposés of corruption in high places—especially the attitude of being "above the law"—have probably made all public officials more conscious of the ethics of their behavior. Last but not least, police administrators have increasingly taken a very stern disciplinary posture towards some of these traditional police values and gone to extraordinary lengths to try to counteract them.

Consider the paramount value of loyalty. Police reformer August Vollmer described it in 1931 as the "blue curtain of secrecy" that descends whenever a police officer does something wrong, making it impossible to investigate misconduct. Yet in the past decade, police officers in Cincinnati, Indianapolis, New York, and elsewhere have given reporters and grand juries evidence about widespread police misconduct. In New York, police officers have even given evidence against their colleagues for homicide, leading to the first conviction there (that anyone can recall) of a police officer for murder in the line of duty. The code of silence may be far from breaking down, but it certainly has a few cracks in it.

The ethics of rewards have certainly changed in many departments over the past decade. In the wake of corruption scandals, some police executives have taken advantage of the breakdown in loyalty to assign spies, or "field associates," to corruption-prone units in order to detect bribe-taking. These officers are often recruited for this work at the police academy, where they are identified only to one or two contacts and are generally treated like any other police officer. These spies are universally hated by other officers, but they are very hard to identify. The result of this approach, along with other anti-corruption strategies, has been an apparent decline in organized corruption.[9]

The ethics of force are also changing. In the wake of well-publicized federal prosecutions of police beatings, community outrage over police shootings, and an explosion in civil litigation that has threatened to bankrupt some cities, the behavior and possibly the attitude of the police in their use of force have generally become more restrained. In Los Angeles, Kansas City, Atlanta, New York, Chicago, and elsewhere, the number of killings of citizens by police has declined sharply.[10] Some officers now claim that they risk their lives by hesitating to use force out of fear of being punished for using it. Even if excessive use of force has not been entirely eliminated, the days of unrestrained shooting or use of the "third degree" are clearly gone in many cities.

The increasing external pressures to conform to legal and societal values, rather than to traditional police values, have generated increasing conflict among police officers themselves. The divide-and-conquer effect may be seen in police officers' unwillingness to bear the risks of covering up for their colleagues, now that the risks are much greater than they have been. Racial conflicts among police officers often center on these values. At the national level, for example, the National Organization of Black Law Enforce-

ment Executives (NOBLE) has been battling with the International Association of Chiefs of Police (IACP) since at least 1979 over the question of how restrictive police department firearms policies should be.

These conflicts should not be over-emphasized, however. The learning of police ethics still takes place in the context of very strong communication of traditional police values. The rising conflicts are still only a minor force. But they are at least one more contingency affecting the moral choices police officers face as they progress through their careers, deciding which values to adopt and which ethical standards to live by.

The Police Officer's Moral Career

There are four major aspects of moral careers in general that are directly relevant to police officers.[11] One is the *contingencies* the officer confronts. Another is the *moral experiences* undergone in confronting these contingencies. A third is the *apologia*, the explanation officers develop for changing the ethic principles they live by. The fourth and most visible aspect of the moral careers of police officers is the *stages of moral change they go through*.

Contingencies

The contingencies shaping police moral careers include all the social pressures officers face to behave one way rather than another. Police departments vary, for example, in the frequency and seriousness of the rule-breaking that goes on. They also vary in the openness of such rule-breaking, and in the degree of teaching of the *skills* of such rule-breaking. It is no small art, for example, to coax a bribe offer out of a traffic violator without directly asking for it. Even in a department in which such bribes are regularly accepted, a new officer may be unlikely to adopt the practice if an older officer does not teach him or her how. In a department in which older officers explicitly teach the techniques, the same officer might be more likely to adopt the practice. The difference in the officer's career is thus shaped by the difference in the contingencies he or she confronts.

The list of all possible contingencies is obviously endless, but these are some of the more commonly reported ones:

- the values the FTO teaches
- the values the first sergeant teaches
- the kind of citizens confronted in the first patrol assignment
- the level of danger on patrol
- whether officers work in a one-officer or two-officer car (after the training period)
- whether officers are assigned to undercover or vice work
- whether there are conflicts among police officers over ethical issues in the department
- the ethical "messages" sent out by the police executive
- the power of the police union to protect officers from being punished
- the general climate of civic integrity (or lack of it)
- the level of public pressure to control police behavior

Contingencies alone, of course, do not shape our behavior. If we were entirely the products of our environment, with no freedom of moral choice, there would be little point in writing (or reading) books on ethics. What contingencies like these do is push us in one direction or another, much like the waves in the ocean. Whether we choose to swim against the tide or flow with the waves is up to each of us.

Moral Experiences

The moral experience is a major turning point in a moral career. It can be an agonizing decision about which principles to follow or it can be a shock of recognition as you finally understand the moral principles implicit in how other people are behaving. Like the person asleep on a raft drifting out to sea, the police officer who has a moral experience suddenly discovers where he or she is and what the choices are.

Some officers have had moral experiences when they found out the system they worked for was corrupt: when the judge dismissed the charges against the son of a powerful business executive, or when a sergeant ordered the officer not to make arrests at an illegal after-hours bar. One leading police executive apparently went through a moral experience when he was first assigned to the vice squad and saw all the money that his colleagues were taking from gamblers. Shocked and disgusted, he sought and obtained a transfer to a less corrupt unit within a few weeks.

Other officers have had moral experiences in reaction to particular incidents. One Houston police rookie was out of the academy for only several weeks when he witnessed a group of his senior colleagues beat up a Mexican-American, Joe Campos Torres, after he resisted arrest in a bar. Torres drowned after jumping or being pushed from a great height into a bayou, and no one knew how he had died when his body was found floating nearby. The officer discussed the incident with his father, also a Houston police officer, and the father marched the young officer right into the Internal Affairs Division to give a statement. His testimony became the basis of a federal prosecution of the other officers.

Other officers may have a moral experience when they see their ethics presented in public, outside the police culture. New York City police captain Max Schmittberger, for example, who had been a bagman collecting graft for his superiors in New York's Tenderloin district, was greatly moved by the testimony of prostitutes he heard at the hearings of the Lexow Committee investigating police corruption in 1893. He told muckraking reporter Lincoln Steffens that the parade of witnesses opened his eyes to the reality of the corruption, so he decided to get on the witness stand himself to reveal even more details of the corruption.

No matter what contingencies occur to prompt a moral experience, the police officer faces relatively few choices about how to react. One option is to drift with the tide, letting things go on as they have been. Another option is to seek an escape route, such as a transfer, that removes the moral dilemma that may prompt the moral experience. A third option is to leave police work altogether, although the financial resources of police officers are not usually great enough to allow the luxury of resigning on principle. The fourth and most difficult option is to fight back somehow, either by blowing the whistle to the public or initiating a behind-the-scenes counterattack.

Not all moral experiences are prompted by criminal acts or even by violations of rules and regulations. Racist jokes or language, ethnic favoritism by commanders, or other issues can also prompt moral experiences. With some officers, though, nothing may ever prompt a moral experience; they may drift out to sea, or back to shore, sound asleep and unaware of what is happening to them.

Apologia

For those officers with enough moral consciousness to suffer a moral experience, a failure to "do the right thing" could be quite painful to lie with. "Even a bent policeman has a conscience," as a British police official who resigned on principle (inadequate police corruption investigations in London) once observed.[12] In order to resolve the conflict between what they think they should have done and what they actually did, officers often invent or adopt an acceptable explanation for their conduct. The explanation negates the principle they may have wished they actually had followed, or somehow makes their behavior consistent with that principle.

Perhaps the most famous apologia is the concept of "clean graft": bribes paid to avoid enforcement of laws against crimes that don't hurt people. Gambling and prostitution bribes were traditionally labeled as "clean graft," while bribes from narcotics pushers were labeled "dirty graft." (As narcotics traffic grew more lucrative, however, narcotics bribes were more often labeled "clean.")

The apologia for beating a handicapped prisoner in a moment of anger may draw on the police value system of maintaining respect for authority and meting out punishment because the courts will not. The apologia for stopping black suspects more often than white suspects may be the assumption that blacks are more likely to be guilty. No matter what a police officer does, he or she is apt to find *situationally justified* reasons for doing it. The reasons are things only the officer can understand because only the officer

knows the full story, all the facts of the *situation*. The claim of situational expertise, of course, conveniently avoids any attempt to apply a general moral principle to conduct. The avoidance is just as effective in the officer's own mind as it would be if the apologia were discussed with the officer's spouse, clergyman, or parents.

Perhaps the most important effect of the apologia is that it allows the officer to live with a certain moral standard of behavior, to become comfortable with it. This creates the potential for further apologias about further changes in moral standards. The process can clearly become habit-forming, and it does. The progression from one apologia to the next makes up the stages of moral change.

Stages

The stages of moral change are points on a moral continuum, the different levels of moral improvement or of the "slippery slope" of moral degeneration. Such descriptions sound trite and old-fashioned, but they are commonly used by officers who get into serious trouble—such as being convicted for burglary—to account for their behavior.

The officers caught in the Denver police burglary ring in 1961, for example, appear to have progressed through many stages in their moral careers before forming an organized burglary ring:

1. First they suffered moral experiences that showed them that the laws were not impartially enforced and that judges were corrupt.

2. Then they learned that other police officers were dishonest, including those who engaged in "shopping," i.e., stealing goods at the scene of a nighttime commercial burglary, with the goods stolen by the police thus indistinguishable from the goods stolen by others.

3. They joined in the shopping themselves and constructed an apologia for it ("the insurance pays for it all anyway").

4. The apologia provided a rationale for a planned burglary in which they were burglars ("the insurance still pays for it").

5. The final stage was to commit planned burglaries on a regular basis.

These stages are logically available to all police officers. Many, perhaps most, officers progress to Stage 3 and go no further, just as most professors steal paper clips and photo-copying from their universities, but not books or furniture. Why some people move into the further stages and others do not is a problem for the sociology of deviance, not ethics. The fact is that some officers do move into more serious stages of unethical conduct after most officers have established the custom in the less serious, but still unethical, stages.

Each aspect of police ethics, from force to time to due process, has different sets of stages. Taken together, the officer's movement across all the stages on all the ethical issues makes up his or her moral career in police work. The process is not just one way; offices can move back closer to legal principles as well as away from them. But the process is probably quite connected across different issues. Your moral stage on stealing may parallel your moral stage on force.

Learning Ethics Differently

This article has treated morality as if it were black and white, i.e., as if it consisted of clear-cut principles to be obeyed or dis-obeyed. Many issues in police ethics are in fact clear-cut, and hold little room for serious philosophical analysis. One would have a hard time making a rational defense of police officers stealing, for example.

But what may be wrong with the way police ethics is now taught and learned is just that assumption: that all police ethical issues are as clear-cut as stealing. They are not. The issues of force, time, discretion, loyalty, and others are all very complex, with many shades of gray. To deny this complexity, as the formal approaches of police academies and police rule books often do, may simply en-courage unethical behavior. A list of "dos" and "don'ts" that officers must follow be-cause they are ordered to is a virtual chal-lenge to their ingenuity: catch me if you can. And in the face of a police culture that has already established values quite contrary to many of the official rules, the black-and-white approach to ethics may be naive.

As indicated above, an alternative ap-proach may be preferred. This would con-sider both clear-cut and complex ethical is-sues in the same fashion: examining police problems in the light of basic moral princi-ples and from the moral point of view. While there may be weaknesses in this alternative approach, it may well be the sounder road to ethical sensitivity in the context of individual responsibility.

Notes

1. See John Van Maanen, "On Becoming a Po-liceman," in *Policing: A View from the Street*, eds. Peter Manning and John Van Maanen (Santa Monica, Calif.: Goodyear, 1978).

2. See John McNamara, "Uncertainties in Police Work: The Relevance of Recruits' Back-grounds and Training," in *The Police: Six So-ciological Studies*, ed. David J. Bordeau (New York: Wiley, 1967).

3. Van Maanen, "On Becoming a Policeman," p. 298.

4. Ibid., p. 301.

5. See William Westley, *Violence and the Police* (Cambridge, Mass.: M.I.T. Press, 1970), pp. 159-60.

6. See William Ker Muir, Jr., *Police: Streetcorner Politicians* (Chicago: University of Chicago Press, 1977).

7. See Westley, *Violence*, pp. 48-108.

8. Van Maanen, "On Becoming a Policeman," p. 302.

9. See Lawrence Sherman, "Reducing Police Gun Use" (Paper presented at the Interna-tional Conference on the Management and Control of Police Organizations, Breukelen, the Netherlands, 1980).

10. Ibid.

11. Cf. Erving Goffman, "The Moral Career of the Mental Patient," in *Asylum: Essays on the So-cial Situation of Mental Patients and Other In-mates* (Garden City, N.Y.: Anchor Books, 1961), pp. 127-69.

12. See Sherman, "Reducing Police Gun Use."

22

Drug Use and Drug-Related Corruption of Police Officers

David L. Carter

Until the 1960s, most police corruption, at least in big cities, was associated with the protection of gambling operations, illegal liquor establishments, prostitution, and similar "victimless" activities which were often operated by organized crime groups. In the last few decades, however, drug-related police corruption has probably surpassed these earlier forms of deviance. In this article, David Carter explores the reasons for the increase in drug-related corruption, develops a typology of different forms of corruption, and examines some of the ways that police departments try to minimize this problem. As you read the article, you might think about why otherwise law-abiding police officers would engage in such unethical and illegal behavior, and whether you could resist the temptations that arise in the course of modern-day drug enforcement.

The corruption of police officers is a problem which spans cultures, countries, and generations in that it is based in human weaknesses and motivations. Because even the lowest ranking police officer can exercise wide power and because there are people who want to take advantage of that power, the threat of corruption is inevitable. Administrators must recognize that no matter how aggressively the problem is controlled, investigated and penalized, there will always be someone in the organization who will become susceptible to corruptive influences.

This is not meant to be a cynical view of the problem, but a practical one.

It is the practical administrator who will be the most successful in combating corruption and keeping its influence at a minimum. Denying that the problem exists or failing to investigate it aggressively will result in a more devastating impact. As one police manager told the author,

> We probably could have stopped this problem sooner if we'd been able to accept the fact that we had some [corrupt] officers. As it stands now, the corruption has spread like a bad infection.

While many elements of corruption can be examined, this chapter focuses only on one aspect: that related to drugs.

The Pathology of Corruption

Police corruption includes a wide variety of prohibited behaviors—either crimes or departmental rule violations—committed under the auspices of a police officer's position. Goldstein defined corruption as

> . . . acts involving misuse of authority by a police officer in a manner designed to produce personal gain for himself or others. [It] is not limited to monetary gain, because gain may be in the form of services rendered, status, influence, prestige, or future support for the officer or someone else. (1975:3-5)

Important elements of this definition are "police authority" and "personal gain." Thus, corruption involves some type of transaction between the officer and another person. The nature of that transaction can be complex and circumstances will vary significantly. Particularly problematic in some cases of drug-related corruption is determining when both of these elements exist together.

The cause of corruption is not a simple issue. There is always the proverbial "bad apple" who somehow slipped through the department's selection process. However, more disturbing are the cases of officers who have good work records and appear dedicated yet they slip into a mode of corrupt behavior. Administrators are frequently at a loss to explain how this occurred to a "good officer." Many factors could contribute to this, including:

- Greed
- Personal motivators such as ego, sex, or the exercise of power
- Tolerance of the behavior by the community
- Socialization from peers and/or the organization
- Inadequate supervision and monitoring of behavior
- Lack of clear accountability of employees behavior
- No real threat of discipline or sanctions

No single factor is likely to "cause" corrupt behavior. Instead, the behavior appears to evolve from the interactive effects of several of these variables.

A Typology of Drug-Related Corruption

Drug-related corruption of police officers is particularly problematic. While overall incidents of corruption appears to have declined, the cases of drug-related corruption have notably increased. The reasons are complex and offer challenges for the police and community together in order to minimize their impact. To better understand the breadth of the problem, the author has developed the following typology.

Type 1 Drug Corruption: In Search of Illegitimate Goals

The Type 1 goals are defined as "illegitimate" in that an officer is seeking to use his/her position as a police officer simply for personal gain. Examples of this type of corruption would include:

- Giving information to drug dealers about investigations, undercover officers, names of informants, planned raids and so forth in exchange for a monetary payment.
- Accepting bribes from drug dealers in exchange for actions such as non-arrest, evidence tampering, perjury, or contamination of evidence.

- Theft of drugs by an officer from the police property room or laboratory for personal consumption or sale of the drug.
- The "seizure" of drugs without arresting the person possessing the drugs with the officer's intent of converting the drugs to personal use.
- Taking the profits of drug dealers' sales and/or their drugs for resale.
- Extorting drug traffickers for money or property in exchange for non-arrest or non-seizure of drugs.

Research by the author indicates that there are two distinct behavioral cycles—not necessarily mutually exclusive—motivating Type 1 corrupt acts. These motivations are classified as "cycles" because of a distinct recurring and reinforcing process. For example, after an officer's initial corrupt act he/she would fear being detected. After the fear decreased and another opportunity occurred, the officer would perform another improper act. Again, a period of fear of apprehension—albeit a shorter one—followed by another incident. The failure of being detected apparently reinforces the officer's feeling of invulnerability from detection. As time increases, the frequency of misconduct would cyclically increase until an undefined saturation point is reached and the officer feels that no further risks could be taken.

User-Driven Cycle. In these cases an officer starts as a "recreational" user of drugs, typically buying the substances for personal consumption from a dealer. The officer's behavior evolves to a point when he/she decides that instead of buying the drugs they can be "confiscated" from users/dealers or taken from the police property room. This decision appears to be the product of several factors which interact. One is the increasing cost of drug use. A second factor is opportunity: the officer concludes that it is cheaper to convert seized drugs for personal use rather than to buy them. Finally, officers begin to worry that their occupational identity may be discovered by drug dealers (if not already known) leading to blackmail.

Profit-Driven Cycle. Officers involved in this form of corruption include both users and non-users of drugs. The intent in this form of corruption is purely monetary. The primary motivation for becoming corrupt is the vast amount of unaccountable and untraceable money involved in the illicit drug trade coupled with the opportunity, by virtue of police authority, to seize these monies. This is further compounded by the fact that the source of the money is illegal activity. During the course of research on the topic, officers involved in corruption tended to make comments along the line that "it's not fair" or "it's not right" that drug traffickers had far more money than the officers who were "working for a living" or who were "risking their lives."

To give perspective on the amounts of money involved, one former undercover narcotics investigator now assigned to a task force to investigate drug corruption stated, "When you're looking at on-going [drug] deals of even medium to small size quantities, $100,000 is a small score for a bribe in drug trafficking today." In another case, ten officers from one police department made two robberies of cocaine from drug traffickers. In just these two robberies, the officers made over $16 million among them. The amounts of money are staggering—and tempting.

Type 2 Drug Corruption: In Search of Legitimate Goals

Strikingly different is the second form of corruption—in search of legitimate goals. Since corruption is the abuse of one's position for personal gain, it may be argued that, in the case of drug corruption, "gain" is not only money, tangible goods, and services but may also be an organizational benefit—perhaps a form of "winning" or "revenge." Examples of Type 2 corrupt behavior include:

- False statements to obtain arrest or search warrants against "known" drug dealers/traffickers.

- Perjury during hearings and trials of drug dealers.

- "Planting" or creating evidence against "known" drug dealers.

- Overt and intentional entrapment.

- Falsely spreading rumors that a dealer is a police informant thus placing that person's safety in jeopardy.

The characterization of "legitimate goals" is from the perspective of the officer. There are persons whom officers "know" are involved in drug trafficking, however, the police are consistently unable to obtain sufficient evidence for arrest. Similarly, there are "known" criminals which have been found not guilty in court because the government has not been able to prove its case—frequently because evidence has been excluded on "technicalities." The officers see these recurring circumstances and become frustrated because the trafficker is "beating the system." This is compounded by the tendency to perceive legal strategies during hearings and trials as "unfair manipulation of the law" by attorneys.

The Type 2 corrupt officer's self-determined goal is to prosecute and incarcerate the drug traffickers. However, Type 2 corruption occurs when the attempt to accomplish this *legitimate goal* is through *illegitimate means*. When the goal (conviction) is achieved the officer receives the satisfaction that he/she "won." This form of revenge is psychologically rewarding and, obviously, improper.

It is argued that in the case of Type 2 corruption, the acts are not only for the personal psychological gain of the officer but also in support of organizational goals through which the officer may be rewarded by commendations, promotions, and/or recognition. It may also be argued that this form of corruption is for organizational gain via the arrest and prosecution of known serious, often dangerous, drug traffickers.

Type 2 corruption is further compounded because this behavior is not traditionally perceived as being corrupt. There is a degree of informal organizational tolerance for behavior which gets "known" traffickers off the street or seizes the traffickers' cache of drugs. This tolerance complicates the determination of wrongdoing and undermines the commitment toward integrity which was discussed in the previous section.

An officer's exposure to drug-related situations as well as the opportunity for either type of corruption will be largely dependent on the officer's assignment. While the opportunity for corruption may be found in many assignments, clearly patrol officers and drug investigators have the greatest exposure to corruption-related situations.

Illicit Drug Use by Police Officers

Just as drug-related corruption has surfaced, the problem of employee drug use has emerged in law enforcement (just as it has in virtually every other occupation.) While instances of alcohol abuse have been well documented as they relate to police officers, scrutiny of drug effects, other than alcohol, have been less prevalent. The obvious distinction between alcohol and illicit substances is the unlawful nature of the latter. Not only must concern be directed toward the behavioral effects associated with drug use, but also the abrogation of duty and trust by the officer who has violated the law through drug possession. Furthermore, concern must be given to the threat posed by the association with drug dealers—this alone can place an officer in a compromising position.

Recreational Drug Use

The most frequent issue related to officer drug abuse is "recreational" use. Recreational use of drugs is a somewhat broad characterization. Admittedly, it is a term which may not be completely inclusive of all drug use, particularly in cases of addiction. For the present discussion, recreational use is defined as drug use that does not involve corruption and where use was initially a product of the desire to experience the expected exhilaration, psychoactive effects, physiological effects and/or mood changes associated with drug consumption. Under this definition, drug use may include both on-duty and off-duty use of illicit narcotic and non-narcotic controlled substances as long as corruption is not involved.

On-Duty Drug Use

The extent of on-duty drug use by officers is simply not known. An intuitive assumption is that some on-duty use occurs; however, it appears to be relatively rare. When it does occur, the potential ramifications are widespread. The most serious implication is that an officer may use deadly force or be involved in a traffic accident while under the influence. Other effects of on-duty use include poor judgment in the performance of the officer's duties, an increase in behavior related to liability risks, participation in other forms of misconduct, and having a negative influence on co-workers and the community with whom the officer has contact.

In one case the author discovered during the course of research on the topic, a patrol officer in a major midwestern city was found using cocaine while on duty. During the internal affairs investigation the officer admitted he had regularly used cocaine on-duty for over one year. The officer said he felt co-workers would be able to tell from his behavior when he was "high," so each time after he "snorted" cocaine he would "chase it" with whiskey. He knew fellow officers would "cover for him" if they thought he was an alcoholic, therefore, he masked the cocaine's behavioral influences with the odor of alcohol. This experience, which provides insight into the occupational culture of policing, serves as an extreme example of how on-duty substance abuse can occur without being discovered.

On-duty drug use can also occur if the problem becomes systemic within the work group. In one moderate-sized midwestern city, about thirty officers were identified as being involved in a "user's ring" (most of whom did not use drugs on-duty.) Drug use became so pervasive that there was tolerance for its use, even on-duty. While some officers in the group did not like the on-duty use, they would not inform on those using drugs during working hours because of the strong implication they would be discovered as a drug user, albeit during off-duty hours. The implication from this experience is that in light of the police subculture, if off-duty use becomes pervasive, there is an increased likelihood of on-duty use among the officers involved.

In perhaps the only empirical study of the subject, Peter Kraska and Victor Kappeler discovered on-duty drug use during the course of working with a southwestern police department on another project. Through the use of unstructured self-report interviews, departmental records, and personal observations they found that 20 percent of the officers in the department used marijuana while on-duty twice a month or more. Another 4 percent had used marijuana at least once while on-duty. Moreover, 10 percent of the officers reported they had used non-prescribed controlled substances (including hallucinogenic drugs, stimulants, or barbiturates) while on-duty. (This may not be an additional 10 percent of the officers; it may include some of the marijuana users.) Most of the officers involved in this behavior were between the ages of 21 and 38 and had been police officers for 3 to 10 years.

One may hope that the high incidence of on-duty drug use found in this study was an exceptional occurrence. If not, the problem may be greater than we believe. Certainly, the findings dispel the myth that drug use is a problem found only in the police departments of the nation's largest cities. Based on this, and other research, it is also reasonable to assume that those agencies which have had more serious drug-related problems— notably corruption—have also experienced on-duty drug use.

Drugs of Choice

In cases where police drug use has been documented, marijuana appears to be the most common drug used. The preference for marijuana is most likely because of its comparatively minor addictive nature, its limited long-term effects, the ease of obtaining it, its comparatively low cost, and, importantly, the lesser social stigma associated with the use of marijuana when compared with other drugs. Cocaine is clearly the second most frequently used drug and appears to be fairly prevalent. The best explanation for this seems to be its availability, its prevalent use in many social situations, and the generally greater sense of exhilaration provided by cocaine compared to marijuana.

The is also some evidence of abuse of nonprescribed or falsely prescribed pharmaceutical substances. Amphetamines and barbiturates fall into this category typically where

officers have used the drugs as a way of coping with various personal problems. In some cases, stimulants have been used to help keep officers "alert" (or awake) when they have been working excessive hours in a second job or going to school. This form of substance abuse appears to have different dynamics than the marijuana or cocaine use. Interestingly, officers showed greater tolerance for protecting officers who used amphetamines and barbiturates as opposed to other controlled substances, despite the fact the use of those substances are illegal. There were no indications of a significant problem with synthetic hallucinogenic drugs or heroin.

As a final note, some police administrators have expressed concern that an increasing number of officers may be using illicit anabolic steroids. Their concern, while somewhat focused on the illegal use, is primarily directed toward the reported behavioral effects of steroids. Specifically, some research has indicated that regular steroid users become violent and aggressive. The implications of these effects in law enforcement are obvious. Interestingly, new police programming may indirectly contribute to this problem. With more departments participating in competitive physical competitions, such as the Police Olympics, which include weight lifting, martial arts, running, and similar activity, in addition to rewarding physical fitness, the appeal of the conditioning effects of steroids is powerful. This is an important area for police executives to carefully explore.

Substance Abuse as a Job-Related Condition

Questions have arisen of whether officer drug use could be a job-related condition. There have been two primary arguments on which this assertion is based: police stress and the officer's job assignment.

The rationale the stress argument posits is that as a result of the high levels of stress in policing, some officers have resorted to drug use as a coping mechanism. Despite the wide array of research on police stress there is no scientific evidence to support this claim. In fact, the author would argue that drug abusing officers would experience *greater stress* since there is always the fear that an officer's drug abuse may be discovered. This, of course, would likely end in discipline or termination. If stress was, in fact, a major cause of police drug use, then it is likely that higher levels of drug use would have been discovered over the past two decades. Furthermore, evidence from police disciplinary actions and labor arbitrations where officer drug use is at issue does not suggest that stress was a cause.

The second issue of job-relatedness is more problematic. This argument states that officers who are working undercover drug investigations with frequent and on-going exposure to drugs may become socialized in the "drug culture." That is, constant interaction in the environment of drug use and transactions reduces the adverse socio-moral implications of drug consumption while at the same time reinforcing the permissibility of its use.

It is clear that undercover officers do, in fact, become socialized into the drug culture based on language, dress, and other behaviors which carry over to the officer's off-duty time. Officers who work undercover in prostitution, gambling, and bootlegging tend to diminish the social impact and "wrongfulness" of these behaviors. Given these factors and our knowledge about the socialization process in general, it is reasonable to assume that officers could be similarly assimilated into the drug culture. This is reinforced by the knowledge that if an officer is going to be accepted into a social group, he/she must appear to ascribe to that group's norms. While the process may begin as a masquerade for the officer, constant exposure to the culture combined with the stress of the environment may reasonably lead to acceptance of drug use (and other improper behaviors) at the social level even though the officer recognizes that they should not be accepted at the legal level. Generally, the longer an officer is in such an environment the more acceptable that group's values and norms become. While empirical research is virtually non-existent on this issue, anecdotal evidence from research conducted by the author gives credence to this process occurring.

The Corruption-Cultural Milieu of Police

Despite the significant differences in the motivations and behaviors involved in the different forms of corruption and drug use, the author has observed eight operational constructs which permeate each type of corruption. These factors appear to have cumulative interactive influences which continually reinforce each type of behavior. That is, left uncontrolled, these factors can contribute to an environment wherein corruption will flourish.

Opportunity Structure

In situations that confront police officers in their positions of authority, there are opportunities for them to "profit" from the exercise of their authority. Barker (1994) observed that the opportunity structure provides the police officer with many situations to observe and/or participate in a wide range of illicit activities. In addition, the police come into contact with many people who are criminal (or on the periphery of criminality) during the officers' normal work routine under conditions of little or no supervision. Kraska and Kappeler observed that three variables related to the opportunity structure of policing add to the police officers' vulnerability. First is the duration and intensity of exposure to the criminal element of a society. Second is the police officer's relative freedom from supervision. Third is the uncontrolled availability of contraband and opportunities to convert situations (such as the investigation of a burglary at a business) to personal gain with minimal risks. The corrupt officer is one who exploits these opportunities.

Abrogation of Trust

Based on the literature of police ethics, organizational values, labor arbitrations, and case law, it is clear that there is a higher standard of integrity required of police officers than of the "average citizen" (Carter, 1988). The essence of that standard is reflected in the officer's oath of office and the concomitant trust citizens place in police officers as a result of their unique authority. On the matter of corruption Klockars has emphasized that, "What is corrupted in police corruption is the special trust police enjoy by virtue of their occupation" (1983:334). Trust is misplaced because of officers' law violations and/or the failure of officers to afford due process and equal protection to citizens is a fundamental abrogation of lawful duties. Because of the critical public safety role the police hold in our global societies, the trust given to a police officer's position is one which should be carefully upheld.

Rationalization

A telling remark by a police officer interviewed by the author sheds light on how corrupt behavior is rationalized. The officer, who had taken money from a drug dealer, simply observed that "it was just drug money," implying that there was a different standard for the taking of illegally earned money compared to lawfully obtained wealth. Another common rationalization is that corruption "was not hurting anyone," again with the implication that there is a different standard of equity or justification when money is taken from a "known criminal" than other persons. Perhaps because in the back of their minds officers recall their oath of office, they tend to rationalize their corrupt acts.

Invulnerability Factor

Essentially, this is the perception that because of an officer's position and authority, he/she will not be implicated in the misconduct. The officer's easy access to information, camaraderie, and the power to influence others contribute to this perception. Perhaps the epitome of this factor can be illustrated in one officer's statement: "Who's going to take the word of a [criminal] over a cop?" The officer felt he was "safe"—invulnerable from allegations by criminals—and would not be caught.

The 'Code of Secrecy'

The literature on policing has thoroughly examined the "code of secrecy" within the police culture (see Barker and Carter, 1994; Blumberg and Niederhoffer, 1985; Kennedy, 1977). The "code," although it has variations, is generally described as a cultural norm that prohibits the discussion of "secrets" and behaviors with those outside of the defined social group (which may vary, depending on the social group). The group's parameters may be defined by shift, assignment, rank, or simply employment by a police organization. The parameters may also be defined on the basis of participation in the occupational group activities. That is, an officer who does not subscribe to the "code" or adhere to its rules may be ostracized from the social group. The influence of peer pressure to "belong" and the social sanctions associated with ostracism make the "code" a powerful cultural dynamic.

Despite the seriousness of police corruption, there still appears to be some reluctance to inform on such officers. When corruption was mentioned by officers who were interviewed in the author's research, the honest officers simply tended to disassociate themselves but not report the corrupt officer to the department. Interestingly, an officer who informs on a fellow officer may be labeled a "rat" who cannot be trusted. The "rat" may even experience more ostracism than the officers involved in the corrupt behavior (see McAlary, 1987; Knapp Commission, 1973). In one city, an officer who was not involved in any form of misconduct observed another officer taking a bribe. The "straight" officer did not report the corrupt officer nor did he say anything about the bribe until he was interviewed by Internal Affairs during an investigation of the corrupt officer. When asked why the officer had not come forward, the Internal Affairs investigator stated,

> . . . he didn't fear getting shot, he didn't fear getting hurt [on the job]; he *did* fear the repercussions of turning in a fellow officer even under these circumstances.

Market Forces

Just as market forces can drive an economy, they can also influence corrupt behavior. Police officers control the commodity of "police authority." Whether the officer independently decides to exercise authority unlawfully (such as taking money from a drug dealer) or whether the officer is induced to a corrupt act by another person, depends to some extent on the risk-benefit ratio. Even the most honest officers have been tempted on occasion to commit a corrupt act. If an officer has the opportunity to "earn" two or three times his annual salary through one corrupt act, temptation becomes stronger. The officer will weigh the risks and benefits of the situation—sometimes even momentarily—to decide his course of action. Included in this "weighing" process are social responsibility, ethical standards, peer influences, and different potential ramifications of the act. Hopefully, the proper factors will weight the scale in that direction. In too many cases, however, officers have succumbed to the temptation, deciding the benefits outweigh the risks.

Inadequate Organizational Controls

Many police organizations simply have not provided sufficiently rigorous supervision and training on matters related to the dynamics of corruption. Similarly, insufficient investigative audit controls are used to monitor case development and officer behavior. Following the review of an extensive drug corruption problem in one city, the police department implemented a new anti-corruption program. The Deputy Chief, in commenting on the program, said,

> We found we had to go back to the basics. We simply did not have enough accountability nor enough training. We were lax, putting these things on the back burner so we could concentrate on crime and handling calls. It's apparent we paid dearly for that misjudgment.

Persistence of the Corruptive Patterns

Even with the threat of investigation and the self-awareness of one's misconduct, it appears extraordinarily difficult for an officer to stop his/her corrupt behavior once it is started. Following this line of thought, Goldstein noted what he called the "addictive element" of corruption: "Once an officer has agreed to accept the [personal gain] of corruption, he usually becomes addicted to the system" (1975:27). Stated differently, corruption becomes habitual. This author argues that this "corruptive habit" has a reinforcing effect in that the officer must further rationalize his/her behavior when the opportunity arises for a cor-

rupt act. Similarly, because of the difficulty of breaking out of the patterns, the feeling of invulnerability must be heightened.

Policy Implications

Police managers need to be certain that there is effective supervision of officers. This includes frequent interaction between the supervisor and subordinate and stringent requirements of accountability on behalf of the officer. In police organizations where corruption is known to be a chronic problem, special supervisory vigilance should be in place. Supervisors should be trained in the "behavioral signs" of corrupt behavior and be required to monitor behavior in circumstances or at crime scenes where opportunities for corruption are highest. Aggressive supervision can be both a preventive policy and a tool to detect corruption.

Training and reinforcement of ethics and professional responsibilities should be provided in periodic training sessions to officers of all ranks. The police organization should articulate organizational values and ensure those values permeate all policies, procedures, and supervisory actions. Training and supervision should also reinforce the officers' role and responsibility to equitably enforce the law, emphasizing that all people are treated the same regardless of whether they are law abiding citizens or "known criminals." Policies and procedures should clearly reflect this position.

A timely and aggressive internal investigations process and discipline system can reduce impressions of "invulnerability" by officers as well as increase the perception of risk associated with corrupt behavior. If an employee understands the department will not tolerate corruption and this is reinforced by a reputation of aggressive internal controls, then the invulnerability factor will be significantly reduced.

The department needs to have an open environment where communications between personnel at all ranks is open and invited. Having an open organization minimizes the need for "secrets." Similarly, supervisors who engender open communications and trust will minimize the effects of the "code of secrecy" as manifest through peer pressure. In addition, having a mechanism for "rumor control" can minimize gossip and misperceptions which, in turn, reduces the environment of secrecy. Finally, through effective leadership and expectations of responsible, ethical behavior, an environment of professional accountability will emerge which reduces reliance on the "code of secrecy."

The department must be particularly sensitive to areas of police behavior which are uniquely vulnerable to corrupt behavior. Constant scanning of the environment to identify corruptive risks should be done in order to counteract those factors. Increasing risk of detection and certainty of punishment should be a paramount factor. The inculcation of values and reinforcement of social responsibility should be done on an on-going basis. Finally, all policies related to the identification, investigation, and adjudication of police misconduct should be periodically reviewed to ensure they are being followed and are consistent with contemporary issues, practices, problems and law.

A Further Perspective on Policy

Understanding factors that motivate officers to become involved in corrupt acts can aid the implementation of both preventive and detection programs. Similarly, understanding factors which contribute, even indirectly, to the potential for corruption can facilitate organizational responses to counteract negative trends.

A consistent finding of the author's research was that organizations—when initially confronted with evidence of corruption—tended to *deny* the problem, creating an obstacle to effective policy development. Another consistent issue was the effect of the police working environment on officer misconduct. The concern was that if an officer's misbehavior was significantly influenced by the occupational environment, policy responses would have to deal with this. Both of these issues warrant greater attention.

Organizational Denial

As noted above, when confronted with indications that police officers are involved in corruption, there is a tendency of administrators to deny the problem. Typically, the denial is not to avoid negative publicity nor is it to "cover up" the problem. Rather, the denial occurs because administrators have difficulty believing that officers are involved in corrupt behavior (Carter and Stephens, 1988).

When asked about drug corruption, comments from police administrators were "I can't believe it," "I can't understand it," and "The allegations can't be true." One administrator stated,

> The last problem I ever thought I'd face is my officers robbing drug dealers *for drugs*. I mean, the reports are here—it's in black and white—but my mind just can't accept it. I don't know if I let [the officers] down or they let me down. Something definitely went wrong in the system somewhere.

This reaction reflects two important things. First, it clearly illustrates the denial, which is a manifestation of the organizational trauma associated with officer corruption. On this subject a captain, who was a 24-year municipal police veteran, stated "I guess I'm just from another generation—I just don't understand [it.]"

A second reaction is what might be categorized as organizational confusion and the lack of preparation to mange corruption problems. Many police departments have generic disciplinary procedures and codes of conduct, but tend to have inadequate policies, procedures, training, supervision, support resources, and administrative control to detect and respond to officer corruption. The lack of planning for potential corruption tends to contribute to programming that is reactive, based on intuitive and emotional reasoning rather than a fully outlined strategy to deal with the problem. As a result, the problem lingers and conflicts occur regarding what the department should do to resolve the situation.

While departments were not eager to publicize their corruption problems, they typically did not mislead the media. In some circumstances, conflicting reports were given from the police department. However, this appeared to occur because the department did not have a complete grasp of the problem and organizational denial tended to cloud its objectivity.

Environmental Factors

Early theories of corruption viewed it "as a result of interaction between the police organization and its environment [with] the causal emphasis placed on the environment" (Sherman, 1983:369). The environment encompasses the organizational and social dynamics of the police officer's work life. It is a variable that includes the community political organization, the structure of local government, norm conflicts, and the values of the local culture. Similarly, Goldstein's observation on the police officer's working environment was that,

> [the] average police officer . . . sees the worst side of humanity. He is exposed to a steady diet of wrongdoing. He becomes intimately familiar with the ways people prey on one another. In the course of this intensive exposure he discovers that dishonesty and corruption are not restricted to those the community sees as criminal. He sees many individuals of good reputation engaging in practices equally dishonest and corrupt. (1975:25)

In light of the literature on environmental causes of misbehavior and inferences from the impact of occupational socialization on an individual's behavior, a critical question could reasonably be asked: If the officer is policing an environment where crime is prevalent and the people with whom the officer has the most frequent contact are criminal or social problems, might this be an influence on the officer's behavior? The answer is not definitive, however, such a circumstance is an important variable which appears to have a contributing influence.

As one illustration, the greatest potential for drug-related police corruption exists for narcotics and vice officers. They receive even less supervision than patrol officers and are not only constantly exposed to the "drug culture" but are also expected to participate in that culture as a charade. In the gamesmanship of undercover work, some officers tend to confuse their own cultural norms with the norms of the criminal culture they have pene-

trated. The buying and selling of drugs becomes second nature, as does the language and social perspective (i.e., values and norms) of that culture.

In one case, the author spoke with an undercover narcotics officer about the practice of "simulation"—that is, pretending to smoke marijuana during the course of an undercover assignment as a means to help legitimize the officer's role. The officer reported that

> Simulation is crap—any user knows if you're smoking or faking, and you can bet they're watching the new guys to see if you're taking a real hit. If I'm at a [drug] deal and I try to simulate, I might as well be wearing a sign that says COP. . . . So you've got to take a real hit to sell yourself. Anyway, it's just a hit of marijuana—it's got less bite than tequila.

The officer went on to report that he, along with another undercover narcotics officer, had smoked marijuana—which they had seized during their undercover work—while off-duty. Perhaps what was most striking about the officer' statements was that he did not appear to recognize the serious impropriety of his acts. In fact, he implied that his department should permit undercover drug officers to smoke marijuana in the course of investigations to help maintain their credibility. In the author's opinion, this officer's occupational environment contributed to his misconduct; however, it is impossible to assign a causal weight to such environmental factors.

When this officer's statement was told to a police supervisor from another agency (who formerly worked undercover narcotics), the supervisor stated: "That guy's got a problem. He's been in too long without anybody keeping an eye on him." It is not argued here that the environment has a wholesale influence on undercover officers. Rather, the environment must be viewed in light of individual socialization and organizational factors which influence behavior.

How can the environmental variable be dealt with in dealing with a corrupt officer? Should the police department share some of the responsibility for the officer's wrongdoing? Do these environmental factors mitigate the officer's liability for corrupt acts? These are difficult questions which require closer direct examination of social, legal, moral, and administrative issues. With respect to the control of these factors, Manning observed,

> It is very simple at one level: control the targets, the money, the evidence, the informants and train and supervise the officers. At another level [this] is very difficult to carry off because the individual officer-based model predominates. (1983)

According to Stoddard, the inference to be drawn from these environmental factors is that we should ". . . see police corruption as something that is not an individual problem but a problem of the occupation and its organization; something in the nature of police work itself" (1983:334).

Control of Corruption

Based on a wide array of literature and the causes enumerated above, there are a number of factors which can be introduced to minimize and control corruption.

Leadership by the Chief of Police

The police chief must establish a clear standard for the department that corruption will not be tolerated in any form. Corruption must be defined for the officers so there is no question about those acts which are prohibited. It must also be clear that officers are expected to act in a lawful and ethical manner which includes reporting officers involved in corrupt behavior (i.e., breaking the "code of secrecy"). Furthermore, the chief must be firm in the commitment that disciplinary action and criminal prosecution will be swiftly and surely taken against offending officers.

Management and Supervision

Managers and supervisors have the responsibility to reinforce the chief's tone of integrity, commend officers for ethical behavior, and lead by example. Supervisors and managers must also monitor officers, particularly those in assignments which are of a higher risk for corruption, to ensure their behavior is lawful. When any suspicion arises about a subordinate's behavior, the manager or supervisor must take immediate action to resolve the questions.

Supervisory Training

Supervisors need to receive training on such areas as recognizing the signs of corruption, employee assessment, and inculcating values in subordinates. Too often supervisors are given these responsibilities, but are not told how to fulfill them. In-service training must also include "updates" on police policy, liability law, and related factors which change in the policing environment.

Organizational Control and Information Management

The department should establish a system which monitors officer behavior to ensure all police personnel are following procedures related to stops, detention, arrests, storing evidence and recovered property, conducting computer checks, and any other aspect of police procedure which is subject to abuse. Irregularities should be more closely examined, particularly where patterns of irregularities exist. All suspicious activities should be documented and investigated according to established internal investigations policy.

Internal Auditing and Informants

Two corruption-related problems arise with informants: The improper use of departmental money to pay informants and the use of informants to perform improper acts on behalf of the officer. To avoid these problems, careful controls must be in place to audit both money and interaction between officers and informants. Any "secret" or "confidential" funds for informants and undercover operations must have rigid controls for accountability.

Internal Affairs

The police Internal Affairs function is designed to investigate allegations of wrongdoing by police officers. Internal Affairs investigators must be familiar with the different types of corruption which occur, how to investigate corruption cases, and to be vigilant in their investigations. Too frequently, these cases are difficult to investigate because of the unwillingness of people to testify.

Drug Enforcement Units

As noted previously, because of the vast amounts of money involved in unlawful drug transactions, officers working in Drug Enforcement Units are particularly susceptible to corruption. Supervision, audit controls, and a policy of regular personnel turnover in these units will help reduce the potential for corruption.

Evidence Handling and Storage

While most police departments have procedures for marking and storing evidence to maintain the chain of custody for evidence in court, these procedures typically do not provide a comprehensive control of evidence. Procedures must be established to comprehensively control property beginning with the time it is seized, not when it arrives at the police station. Supervisors should also monitor officer conduct when property is seized. Care should also be taken to periodically monitor property in storage to ensure it has not been tampered with.

An Early Warning System

Based on the research related to officer corruption, certain behaviors have emerged which are indicative of misconduct. Purchases which appear to be beyond the officer's financial means, changes in the officer's social behavior, and allegations from informants that an officer might be "on the take" are illustrations of these indicators. Utilizing these types of information, the department may develop an "Early Warning System" which monitors the indicators—particularly for officers in highly susceptible assignments. In this way, corruption can be dealt with before it becomes extensive. Moreover, such a system may serve a preventive role as well.

Training

Officer training on matters related to corruption, integrity, ethics, and social responsibilities should be provided on a periodic basis to keep awareness of the problem omnipresent. For officers working in undercover assignments, training should be provided which explicitly addresses the threats of corruption in the assignment, how to avoid corruption, and actions to take when corruptive advances are made toward the officer.

Discipline

When officers are found to have been involved in corruption, discipline should be swift, sure, and substantial. This reinforces the chief's commitment to having a "clean" department and shows that there will be no toleration for corrupt behavior.

Corruption, perhaps more than any form of misconduct, undermines the public confidence in the police. It represents a complete violation of the public trust and an absolute abuse of the authority the public has vested in officers. When corruption flourishes in a department, the integrity of the entire police department is drawn into question. As a result, stringent controls play an important role in maintaining public confidence and effectiveness of the policing function.

References

Alpert, Geoffrey P. and Roger C. Dunham. 1992. *Policing Urban America*. 2d. ed. Prospect Heights, IL: Waveland Press.

Barker, Thomas. 1994. "Peer Group Support for Occupational Deviance." In Thomas Barker and David L. Carter, *Police Deviance*. 3d ed. Cincinnati, OH: Anderson Publishing Company.

Blumberg, Abraham and Elaine Niederhoffer (eds.) 1985. *The Ambivalent Force*. 3d ed. New York: Holt, Rinehart and Winston.

Carter, David L. 1990. "An Overview of Drug-related Misconduct of Police Officers: Drug Abuse and Narcotic Corruption." In Ralph Weisheit, *Drugs and the Criminal Justice System*. Cincinnati, OH: Anderson Publishing Company.

Carter, David L. 1990. "Drug-Related Corruption of Police Officers: A Contemporary Typology." *Journal of Criminal Justice*. 18:85-98.

Carter, David L. 1988. *Controlling Off-Duty Behavior: Higher Standards of Integrity for the Police*. Paper presented at the annual meeting of the Academy of Criminal Justice Sciences. San Francisco, California.

Carter, David L. and Darrel Stephens. 1988. *Drug Abuse by Police Officers: An Analysis of Critical Policy Issues*. Springfield, IL: Charles C. Thomas, Publisher.

Commission to Investigate Allegations of Police Corruption and the City's Anti-Corruption Procedures. (Knapp Commission.) 1973. *Report of the Commission*. New York: George Braziller.

Dombrink, John. 1994. "The Touchables: Vice and Police Corruption in the 1980s." In Thomas Barker and David L. Carter, *Police Deviance*. 3rd ed. Cincinnati, OH: Anderson Publishing Company.

Goldstein, Herman. 1975. *Police Corruption: A Perspective on its Nature and Control*. Washington, DC: Police Foundation.

Klockars, Carl (ed.) 1983. *Thinking About Police: Contemporary Readings*. New York: McGraw-Hill.

Kenney, Dennis J. and James O. Finckenauer. 1995. *Organized Crime in America*. New York: Wadsworth Publishing Company.

Kraska, Peter and Victor Kappeler. 1988. "A Theoretical and Descriptive Examination of Police On-Duty Drug Use." *American Journal of Police*. 7:60.

Sherman, Lawrence. 1983. "Scandal and Reform." In Carl Klockars, *Thinking About Police: Contemporary Readings*. New York: McGraw-Hill.

Stoddard, E.R. 1983. "Blue Coat Crime." In Carl Klockars, *Thinking About Police: Contemporary Readings*. New York: McGraw-Hill.

23

Exploring Police Sexual Violence Against Women*

*Peter B. Kraska and
Victor E. Kappeler*

Kraska and Kappeler identify and discuss several variations of a little-examined form of police deviance, which they term police sexual violence. This type of behavior combines the phenomenon of male sexual violence against women with the question of police abuse of their authority for personal gain or satisfaction. In a traditionally male-dominated society and an even more male-dominated profession (policing), perhaps some incidence of this kind of deviance should not be surprising. But the authors demonstrate that its occurrence is far from rare. Why do you think that an important topic such as this has received so little attention? What steps do you think should be taken to minimize, if not eliminate, this serious form of police deviance?

This study identifies and examines an unexplored criminological phenomenon, termed here police sexual violence. Analysis and interpretation of quantitative data and case studies are used to explore the subject. Two data sets, one from federal litigation cases and the other from a media source, provide the material for examining the known incidence, distribution, and nature of this form of police crime and sexual violence against women. The data include 124 cases of police sexual violence; 37 of these are sexual assault and rape cases committed by on-duty police officers against female citizens. The analysis of case studies draws on and inte-

grates feminist and police studies literature, allowing for the development of a police sexual violence continuum and the exploration of theoretical, conceptual, and practical issues. The conclusion explores the cultural and structural context within which police sexual violence against women occurs.

Criminologists' study of crime has yielded two critical realizations. First, crime crosses all economic, social, and occupational strata. The traditional criminological focus on lower-class, "predatory" street criminals is shifting to offenders within professions and institutions often held in high esteem by the public, such as religious leaders, physicians, corporate executives, government officials, and family members. One of the most persuasive examples of the ubiquitous nature of wrongdoing comes from the study of lawbreaking within the societal institution mandated with enforcing the criminal law. Interest in police crime has risen since the Rodney King episode and the Mollen Commission's rediscovery of corruption in the New York City Police Department.

Preoccupation with street crime has also, in the past, inhibited our attention to persons *victimized* by crime. This is especially true for those who suffer violence occurring in the family, in interpersonal relationships, and in the workplace. Years of research and scholarship have been required to reconceptualize these offenses as serious crime rather than private or personal matters. This reconceptualization has led to a second critical realization: these offenses are often committed against women not at random, but systematically, because of their status as women (Bart and Aloran 1993; Caufield and Wonders 1994; Dobash and Dobash 1992; Kelly 1988; Russell 1982; Stanko 1985). Feminist scholarship is significantly affecting how the academic community views crime, particularly violence against women; yet the undertaking to legitimate the study of gender as a crucial component in the crime dynamic continues (Caufield and Wonders 1994; Daly and Chesney-Lind 1988; Simpson 1989).

Incorporating these realizations allows exploration of an important instance of neglecting the "female" component in police crime. From the research and literature on excessive

---

*This is a revised version of a paper presented at the 1992 annual meetings of the American Society of Criminology, held in New Orleans.

use of force, one would assume that police commit unjustifiable acts of violence only against men, and that women suffer no *direct* and systematic mistreatment at the hands of police officers (Alpert and Fridell 1992; Friedrich 1980; Fyfe 1978; Geller and Karales 1981; Geller and Scott 1991). This neglect, a result of research orientation as well as oversight, is inconsistent with the international literature, in which police mistreatment of women (particularly sexual violence) is receiving widespread attention (Amnesty International 1991; Chapman 1991; Women's Rights Project 1992). Noting this omission, our research identifies and examines what we will call "police sexual violence"(PSV) against women. PSV not only identifies a unique and potentially important criminological phenomenon; in addition, it is significant because it theoretically informs both feminist and police studies. Balancing these two often incompatible sources of literature creates difficulties, even in appropriately labeling the phenomenon under study. Although we are examining males' behavior, we also recognize PSV as a form of women's victimization (Reinharz 1992).

Women and the Police: Reviewing the Literature

Historically the police have viewed women as marginal to the police role and function. Early in the twentieth century, women were first allowed to perform police functions associated with social work, but even as late as 1971, only 10 or 11 women in the entire United States were patrol officers (Garmire 1978). Although the number of women on patrol has increased (Carter, Sapp, and Stephens 1989; Reaves 1992a) and several studies affirm their competence (Hale and Wyland 1993), the integration of women into paramilitary police organizations still meets with opposition (Christopher Commission 1992; Hale and Wyland 1993; Martin 1990; Rafford 1989). Public policing continues to be a predominantly male institution, not only in whom it employs but also in the ideology and culture from which it operates (Hunt 1990; Rafford 1989; Roberg and Kuykendall 1993; Young 1991).

Male exclusivity in policing often clashes with the interests of women as 1) victims of crime, 2) coworkers, and 3) law-breakers (Moyer 1992; Rafford 1989; Stanko 1989). Our purpose here is to examine the literature from feminist and police studies that explores the relationship between women and police, especially as it pertains to PSV against women.

Police Deviance Literature

In the past three decades, research on police corruption, deviance, and misconduct has proliferated. This research has taken the form of government reports (Christopher Commission 1992; Knapp Commission 1972) as well as independent research (Barker 1977; Carter 1990; Sherman 1974; Stoddard 1968; Westley 1970). Historically, however, most of the literature focused on police corruption as opposed to police deviance. Only recently has deviance not associated with corruption received scholarly consideration (Barker 1978; Carter 1990; Hunt 1990; Kraska and Kappeler 1988; Sapp 1986). These studies reveal a consistent pattern of misconduct that contradicts traditional conceptualizations of police corruption.

The police literature that alludes to PSV addresses the phenomenon as "police sexual misconduct," emphasizing the on-duty "consensual sex" activities of a male officer with a female citizen (Barker 1978; Lagrange 1993). One study surveyed 43 officers in a southern city and found that the proportion of officers in that department perceived as having sex on duty was almost 32 percent (Barker 1978). That study makes clear why many researchers and most police organizations emphasize consensual sex rather than instances of PSV.

> The police officer comes into contact with a number of females during his routine patrol duties. These contacts occur under conditions which provide numerous opportunities for illicit sex. . . . The officer also has the opportunity to stop a number of women coming home after a night of drinking. An intoxicated female may decide that *her sexual favors* are a small price to pay in order to avoid arrest for driving while intoxicated. . . . The woman may also be coerced into the act

by a "rogue" officer, but on numerous occasions the woman is more than a willing partner. . . . There are also a number of women who are attracted to the uniform or the aura of the occupation (Barker 1978:266; emphasis added).

Similarly, an author of a recent police textbook writes that "police officers are subjected to incredible temptation to deviate. . . . the opportunities for easy money, drugs, and sex are seemingly endless. . . . " (Lagrange 1993: 235).

The opportunity structure that facilitates police deviance is certainly an element in understanding police crime. Yet much of the policing literature assumes implicitly that police are a desired sexual commodity who are routinely tempted by women willing to trade "sexual favors" for leniency (see, for example, Sapp 1986). This "consensual sex" assumption inhibits alternative, more victim-based conceptualizations of police sexual violence. The view of this phenomenon as a problem of sexual favors assumes tacitly that deviant police are passive actors who are "corrupted," rather than active "corruptors." More important, it undermines the recognition of "police sexual deviance" as violent crime committed against women by relegating it to "sexual favors;" as a result, the coercive nature of these encounters is masked. This assumption of consensual sex also reinforces the untested notion that only the rogue, aberrant officer would use direct coercion, force, or the authority of the badge in such encounters. The "rogue" argument has been dispelled in the best of the police literature (Sherman 1974, 1978; Stoddard 1968; Westley 1953, 1970). Collectively, this thinking promotes a lack of serious attention to the phenomenon, promotes a conceptualization of police sexual deviance that denies the violence associated with sexual victimization, and negates the possibility of a systematic or occupationally generated form of police victimization of women.

A close reading of Sapp's (1986) study raises questions about the assumption that PSV is an occasional act committed by rogue officers. This is perhaps the only research in either the policing literature or women's studies which directly addresses several types of

PSV against women. Sapp collected interview data from "several hundred" (the actual number not specified) law enforcement officers in seven states. Although the study suffers from the usual limitations associated with informal interviewing, the findings reveal a clear pattern of what Sapp termed "police sexual harassment" of female citizens. One interviewee describes the phenomenon.

> You bet I get (sex) once in a while by some broad who I arrest. Lots of times you can just hint that if you are taken care of, you could forget about what they did. One of the department stores here doesn't like to prosecute. . . . If it's a decent looking woman, sometimes I'll offer to take her home and make my pitch. Some of the snooty, *high class broads* turn on *real quick* if they think their friends and the old man doesn't have to find out about their shoplifting (Sapp 1986:88; emphasis added).

Drawing from traditional policing literature, Sapp contends that the combination of unique opportunity, police power and authority, and the relative isolation of police-citizen encounters all facilitate sexual harassment of female citizens by police (Kappeler, Sluder, and Alpert 1994). Sapp traces the lack of recognition of this phenomenon, and the lack of institutional will to control it, to agency apathy, which he characterizes as a dangerously unenlightened "boys will be boys" attitude among police administrators and supervisors. His research, however, does not explore the possibility that within this environment of willing women ("high class broads turn on real quick"), male police officers may use even more overt forms of coercion through the use or threat of physical force, along with the authority of the uniform and the badge, to sexually harass, assault, or even rape female citizens. In addition, in some instances of sexual violation, the officer may not be pursuing a consensual sexual encounter, but may use police authority solely for sexual degradation or humiliation.

Feminist and Women's Studies Literature

The questionable assumptions found in the policing literature are not evident in the international human rights literature (Chapman 1991). Amnesty International and the division of Human Rights Watch have both recognized PSV against women as a serious human rights problem (Amnesty International 1991; Women's Rights Project 1992). The report by Human Rights Watch on the Pakistani police found that "more than 70 percent of women in police custody are subjected to physical and sexual abuse by law enforcement agents, yet not a single police official has been subjected to criminal penalties for such abuse" (Women's Rights Project, 1992:2). A 1991 Amnesty report notes the systematic police abuse of women in countries around the world, including acts such as rape, sexual humiliation through frequent and unnecessary strip-searches, the use of police power and privilege to gain sexual advantage, and degrading verbal abuse.

The human rights literature on violence against women constitutes the only definite examination of PSV against female citizens. Historically, feminist literature has focused on how legal institutions, specifically the police, have mistreated women as victims of men's violence (Daly and Chesney-Lind 1988; Lafree 1981; Radrod 1989; Simpson 1989). Although we will not review this expansive literature here, we will consider a more direct form of PSV—occupational sexual harassment—for two reasons. First, it provides a well-documented instance of male police officers sexually harassing women. Second, it furnishes an instructional theoretical account of sexual harassment in police agencies that might be applicable to the police harassment of female citizens not working in policing organizations.

Since women's entry into policing in the mid-1970s, researchers have examined the problem of sexual harassment of female police employees (Hale and Wyland 1993; Martin 1980, 1990). Sexual harassment constitutes the most conspicuous warning to women that they do not belong in any substantive way to this male-dominated occupation (Hale and Wyland 1993; Martin 1992). Susan Martin (1990:290) found that "most women officers have experienced both sex discrimination and sexual harassment." Her most recent research finds that of 70 female officers interviewed,

two-thirds of the women identified at least one instance of sex discrimination and 75 percent reported instances of sexual harassment on the job. . . . Descriptions of the harassment faced by the first group on women on patrol indicated that frequently it was blatant, malicious, widespread, organized, and involved supervisors, occasionally it was life-threatening (Martin 1992.290).

Those who attempt to explain what underlies this harassment reach the same conclusion as those who scrutinize police-biased handling of violence against women in general: the cause is a sexist, highly masculine organizational ideology. Some observers have made note of the ideology (Christopher Commission 1992, Harris 1973), but researching this aspect of police culture is a relatively new undertaking. Probably the two most revealing works are those by Hunt (1990) and Young (1991). Using qualitative data collected from 18 months of fieldwork, Hunt (1990) examined the underlying logic of sexist ideology in a large urban police department. She excavates the components of a sexist police culture, highlighting (among other things) how the constructed image of the "moral woman" threatens the secret amoral world of male policing, and how policemen use degradation and humiliation to neutralize the perceived power that policewomen have or might obtain in the organization. Her conclusion has important implications for PSV against women:

> [I]t is important to acknowledge that sexism is not simply a product of sex role learning but it has a deep structure which is articulated in every aspect of the police world. As such, it is organizationally crucial to the practice of policing as well as the occupational identity of individual police (Hunt 1990:26).

Young (1991) reaches similar conclusions when examining anthropologically his 30 years of law enforcement experience in England. He likens police culture to that found in other all-male organizations, where shared values combine to form a "cult of masculinity" used as a legitimating ideology to denigrate and deny the value of women. His work exposes the consequences for women within the organizations: "My own observations suggest that policemen are overtly and consistently hostile towards women in 'the job,' and that the social control of these women is inevitably a burning issue" (Young 1991:193). Thus, the link between the institutionalized sexist ideology of the police and occupational sexual harassment is well established. Our research asks whether this cultural environment also operates outside the police organization, affecting some police officers' willingness to sexually harass, humiliate, and violate female citizens.

The policing literature assumes that "police sexual misconduct" most often involves "consensual sex," sexual favors, and rogue officers; the feminist literature makes clear that the traditional police culture, along with the occupational role and structural position of the police, may provide the appropriate organizational and cultural context for PSV against women. Thus instances of this phenomenon, if discovered, would be consistent with both the policing and the feminist literature reviewed here. In exploratory fashion, our research addresses two preliminary points. First, by using two incidence-based data sets, one from federal litigation cases and the other from media accounts, we inquire into the known scope and distribution of PSV. Second, to understand the nature of this phenomenon and how it informs and is informed by the existing feminist and policing literature, we develop a PSV continuum using illustrative case examples.

Methodology: The Double Bind of Secrecy

The difficulty of acquiring knowledge on this sensitive topic cannot be overstated. The wall of secrecy in policing, which conceals these crimes ("the blue wall of silence"), forms a difficult barrier for the researcher (Manning 1978; Skolnick 1966; Westley 1953). Even in the infrequent cases where some sort of wrong-doing becomes departmental knowledge, it is almost impossible to obtain information without a court order or a covert and perhaps ethically problematic research design. (Even the Christopher Commission could not access the personnel files of the officers involved in the Rodney King beating).

The secrecy bind only magnifies when one looks to the other potential source of data—those victimized by PSV. Victims of sexual violence in general have few incentives to pursue a formal complaint, as well as many disincentives including the fear of being blamed for the incident and the fear of not being believed. Not being believed and "the fear of depersonalizing and humiliating institutional procedures and interpersonal hassles to which victims of sexual violence are frequently subject" may be intensified when the offender is a police officer (Schneider 1993:57). In short, the "blue wall of silence" and the barriers to reporting combine to form a double bind of secrecy that makes data virtually unavailable to researchers.

Therefore we relied on cases in which victims overcame these obstacles and made public their victimization. Three avenues of public disclosure are possible: a formal complaint filed with the police department, the filing of a criminal complaint or a lawsuit against the officer and the department, and the disclosure of the incident to the press. We first collected data for this study using media accounts of PSV found in a national newspaper between 1991 and the first six months of 1993.[1] Second, we examined all published cases decided by the Federal District Courts between 1978 and 1992 in which the police were sued under 42 U.S.C. Section 1983, alleging some form of sexual violence.[2] These data are limited in that they include only reported incidents of PSV that reached the media, or cases pursued by a plaintiff in the federal courts. Thus our data provide only an indication of how often someone goes public with a complaint; they can tell us little about the upper range of the frequency of PSV. Finally, we use relevant comments derived from interviews with key criminal justice personnel, police officers, lawyers, and rape crisis workers to illuminate the nature of PSV against women.[3]

To establish a coding system for these cases, we examined the existing literature on violence against women and on police deviance, and made an initial coding of randomly selected cases. We coded the manifest content of each case in a stratified random sequence to distribute any coder bias. We developed a data classification system to enable the content analysis to determine the variety of PSV, geographic and demographic descriptors, political subdivision and employing agency, and the organizational position of the offending law enforcement officer.

We use illustrative cases in the second part of this study to examine the range of behaviors and the nature of PSV incidents. As Reinharz (1991) notes, case studies are an important tool for exploring relevant issues, examining relationships between factors, developing potential theories and concepts, and understanding the nuances of an unexplored, difficult-to-research phenomenon. This method highlights these dimensions inductively, following a long-standing epistemological tradition of developing "grounded theory" (Glaser and Strauss 1965).

We found a diverse range of incidents constituting "police sexual violence," which required a definition that could encompass different police behaviors. Drawing heavily on the work of Kelly (1988), our definition includes *those situations in which a female citizen experiences a sexually degrading, humili-ating, violating, damaging, or threatening act committed by a police officer through the use of force or police authority.* As Kelley (1988:40) points out, this definition of sexual violence makes no direct reference to the "imputed intentions of the violator." This point is important because an officer ordering a body-cavity search in the back of a patrol cruiser may not overtly intend sexual humiliation, but that may be the effect nonetheless.[4]

Findings and Analysis

A Continuum of Police Sexual Violence

Instances of PSV examined ranged from invasions of privacy of a sexual nature to forcible rape. Consequently we conceptualized PSV on a continuum to avoid focusing only on extreme incidents. The continuum also allows us to explore the sociostructural links between these different forms of violence (Ahluwalia 1992; Kelly 1988). It is based on the "obtrusiveness" of the police behavior, and ranges from unobtrusive to obtrusive to criminal (see Table 23.1). "Unobtrusive" behavior includes behaviors such as voyeurism, viewing sexually explicit photographs or videos of crime victims, and other

Table 23.1
A Continuum of Police Sexual Violence

Continuum Category	Range of Behaviors	Institutional or Cultural Support	Operational Justification	Range of Legal Sanctions
Unobtrusive Behavior	Viewing victims, photographs, and sexually explicit videos, invasions of privacy, secondary victimization	Possible institutional and cultural	Crime control investigation, examine evidence, review evidence for case preparation	Civil lawsuit
Obtrusive Behavior	Custodial strip searches, body cavity searches, warrant-based searches, illegal detentions, deception to gain sexual favors, provision of services for sexual favors, sexual harassment	Possible institutional and cultural	Preservation of evidence, ensure security, control contraband, law enforcement, hampers enforcement efforts, necessary for covert investigations	Civil lawsuit to possibly criminal
Criminal Behavior	Sexual harassment, sexual contact, sexual assault, rape	Linked to institutionalized police characteristics	None	Civil lawsuit to criminal

Table 23.2
Frequencies of Police Sexual Violence, by Continuum Categories

Continuum Category	News Source		Federal Litigation Cases		Total	
	(f)	%	(f)	%	(f)	%
Unobtrusive	4	12.1	9	9.9	74	59.7
Obtrusive	7	21.2	67	73.6	13	10.5
Criminal	22	66.7	15	16.5	37	29.8
Total	33	100	91	100	124	100

Table 23.3
Frequencies of Police Sexual Violence, by Offense Type

Type of Offense	News Source		Federal Litigation Cases		Total	
	(f)	%	(f)	%	(f)	%
Violation of Privacy	10	30.3	8	8.8	18	14.6
Strip Search	2	6	67	73.6	69	55.6
Sexual Assault	12	36.4	8	8.8	20	16.1
Rape	9	27.3	8	8.8	17	13.7
Total	33	100	91	100	124	100

invasions of privacy. Obtrusive sexual behavior includes unnecessary, illegal, or punitive pat-down searches, strip searches, body-cavity searches, the provision of police services or leniency for sexual advantage, the use of deception to gain sexual advantage from citizens, and some instances of sexual harassment.[5] Criminal behavior involves certain instances of sexual harassment, sexual assault, and rape.

Known Incidence and Distribution

We found a total of 124 cases of police sexual violence (see Tables 23.2 and 23.3). Thirty-three of these came from a single national news source between January 1991 and June 1993; 91 came from the legal database mentioned above (there is no overlap between cases reported from each source). Although the federal litigation data begin in 1978, almost 51 percent of the cases have been filed since 1988. Among these federal cases, 10 percent (n=9) involved unobtrusive PSV incidents, 74 percent (n=67) obtrusive incidents, and 16.5 percent (n=15) criminal behavior. About 9 percent (n=8) were rapes, 9 percent (n=8) were sexual assaults, and 9 percent (n=8) were violations of privacy (n=8). The remaining cases, 74 percent (n=67), involved the use of strip or body-cavity searches by the police. Most cases involved only one officer; however, 11 percent of the incidents involved two or more officers. Eighty-seven percent of the violations were committed by line officers; administrative personnel were involved in 12 percent of the cases.

The 67 victims of strip and body-cavity searches had been charged with relatively minor legal infractions; in fact, 78 percent (n=45) had been charged with either misdemeanor crimes or mere traffic violations. Only 22 percent (n=13) of the women subjected to this police practice had been charged with a felony violation; most of these cases did not involve violations that would justify the use of an intrusive search. Police lost 69 percent of the claims brought against them, an extremely high percentage compared with all other areas of civil litigation: the police generally lose fewer than 10 percent of such actions (Kappeler 1993; Kappeler, Kappeler, and del Carmen 1993). A civil judgment against the police was not a sufficient deterrent: many of the cases were brought against recidivist police organizations that refused to change their practices. Indeed, the legal system provided little incentive to curb the unlawful use of strip and body-cavity searches—the average damage award against a police organization was only $27,182. This figure is more than $100,000 below the average damage award level against the police for the use of excessive force (Kappeler et al. 1993).

In the data from the national news source, only 2 cases, or 6 percent of all the cases, involved strip searches. The relative absence of reports of illegal strip searches probably reflects what the media deem newsworthy. The bulk of these cases were sexual assaults (n=12) and rape (n=9), constituting almost 64 percent of all the instances of PSV. In contrast to the federal cases, the media tended to focus on the extreme instances of PSV: 12 percent (n=4) of these cases involved PSV incidents that fell within the "unobtrusive" segment of the continuum, 21 percent (n=7) were obtrusive, and 67 percent (n=22) were criminal. About 16 percent of these cases involved two or more officers; 84 percent involved a single officer. Nearly 30 percent (n=10) of the violations were committed by administrative personnel (chief, captain, sergeant, and sheriff), and the remaining 70 percent by line officers.

When we combined the two data sets, we found 37 cases of either rape or sexual assault by a police officer, or 30 percent of the incidents. Administrative and supervisory personnel were involved in 16 percent (n=20) of all cases; 12 percent (n=15) involved two or more officers. Therefore the notion of the "rogue" line officer is challenged. Moreover, several cases involved law enforcement personnel from agencies in different political jurisdictions, acting in concert (see illustrative case below under "secondary victimization").

How were these incidents of PSV distributed geographically and by political jurisdiction? Both data sets revealed that defendants from municipal law enforcement were involved in 64.5 percent of the cases (n=80), officers from sheriff's departments in 21 percent (n=26), officers from different political jurisdictions in 6.5 percent (n=8), and state and federal officers in 8 percent (n=10) (see Table 23.4). The proportions of cases coming from different agency levels are similar to the proportions of officers employed at these levels (see Reaves 1992a, 1992b). Geographically, instances of PSV were reported in 31 of the 50 states and were dispersed throughout all regions.

Interpreting Exploratory Data

These data must be interpreted cautiously because of their exploratory nature and the double bind of secrecy. Either to reject their significance or to claim that PSV is a pervasive problem is to overstep the exploratory nature of this research. Because of the methodology employed, however, these 124 cases may represent only the tip of the iceberg. Two factors support our claim. First, the policing and feminist literature reviewed earlier identify not only a clear precedent for police sexual violence against women, but also an organizational, structural, and cultural environment favoring this form of victimization. Second, even if one considers only the most extreme form of PSV (rape), the research suggests a pattern in several geographical areas whereby the reporting of police rape by a single victim brought forth three to five additional victims, usually raped by different officers. This pattern was found in Dallas, in

Table 23.4
Frequencies of Police Sexual Violence, by Political Jurisdiction

Political Jurisdiction	News Source		Federal Litigation Cases		Total	
	(f)	%	(f)	%	(f)	%
Municipal	24	72.8	59	64.8	83	66.9
County	6	18.2	21	23.1	17	21.8
State	1	3	0	0	1	.8
Federal	1	3	2	2.2	3	2.4
Multi-jurisdictional	1	3	8	8.8	9	7.3
Other	0	0	1	1.1	1	.8
Total	33	100	91	100	124	100

several areas in southern California, in Houston, and in Maryland (Boyer, 1992; Ford 1992; Makeig 1993; O'Conner 1993; Platte 1991; Shen 1990). In 1992 alone, for example, four alleged victims of police rape surfaced in Dallas; each victim accused a different officer. The clinical supervisor of a Dallas rape crisis center subsequently reported that their organization assists two or three women a year who have been raped by on-duty Dallas police officers. These women have not reported the incident to the police because "they're afraid of retaliation" (O'Conner 1993:274). Again, the data presented here include only those incidents in which victims overcame reporting obstacles and made a formal complaint; most likely, these constitute only a small percentage of the actual cases.

Illustrative Cases, Issues, and Interpretations

We identify an entire range of behaviors (unobtrusive to obtrusive to criminal) as police sexual violence. A continuum counters the tendency to view the more extreme forms of sexual violence as aberrations, which severs them from their common structural and cultural bases. In examining actual cases of PSV along the continuum, the objective is to analyze, in exploratory fashion, the relevant theoretical, conceptual, and practical issues.[6] In this way the phenomenon can inform feminist and policing studies, while the literatures in those areas can aid in understanding this form of violence against women and police crime.

Unobtrusive: Secondary Victimization. The cases in this section include instances of PSV that fall on the least obtrusive end of the continuum. In these cases, the police violate a victim's privacy rights—a type of "secondary victimization." In *DiPalma v. Phelan* (1992), for instance, a 16-year-old female reported to the police that she had been sexually abused by her father. The police department assured her that if she signed a supporting deposition, her wish to remain anonymous to anyone unconnected with the criminal investigation would be honored. Her father pleaded guilty to the charges. Because he was employed by the municipality, the Town Board requested all documentation about the case. Despite the promise of confidentiality and the highly sensitive information in the police file, the police cooperated with the Town Board and released the information. The State Supreme Court dismissed the young woman's cause of action because "neither case law nor statute clearly establishes that a sex crime victim's constitutional right to privacy is violated by the disclosure of her identity."

Although this case does not involve violent physical contact, it demonstrates deception by police and a lack of sensitivity, which resulted in "official" victimization. The judiciary sanctioned this form of secondary police victimization, an indication of possible institutionalization of this practice. It is also significant that the violation occurred in the administrative setting of both the police institution and municipal government; it was not the act of a rogue officer.

James v. City of Douglas (1991) demonstrates a more direct form of police victimization in which deception was used to gain a crime victim's confidence and then to violate her privacy. Celeste James went to the police with allegations that her business partner was attempting to extort insurance money by threatening to show her family a videotape of herself and her business partner engaged in sexual activity. The tape was made without her knowledge or consent. She expressed her reluctance to cooperate with the investigation because of the embarrassing nature of the tape. The police assured James repeatedly that if she cooperated, they would handle the tape discreetly. The tape, once confiscated by the police, was handled otherwise: several police officers at the scene of the search viewed it in its entirety; no one ever logged it in as evidence; and copies were made and circulated throughout much of the department. During one of the "viewings," the chief of police, the assistant chief, the sheriff of the county, and a sheriff's deputy were all present. The court ruled that the showing of the videotape violated a "clearly established constitutional right to privacy."

This case, in which officers engaged collectively in a contemporary form of voyeurism, points to the cultural acceptance, throughout the rank structure of these particular agencies, of violating a female crime victim's trust. Sapp (1986) lists voyeurism as one way in which some "sexually deviant" officers entertain themselves while on duty. This case illustrates the unique access of the police to such private material, and how responsibly they handle female victims of sexual violence. Men's "sexual access" to women (Kelly 1988) and the police handling of male violence against women (Dobash and Dobash 1992) are both important issues in feminist scholarship.

Obtrusive: Strip and Body-Cavity Searches. In moving along the PSV continuum to the "obtrusive" category, it is important to note again that the human rights literature recognizes the police abuse of strip and body-cavity searches as a serious and prevalent form of PSV. Almost 74 percent of the federal litigation cases examined here involved the alleged illegal use of strip body-cavity searches; the police lost nearly 70 percent of these cases.

The police examination of a female's body and body cavities is extremely intrusive and violating. Because of "operational necessities," however, the police can engage legally in many behaviors that would be considered criminal if performed in a different context (Brodeur 1981). For the recipients of a body-cavity search, however, context and pretenses of operational justification mean little.

The plaintiffs in the following cases likened the experience to "rape" and "being violated in the most extreme way." Technically, the legality of a search depends not on its effect on the recipient but on whether the police conducted the search out of "necessity," based it on reasonable suspicion, and conducted it within constitutional guidelines. The following cases illustrate how the police sometimes employ this tactic for their own pleasure or to sexually degrade, humiliate, or intimidate women.

In Rodriguez v. Fuetado (1991), the police were clearly more interested in degradation and intimidation than in collecting incriminating evidence. They suspected Rodriquez of trafficking in illegal drugs and sought a warrant, which a judge approved, to search her vagina for narcotics. The police appeared at her residence late at night, forced the door

open, and found her and her husband sleeping in bed (an unlikely occasion for harboring drugs in a body cavity). The police told Rodriquez that they had a warrant to search her vagina, and repeatedly demanded that she reach in and "take out the stuff." When she refused to cooperate, the police drove her to the local hospital. Rodriquez still protested the search; under duress and coercion, the physician on duty put on rubber gloves and proceeded to insert a probe into the plaintiff's vagina. He then removed the probe, placed one hand on the plaintiff's stomach, and inserted his fingers or some other instrument far into her vagina. No drugs were found. The courts ruled against the plaintiff, but did claim that they were "deeply troubled" by the search. The fact that the plaintiff was taken to the hospital by the police in the middle of the night to have her vagina searched raises, at the very least, the possibility that the police were more interested in intimidating the plaintiff than they were in finding narcotics. It is difficult to imagine a more intrusive, humiliating, and demeaning search. . . . Interestingly, the court did not mention the propriety of the judge's actions in issuing a warrant for this invasive search, or in failing to limit the fashion in which it was conducted.

More controversial are cases in which the police conduct "investigatory strip searches" in the field. The court ruled only partially against the police in *Timberlake v. Benton* (1992). In this case, two teenage females were driving a truck owned by a relative suspected of drug trafficking. Even though the police had no information linking the two women to the illegal distribution of drugs, the "drug task force" supervisor (a male) ordered a female officer to conduct a complete strip and body-cavity search in the back seat of a patrol cruiser. The female suspects stripped; they were ordered onto their hands and knees with their posteriors facing the open doorway and highway in *plain* sight of male officers at the scene. The drug enforcement officer hinted at his motive for the search when he threatened the women with future strip searches unless they provided information about their relative. The court ruled that the women were not entitled to punitive damages but that the police might be liable for injuries resulting from the search. The court also noted that this police department had a history of conducting illegal "non-custodial investigatory strip searches."

These cases raise several important issues. Illegal strip and body-cavity searches have remained civil rights violations rather than crimes, even though the law allows excessive force by police to be conceptualized as both a civil and a criminal act. One could argue that the differential treatment of these cases by the judiciary serves to condone these practices. One lawyer who specializes in suing the police sheds light on the difficulty of such cases: "We don't like strip search cases. . . . What you have to remember is that there are no damages when cops search suspects and the courts are unwilling to allow punitive awards in these situations. . . . These police practices cannot be explained away as the rogue cop circumventing the law for personal gain. Brodeur's (1981:135) insight about other forms of police organizational deviance applies here: "It is a mistake to hold that it is for the most part informal practices that circumvent the law. These practices are to a significant extent grounded in the law." The judiciary in *Rodriguez* not only failed to rule against the police department, but also approved of the search by issuing the warrant. Because the police are in a unique position to conduct searches of a person's most private physical self, one would think that stringent constitutional constraints would be in place. In practice, however, our data suggest that police organizations routinely disregard the rule of law, opting to absorb the token damage awards that juries are likely to impose.

That component of the masculine belief system in policing which supports unnecessary strip and body-cavity searches may also exist in the judiciary and the bar. The legal and media cases used here demonstrate a sexist, culturally based belief held by some police, judges, and lawyers that women are capable of carrying drugs and weapons inside their body cavities, and do so regularly. As one Ohio Supreme Court justice wrote: "Even if Ficker had been concealing contraband . . . it would require a quantum leap in logic to conclude that such contraband would be routinely carried within a body cav-

ity" (*Fricker v. Stokes*, 1986:206). Unlike forms of "deviance," therefore, this form of police wrongdoing leads us to ask to what degree this type of PSV is linked to legal, organizational and cultural elements of the police and justice system.

Obtrusive Criminal: Police Sexual Harassment. Police sexual harassment falls into the gray area between the "obtrusive" and the "criminal" categories. Such harassment of female citizens in itself, unlike harassment in the workplace, is not directly proscribed by law; even in its most serious forms, it is rarely handled as "crime," by a police department or the criminal justice system. As evidenced by the cases cited below, however, certain behaviors involved in police sexual harassment could be defined as crime, such as false imprisonment, battery, or sexual abuse.

U.S. v. Langer (1992) illustrates a typical instance of police sexual harassment. A patrol sergeant employed by a municipal police department was convicted of stopping and detaining five female drivers, one of them on two occasions. Each stop was made at night on a deserted stretch of highway, under the pretense of enforcing drunk driving laws. The officer usually informed the women that they needed a ride home. One of his victims was a 19-year-old female, whom he falsely accused of driving while intoxicated. He insisted on taking her for a ride in his patrol car to "sober her up." After driving around for some time, the sergeant pulled his patrol car into a deserted spot overlooking a lake. He then told his detainee that she was very understanding and attractive, and that he wanted to take her out. After she declined, stating that she had a boyfriend, the officer persisted in questioning her about her relationship with her boyfriend. She asked to be taken back to her car; the officer refused, and instead drove her to a diner. He repeatedly refused her requests to be released, but eventually released her. In the woman's words. "He walked me to my car and I took my keys and I opened the lock, and he opened up my car door for me, and when I turned around to get into the car, he grabbed me by the shoulders and pushed me against the car with his body and kissed me." The sergeant subsequently called her several times and left messages on her answering machine.

With only slight changes, the same scenario would be standard fare in depicting interactions between police and female citizens in popular entertainment. A male police officer pulls over a female who attracts him and coyly threatens her with a traffic ticket, while they deliver sexual innuendoes to one another. In another common depiction, a male police officer assigned to protect a vulnerable woman exploits his position as an occasion for romance. These customary portrayals are important because they point to society's acceptance of male police officers' using state authority and power to pursue women sexually. Yet none of the cases examined here displays a female who reciprocated with sexual innuendo or banter, or seemed willing to offer "sexual favors." In a sexist organization, this broader cultural support may have real-world consequences. Sapp's (1986) research identified police sexual harassment as a pervasive and tolerated form of police misconduct.

The same behavior—exploiting a gender-based power difference to make sexually demeaning or suggestive remarks under the threat of a sanction—certainly would constitute sexual harassment or extortion in the workplace (MacKinnon 1979). Feminist scholars are exploring contexts beyond the workplace in which sexual harassment takes place, such as doctor/patient or professor/student (Belknap and Erez forthcoming). The sexual harassment of women by male police officers is particularly significant: the often-discussed power differential exists not only because the harasser is male, but also because he has the state-sanctioned power to detain, arrest, and use physical force if the female does not cooperate. Unlike the college professor, the physician, or even the employer, the police officer can invoke operational necessity, sometimes with institutional support, to engage in a range of potentially abusive behaviors, most significantly the legitimate use of violence. This extreme difference in power helps us understand police rape, the most extreme form of PSV.

Criminal: Police rape. Rape falls at the extreme end of the PSV continuum. In several cities and states (discussed earlier), the discovery that police officers have raped female citizens while on duty causes outrage among some, disbelief among others, and shock among nearly all people. This type of crime raises many important theoretical and legal issues.

We found an obvious pattern when reviewing the rape cases cited here. The incidents resemble the sexual harassment case cited above, in that they involve a police officer who pulls over a female citizen for some traffic violation (generally driving under the influence), threatens her with arrest, and takes her to a secluded location for some outwardly legitimate reason. The difference here is that the police officer then rapes his victim.

A 33-year-old veteran officer in southern California, for example, used to lie in wait for women outside bars and restaurants, pull them over on false charges, convince them that they were about to be arrested, follow them to a secluded spot (a remote lake), and then rape them in the back seat of his patrol car. The police suspected that over the years, this may have happened to numerous women with no serious departmental inquiry. Only three women of the 30 interviewed eventually came forward with charges (Ford 1992).

In Houston in 1992, several women made claims against a Houston police officer; only one resulted in prosecution. This case involved a 23-year-old woman who worked for an attorney. Earlier on the evening of the arrest, she had been at a nightclub. The officer pulled her over, said he smelled alcohol on her breath, and took her driver's license and insurance card "[Officer] Potter told her to follow him to a nearby parking garage that he called his 'sleeping spot.'" In the victim's words, "'I was real apprehensive and frightened, but he just started asking about my background and family. I thought he was just going to write out the ticket in the car and let me go.'" (Zuniga 992:15A). Instead the officer made sexually degrading comments and ignored her pleas for freedom. He then ordered her out of the patrol car and told her: "'You could go to jail and get raped by the (blacks) or would you rather bend over or lay down?'" (Zuniga 1992:15A). The police officer then raped her over the hood of the patrol car. Afterward he apologized for having to leave because he was 30 minutes late to his last call. The woman returned home, called a rape crisis hotline, and then went to the hospital for a rape examination.

The real significance for this study is that these particular officers, as members of the select group of persons empowered to enforce the state's laws and protect the citizens, exploited their unique access to female citizens, and their power and authority as police, to engage in sexually violent behavior.

Also important is the pattern of raping women who are out late at night and suspected of being intoxicated. As one officer told the first author during the data collection stage, he and five other officers in his department routinely go out "bimbo-hunting": they wait outside the bars, pull over women who "should be home with their boyfriends," and sexually harass them. Part of the logic of sexism is that women are expected to abide by certain norms of feminine sexuality and to remain in their "proper place" (Hatty 1989; Scully 1990). A police officer told Hatty (1989:79), "I see a lot of women who are drunk all the time. They're just sluts. They should be looking after their kids." The predatory dynamic here might include the sexist belief among some police that women who go drinking and who frequent bars have a lower status, possibly so low as to be "police property," and therefore are subject to victimization and/ or open to sexual extortion (Lee 1981).[7]

Another important concern here is that the difficulties faced by women in reporting sexual violence in general may only be intensified when the offender is a police officer. In 1991 the California Supreme Court awarded $150,000 to a woman raped by an on-duty police officer 10 years earlier. (The officer served 18 months in prison.) The woman hoped the ruling would encourage other victims of police rape to overcome their fear of reporting. As she stated, "I was afraid at the time that no one would believe me." Several cases demonstrate that this fear may not be unfounded.

In *Parrish v. Lukie* (1992), Officer Lukie drove a female detainee to an isolated portion of North Little Rock and forced her to per-

form oral sex. The police were aware of Lukie's history of sexually assaulting women on the job, but no action was ever taken. The court ruled:

> [W]e find overwhelming evidence to support the jury's finding that North Little Rock police officers operated in a system where reports of physical or sexual assault by officers were discouraged, ignored, or covered up.

As with sexual violence against women in general, the difficulty for several victims of police rape was presented by the courts, even when the police took the complaint seriously. In a period of only 11 months, four different Dallas police officers were accused of raping female citizens. Three of the cases went to the grand jury, with the Dallas police department asking for an indictment of rape; all of these cases were reduced to the misdemeanor offense of "official oppression." The jury, guided by the prosecutor, determined that the cases lacked the legal requirement of "use of force." In each case, police officers pulled over women on false traffic violations and sexually assaulted them. The juries did not find evidence of coercion because the women did not attempt to leave the scene of the incident, or did not "fight back."

One victim's account reveals the reason. After an evening at a nightclub with her two daughters, she was pulled over by a Dallas police officer for driving while intoxicated.

> He said, "I want you to step out. . . ." He grabbed me by the elbow and led me between the two cars. . . . The whole time I was intimidated. I was really scared of this man; there was just something about him. He made me feel like I was going to comply no matter what. He had the authority. At that point, I lost it. I was in this man's control. For me to holler, to try to run away on foot, wouldn't have done any good. We were out in an empty parking lot at two in the morning. What was I going to do? Run to the police station?. . . He unzipped my pants and pulled them down to my hips. Then he grabbed me by my arm again and flung me around. I thought, "My God, this man is going to sodomize me." I've never been sexual that way. I'm Hispanic and we don't do this. . . . Nothing was being said by this man.

Nothing was talked about. . . . (O'Conner 1993:231).

Some feminist scholars place the male ability to use force and coercion at the center of their analysis of crimes against women and their oppression (see Kelly 1988). The above account illustrates how the assaulting police officer's possession of state-sanctioned power, along with the power of being male, rendered overt force unnecessary. As Hannah Ardent states, "[F]orce is only used when power is in jeopardy" (Kelly 1988:22). Because the criminal and the civil law have failed to extend their conceptualization of coercion or force to women's victimization at the hands of the police, several women's groups are advocating a new law in Texas which would classify a police officer's uniform and badge as an instrument of force. As in the ruling in *Miranda v. Arizona* (1966), this law would assume that the authority of the police when detaining a suspect inherently creates the threat of force.

Conclusion: Building Links Along the Continuum

The extreme power differential between policemen and female citizens comprises only one of several links connecting the various forms of PSV against women. Others are a sexist organizational ideology, judicial and legal support or tolerance for some types of PSV, and the structural position of the police.

In this paper we examine a unique form of police crime and violence against women. Two literatures—police studies and feminist studies—are most appropriate for contextualizing theoretically the range of behaviors defined here as PSV against women. The policing literature focuses mainly on on-duty consensual sex; feminist studies primarily examine "secondary victimization" of women by the police. The only direct examination of PSV is found in the descriptive international human rights literature. The feminist and the policing literature overlap in their examination of male police officers sexually harassing female police and citizens; they also expose a cultural and structural setting conducive to PSV. The policing literature allows for the conceptualization of power, authority, and opportunity, but generally masks the gender bias of the police occupation and the law with discussions of aberrant officers, sexual favors, and consenting females. The feminist literature illuminates the bias and the systemic differential treatment of citizens based on gender, but fails to fully recognize the nuances of police power, authority, and opportunity as they influence police crime.

The dual elements of police secrecy and reporting obstacles for victims inhibit the type of data available on this sensitive topic. Our research has provided an exploratory examination of the known incidence and nature of the many forms of PSV through a database of federal litigation, media cases, and interviews.

A critical element throughout the PSV continuum is the sexist nature of the conventional police culture. Feminist studies have discussed at length how a sexist organizational ideology in a police department can harm female victims of crime, coworkers, and lawbreakers. As Hunt (1990) found, sexism is a deep structure within policing, manifested in the "occupational identity of individual police." Other feminist studies have discovered that a sexist culture in any organization which has access to women can constitute a governing structural factor in sexual violence. Martin and Hummer (1989) examined the conditions and processes in college fraternities which facilitate sexual violence against women. Copenhaver and Grauerholz's statement about their research succinctly highlights the parallel between fraternities and police organizations:

> Martin and Hummer's research provides insight into how social institutions such as fraternities encourage sexual violence against women. Fraternities norms and practices, especially the preoccupation with loyalty, group protection and secrecy, use of alcohol, involvement in violence and physical force . . . create an atmosphere conducive to sexual violence against women (1991:31).

Our research exposes a darker consequence of this ideological environment. It supplements a growing realization in police studies, largely due to feminist scholarship, that police studies should involve another significant "ism"—beside racism, cynicism, and isolationism—necessary for an understanding of police crime and culture (Hunt 1991, Young 1991; Roberg and Kuykendall 1993). Police academics and some police agencies are beginning to recognize the importance of addressing this aspect of policing.

> Departments must attempt to accelerate change with respect to the traditional sexist police culture. Although some significant strides have been made with respect to de-emphasizing the highly militaristic/masculine approach to police organization and management over the past decade, such traditions are firmly entrenched and difficult to overcome. (Roberg and Kuykendall 1993:405)

Another common element on the PSV continuum is the structural position and situational opportunity of the police to commit acts of PSV. The police possess exceptional access to women, often in situations with little or no direct accountability. Each form of PSV examined here—invasion of privacy, strip and body-cavity searches, sexual harassment, and rape—involves exploitation of this privileged position by both patrol officers and administrative personnel. Strip and body-cavity searches are especially relevant because they have organizational and institutional support.

The structural position of police in society includes their occupational role as trusted "citizen protectors." Because women's personal safety and their fear of sexual violence are fundamental issues in feminist studies (Ahluwalia 1992; Stanko 1991), PSV adds a critical dimension to the ambivalence in the literature about relying on the police and criminal justice system to "protect" women (Caufield and Wonders 1993; Edwards 1990; Mein and Kress 1976; Rafford 1989; Thorton 1991). As several authors point out, violence against women is committed most often by those to whom women turn for protection (Stanko 1993). Each instance of PSV in this study adds credibility to this feminist insight.

These sociocultural links demonstrate the importance of conceptualizing PSV on a continuum. In this way we can avoid viewing police crime as simply an aberration committed by a rogue officer; we can place it within an entire range of less obtrusive behaviors, all of which have common structural and cultural roots. The concept of the continuum also allows for the recognition that PSV in some forms may be institutionally supported, and in other forms may be connected to institutionalized characteristics of the police (see Table 1). The intellectual environment in crime and justice studies is ripe for scrutinizing more closely the crime committed by the institution ostensibly designed to control it, and the critical role gender bias plays.

Notes

1. The newspaper source in the "Across the Nation" section of *USA Today*, supplemented, when practical, by the collection of local newspaper accounts of these incidents. We realize the limitations in using newspaper accounts but, as Marx observes, "media accounts are too often ignored by academic analysts. I have found them an invaluable source of cases, ideas, and questions" (1988:xxi).

2. These data were extracted from a larger data set of published cases decided by the Federal District Courts and associated with police liability. Only about 12 percent of civil rights cases decided by the courts are actually published (Olson 1992).

3. We conducted formal and informal interviews during a two-year period. These included interviews with victims of PSV (n=5), members of the media reporting on PSV (n=3), police officials (n=15), police officers who have engaged or currently are engaging in PSV (n=6), and lawyers involved in litigating PSV (n=6). We conducted these interviews to educate ourselves about this phenomenon, not as the empirical foundation for this research.

4. One shortcoming of this definition is that it may not include those instances of PSV which were degrading and exploitative, but were not perceived as such by the victim. One such case occurred in Florida, where several deputy sheriffs exchanged sex for extra security with a mentally disturbed late-night clerk at a Circle K store ("Florida Deputies" 1990).

5. See Marx (1992) for an excellent discussion of the police use of sex and deception in law enforcement.

6. We selected cases that illustrated the upper and lower bounds of the continuum categories, and that provided detailed descriptions of the facts and circumstances in the cases. Several other cases in the litigation database would have served equally well.

7. Although in this research we could not account for the race of the officers and the victims, the Dallas anecdote near the end of this section illustrates the possibility that the dynamic of lowering the victim's status may include the victim's race as well as "a female drinking late at night." See Sims (1976) for an instance of sexual abuse, by the justice system, of black females in a southern jail.

References

Ahluwalia, S. (1992) "Counting What Counts: The Study of Women's Fear of Crime." In J. Lowman and B.D. Maclean (eds.) *Realist Criminology: Crime Control and Policing in the 1990s*, pp. 246-263. Toronto: University of Toronto Press.

Alpert, G. and L. Fridell (1992) *Police Vehicles and Firearms: Instruments of Deadly Force*. Prospect Heights, IL: Waveland.

Amnesty International (1991) *Women in the Front Line: Human Rights Violations against Women*. New York: Amnesty International Publications.

Barker, T. (1977) "Peer Group Support for Police Occupational Deviance." In T. Barker and D. Carter (eds.), *Police Deviance*, pp. 9-21. Cincinnati: Anderson.

—— (1978) "An Empirical Study of Police Deviance Other Than Corruption." *Journal of Police Science and Administration* 3:264-72.

Bart, P.B. and E.G. Moran, eds. (1993) *Violence against Women: The Bloody Footprints*, Newbury Park, CA: Sage.

Belknap, J. and E. Erez (forthcoming) "Redefining Sexual Harassment: Confronting Sexism in the 21st Century." *The Justice Professional*.

Boyer, E.J. (1992) "Rape Claim Twisted, Officer Says." *Los Angeles Times*, February 13, pp. B3, B14.

Brodeur, J.P. (1981) "Legitimizing Police Deviance." In C.D. Shearing (ed.), *Organizational Police Deviance*, pp. 127 -160. Boston: Butterworth.

Carter, D.L. (1990) "Typology of Drug Corruption." *Journal of Criminal Justice* 2:85-98.

Carter, D.L., A.D. Sapp, and D.M. Stephens (1989) *The State of Police Education: Policy Direction for the 21st Century*. Washington, DC: Police Executive Research Forum.

Caulfield, S.L. and N.A. Wonders "Personal AND Political: Violence against Women and the Role of the State." In K.D. Tunnell (ed.), *Political Crime in Contemporary America: A Critical Approach* pp. 79 -100 New York: Garland.

—— (1994) "Gender and Justice: Feminist Contributions to Criminology." In G. Barak (eds.), *Varieties of Criminology: Readings from a Dynamic Discipline*, pp. 213 -230. Westport, CT: Praeger.

Chapman, J.R. (1991) "Violence against Women as a Violation of Human Rights." *Social Justice* 2:54 -70.

Christopher Commission (1992) *Report of the Independent Commission on the Los Angeles Police Department*. Los Angeles: Christopher Commission.

Copenhaver, A. and E. Grauerholz (1991) "Sexual Victimization among Sorority Women: Exploring the Link between Sexual Violence and Institutional Practices." *Sex Roles* (1/2:31-41.

Daly, K. and M. Chesney-Lind (1988) "Feminism and Criminology." *Justice Quarterly* 4:497-538.

Dobash, R.E. and R.P. Dobash (1992) *Women, Violence and Social Change*. New York: Routledge.

Edwards, S. (1990) "Violence against Women: Feminism and the Law." In A. Morris and L. Gelsthorpe (eds.), *Feminist Perspectives in Criminology*, pp. 71-101. Philadelphia: Open University Press.

"Florida Deputies Accused in Security for Sex Plot." (1990) *Crime Control Digest*, December 31, p. 5.

Ford, A. (1992) "Deputy Accused of Sex Assaults on Duty." *Los Angeles Times*, October 21, p. A95.

Friedrich, R.J. (1980) "Police Use of Force: Individuals, Situations, and Organizations." *Annals of the American Academy of Political and Social Sciences* 452:8297.

Fyfe, J.J. (1978) "Shots Fired: Examination of New York City Police Firearms Discharges." Doctoral dissertation, State University New York, Albany.

Garmire, B.L. (1978) *Local Government, Police Management*. Washington, DC: International City Management Association.

Geller, W.A. and K.J. Karales (1981) "Split-Second Decisions: Shootings of and by Chicago Police." Chicago: Chicago Law Enforcement Study Group.

Geller, W.A. and A. Scott (1991) "Deadly Force: What We Know." Washington, DC: Police Executive Research Forum.

Glaser, B. and A. Strauss (1965) "The Discovery of Substantive Theory: A Basic Strategy Underlying Qualitative Research." *The American Behavioral Scientist* 6:5 -12.

Hale, D.C. and S.M. Wyland (1993) "Dragons and Dinosaurs: The Plight of Patrol Women." *Police Forum* 3:1-8.

Harris, R. (1974) *The Police Academy: An Insider's View*. New York: Wiley.

Hatty, S. E. (1989) "Policing and Male Violence in Australia." In J. Hanner, J. Radford and S.A. Stanko (eds.), *Women, Policing, and Male Violence: International Perspectives*, pp. 70-89. New York: Routledge.

Hunt, J.C. (1990) "The Logic of Sexism among Police." *Women and Criminal Justice* 2:3-30.

Kappeler, V. E. (1993) *Critical Issues in Police Civil Liability* Prospect Heights, IL: Waveland.

Kappeler, V.E., S.F. Kappeler, and R.V. del Carmen (1993) "A Content Analysis of Police Civil Liability Cases: Decisions of the Federal District Courts, 1978-1990." *Journal of Criminal Justice* 21:325-37.

Kappeler, V.E., R. Sluder, and G.P. Alpert (1994) *Forces of Deviance: Understanding the Dark Side of Policing*. Prospect Heights, IL: Waveland.

Kelly, L. (1988) *Surviving Sexual Violence*. Cambridge, UK: Polity.

Klein, D. and J. Kress (1976) "Any Women's Blues: A Critical Overview of Women, Crime and the Criminal Justice System." *Crime and Social Justice* 5:34-49.

Knapp Commission (1972) *The Knapp Commission Report on Police Corruption*. New York: George Brasiller.

Kraska, P.B. and V.E. Kappeler (1988) "A Theoretical and Descriptive Examination of Police On-Duty Drug Use." *American Journal of Police* 1:1-36.

Lafree, G.D. (1981) "Official Reactions to Social Problems: Police Decisions in Sexual Assault Cases." *Social Problems* 5:582-94.

Lagrange, R.L. (1993) *Policing American Society*. Chicago: Nelson-Hall.

Lee, J.A. (1981) "Some Structural Aspects of Police Deviance in Relations with Minority Groups." In C.D. Shearing (ed.), *Organizational Police Deviance*, pp. 49-82. Boston: Butterworth.

MacKinnon, K. (1979) *Sexual Harassment of Working Women*. New Haven: Yale University Press.

Makeig, J. (1993) "Officer to Serve Time for '88 Rape." *Houston Chronicle*, February 26, p. A26.

Manning, P.K (1978) "The Police: Mandate, Strategies and Appearances." In L.K. Gaines and T. Ricks (eds.), *Managing the Police Organization*, pp. 22-49. St. Paul: West.

Martin, S.E. (1980) *Breaking and Entering: Policewomen on Patrol*. Berkeley: University of California Press.

—— (1990) *On the Move: The Status of Women in Policing*. Washington, DC: Police Foundation.

—— (1992) "The Changing Status of Women Officers: Gender and Power in Police Work." In I.L. Moyer (ed.), *The Changing Role of Women in the Criminal Justice System*, pp. 281-305. Prospect Heights, IK: Waveland.

Marx, G.T. (1988) *Undercover: Police Surveillance in America*. Berkeley: University of California Press.

—— (1992) "Under-the-Covers Undercover Investigations: Some Reflections on the State's Use of Sex and Deception in Law Enforcement." *Criminal Justice Ethics* (Winter/Spring): 13-24.

Moyer, I.L. (1992) "Police/Citizen Encounters: Issues of Chivalry, Gender and Race." In I.L. Moyer (ed.), *The Changing Role of Women in the Criminal Justice System*, pp. 60-80. Prospect Heights, IL: Waveland.

O'Conner, C. (1993) "Explosive Charges of Cops Who Rape." *Glamour*, March, pp. 231, 274-78.

Olson, S.M. (1992) "Studying Federal District Courts through Published Cases: A Research Note." *Justice System Journal* 3:782-99.

Platte, M. (1991) "Officer Suspected of Rape Probably Knew of Stakeouts." *Los Angeles Times*, August 17, pp. A26.

Radford, J. (1989) "Women and Policing: Contradictions Old and New." In J. Hanner, J. Radford and E. A. Stanko (eds.), *Women, Policing, and Male Violence: International Perspectives*, pp. 13-45. New York: Routledge.

Reaves, B.A. (1992a) *State and Local Police Departments, 1990* Washington, DC: Bureau of Justice Statistics, U.S. Department of Justice.

—— (1992b) *Sheriff's Departments, 1990*. Washington, DC: Bureau of Justice Statistics, U.S. Department of Justice.

Reinharz, S. (1992) *Feminist Methods in Social Research*. New York: Oxford University Press.

Roberg, R.R. and J. Kuykendall (1993) *Police and Society*. Belmont, CA: Wadsworth.

Russell, D. (1982) *Rape in Marriage*. New York: Collier.

Sapp, A. (1986) "Sexual Misconduct by Police Officers." In T. Barker and D. Carter (eds.), *Police Deviance*, pp. 83-95. Cincinnati: Anderson.

Schneider, B.E. (1993) "Put Up and Shut Up: Workplace Sexual Assaults." In P.B. Bart and E.G. Moran (eds.), *Violence against Women: The Bloody Footprints*, pp. 57-72. Newbury Park, CA: Sage.

Scully, D. (1990) *Understanding Sexual Violence*. New York: Routledge.

Shen, F. (1990) "Veteran Arundel Officer Charged with Rape in Car." *Washington Post*, February 20, pp. 17A.

Sherman, L.W. (1974) *Police Corruption: A Sociological Perspective*. Garden City, NY: Doubleday.

—— (1978) *Scandal and Reform: Controlling Police Corruption*. Berkeley: University of California Press.

Simpson, S.S. (1989) "Feminist Theory, Crime, and Justice." *Criminology* 4:605-31.

Sims, P. (1976) "Women in Southern Jails." In L. Crites (ed.), *The Female Offender*, pp. 137-148. Lexington, MA: Heath.

Skolnick, J.H. (1966) *Justice without Trial: Law Enforcement in a Democratic Society*. New York: Wiley.

Stanko, E.A. (1985) *Intimate Intrusions*. London: Unwin Hyman.

—— (1991) "State Supreme Court Holds Los Angeles Liable for Rape by Officers." *Los Angeles Times*, September 8, p. 17.

—— (1989) "Missing the Mark? Police Battering." In J. Hanmer, J. Radford, and E.A. Stanko (eds.), *Women, Policing, and Male Violence: International Perspectives*, pp. 46-69. New York: Routledge.

—— (1991) "When Precaution Is Normal: A Feminist Critique of Crime Prevention." In A. Morris and L. Gelsthorpe (eds.), *Feminist Perspectives in Criminology*, pp. 173-83. Philadelphia: Open University Press.

—— (1993) "Ordinary Fear Women, Violence and Personal Safety." In P.B. Bart and E.G. Moran (eds.), *Violence against Women: The Bloody Footprints*, pp. 155-64. Newbury Park, CA: Sage.

Stoddard, E.R. (1968) "The Informal Code of Police Deviancy: A Group Approach to Blue-Coat Crime." *Journal of Criminal Law, Criminology, and Police Science* 59:201-13.

Thorton, M. (1991) "Feminism and the Contradictions of Law Reform." *International Journal of the Sociology of Law* 19:453-74.

Westley, W.A. (1953) "Secrecy and the Police." *Social Forces* 34:254-57.

—— (1970) *Violence and the Police: A Sociological Study of Law, Custom, and Morality*. Cambridge, MA: MIT Press.

Women's Rights Project (1992) *Double Jeopardy: Police Abuse of Women in Pakistan*. New York: Human Rights Watch.

Young, M. (1991) *An Inside Job: Policing and Police Culture in Britain*. Oxford: Clarendon.

Zuniga, J.A. (1992) "HPD Officer Is Indicted in Sex Attack." *Houston Chronicle*, December 19, pp. 29, 15A.

Cases Cited

DiPalma v. Phelan, 57 F. Supp. 948 E.D.N.Y. (1992)

Tricker v. Stokes, 22 St. 3d 202 (Ohio 1986)

James v. City of Douglas, GA, 941 F.2d 1539, 11th Cir. (1991)

Miranda v. Arizona, 384 U.S. 436 (1966)

Parrish v. Lukie, 963 F.2d, 8th Cir. (1992)

Rodriguez v. Fuetado, 575 F. Supp. 1439 Mass. (1991)

Timberlake by Timberlake v. Benton, 786 F. Supp. 676, M.D. Tenn. (1992)

U.S. v. Langer, 958 F.2d 522, 2nd Cir. (1992)

24

Fluffing up the Evidence and Covering Your Ass: Some Conceptual Notes on Police Lying

*Tom Barker and
David Carter*

Police deviance is not limited to corruption and brutality. One activity frequently pointed to is police lying. This is an interesting phenomenon for several reasons: (1) police routinely encounter suspects and other citizens who lie to them, making their jobs more difficult; (2) police credibility in court is based on the assumption that police officers will not lie under oath; and (3) police department rules typically require officers to tell the truth during internal investigations or else face severe discipline. In spite of all this, Barker and Carter show in their article that some forms of police lying, in both legal and administrative arenas, are common. Why is this true, do you think? Is it a serious problem, or just something we should chalk up to human behavior? What steps could be taken to reduce this form of police deviance?

Introduction

Lying and other deceptive practices are an integral part of the police officer's working environment. At first blush, one's reaction to this statement might be rather forthright. Police officers should not lie. If you can't trust your local police who can you trust. However, as with most issues the matter is not that simple.

We are all aware that police officers create false identities for undercover operations. We know that they make false promises to hostage takers and kidnappers. We also know officers will strain the truth in order to spare the feelings of a crime victim and his/her loved ones. Police officers are trained to lie and be deceptive in these law enforcement practices. They are also trained to use techniques of interrogation which require deception and even outright lying.

Police officers learn much of this in the police academy. Where they are also warned about the impropriety of perjury and the need to record all incidents fully and accurately in all official reports. The recruit learns that all rules and regulations must be obeyed. He/she learns of the danger of lying to internal affairs or a supervisor. The recruit is told to be truthful in his dealings with the noncriminal element of the public in that mutual trust is an important element in police community relations. Once the recruit leaves the academy—and in some departments where officers work in the field before attending rookie school—the officer soon learns from his/her peers that police lying is the norm under certain circumstances.

Our purpose is to discuss the patterns of lying which might occur in a police organization, the circumstances under which they occur and the possible consequences of police lying.

Taxonomy of Police Lies

Accepted Lying. Certain forms of police lying and/or deception are an accepted part of police officers working environment. The lies told in this category are accepted by the police organization because they fulfill a defined police purpose. Administrators and individual police officers believe that certain lies are necessary to control crime and "arrest the guilty." In these instances the organization will freely admit the intent to lie and define the acts as legitimate policing strategies. On face value, most would agree with the police that lies in this category are acceptable and necessary. However, a troubling and difficult question is "to what extent, if at all is it *proper* for law enforcement officials to employ trickery and deceit as part of their law enforcement practices (Skolnick, 1982, italics added)?" As we shall see, the answer to this question is not so easy. Acceptable lies may be very functional for the police but are they always proper, moral, ethical, and legal?

The most readily apparent patterns of "accepted" police lying are the deceptive practices that law enforcement officers believe are necessary to perform undercover operations or detect other forms of secret and consensual crimes. Police officers engaged in these activities must not only conceal their true identity but they must talk, act and dress out of character, fabricating all kinds of stories in order to perform these duties. One could hardly imagine that FBI Special Agent Joseph Pistone could have operated for six years in the Mafia without the substantial number of lies he had to tell (Pistone, 1987). However, the overwhelming majority of undercover operations are not as glamorous nor as dangerous as working six years with the Mafia or other organized crime groups. The most common police undercover operations occur in routine vice operations dealing with prostitution, bootlegging, gambling, narcotics, bribery of public officials (e.g. ABSCAM, MILAB, BRILAB) and sting operations.

These deceptive practices in undercover operations are not only acceptable to the law enforcement community but considered necessary for undercover operations to be effective. Nevertheless, such activities are not without problems. The "Dirty Harry" problem in police work raises the question as to what extent morally good police practices warrant or justify ethically, politically or legally suspect means to achieve law enforcement objectives (Klockars, 1980). Marx also raises the issue that many of the tactics used by law enforcement officers in such recent undercover operations as ABSCAM, MILAB, BRILAB, police run fencing or sting operations and anti-crime decoy squads may have lost sight of "the profound difference between carrying out an investigation to determine if a suspect is, in fact, breaking the law,

and carrying it out to determine if an individual can be induced to break the law (Marx, 1985: 106)." One Congressman involved in the ABSCAM case refused the first offer of cash bribe to only later accept the money after federal agents, concluding that he was an alcoholic, gave him liquor (Marx, 1985: 104).

Encouraging the commission of a crime may be a legally accepted police practice when the officer acts as a willing victim or his/her actions facilitate the commission of a crime which was going to be committed in the first place. However, it is possible for "encouragement" to lead the suspect to raise the defense of entrapment. According to *Black's Law Dictionary* entrapment is "the act of officers or agents of the government in inducing a person to commit a crime not contemplated by him, for the purpose of instituting a criminal prosecution against him (277)." For the defense of entrapment to prevail the defendant must show that the officer or his/her agent has gone beyond providing the encouragement and opportunity for the commission of a crime and through trickery, fraud or other deception has induced the suspect to commit a crime. This defense is raised far more times than it is successful because the current legal criteria to determine entrapment is what is known as the subjective test.

In the subjective test the predisposition of the offender rather than the objective methods of the police is the key factor in determining entrapment (Skolnick, 1982; Marx, 1985; Stitt and James, 1985). This makes it extremely difficult for a defendant with a criminal record to claim that he/she would not have committed the crime except for the actions of the officer. The "objective test" of entrapment raised by a minority of the Supreme Court has focused on the nature of the police conduct rather than the predisposition of the offender (Stitt and James, 1985). For example, the objective test probably would examine whether the production of crack by a police organization to use in undercover drug arrests is proper and legal. According to an Associated Press story the Broward County Florida Sheriff's Department, not having enough crack to supply undercover officers, has started manufacturing their own. The sheriff's department chemist has made at least $20,000 worth of the illegal substance. Local defense attorneys have raised the issue of entrapment. In fact, one public defender stated:

> I think there's something sick about this whole system where the police make the product, sell the product and arrest people for buying the product (*Birmingham Post-Herald*, April 19, 1989: B2).

The issue of deception aside, this practice raises a number of ethical and legal issues concerning police practices. At what point do we draw the line to make a police undercover operation convincing?

In addition to the accepted practices of lying and deception required for undercover operations, members of the police community often believe that it is proper to lie to the media or the public when it is necessary to protect the innocent, protect the image of the department or calm the public in crisis situations. The department's official policy may be one of openness and candor when dealing with the media. However, as a practical matter members of the department may deny the existence of an investigation or "plant" erroneous information to protect an on-going investigation (i.e., disinformation). The untimely revelation of acts may alert the suspects and drive them underground or cause them to cease their illegal activities. Nevertheless, one could argue that public exposure of certain criminal activities or the possibility of them might decrease the risk of injury to persons or property. This issue was raised in the recent terrorist bombing of PanAm Flight 103 over Lockerbie, Scotland. What was the best course of action? Tell the public of all threats against airlines—most of which were unfounded—and create fear? Or keep all threats confidential and hope that airline and government officials effectively deal with the threats?

In some crimes, such as kidnaping, the publication of accurate information or any information at all might lead to the murder of the victim. Therefore, under these circumstances police administrators might view lies told to protect the victim as perfectly acceptable and necessary.

Police administrators are well aware of the possibility that the entire organization may be labeled deviant because of the deviant acts of its members. The "rotten apple theory" of police corruption has often been used as an impression management technique by police administrators who are aware of this possibility (Barker, 1977). It is easier to explain police deviance as a result of individual aberrations than admit the possibility of systemic problems and invite public scrutiny. However, candor and public scrutiny may be the best way to insure that corruption and other forms of police deviance do not occur or continue in an organization (see Cooper and Belair, 1978).

Thus, accepted lies are those which the organization views as having a viable role in police operations. The criteria for the lie to be accepted is:

> It must be in furtherance of a legitimate organizational purpose.
>
> There must be a clear relationship between the need to deceive and the accomplishment of an organizational purpose.
>
> The nature of the deception must be one wherein officers and the management structure acknowledge that deception will better serve the public interest than the truth.
>
> The ethical standing of the deception and the issues of law appear to be collateral concerns.

Tolerated Lying. A second category of police lies are those which are recognized as "lies" by the police organization but are tolerated as "necessary evils." Police administrators will admit to deception or "not exactly telling the whole truth" when confronted with the facts. These types of situational or "white" lies are truly in the gray area of propriety and the police can provide logical rationales for their use. When viewed from an ethical standpoint they may be "wrong" but from the police perspective they are necessary (i.e., tolerated) to achieve organizational objectives or deal with what Goldstein has termed the basic problems of police work (Goldstein, 1977: 9).

The basic problems of police work arise from the mythology surrounding police work; e.g., statuses usually require and the public expects the police to enforce all the laws all the time, the public holds the police responsible for preventing crime and apprehending all criminals, the public views the police as being capable of handling all emergencies, etc. (Goldstein, 1977). Most police administrators will not publicly admit that they do not have the resources, the training or the authority to do some of the duties that the public expects. In fact, many police administrators and police officers lacking the education and insight into police work would be hard pressed to explain police work, particularly discretionary decision making to outside groups. They therefore resort to lies and deception to support police practices.

Police administrators often deny that their departments practice anything less than full enforcement of all laws rather than attempt to explain the basis for police discretionary decisions and selective enforcement. We continually attempt to deal with social problems through the use of criminal sanctions and law enforcement personnel. Mandatory sentencing for all offenders committing certain felony and misdemeanor offenses is often seen as a panacea for these offenses. For example, in recent years many politically active groups such as Mothers Against Drunk Drivers (M.A.D.D.) have pressured legislators for stronger laws with mandatory enforcement in drunk driving cases. However, their sentiment in cases not involving accidents may not be shared by the general public (Formby and Smykla, 1984) or the police. One can only speculate as to the number of discretionary decisions still being made by police officers in D.U.I. offenses in departments where full enforcement is the official policy. One of the authors learned of an individual who had two D.U.I. offenses reduced and asked a police supervisor about it.

Barker: The chief has said that all D.U.I. suspects are charged and those over the legal blood alcohol level never have the charge reduced. In fact, he said this at a M.A.D.D. meeting. Yet, I heard that (____) had two D.U.I. offenses reduced.

Supervisor: That is true Tom. However, (____) is helping us with some drug cases. M.A.D.D. may not understand but they do not have to make big busts.

The point of note is that the police, in response to political pressure, make a policy on DUI cases and vow that the policy will be followed. However, in this case, that vow is not true. The police made a discretionary judgement that the assistance of the DUI offender in drug investigations was of greater importance than a DUI prosecution. Thus, this policy was tantamount to a lie to the M.A.D.D. membership—a lie tolerated by the police department.

The public also expects the police to handle any disorderly or emergency situations. The American public believes that one of the methods for handling any problem is "calling the cops" (Bittner, 1972). However, in many of these order maintenance situations the police do not have the authority, resources or training to deal with the problem. They often face a situation "where something must be done now" yet an arrest is not legally possible or would be more disruptive. The officer is forced to reach into a bag of tricks for a method of dealing with the crisis. Lying to the suspects or the complaints is often that method. For example, police officers may tell noisy teenagers to move along or be arrested when the officers have neither the intention nor the legal basis for an arrest. They often tell complainants that they will follow up on their complaint or turn it over to the proper agency when they have no intention of doing it. The police see these lies as a way of handling "nusiance work" that keeps them from doing "real police work" or as a way of dealing with a problem beyond their means. In these cases, the lie is used as a tool of expediency—arguably an abuse of police discretion but one which is tolerated.

In domestic disturbances police officers face volatile situations where the necessary conditions for an arrest often are not present. Frequently there is a misdemeanor where the officer does not have a warrant, an offense has not been committed in his/her presence and the incident occurred in a private residence. However, the officer may feel that something must be done. Consequently, the officer may lie and threaten to arrest one or both combatants, or talk one of the parties out to the street or the patrol car to discuss the incident and arrest them for disorderly conduct or public intoxication when they reach public property. Another option is to make an arrest and lie about the circumstances in order to make the arrest appear legal. Obviously, the latter strategy will not be a tolerated pattern of lying. It would fall into the pattern of deviant lying to be discussed later.

Officers soon learn that the interrogation stage of an arrest is an area where certain lies are tolerated and even taught to police officers. The now famous *Miranda v. Arizona* case decided by the U.S. Supreme Court in 1966 quoted excerpts from Inbau and Reid's *Criminal Interrogation and Confession* text to show that the police used deception and psychologically coercive methods in their interrogation of suspects (George, 1966: 155-266). The latest edition of this same text gives examples of deceptive and lying practices for . . . skilled interrogators to engage in (Inbau, Reid, Buckley, 1986).

As an illustration of these techniques, the reader is told that the interrogator should put forth a facade of sincerity so convincingly that "moisture may actually appear in his eyes" (p. 52). Another recommended effective practice of deception is that the interrogator have a *simulated* evidence case folder on hand during the course of the interrogation if an actual case file does not exist (p. 54). The interrogator may also make inferences such as a large number of investigators are working on the case and drew the same evidentiary conclusion about the suspect's guilt, even if, in reality, the interrogator is the only person working the case (p. 85). The inference is that the case against the suspect is strong because of the number of people involved in the investigation and the consequent weight of the evidence.

One particularly troublesome piece of advice for interviewing rape suspects is that:

> Where circumstances permit, the suggestion might be offered that the rape victim had acted like she might have been a prostitute and that the suspect had assumed she was a willing partner. In fact, the interrogator may even say that the police knew she had engaged in prostitution on other occasions. . . (p. 109)

As a final illustration, the book notes that an effective means to interrogate multiple suspects of a crime is "playing one offender against the other." In this regard it is suggested that the "interrogator may merely imitate to one offender that the other has confessed, or else the interrogator may actually *tell* the offender so" (emphasis added, p. 132).

It is difficult to say whether or not these tolerated forms of lying are "wrong"—many investigators would argue that they are not really "lies" but good interrogation techniques. One could also argue that the ends justify the means as long as the actions of the officers are not illegal. However, one can hypothesize that deception in one context increases the probability of deception in other contexts (cf, Skolnick, 1982: Stitt and James, 1985). As a veteran police officer told one of the authors while they were discussing ways to convince a suspect to agree to a consent search:

> Barker: That sure sounds like telling a lot of lies.
>
> Officer: It is not police lying; it is an art. After all the criminal has constitutional protection. He can lie through his teeth. Why not us? What is fair is fair.

This attitude, which is borne in the frustrations of many officers, sets a dangerous precedent for attitudes related to civil liberties. When law enforcement officers begin to tolerate lies because it serves their ends—regardless of the constitutional and ethical implications of those lies—then fundamental elements of civil rights are threatened.

Deviant Police Lies

The last example raises the possibility of the third category of police lying—deviant lies. After all "he [the suspect] can lie through his teeth. Why not us?" Deviant police lies are those which violate substantive or procedural law and/or police department rules and regulations. The deviant lies which violate substantic or procedural law are improper and should not be permitted. However, organization members (including supervisors), and other actors in the criminal justice system are often aware of their occurrence.

Noted defense attorney Alan Dershowitz states that police lying is well known by actors in the criminal justice system. He clearly illustrates these as the "Rules of the Justice Game." In part, the rules include:

Rule IV: Almost all police lie about whether they violated the Constitution in order to convict guilty defendants.

Rule V: All prosecutors, judges, and defense attorneys are aware of Rule IV.

Rule VI: Many prosecutors implicitly encourage police to lie about whether they violated the Constitution in order to convict guilty defendants.

Rule VII: All judges are aware of Rule VI.

Rule VIII: Most trial judges pretend to believe police officers who they know are lying.

Rule IX: All appellate judges are aware of Rule VIII, yet many pretend to believe the trial judges who pretend to believe the lying police officers (Dershowitz, 1983: xxi-xxii).

This may be an extreme position. However, other criminal defense attorneys believe that the police will lie in court. In fact, one study concluded that "the possibility of police perjury is a part of the working reality of criminal defense attorneys" (Kittel, 1986: 20). Fifty-seven percent of the 277 attorneys surveyed in this study believed that police perjury takes place very often or often (Kittel, 1986: 16). Police officers themselves have reported that they believe their fellow officers will lie in court (Barker, 1978). An English barrister believes that police officers have perjured themselves on an average of three out of ten trials (Wolchover, 1986).

As part of the research for this chapter, one of the authors asked an Internal Affairs (IA) investigator of a major U.S. police department about officer lying:

Carter: During the course of IA investigations, do you detect officers lying to you?

IA Investigator: Yes, all the time. They'll lie about anything, everything.

Carter: Why is that?

IA Investigator: To tell me what I want to hear. To help get them out of trouble. To make themselves feel better—rationalizing I guess. They're so used to lying on the job, I guess it becomes second nature.

An analysis of deviant lies reveals that the intent of the officer in telling deviant lies may be either in support of perceived legitimate goals, or illegitimate goals.

Deviant Lies in Support of Perceived Legitimate Goals

The deviant lies told by the officer to achieve perceived legitimate goals usually occur to "put criminals in jail," prevent crime, and perform various other policing responsibilities. The police officer believes that because of his/her unique experiences in dealing with criminals and the public he/she knows the guilt or innocence of those they arrest (Manning, 1978). Frequently, officers feel this way independently of any legal standards. However, the final determination of guilt or innocence is in the Judicial. The officer(s), convinced that the suspect is factually guilty of the offense, may believe that necessary elements of legal guilt are lacking, e.g., no probable cause for a "stop", no elements of legal guilt are lacking, e.g., no probable cause for a "stop", no Miranda warning, not enough narcotics for a felony offense, etc. Therefore, the officer feels that he/she must supply the missing elements. One police officer told one of the authors that it is often necessary to "fluff up the evidence" to get a search warrant or insure conviction. The officer will attest to facts, statements, or evidence which never occurred or occurred in a different fashion. Obviously when he/she does this under oath, perjury has then been committed. Once a matter of record, the perjury must continue for the officer to avoid facing disciplinary action and even criminal prosecution.

Recently, charges were dropped against an accused cop killer and three Boston police officers were suspended with pay pending a perjury investigation. The perjury involved a Boston detective who "invented" an informant. The detective maintained that the informant gave critical information which was cited in the affidavit for a search warrant (*New York Times*, 1989: K9). The "no knock" search warrant's execution led to the death of a Boston detective. Similarly, the officer(s) who lies in these instances must employ creative writing skills in official reports to ensure that the written chronology of events are consistent with procedures regardless of what actually occurred.

These lies are rationalized by the officer because they are necessary to ensure that criminals do not get off on "technicalities." A central reason for these deviant lies is officer frustration. There is frustration with the criminal justice system because of the inability of courts and corrections to handle large caseloads. Frustration with routinized practices of plea negotiations and intricate criminal procedures which the officer may not fully understand. The officer sees the victims of crimes and has difficulty in reconciling the harm done to them with the wide array of due process protections afforded to defendants. Nevertheless, the officer has fallen into "the avenging angel syndrome" where the end justifies the means. The officer can easily rationalize lying and perjury to accomplish what is perceived to be the "right thing." The officer's views are short-sighted and provincial. There is no recognition that such behavior is a threat to civil liberties and that perjury is as fundamentally improper as the criminal behavior of the accused.

Deviant Lies in Support of Illegitimate Goals

Lies in this category are told to effect an act of corruption or to protect the officer from organizational discipline or civil and/or criminal liability. Deviant lies may be manifest in police perjury as the officer misrepresents material elements of an arrest or search in order to "fix" a criminal prosecution for a monetary reward. Lying and/or perjury in court is an absolute necessity in departments where corrupt acts occur on a regular basis. Sooner or later every police officer who engages in corrupt acts or observes corrupt acts on the part of other officers will face the possibility of having to lie under oath to protect him/herself or fellow officers. Skolnick has

suggested that perjury and corruption are both systematic forms of police deviance which occur for the same sort of reason: "police know that other police are on the take and police know that other police are perjuring themselves" (Skolnick, 1982: 42).

It is also possible that other forms of police deviance will lead to deviant lying. For example, the officer who commits an act of police brutality may have to lie on the report to his/her supervisor and during testimony to avoid the possibility of criminal sanction, a civil lawsuit or department charges. The officer who has sex on duty, sleeps or drinks on duty may have to lie to a supervisor or internal affairs to avoid department discipline. The officer who causes an injury or death to a suspect which is not strictly according to law or police policy may have to lie to protect himself or his fellow officers from criminal and/or civil liability.

As an illustration, one of the authors assisted a police department which was under a federal court injunction related to an extensive number of civil rights violations for excessive force and harassment. During one series of inquiries, the following conversation occurred:

> Carter: Did you ever talk to other accused officers before giving your deposition in these cases?
>
> Officer: Of course. [NOTE: The tone of the response was almost incredulous.]
>
> Carter: Would you discuss the facts of the allegation?
>
> Officer: Sure. We had to be sure our stories were straight.

Other implications from these statements and the continued conversations were clear: officers were willing to lie during the sworn deposition to protect themselves and others. They would swear to the truth of facts which were plainly manufactured for their protection. Moreover, their remorse was not that they lied, but that they got caught in misconduct. Similarly, a police chief in West Virginia recently told a federal judge he lied to investigators in order to cover up for four officers accused of beating handcuffed prisoners (*Law Enforcement News*, March 15, 1989,

p. 2). Again, the illegitimate goal of "protection" surfaces as a motive for lying.

The typical police bureaucracy is a complex organization with a myriad of rules and regulations. The informal organization, including many supervisors, overlooks these rules until someone decides to "nail someone." Given the plethora of rules and regulations in most large urban police departments it is virtually impossible to work a shift without violating one. It may be common practice to eat a free meal, leave one's beat for personal reasons, not wear one's hat when out of the car, to live outside the city limits, etc. All of these acts may be forbidden by a policy, rule or regulation. When a supervisor decides to discipline an officer for violating one of these acts, the officer, and often fellow officers, may resort to lies to protect themselves and each other. After all, such "minor" lies are inherent in the "Blue Code" Manning observes that rule enforcement by police supervisors represents a mock bureaucracy where ritualistic and punitive enforcement is applied after the fact (Manning, 1978). The consequences of these seemingly understandable lies can be disastrous when discovered. The officer(s) may be suspended, reduced in rank or dismissed. The same organization whose members routinely engage in acceptable, tolerated and deviant lying practices can take on a very moralistic attitude when it discovers that one of its own has told a lie to avoid internal discipline. Nevertheless, the lies told in these examples are told in support of the illegitimate goal of avoiding departmental discipline.

Conclusion

The effects of lying, even those which are acceptable or tolerated, are multi-fold. Lies can and do create distrust within the organization. When the public learns members of the police lie or engage in deceptive practices this can undermine citizen confidence in the police. As we have seen some police lies violate citizens' civil rights and others are told to cover up civil rights violations. Police lying contributes to police misconduct and corruption and undermines the organization's discipline system. Furthermore, deviant police lies undermine the effectiveness of the criminal justice system.

What should the organization do to deal with the reality of police lies? An important first step is to establish a meaningful code of ethics and value statements for the organization. Importantly this should go beyond the development of documents. The operational and managerial levels of the police department must know that the code of ethics and value statements are guides to police moral and ethical behavior. They should never become another set of rules and procedures to be used when necessary to "nail someone." Once ethics and values are embodied, it is essential to develop a support structure consisting of directives, training and supervision. This will create a moral environment throughout the organization and establish parameters of acceptable behavior giving notice to employees about expectations of management.

References

Barker, T. 1978. "An Empirical Study of Police Deviance Other Than Corruption," *Journal of Police Science and Administration*: 6: 3: 264-272.

——. 1977. "Peer Group Support for Police Organizational Deviance," *Criminology* 15: 3: 353-366.

Bittner, E. 1972. *The Functions of the Police in Modern Society*, Washington, D.C., U.S. Government Printing Office.

Birmingham Post-Herald, 1989. "Sheriff's Chemist Makes Crack," April 19: B2.

Black, H. C. 1983. *Black's Law Dictionary, Abridged Fifth Edition*. West Publishing Co.: St. Paul, MN.

Cooper, G. R. and Robert R. Belair, 1978. *Privacy and Security of Criminal History Information: Privacy and the Media*, U.S. Department of Justice. Washington, D.C., U.S. Government Printing Office.

Dershowitz, A. M., 1983. *The Best Defense*, Vintage Books: New York.

Formby, W. A. and John O. Smykla. 1984. "Attitudes and Perception Toward Drinking and Driving: A Simulation of Citizen Awareness." *Journal of Police Science and Administration*, 12: 4: 379-384.

George, J. B. 1966. *Constitutional Limitations on Evidence in Criminal Cases*. Institute of Continuing Legal Education: Ann Harbor, MI.

Goldstein, H. 1977. *Policing A Free Society*. Ballenger Publishing Company, Cambridge, Mass.

Inbau, F. E., J. E. Reid and Joseph P. Buckley, 1986. *Criminal Interrogation and Confessions* 3rd Ed., Williams and Wilkins: Baltimore, MD.

Kittel, N. G. 1986. "Police Perjury: Criminal Defense Attorneys' Perspective," *American Journal of Criminal Justice* XI: 1: 11-22. (Fall).

Klockars, C. B. 1980. "The Dirty Harry Problem," *The Annals*, 452: 33-47 (November).

Law Enforcement News, 1989. March 15: 2. Manning, P. K.

——. 1978. "Lying Secrecy and Social Control" in Peter K. Manning and John Van Maanen (Eds.) *Policing: A View From The Street*, Goodyear Publishing Co.: Santa Monica, CA: 238-255.

Marx, G. T. 1985. "Who Really Gets Stung? Some Issues Raised By The New Police Undercover Work," in Elliston, F. A. and Michael Feldberg (Eds.) *Moral Issues in Police Work*. Rowan and Allanheld: Totowa, NJ.

New York Times, 1989. "Dead Officer, Dropped Charges: A Scandal in Boston," March 20: K9.

Pistone, J. D. 1987. *Donnie Brasco: My Undercover Life in the Mafia*. Nail Books: New York, NY.

Skolnick, J. 1982. "Deception By Police," *Criminal Justice Ethics*, 1(2),: 40-54 (Summer/Fall).

Stitt, B. G. and Gene G. James, 1985. "Entrapment An Ethical Analysis" in Elliston, F. A. and Michael Feldberg (Eds.), *Moral Issues in Police Work*. Rowman and Allanheld: Totowa, NJ.

Wolchover, D. 1986. "Police Perjury in London." *New Law Journal*: 180-184 (February).

Part VII

Administration and Management

Police departments are organizations, with missions, goals, structures, managers, workers, and clients. The top managers of police agencies are usually the ones held most accountable for the organization's effective performance and respectable public image. These top administrators, whether chiefs, commissioners, superintendents, directors, or sheriffs, have two sets of obligations: one internal, concerned with running the organization, and one external, concerned with the organization's "environment." The internal role involves such activities as organizing, staffing, directing, and controlling. The external role involves dealing with important outside forces that affect the police agency, such as politicians, the community, the media, judges, prosecutors, and the like. Some important management functions span the internal and external roles, including planning and leading.

How best to administer and manage police agencies has long been debated. From the 1950s through the 1970s, police administration tended to emphasize the internal role and favored more centralized, specialized, and formalized approaches. Police departments became more bureaucratized, with more levels of hierarchy, more special units, and more written policies, procedures, rules, and regulations. The goal of good human relations in the management

of people was often stated, but the typical police department could still be characterized as a "punishment-oriented bureaucracy," and police employees usually rated their bosses as controlling and unsympathetic.

In the 1980s and 1990s, perhaps due to the popularity of community policing, police administration has devoted more attention to its external role. Police executives as well as police officers have become more fully engaged with citizens, and collaboration among all government agencies, including the police, is increasingly emphasized. Police managers also seem more willing to adopt the role of the community's leader, instead of merely reacting to its current interests and agendas. Internally, there has been greater emphasis on decentralization, flattening the hierarchy, de-specialization, and empowerment of employees, although far more police agencies might talk about doing these things than will actually implement them in significant ways.

The articles in this section examine these administrative and managerial issues in depth. The first article explores the matter of organizational control within police agencies, pointing out that different aspects of police work and different types of police behavior might be better controlled using different methods. This may seem like common sense, but in fact police organizations have traditionally leaned toward monolithic, one-dimensional control strategies. The second article addresses a related concern—just what empowerment of police officers really means, and whether citizens really want to have less control over such powerful actors. The third article assesses a new and long-awaited approach to police organizational reform, accreditation, and questions whether its approach is compatible with community policing.

The final article in this section adopts a somewhat different approach, called the institutional perspective, in order to seek a more sophisticated understanding of the behavior of police organizations themselves: why they succeed and fail, how they protect themselves from external threats, and so forth. This approach provides some interesting insights and allows scholars to compare more systematically police agencies and other types of organizations. ✦

25

Developing Police Policy: An Evaluation of the Control Principle

Geoffrey P. Alpert and
William C. Smith

As demonstrated in Part VI, police officers have considerable power and authority, which they sometimes abuse. In addition, like all employees they sometimes make poor decisions and they sometimes do not work as hard as they should. Thus, police departments, like other types of organizations, seek to exert control over their employees. In police agencies, forms of organizational control have traditionally included supervision, written guidelines, and formal discipline for rule violations. These traditional control mechanisms are reviewed in this article, as well as alternatives that might be employed. Alpert and Smith provide as well-reasoned discussion about different types of control and how they might best be applied to police behavior. As you read the article, consider the organizational control options from your standpoint as a citizen who might be subject to police authority, and also from the point of view of police officers who would like to have some freedom and flexibility in their work and a sense of justice in organizational discipline.

Law enforcement is a paradigm of operational control. Virtually every aspect of policing is subject to some combination of either law policy, guideline, directive, rule or general order. By the very nature of the police function, such a tight rein appears to be criti-cally necessary. Conventional wisdom is that police agencies must exercise strict control over their officers. As policing has become more complex there has been a tendency to overregulate the officers' actions. Creating complex policies, procedures and rules has become the customary method of controlling the discretion of police officers. It is the purpose of this paper to explore the context and role of police policy making and to address the need to authorize discretion rather than strictly control officers' behavior in many areas of policing. The first section describes the legal parameters of policy and the differences among policies, procedures and rules. The second section reviews the areas that need strong policies and the areas that need only broad guidance. The third section includes a brief comment on the need to assess policies. The final section includes examples of the components of policy.

Legal Parameters of Policy

The primary mission of police is the protection of life. However, it would be naive to regard policy making as driven only by that altruistic principle. Other forces, including public preferences, the desire for uniform quality of performance and liability prevention all direct policy. Realistically, the police policy making process is governed by the principles of risk management and liability.

The history of policy making has been one of reaction. Traditionally, policies have been produced in a response to a problem. In recent years, however, policy makers have received a backhanded judicial incentive to review and revise their policies. When the U.S. Supreme Court in *City of Canton, Ohio v. Harris* (1989) recognized "deliberate indifference" as the benchmark for municipal policy deficiencies, it created a financial necessity for agencies to review, revise and sometimes develop policies (Alpert, 1989).

To understand the judicial incentive, a quick review of the history of police civil liability is necessary. Until the early 1960s, police civil liability was unremarkable and basically limited to claims of negligence (Kappeler, 1993 and del Carmen, 1991). The United States Supreme Court's decision in

Monroe v. Pape (1961) had effectively alleviated concerns held by municipalities that they were proper defendants for citizens' civil rights claims brought under 42 U.S.C. Section 1983. This atmosphere continued until the Court's 1978 decision in *Monnell v. New York City Department of Social Services* (1978). The Court in *Monnell* effectively overruled *Pape* and opened the floodgates for Section 1983 actions against municipalities, thereby giving plaintiffs access to the deep pockets of the local treasury. The linchpin of the *Monnell* decision was that the policy of a municipality, as a moving force behind a plaintiffs injury, could result in municipal liability. In essence, the courts were evaluating the behavior of the police and were involved in judicial rule making (Alpert and Haas, 1984). Since *Monnell*, additional refinements of the "policy" rule have resulted in municipal liability concerns regarding police "custom" and "practice."

Noteworthy among these refinements are cases which have held that an elected county prosecuting attorney who provided advice to the police is a "policy maker" of a county for purposes of attaching liability (*Pembaur v. City of Cincinnati*, 1986) and one in which an unchecked pattern of violence was held to be attributable to a sheriff's policy of inadequate training (*Davis v. Mason County* 1991).

Although local municipalities have been put under great pressure to address policy issues, state agencies and their employees have felt some sense of insulation from the threat of lawsuits brought pursuant to Section 1983. This belief has persisted even through the Supreme Court's enthronement of the "deliberate indifference" standard in *City of Canton v. Harris* (1989). The sense of security was brought about by the ostensible protection of the Eleventh Amendment which precludes suits against states in a federal court and by judicial interpretations that extended the protection to federally created causes of action that could be brought in state court. Indeed, the Supreme Court held as recently as 1989 in *Will v. Michigan Department of State Police* that state actors in their official capacities enjoyed immunity from suit under Section 1983 even when brought in state court. Prior to *Will*, the holding in *Howlett v. Rose*

(1987) conferred the same immunity in federal court Section 1983 actions. As a result of this reasoning, state law enforcement officials and their officials have enjoyed greater immunity than their local law enforcement counterparts in Section 1983 cases where "official capacity" actions have been involved.

The 1990s, however, have brought about a rethinking of the status of such immunity. In *Hafer v. Melo* (1991), the United States Supreme Court allowed an elected official to be sued under Section 1983 for what were alleged by her to be "official capacity" actions. The significance of the case lies in its discussion of the distinctions between actions taken in a personal capacity and those performed in official capacity. The operational consequence of the case is pressure on all law enforcement executives to review their various methods of control, including policies, lest such control methods be deemed to constitute personal capacity actions.

Policies, Procedures and Rules

A *policy* is not a statement of what must be done in a particular situation but it is a statement of guiding principles that must be followed in activities that fall within either specific organizational objectives or the overall police mission. A policy is a guide to thinking. A *procedure* is the method of performing a task or a manner of proceeding on a course of action. It differs from policy in that it specifies action in a particular situation to perform a task within the guidelines of policy. A procedure is a guide to action. A *rule* is a managerial mandate that either requires or prohibits specified behavior. A rule is a mandate to action. These various control mechanisms are designed to address a multitude of needs, including the need for regulation and uniformity of police activities.

The National Advisory Commission on Criminal Justice Standards and Goals, *Report on Police* (1973:54) provides an excellent discussion of the differences among written policies, procedures and rules.

> Policy is different from rules and procedures. Policy should be stated in broad terms to guide employees. It sets limits of discretion. A policy statement deals with

the principles and values that guide the performance of activities directed toward the achievement of agency objectives. A procedure is a way of proceeding—a routine—to achieve an objective. Rules significantly reduce or eliminate discretion by specifically stating what must and must not be done.

As an example, this notion has been translated by the Metro-Dade Police Department in Miami, Florida which has defined policy as, ". . . principles and values which guide the performance of a departmental activity. Policy is not a statement of what must be done in a particular situation; rather, it is a statement of guiding principles which should be followed in activities which are directed toward attainment of objectives" (1989:5).

These directives, in varying degrees, establish discretionary parameters for officers to perform day-to-day operations in a manner consistent with the philosophy of the administration and command staff. Policies, based upon relevant laws and philosophy, serve to control officers' behavioral choices.

The Need for Control in Police Activities

Law enforcement agencies must have rules, regulations, training, supervision and structured accountability to guide and control the broad discretionary powers of their officers. However, as officers are confronted daily with a variety of complex situations, discretion is necessary (Adams, 1990). Discretion must be guided by legal strictures and administrative philosophy rather than by adrenaline-charged, split-second decisions. Written and enforced directives are necessary for the proper management of law enforcement functions because of the structural, personal and situational factors that affect behavioral choices. These directives are formulated by determining objectives and identifying the principles or ideas that will best guide the officer in achieving them (Alpert and Dunham, 1992).

The objectives and methods of police departments are affected by the laws, the communities they serve, their parent political system, the fraternal associations, unions, pro-

fessional police associations and other general and special interest groups (Sheehan and Cordner, 1989:465). A policy indicates to the officers and the public the agency's philosophy in the area of concern and also provides a set of standards by which it can be held accountable (see Alpert and Dunham, 1992). As James Auten (1988:1-2) has noted:

> To do otherwise is to simply leave employees "in the dark" in the expectation that they will intuitively divine the proper and expected course of action in the performance of their duties. . . . Discretion must be reasonably exercised within the parameters of the expectations of the community, the courts, the legislature and the organization, itself.

Similarly, Robert Wasserman informs us (1982:40):

> . . . When written policy statements are not available (or not well disseminated), the police agency and the administration run considerable risk that some police actions will be completely alien to a segment of the community. This result can be aggravated conflict between police and the community, resulting in political demands for major measures to ensure accountability on the part of the police organization.

Wasserman warns the police administrators to create and disseminate policy directives before a problem occurs and the public holds the police and other government officials accountable. Policies and procedures must cover general duties and obligations as well as methods to achieve them. In other words, law enforcement agencies must have regulations, provide training and supervision and hold officers accountable for their actions.

Deciding upon which activities and tasks require strong control or fundamental guidance requires a comprehensive understanding of the role and function of police in society. One aspect of that insight is the increasing educational level of the police. During the past few years, more educated persons are joining the police force and many officers are raising their level of education. At a time when police are becoming more educated, the requirements of the police are becoming more complicated. No longer do the police simply respond to calls for service. The renewed emphasis on community-oriented policing and problem-solving policing requires officers to think and plan rather than just respond (Alpert and Dunham, 1992). That is, officers are being educated and trained to use good judgment and discretion in many situations. However, in some critical areas, officers need strong policies and training.

Identification of Policy Areas

There is little doubt that some police activities require closer supervision and control than others. Although much of the police function may occur in areas of high public visibility, neither logic nor necessity mandate that every activity or decision be subject to strict agency directive or control. The crucial task is to identify those behaviors that should be value-driven and those that must be control-driven. Obviously, behavior which, if improperly carried out, is likely to result in severe injury or death, must be subject to control-driven policies.

David LaBrec (1982) has designed a graphic that helps to explain the categories of risk. Simply put, the police functions that are high-risk and low frequency require strong policies, formal procedures and explicit rules. The high-frequency, low-risk functions can be discharged with minimal guidance and a strong system of shared values (see Greene et al., 1992). The use of force or deadly force can be considered a high-risk, low-frequency activity, and police pursuit driving be considered a high-risk, high-frequency activity (Alpert and Fridell, 1992). These functions require the most extensive policies, training and overall guidance (Alpert and Smith, 1991).

There are police activities that require specific direction but not to the extent required for use of deadly force or pursuit driving. In fact, some of these activities if subjected to a strict control policy may result in officer behavior which is detached, dispassionate or cold. For example, police response to domestic violence incidents requires not only tact but the ability to read a situation and respond in the interests of all parties. Such a compli-

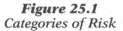

Figure 25.1
Categories of Risk

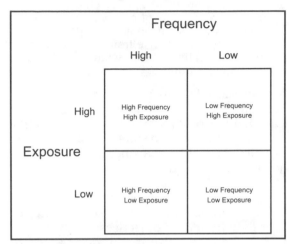

cated behavioral scenario would be virtually impossible to regulate by a strict control policy. However, certain important procedural issues must be controlled by this type of policy, including statutory requirements concerning the timing and substance of the police response to a domestic abuse call, arrest requirements as well as the coordination of efforts among officers, investigators and victim service agencies (Buzawa and Buzawa, 1992).

Many of these police tasks must be considered as an art, requiring a fluid response and not a mechanical reaction. Policing requires a variety of behavioral alternatives. That is, officers need wide discretion in those areas of their work not directly and immediately involved in the protection of life or defense against injury. Discretion must not be based on "gut reaction" or a whim, but requires extensive quality pre-service and in-service training. In order for officers to choose an appropriate response (discretionary choice), he or she must be trained in the options available. A critical part of the training must focus on ethics, values and morals. Value-driven guidelines are preferred in areas not directly involved in the protection of life or defense against injury (Greene et al., 1992).

An example of a police function requiring only summary guidance is telephone contact with the public. Police administrators have no need to instruct their officers and civilians who answer the telephone to read a written statement. They should, however, require officers to be pleasant, cooperative and provide assistance. Further, a policy in this area should direct the officer or civilian to collect certain information. The Metro-Dade Police Department (1989:32) provides the following direction:

> Telephone Communications: The telephone is the primary method by which police services are requested. All incoming telephone calls must be answered promptly to provide the desired quality of service.

> Telephone Courtesy: When answering the telephone, an employee should identify the unit and himself, and ask to be of assistance. Employees should make every attempt to supply requested information and assistance or refer party to proper agency.

Answering the telephone is a high-frequency, low-risk function. Obviously, officer discretion is important as long as it fits within the general guidelines of the agency. The examples of force, response to domestic violence and answering the telephone establish points on a policy-control continuum.

Police agencies must determine which functions require the most stringent control and which require structured guidelines or summary guidance only. Using examples discussed above, Figure 25.2 provides an illustration of the continuum of policy control.

Figure 25.2
Continuum of Policy

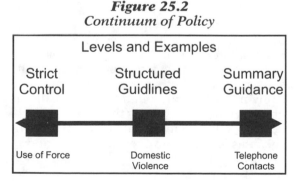

A valuable example of this determination process can be taken from private industry. Private companies are increasingly minimizing formal rules and placing importance on value training and discretionary behavior

(Cordner, 1989). Moore and Stephens (1991) suggest more reliance on what Kenneth Andrews labeled "The Corporate Strategy" (Andrews, 1980). This strategy refers to the identification of an objective(s), design of the organizational character and allocation of resources to achieve the objectives under potentially adverse circumstances. While there are numerous differences between the public and private sectors which complicate the transfer of technology and operational philosophies, private enterprise offers an innovative direction worthy of analysis (Cordner, 1989 and Moore and Stephens, 1991).

Concepts derived from the private sector transferred to police management would raise the following issues. Officer discretion is appropriate if defensible and valid hiring and fitness-for-duty evaluations are employed. Focus in training should be shifted to allow officers greater creativity in dealing with "non-textbook" scenarios where human emotion, pride or dignity are at issue. It is critical that police officers learn to deal with members of the public as fellow human beings rather than as participants in situations. It is necessary not to program an officer's response to a preconceived scenario but permit a response that incorporates training and preparation. In other words, the control principle must not be permitted to escape its bounds and take reason and compassion hostage. Perhaps the area of policing in which there is the greatest need for control is the use of force.

An Example of Force

In 1970, Egon Bittner noted that the unique feature of the police is their power to use force and deadly force limited only by law and policy. Further, the significance of this power, he argued, includes its omnipresent potential and threat. No other occupational group possesses this authority. Although police use of physical force is not a frequent event, its abuse is by any human means irreversible and by any legal means incapable of compensation. In other words, it is the classic low-frequency, high-risk event (see Friedrich, 1980 and Fyfe, 1988).

Although a relatively low-frequency event, accusations of excessive force are among the most common and highly visible complaints made against police officers. The proliferation of control mechanisms in this and other areas has been fueled by the nature and ever-increasing number of civil liability actions filed against the police (i.e., Rodney King). The absence of meaningful policy and training in critical function areas may serve as an invitation to sue where the absence is proximately related to a plaintiff's injury. Other explanations for increased control range from the traditional and generalized perception of need by the command staff to specific needs including administrative discipline and the accreditation movement. In effect, it could be safely said that the extent of policy within a police agency is linked to the intensity of its mission and its potential exposure to liability. In sum, the police who are given the authority to use force over others must be subject to significant restraint in its application.

Officer discretion must be guided by implementing a structured policy and providing extensive and continuous training to remove the need to make split-second decisions. This discretion may be cultivated by the following strategies: the articulation and acceptance of organizational values, internal inspections and audits of incidents, community feedback, an interactive style of policing and an appropriate system of discipline (Alpert and Dunham, 1992 and Alpert and Fridell, 1992).

An unintended consequence of strict control policies, however, is their expansion into areas where such structure may be disadvantageous to both law enforcement and the public it serves (Cordner, 1989). Cordner notes that "The prevailing wisdom in modern police administration is that policies and rules are needed to govern every contingency and every substantial aspect of operation and management" (1989:17). The critical question becomes: Is a strict-control policy model effective for all behavior or has the current trend of developing policies for most police functions set forth on a faulty premise?

Proposing Boundary Limitations

As discussed above, the use of deadly force may be low-frequency but is high-risk. The current paranoia over civil liability and the need to improve relations with members of the community have caused many police agencies to implement a strong system of oversight and superficial accountability of daily police operations. On the one hand, some policy makers, by addressing each important police function, believe that they are insulated from personal or institutional liability. On the other hand, some believe this strategy merely decreases officers' discretion without any corresponding immunity (see del Carmen, 1991). From either position, a strong-control form of management ignores a critical aspect of the police function: human interaction. Further, a program of extensive regulation by policy likely conveys to officers a message of distrust and engenders a stifling of creativity. The critical issue is to identify the acceptable limits for strict-control mechanisms.

Proposed boundaries may be drawn at those activities that are oriented *to protection of life and defame against injury*. While the principal mission of the police is the protection of life, not every activity in the duty day is directed toward this goal. A useful inquiry in identifying those police functions that are life-preserving and that defend against injury is accomplished by asking whether the activity involved will likely cause severe injury or death if improperly discharged. In other words, a behavioral threshold should be created so that, once crossed, strict control would be appropriate. This concept, in its purest sense, should create little controversy; for it is precisely the approach that is underscored in the majority of police agencies. For example, few would argue with the view that the discharge of a firearm, vehicular pursuit of an offender, or the use of a baton or Taser must be subject to strenuous control. The stark reality is that such behaviors are relatively infrequent although their criticality is great. What is proposed is that police officers be afforded the opportunity in less than critical areas, such as the ones mentioned above, to participate in a belief system where their discretionary actions reflect a legitimate desire to serve the public.

Recently, Cohen and Feldberg (1991:148-149) identified three factors that provide police officers with sufficient information to operate successfully in a law-enforcement agency.

The practical ingredients and individual needs in order to have free moral choice in matters of professional conduct are an understanding of the values that inform his or her profession, the intention to live up to the values and an environment that supports those values and discourages behavior that is contrary to them.

Basically, appropriate departmental policies, training and a powerful accountability or disciplinary system will create an environment that establishes the mission and philosophy of the agency. If an officer is trained in those values and guidelines and chooses to follow them, he or she will be able to use discretion appropriately. Hopefully, this training and understanding will help officers make the appropriate behavioral choices and mirror what Cohen and Feldberg have called the "free moral choice in matters of professional conduct" (1991:148).

Assessing the Effectiveness of Policies

Police officers perform a wide variety of functions and the agencies in which they work are traditionally organized in a para-military structure with a specific chain-of-command. This structure and function suggests a need for a strong-control type of management. The evolution of many policy manuals is based upon the negative reinforcement of behavior. Many policy directives are stated negatively and it is often difficult to measure their effectiveness as police performance measures are typically based upon positive behaviors. The difference between what is measurable and the behavior recommended by the majority of policies creates serious "bean-counting" or methodological problems for evaluation (see Spelman, 1988). As Cordner notes (1989:19), "No experiments have been conducted to test the effectiveness of written rules and guidelines. There simply is not much agreement about how to define or measure the effectiveness of a police agency."

Rather than evaluate the effectiveness of a proposed policy, many administrators have made policy changes as a response to officers' mistakes. This process has created in many agencies a compilation of guidelines, regula-

tions and rules that prohibit behavior that has been found inappropriate or in violation of the law. Some aspects of policy or a rule may be attributed to a specific officer or situation. Often, these rules are fondly named after the officer or event.

While this approach appears solid, it creates a situation that may be too limiting and challenges officers to circumvent the language of the policy. In other words, control-oriented management can lead to a macro-management approach by always limiting behavioral alternatives with rules.

A superficial assessment of this "prohibition" approach may yield a positive result. However, an in-depth analysis would likely come to a different conclusion. The consequences of the approach are a loss of police services, reduced morale among the officers and an environment that stifles creative police work. Gary Cordner notes (1989:18):

> The question of most importance is whether extensive written directives make police organizations more effective. Do rules and regulations improve the quality of police service? Do they contribute to police goal attainment?

These questions raise very important issues that remain unanswered. The next section addresses the elements that should be included in an appropriate and defensible policy.

Elements of Model Policies

The development of police policies should reflect the values of the command staff *and community* and should include input from officers at all levels. Policies should incorporate the following principles:

1. Be workable in real-world situations;

2. be adaptable to training;

3. be written in a positive manner;

4. refer to or incorporate relevant laws;

5. be pre-tested to assure that all officers understand the specific intent and consequences of non-compliance;

6. include in-service training, as a matter of record, for all officers and supervisors; and

7. provide examples of behavior.

Many departmental policies have been developed properly, include these principles and provide excellent direction and guidance to their officers. Other agencies do not have policies or have such weak policies that they provide no real direction. As a response to the problems of developing and refining policies, the International Association of Chiefs of Police (IACP) established a National Law Enforcement Policy Center. Through the auspices of the Center, the IACP developed the most comprehensive compilation of model policies and background papers (Issues and Concepts) justifying their views (National Law Enforcement Policy Center, 1991). This compilation includes policies on some of the most difficult issues facing law enforcement in the 1990s. The model policies include protection of life issues with little discretion such as the use of force, deadly force and pursuit driving as well as areas permitting wide discretion such as a policy to control a confidential fund.

The model policies were developed to provide general guidance. A disclaimer states that the models must be reviewed and adjusted to individual departments. The requirement to adjust these models must be emphasized. Different jurisdictions and environments need different direction to produce the best policing. However, any agency would benefit from the outline and background papers prepared by the Policy Center. Fortunately, there are many commonalities among police policies for high-risk activities. These include a policy's *first* principle, that an officer's primary responsibility is to protect lives. As many police activities are potentially dangerous and because officers are likely to react to the heat of the moment, an overall *MISSION STATEMENT* must be included as a first element and as a reminder in policies guiding high-risk activities. Beyond the mission statement, the IACP models provide an excellent design for developing an agency's policy. For example, the model policy regarding use of force is detailed and includes the following headings or elements:

A. Purpose

B. Policy (statement of philosophy)

C. Definitions

D. Procedures

1. parameters for use of deadly force;

2. parameters for the use of nondeadly force;

3. training and qualifications;

4. reporting uses of force; and

5. departmental response (administrative review).

By adding a mission statement to this outline, a department will have an excellent foundation for a policy. It is important to acknowledge the threat that new policies may have on some departments' officers.

If a new philosophy is incorporated in a policy or a more structured response is required from an officer, effective training to the policy is required. Effective training may include the reading, understanding and discussion of a policy for low-risk activities. However, in high-risk activities, beyond the understanding of the language of the policy, practice and simulation or role-playing decision-making skills may be necessary to avoid what the United States Supreme Court has called, "deliberate indifference."

Accountability

Just as police policies are divided among several levels based upon their consequences, accountability of officers must also be structured. Officers who make contact with citizens are usually asked to take notes on the meeting to preserve any information that was provided. Officers who are involved in automobile accidents will have to complete a mandated accident reporting form. Officers who must control a suspect with force to effect an arrest should be responsible for completing a "control of persons" report. If deadly force is used, an officer must complete a form describing the why, where and how. It is important to hold accountable any officer who has been involved in some low-risk and all high-risk activities. Writing an analytical critique is the first step. This process serves several purposes: *first*, the information contained in a critique can help determine if the action was necessary and conducted within the departmental policy; *second*, critiques will help determine if specific training is needed; *third*, critiques will help determine if a change in policy is needed; and *fourth*, an analysis of the data generated in these reports will reveal trends and demonstrate specific risk factors. As a second step, the agency must assign supervisory personnel to evaluate these reports and determine if a violation has occurred and suggest that the officer face disciplinary action.

An agency's disciplinary system is a critical reinforcer of its policies and rules. It is important that an agency's policies are followed and that an appropriate disciplinary scheme is established for violations. An important function of the disciplinary action is the message that is sent to others when an officer is disciplined or when he or she is *not* disciplined for a policy violation. All officers must understand the importance of the rules and regulations and the consequences for violating them. For example, if an officer is involved in a preventable accident, it is important to have a disciplinary scheme established. The first violation may result in a letter to the file while a second violation may require some remedial training. A third violation may result in a change of duty so the individual does not have an opportunity to use force to control a suspect. At some point a department will have to take more drastic action and those steps must also be made known to the officers. A policy without a disciplinary system will not be taken as seriously as one which includes a system of discipline. Similarly, a disciplinary system that can be subverted or manipulated will not serve as a deterrent. There is no room for "winking" at a violation and excusing poor judgment or deliberate actions which results in a violation of policy.

This concept has been summarized by The United States Commission on Civil Rights which found that (1981:158):

> Once a finding sustains the allegation of wrongdoing, disciplinary sanctions commensurate with the seriousness of the offense that are imposed fairly, swiftly, and consistently will most clearly reflect the commitment of the department to oppose police misconduct. Less severe action such as reassignment, retraining, and psychological counseling may be appropriate in some cases.

Conclusion

Creating meaningful mechanisms of control, including the development of police policies is a process of integrating a wide variety of interests. To be effective, policy must address the legitimate concerns of the public as well as the law. In balancing these issues, due attention must be paid to future flexibility and the process of refinement and change.

Police activities range from low-criticality to high-criticality and low-frequency to high-frequency. Police officials must identify which activities require strict control-oriented policies and which require only summary guidance. In other words, the style of policy will vary according to a continuum of control. In addition, there must be training to the policy, control and supervision of the activities and a system of discipline that holds the officers and agency accountable for the behavior.

The determination of the type of policy to be employed in any given duty function must be based upon the command staff's realization and understanding of law enforcement as a service to the public. Investiture of discretion to officers in low criticality areas after proper training in ethics, values and morals may go a great distance in bridging intermittent gaps between the police and the community. By the same token, high criticality functions will necessitate strict-control policies to guide them to protect the public safely in an effective and efficient manner.

References

Adams, T. (1990). *Police Field Operations*. Englewood Cliffs, NJ: Prentice-Hall.

Alpert, G. (1989). "*City of Canton v. Harris* and the Deliberate Indifference Standard." *Criminal Law Bulletin*, 25: 466-472.

Alpert, G. and R. Dunham (1992). *Policing Urban America*. Prospect Heights, IL: Waveland Press.

Alpert, G. and L. Fridell (1992). *Police Vehicles and Firearms: Instruments of Deadly Force*. Prospect Heights, IL: Waveland Press.

Alpert, G. and K. Haas (1984). "Judicial Rulemaking and the Fourth Amendment: Cars, Containers and Exclusionary Justice." *Alabama Law Review*, 35: 23-61.

Alpert, G. and W. Smith (1991). "Beyond City Limits and into the Wood(s): A Brief Look at the Policy Implications of *City of Canton v. Harris* and *Wood v. Ostrander*." *American Journal of Police*, 10:19-40.

Andrews, K. (1980). *The Concept of Corporate Strategy*. Chicago, IL: Irwin.

Auten, J. (1988). "Preparing Written Guidelines." *FBI Law Enforcement Bulletin*, 57:1-7.

Bittner, E. (1970). *The Functions of Police in Modern Society*. Rockville, MD: National Institute of Mental Health.

Brooks, L. (1989). "Police Discretionary Behavior: A Study of Style." In R. Dunham and G. Alpert (eds.), *Critical Issues in Policing*. Prospect Heights, IL: Waveland Press.

Brown, M. (1981). *Working the Street: Police Discretion and the Dilemmas of Reform*. New York, NY: Russell Sage Foundation.

Buzawa, E. and C. Buzawa (1992). *Domestic Violence: The Criminal Justice Response*. New York, NY: Greenwood Press.

Cohen, H. and M. Feldberg (1991). *Power and Restraint: The Moral Dimension of Police Work*. Westport, CT: Praeger.

Cordner, G. (1989). "Written Rules and Regulations: Are They Necessary?": *FBI Law Enforcement Bulletin*, July: 17-21.

Davis, K. (1975). *Police Discretion*. St. Paul, MN: West Publishing.

del Carmen, R. (1991). *Civil Liabilities in American Policing*. Englewood Cliffs, NJ: Brady.

Friedrich, R. (1980). "Police Use of Force: Individuals, Situations and Organizations." *Annals of the American Academy of Political and Social Science*, 452: 82-97.

Fyfe, J. (1988). *The Metro-Dade Police—Citizen Violence Reduction Project*. Washington, DC: Police Foundation.

Greene, J., G. Alpert, and P. Styles. "Values and Culture in Two American Police Departments: Lessons from King Arthur." *Contemporary Criminal Justice*, 8:183-207.

Kappeler, V. (1993). *Critical Issues in Police Civil Liability*. Prospect Heights, IL: Waveland Press.

LaBrec, D. (1982). "Risk Management: Preventive Law Practice and Practical Risk Management Methods for the 1980s." Paper presented to the Annual Meeting of the National Institute of Municipal Law Officers, Miami, FL.

Metro-Dade Police Department (1989). *Metro-Dade Police Department Manual—Part 1*. Dade County Florida.

Moore, M. and D. Stephens (1991). *Beyond Command and Control: The Strategic Management of Police Departments*. Washington, DC: Police Executive Research Forum.

National Advisory Commission on Criminal Justice Standards and Goals (1973). *Report on Police*. Washington, D.C.: U.S. Government Printing Office.

National Law Enforcement Policy Center (1991). *A Compilation of Model Policies*. Arlington, VA: National Law Enforcement Policy Center.

Sheehan, R. and G. Cordner (1989). *Introduction to Police Management*. Cincinnati, OH: Anderson Publishing Co.

Spelman, W. (1988). *Beyond Bean Counting*. Washington, D.C.: Police Executive Research Forum.

United States Commission on Civil Rights (1981). *Who is Guarding the Guardians?* Washington, D.C.: U.S. Government Printing Office.

Wasserman, R. (1982). "Government Setting." In B. Garmire (ed.), *Local Government Police Management. Second Edition*. Washington, D.C.: International City Management Association.

Cases

City of Canton, Ohio v. Harris, 489 U.S. 378 (1989).

Davis v. Mason County 927 F.2d 1473 (9th Cir. 1991).

Monroe v. Pape, 365 U.S. 167 (1961).

Monnell v. New York City Department of Social Services, 436 U.S. 658 (1978).

Pembaur v. City of Cincinnati, 475 U.S. 469 (1986).

Will v. Michigan Department of State Police, 491 U.S. 58 (1990).

Howlett v. Rose, 469 U.S. 356 (1990).

26

Empowering Police Officers: A Tarnished Silver Bullet?

*Larry K. Gaines and
Charles R. Swanson*

One of the great buzzwords of modern management, and a commonly recommended characteristic of community policing, is "empowerment." Generally, the idea is to empower employees to make decisions, use their creativity, and act more independently, all to the greater benefit of the organization, in return for which the employees themselves will enjoy a heightened sense of achievement and job satisfaction. The willingness of police commanders and supervisors to empower their subordinates is questionable. Also in question is the wisdom of further empowering police officers who already have broad discretion and the power of life and death. In this article, Gaines and Swanson raise these issues and discuss them pragmatically. You might want to consider, as a citizen who might be stopped or questioned, just how much you want to see police officers "empowered." Don't forget, though, that you might also be a homeowner who would like to see the police "empowered" to solve problems in your neighborhood. On balance, how do you see this issue of police empowerment?

The idea of community policing rests with Goldstein (1979, 1990) who postulated that the police response to crime and disorder was superficial and bureaucratic in that the police typically responded to problems rather than attempting to resolve problems. He also suggested that the police, if they are to be successful, must engage the community and its citizens in order to develop a more comprehensive, workable solution to problems. Hence, the two defining elements of community policing are community partnership and problem-solving (Bureau of Justice Assistance 1994). Immediately following Goldstein's groundbreaking work there was considerable confusion about the nature of community policing. The confusion revolved around whether community policing was a philosophy, strategy, or group of tactics. There was a proliferation of work which suggested that it was all of the above.

Cordner (1995) attempted to clarify the debate by demonstrating how community policing cuts across the complete spectrum of police management and operations. He insinuated that if community policing is to be implemented successfully, it must become an integral part of every aspect of the police organization. Introspectively, most police departments have been unable to muster the wherewithal to comprehensively implement community policing and have adopted it piecemeal. This has resulted in a patchwork of programming and philosophies. For example, McEwen (1994) found that Drug Awareness and Resistance Education (DARE) programs and neighborhood watches were the two most commonly implemented community policing programs. Both of these programs pre-date community policing which, to some extent, may demonstrate the confusion associated with implementing community policing and a possible lack of new, innovative programming (tactics) as a result of it. There has also been a tendency to label all sorts of pre-existing programs as part of a department's community policing strategy (McEwen 1994; Zhao & Thurman 1997).

There is a significant contingency who recognize that a new management structure is required if community policing is to be effectively implemented (Goldstein 1990; Peak & Glensor 1996). Many would call for a police department which adheres to a participative management style (Roberg & Kuykendall 1990; Witte, Travis, & Langworthy 1989), while others correspondingly call for police managers to abdicate power through decentralization and empowerment of subordinates (Brown 1989). Those calling for change generally deplore the idea of the quasi-military model in law enforcement and believe that change will ultimately result in a police agency which is more effective across a variety of fronts.

Pronouncements of participation and empowerment generally elicit strong images about the police organization. They represent an idea which is antithetical to past and many current organizational arrangements. To this end, they represent a broad brush attack on police management as we currently know it. It seems that change is unquestionably desirable for the modern, community policing department.

It is the thesis of this paper, however, that participative and empowerment prescriptions represent general ideas which may be of minimum value when examining the modern police organization. If we examine the repeated calls for participation and empowerment more closely, we find that their symbolism results in several assumptions about modern management: (1) the quasi-military model is inappropriate for policing; (2) modern police administration is quasi-militaristic and authoritarian; (3) employees desire to be empowered; and (4) human relations theories, the embodiment of participation and empowerment, represents a more viable, workable model.

The following sections will explore these assumptions. It should be recognized that there exist few comprehensive examinations of the police organization (cf. Langworthy 1986), and we tend to discuss the police organization in general or theoretical terms which often are based on impressions, rather than observed fact.

The Quasi-Military Model is Inappropriate for Policing

The quasi-military model of police management is rooted in classical organizational theory. Classical theory equates to structure and control. It creates a rational organization whereby activities are ordered and people report to superiors in a monolithic rank structure. It emphasizes efficiency and productivity, with minimum consideration for employ-

ees. Critics are quick to point out that it is demoralizing to employees (Angell 1978); it tends to concentrate inward neglecting the larger organizational environment (Cordner 1978); and it tends to concentrate on the trappings of power and authority as opposed to productive outputs such as services and products (Guyot 1979).

Some, however, would argue that bureaucracy or the quasi-military model is the only manner by which to manage large organizations (Goodsell 1985). That is, a consultative or participative form of management can easily be used in small police department or an engineering consulting firm, but large organizations such as the New York City Police Department or the Chicago Police Department require the employment of bureaucratic organizational principles. Large organizations require rationality.

Second, the bureaucratic organization very likely is the most effective management structure with which to deliver services. In an analysis of empirical studies, Goodsell (1985) found that bureaucracies were fairly effective, contrary to their critics. He argues that critics frequently highlight cases which have been mishandled by bureaucrats, but these critics seldom give due consideration to the multitude of cases which are handled efficiently and effectively. Indeed, all management formats will produce errors or mistakes. There is not sufficient evidence to support that other organizational forms are any more effective than bureaucracies. To this end, Parrow (1972: 6-7) notes:

> . . . the extensive preoccupation with reforming, "humanizing," and decentralizing bureaucracies, while salutary, has served to obscure from organizational theorists the true nature of bureaucracy and has diverted us from assessing its impact on society. The impact on society in general is incalculably more important than the impact upon the members of a particular organization . . . bureaucracy is a form of organization superior to all others we know or can hope to afford in the near and middle future; the chances of doing away with it or changing it are probably non-existent in the rest of this century.

There also is a body of research and theory known as contingency theory which hypothesizes that there is no one best way to manage, and bureaucracy and participation are equally appropriate under the right conditions. For example, Burns and Stalker (1961) examined about 20 firms in Great Britain and found that those operating in relatively stable environments adopted a mechanistic organizational structure (bureaucratic), while those facing unstable environments adapted by using organic structures (participative). Similarly, Woodward (1965) found that mechanistic structures were more appropriate for mass-production work settings, while organic systems were appropriate for non-repetitive work environments. This body of literature seems to indicate that some segments of a police organization may be more effective if organized using bureaucratic principles, while other segments may be better served if a participative style were used.

In summary, there is evidence that the quasi-military model is necessarily authoritarian. Bureaucracy's track record certainly is not as discouraging as its critics would suggest. In fact, the evidence insinuates that it is more appropriate under certain conditions. These conditions can undeniably be applied to law enforcement. For example, a mechanical structure may be best suited for police units such as: records, communications, traffic, juvenile, and patrol. Organic structures may be more suitable for units such as criminal investigation, drug investigation, and planning. Although the placement of particular units within the mechanistic-organic schema can be debated, the appropriateness of both organizational forms in a police organization appears to be reasonable.

Modern Police Administration is Quasi-Militaristic and Authoritarian

The call for police managers to empower their subordinates beckons a need to depart from some current arrangement. In other words, pronouncements to empower subordinates symbolically infers that there currently is a dearth of empowerment in police departments and that they remain quasi-militaristic. Moreover, there are those who proclaim that police management remains unduly authoritarian and counterproductive (Souryal 1995). Proponents of empowerment seem to suggest that power and authority remain centrally located within police organizations and mid-level managers have little discretion to deal with problems and issues.

The police, historically, have adhered to a quasi-military model of organization. The Metropolitan Police Act of 1829 created the London Metropolitan Police, the first modern police department, and it was organized along a military model (Reith 1975). The professional era of police management of the 1950s evolved around the quasi-military or bureaucratic model in which organization and management was necessary to reform policing and reduce the degree of corruption which was inherent to policing at the time. Today, many vestiges of the military, e.g., hierarchy, military titles, specialization, etc., remain a part of law enforcement.

However, it seems unreasonable to compare today's police organization with the military, even though they tend to use some of the same nomenclature and share similar hierarchical arrangements. Police officers have substantial discretion in how they operate (Lipsky 1980; Brooks 1997), while soldiers do not. Even though managers and supervisors attempt to control officers' discretion, officers retain substantial latitude in how they handle many of the tasks to which they are assigned. Indeed, police managers tend to give minimal attention to most activities when it comes to controlling discretion except high liability areas and areas of great public concern (Alpert & Smith 1994). The same latitude often is given to supervisors and middle managers. In essence, police behavior at all levels cannot be absolutely controlled, nor are there extensive efforts to control it; efforts are made to control only the important or critical areas.

Police administration has not operated in a management void. Beginning with the 1970s, police administration has undergone a number of gradual changes. These changes occurred on two fronts. First, a number of police departments experimented with team policing. A central element in many of the team policing projects was to use small teams of police officers, as opposed to large bureaus, to provide a wide variety of police services. Important traits of team policing were: decentralized decision making, small groups, and reduced hierarchy (Gay et al. 1977). About the same time, a number of departments attempted to allow officers and mid-level managers to have greater input into decision making, especially at the operational levels (Tenzel, Storms, & Sweetwood 1976). A large number of departments even used quality circles to involve subordinates in decision making (Hatry & Greiner 1986). There has been substantial experimentation with participatory measures, and it is safe to say, that they remain present in a large number of police departments throughout the United States (Toch 1997).

When police departments are characterized as being authoritarian, such a statement implies that authoritarianism is prevalent throughout the department. A small department may consistently have one management style throughout, but it is doubtful that large agencies do. For example, it is very likely that drug unit commanders have greater latitude in targeting possible offenders and enforcement tactics used compared to patrol commanders. Moreover, individual investigators would have substantial input into the decision making processes, whereas officers in patrol areas do not. There are differences in how individual units are managed within every police department, and these differences are dictated by the nature of the assignment, commanders' personal management style, and the larger organizational environment.

Many students of police administration maintain that policing is reactive, and if this is correct to any degree, it may be that the best way to describe much of police administration is that it is somewhat laissez-faire with the trappings of being quasi-militaristic or bureaucratic. This presumption is further supported by the fact that police departments, particularly larger departments, tend to react to environmental problems, which is characteristic of laissez-faire organizations, as opposed to proactively dealing with issues before they manifest into problems. An efficient military organization would more effectively and timely address incipient problems.

If there is even a modicum of laissez-faire style, then the idea of a highly controlled police organization becomes somewhat questionable.

Another issue which begs to be raised concerns the differences in police administration compared to management practices in other units of government, business, and industry. Are police organizations administered differently than fire departments, social service delivery agencies, state banking commissions, or environmental control agencies? How different are Proctor and Gamble, Toyota, or any Fortune 500 company's operations from police administration? These entities all use matrix forms of organization whereby all styles of leadership and organization are used, and they very likely have some areas or units where empowerment prevails, while a quasi-militaristic or bureaucratic form of management is practiced elsewhere. Along these lines, although a factory may practice quality circles, the overall management practices may remain quasi-militaristic.

Employees Desire to Be Empowered

The idea of empowerment assumes that subordinates have a desire to accept more responsibility, but are not given the opportunity to do so. Although this position assumes that police subordinates desire to change and accept more responsibility through empowerment, this presumption is not always correct because most employees resist change. Greene, Bergman, and McLaughlin (1994), for example, studied the implementation of community policing in Philadelphia, reporting resistance at all levels, including rank-and-file officers. Working arrangements and conditions become habits, and workers are very reluctant to change these habits (Greenberg & Barron 1995).

In formulating his idea of community policing, Goldstein (1979, 1990) criticized the police for providing only a superficial response to most calls-for-service. He postulates that the police should attempt to identify problems once on-the-scene as opposed to providing only a minimal effort at problem identification, which occurs in the majority of cases. This means that police officers should be expected to do "more" at the scene, and supervisors should attempt to ensure that officers have the capacity to deal with problems and in fact deal with them effectively. If this occurs, officers and supervisors will have to work harder, involving substantial interaction with clients, increasing efforts to search for alternative solutions, and devoting considerable effort to ensure that alternatives are implemented properly and problems solved. There certainly are institutional barriers such as issues relating to workload, the queuing of calls, and tools available to police officers, which prevent officers from more effectively dealing with calls, but individual officer resistance may be the greatest barrier.

Even though police administrators may wish that subordinates exert greater efforts, subordinates may not be inclined to do so. Reuss-Ianni (1983) found New York police officers to have a value system which made them highly resistant to change and new responsibilities. Lurigio and Skogan (1994) found Chicago officers who were involved in a community policing program to be ambivalent about new tasks and responsibilities. Likewise, Lord (1996) found officers and sergeants in Charlotte-Mechlenburg County show manifestations of stress when implementing community policing. Finally, unions tend to be highly resistant to the idea of change, particularly the type of change associated with community policing (Greene, Bergman, & McLaughlin 1994).

In all fairness, however, the argument that police subordinates are or may not be receptive to assuming new responsibilities may be as narrow-minded as asserting that police administration is quasi-militaristic. Crank (1997) in a recent examination of police culture, noted that police officers and the police culture in general consists of values which emphasize "doing a good job." Wycoff and Skogan (1994) found that Madison, Wisconsin police officers expressed a weak interest in accepting additional tasks. The degree to which a police department's culture is open to new assignments and ideas runs the complete gamut of closedness–openness. Although management style is very likely a factor in the equation, there certainly are many other factors. In other words, management style most likely will account for only a portion of employee resistance.

Command, Accountability, and Empowerment

The preceding sections examined police administration as it relates to the idea of participation and empowerment, the purpose of which was to dispel the view that law enforcement agencies are uniform in organization and management. It also attacked the notion that all police departments are authoritarian, quasi-militaristic monoliths. To the contrary, police organizations have evolved substantially over the past three decades (Toch 1997). Some have more participative management systems than others, and there is substantial variability of managerial style within individual police departments.

The thesis of this paper is that empowerment is not necessarily where management must divest itself of some measure of power and authority and deliver it to lower level subordinates, but that empowerment is a process of delegating general and specific responsibilities and authority to subordinates and holding them accountable for their accomplishments. In other words, empowerment is a process whereby administrators not only relinquish power and authority, but in many instances they must force it upon lower level managers. The failure to empower subordinates is not vested solely with administrators, but fault lies throughout the organization. Working arrangements in most departments are historical in nature, and getting personnel and units actively involved in community policing functions may be very difficult (Greene, Bergman, & McLaughlin 1994). The question then arises, "how can community policing be implemented, especially at lower strata within the police organization?"

Perhaps, the context of this question can best be explored by first examining how community policing generally has been implemented. There is some evidence that many departments have operationally defined it as the programs and strategies which have been implemented (McEwen 1994). That is, operationally, community policing has come to be defined as the sum of its parts. A particular department's community policing initiative is constituted by the programs it has implemented. This allows every police department to characterize itself as a community policing department, regardless of what it is doing. Indeed, just about every police department has attached the community policing label to its activities. This phenomenon may be the result of anecdotal reports, increased public attention on community policing, and the availability of federal monies as opposed to a general recognition that community policing works or is actually being implemented.

Cordner (1995) provides some insight into implementation when he discussed it as an organization-wide process. Using this perspective, it becomes fairly obvious that its implementation can be treated no differently than any other organization-wide change. It infers that focusing on participative management and empowerment exclusively will not result in a long-term, successfully implemented program. It also means that community policing is an organization-wide phenomenon which includes administrative participation. Administrators play a key role in the successful implementation of community policing because they must develop and implement a comprehensive plan of what community policing means to the community and department, and administrators must remain intimately involved because ultimately they are the ones who are held accountable if community policing or any other strategy or tactic fails.

Implementing Community Policing as Change

Planned change in an organization can be radical where large amounts of change are introduced rather quickly, or it can be planned incremental change. Perhaps, the best way to approach implementation of community policing is as planned incremental change, especially considering that it is extremely difficult to implement radical change in large organizations. Planned incremental change is less disruptive to the organization. Even though the change is piecemeal, it nonetheless can be comprehensive. Comprehensive change must focus on: (1) goals and strategy, (2) people, (3) services, and (4) technology (Hodge, Anthony, & Gales 1996).

Goals and Strategy

As noted above, the two essential elements of community policing are community partnerships and problem-solving. These two elements represent a move whereby the police respond to the community more effectively when providing services, maintaining order, and enforcing the law. For the most part, community policing has not changed law enforcement goals. It has caused police administrators to scrutinize what their officers are doing and attempt to make improvements, especially in terms of service quality. The police still provide services, maintain order, and enforce the law, but the two principle vehicles for doing so are community partnerships and problem-solving.

Administrators must ensure that all levels of the department respond to changes in strategy and philosophy. This is done through direction and policy formulation. Direction and policies set the tone for the organization and are extremely crucial when change is first initiated. That is, when change is first initiated, lower level employees often experience role ambiguity and confusion. Administrators must ensure that mechanisms are in place which provide subordinates adequate guidance. Direction and policies become less important once the change is fully incorporated in the organization.

People

If community policing is to succeed, traditional human resource systems must be altered to ensure that the proper personnel are recruited and selected, they are properly trained, and they receive the support necessary to do the job once hired and deployed. For example, Himelfarb (1997) completely restructured the training regime for the Royal Canadian Mounted Police (RCMP) so that Mounties would give greater consideration to citizen-clients and more comprehensively address problems. The Houston Police Department developed a cascading training program for each rank level to provide all officers a clearer idea of how community policing affects performance and responsibilities

(Kelling & Bratton 1993). Although officers should be exposed to a comprehensive training program which informs them of their responsibilities and authority, in many training programs, community policing has been unfortunately discussed in general terms, which is of little utility to most officers. Training and direction must be grounded in the realities of the new job.

Services

Community policing drastically alters how the police should view responding to the community. As discussed above, problem-solving requires that the police treat and resolve problems rather than superficially attend to citizen calls and requests. Many departments have adopted the SARA model for accomplishing this task: scanning, analysis, response, and assessment (Eck & Spellman 1987). The important point is that the police must go beyond answering calls and substantively address pertinent activities or problems. This will necessitate officers spending more time at calls, obtaining support from other units within the department, and in some cases, using other governmental agencies as well as private agencies to solve problems.

Whereas problem-solving describes how the police should provide services, the idea of community partnerships gives service delivery the correct contextual foundation. Traditional police departments operated as a closed system (Cordner 1978), whereby the police, not citizens, determined goals and objectives. Over time, the police have come to recognize that citizens have a legitimate right to have direct input into police goals and objectives, and indeed, the police are constituted to serve the public. This has operational meaning at two levels. First, the police must recognize that the community and constituent groups within the community have different needs, and the police must respond to these differential needs. Second, in actuality, citizens who call the police are clients, and they should be treated accordingly. Quality should not be measured by the number of calls answered by the police, but rather by the level of service and client satisfaction.

Technology

Perhaps, there is no other governmental agency which collects more information than the police. The police are masters at taking reports. Unfortunately, these data are seldom used to their fullest extent for strategic and tactical purposes. The police, through their computer information systems, must search for problem areas in terms of trends and relationships (Gaines, Angell, & Southerland 1991). Police information systems are one of the best mechanisms to scan the environment for problems. Once problems are identified, the data can be used to assist in tailoring police tactics. These information systems can also be used in assessing whether tactics successfully addressed a problem. Problem-solving is focused police work, and information is necessary to develop the focus.

Conclusion

The purpose of this paper was to provide a comprehensive examination of how community policing should be implemented. Heretofore, many implementation discussions have focused on participation and empowerment. Without a question, these management strategies are important to the successful implementation of community policing, but it must be remembered that they represent a part, not the whole, when implementing community policing. Community policing is an organization-wide program which requires a comprehensive change strategy. Even though it can be done incrementally, it must nonetheless be done comprehensively.

Administrators must conceive a strategy which touches every unit and officer. The strategy must to some extent describe the new roles assumed by officers as a result of community policing. Administrative mechanisms, whether total quality management, management by objectives, or another management configuration, must be implemented to assure that officers assume new roles and responsibilities. If administrators implement community policing haphazardly and not systemically, it will eventually fail as have a number of other police innovations (Gaines 1994).

References

Alpert, G. & Smith, W. 1994. "Developing Police Policy: An Evaluation of the Control Principle." *American Journal of Police, 13* (2), pp. 1-20.

Angell, J. 1978. "Toward an Alternative to the Classic Police Organizational Arrangements." In L. Gaines & T. Rick (Eds.), *Managing the Police Organization*, pp. 103-119. St. Paul: West.

Bracey, D. 1992. "Police Corruption and Community Relations: Community Policing." *Police Studies, 15*(4), pp. 179-183.

Brooks, L. 1997. "Police Discretionary Behavior: A Study of Style." In R. Dunham & G. Alpert (Eds.), *Critical issues in policing: Contemporary readings*, pp. 149-166. Prospect Heights, IL: Waveland.

Brown, L. 1989. "Community Policing: A Practical Guide for Police Officials." *Perspectives on Policing*, No. 12. Washington, D.C.: NIJ.

Bureau of Justice Assistance. 1994. *Understanding Community Policing: A Framework for Action.* Washington, D.C.: Bureau of Justice Assistance.

Burns, T., & Stalker, G. 1961. *The Management of Innovation.* London: Tavistock.

Cordner, G. 1978. "Open and Closed Models of Police Organizations: Traditions, Dilemmas, and Practical Considerations." *Journal of Police Science and Administration, 6*, pp. 22-34.

Cordner, G. 1995. "Community Policing: Elements and Effects." *Police Forum, 5*(3), pp. 1-7.

Crank, J. 1997. "Celebrating Agency Culture: Engaging a Traditional Cop's Heart in Organizational Change." In Q. Thurman & E. McGarrell (Eds.), *Community Policing in a Rural Setting*, pp. 49-58. Cincinnati: Anderson.

Eck, J., & Spellman, J. 1987. "Who Ya Gonna Call? The Police as Problem Busters." *Crime and Delinquency, 33*, pp. 31-52.

Gaines, L. 1994. "Community-Oriented Policing: Management Issues, Concerns, and Problems." *Journal of Contemporary Criminal Justice, 10*(1), pp. 17-35.

Gaines, L., Angell, J., & Southerland, M. 1991. *Police Administration.* New York: McGraw-Hill.

Gay, W., Woodward, J., Day, T., O'Neil, J., & Tucker, C. 1977. *Issues in Team Policing: A Review of the Literature.* Washington, D.C.: National Institute of Justice.

Goldstein, H. 1979. "Improving Policing: A Problem-Oriented Approach." *Crime and Delinquency, 25*, pp. 236-258.

Goldstein, H. 1990. *Problem-Oriented Policing.* New York: McGraw-Hill.

Goodsell, C. 1985. *The Case for Bureaucracy.* (2nd ed.). Chatham, NJ: Chatham House.

Greenberg, J. & Barron, R. 1995. *Behavior in Organizations.* (5th Ed.). Englewood Cliffs, NJ: Prentice-Hall.

Greene, J., Bergman, W., & McLaughlin, E. 1994. "Implementing Community Policing: Cultural and Structural Change in Police Organizations." In D. Rosenbaum (Ed.), *The Challenge of Community Policing: Testing the Promises*, pp. 92-109. Thousand Oaks, CA: Sage.

Guyot, D. 1979. "Bending Granite: Attempts to Change the Rank Structure of American Police Departments." *Journal of Police Science and Administration, 7*, pp. 253-284.

Hatry, H., & Greiner, J. 1986. *Improving the Use of Quality Circles in Police Departments.* Washington, D.C.: National Institute of Justice.

Himelfarb, F. 1997. "RCMP Learning and Renewal: Building on Strengths." In Q. Thurman & E. McGarrell (Eds.), *Community Policing in a Rural Setting*, pp. 33-40. Cincinnati: Anderson.

Hodge, B., Anthony, W., & Gales, L. 1996. *Organization Theory: A Strategic Approach.* Upper Saddle River, NJ: Prentice-Hall.

Kelling, G., & Bratton, W. 1993. *Implementing Community Policing: The Administrative Problem.* (Perspectives on Policing), No. 17. Washington, D.C.: National Institute of Justice.

Langworthy, R. 1986. *The Structure of Police Organizations.* New York: Praeger.

Lipsky, M. 1980. *Street-Level Bureaucracy: Dilemmas of the Individual in Public Services.* New York: Russell Sage Foundation.

Lord, V. 1996. "An Impact of Community Policing: Reported Stressors, Social Support, and Strain Among Police Officers in a Changing Police Department." *Journal of Criminal Justice, 24*, pp. 503-522.

Lurigio, A., & Skogan, W. 1994. "Winning the Hearts and Minds of Police Officers: An Assessment of Staff Perceptions of Community Policing in Chicago." *Crime and Delinquency, 40*, pp. 315-330.

McEwen, T. 1994. *National Assessment Program: 1994 Survey Results.* Washington, D.C.: National Institute of Justice.

Parrow, C. 1972. *Complex Organizations: A Critical Essay.* Glenview, IL: Scott, Foresman, and Company.

Peak, K., & Glensor, R. 1996. *Community Policing and Problem Solving: Strategies and Practices.* Upper Saddle River, NJ: Prentice-Hall.

Reith, C. 1975. *The Blind Eye of History.* (Reprint ed.). Montclair, NJ: Patterson-Smith.

Reuss-Ianni, E. 1983. *Two Cultures of Policing: Street Cops and Management Cops.* New Brunswick, NJ: Transaction.

Roberg, R., & Kuykendall, J. 1990. *Police Organization and Management: Behavior, Theory, and Processes.* Pacific Grove, CA: Brooks/Cole.

Souryal, S. 1995. *Police Organization and Administration.* Cincinnati: Anderson.

Tenzel, J., Storms, L., & Sweetwood, H. 1976. "Symbols and Behavior: An Experiment in Altering the Police Role." *Journal of Police Science and Administration, 4,* pp. 21-27.

Toch, H. 1997. "The Democratization of Policing in the United States: 1895-1973." *Police Forum, 7*(2), 1-8.

Witte, J., Travis, L., & Langworthy, R. 1989. "Participatory Management in Law Enforcement: Police Officer, Supervisor and Administrator Perceptions." *American Journal of Police, 9*(4), 1-24.

Woodward, J. 1965. *Industrial Organization: Theory and Practice.* London: Oxford University Press.

Wycoff, M., & Skogan, W. 1994. "The Effect of a Community Policing Management Style on Officers' Attitudes." *Crime and Delinquency, 40,* pp. 371-383.

Zhao, J., & Thurman, Q. 1997. "Facilitators and Obstacles to Community Policing in a Rural Setting." In Q. Thurman & E. McGarrell, (Eds.), *Community Policing in a Rural Setting,* pp. 27-32. Cincinnati: Anderson.

27

Community Policing and Police Agency Accreditation

Gary W. Cordner and Gerald L. Williams

For years, many people in the police field yearned for national standards that could be used to upgrade the consistency and dependability of American policing. Such a body of standards was finally created in 1979, along with an organization (CALEA—the Commission on Accreditation for Law Enforcement Agencies) to administer the standards for police departments volunteering to pursue accredited status. The standards and the accreditation process have been controversial, however. The most recent controversy is whether these standards support or inhibit the implementation of community policing. In their article, Cordner and Williams report on a national study that focused on the compatibility of accreditation and community policing. As you read the article, think about whether the accreditation system should or should not be revised to make it more supportive of community policing. What would be the pros and cons of such a revision?

Community policing and law enforcement agency accreditation are two of the most significant police reform initiatives of the late 20th century. Whether these two major developments, one primarily operational and the other mainly administrative, are compatible or in conflict emerged as a serious issue in the late 1980s and early 1990s (Behan 1992;

Oettmeier 1993; Sykes 1994; Watson and Williams 1991). The spectacular rise in popularity of community policing in the middle 1990s has made this question that much more timely and important.

The accreditation program, begun in 1979, is based on a manual of standards and is administered by the Commission on Accreditation for Law Enforcement Agencies (CALEA). This nonprofit organization's governing body consists of 21 members, 11 of whom are law enforcement practitioners and 10 of whom represent other areas of government and the private sector. The process of accreditation involves a self-study phase and an on-site assessment, with final decisions about granting accredited status made by the full Commission (Behan 1989; Greenberg 1989; Mastrofski 1986). Maintaining accredited status then requires reaccreditation every three years. The accreditation standards (currently numbering 436) underwent a substantial review and revision during 1993–1994.

Community policing (COP), with roots in such earlier developments as police-community relations, team policing, crime prevention, and the rediscovery of foot patrol, has become the dominant new strategy of policing. It is now seen almost universally as the most effective method available for improving police-community relations. Proponents also believe that it will ultimately prove to be an effective crime control strategy. Indicative of its stature in the 1990s, community policing is required of the 100,000 new police officers funded by the Crime Bill passed in 1994 by the U.S. Congress.

Any study that involves community policing has definitional and measurement challenges. In the initial stages of the project, we were primarily guided by the works of Trojanowicz and Bucqueroux (1990), Skolnick and Bayley (1986), and Goldstein (1990) in identifying key characteristics of community policing and problem solving. Later, we relied on works by Greene and Mastrofski (1988) and by Rosenbaum (1994) to identify key conceptual and implementation issues. Ultimately, we focused on specific aspects of community policing in our case study sites using a typology of elements and dimensions developed by Cordner (1995).

The issue of compatibility between accreditation and COP takes several forms, but largely comes down to two questions about direct and indirect impact:

- **Direct Impact**—Are the police *operations* requirements of accreditation compatible with community policing?

- **Indirect Impact**—Are the police *administration* requirements of accreditation compatible with community policing?

The accreditation standards might avoid any direct or indirect incompatibility with COP by virtue of being neutral, flexible, or simply not very demanding. Alternatively, *direct* conflict or support might arise to the degree that the accreditation standards require or encourage particular approaches to the delivery of police services to the public. The standards might discourage such operational tactics as partnerships with the community and collaborative problem solving, for example, or they might encourage them. Similarly, *indirect* conflict or support might arise to the extent that the standards mandate a specific approach to organizing and managing police agencies. For example, the accreditation standards might discourage citizen input into police policies and priorities or discourage employee empowerment, or they might encourage such administrative practices.

Design of the Study

This study examined the compatibility of community policing and accreditation by using three principal research strategies:

1. **Content Analysis:** separate content analyses of the 897 accreditation standards in effect at the end of 1992 and the revised set of 436 standards published in 1994. Each content analysis was done in three stages: first, three researchers independently coded each standard, then a consensus coding was reached, and then the coding of all standards was reviewed for internal consistency. The standards were coded on 27 variables derived from the literature on community policing and police administration.

2. **Expert Surveys:** a survey sent to the CEOs of 12 case study sites and 12 other "expert" practitioners and academics selected because they had expressed, in person or in published works, particular views about the substantive impact of accreditation or about the implications of accreditation for community policing. The survey sought these experts' evaluations of 14 hypotheses about the intersection of community policing and accreditation.

3. **Case Studies:** case studies of 12 law enforcement agencies that were accredited and also engaged in some form of community policing. Other criteria used in the site selection process included agency size, population diversity, agency type, and regional variation. Each site was visited twice during the study, once for a general overview and once to focus on some specific aspect of community policing. Substantial documentation was also gathered at each site.

Findings

The major findings from each of the three research strategies were as follows:

- **Content Analysis**—(1) the accreditation standards do not directly conflict with COP, but neither do they provide strong support for community-oriented or problem-oriented police operations; (2) the standards support a traditional, formalistic approach to police administration, yet they do not particularly require centralization, specialization, or more hierarchy; and (3) the standards are written in such a way that they are overwhelmingly process-oriented rather than outcome-oriented. As such, their real impact on the quality and nature of police services delivered to citizens is inherently problematic.

- **Expert Surveys**—(1) neither the 12 case study site CEOs nor the outside experts expressed much support for the likelihood of direct conflict between accreditation and community policing; (2) the outside experts did express support for several varieties of indirect conflict, though, whereas the CEOs thought even indirect conflict was unlikely.

- **Case Studies**—(1) very little evidence of conflict between accreditation and COP was uncovered in any of the case study sites. Some site representatives saw the two reforms as essentially independent while others felt strongly that their accreditation efforts had supported their community policing efforts.

The information derived from these research strategies can be synthesized and further used to evaluate 14 specific hypotheses about possible relationships between community policing and accreditation. These hypotheses posit a wide range of potential direct and indirect effects.

H1: The Anti-COP Hypothesis

Little or no support was uncovered for the hypothesis that accreditation *directly* conflicts with community policing. The accreditation standards do not prohibit community-oriented initiatives nor do they require activities that most COP advocates would shun. All of the case study site chiefs and 70% of the outside experts disagreed with the anti-COP proposition. Very little evidence was found in the case studies of direct conflict between community policing and accreditation.

H2: The Anti-POP Hypothesis

Similarly, little or no evidence was found to support the argument that accreditation *directly* conflicts with problem-oriented policing (POP). The standards do not prohibit taking a problem-oriented approach, although they definitely reflect much more of an incident-oriented view of policing. Neither the chiefs nor the outside experts indicated much support for the anti-POP hypothesis, and no evidence for it was found in the case studies.

H3: The Rigid Bureaucracy Hypothesis

Some support was found for the proposition that accreditation creates a formal administrative/management system that interferes with COP/POP. The predominant characteristic of the standards is that they require formalization, especially written directives. The standards also tend to support functional specialization of personnel, administrative accountability, and some limits on police officer discretion. Four of the 10 outside experts agreed with the hypothesis: Herman Goldstein worried that accreditation "in its totality and especially its emphasis, creates an attitude and environment that stands in the way of developing COP/POP."

The evidence for this rigid bureaucracy hypothesis is mixed, however. Although they strongly support formalization, the standards do not particularly encourage centralization, specialized units, or more hierarchy. Moreover, several chiefs and outside experts emphasized that all organizations need some structure and parameters. And as then-Chief Michael Gambrill from Baltimore County, Maryland argued, "a formal administrative/management system is not the issue that creates the rigid bureaucracy. It is the degree of rigidity with which the structure is created and maintained that creates conflicts."

H4: The Efficiency Hypothesis

Some support was also found for the view that accreditation tends to focus administrative attention on internal organizational matters instead of on substantive problems in the community. The vast majority of the standards (80%+) pertain more to administration than to operations. Twice as many of the outside experts agreed as disagreed with the hypothesis: James Fyfe expressed his dismay that "CALEA standards do not focus more directly on the direct delivery of police services."

All of the case study site chiefs disagreed with the hypothesis, though. Their view, similar to that expressed above in response to the rigid bureaucracy hypothesis, is that police departments have to focus considerable attention inwardly on administrative issues and problems, and that accreditation helped them do that more effectively. Generally, these CEOs agreed with the first part of the hypothesis, that the focus of accreditation is internal, but did not feel that this deflected attention away from substantive problems in the community.

H5: The Thin Blue Line Hypothesis

Little evidence was found in support of the hypothesis that accreditation emphasizes police responsibility and accountability to the detriment of community input. The standards do emphasize managerial accountability for a variety of administrative matters within police organizations, but they do not prohibit citizen input and in fact encourage such input with several standards. The type of accountability addressed by the standards generally pertains to internal administrative processes; the standards are largely silent about accountability for community conditions, discretionary decisions, or similar issues about which citizen input would be most germane. No chiefs and only three experts agreed with the hypothesis, but in his comments James Fyfe did lament the fact that real accountability to the public was not stressed more in the accreditation standards and process.

H6: The Style Over Substance Hypothesis

Mixed support was found for the hypothesis that accreditation emphasizes process to the detriment of outcomes. Few of the CALEA standards (less than 5%) specify an outcome or even a standard of care that must be met—rather, they typically require that a written directive or other organizational process be in place. The underlying assumption, apparently, is that if a police agency runs itself according to these accepted processes, good outcomes will happen. This would seem to be a risky assumption, however. Moreover, the gulf between accreditation and what actually happens on the street and in the community might contribute to the view that accreditation is just not that important or relevant in the age of community policing.

Almost all of the chiefs defended this characteristic of the accreditation standards, though. Phil Keith of Knoxville, Tennessee, for example, argued that "it is the agency's responsibility to follow through and be concerned with outcomes." And as Larry Hoover noted, this focus on process rather than outcome is not peculiar to law enforcement, but rather common to accreditation in most fields.

H7: The Incident-Driven Hypothesis

Some support was found for the proposition that accreditation reflects an incident-oriented perspective on policing to the detriment of the problem-oriented approach. Those standards that express any perspective on the nature of police work (about 20% of the total) are 4-5 times more likely to be incident-oriented than problem-oriented. The outside experts were split over whether this interfered with POP efforts, though, and the site chiefs did not believe it did. No evidence was found in the case studies that problem-solving was significantly inhibited by accreditation.

H8: The Professional Model Hypothesis

The accreditation program was developed during the heyday of the professional model. The standards, taken in their entirety, reflect this lineage in their emphasis on formalization, their focus on administrative matters, and their incident-oriented view of police work. As Jack Greene commented, "it is simply in their nature."

The real issue is whether this characteristic interferes with community policing. The site chiefs did not think so, while the majority of the outside experts did. This disagreement probably parallels those discussed earlier in regard to the rigid bureaucracy and efficiency hypotheses. Some observers see the professional model as the infrastructure or even the launching pad for community policing, while others see it more as a swamp from which police departments must first escape before implementing meaningful COP initiatives.

H9: The Scarce Resources Hypothesis

This hypothesis posits that accreditation and COP compete within police agencies for scarce resources and for managerial attention. The implication is that the two initiatives may be programmatically compatible, but nevertheless in conflict because of their cost and complexity. A good bit of support for this proposition was expressed by chiefs and outside experts, although few saw this conflict as irreconcilable or necessitating a choice between the two. Chief Lorne Kramer from Colorado Springs observed that "even though they do compete for resources, the benefits of both are substantial and worth the investment."

H10: The Police Politics Hypothesis

Relatively little support was uncovered for the police politics hypothesis, which holds that conflict between accreditation and community policing occurs, not for programmatic reasons, but because the two reforms tend to draw allegiance from competing interest groups within individual police agencies and within the police industry generally. David Carter noted that "both are in advocacy roles, so one should expect competition," but seemed to reflect the majority view that such competition was not overly divisive or threatening to either initiative. Little evidence was found in the case study sites that community policing and accreditation created warring camps or were even the symbolic battle flags of competing factions.

H11: The Support Hypothesis

A number of accreditation standards were found to directly *support* elements of community policing, although, as indicated above, the standards in their entirety reflect the professional model of policing. A solid minority (about 40%) of both the site chiefs and outside experts thought that accreditation supported COP, but the majority of each group disagreed. As will be indicated below, there is probably more evidence that the accreditation process and standards are neutral and/or flexible than that they directly support community policing.

H12: The Neutrality Hypothesis

The content analysis concluded that the vast majority of the standards were essentially neutral toward community policing, at least on their face. The site CEOs tended to agree, but the outside experts did not. Gary Sykes commented that the accreditation standards "carry with them a set of assumptions about how the agency should be managed and . . . presume a hierarchical organization and bureaucratic culture." Chief Thomas Koby from Boulder, Colorado concurred: "It further institutionalizes a functional management model in a profession that is service based."

These comments once again illustrate a significant cleavage in thinking about the accreditation vs. COP issue. Some observers view the latent professional model characteristics (both organizational and operational) of accreditation as far from neutral and as contradictory to community policing. Others see the standards as neutral because they simply require administrative structure and consistency while leaving issues of policing philosophy and strategy up to each department.

H13: The Flexibility Hypothesis

A majority of both the chiefs and the experts agreed with the hypothesis that police agency accreditation has no direct effect on community policing because of the flexibility of the standards. As the chief from Baltimore County noted, "if this weren't true, we would not be able to do both as we have done for years." The content analysis supported this view, as few of the standards were judged to be very restrictive and few directly supported either COP or any other strategy of policing.

H14: The Null Hypothesis

This hypothesis expresses the skeptical view that perhaps (1) accreditation is such a paper tiger that it has no real impact, or (2) community policing is so much more rhetoric than reality that it has no real impact, or (3) both. If any of these three propositions is correct, then we would not expect to find much conflict between accreditation and community policing, because there would be so little substance over which to fight.

Most of the site chiefs and other experts disagreed with this hypothesis. Many echoed the comments of the chief from Colorado Springs: "Both of these philosophies and styles of management have numerous and varied benefits which do not only improve services, address critical issues, solve problems and limit liability exposure but are capable of working together with minimal conflict." The strongest supporter of the null hypothesis was Stephen Mastrofski, who acknowledged the potential of both accreditation and community policing but doubted that either had yet had much impact "at the 'technical' level where the department's work gets done."

The content analysis and case studies provided some support for the accreditation side of the null hypothesis, in three ways. First, as noted, the standards are overwhelmingly process-oriented and administratively-focused. This increases the "paper tiger" possibility—that the reality of accreditation is in the files, not on the street. Second, many of the case study sites indicated that they had not had to make many significant changes in the way they did business in order to become accredited—they simply had to codify and document what they were already doing. Third, in most of the sites ordinary police officers expressed little familiarity with accreditation and cited little evidence that it had affected their work, either positively or negatively.

Conclusion

Table 27.1 summarizes the degree of support found for each of the 14 different hypotheses concerning the relationship between community policing and accreditation.

Based on all of the data from the content analyses, expert survey, and case studies, we would answer four commonly-asked questions about the intersection of community policing and accreditation as follows:

1. Are accreditation and community policing compatible? *Yes.*

2. Do accreditation and community policing conflict? *Not directly, but there are some indirect tensions and strains between these two reform initiatives.*

3. Does accreditation support community policing? *Yes, but only to a limited extent.*

4. Did any of this change with the 1994 "top-down" revision of the CALEA standards? *Not much.*

In addition, four other conclusions about the relationship between community policing and accreditation seem to be supported by the research conducted for this study:

Table 27.1
Summary of Support for 14 Hypotheses About the Relationship Between Community Policing and Accreditation

Hypotheses	Support
The Anti-COP Hypothesis: accreditation directly conflicts with COP	little or no support
The Anti-POP Hypothesis: accreditation directly conflicts with POP	little or no support
The Rigid Bureaucracy Hypothesis: accreditation creates formality which interferes with COP	some support—mixed opinion
The Efficiency Hypothesis: accreditation's internal focus deflects attention from substantive problems in the community	some support—mixed opinion
The Thin Blue Line Hypothesis: accreditation emphasizes accountability within the organization to the detriment of accountability to the community	little support
The Style Over Substance Hypothesis: accreditation focuses attention on process rather than outcomes	some support—mixed opinion
The Incident-Driven Hypothesis: accreditation takes an incident-oriented view to the detriment of the problem-oriented approach	some support—mixed opinion
The Professional Model Hypothesis: accreditation implicitly favors the professional model over COP	some support—mixed opinion
The Scarce Resources Hypothesis: accreditation and COP compete for resources and attention	general support
The Police Politics Hypothesis: supporters of COP and accreditation compete for status and influence	little support
The Support Hypothesis: accreditation directly supports COP/POP	some support—mixed opinion
The Neutrality Hypothesis: accreditation is neutral toward COP/POP	some support—mixed opinion
The Flexibility Hypothesis: accreditation does not interfere with COP/POP because of the flexibility of the standards	general support
The Null Hypothesis: no conflict because one or the other (or both) of accreditation and COP has no impact	some support—but not from chiefs or experts

1. Whether one sees conflict between COP and accreditation depends significantly on one's view of community policing—especially whether it is seen as a relatively modest departure from the professional model or a more radical departure.

2. A lot also depends on one's philosophy of organization and management. Accreditation clearly emphasizes formalization, for example—but whether this is seen as providing helpful guidance or as strangling creativity varies widely.

3. The effect of accreditation on a police organization and on community policing depends in part on *how* it is implemented. It may include an intense self-study or it may be merely a paper exercise; it may include widespread participation from throughout the agency or it may be imposed top-down; it may incorporate meaningful community participation or it may be pursued more as a public relations and marketing exercise; and so on.

4. How these two initiatives actually intersect varies from one department to the next and is affected by such things as agency size, sequencing, labor-management relations, pre-existing administrative and operational practices, and other idiosyncratic factors.

One might ask, what does the law enforcement agency accreditation program stand for? Presently, it stands more for administrative efficiency than for anything else—and this is by conscious design. An important question facing CALEA and the police field is whether the time has come to alter the program's quasi-neutral (on the surface, but with clear latent allegiance to the professional model), flexible nature to make it more supportive of community policing. Advocates of this change argue that it would benefit the community and add more substance and value to the accreditation process. Opponents worry that such a change would reduce the flexibility of the standards and also set a precedent for accreditation to embrace each decade's most popular policing strategy.

A related but separate dilemma facing CALEA is whether the standards could and should be focused less on internal administrative processes and more on operations, standards of care (especially related to encounters with the public), and outcomes. It seems clear that many standards could easily be revised to be less process-oriented and more output- or outcome-oriented. If this was done, the standards would have more substance and would be more closely connected to things that really matter to the public. However, it would become much more difficult for on-site assessors and CALEA to verify compliance with such standards (or, more likely, to verify that departments were doing everything within reason to produce the specified output, meet the standard of care, or achieve the specified outcome). Standards of this sort might also be more challenging and threatening to police agencies, and denial of accreditation might become more common.

CALEA needs assistance in wrestling with these practical and philosophical dilemmas. Over time, the accreditation process and standards have come to be seen as the domain and property of CALEA staff and constituent accredited agencies (410 as of September 1996) to a greater degree than is probably healthy. Also, CALEA has experienced some distress due to conflicts among its original sponsoring organizations. As a result, a degree of defensiveness and a reactive posture have developed. This situation makes it unlikely that major shifts in focus and emphasis, such as those suggested above, will be given meaningful consideration.

Three responses to this situation may be worthy of consideration. First, CALEA ought to make an effort to improve its own research and development capacity, in order to heighten the amount of attention given to current standards, new standards, and the bigger picture, and to establish a more proactive posture toward ongoing changes in policing. Second, CALEA's sponsoring organizations ought to play more active roles in the big-picture issues surrounding law enforcement agency accreditation and rededicate themselves to the notion that accreditation is about efficiency *and* effectiveness. Finally, everyone concerned about the future of American policing (including academics, elected officials, and community leaders) should pay more attention to these accreditation issues and should participate more actively in the debate over CALEA's direction and focus.

Note

Preparation of this chapter was supported, in part, under award #92-IJ-EX-KO38 from the National Institute of Justice, U.S. Department of Justice. Points of view in this document are those of the authors and do not necessarily represent the official position of the U.S. Department of Justice.

References

Behan, Cornelius J. 1989. "The Accreditation Process." In James J. Fyfe, ed., *Police Practice in the '90s: Key Management Issues.* Washington, DC: International City Management Association, pp. 124-134.

——. 1992. "Allies, Not Adversaries: Accreditation and Community Policing." *Commission Update* (September): 1. Fairfax, VA: CALEA.

Cordner, Gary W. 1995. "Community Policing: Elements and Effects." *Police Forum* 5, 3 (July): 1-8.

Goldstein, Herman. 1990. *Problem-Oriented Policing.* New York: McGraw-Hill.

Greenberg, Sheldon. 1989. "Police Accreditation." In Dennis Jay Kenney, ed., *Police & Policing: Contemporary Issues.* New York: Praeger, pp. 247-256.

Greene, Jack R. and Stephen D. Mastrofski, eds. 1988. *Community Policing: Rhetoric or Reality?* New York: Praeger.

Mastrofski, Stephen. 1986. "Police Agency Accreditation: The Prospects of Reform." *American Journal of Police* 5, 2: 45-81.

Oettmeier, Timothy N. 1993. "Can Accreditation Survive the '90s?" In John W. Bizzack, ed., *New Perspectives on Policing.* Lexington, KY: Autumn House Publishing, pp. 96-112.

Rosenbaum, Dennis P., ed. 1994. *The Challenge of Community Policing: Testing the Promises.* Thousand Oaks, CA: Sage.

Skolnick, Jerome H. and David H. Bayley. 1986. *The New Blue Line: Police Innovation in Six American Cities.* New York: Free Press.

Sykes, Gary W. 1994. "Accreditation and Community Policing: Passing Fads or Basic Reforms?" *Journal of Contemporary Criminal Justice* 10, 1: 1-16.

Trojanowicz, Robert and Bonnie Bucqueroux. 1990. *Community Policing: A Contemporary Perspective.* Cincinnati, OH: Anderson.

Watson, Elizabeth M. and Gerald L. Williams. 1991. "Community Policing and Law Enforcement Accreditation: Emerging Issues." In William A. Geller, ed., *Local Government Police Management,* 3rd edition. Washington, DC: International City Management Association, pp. 392-393.

Reprinted from Gary W. Cordner and Gerald L. Williams, "Community Policing and Police Agency Accreditation." National Institute of Justice Executive Summary, 1997. ✦

28

An Institutional Perspective of Policing

John P. Crank and
Robert Langworthy

Most literature on police administration is composed of normative and prescriptive ideas borrowed from business administration and public administration and aimed at helping police managers run their agencies more effectively. This article, however, is part of a much smaller tradition that simply tries to explain what makes police organizations "tick," that is, why do they behave the way they do? Moreover, rather than taking the highly rationalistic (and naïve) view that police organizations behave as they do simply to accomplish their objectives, Crank and Langworthy adopt a more naturalistic approach, known as the "institutional perspective." This approach has great promise for helping us understand the trials and tribulations of police organizations over time. As you read about the role of myths, rituals, crises, and the organizational environment, think about how this approach fits police departments with which you are familiar.

I. Introduction

A. Overview

This article is about the institutional environment of American municipal police departments and the way in which that environment influences the departments' organization and activity. This institutional orientation differs from the normative focus of traditional theories of police department organization. This normative focus has concentrated on rational considerations of efficiency and effectiveness of police departments' organizational structures, policies and operational strategies as gauged by technical outputs, such as the production of arrests.[1]

In contrast, the institutional perspective presented here focuses on powerful myths produced by broad processes in a police department's institutional environment and looks at the influence these myths have on the formal structure and activities of particular organizational elements within the department. By successfully incorporating institutional myths into its formal structures and activities, other relevant actors in its institutional environment perceive that a police department is legitimate.[2] A fundamental interest in survival leads police departments to "accede to the demands of other actors" on whom departments depend for legitimacy, and with the receipt of legitimacy, the continued flow of resources for organizational survival.[3] However, at times, entities confront conflicting myths in their institutional environments.[4] Utilizing the perspective of Meyer and Scott, this article suggests that a municipal police department develops "treaties between contending legitimations" when it encounters conflicting myths in its institutional environment.[5] Even with such treaties, conflicts may intensify into a crisis in which a department loses its legitimacy within its institutional environment. Consonant with the institutional perspective, such a legitimacy crisis is resolved ceremonially through a ritual, which combines the public degradation of the department and the removal and replacement of the disgraced chief of police by a new chief with a "legitimating" mandate.

B. Relation to Other Approaches

Literature on the organizational structure of municipal police departments has traditionally been normative, advocating particular types of structures to achieve organizational goals.[6] According to this literature, particular types of structures and operational strategies enhance the efficiency and/or effectiveness of the police department's pursuit of desired goals. Reform-minded policymakers have endeavored to identify organizational structures that facilitate the production of outputs consistent with particular departmental goals.[7] Organizationally-based reform efforts, however, seldom have achieved the desired goals, leading to declarations that "reform had come to a standstill,"[8] frustration over the intransigence of the police to change[9] and calls for the critical re-evaluation of "normative theories" linking organizational structures to desired outputs.[10]

The disappointments with the results of police organizational reform has prompted inquiries into the constraining influence of characteristics of a police organization's environment on attempts to change its structure and activities.[11] This article complements and extends that progression of environmental analysis by considering the influence that characteristics of a police department's institutional environment have on organizational structure and activity. The institutional focus of this article reveals the influence of resurgent interest in the relationship between the institutional characteristics of an organization's environment and its structures and activities.[12] One result of that renewed interest is an appreciation of the pronounced degree to which the organization and activity of a public sector agency is influenced by the institutional features of its environment.[13] Even though police departments are quintessential public sector agencies, efforts to assess them using an institutional perspective are almost nonexistent.[14] Consequently, this article represents a preliminary attempt to delineate conceptually the institutional environment of policing and to identify some important elements in that environment.[15]

II. Municipal Police Environments

The central view of this article is that the organization and practice of municipal police work occurs in an environment saturated with institutional values. As a result of this environmental context, police practices and organizational structures cannot be understood either simply in terms of production economies or so solely from the perspective of technical efficiency and effectiveness. A police organization does not create a product which is "exchanged in a market such that organizations are rewarded for effective and efficient control of the work process."[16] Consequently, assessments of police activity that employ efficiency and effectiveness criteria have limited utility in the understanding of the structure and activities of a police department.

Instead, a police department participates with other powerful actors, called sovereigns, in an institutional environment, and it receives legitimacy from these sovereigns.[17] Sovereigns are other actors whose views are significant, that is, they are entities that have the capacity to affect the fundamental well-being of a police organization. When the department conforms to institutional expectations of what the appropriate structures and activities for a police department are, a police department is recognized by those sovereigns within its institutional environment as a legitimate or true police agency. In other words, it looks like a police agency should look, and it acts like a police agency should act. Consequently, to secure the continued well-being of the department, the organizational forms and practices of police departments tend to conform to broad, institutionally accepted norms.[18] Thus, the elaboration of police organizational structure and the selection of particular goals, operational strategies and departmental policies represent the department's efforts to establish and maintain organizational legitimacy and via that legitimacy, the police department insures the continued flow of resources needed for long-term well-being and survival.[19] Simply put, a police department's organizational structure, policies and operational strategies have a great deal to do with institutional values in its environment and very little to do with production economies or technical capabilities.

Diverse aspects of policing reveal the extent to which the organizational structure and activities of a police department are affected by its institutional environment. The following are some examples that highlight the influence of the institutional environment on police appearance, specialized law enforcement units and two common police practices.

Example 1: Police Appearance

To be recognized as police by the community, police department personnel must conform to broad, institutionally derived expectations about the appropriate appearance of police. Among those expectations are appropriate titles, uniforms, badges and insignia indicating rank, department and assignment, all of which ceremonially verify that a police officer *is* a police officer. Failure to conform to institutional expectations of appropriate police appearance may result in a loss of "legitimacy." That is, the public or other powerful actors in the institutional environment may simply refuse to accept the police as police.

For example, in 1970, the Lakewood (Colorado) Police Department entitled itself the "Lakewood Department of Public Safety," adopted non-traditional rank designations (*e.g.*, field advisor for sergeant, and senior field advisor for lieutenant) and wore blazers for uniform dress. By 1973, however, the department had abandoned these changes and reverted to a "police" title and traditional ranks, insignia and dress. The use of a "public safety" title and non-traditional ranks, insignia and dress had generated both confusion and embarrassment in contacts with other agencies and with the public.[20] Moreover, other police agencies with which the Lakewood Police Department had ongoing contact stopped sharing information with them. Lakewood lost its legitimacy in the eyes of the public and other police agencies.

This example illustrates that a "police" title and traditional ranks, insignia and uniforms are important symbols that provide legitimacy in the institutional environment of a police department. Abandoning these symbols ultimately may subvert a department's legitimacy with particular sovereigns, such as the general public and other police agencies. In this case, Lakewood restored legitimacy after hiring a new police chief with a mandate to return the department to traditional modes of police dress.[21]

Example 2: Specialized Law Enforcement Units

The following example suggests that the elaboration of organizational structure is determined by institutional expectations of what the police *should* do, rather than practical considerations of what they *actually* do. Law enforcement is perceived as a highly legitimate police activity by the public and its elected representatives.[22] Consequently, police budgets tend to be justified in terms of the need for greater levels of law enforcement, and police departments tend to become functionally complex in the number and specialization of its crime-fighting units.[23] But, this organizational complexity is ceremonial: instead of evolving because additional specialization actually improves efficiency and effectiveness, the elaborate structure has developed in response to what a department should look like to sovereigns in its institutional environment (primarily the public and its elected representatives). It is thus common to find urban police departments with specialized crime units such as burglary, DUI, auto theft, fraud, gangs, assault, homicide, robbery, juveniles, vice and narcotics.[24]

The specialization itself is perceived by the sovereigns as essential to the "war against crime." That is, because of the influence of these sovereigns, organizational structure has elaborated in the direction of specialized crime-fighting units. Yet such specialization is inconsistent with the tasks actually undertaken by police departments. Research on the variety of activities performed by police has shown that only a relatively small proportion of police work actually involves true law enforcement; the bulk of customary police work typically involves such activities as community service, crime prevention and maintenance of order.[25] The elaborate organizational structure emphasizes law enforcement activities, reinforcing the police department's institutional image as a "crime fighter," in spite of inconsistencies between that image and the actual work of the department.[26]

Example 3: Preventive Patrol and Rapid Response Systems

Finally, technical rules that are initially introduced for reasons of effectiveness may themselves become institutionalized.[27] Two related technical procedures that have become institutionalized are motorized random preventive patrol and rapid response systems (based on automatically routing 911 emergency telephone calls). Motorized random preventive patrol was introduced in the 1920s as a crime prevention strategy.[28] Subsequent adoption of this crimefighting strategy among police organizations, however, suggests that its diffusion across the American municipal landscape is more consistent with processes of institutional diffusion than with department-by-department evaluations of its effectiveness in law enforcement or crime prevention.[29] Today, this strategy is widely used in spite of an increasing body of evidence that shows random preventive patrol is not effective in preventing crimes or producing arrests.[30] In other words, the use of random preventive patrol displays to the institutional audience, and particularly to sovereigns, that a particular police department behaves like police organizations should behave in this specific technical area; conformity with the expected institutional norm is more important than whether the specific practice itself actually contributes to better policing.

As a complement to motorized preventive patrol, rapid response (911) systems have been promoted as a means for quick response to emergency calls from the public.[31] However, as with random preventive patrol, there is scant evidence that 911 systems are effective in either crime prevention or law enforcement.[32]

Furthermore, since a 911 system coupled with motorized preventive patrol absorb a substantial portion of a police department's limited manpower and budget resources, they impair a department's ability to try alternative patrol or crime prevention strategies.[33] Yet despite that impairment and the doubts about their effectiveness, the use of 911 systems in conjunction with random preventive patrol continues to be widespread.[34]

Why do these two procedures, designed for purposes of technical effectiveness, persist with such vigor despite their apparent failure to improve actual policing? Because they have extraordinary legitimacy with the public. As Skolnick and Bayley note, "People expect a patrol car to come whenever they need police help. They complain bitterly when it doesn't arrive instantaneously."[35] In other words, rapid response systems have become an important ritual of contemporary policing; they ceremonially demonstrate the legitimacy of the public's reliance on the police. Failure to provide rapid response to calls for assistance may bring the department under the scrutiny of important sovereigns such as the press, mayor or city council. These sovereigns may raise the specter that the police are not fulfilling their mandate to protect the public; ultimately they may envelop the police department in a full-blown legitimation crisis. Thus, even though the rituals of 911 systems and random preventive patrol may be neither effective nor efficient as law enforcement or crime prevention strategies, they provide ceremonial evidence that a police department behaves as it should. The ceremonial evidence consists of visibly displacing patrol cars on the streets and using elaborate charts and measures for tracking response time to citizen calls for assistance. Failure to sustain these important rituals may result in the de-legitimation of a police department.

These examples highlight some of the diverse ways in which a police department is affected by its institutional environment. The remainder of the article is an initial attempt to construct an institutional theory of police organizations. A fuller institutional theory of policing will develop only over time through the process of scholarly debate and discussion. We hope that the following preliminary ideas will help promote that process.

III. Toward an Institutional Theory of Police Organizations

A. Institutionalism

The idea of an institutionalized organization, in the broadest sense, means that "organizational forms and behaviors take the form that they do because of prevailing values and beliefs that have become institutionalized."[36] Institutionalized organizations, because they embody prevailing values and beliefs, cease to be "mere engines" of bureaucratic efficiency; they are recognized as valued natural communities, whose "self-maintenance becomes an end in itself."[37]

This article borrows extensively from Meyer and Rowan's discussion of institutionalized organizations to describe the institutional environment of policing and its influence on the organization and operation of a police department.[38] Meyer and Rowan maintain that institutionalized organizations are constructed of "widespread understandings of social reality,"[39] which they called myths. Here, "myth" means that these understandings of social reality are perceived to be more important than any particular individual or organization and have an intrinsic quality of "truth" or "rightness" about them. The dress code of the police, police budgets, random motorized patrol and rapid response discussed above each represent powerful institutional myths in that they are typically seen as so integral to policing that their truth is beyond question. Such myths are incorporated into the organization as particular structures or operational strategies that are carried out by members of the organization in a "dramaturgy of exchange" to "gain acceptance from major participants in the inter-organizational environment."[40] These ritual activities of significance ceremonially demonstrate to other institutional participants that the police organization *looks like* or *acts like* a police department and thus deserves continued support *qua* a police department. In the following sections, we discuss the evolution of institutional myths that bear on police departments and the relationship between these myths and elements of police organizational structure and activity.

B. Myth and Myth-Building in the Institutional Environment

Three broad historically based processes may be described as institutional myth-builders.[41] These processes, adapted for the analysis of police organizations, are here called (1) official legitimacy, (2) elaboration of relational networks and (3) organizational institutional reactivity. These historical processes reveal the influence of organizations and powerful individuals as agents in the construction of institutional myths.[42] Discussions and examples of each of these are presented below, with the caveat that the processes described here are ideal types. Thought-

ful consideration of the examples presented below suggests that these processes, though analytically distinct, tend to overlap in particular situations.

1. Official Legitimacy. A powerful source of institutional myths are those that are incident to official legitimacy. As Meyer and Rowan note, judicial authorities may create legal mandates, administrative agencies may establish rules of practice, and occupations may require licenses or rules.[43] This type of myth represents a coercive aspect of legitimacy. Environmental sovereigns may literally force legitimacy on a particular organization when it has not provided a satisfactory legitimating account of itself.[44] Many aspects of police activity and organizational structure are linked to institutional myths that derive from this process. The following are several examples in which police organizations are forced to accede to officially accepted practices in order to retain legitimacy.

Example 1: Civil Service. A potent institutional myth that carries the weight of official legitimacy is civil service. Here, the institutional myth is that civil service is the appropriate organizational form for police personnel systems. Introduced during the reformist era in the late 1800s, civil service statutes provided police departments with written standards for hiring, promotion and review of police personnel.[45] Research has suggested that civil service emerged as a powerful institutional form in its own right, diffusing widely across the municipal landscape independent of its early reform base.[46] The wide diffusion of civil service may have occurred so thoroughly because it was an integral component of the institutionalization of the rational bureaucratic form of organization in municipal government.[47] Civil service has subsequently become a highly institutionalized form for defining the relations among police personnel. Today, the use of civil service personnel systems in police departments is so entrenched and institutionally universal that efforts to change police personnel policies have been compared to "bending granite."[48]

Example 2: Due Process. A second example is the power of legal mandate that resulted from the Supreme Court decisions handed down by the Warren Court in the 1960s. This period produced a myth that, in encounters between the police and the public, ceremonial rituals demonstrating police observance of due process actually produce justice. Decisions such as *Miranda v. Arizona*[49] emphasized the individual's constitutional protections as a legal element which police must formally incorporate into arrest activity. The ceremonial invocation of these protections in police arrest and interrogation demonstrates to the courts that the police are legitimately acting as they should. This ceremony may involve the ritual presentation of symbolic totems of the state's power, such as two-by-three inch embossed plastic cards with *Miranda* rights printed in both English and Spanish, which are given to suspects at the time of an arrest. Another example of this ceremony occurs when state police agencies invoke the ritual of signature by having a Hispanic suspect sign a document, printed in English on one side and Spanish on the other, indicating that a suspect has agreed to a vehicular search for contraband following a routine traffic stop.

Example 3: Credentialing. A final example concerns legitimacy derived from credentialing police officers. The myth is that only individuals who have completed formal training are indeed "police." That is, as a result of the formal credentialing process, credentialed officers are recognized by sovereigns as legitimate police representatives. Likewise, officers who do not receive credentialed training, often described as part-time or auxiliary police officers, lack legitimacy and are not considered "real police." The following illustrates the implications of this credentialing process for organizational legitimacy. In statewide hearings[50] sponsored by the Illinois State Police Training Board in 1988, the Secretary of the Southern Illinois Fraternal Order of the Police openly and aggressively attacked the practice of using less expensive, part-time police who had not received state-licensed training. Many small police departments had adopted this practice. The Secretary's challenge centered on the part-time officers' lack of credentialed training and raised the specter of devastating litigation if non-credentialed officers were involved in a police shooting or civil rights violation. In other words, police officers who have not been ceremonially credentialed as police may lack legitimacy with the courts, and their behavior may subsequently provide the basis for devastating litigation against the police department and the municipality.

Such litigation has occurred. In 1984, Walter DeBow was severely beaten by another inmate in the East St. Louis jail.[51] He subsequently filed a negligence suit against the city and the police department, charging that the jail was not staffed with properly trained police. He was awarded $3.4 million, and the city defaulted on paying the judgment. He subsequently sued East St. Louis for city property, and in September 1990, he was "awarded the deed to one of East St. Louis's finest buildings, the four-year old municipal building."[52] This example also reveals the coercive power of official legitimacy. Failure of the police to properly credential their officers may have a devastating impact, not only on the police department, but also on its primary benefactor and powerful sovereign, the city municipal government.

2. Elaboration of Relational Networks. Another process by which institutional myths evolve is through the elaboration of relational networks. The elaboration of relational networks refers to the process by which increases in connectedness between spheres of activity in a particular institutional environment result in new organizational elaboration in the form of structures, procedures or policies.[53] Connectedness refers to formal and informal linkages or "transactions tying organizations to one another."[54] This is similar to the concept of environmental turbulence, which describes the level of causal interconnection within the environment.[55] According to this idea, the intersection of previously unconnected spheres of activity, or increases in levels of activity between connected spheres of activity, results in new organizational forms and beliefs defining the relations between the spheres of activity. As relations endure and solidify, the emergent forms and beliefs can achieve mythical status, ceremonially reaffirming the relationship between those spheres. The following examples suggest this process.

Example 1: Organized Labor and Police Reform. The connectedness between police departments and organized labor bodies, has contributed to the formalization of police personnel policies and contract negotiation procedures. It also has contributed to the contemporary myth that line-level police work is and should be highly discretionary. The intersection of police and organized labor, though initially occurring in the early 1900s, gained momentum in the years after World War II. During that era, the expansion of union and nonunion labor representation in police departments increased the influence of line officers on departmental affairs. Also, the expansion of organized labor activity into the sphere of police activity was associated with a fundamental shift in police reform.[56] The shift focused away from reform, in terms of organizational restructuring (for purposes of control of line officer behavior), and toward the opposite—reform in terms of the provision of line officer autonomy or discretion.[57] Today, the idea that discretion is inherent in the police role and, moreover, *should* be a part of the police role[58] is becoming institutionalized in part because of the elaboration of police relational networks to include labor representation. This example suggests that both organizational structure and line-level role characteristics have been affected by the intersection of the spheres of activity of unions and police organizations.

Example 2: Value of Innovation. This example describes an elaboration of the law-enforcement network that produced a myth which seemingly contradicts ideas of institutionalization. The establishment of relations between three broad institutional sectors has created the myth that innovative experimentation can be done and is good. The emergence of this myth derives from the intersection of the police, higher education and the federal government sectors; it was initiated bv the Omnibus Crime Control and Safe Streets Act of 1968.[59]

The Omnibus Crime Contral and Safe Streets Act was passed in 1968 in response to national concern over increasing crime. The Omnibus Act provided a mechanism, the Law Enforcement Assistance Administration (LEAA), for the disbursement of grant monies from the federal sector to state planning agencies, which then distribute grant monies to regional planning units, often comprised of local police agency personnel.[60]

The LEAA purposefully opposed categorical grant applications; instead, it insisted that the redistribution of federal grants be linked to program innovation. As Feely and Sarat noted, "The [Omnibus] Safe Streets Act required the federal government to demand innovation in criminal justice policy and state and local governments to respond to those demands. . . . The message of the act was simple—money would be given, innovation produced."[61]

Innovative programs, such as team policing, decentralized organizational structures, directed patrol and mini-stations, enabled police departments to secure otherwise scarce resources during the early and mid-1970s when many municipalities faced significant fiscal hardships. Thus, the idea of innovation emerged as a potent contemporary myth in the institutional environment of policing. The adoption of such innovative programs into police organizational structure and activity provided ceremonial evidence that police departments were responding to their problems appropriately, because innovation had become legitimate in the eyes of a powerful benefactor, the federal government. This example suggests that many innovative police organizational structures (*e.g.*, research and development units, police teams, niini-stations), strategies (*e.g.*, crime prevention through community mobilization) and operations (*e.g.*, directed patrol) emerged in part in response to the powerful contemporary myth of innovation.

Research skills needed to implement and evaluate these innovative programs were sought among university academicians, who provided the stamp of scientific objectivity to police research and related organizational innovation. In this way, a complex network of relationships linking the police, higher education and the federal government has led to the institutionalization of an important contemporary myth—innovation is good for police and can contribute to the police department's ability to solve both criminal and social problems.

3. Organizational-Institutional Reactivity. The third source of institutional myth derives from the way in which police leadership is involved in the myth-building process.

According to this notion powerful police departments, police professional associations and executive police leadership are actively engaged in constructing and shaping of myths in their institutional environment.[62] The following examples suggest ways in which police departments and organizations and their leaders have themselves been involved in institutional myth-building.

Example 1: Professional Organizations. The International Association of Chiefs of Police, together with the more recent emergence of other professional organizations involving police personnel, such as the International Association of Police Planners, the Academy of Criminal Justice Sciences[63] and the Police Executive Research Forum, have provided the police profession with occupationally-based fora actively engaged in shaping its institutional environment. These organizations have not simply provided fora for the exchange of ideas but have also provided a mechanism—professional associations—for the anointing of particular technical procedures as orthodoxy. These powerful professional associations thus become agents of institutionalization.[64]

Example 2: Influential Leadership. An example of how a powerful police executive can contribute to the institutionalization of particular police practices is that of August Vollmer and his efforts to institutionalize the Uniform Crime Reports. August Vollmer, widely recognized as the patriarch of police professionalism, has had a broad impact on police activities nationally and was instrumental in establishing many police practices that have subsequently achieved mythical stature. Vollmer's broad influence is revealed in the establishment of the Uniform Crime Reports (UCR).[65] Vollmer initially proposed the UCR as a method to track crime in the United States. Today, the ritual of data collection for the UCR is accomplished by tens of thousands of reporting districts across the country, all of which use similar offense classifications for the labeling of reported and cleared crime. Thus, a particular technique for measuring crime has become institutionalized as a means of assessing whether a police department acts (*i.e.*, making arrests) as a police organization is supposed to act. In spite of a great deal of contemporary evidence that the Uniform Crime Reports tell us very little about actual crime, attention to UCR data collection provides a police organization with ceremonial evidence that the organization is doing something about crime.[66]

August Vollmer's influence among the police also reveals how executive leadership can contribute to the institutionalization of technical procedures. Vollmer advocated applying technology to police work.[67] He expounded on the importance of scientific technologies for crime control, introduced the first scientific crime control laboratory in the United States in 1916 and the first lie detector machine for use in criminal investigation in 1921.[68]

Vollmer's reform advocacy gained a national audience, and his conception of scientific crime control diffused and became institutionalized. Today scientific crime control applications encompass such diverse areas as fingerprinting, DNA testing, weaponry, sophisticated communications systems, widespread use of mobile traffic units and computerization, including computer links inside patrol cars.

Example 3: Crime-Fighting Image. Next is an example of how myth-building by police leadership can affect organizational structure. Though there was movement at the turn of the century to clarify the role of police in terms of law enforcement,[69] the 1930s was the era in which the police role came to be seen in terms of law enforcement.[70] Police leadership that encouraged the crime-fighting orientation included O. W. Wilson and J. Edgar Hoover.[71] This change toward crime prevention has been described as an institutional-level change.[72] That this image was developed to serve the needs of the police has been noted: Manning has argued that the crime-fighter image was constructed by the police to gain the public confidence, and Klockars has referred to the image of the crimefighting "professional" as a circumlocution.[73] Nevertheless, the rise in reported serious crime from the 1930s to the early 1980s magnified in the public mind the importance of law-enforcement activities and further reinforced the public perception of the primary role of police as law enforcement. Thus, since the turn of the century, the structures of police departments have been organized around crime-fighting activity, even though, as noted previously, only a small proportion of police activity, including the activity of patrol officers in urban areas with high crime rates, directly involves crimefighting. Today, efforts by police administrators to acquire increased budgets are invariably justified on the basis of a perceived need to improve crime-fighting capabilities.[74] This example suggests that police organizational structure is *enabled* by institutionalized expectations (which are influenced by important police actors) that the principal activity of the police is law enforcement.

IV. Legitimacy Crises

A. *Legitimacy Challenged.* The preceding described three broad processes of institutional myth-building and provided examples of how myths are incorporated into elements of police organizational structure and activity. From an institutional perspective, organizational legitimacy derives from the organization's success in incorporating institutional myths into its formal structure and activities. However, it is possible for an organization to be faced with conflicting myths in its institutional environment.[75] Such a conflict is called a legitimation conflict; it represents a collision between different sovereigns' conceptions of legitimate policing. Conflicts at this level may bring into question the fundamental legitimacy of a police department.

The organizational response to a legitimation conflict is ceremonial: structures and policies are developed that display to sovereigns that the organization is responding to the conflict. Thus, aspects of organizational structure, policies or procedures are developed as "treaties between contending legitimations"[76] that flow from different sovereigns. Two areas of organizational structure and associated policy—personnel procedures and internal review—are presented as exam-

ples of treaties that derive from conflicts over personnel policy and police behavior.

Example 1: Personnel Policies. Intradepartmental conflicts between supporters of old-style police professionalism and advocates of affirmative action personnel policies have created legitimation conflicts for police departments. Focused on the differing conceptions of what was an appropriate personnel policy for a police department, these conflicts have been resolved by treaties in the form of department structure and personnel procedures. The police professionalism movement supported civil service type personnel procedures because these procedures removed decisions over the hiring, evaluation and firing of personnel from the control of political machines. The personnel procedures advocated by the professionalism reformers in support of the goal of departmental autonomy included establishing rigorous, objective hiring criteria and recruiting from outside the service area if necessary to satisfy the criteria.

However, during the 1970s, politically empowered minority groups began to challenge the legitimacy of civil-service type personnel policies. These groups advocated use of personnel procedures that promoted balanced representation of community demographics in a department and affirmative action hiring strategies.[77] Such challenges, reflecting the political empowerment of minority groups, attained the status of legitimation conflicts; in response, accommodating departmental structures and procedures emerged. For example, Skolnick and Bayley discuss the way in which the police chief redesigned the Oakland, California, police department's personnel hiring and promotional procedures in 1974 to respond to the concerns of both the Police Officer's Association and the Black Police Officer's Association.[78]

Also, many police departments have added affirmative action units,[79] created non-sworn positions[80] and modified their organizational charts in attempts to respond to conflicts over personnel policies.[81] All of these actions represent treaties in which the police department ceremonially acknowledged important sovereigns with differing legitimating accounts of appropriate personnel policy.

Example 2: Control Over Police Behavior. Internal review boards (as contrasted with external review boards) represent another example of how organizational structure represents a treaty among the contending legitimations that flow from powerful sovereigns. In this case, the sovereigns are the police department itself, the police union and labor representatives, and mobilized public opinion. Complex and highly ritualized internal review procedures have emerged to provide a ceremonial organizational response to public concerns over the ability of the police to police themselves. Such formal assessments of officers' behavior may even be mandatory in some situations, such as when a police officer fires a weapon in the line of duty. Moreover, the internal review procedures are often complex and time-consuming. Yet, despite this organizational elaboration of procedures in internal review, the penalties resulting from internal review are typically mild and infrequently imposed.[82] Rather than being seen as an effective control over police behavior, the internal review process may be better described as a ceremonial ritual whose purpose is to act as a treaty among contending legitimations of police behavior. Thus, the function of an internal review board is not only to avoid the bitter divisiveness and disruption that an external review board (with its civilian members) creates among police executives, public officials and line officers, but also to help protect against the public degradation of the police department.[83]

As suggested above, organizations adapt in order to accommodate challenges to their legitimacy. There are also occasions, however, when organizational legitimacy is simply lost.

B. Legitimacy Lost and Regained. In many ways, police organizations resemble what Meyer and Zucker describe as permanently failing organizations: they appear to career from crisis to crisis; and by virtually any external criteria of efficiency, they do not perform well.[84] Yet, only rarely do police departments fail to survive, in the sense of actually being abandoned by their communities.[85]

Nevertheless, police departments can lose legitimacy. In the institutional model, the loss of legitimacy is itself a ceremonial process, marked by rituals of moral degradation, and removal and replacement of the police chief executive in order to regain institutional legitimacy. The moral degradation of a police department and the firing of its police chief is inevitably a highly ceremonial event staged in a public arena, even though the incident that provoked the degradation and removal may be something over which the chief had little or no control. A precipitating incident might be any of a number of different occurrences, such as a line officer who used too much coercion in a street encounter, departmental corruption uncovered by the press, the mayor's dissatisfaction with the production of arrests or newly elected leadership with a mandate to "get tough on crime."[86]

All of these circumstances may provide occasions for the ceremony of public degradation and removal of a police chief, even though it is often unclear whether the chief actually could have prevented the events that precipitated the legitimation crisis. Regardless, as a result of the precipitating events, the police department faces a non-resolvable legitimation crisis and consequently suffers a loss of legitimacy in the eyes of its sovereigns. Then the cathartic ritual of departmental degradation, removal of a police chief and replacement with a new chief takes place. The ritual is a ceremonial act designed to re-establish the legitimacy of the police department to the dissatisfied sovereigns. The installation of a replacement chief (the symbolic head of the department) with a new (legitimating) mandate can appease the alienated sovereigns, who are dissatisfied with the current legitimating account of the department.

An example of such a legitimation crisis involves the recent controversy over an incident involving the Los Angeles Police Department. On March 3, 1991, several Los Angeles police officers were videotaped beating a black motorist. Subsequent national media exposure of the videotape invoked responses from the full panoply of sovereigns in the institutional environment of the Los Angeles Police Department. The focus of attention for this incident rapidly shifted from the officers, four of whom faced criminal charges, to

Chief of Police Daryl F. Gates. Calls for the removal of Chief Gates came from institutional sovereigns such as the mayor, members of the City Council, representatives of the business community and the California Chapter of the American Civil Liberties Union.[87] The media, providing repeated national showings of the videotape, was an agent for the mobilization of public opinion against Chief Gates. Within the department, however, Gates gathered support from important police representatives.[88] Moreover, his position was protected by Civil Service and provided him with virtually unlimited tenure.

The depth of the legitimation conflict proved too great for Gates to withstand. In the wake of the controversy, Chief Gates and Mayor Bradley jointly selected a panel of experts, called the Christopher Commission,[89] headed by former Deputy Secretary of State Warren Christopher. The published findings of the commission recommended that Chief Gates retire from office and announce his tentative retirement if a satisfactory successor has not been chosen by then. On April 16, 1992, the *Los Angeles Times* announced that Philadelphia Police Commissioner Willie L. Williams would succeed "embattled" Chief Gates as the department's top official.[90] On the same day the announcement was made, Gates' degradation continued: in a closed and contentious meeting with the powerful Los Angeles City Council, Chief Gates was questioned regarding a series of lawsuits over alleged police misbehavior.[91]

Gates announced his retirement at the end of June 1992. With his replacement, the ritual of public degradation, removal and replacement will conclude; Willie Williams will assume stewardship of the department, and do so with a new (legitimating) mandate. Part of his legitimating mandate is revealed in his reputation as a strong chief who is tough on police abuse, and part lies in who he is—an outsider, the first to head the department in forty years.[92] Thus, with the hiring of Williams, the cathartic cycle of legitimation lost and ceremonially regained is completed, and legitimacy lost will be restored.

V. Conclusions

Why do police departments persist in American municipalities? It is not because they produce some clearly defined, measurable and highly marketable output. Indeed, there is little consensus on precisely what it is that police departments *should* be doing. Nevertheless, police departments have proven to be remarkably stable institutions. They are perceived as so endemic to city life that the elimination of a municipal police department is, for most people, unthinkable. Their persistence has occurred because they embody broad institutional values and are thus recognized as a part of the natural order of things. As such, their organizational right to exist is beyond question. They are institutionalized organizations.

In this article, we have endeavored to demonstrate some of the ways in which an institutional perspective may provide insight into the activities and organization of American municipal police departments. We suggest that police organizations do not achieve legitimacy through their ability to participate in a technical environment; rather, they are institutionalized organizations that "turn [their] back on a technical core in order to concentrate on conforming to [their] institutional environment."[93] Using numerous examples, we have suggested ways in which police organizations conform to their institutional environment. Through ceremonial displays of legitimacy, that is, by incorporating into their organizational structure or displacing in formalized activities broad institutional myths, police organizations are able to survive, regardless of the organization's ability to produce a clearly defined or economically marketable product.

This article has presented a picture of a police department that is so interpenetrated by elements of its institutional environment that the idea of formal boundaries separating the department from its institutional environment is itself problematic. If, as Meyer and Rowan suggest, both organizations and their institutional environments "reflect socially constructed reality,"[94] then a clear notion of a bounded police department, somehow distinct from but linked through boundary-maintenance mechanisms to its environment, cannot be sustained.

The institutional perspective is not simply a constraint theory of organizational structure and activity; it is also an enabling theory of structure and activity. That is, the structure and activity of police organizations are not simply constrained by variable features in their environment. Rather, they are both constrained and enabled by their institutional environment, or as Meyer and Rowan suggest, by realizations of their institutional environments.[95]

By acknowledging the contribution of the wider institutional environment to both constrain and enable variation in a police department's organization and activities, we have opened a Pandora's Box of analytic complexity:

> Organizations are affected by the structure of relations of the interorganizational systems in which they are embedded, and these systems are in turn affected by the societal systems in which they are located, and these systems are affected by the world system in which they are located. All of these systems are evolving over time, and each is comprised of elements created at differing points of time.[96]

Thus, institutional perspectives of organizations that have the capacity to become complex leave one with the tautological conclusion that everything causes everything else. Nevertheless, the idea that police are responsible for the efficient and effective production of technical outputs, such as arrests, should be abandoned. As a replacement, the institutional perspective suggests that a police department's activities in response to crime are determined, not in terms of the effective crime prevention or crime fighting, but rather in response to crime as it is perceived by sovereigns in its institutional environment.

For example, the mythical importance that index crimes[97] have achieved in comparison to other categories of crime can be traced to the construction of those crime categories by August Vollmer and, by implication, to the institutional myth-building process called institutional-organizational reactivity.[98] In other words, what are referred to as index crimes are more clearly institutional rather than technical constructs, and the importance that the police and the public (who receive information on index crimes from the police) place on these specific categories of crime can be attributed to their mythical potency in the institutional environment of policing.

The institutional perspective presented in this article suggests that there are values, beliefs and norms in the institutional environment of policing that are embodied in powerful myths that organizations ceremonially incorporate into structure and activity. At the same time, this article has endeavored to describe an institutional environment of policing that is not simply static, but is also remarkably fluid. As such, this article has presented an institutional perspective in terms of broad social processes that contain change dynamics as well as elements of stasis. Change dynamics in this article are described primarily in terms of powerful actors or organizations representing the police that are capable of reacting back onto and modifying their institutional environment. From this, four areas of future research are suggested.

First, detailed case studies may provide further insight into the relationship between particular organizations and institutional features of their environment. This would provide a clarification of the influence of specific institutional sovereigns over particular organizations, and the way in which the influence of these sovereigns is ceremonially acknowledged by particular organizations.

Second, we have proceeded on the premise that police organizations are so highly institutionalized that issues of efficiency and effectiveness in the production of technical outputs are virtually irrelevant to their organizational well-being. However, we believe that future research should not view police organization and behavior only in terms of its wider institutional environment. There is a technical core to police work, and research should assess the interplay among technical and institutional dynamics in the production of police structure and activity.

Third, the institutional environment of police organizations has been taken as a given: where changes in the institutional environment are discussed, they appear to be described as minor perturbations within a powerful and pervasive institutional environment. Yet, an examination of the history of policing suggests that this may not be the case. Municipal police organizations are of relatively recent origin in the United States. It was not until 1854, for example, that Philadelphia abandoned their nightwatchman system and put in place a full-time police department.[99] An implication and suggestion for future research is that the institutional environment of police organizations may be, over time, capable of dramatic transformation, and institutional analyses should attend to broad changes that may occur in that environment.

A final area of suggested inquiry is that of institutional isomorphism. Institutional theorists suggest that contemporary forces in American society are contributing to a dramatic isomorphism in organizations that participate in the same institutional sector.[100] Yet, observers of the police remark on the dramatic changes in the organization and behavior of contemporary policing.[101] Efforts to reconcile these opposing perspectives may both provide insight into the police and contribute to the understanding of institutional processes.

Notes

1. *See* Larry K. Gaines et al., *Police Administration* (1991); Orlando W. Wilson & Roy C. Mclaren, *Police Administration* (4th ed. 1977).

2. *See* John W. Meyer & Brian Rowan, "Institutionalized Organizations: Formal Structure as Myth and Ceremony", 83 Am. J. Soc. 340, 348 (1977).

3. Paul DiMaggio, "Interest and Agency in Institutional Theory," in *Institutional Patterns and Organizations: Culture and Environment* 3, 8 (Lynne G. Zucker ed., 1988).

4. *See* John W. Meyer & W. Richard Scott, "Centralization and the Legitimacy Problems of Local Government, in *Organizational Environments: Ritual and Rationality* 199 (John W. Meyer & W. Richard Scott eds., 1983).

5. *Id*. at 210.

6. *See* Robert H. Langworthy, "Organizational Structure" in *What Works in Policing* 87 (G. Cordner & D. Hale, eds., 1992); Robert H.

Langworthy, *The Structure of Police Organizations* (1986).

7. *Id*. at 89-92. For an example of a text that links organizational structure and productive function, *see* Wilson & McLaren, *supra* note 1.

8. Robert M. Fogelson, *Big-City Police* 295 (1977).

9. *See* Gary W. Sykes, "The Functional Nature of Police Reform: The 'Myth' of Controlling the Police," in *Critical Issues in Policing* 286 (Roger G. Dunham & Geoffrey P. Alpert eds., 1989); Dorothy Guyot, "Bending Granite: Attempts to Change the Rank Structure of American Police Departments, in *Police Administrative Issues; Techniques and Functions* 43 (Mark R. Pogrebin & Robert M. Regoli eds., 1986).

10. See Robert H. Langworthy, "Wilson's Theory of Police Behavior: A Replication of the Constraint Theory", 2 *Justice Quarterly* 89 (1985).

11. See, e.g., Dorothy Guyot, *supra* note 9. The research that has provided insights into ways that various environments affect police organizational structures and activities is represented by the following. Langworthy and Crank examined linkages between police organizational structures and environmental factors. *Langworthy*, *supra* note 6, at 97-125; John P. Crank, "The Influence of Environmental and Organizational Factors on Police Style in Urban and Rural Environments," 27 *J. Res. in Crime & Delinquency* 166 (1990). Slovak and Swanson employed multivariate models to assess the impact of environmental factors on variation in police style. Jeffrey S. Slovak, *Styles of Urban Policing: Organization, Environment and Police Styles in Selected American Cities* (1986); Cheryl Swanson, "The Influence of Organization and Environment on Arrest Policies in Major U.S. Cities" 7 *Pol'y Stud. J.* 399 (1978). Kowalewski et al. and Meagher assessed the implications of a rural location on police operations. David Kowalski et al., "Police Environments and Operational Codes: A Case Study of Rural Setting," 12 *J. Police Sci. & Admin.* 363 (1984); M. Steven Meagher, "Police Patrol Styles: How Pervasive is Community Variation?", 13 *J. Police Sci. & Admin.* 36 (19-85).

12. For a discussion of the recent interest in institutional theory, *see The New Institutionalism in Organizational Analysis* 1-40 (Walter Powell & Paul J. DiMaggio eds., 1991). *See also Institutional Patterns and Organizations: Culture and Environment* (Lynne G. Zucker ed., 1988); R. Richard Ritti & Jonathan H. Silver, "Early Processes of Institutionalization: The

Dramaturgy of Exchange in Interorganizational Relationships," 31 *Admin. Sci Q.* 25 (1986); W. Richard Scott, "Systems Within Systems: The Mental Health Sector," 28 *Am. Behavioral Scientist* 601 (1985); Paul DiMaggio & Walter W. Powell, "The Iron Cage Revisited: Institutional Isomorphism and Collective Rationality in Organizational Fields," 48 *Am. Soc. Rev.* 147 (1983).

13. See Frank R. Dobbins et al., "The Expansion of Due Process in Organizations," in *Institutional Patterns and Organizations: Culture and Environment* 71 (Lynne G. Zucker ed., 1988); Edward Shils, *Center and Periphery: Essays in Microsociology* (1975).

14. Two recent exceptions to the general absence of institutional analysis are noteworthy. Crank et al. presented an analysis of local and centrist sovereignty in the institutional environment of police organizations. John P. Crank et al., "Sovereigns in the Institutional Environment of Police Organizations," Paper Presented at the Annual Meeting of the Academy of Criminal Justice Sciences (1990). Mastrofski et al. assessed the relative efficacy of three models of organizational structure—the rational model, the constrained rational model and the loosely coupled model—for explaining DUI arrests, Stephen D. Mastrofski et al., "Organizational Determinants of Police Discretion: The Case of Drinking - Driving," 15 *J. Crim. Just.* 387 (1987). The present article draws from the same theoretical tradition as these works and simply attempts to broaden the conceptualization of a police department as a participant in an institutional environment.

15. Though not presented explicitly as institutional theory, the writings of Peter Manning anticipate much of the conceptual development of police organizations presented here. See Peter K. Manning, *Police Work* ch. 4 (1977). Manning argues, for example, that police use particular technologies and tactics symbolically to provide a particular or, in our words, ceremonial image of police organization and activity to the public. See Peter K. Manning, "The Police: Mandate, Strategies, and Appearances," in *Policing: A View From the Street* 7-31 (Peter K. Manning & John Van Maanen eds., 1978). As Manning, notes, "The police have developed and utilized [such] strategies . . . for the purpose of creating . . . the appearance of managing their troublesome mandate." *Id.* at 23.

16. Richard Scott & John W. Meyer, "The Organization of Societal Sectors," in *Organizational Environments: Ritual and Rationality* 129, 140 John W. Meyer & W. Richard Scott eds., 1983).

17. Meyer & Scott, *supra* note 4, at 201-02. Sovereigns are agents of authority that are capable of influencing department policy, withholding information or disrupting the flow of resources via such means as litigation, municipal funding or research support for program development; they also may movilize public sentiment or embarrassing media exposure. *Id.* Examples of sovereigns in the institutional environment of police organizations include the city council, mayor, police unions, empowered minority groups, the courts and the voting public.

18. DiMaggio, *supra* note 3, at 9.

19. See Meyer & Rowan, *supra* note 2, at 352.

20. Guyot, *supra* note 9, at 58.

21. *Id.*

22. Manning, *supra* note 15, at 13.

23. *Id.*

24. *See*, for example, the organizational chart for the Kansas City Police Department in Samuel Walker, *The Police in America* 80-81 (1st ed. 1983).

25. *Id.* at 18, 19; Albert Reiss, Jr., *The Police and the Public* 70-71 (1972).

26. Manning, *supra* note 15, at 30.

27. Meyer & Rowan, *supra* note 2, at 344.

28. Samuel Walker, *A Critical History of Police Reform* 136 (1977).

29. See Pamela S. Tolbert & Lynne G. Zucker, "Institutional Sources of Change in the Formal Structure of Organizations: The Diffusion of Civil Service Reform," 1880-1935, 28 *Admin. Sci. Q* 22, for a discussion of the process of the institutional diffusion of due process in the United States.

30. See Kelling et al., for a report of the first systematic evaluation of random preventive patrol. George Kelling et al., *The Kansas City Preventive Patrol Experiment: A Technical Report* 142, 271 (Police Foundation 1974). It concluded that random preventive patrol had no significant impact on crime, citizen perception of police service or citizen fear of victimization. *Id.*

31. Samuel Walker, *The Police in America: An Introduction* 92 (2d ed. 1992).

32. *See* Jerome H. Skolnick & David H. Bayley, *The New Blue Line: Police Innovation in Six American Cities* 5 (1986).

33. Herman Goldstein, *Problem-Oriented Policing* 20 (1990).

34. Walker notes that approximately 80% of big-city police departments use 911 systems. Walker, *The Police in America supra* note 31, at 92.

35. Skolnick & Bayley, *supra* note 32, at 28.

36. Richard H. Hall, *Organizations: Structure, Process, and Outcomes* 313 (4th ed. 1987).

37. Philip selznick, *Leadership in Administration* 17 (1957). The idea of a valued, natural community is suggested by the police recruitment process. Among recruits, policing is not simply a vocation; recruits believe in the contribution that policing makes to society and that policing is an avocation. New recruits are made to believe that they are participating in an important endeavor and that they are joining an elite and special occupation. John Van Maanen, "Observations on the Making of Policemen," in *The Ambivalent Force* 93-94 (Abraham Blumberg & Elaine Niederhoffer eds., 3d ed. 1985).

38. *See* Meyer & Rowan, *Supra* note 2.

39. *Id.* at 343.

40. Ritti & Silver, *supra* note 12, at 26.

41. Meyer & Rowan, *supra* note 2, at 347.

42. *Id.* This perspective differs from classic formulations of institutional theory in which institutions were perceived to be independent of human agency. Contemporary institutional theory has recognized the importance of powerful actors in the institutionalization process. For a discussion of the issue of agency, *see* DiMaggio, *supra* note 3.

43. Meyer & Rowan, *supra* note 2, at 347.

44. DiMaggio & Powell, *supra* note 12, at 150-52.

45. Walker, *supra* note 28.

46. For a discussion of the process of institutional diffusion, *see* Dobbins et al., *supra* note 13. Tolbert and Zucker suggest that the adoption of civil service reforms was effected at the outset by changing city demographics and local political culture. Tolbert & Zucker, *supra* note 29, at 22-24. However, later patterns of reform were unrelated to these characteristics. They concluded that the dissemination of civil service across the American municipal landscape occurred because of "institutional definitions of the legitimate structural form for municipal administration." DiMaggio & Powell, *supra* note 12, at 149.

47. Meyer & Rowan, *supra* note 2, at 345.

48. Guyot, *supra* note 9.

49. *Miranda v. Arizona*, 384 U.S. 436 (1966).

50. Statewide hearings were held by the Illinois Local Government Law Enforcement Officers Training Board in 1988 to provide a public forum for the discussion of minimum pre-service training standards for part-time police. These hearings were held in Rockford (March 24), Collinsville (March 29), Springfield (March 31) and Rosemont (April 7).

51. "City Hall No Longer City's," *N.Y. Times*, Sept. 29, 1990, at 8.

52. *Id.*

53. DiMaggio & Powell, *supra* note 12, at 148.

54. *Id.*

55. Hall, *supra* note 36.

56. Fogelson, *supra* note 8, at 193-218.

57. Jerome Skolnick, *Justice Without Trial*, 235-36 (2d ed. 1975).

58. *See* Gary W. Sykes, "Street Justice: A Moral Defense of Order-Maintenance Policing," 3 *Just. Q.* 497 (1986) and James Q. Wilson & George L. Kelling, "Police and Neighborhood Safety: Broken Windows," *Atlantic Monthly*, March 1982, at 29 for discussions of discretion, order-maintenance activities and community protection. In brief, both of these perspectives argue that line-level discretion in arrest decisions is necessary for the protection of communities against criminal invasion.

59. 42 U.S.C. 3758 (1968).

60. Malcolm M. Feely & Austin D. Sarat, *The Policy Dilemma: Federal Crime Policy and the Law Eforcement Assistance Administration*, 1968-1978, at 46-47 (1980).

61. *Id.* at 45-60.

62. Meyet & Rowan, *supra* note 2, at 348.

63. The Academy is a professional organization representing both practitioners and academicians.

64. DiMaggio & Powell, *supra* note 12, at 152-53.

65. Walker, *supra* note 28, at 155-56.

66. Manning, *supra* note 15, at 130-32.

67. Gene Edward Carte, "August Vollmer and the Origin of Police Professionalism," in *Police Admin. Issues* 3 (Mark R. Pogrebin & Robert Nl. Regoli eds., 1986).

68. *Id.* at 6.

69. Walker, *supra* note 28, at 47.

70. *Id.* at 139-66.

71. *Id.* at 139.

72. As Walker notes, "The Federal Bureau of Investigation suddenly emerged as a major factor in policing. Accompanying this institutional change was an even more profound intellectual reorientation: the 1930s marked the flowering of the crime-fighting role-image of the police." *Id.* at 151.

73. Manning, *supra* note 15, at 15-16; Carl B. Klockars, "The Rhetoric of Community Policing," in *Thinking About Police* 534-35 (Carl B. Klockars & Stephen D. Mastrofski eds., 2d ed. 1991).

74. Klockars, *supra* note 73, at 532-35.

75. Meyer & Scott, *supra* note 4, at 202. Organizational attainment of legitimacy from relevant actors in their institutional environment is called an organization's "cultural theory." An organization's cultural theory is defined as "the extent to which the array of established cultural accounts provides explanations for its existence, functioning, and jurisdiction, and lack or deny alternatives." *Id.* at 201. In other words, an organization has attained perfect cultural theory when it has unquestioned legitimacy in all areas of its institutional environment.

76. *Id.* at 210.

77. Walker, *supra* note 31, at 314-15.

78. Skolnick & Bayley, *supra* note 32, at 152-55.

79. According to Walker, affirmative action "means that an employer must take *positive steps* (hence: affirmative action) to remedy past discrimination." Walker, *supra* note 31, at 315.

80. Ostrom, Parks and Whitaker define sworn police as "any individual given extraordinary power of arrest by virtue of statutory or other legally valid authorization." Eleanor Ostrom et al., *Patterns of Metropolitan Policing* 331 (1978). Non-sworn police positions are those that do not include the authority to arrest.

81. Guyot, for example, describes such strategies as opening management positions to nonsworn officers, removing middle-management positions, adding the rank of Master Police Officer and elaborating each rank with multiple in-rank classifications to increase opportunities for advancement. Guyot, *supra* note 9, at 43, 55, 57, 59.

82. Warren Christopher & The Independent Commission in the Los Angeles Police Department, *Report of the Independent Commission on the Los Angeles Police Department* 153-79 (1991).

83. For a discussion of conflicts among the public and the police that emerged when three cities attempted to put into place boards with the power of civilian review over the police, *see* Stephen C. Halpern, "Police Empoyee Organizations and Accountability Procedures in Three Cities," 8 *Law & Soc. Rev. 561 (1974). To describe organizational structure or activity as cermonial is not to negate the value or importance of that structure or activity. Because police organizations operate in a highly institutionalized environment, their success is contingent on ceremonial recognition of institutionalized values.*

84. The idea of permanently failing organizations is developed by M. Meyer and Zucker. The essence of their position is that particular organizations survive, in spite of a track record of questionable success in terms of technical criteria of efficiency and effectiveness, because of their ability to respond to the expectations of their institutional environment. Marshall W. Meyer & Lynne Zucker, *Permanently Failing Organizations* (1989).

85. The 1970s witnessed a dramatic increase in the number of municipal governments which replaced traditionally separate police and fire agencies with consolidated agencies. These agencies, called Public Safety Departments, consisted of line personnel who were cross-trained in both law enforcement and fire suppression. Often implemented for reasons of efficiency and economy, these agencies confronted broad-based legitimacy challenges, and many subsequently have been abandoned in favor of traditionally separate police and fire organizations in the delivery of both police and fire services. Assessments of this phenomenon are discussed in John P. Crank & Diane Alexander, "Opposition to Public Safety: An Assessment of Issues Confronting Public Safety Directors," 17 *J. Pol. Sci. & Admin.* 55 (1989); Charles Coe & Joel Rosch, "Benefits and Barriers to Police-Fire Consolidation," 15 *J. Pol. Sci. & Admin.* 216 (1987).

86. Robert M. Regoli et al., Career Stage and Cynicism for a National Sample of Police Chiefs, Paper presented at the Annual Meeting of the Academy of Criminal justice Sciences (1989).

87. Hector Tobar, "Gates Offers Plan to Revive Confidence in the LAPD," *L.A. Times*, March 28, 1991; at A1; Glenn F. Bunting, "Woo Says

Gates Should Quit or Be Fired," *L.A. Times*, March 28, 1991, at Bl.

88. Jesse Katz, "Gates Should Stay, Hahn Says," *L.A. Times*, March 31, 1991, at B5.

89. *See supra* note 84.

90. David Ferrell & Josh Meyer, "Officers Are Divided on Department's New Boss," *L.A. Times*, April 16, 1992, at Al.

91. *Id.*

92. *Id.*

93. John W. Meyer et al., "Institutional and Technical Sources of Organizational Structure: Explaining the Structure of Educational Organizations," in *Organization and the Human Services* 151, 153 (H. Stein ed., 1981).

94. Meyer & Rowan, *supra* note 2, at 346.

95. *Id.*

96. Scott & Meyer, *supra* note 16, at 174.

97. Manning, *supra* note 15, at 20. Index crimes are a classification used to indicate eight types of legally serious crime and are collected by the FBI by state reporting districts.

98. See supra part III.B.3.

99. Michael Feldberg, *The Turbulent Era: Riot and Disorder in Jacksonian America* 114 (1980).

100. DiMaggio and Powell suggest that there is a "startling homogeneity of organizational forms and practices" within organizational fields, and describe broad contemporary mechanisms of institutional isomorphic change. DiMaggio & Powell, *supra* note 12, at 148.

101. Skolnick and Bayley identify four areas of contemporary change in police organizational structure and activity: police-community reciprocity, civilianization, reorientation of patrol, and areal decentralization of command. Kenneth Newman has described contemporary change as a "sea-change" that is roughly described by the rubric "mobilization of the citizenry for its own defense." Skolnick & Bayley, *supra* note 32, at 210-20; "Debating the Evolution of American Policing," in *Perspectives of Policing* #5 232 (Francis X. Hartman ed., 1988).

Part VIII

Contemporary Issues

The range of contemporary issues facing the police is formidable. Consider such issues as high-speed pursuits, use of physical fitness and intelligence tests in hiring, requirements that police officers have college degrees, increasing cultural diversity in the work force and in society, computer crime, gangs, domestic and international terrorism, the globalization of organized crime, police aid to developing democracies, and so on. Because police organizations keep changing, technological developments occur more and more swiftly, and society keeps evolving, there should never be a shortage of new and interesting problems facing police or police administration.

The readings in this section explore just a sampling of contemporary issues and problems in the police world. The first article presents the Christopher Commission's findings and recommendations following the highly publicized Rodney King beating in Los Angeles. The beating was probably a relatively unremarkable occurrence in the annals of police brutality, except that it was captured on video tape and played countless times on television for all the world to see.

The second article reviews a variety of evidence on the most extreme form of police authority, the use of deadly force. We grant police officers the authority to use deadly force in certain situations out of necessity, but it is the rare occasion when the use of such force is not accompanied by controversy and claims that lesser force would have sufficed.

The third article describes an apparent recent trend toward the militarization of policing, including police use of weapons, uniforms, tactics, and training that we have traditionally associated more with the military than with the police. Taken together, these three articles remind us that the capacity and license to use force remain at the core of the police role and at the center of many political and social disputes about proper and improper policing.

The fourth article in this final section addresses the trials and tribulations faced by women trying to enter the traditionally masculine world of policing. Pioneers always face difficulties and challenges, but women police today still encounter resistance from male officers, more than 20 years after women on patrol became fairly commonplace in many jurisdictions. It will be interesting to see, in this new era of deemphasized affirmative action, and with the employment of women in the military apparently undergoing increased scrutiny, how current and future generations of women police officers will fare. ✦

29

Report of the Independent Commission on the Los Angeles Police Department

The Christopher Commission

W*ho does not remember the videotaped beating of Rodney King by officers of the Los Angeles Police Department, or the subsequent trials and associated civil disorder? Few individual police-related events have aroused as much national attention or discussion; the mere mention of Rodney King communicates volumes. This article presents the summary report of the Commission that was created to examine the LAPD in the wake of the incident. As you will see, the report identifies many shortcomings in the department and recommends substantial changes. Do you think that these changes, if fully implemented, would accomplish the objective of reforming the LAPD? Do you think they went too far, or not far enough?*

Summary of the Report

T he videotaped beating of Rodney G. King by three uniformed officers of the Los Angeles Police Department (LAPD), in the presence of a sergeant and with a large group of other officers standing by, galvanized public demand for evaluation and reform of police procedures involving the use of force. In the wake of the incident and widespread outcry, the Independent Commission on the Los Angeles Police Department was created. The Commission sought to examine all aspects of

the law enforcement structure in Los Angeles that might cause or contribute to the problem of excessive force. The Report is unanimous.

The King beating raised fundamental questions about the LAPD, including:

- the apparent failure to control or discipline officers with repeated complaints of excessive force
- concerns about the LAPD's "culture" and officers' attitudes toward racial and other minorities
- the difficulties the public encounters in attempting to make complaints against LAPD officers
- the role of the LAPD leadership and civilian oversight authorities in addressing or contributing to these problems

These and related questions and concerns form the basis for the Commission's work.

Los Angeles and Its Police Force

The LAPD is headed by Police Chief Daryl Gates with an executive staff currently consisting of two assistant chiefs, five deputy chiefs, and 17 commanders. The City Charter provides that the Department is ultimately under the control and oversight of the five-member civilian Board of Police Commissioners. The Office of Operations, headed by Assistant Chief Robert Vernon, accounts for approximately 84% of the Department's personnel, including most patrol officers and detectives. The Office of Operations has 18 separate geographic areas within the City, divided among four bureaus (Central, South, West and Valley). There are currently about 8,450 sworn police officers augmented by more than 2,000 civilian LAPD employees.

While the overall rate of violent crime in the United States increased three and one-half times between 1960 and 1989, the rate in Los Angeles during the same period was more than twice the national average. According to 1986 data recently published by the Police Foundation, the Los Angeles police were among the busiest among the officers in the nation's largest six cities. As crime rates soar, police officers must contend with more and more potential and actual violence each day. One moment officers must confront a life-threatening situation; the next they must deal with citizen problems requiring understanding and kindness. The difficulties of policing in Los Angeles are compounded by its vast geographic area and the ethnic diversity of its population. The 1990 census data reflect how enormous that diversity is: Latinos constitute 40% of the total population; Whites 37%; African-Americans 13%; and Asian/Pacific Islanders and others 10%. Of the police departments of the six largest United States cities, the LAPD has the fewest officers per resident and the fewest officers per square mile. Yet, the LAPD boasts more arrests per officer than other forces. Moreover, by all accounts, the LAPD is generally efficient, sophisticated, and free of corruption.

The Problem of Excessive Force

LAPD officers exercising physical force must comply with the Department's Use of Force Policy and guidelines, as well as California law. Both the LAPD Policy and the Penal Code require that force be reasonable: the Policy also requires that force be necessary. An officer may resort to force only where he or she faces a credible threat, and then may use only the minimum amount necessary to control the suspect.

The Commission has found that there is a significant number of LAPD officers who repetitively misuse force and persistently ignore the written policies and guidelines of the Department regarding force. The evidence obtained by the Commission shows that this group has received inadequate supervisory and management attention.

Former Assistant Chief Jesse Brewer testified that this lack of management attention and accountability is the "essence of the excessive force problem . . . We know who the bad guys are. Reputations become well known, especially to the sergeants and then of course to lieutenants and the captains in the areas . . . But I don't see anyone bring these people up . . ." Assistant Chief David Dotson testified that "we have failed miserably" to hold supervisors accountable for excessive force by officers under their command. Interviews with a large number of present and former LAPD officers yield similar

conclusions. Senior rank-and-file officers generally stated that a significant number of officers tended to use force excessively, that these problem officers were well known in their divisions, that the Department's efforts to control or discipline those officers were inadequate, and that their supervisors were not held accountable for excessive use of force by officers in their command.

The commission's extensive computerized analysis of the data provided by the Department (personnel complaints, use of force reports, and reports of officer-involved shootings) shows that a significant group of problem officers poses a much higher risk of excessive force than other officers:

- Of approximately 1,800 officers against whom an allegation of excessive force or improper tactics was made from 1986 to 1990, more than 1,400 had only one or two allegations. But 183 officers had four or more allegations, 44 had six or more, 16 had eight or more, and one had 16 such allegations.

- Of nearly 6,000 officers identified as involved in use of force reports from January 1987 to March 1991, more than 4,000 had fewer than five reports each. But 63 officers had twenty or more reports each. The top 5% of the officers (ranked by number of reports) accounted for more than 20% of all reports.

Blending the data disclosed even more troubling patterns. For example, in the years covered, one officer had 13 allegations of excessive force and improper tactics, 5 other complaint allegations, 28 use of force reports, and 1 shooting. Another had 6 excessive force/improper tactic allegations, 19 other complaint allegations, 10 use of force reports, and 3 shootings. A third officer had 7 excessive force/improper tactic allegations, 7 other complaint allegations, 7 use of force reports, and 1 shooting.

A review of personnel files of the 44 officers identified from the LAPD database who had six or more allegations of excessive force or improper tactics for the period of 1986 through 1990 disclosed that the picture conveyed was often incomplete and at odds with contemporaneous comments appearing in complaint files. As a general matter, the performance evaluation reports for those problem officers was very positive, documenting every complimentary comment received and expressing optimism about the officer's progress in the Department. The performance evaluations generally did not give an accurate picture of the officers' disciplinary history, failing to record "sustained" complaints or to discuss their significance, and failing to assess the officer's judgment and contacts with the public in light of disturbing patterns of complaints.

The existence of a significant number of officers with unacceptable and improper attitude regarding the use of force is supported by the Commission's extensive review of computer messages sent to and from patrol cars throughout the City over the units' Mobile Digital Terminals (MDTs). The Commission's staff examined 182 days of MDT Transmissions selected from the period from November 1989 to March 1991. Although the vast majority of messages reviewed consisted of routine police communications, there were hundreds of improper messages, including scores in which officers talked about beating suspects: "Capture him, beat him and treat him like dirt . . ." Officers also used the communications systems to express their eagerness to be involved in shooting incidents. The transmissions also make clear that some officers enjoy the excitement of a pursuit and view it as an opportunity for violence against a fleeing suspect.

The patrol car transmissions can be monitored by a field supervisor and are stored in a database where they could be (but were not) audited. That many officers would feel free to tape messages about force under such circumstances suggests a serious problem with respect to excessive force. That supervisors made no effort to monitor or control those messages evidences a significant breakdown in the Department's management responsibility.

The Commission also reviewed the LAPD's investigation and discipline of the officers involved in all 83 civil lawsuits alleging excessive or improper force by LAPD officers for the period 1986 through 1990 that resulted in a settlement or judgment of more than

$15,000. A majority of these cases involved a clear and often egregious officer misconduct resulting in serious injury or death to the victim. The LAPD's investigation of these 83 cases was deficient in many respects, and discipline against the officers involved was frequently light and often nonexistent.

While the precise size and identity of the problem group of officers cannot be specified without significant further investigation, its existence must be recognized and addressed. The LAPD has a number of tools to promote and enforce its policy that only reasonable and necessary force be used by officers. There are rewards and incentives such as promotions and pay upgrades. The discipline system exists to impose sanctions for misconduct. Officers can be reassigned. Supervisors can monitor and counsel officers under their command. Officers can be trained at the Police Academy and, more importantly, in the field, in the proper use of force.

The Commission believes that the Department has not made sufficient efforts to use those tools effectively to address the significant number of officers who appear to be using force excessively and improperly. The leadership of the LAPD must send a much clearer and more effective message that excessive force will not be tolerated and that officers and their supervisors will be evaluated to an important extent by how well they abide by and advance the Department's policy regarding use of force.

Racism and Bias

The problem of excessive force is aggravated by racism and bias within the LAPD. That nexus is sharply illustrated by the results of a survey recently taken by the LAPD of the attitudes of its sworn officers. The survey of 900 officers found that approximately one-quarter (24.5%) of 650 officers responding agreed that "racial bias (prejudice) on the part of officers toward minority citizens currently exists and contributes to a negative interaction between police and community." More than one quarter (27.6%) agreed that "an officer's prejudice towards the suspect's race may lead to the use of excessive force."

The Commission's review of MDT transmissions revealed an appreciable number of disturbing and recurrent racial remarks. Some of the remarks describe minorities through animal analogies ("sounds like monkey slapping time"). Often made in the context of discussing pursuits or beating suspects, the offensive remarks cover the spectrum of racial and ethnic minorities in the City ("I would love to drive down Slauson with a flame thrower . . . we would have a barbecue"; "I almost got me a Mexican last night but he dropped the damn gun too quick, lots of wit"). The officers typing, the MDT messages apparently had little concern that they would be disciplined for making such remarks. Supervisors failed to monitor the messages or to impose discipline for improper remarks and were themselves frequently the source of offensive comments when in the field.

These attitudes of prejudice and intolerance are translated into unacceptable behavior in the field. Testimony from a variety of witnesses depict the LAPD as an organization with practices and procedures that are conducive to discriminatory treatment and officer misconduct directed to members of minority groups. Witnesses repeatedly told of LAPD officers verbally harassing minorities, detaining African-American and Latino men who fit certain generalized descriptions of suspects, employing unnecessarily invasive or humiliating tactics in minority neighborhoods and using excessive force. While the Commission does not purport to adjudicate the validity of any one of these numerous complaints, the intensity and frequency of them reveal a serious problem.

Bias within the LAPD is not confined to officers' treatment of the public, but is also reflected in conduct directed to fellow officers who are members of racial or ethnic minority groups. The MDT messages and other evidence suggest that minority officers are still too frequently subjected to racial slurs and comments and to discriminatory treatment within the Department. While the relative number of officers who openly make racially derogatory comments or treat minority officers in a demeaning manner is small, their attitudes and behavior have a large impact because of the failure of supervisors to enforce vigorously and consistently the Department's policies against racism. That failure conveys to minority and non-minority officers alike the message that such conduct is in practice condoned by the Department.

The LAPD has made substantial progress in hiring minorities and women since the 1981 consent decree settling discrimination lawsuits against the Department. The effort should continue, including efforts to recruit Asians and other minorities who are not covered by the consent decree. The Department's statistics show, however, that the vast majority of minority officers are concentrated in the entry-level police officer ranks in the Department. More than 80% of African American, Latino and Asian officers hold the rank of Police Officer I-III. Many minority officers cite white dominance of managerial positions within the LAPD as one reason for the Department's continued tolerance of racially motivated language and behavior.

Bias within the LAPD is not limited to racist and ethnic prejudices but includes strongly felt bias on gender and sexual orientation. Current LAPD policy prohibits all discrimination, including that based on sexual orientation. A tension remains, however, between the LAPD's official policy and actual practice. The Commission believes that the LAPD must act to implement fully its formal policy of nondiscrimination in the recruitment and promotion of gay and lesbian officers.

A 1987 LAPD study concluded that female officers were subjected to a double standard and subtle harassment and were not accepted as part of the working culture. As revealed in interviews of many of the officers charged with training new recruits, the problem has not abated in the last four years. Although female LAPD officers are in fact performing effectively, they are having a difficult time being accepted on a full and equal basis.

The Commission heard substantial evidence that female officers utilize a style of policing that minimizes the use of excessive force. Data examined by the Commission indicate that LAPD female officers are involved in use of excessive force at rates substantially below those of male officers. Those statistics, as confirmed by both academic studies and anecdotal evidence, also indicate that women officers perform at least as well as their male counterparts when measured by traditional standards.

The Commission believes that the Chief of Police must seek tangible ways, for example, through the use of the discipline system, to establish the principle that racism and bias based on ethnicity, gender, or sexual orientation will not be tolerated within the Department. Racism and bias cannot be eliminated without active leadership from the top. Minority and female officers must be given full and equal opportunity to assume leadership positions in the LAPD. They must be assigned on a fully nondiscriminatory basis to the more desirable, "coveted" positions and promoted on the same nondiscriminatory basis to supervisory and management positions.

Community Policing

The LAPD has an organizational culture that emphasizes crime control over crime prevention and that isolates the police from the communities and the people they serve. With the full support of many, the LAPD insists on aggressive detection of major crimes and a rapid, seven-minute response time to calls for service. Patrol officers are evaluated by statistical measures (for example, the number of calls handled and arrests made) and are rewarded for being "hardnosed." This style of policing produces results, but it does so at the risk of creating a siege mentality that alienates the officer from the community.

Witness after witness testified unnecessarily aggressive confrontations between LAPD officers and citizens, particularly members of minority communities. From the statements of these citizens, as well as many present and former LAPD officers, it is apparent that too many LAPD patrol officers view citizens with resentment and hostility; too many treat the public with rudeness and disrespect. LAPD officers themselves seem to recognize the extent of the problem: nearly two-thirds (62.9%) of the 650 officers who responded to the recent LAPD survey expressed the opinion that "increased interaction with the community would improve the Department's relations with citizens."

A model of community policing has gained increased acceptance in other parts of the country during the past 10 years. The community policing model places service to the public and prevention of crime as the primary role of the police in society and emphasizes problem solving, with active citizen involvement in defining those matters that are important to the community, rather than arrest statistics. Officers at the patrol level are required to spend less time in their cars communicating with other officers and more time on the street communicating with citizens. Proponents of this style of policing insist that addressing the causes of crime makes police officers more effective crime-fighters, and at the same time enhances the quality of life in the neighborhood.

The LAPD made early efforts to incorporate community policing principles and has continued to experiment with those concepts. For example, the LAPD's nationally recognized DARE program has been viewed by officers and the public alike as a major achievement. The LAPD remains committed, however, to its traditional style of law enforcement with an emphasis on crime control and arrests. LAPD officers are encouraged to command and confront, not to communicate. Community policing concepts, if successfully implemented, offer the prospect of effective crime prevention and substantially improved community relations. Although community-based policing is not a panacea for the problem of crime in society, the LAPD should carefully implement this model on a City-wide basis. This will require a fundamental change in values. The Department must recognize the merits of community involvement in matters that affect local neighborhoods, develop programs to gain an adequate understanding of what is important to particular communities, and learn to manage departmental affairs in ways that are consistent with the community views expressed. Above all, the Department must understand that it is accountable to all segments of the community.

Recruitment

Although 40% of the candidates for admission to the Police Academy are disqualified as a result of psychological testing and background investigation, the Commission's review indicated that the initial psychological evaluation is an ineffective predictor of an applicant's tendencies toward violent behavior and that the background investigation pays too little attention to a candidate's history of violence. Experts agree that the best predictor of future behavior is previous behavior. Thus, the background investigation offers the best hope of screening out violence-prone applicants. Unfortunately, the background investigators are overworked and inadequately trained.

Improved screening of applicants is not enough. Police work modifies behavior. Many emotional and psychological problems may develop during an officer's tenure on the force. Officers may enter the force well-suited psychologically for the job, but may suffer from burnout, alcohol-related problems, cynicism, or disenchantment, all of which can result in poor control over their behavior. A person's susceptibility to the behavior-modifying experiences of police work may not be revealed during even the most skilled and sophisticated psychological evaluation process. Accordingly, officers should be retested periodically to determine both psychological and physical problems. In addition, supervisors must understand their role to include training and counseling officers to cope with the problems policing can often entail, so that they may be dealt with before an officer loses control or requires disciplinary action.

Training

LAPD officer training has three phases. Each recruit spends approximately six months at the Police Academy. The new officer then spends one year on probation working with more experienced patrol officers who serve as Field Training Officers (FTOs). Thereafter, all officers receive continuing training, which includes mandatory field training and daily training at roll call. The Commission believes that in each phase of the training additional emphasis is needed on the use of verbal skills rather than physical force to control potentially volatile situations and on the development of human relationship skills.

The quality of instruction at the Police Academy is generally impressive. However, at present the curriculum provides only eight hours in cultural awareness training. No more than one and one-half hours is devoted to any ethnic group. Substantially more training on this important topic is essential. In addition, the Academy's current Spanish language program needs to be reviewed and current deficiencies corrected. Officers with an interest in developing broader language skills should be encouraged to do so.

Upon graduation the new officer works as a "probationary officer" assigned to various field training officers. The FTOs guide new officers' first contacts with citizens and have primary responsibility for introducing the new probationers to the culture and traditions of the Department. The Commission's interviews of FTOs in four representative divisions revealed that many FTOs openly perpetuate the siege mentality that alienates the patrol officers from the community and pass on to their trainees confrontational attitudes of hostility and disrespect for the public. The problem is in part the result of flaws in how the FTOs are selected and trained. The hiring of a very large number of new officers in 1989, which required the use of less experienced FTOs, greatly exacerbated the problem.

Any officer promoted to Police Officer III by passing a written examination covering Department policies and procedures is eligible to serve as an FTO. At present there are no formal eligibility or disqualification criteria for the FTO position based on an applicants' disciplinary records. Fourteen of the FTOs in the four divisions the Commission studied had been promoted to FTO despite having been disciplined for use of excessive force or use of improper tactics. There also appears to be little emphasis on selecting FTOs who have an interest in training junior officers, and an FTO's training ability is given little weight in his or her evaluation.

The most influential training received by a probationer comes from the example set by his or her FTO. Virtually all of the FTOs interviewed stated that their primary objective in training probationers is to instill good "officer safety skills." While the Commission recognizes the importance of such skills in police work, the probationers' world is quickly divided into "we/they" categories, which is exacerbated by the failure to integrate any cultural awareness or sensitivity training into field training.

The Commission believes that, to become FTOS, officers should be required to pass written and oral tests designed to measure communications skills, teaching, aptitude, and knowledge of Departmental policies regarding appropriate use of force, cultural sensitivity community relations, and nondiscrimination. Officers with an aptitude for and interest in training junior officers should be encouraged by effective incentives to apply for FTO positions. In addition, the training program for FTOs should be modified to place greater emphasis on communication skills and the appropriate use of force. Successful completion of FTO School should be required before an FTO begins teaching probationers.

Promotion, Assignment, and Other Personnel Issues

In the civil service process for promotion of officers in the LAPD, the information considered includes performance evaluations, educational and training background, and all sustained complaints. The number and nature of any "not sustained" complaints, however, are not considered. The Commission recommends that a summary of not sustained complaints be considered in promotion decisions, as well as in paygrade advancements and assignments to desirable positions that are discretionary within the LAPD and outside of the civil service system.

This is not to say that a past complaint history, even including a sustained complaint for excessive force, should automatically bar an officer from promotion. But there should be a careful consideration of the officer's complaint history including a summary of not sustained complaints, and particularly multiple complaints with similar fact patterns.

Complaint histories should also be considered in assignment of problem officers who may be using force improperly. For example, a problem officer can be paired with an officer with excellent communication skills that

may lessen the need for use of force, as opposed to a partner involved in prior incidents of force with that problem officer. Another example is assignments to the jail facilities where potential for abuse by officers with a propensity to use excessive force is high. As several incidents examined by the Commission made clear, transfer of an officer to another geographical area is not likely to address a problem of excessive force without other remedial measures such as increased supervising, training, and counseling.

Since 1980 the Department has permitted police officers working in patrol to select the geographic area or division for their patrol assignment subsequent to their initial assignment after completion of probation. As a result sergeants and patrol officers tend to remain in one division for extended periods. The Commission believes that assignment procedures should be modified to require rotation through various divisions to ensure that officers work in a wide range of police functions and varied patrol locations during their careers. Such a rotation program will increase officers' experience and will also enable the Department to deploy police patrols with greater diversity throughout the City.

Under the current promotion system officers generally must leave patrol to advance within the Department. Notwithstanding the importance of the patrol function, therefore, the better officers are encouraged to abandon patrol. To give patrol increased emphasis and to retain good, experienced officers, the LAPD should increase rewards and incentives for patrol officers.

Personnel Complaints and Officer Discipline

No area of police operations received more adverse comment during the Commission's public hearings than the Department's handling of complaints against LAPD officers, particularly allegations involving the use of excessive force. Statistics make the public's frustration understandable. Of the 2,152 citizen allegations of excessive force from 1986 through 1990, only 42 were sustained.

All personnel complaints are reviewed by a captain in the LAPD's Internal Affairs Division (IAD) to determine whether the complaint will be investigated by IAD or the charged officer's division. Generally, IAD investigates only a few cases because of limited resources. Wherever investigated, the matter is initially adjudicated by the charged officer's division commanding officer, with a review by the area and bureau commanders.

The Commission has found that the complaint system is skewed against complainants. People who wish to file complaints face significant hurdles. Some intake officers actively discourage filing by being uncooperative or requiring long waits before completing a complaint form. In many heavily Latino divisions, there is often no Spanish speaking officer available to take complaints.

Division investigators are frequently inadequate. Based on a review of more than 700 complaint investigation files, the Commission found many deficiencies. For example, in a number of complaint files the Commission reviewed, there was no indication that the investigators had attempted to identify or locate independent witnesses or, if identified, to interview them. IAD investigations, on the whole, were of a higher quality than the division investigations. Although the LAPD has a special "officer involved shooting team," the Commission also found serious flaws in the investigation of shooting cases. Officers are frequently interviewed as a group and statements are often not recorded until the completion of a "pre-interview."

The process of complaint adjudication is also flawed. First, there is no uniform basis for categorizing witnesses as "independent" or "non-involved" as opposed to "involved," although that distinction can determine whether a complaint is "not sustained" or "sustained." Some commanding officers also evaluate witnesses' credibility in inconsistent and biased ways that improperly favor the officer. Moreover, even when excessive force complaints are sustained, the punishment is more lenient that it should be. As explained by one deputy chief, there is greater punishment for conduct that embarrasses the Department (such as theft or drug use) than for conduct that reflects improper treatment of citizens. Statistical data also support the inference that the Department treats excessive force violations more leniently than it treats other types of officer misconduct.

Perhaps the greatest single barrier to the effective investigation and adjudication of complaints is the officers' unwritten code of silence: an officer does not provide adverse information against a fellow officer. While loyalty and support are necessary qualities, they cannot justify the violation of an officer's public responsibilities to ensure compliance with the law, including LAPD regulations.

A major overhaul of the disciplinary system is necessary to correct these problems. The Commission recommends creation of the Office of Inspector General within the Police Commission with responsibility to oversee the disciplinary process and to participate in the adjudication and punishment of the most serious cases. The Police Commission should be responsible for overseeing the complaint intake process. Citizens must believe they can lodge complaints that will be investigated and determined fairly. All complaints relating to excessive force (including improper tactics) should be investigated by IAD, rather than at the involved officer's division, and should be subject to periodic audits by the Inspector General. While the Chief of Police should remain the one primarily responsible for imposing discipline in individual cases, the Police Commission should set guidelines as a matter of policy and hold the Chief accountable for following them.

Structural Issues

Although the City Charter assigns the Police Commission ultimate control over Department policies, its authority over the Department and the Chief of Police is illusory. Structural and operational constraints greatly weaken the Police Commission's power to hold the Chief accountable and therefore its ability to perform its management responsibilities, including effective oversight. Real power and authority reside in the Chief.

The Chief of Police is the general manager and chief administrative officer of the Police Department. The Police Commission selects the Chief from among top competitors in a civil service examination administered by the Personnel Department. Candidates from outside the Department are disadvantaged by the city charter provisions and seniority rules.

The Chief's civil service status largely protects him or her from disciplinary action or discharge by giving him a "substantial property right" in his job and declaring that he cannot be suspended or removed except for "good and sufficient cause" based upon an act or omission occurring within the prior year. In addition, recently enacted Charter Amendment 5 empowers the City Council to review and override the actions of the City's commissioners, including the Police Commission.

The Police Commission's staff is headed by the Commanding Officer, Commission Operations, a sworn LAPD officer chosen by the Police Commission, who normally serves in that post for two to three years. Because the Police Commission depends heavy on the Commanding Officer to review information received from the Department to identify issues, it must also rely on his willingness to criticize his superior officers. However, he lacks the requisite independence because his future transfer and promotion are at the discretion of the Chief of Police, and he is part of the Chief's command structure as well as being answerable to the Police Commission.

The Police Commission receives summaries, prepared by the Department, of disciplinary actions against sworn officers, but cannot itself impose discipline. The summaries are brief and often late, making it impossible for the Police Commission to monitor systematically the discipline imposed by the Chief in use of force and other cases.

The Commission believes that the Department should continue to be under the general oversight and control of a five-member, part-time citizen Police Commission. Commissioner's compensation should be increased substantially. They should serve a maximum of five years with staggered terms. The Police Commission's independent staff should be increased by adding civilian employees, including management auditors, computer systems data analysts, and investigators with law enforcement experience. It is vital that the Police Commission's staff be placed under the control of an independent civilian Chief of Staff, a general manager level employee.

The Chief of Police must be more responsive to the Police Commission and the City's elected leadership, but also must be protected against improper political influences. To achieve this balance, the Chief should serve a five-year term, renewable at the discretion of the Police Commission for one additional five-year term. The selection, tenure, discipline, and removal of the Chief should be exempted from existing civil service provisions. The Chief should be appointed by the Mayor, with advice from the Police Commission and the consent of the City Council after an open competition. The Police Commission should have the authority to terminate the Chief prior to the expiration of the first or second five-year term, but the final decision to terminate should require the concurrence of the Mayor and be subject to a reversal by vote of two-thirds of the City Council.

Implementation

Full implementation of this Report will require action by the Mayor, the City Council, the Police Commission, the Police Department, and ultimately the voters. To monitor the progress of reform the City Council should require reports on implementation at six month intervals from the Mayor, the Council's own Human Resources and Labor Relations Committee, the Police Commission, and the Police Department. The Commission should reconvene in six months to assess the implementation of its recommendations and to report to the public.

Chief Gates has served the LAPD and the City 42 years, the last 13 years as Chief of Police. He has achieved a noteworthy record of public service in a stressful and demanding profession. For the reasons set forth in support of the terms, the recommendation that the Chief of Police be limited to two five-year terms, the Commission believes the commencement of a transition in that office is now appropriate. The Commission also believes that the interests of harmony and healing would be served if the Police Commission is now reconstituted with members not identified with the recent controversy involving the Chief.

More than any other factor, the attitude and actions of the leaders of the Police Department and other City agencies will determine whether the recommendations of this Report are adopted. To make genuine progress on issues relating to excessive force, racism, and bias, leadership must avoid sending mixed signals. We urge those leaders to give priority to stopping the use of excessive force and curbing racism and bias and thereby to bring the LAPD to a new level of excellence and esteem throughout Los Angeles.

30

Police Use of Deadly Force: Research and Reform

James J. Fyfe

The ultimate form of police authority is the use of deadly force. Police use of deadly force has always been limited, of course, but as Jim Fyfe shows in this article, growing concern and consequent tightened restrictions began to surface in the 1960s. Fyfe, perhaps the leading expert on this subject, traces these changing practices and also demonstrates that the amount and circumstances of police shooting vary over time and, even more, how much they vary from city to city. You should be surprised by how much homicides-by-police vary between Buffalo and Rochester in the Northeast, Milwaukee and St. Louis in the Midwest, Charlotte and Jacksonville in the South, and Sacramento and Long Beach in the West, to provide just a few examples. What do you think accounts for these differences? What can be done to reduce the overall use of police deadly force?

Most social science writing opens with a testament to the seriousness of the problem under study and a lament about the absence of prior related research. Where police deadly force is concerned, however, documenting the seriousness of the subject matter is no challenge: the police are the only American public servants authorized routinely to make quick, unilateral, and irreversible decisions that are likely to result in the deaths of other Americans.[1]

When police officers fire their guns,[2] the immediate consequences of their decisions are realized at the rate of 750 feet per second and are beyond reversal by any level of official review. As most police recruits learn in the academy, the cop on the street—who, with the corrections officer, generally can boast of fewer academic and training credentials than any other criminal justice official—carries in his holster more power than has been granted the Chief Justice of the Supreme Court. When used injudiciously, this power has led to riot and additional death, civil and criminal litigation against police and their employers, and the ousters of police chiefs, elected officials, and entire city administrations. Even when used with great restraint, police deadly force has created polarization, suspicion, and distrust on the part of those who need the police most.

Because this is a review essay and reexamination of existing data rather than a report on new research, it provides only limited opportunity for breast beating about scholarly indifference: one cannot agree to write a review essay without a sizable body of literature to review. Still, *sizable* is a relative term; the existing research on the only unilateral life-or-death decision available to any American criminal justice official is the work of only a few individuals, and is dwarfed by the volume of studies on most other (and less critical) decision points in the criminal justice process. My dining-room table could accommodate easily the number of contemporary social scientists who have devoted any serious attention to police deadly force.

This is not to say that earlier researchers answered all the questions: 20 years ago, those who had studied deadly force could have been driven to dinner in the back seat of a compact car. Until the late 1960s, when two presidential commissions reported that police shootings were the immediate precipitants of many of that era's urban riots (National Commission on Civil Disorders 1968: 17-53) and that officers generally received little guidance in use of deadly force (President's Commission 1967: 188-89), the professional criminal justice community and most of the public paid little heed to how wisely or how well this power was exercised and controlled.[3] Criminology and criminal justice scholars apparently did not notice that police officers in most states were authorized by law and by their departments to kill people whom they suspected of bicycle theft;[4] with the slight exceptions noted, they left us no clue as to how often or in what circumstances the police shot suspected bicycle thieves or anybody else. The practitioners who wrote books for police chiefs offered advice on training officers how to shoot, but generally ignored questions of when—and when not—to shoot.

Before that period, as far as I can determine, there existed only two empirical studies of police deadly force incidents. Gerald Robin (1963) analyzed all fatal shootings by Philadelphia police during the 11 years from 1950 through 1960, and also obtained some comparative statistics from several other cities. The American Civil Liberties Union (1966) found that police in an unnamed city had discharged their firearms more than 300 times in two years, and that more than one-third of these incidents were precipitated by vehicle chases involving juvenile suspects. In his *Police Administration*, almost certainly the most widely read police text of the time, O. W. Wilson (1963) said nothing about police deadly force or firearms except to suggest locations and safety precautions for shooting ranges and weapons storage cabinets (443-44). *Municipal Police Administration*, the International City Management Association's voluminous guide for police chiefs, said only the following before recommending specifications for weapons:

> A firearm allows the officer to protect himself and at the same time extend his usefulness into space as well as his skill and effectiveness of his weapon permit. How wisely this power is used depends upon the officer, his training, and established procedures and policy. The weapon only projects the long arm of the law as it is enforced by individuals (Eastman 1961: 444).

In the years since Robin's work was published and, more significantly for public policy, since the Presidential Task Force on the Police (President's Commission 1967: 189-90) examined and commented on police power to kill, a comparative boom has taken place in the literature of deadly force. Even so, because the police rarely have been asked

to report to public officials about how they use this power, and because few scholars have persuaded the police to be more forthcoming, there is much that we do not know. Thus my excoriation of scholars' past failure to study deadly force is also an exhortation to future research. Deadly force is a serious subject that deserves greater scholarly interest than it has received.

The Emergence of a Problem

Although Robin's 1963 study was the first systematic look at the use of deadly force, it had little apparent effect on either scholars or officials.[5] The subject did draw attention a year later when the first of the major urban disorders of the 1960s, in Harlem and in Bedford-Stuyvesant, followed immediately upon the fatal shooting of a 15-year-old black boy who reportedly attacked an off-duty police lieutenant with a knife.[6] Soon it became apparent, as the National Advisory Commission on Civil Disorders (the "Kerner Commission") reported four years later, that this pattern would not remain unique to New York. In May 1966, a year after Los Angeles had suffered its Watts riot, the Commission reported that the accidental shooting death of a young black man led to renewed demonstrations and increased tensions in that city (1968: 38). In 1967 the National Guard was called in to restore order at Jackson State College in Mississippi after police attempts to disperse a crowd resulted in the shootings of three blacks, one of whom was killed (1968: 41). The 1967 Tampa riots were triggered by the fatal police shooting of a black youth who was fleeing from the scene of a burglary (1968: 42). The Commission also wrote that "only the dramatic ghetto appearance of mayor Ivan Allen, Jr., had averted a riot" in Atlanta in 1966 (1968: 53).

Legal and Administrative Controls on Deadly Force

President Johnson's other major blue-ribbon panel, the President's Commission on Law Enforcement and Administration of Justice, looked carefully at police-community relations. In the report of its Task Force on the Police—which, in my view, remains the single most significant and most influential contribution to American police policy and practice to date—the Commission made clear its dismay at the virtual absence of administrative policies to guide police officers' decisions to use deadly force (President's Commission 1967: 189-90). In a report to the Commission, Police Task Force chair Samuel Chapman cited the full text of one unnamed police department's policy on use of firearms as an illustration of the need for direction in this most critical matter of police discretion:

> Never take me out in anger; never put me back in disgrace (Chapman 1967).

Chapman also saw to it that the final report of the Task Force included a model administrative policy on use of firearms (President's Commission 1967:188-89). This was not the first time he had championed this cause; in 1963 he and Thompson Crockett reported on a 1961 survey of 71 Michigan police departments serving populations of 10,000 or more. They found that

> 54 per cent (27 of 50) of the agencies furnishing information had no written policies in effect to govern the use of firearms. These twenty-seven departments, which relied upon "oral policy", were asked to indicate the main points of oral instructions given to their officers regarding when to use firearms. Of the twenty-seven, only five departments mentioned such basic situations as self-defense and fleeing felons where firearms may be used. Thus, based on the reported practice in these Michigan cities, it would appear reasonable to regard with grave reservation that suitability of relying singularly upon "oral policy" (Chapman and Crockett 1963:42).[7]

Further:

> "[W]hen to fire" is frequently trusted to the "judgment" or "discretion" of officers as individuals . . . (1963:41)

The consequence is that while officers know *how* to care for and use their firearms, many have little or no understanding of *when* the weapon may be employed. This paradox is similar to teaching an employee how to maintain and drive an automobile while neglecting to instruct him on the subject of mo-

tor vehicle regulations. It might be argued, as it often is in the case of firearms regulations, that the driver's "common sense," coupled with a warning not to crash into anybody unless absolutely necessary, would suffice to enable the driver to operate his vehicle at large on the highways. This argument conveniently ignores the fact that driving regulations, like firearms regulations, are not based entirely on "common sense" or personal safety (Chapman and Crockett 1963:41; emphasis in original).

Breadth of Law. In the absence of such policies, police shooting discretion generally was limited only by state criminal statutes or by case law defining justifiable homicide. These laws have several inadequacies. First, even the most restrictive state laws permit police to use their weapons in an extremely broad range of situations. Every state historically has permitted police officers to use deadly force to defend themselves or others against imminent death or serious physical harm, a provision that cannot be debated seriously. Indeed, except that generally they are obliged to attempt to retreat to safety before resorting to deadly force, American citizens enjoy the same justification for homicide (see, for example, New York Penal Law 1967). Because we ask the police to put their lives on the line in our behalf, it follows that they should enjoy this slight advantage over the rest of us.

Yet many states also have codified some variant of the common-law "fleeing felon" rule, which authorizes use of deadly force as a means of apprehending persons fleeing from suspected felonies. The Tennessee statute that eventually became the focus of *Tennessee v. Garner* (1985), illustrates the broadest category of such laws:

> Resistance to Officer—If after notice of the intention to arrest the [felony] defendant, he either flees or forcibly resists, the officer may use all the necessary means to effect the arrest (Tennessee Code Annotated sec. 40-7108:55).

The breadth of such "any *fleeing* felon" statutes perhaps was questioned first by Mikell, who queried the American Law Institute:

May I ask what we are killing [the suspect] for when he steals an automobile and runs off with it? Are we killing him for stealing the automobile? . . . It cannot be . . . that we allow the officer to kill him because he stole the automobile, because the statute provides only three years in a penitentiary for that. Is it then . . . for fleeing that we kill him? Fleeing from arrest . . . is punishable by a light penalty, a penalty much less than that for stealing the automobile. If we are not killing him for stealing the automobile and not killing him for fleeing, what are we killing him for? (American Law Institute 1931: 186-87)[8]

Years later, apparently unaware that the fleeing felon laws of about one-half the states fit precisely the specifications he deplored, Chief Justice Burger mused:

I wonder what would be the judicial response to a police order authorizing "shoot to kill" with respect to every fugitive. It is easy to predict our collective wrath and outrage. We, in common with all rational minds, would say that the police response must relate to the gravity and need; that a "shoot" order might conceivably be tolerable to prevent the escape of a convicted killer but surely not for car thieves, pickpockets, or a shoplifter (*Bivens v. Six Unknown Agents* 1971, W. Burger, C.J., dissenting).

The History of Deadly Force Law. The history of the *any* fleeing felon laws that Chief Justice Burger regarded as outrageously hypothetical in 1971 (but which he voted subsequently to affirm in joining the *Garner* dissent) has been well documented in other places (Boutwell 1977; Fyfe 1981a; Rummel 1968; Sherman 1980), and needs be traced here only briefly. It dates back to the English Middle Ages, when virtually all felons were punished by death after trials that paid little heed to current standards of due process or to the distinctions that have been drawn between factual and legal guilt. At that time, if the suspect had committed the felony, he almost certainly would be convicted; if convicted, he almost certainly would be executed. Thus, for all practical purposes, it made little difference whether the felon died

during pretrial flight or at the hands of the executioner.

The manner in which felony suspects are pursued and apprehended also has changed in important ways over the centuries. When the fleeing felon rule originated, those who typically pursued felons were ordinary male citizens who were obliged by law to respond to the *hue and cry* and to join in pursuit. Because they were usually armed only with clubs or knives, discharging their duty to arrest compelled them to overpower physically people who knew that arrest was likely to result in execution. These circumstances also are a far cry from more modern applications of the fleeing felon rule. The officer involved in *Garner*, for example, fired his fatal shot from the relative safety of 30 feet at the back of an unarmed, 5'4", 100-pound juvenile burglary suspect who, if apprehended alive, would likely have been sentenced to probation.[9]

Debates about the merits of the *any* fleeing felon laws came to an abrupt end in 1985, when the Supreme Court ruled in *Garner* that the Tennessee statute, when applied against unarmed, nondangerous fleeing suspects, violated the Fourth Amendment's guarantees against unreasonable seizure.[10] In his opinion for the majority, Justice White wrote that deadly force was a constitutional means of effecting arrest only when a felony "suspect threatens the officer with a weapon or there is probable cause to believe that he has committed a crime involving the infliction or threatened infliction of serious physical harm" (*Tennessee v. Garner*, 471 U.S. at 4). This decision affects the laws not only of the 23 states that followed the broad *any* fleeing felon rule; because Garner was a suspect in a nighttime residential burglary, it also affects the laws of several other states that included this offense under the limited category of offenses justifying deadly force for purposes of apprehension.[11]

The Law as a Control on Professional Discretion. Although *Garner* moots some of the arguments about the great breadth of deadly force statutes, it does little to ameliorate a second and more general limitation of law in describing police shooting discretion: in no field of human endeavor does the criminal law alone define adequately the parameters of acceptable occupational behavior. In the course of their work, doctors, lawyers, psychologists, professors, soldiers, nursing home operators, truck drivers, government officials, and journalists can do many outrageous, unacceptable, and hurtful things without violating criminal law. In exchange for the monopolies on the activities performed by those in their crafts, the most highly developed of these professions keep their members' behavior in check by developing and enforcing codes of conduct that are both more specific and more restrictive than are criminal definitions. Who would submit to treatment by a surgeon whose choices in deciding how to deal with patients were limited only by the laws of homicide and assault?

Apply that logic to use of police firearms. Even post-*Garner*, no state law tells officers whether it is advisable to fire warning shots into the air on streets lined by high-rise buildings. The law provides no direction to officers who must decide quickly whether to shoot at people in moving vehicles and thereby risk turning them into speeding unguided missiles. The law related to police use of force, in short, is simply too vague to be regarded as a comprehensive set of operational guidelines.[12]

Resistance to Rule Making Regarding Deadly Force

Even so, many police administrators did not act on policy recommendations like Chapman's until their officers had become involved in shootings that (although noncriminal) generated community outcries and crises (Sherman 1983). Their sometimes vigorous resistance to change was rooted in many considerations. First, police authority to restrict shooting discretion more tightly than state law was uncertain. In 1971, for example, the Florida Attorney General issued a written opinion that administrative policies overriding the state's any fleeing felon law were legally impermissible (Florida Attorney General 1971:68-75); this narrow view of the separation of powers has been cast aside since in favor of more realistic interpretations of police chief's administrative prerogatives. In addition, apparently on the theory

that jurors were unlikely to find police behavior unreasonable unless officers had violated their own departments' formal rules and policies, some police officials refrained from committing deadly force policies to paper. Time also has shown that this rather self-serving attempt to avoid accountability and liability was counterproductive: jurors don't need a piece of paper to tell them whether an individual officer acted reasonably, but typically they do find that a police department's failure to provide officers with such paper is inexcusable.[13] Finally, many police officers feared that restrictive deadly force policies would endanger the public and the police; by removing whatever deterrent value inhered in the fleeing felon rule, such policies would result in an increase in crime and a decrease in police ability to apprehend fleeing criminals. Indeed, even when research suggested that this was not the case (Fyfe 1979), many police chiefs continued to regard restrictive deadly force policies as invitations to public accusations that they were "weak on crime" or had "handcuffed the police."[14]

By now, however, the question of whether police should promulgate restrictive deadly force policies has been answered in the affirmative; at least among larger agencies, it is the rare department whose manual does not include, such a policy.[15] Social science research has played some part in easing police resistance to formulation of deadly force policy, and in the Supreme Court's *Garner* decision as well. Thus it is time now to turn from discussions of law and policy to consideration of what that research has shown.

Research on Deadly Force and its Implications

Sources of Data

In a democracy that counts executions carefully and tries to keep close count of the political prisoners held by foreign governments, one might expect to find accurate data on the number of Americans who become subjects of police deadly force. Yet in an omission that can be defined only as inexcusable, no federal agency has ever collected or published such data nationwide. Amid their

Table 30.1
Injuries Sustained by Persons Shot by Police

Source, City, and Time Period	Fatal Wound	(IACP)*	Nonfatal Wound
Blumberg (1981)			
Atlanta, 1971-78	37.8%		62.2%
	(n = 70)	(n = 65)	(n = 115)
Kansas City, 1969-78	36.0%		64.0%
	(36)	n/a	(64)
Fyfe (1980)			
Philadelphia, 1975-78	21.2%		78.8%
	(70)	(70)	(260)
Fyfe (1988)			
New York, 1971-75	35.6%		64.4%
	(323)	(323)	(584)
Geller and Karales (1981)			
Chicago, 1974-78	25.5%		74.5%
	(132)	(130)	(386)
Horvath and Donahue (1982)			
Detroit, 9/1/76-8/31/81	33.6%		66.4%
	(79)	(100)	(159)
Meyer (1980)			
Los Angeles, 1974-78	41.7%		58.3%
	(128)	(130)	(181)
Milton et al. (1977)			
Birmingham, 1973-74	26.8%		72.2%
	(11)	(4)	(30)
Detroit, 1973-74	29.1%		70.1%
	(52)	(56)	(127)
Indianapolis, 1973-74	36.1%		63.9%
	(13)	(0)	(23)
Kansas City, 1973-74	23.1%		76.9%
	(6)	(8)	(20)
Oakland, 1973-74	23.5%		76.5%
	(4)	(1)	(13)
Portland, 1973-74	33.3%		66.7%
	(3)	(4)	(6)
Washington, D.C., 1973-74	31.4%		68.6%
	(22)	(24)	(48)
Totals	31.5%		68.5%
	(970)		(2113)

* Fatal woundings according to Matulia (1985: A-3, A-4); all data for 1970 through 1974 are derived from Federal Bureau of Investigation Supplementary Homicide Reports.

statistics on crimes reported and solved, calls received, tickets issued, and assaults on officers, even the glossiest police department annual reports rarely include any information on the frequency or the circumstances of police use of deadly force.

FBI. The FBI collects voluntarily submitted information on deaths at the hands of the police for its Supplementary Homicide Reports, but (probably because it cannot vouch for the accuracy of this information) the FBI disseminates it only on request and does not mention police deadly force in its annual Uniform Crime Reports. Table 30.1 suggests that the Bureau's doubts are well founded. Only my own work in New York City and Philadelphia shows agreement with data reported in Matulia's study (1985: A-3, A-4); for the years 1970 through 1974, these data consist exclusively of FBI Supplementary Homicide Report statistics.[16]

National Center for Health Statistics. In the absence of national data from any federal criminal justice agency, some researchers (Harring, Platt, Spieglman, and Takagi 1977; Kania and Mackey 1977; Kobler 1975a, 1975b; Robin 1963; Takagi 1974) based their conclusions on annual figures for "death by legal intervention of the police" from the National Center for Health Statistics (NCHS). These reports, compiled from local coroners' diagnoses of causes of death, generally indicate that such deaths number between 200 and 400 annually.

The use of NCHS data in research on deadly force requires two assumptions. First, one must assume that body counts tell us something about the overall frequency of police decisions to use deadly force, most of which result in nonfatal wounds or missed shots. Such extrapolation is hazardous because, as Table 30.1 indicates, the percentage of shootings that result in death varies considerably across jurisdictions. At the extremes, from 1971 through 1975, only one in five (21.2%) of those shot by Philadelphia police succumbed to his or her wounds, whereas more than two in five (41.7%) died among those hit by Los Angeles police bullets between 1974 and 1978. This picture becomes even more muddled when we take into account incidents in which officers shoot and miss their targets entirely. This was the outcome in 48.6 percent of the 1974-1978 Los Angeles incidents studied by Meyer (1980a:103), 68 percent of the 1971-1975 New York (NYPD) shootings that I studied (see Fyfe 1978), 73.1 percent of Chicago shootings from 1975 through 1977 (Geller and Karales 1981:162), and 74.1 percent of the Detroit incidents studied by Horvath and Donahue (1982:185).

Second, one must assume that the NCHS data are accurate. This assumption is wrong, however, as Sherman and Langworthy (1979) demonstrated. Drawing directly from 36 large American police jurisdictions, they obtained data on fatalities resulting from police deadly force during various years between 1966 and 1976. On average, they found that the police figures were about twice as high as those provided to NCHS by local coroners, and that the police/NCHS disparities followed no pattern from which one might easily make cross-jurisdictional generalizations. Because it is safe to assume that the police had the bodies to account for the numbers they provided to Sherman and Langworthy, it is also safe to conclude that far more deaths by legal intervention of the police take place than the NCHS data suggest.

Police-Generated Data. This conclusion is supported by extrapolation from Matulia's (1985) study of justifiable police homicide in the 57 American cities with populations over 250,000. When we set aside his 1970-1974 FBI data on grounds of probable inaccuracy, his police-generated data (Table 30.2) indicate that police in these cities accounted for an average of 260 deaths per year from 1975 through 1983. Because these police departments employ only about one-quarter of all American police officers and are home to less than one-quarter of the country's population, it seems improbable that Matulia is correct when he asserts that they account for approximately 70 percent of total American police homicides (Matulia 1985: vii). Indeed, if the annual rates of fatalities by these officers (means - 2.24 per 1,000 officers; 0.62 per 100,000 population) can be generalized to the rest of the nation, it is likely that the annual number of police homicides in the United States has exceeded 1,000 during recent years.

Table 30.2
Police Homicide in 57 Largest American Cities, 1975-1983

Year	Number[*]	Rate per 1,000 Officers	Rate per 100,000 Population
1975	360	2.95	0.87
1976	268	2.24	0.65
1977	262	2.20	0.64
1978	249	2.14	0.60
1979	289	2.52	0.70
1980	251	2.25	0.61
1981	217	1.95	0.52
1982	211	1.86	0.50
1983	229	2.02	0.54
Totals	2336		
Annual Means	259.5	2.41	0.62

[*] Source: Matulia 1985: A-3 - A-5.

Before rejecting this estimate on the intuitive grounds that police in the volatile cities studied by Matulia are likely to account for a disproportionate number of police homicides, one should take two considerations into account. First, as will be discussed later, there is considerable evidence that (all other things being equal) departments that have carefully restricted officers' shooting discretion are likely to experience fewer police homicides than those that have not. In virtually all of the big departments studied by Matulia such policies were in effect during at least some of the years he studied, but these policies were far less common among smaller agencies. Most recently, for example, Neilsen (1983) found that no written deadly force policies existed in 12 percent of the police agencies and 46 percent of the sheriff's departments that responded to his five-state sample of departments serving populations of 20,000 or more. Second, the association between population size and police homicide rate is far from linear. Indeed, I found that city size was associated only marginally with annual homicide rate per 100,000 population from 1975 through 1983 in the cities studied by Matulia (r=+.06), and that association of city size with annual homicide rate per 1,000 officers was slightly negative (r=-.08).

My estimate of 1,000 deaths per year is highly speculative because qualitative differences exist between policing in America's big cities and in the nation's other police jurisdictions; these differences may affect the probability of police shooting in ways we have not identified. Thus the best that can be said is that even Matulia's data—the most comprehensive ever collected—give us only a limited picture of the extent of police use of deadly force in the United States and include only some unknown fraction of those killed by the police. The good news in Table 30.2 is that the trend of police homicides in the cities studied by Matulia is generally downward.

It is misleading, of course, to treat America's highly decentralized police agencies as a monolith. As Table 30.3 illustrates, Matulia's data include some fascinating variations across regions and cities. Most generally, the data indicate that the probability of officers' being involved in fatal shootings or other forms of homicide was lowest in the northeast (rate=1.39) and greatest in the south (rate=3.10), with considerable variation among the cities within each region.

Explanations of Variations in Police Homicide Rates

In attempts to explain why officers in some police departments are more likely than those in others to use deadly force and to kill, researchers generally have identified two sets of variables as salient. One is environmental and lies beyond the direct control of police administrators; the other is internal and is subject to control by police chiefs. The former category includes such variables as the level of violence among the constituencies of the police and the extent of lawful police authority to use deadly force. Included in the second category are such variables as general police operating philosophies and specific policies, both formal and unstated.

Environmental Explanations. Because police exposure to situations likely to precipitate shooting is presumably greatest where levels of general community violence are high, we would expect to find strong relationships between police homicide rates and measures of community violence and police contact with offenders. Perhaps the first researchers to explore such a hypothesis were Kania and Mackey (1977), who reported

Table 30.3
Mean Annual Rate of Police Homicide per 1,000 Officers by Geographic Region and City, 1975-1983

	Rate per 1,000	Number
Northeast	1.39	480
Boston	1.19	22
Buffalo	0.50	5
Newark	1.90	22
New York	1.36	295
Philadelphia	1.66	116
Pittsburgh	0.81	10
Rochester	1.78	10
North Central	2.24	628
Akron	0.97	4
Chicago	1.71	197
Cincinnati	1.88	17
Cleveland	2.59	44
Columbus	2.94	28
Detroit	3.33	143
Indianapolis	3.75	34
Kansas City	2.71	29
Milwaukee	0.86	16
Minneapolis	1.62	11
Omaha	2.42	12
St. Louis	3.61	64
St. Paul	0.42	2
Toledo	1.86	11
Wichita	4.33	16
South	3.10	477
Atlanta	3.28	37
Baltimore	1.82	53
Birmingham	5.19	31
Charlotte	1.31	7
Jacksonville	7.17	61
Louisville	3.11	20
Memphis	3.75	42
Miami	3.50	25
Nashville	3.28	28
New Orleans	6.80	91
Norfolk	1.68	9
Tampa	3.14	17
Washington	1.55	56
West	2.85	751
Albuquerque	1.94	9
Austin	0.87	4
Dallas	4.32	78
Denver	2.26	28
El Paso	1.88	11
Fort Worth	1.91	12

(Continued on next page)

Table 30.3 (continued)		
	Rate per 1,000	Number
West (continued)		
Honolulu	0.37	5
Houston	4.73	130
Long Beach	6.10	34
Los Angeles	3.05	192
Oakland	5.22	30
Oklahoma City	4.79	30
Phoenix	1.84	27
Portland, OR	0.81	5
Sacramento	0.44	2
San Antonio	2.74	28
San Diego	2.87	32
San Francisco	1.40	22
San Jose	2.62	19
Seattle	1.86	17
Tuscon	3.08	15
Tulsa	3.54	21
Totals	2.24	2336

strong associations between NCHS police homicide rates (however inaccurate) and rates of public homicide and violent crime across the states. In their intercity study, Sherman and Langworthy (1979) found the same kinds of associations between police homicide rates and such measures of potential police-citizen violence as gun density and rates of arrest for all offenses and for violent offenses. Finally, I (Fyfe 1980b) found strong associations between rates of shooting by on-duty officers and rates of public homicide and arrests for violent crime across 20 police subjurisdictions within New York City.

There is a statistically significant association (p=.002) between the police homicide rates shown in Table 3 and the most easily derivable measure of public violence, the corresponding public homicide rates. As even a cursory examination of the table would suggest, however (is New Orleans really four times as violent as Washington DC, for example?), this measure accounts for only 13 percent of the variation in police homicide rates (r=.37; r^2 =.13).

The table also suggests that the second environmental factor, the law of police deadly force, is of little help in explaining variation in police homicide rates. If the law were op-

erative here, one would not expect to find (for example) that officers in Long Beach (rate= 6.10) killed citizens twice as often as their colleagues across the city line in Los Angeles (rate=3.05), or that the police homicide rate in Jacksonville (7.17) was twice as high as in the more notorious Miami (3.50).[17]

Internal Organizational Explanations. Certainly the police reflect the violence of the environments in which they work, and the police are duty bound to operate within the law. Yet the limits of the law have been discussed already, and it is apparent that other things also are at work here. Most specifically, as Uelman (1973) suggested in his research on variations in shooting rates among 50 police departments in Los Angeles County, it is clear that such internal organizational variables as the philosophies, policies, and practices of individual police chiefs and supervisors account for a considerable amount of variation in police homicide rates. Uelman's conclusion has been buttressed by studies (Fyfe 1979; Gain 1971; Meyer 1980b; Milton, Malleck, Lardner, and Abrecht 1977; Scharf and Binder 1983) which report, with varying degrees of rigor and certainty, that reductions in police shooting frequency and changes in police shooting patterns have followed implementation of restrictive administrative policies on deadly force and weapons use.

A Case in Point. Without detailed analysis of the context and content of police officials' utterances and policy statements, it is impossible in an essay of this type to sort out their effects in a manner that would satisfy methodological purists.[18] Even so, the effect of police operating philosophy and policy on police deadly force has been most striking in Philadelphia. There the police commissioner in 1970 and 1971 was Frank Rizzo, the flamboyant hard-liner[19] who went on to serve as mayor from 1972 through 1979. In 1973, when the Pennsylvania legislature modified its deadly force statute to prohibit shooting at fleeing persons who were not suspected of "forcible felonies" (Pennsylvania Statutes Annotated 1973), the Philadelphia Police Department (PPD) abolished its former restrictive policy on deadly force on the grounds that the legislature had not defined "forcible felonies" adequately (see United States Civil

Rights Commission 1979: 181-83, 215-18). From that point until Rizzo left office, PPD adopted an operating style in which police were effectively free to do anything with their guns, as long as they did not use them to resolve their own personal disputes.[20]

Figure 30.1 suggests that some PPD officers took great advantage of this freedom. During 1972, the last full year in which PPD operated under a restrictive deadly force policy, the PPD homicide rate per 1,000 officers was 1.47 (with 12 deaths resulting); the rate jumped to 2.87 (23 deaths) in 1973 and peaked at 3.52 (29 deaths) in 1974. In 1976, when the city was cooperating in a federal court request to develop means of ending abuse of citizens, the police homicide rate dipped briefly to 1.35. In 1977, after the United States Supreme Court dismissed the case that had resulted in this agreement,[21] the rate doubled (deaths rose from 11 to 21). In 1981, the first full year of a new restrictive deadly force policy,[22] the rate decreased to 0.80 and remained relatively low during the next two years. Overall, the PPD police homicide rates were 2.09 while Rizzo was police commissioner, 2.29 while he was mayor, and 1.05 after he was out of office (as compared

to the annual PPD homicide rate of 0.61 over 1950-1960; see Robin 1963).

These are powerful numbers. Indeed, when I attempted to quantify Rizzo's influence over PPD operations (0=Rizzo out of office, policy in place 1980-1983; 1=Rizzo as mayor or commissioner, policy in place 1970-1973; 2-Rizzo as mayor, no policy 1974-1979), I found that the extent of his authority was a strong predictor of the annual PPD police homicide rate ($r=.72$; $p=.002$), and that adding the public homicide rate to this equation added only marginally to predictive ability ($r=.26$; $R=.78$). In short—and except for the bizarre MOVE incident—knowing what Frank Rizzo was doing was far more valuable for estimating the PPD police homicide rate than were data on public homicides.[23]

Elective and Nonelective Shootings

This analysis obviously suffers from the body count flaw; it includes only fatal shootings rather than all incidents of deadly force by PPD officers. Further, although I am convinced otherwise, many researchers will argue that my analyses of PPD homicides may have omitted some critical variable or set of variables. In addition, and if we assume for

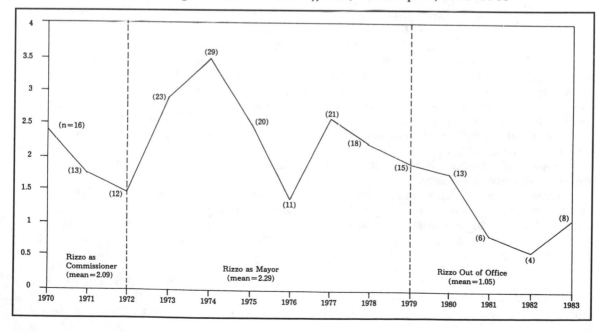

Figure 30.1
Fatal Shootings Per 1,000 Police Officers, Philadelphia, 1970–1983

the moment that I am correct in asserting that Frank Rizzo was *the* critical variable in all Philadelphia police issues during the years in question, analysis of trends in police use of deadly force typically involves far more sophistication than when police or government administrators are as straightforward as Rizzo in espousing and executing their views.

In less extreme cases, examining in detail the circumstances of shootings is perhaps the most direct way to measure the relative effects of organizational and environmental variables on officers' use of deadly force. For these purposes it is useful to conceive of police shootings as incidents on a continuum that runs from *elective* situations, in which officers may decide to shoot or to refrain from shooting at no risk to themselves or of others, to *nonelective* situations, in which officers have no choice but to shoot or to die (see Fyfe 1981c).

By these standards, Edward Garner's death—the shot at the back of the fleeing, unarmed, nonthreatening, property crime suspect who presents no apparent danger to anybody—was the prototypical elective shooting. Shootings such as this are influenced by internal police organizational variables; Garner and others in Memphis were shot in such circumstances because the police department encouraged or tolerated such action. Yet as in the case of the Memphis Police Department in 1979, the police also can put an end to such shootings by simple administrative fiat (Memphis Police Department 1979). Shootings at the other end of the continuum are a different matter; no police department can direct officers to refrain from shooting when failure to do so may mean imminent death. Formal discretionary guidelines are of little relevance in such situations because, by any reasonable standard, the officers involved have only one choice.

Between these two extremes are more ambiguous police shootings that may be influenced to varying degrees by such variables as general organizational culture and the presence or absence of training in tactics. It is my experience, for example, that officers in some departments sometimes find themselves in harm's way because they respond to encouragement, both formal and from peers, to take

charge of threatening situations quickly with as little assistance (and as little inconvenience to colleagues) as possible. In other departments, the operative norm encourages officers to use caution, to take cover, and to search for nonlethal means of resolving potential violence. These mid-range shootings typically involve officers who, for whatever reasons, find themselves dangerously close to individuals who are armed with knives or other weapons, who attempt to run them down with vehicles, or who are determined to overpower them through mere physical force. Thus, in decreasing order of potential lethality, we can derive the following typology of police shootings which will be useful in reexamining data already published elsewhere:

Gun assault: Citizen(s) armed with gun uses or attempts to use it against police.

Knife or other assault: Citizen(s) armed with cutting instrument or other weapon (e.g., bat, chain, club, hammer, vehicle) uses or attempts to use it against police.

Physical assault: Citizen(s) attacks or attempts to attack police with fists, feet, or other purely physical means.

Unarmed, no assault: Unarmed citizen(s) makes no threat and attempts no attack on police or on any other person.

As inexact as this typology may be, it does allow for some assessment of the relative extent to which police shootings are influenced by environmental and internal organizational forces. One would expect, for example, that shootings by officers whose discretion is limited carefully would tend toward the nonelective end of this continuum, and that a great percentage of shootings by officers in less stringently regulated departments would be elective.

This said, we move to Table 30. 4, which demonstrates great variation in the nature of reported shootings across Chicago, New York, and Philadelphia (p.0001). Even though the data included in the table are not absolutely compatible (my coding scheme for New York and Philadelphia includes accidental shootings and others that Geller and Karales [1981] treated separately, and that

Table 30.4
Shooting Incident Types in New York City, Philadelphia, and Chicago

Shooting Type	City		
	New York 1971-1975[a]	Philadelphia 1971-1975[a]	Chicago 1974-1978[b]
Gun Assault	53.0%	39.0%	62.1%
	(n = 481)	(n = 185)	(n = 264)
rate[c]	3.20	4.60	4.02
Knife/Other Assault	34.0%	19.6%	15.3%
	(n =308)	(n = 93)	(n = 65)
rate	2.07	2.32	0.99
Physical Assault	4.5%	16.5%	1.7%
	(n = 41)	(n = 78)	(n = 7)
rate	0.28	1.95	0.11
Unarmed, No Assault	8.5%	24.9%	20.9%
	(n = 77)	(n = 118)	(n = 89)
rate	0.52	2.94	1.36
TOTALS	100.0%	100.0%	100.0%
	(n = 907)	(n = 474)	(n = 497)[d]
rate	6.09	11.82	7.57

chi-square = 216.45
p <.0001

a.Source: Fyfe (1988). Includes all reported incidents in which police officers shot and wounded or killed others.
b.Derived from Geller and Karales (1981:103). Includes the number of persons shot rather than the number of incidents in which persons were shot. Excludes persons shot and wounded or killed for the following reasons:

Reason for shooting	n	rate[c]
Not ascertained	6	0.09
Stray bullet	17	0.26
Mistaken identity	4	0.06
Accidental	52	0.79
Other intentional	7	0.11
Civilian appeared to display an unknown object without pointing it	5	0.08
Civilian appeared to possess an unknown concealed object without pointing it.	7	0.11
Total	98	1.49

c.Mean annual rate per 1,000 officers
d.Total number of incidents in which citizens were shot

are described in Note B of the table), it is clear that shootings occurred in significantly different circumstances in the places and times included in the table. About eight in ten of the shootings in Chicago and New York involved citizens who reportedly attacked officers with guns (Chicago=62.1%; New York=53.0%), or other weapons (Chicago= 15.3%; New York=34.0%), but fewer than six in ten Philadelphia shootings (39.0% guns; 19.6% knives and other) fell into either of these two categories. At the other end of the continuum, the percentage of "unarmed, no assault" incidents in New York City, which operated under an essentially "defense of life only" deadly force policy during much of the period studied (see Fyfe 1979), was considerably smaller than in either Chicago or Philadelphia (8.5% versus 20.9% and 24.9%, respectively), where police were given relatively more freedom to use their guns in elective situations. Therefore, not surprisingly, the rates presented on the table also indicate that the greatest discrepancies among these three police agencies' shooting experiences are found at the elective end of our continuum ("unarmed, no assault" rates for New York, Philadelphia, and Chicago=0.52, 2.94, and 1.36, respectively).

The rates in this table also illustrate the dangers of attempting to describe deadly force in terms of body counts. The three departments included in Table 30.4 do not appear to differ much in regard to deadly force resulting in fatalities (1971-1975 police homicide rates per 1,000 officers=2.39 and 2.42 for New York and Philadelphia; 1974-1978 Chicago rate=1.97). When incidents resulting in nonfatal wounds are added to these figures, however, the differences among these cities grow and change direction (rates=6.09, 7.57, and 11.82 for New York, Chicago, and Philadelphia). In other words, Philadelphia police officers were only slightly more likely than New York or Chicago officers to shoot and kill citizens during the periods included in Table 4, but they were nearly twice as likely to shoot and kill or *wound* citizens. Further, because Chicago police apparently maintained records of missed shots only from 1975 through 1977 (Geller and Karales 1981: 162) and because PPD did not do so at all during the period studied, there is no way to determine with any precision how great these discrepancies might have been if we had been able to include incidents in which officers' bullets failed to hit their targets.

Even so, there is reason to believe that the differences among these cities would be even more striking if such data were available. First, police departments that permit shooting in elective situations are likely to experience high percentages of missed shots. Just as nonelective shootings are extremely dangerous for the officers involved, they are also very dangerous for their opponents. It is far easier to hit someone who is standing eight or ten feet away with a shotgun in his hands than someone who is running away in the dark (see, e.g., Horvath and Donahue 1982:87). Second, such departments also tend to experience high percentages of woundings in relation to fatalities. The four-to-one ratio of nonfatal to fatal wounds noted earlier for Philadelphia (Table 1) did not result from any extraordinary humaneness on the part of PPD officers. It came about because an extraordinary percentage of the people shot at by the

Philadelphia police were running targets; the officers fired at ranges so great that they were unable to hit the center body mass at which they were trained to shoot.

The data in my own work and in Geller and Karales's (1981) study support these assertions. The differences among police homicide rates for these cities are relatively small, but become more marked when nonfatal woundings are added to the equation. Finally, when the 1975-1977 data on all Chicago police shootings at citizens (n=1,145; Geller and Karales 1981:162) are compared to the corresponding 1971-1975 data (n=2,234; Fyfe 1978:390), the derived shooting rates per 1,000 officers differ greatly (Chicago = 29.07; New York = 14.99). It is difficult to imagine that inclusion of data from Philadelphia—where officers had by far the most liberal shooting license among these three cities—would not skew this contrast even further.

Who Gets Shot?

Subjects' Race. Regardless of the care employed in restricting officers' shooting, every study that has examined this issue found that blacks are represented disproportionately among those at the wrong end of police guns. Takagi (1974:29) found that among the 2,441 males reported by NCHS to have been killed by American police officers from 1960 through 1968, 1,188 (48.7%) were black. Using more recent figures from the same data source, Harring et al. (1977) reported that blacks' death rates from police homicide nationwide were nine to ten times as high than those of whites. Even though the data source used by both of these studies was shown subsequently to be inaccurate, the general trend of these findings is consistent with those drawn from data that probably are more reliable.

Robin (1963) reported that 28 of the 32 people (87.5%) shot and killed by Philadelphia police from 1950 through 1960 were black. Knoohuizen, Fahey, and Palmer (1972) found that blacks (then 33 percent of the Chicago population) accounted for 70.9 percent of the 79 deaths caused by intervention of Chicago police during 1969 and 1970. Milton et al. (1977:19-22) reported that 79 percent of those shot by police during 1973 and 1974 in Birmingham, Detroit, Indianapolis, Kansas

City, Oakland, Portland (Oregon), and Washington DC were black, although only 39 percent of the population in those cities was black. Meyer (1980a) found that blacks constituted 55 percent of those shot at by Los Angeles [police] although the city's total population was only 18 percent black. I (Fyfe 1981b) found that in New York City, where 20.5 percent of the population was black, 60.2 percent of those shot at by police from 1971 through 1975 were black, and that there was a strong association (r=.77; see Fyfe 1981c) between police homicide rates and percentage black population across the cities studied earlier by Sherman and Langworthy (1979). Blumberg (1981:155) reported that 78 percent of those shot by Atlanta police from 1971 through 1978 (1970 black population=51.3%) and 62 percent of those shot by Kansas City police from 1969 through 1978 (1970 black population=22.1%) were black. Geller and Karales (1981:119) reported that blacks were more than six times as likely as whites to have been shot by Chicago police from 1974 through 1978. Binder, Scharf, and Galvin (1982: IV, 273) found similar disparities between black shooting subjects and black population in Birmingham (79%:56%), Miami (51%:25%), Newark (78%:58%), and Oakland (79%:47%).

Only the ingenuous and the naive can conclude from these figures that racism is not involved in police use of deadly force. Still, we should not be quick to point accusingly at the police, either individually or as an institution. These racial disparities parallel those found in other social phenomena such as life expectancy, rates of incarceration, unemployment, infant mortality, levels of income, educational attainments, and socioeconomic status (see, e.g., United States Bureau of the Census 1974). Therefore, as in the issue of intercity variations in police shooting rates, we should ask whether and to what extent racially disparate police homicide rates may indicate that police are simply quicker to shoot blacks than whites, or whether these disparate rates may be consequences of racial variations in officers' exposure to situations likely to precipitate shooting.

John Goldkamp (1976) frames this question in terms of two conflicting "belief perspectives." The first asserts that disproportionate minority deaths [result] from both irresponsible use of deadly force by a small minority of police officers and differential administration of law enforcement toward minority citizens (which in effect produces disproportionately high arrest and death rates for minorities in general) (169).

> According to Goldkamp, adherents of Position II hold that the disproportionately high death rates of minorities at the hands of the police can be explained by the disproportionately high arrest rates of minorities for crimes of violence, or by assumptions concerning the suspect's responsibility for his/her own death in violent police-suspect interactions (16).

If the first of these two extreme positions is the more accurate, black overrepresentation among those shot at by police might be reduced by attempting to eliminate racism within policing through improved personnel screening, training, and controls on officers' shooting discretion. The implications of Goldkamp's second belief perspective, however, are far more complex. If racial disparities in police homicide statistics are largely only another manifestation of whatever forces have placed so many blacks on the low end of the American ladder generally, it follows that they can be eliminated only by major social change.

With one exception, empirical tests of these alternative theses generally support Goldkamp's second belief perspective, and offer little evidence in support of assertions that police discriminate with their trigger fingers. Researchers have found close associations between racial distributions of police shooting subjects and measures of the risk of being shot at, such as arrests for murder, robbery, aggravated assault, weapons offenses, and burglary (Harding and Fahey 1973:311), arrests for FBI Crime Index offenses (Binder, et al. 1982; IV, 124, 275), and arrests for violent Crime Index offenses (Fyfe 1981b:93; Meyer 1980a:102; Milton et al. 1977:19-22).

These correlations, of course, tell us little about whether both arrest and deadly force statistics are the results of discriminatory police practices. Thus some researchers also have attempted to determine whether the circumstances in which officers employ deadly force vary by subjects' race. I (Fyfe 1981b) found that in New York City robberies precipitated far more police shootings involving black subjects (45.8%) than white or Hispanic subjects (23.4% and 26.9%). More to the point, I also found that shootings at black subjects were clustered closer to the hazardous end of the elective-nonelective continuum discussed earlier than were shootings at whites. The percentage of black shooting subjects armed with handguns, rifles, machine guns, or shotguns (60.5%) was nearly twice as high as that of whites (35.4%; Hispanics=53.7%); white subjects were unarmed and not assaultive (15.5%) about twice as often as blacks (7.8%; Hispanics=5.1%). Finally, I found that the subjects race made little difference in the percentages of subjects wounded or killed among racial groups.

Blumberg's (1981) findings on this question were similar. Regardless of race, he reported, approximately seven in ten of those shot by Atlanta police and half of those shot by Kansas City police from 1971 through 1978 had attacked officers with weapons. He also found that neither the intensity of officers' responses (measured by the numbers of officers who shot and of police shots fired) nor the consequences of their responses (ratio of nonfatal to fatal wounds) varied by subjects' race. Nor do Binder et al. (1982: IV, 279-99) report measurable variation by subjects' race in Birmingham, Miami, Newark, or Oakland. In those four cities, the percentages of blacks and whites who attacked officers when they were shot were identical (47%), and the percentages of both races who fled (44% for blacks; 42% for whites) were nearly the same.

Geller and Karales (1981:123-25) reported slightly different findings. Their data indicated that nearly six in ten blacks and Hispanics shot by Chicago police (55% and 56% respectively) had used or threatened to use guns against officers, but that blacks also were more likely than whites or Hispanics to have been shot during "flight without other resistance" (blacks= 19%; whites and Hispanics each= 12%).

Meyer's (1980a:105) analysis reported that 28 percent of the 321 blacks shot at by Los Angeles police (LAPD) from 1974 through, 1978 were unarmed, as against 20 percent of 131 whites and 22 percent of 126 Hispanics. Yet far more theoretically and practically interesting than these relatively minor percentage differences are Meyer's (1980a:107) findings concerning LAPD's adjudications of these incidents. The department found that officers had acted against policy and/or were deserving of administrative disapproval in 43 percent of cases involving unarmed Hispanics and 46 percent of cases involving unarmed whites, but in only 33 percent of cases involving unarmed blacks. Stated in another way, 10.8 percent of the cases in which LAPD officers shot at whites involved unarmed subjects and concluded with findings that officers had acted reasonably; the comparable percentage for black subjects is 18.2.

Certainly these cases may vary in ways not captured by Meyer's "unarmed" classification; as he acknowledges, his findings are based on a relatively small number of incidents. Still, as he observed, when the subjects' race was taken into account, LAPD's shooting review process "produced somewhat different results for shootings that may have deserved the closest scrutiny by review boards and are frequently the most controversial" (1980a:107).[24]

Adherents of Goldkamp's first belief perspective on deadly force are likely to interpret these data as a sign that LAPD was consciously more tolerant toward shootings of unarmed blacks than of unarmed whites. This may be the case, but it is also plausible that such a conspiratorial interpretation oversimplifies more subtle and complex phenomena. In Los Angeles, as elsewhere, race and place are associated closely. Blacks generally live and spend their time in ghettos characterized by relatively high rates of crime; whites generally live in and frequent more affluent and less violent areas. In Los Angeles, as elsewhere, ghetto police quickly learn that they work in a violent environment. Their workload is heavier and more demanding than that of their colleagues in country club districts; in my experience, their expectations also differ. Ghetto police officers learn quickly that they can expect anything when they respond to reports of trouble, and usually are very careful to make themselves immune from attack. Officers in outlying police districts, however, find more often that most reports of crimes turn out to be false alarms, and that street fights involve verbal disputes over parking spaces more often than armed combat. Consequently officers in outlying districts typically employ far less often the defensive tactics that are part of the ghetto officer's regular *modus operandi*.

Police brass, who have usually done field police work in a variety of environments, are aware of these differences. As a result, their definitions of reasonableness also may vary with the characteristics of the areas and the people involved in police actions. In Los Angeles, perhaps the city in which one must cross the greatest distances to travel between *safe* and *dangerous* communities, one would expect these differences to be most pronounced. Thus it is not surprising that those who review police shootings may be more likely to give the benefit of the doubt to an officer who misinterpreted a "furtive movement" on the part of a black man in Watts than to an officer who shot a white man in similar circumstances in the San Fernando Valley.

If this interpretation is correct, it leads us to ask whether the people who review police shootings act justifiably if they take place— and therefore race— into account along with citizen and police actions during their deliberations. Meyer's data are far too limited to provide a definitive answer to this question, but even if we allow for such considerations, we risk accusations of hypocrisy if we accuse LAPD of arbitrariness on such grounds. Considerations of place and race are not unique to the police; they reflect the same judgments that many people make when they avoid buying homes or taking late-night strolls in areas like Watts, but do not think twice about engaging in such activities in areas like the Valley. They also reflect the differential expectations of people who are asked for the time on dark inner-city streets and those who have precisely the same experience in suburban shopping malls. In short, as long as some American neighborhoods are perceived *realistically* as dangerous places that should be

avoided whenever possible, we should be neither surprised nor damning if we find that police administrators may take the same considerations into account when judging the actions of officers who are not free to avoid dangerous neighborhoods and who shoot occasionally at the people who live in them. If Meyer's data are not merely accidental, they do show a racist effect in review of LAPD police shootings. This effect, however, may have less connection with arbitrariness on the part of the police than with the fact that the police work in a society that itself is so arbitrary regarding issues of race.

Perhaps the clearest evidence of police arbitrariness in exercise of deadly force is found in my analyses of Memphis police shootings (published in part in Fyfe 1982). There, in examining data obtained by the NAACP Legal Defense Fund in discovery proceedings during the *Garner* litigation, I found that blacks were far more likely than whites to have been shot, or shot at, during elective encounters with police. From 1969 through 1976 (less January 15 to December 31, 1972, a period in which no data were available), Memphis police shot and killed 39 citizens, five of whom were not identified by race. Of the 26 blacks among the remaining 34 subjects, seven (26.9%) were assaultive and armed with guns, as compared to five (62.5%) of the eight whites; 13 blacks (50%) and one white (12.5%) were unarmed and not assaultive when they were killed. When standardized on population, these figures showed that although black Memphians were about twice as likely as whites to be killed when using guns to threaten or fire on police with guns (rates=2.9 and 1.3 per 100,000 population, respectively), they were 18 times as likely as whites to die from police bullets when unarmed, not assaultive, and generally running away. From 1969 through 1974, Memphis police shot at 112 property crime suspects, 96 (85.7%) of whom were black. These figures showed that black property crime suspects were more than twice as likely as white suspects to have been fired at by police (black shooting rate per 1,000 black property crime arrestees=4.3; white rate=1.8). Black suspects were nearly three times as likely as white to have been fired at and missed (black rate=3.2 missed shootings per 1,000 black property crime arrestees; white rate=1.2), six times as likely to have suffered nonfatal bullet wounds during the course of such arrests (black rate=0.6 per 1,000 arrests; white rate=0.1 per 1,000), and slightly more likely to have been shot and killed during officers' attempts to effect property crime arrests (black rate=0.6; white rate=0.5). The numbers also showed that Memphis officers were 15 times more likely to shoot at black property crime suspects (206 shootings per 1,000 officers) than at white property crime suspects (rate=14.3 per 1,000 officers). Overall, therefore, these data suggest that Memphis police used their broad authority to shoot in elective situations when their targets were black, and that typically they refrained from doing so when white subjects were involved.[25]

Who Does the Shooting?

Police work would be far simpler if we were able to distinguish between trigger-happy officers and those unlikely to shoot except under the most extreme provocation. Findings regarding the characteristics of officers involved in shootings are mixed, however; they give little guidance to policy makers beyond the advice that they should avoid hiring or retaining officers with extreme obvious pathologies, and that they should limit shooting discretion carefully so that officers' individual prejudices are given little chance for expression.[26]

Officers' Race. Race is the most hotly discussed officer characteristic related to deadly force. Champions of representativeness in policing (among whom I count myself most enthusiastically) have long argued that one of the most promising routes to reducing police-citizen violence is to increase the percentage of minority officers. Presumably these officers are attuned more closely to the problems and folkways of the minority citizens who are disproportionately the subjects of police deadly force and police attention generally (see, e.g., Clark 1974; Jenkins and Faison 1974; United States Civil Rights Commission 1981: 153-55).

The relevant research, however, does not lead easily to such a simplistic conclusion be-cause the role of officers' race in police shootings is confounded by many other variables. When I first reported that black NYPD officers were about twice as likely as white officers to have shot or shot at citizens (Fyfe 1978:207), I received protest from black friends who were convinced that I was in error and congratulations from other people who were convinced that my findings demonstrated that black officers were quicker on the trigger than whites. Both sides were wrong. My finding demonstrated only that black NYPD officers—both on-duty and off-duty—typically worked and lived in environments that were far more violent than those frequented by white officers. Much of the disparity between black and white NYPD shooting rates was attributable to the fact that black officers were involved in off-duty shootings about six times as often as white officers, largely because black officers more often lived in and frequented the city's high-crime areas. In those areas their chances of encountering situations leading to shooting, justifiable or otherwise, were far greater than those of their suburban-dwelling white colleagues.[27]

Disparities in on-duty shooting rates were attributable largely to racial differences in rank and assignment. One in six white NYPD officers (16.5%) held a supervisory or administrative rank (sergeant or above) in which exposure to street-level violence was limited or nil; fewer than one in 20 black officers (4.6%) held such a position. Among the remaining police officers and detectives, blacks were posted to high-risk assignments far more often than whites; in the final analysis, the shooting rates of black and white patrol officers in New York's euphemistically labeled "high experience precincts," who account for most NYPD shootings, were virtually indistinguishable (white officers' rate over five years = 196.5 per 1,000 officers, with n of 1,265; black rate=198.6, n=204; Hispanic rate=210.2, n=70) (Fyfe 1981d; see also Geller and Karales 1981 for similar findings in Chicago).

This research does not address whether overall police shooting rates would be considerably higher if not for the presence of substantial numbers of minority officers in ghettos. I tend to believe that if inner-city police were still the near lily-white occupying armies characterized so cuttingly by James Baldwin (1962:61-62) a quarter-century ago, considerably more shooting by police would occur in American cities.

Officers' Age. Intuition suggests that older— and presumably less impulsive—officers may be more likely than younger officers to refrain from shooting. I (Fyfe 1978: 356-71), however, found that when the NYPD's 3,000 junior officers were laid off and replaced in the field by 2,200 older officers who had been transferred from nonstreet assignments, the rate of officers' shooting did not decline. Instead the layoffs apparently served only to increase the mean age and length of service of officers involved in line-of-duty shootings. Binder et al. (1982), who found no significant differences between the age distributions of shooters and of nonshooters in the departments they studied, did report that shooters were over-represented among younger officers, but this disparity may be an artifact of age-related variations in assignment and in exposure to potential shooting situations. Blumberg (1983:117-39), in contrast, compared shooters with those who had not fired their guns among Atlanta and Kansas City officers. Even when attempting to control for exposure to risk of shooting, he found that younger officers were somewhat more likely than older officers to have fired their guns.

The Best and the Brightest. The research on officers' intellectual capacity and educational attainment is not much more informative than research on age. Binder et al. (1982) found that shooters were less well educated than nonshooters, but again, their findings may be confounded by educationally related variations in risk. Police officers with college degrees are far more likely to be operating their department's computers than are officers who hold only general equivalency diplomas, and shootings rarely occur inside police headquarters. My analyses of the relationship between officers' IQ scores and NYPD adjudications of shootings (previously unreported) confuse the picture further. I found that the percentage of shootings condemned by the department was about twice

as high among "dull" officers (IQ scores below 90) as among "dull-normal," "normal," or "bright-normal" officers (IQ scores of 90 to 124), but that the percentage of shootings by "very bright" officers (who had scored 125 or higher on test with a maximum score of 133) disapproved by the department also was twice as high as that among their normal and bright-normal colleagues. This finding, too, is related closely to assignment. During the period in question, NYPD's brightest officers typically enjoyed administrative assignments in which the risk of engaging in *legitimate* violence was minimal. Consequently the percentage of their shootings that involved *illegitimate* violence (e.g., off-duty personal disputes) was far higher than among less intellectually gifted officers.

The Twenty-Four-Hour Cop. The issue of off-duty shootings is substantial. Milton et al. (1977:27) reported that 17 percent of the 320 shootings they studied in Birmingham, Detroit, Indianapolis, Kansas City, Oakland, Portland (Oregon), and Washington DC involved off-duty officers. I (Fyfe 1980a) found a similar percentage in New York City, and reported that many of NYPD's off-duty shootings were "bad"; 41.5 percent resulted in administrative condemnations, 3.8 percent were suicide attempts, 12.6 percent were accidents, and even many of those found to be justifiable involved officers who made bad situations worse by resorting quickly to firearms when they found themselves suddenly in the middle of restaurant or bar robberies. Geller and Karales (1981:87) reported that 23 percent of Chicago shootings involved off-duty officers, and (1981:9) that 38 percent (*n*=71) of the Chicago officers who were shot during the period they studied were shot by themselves or by other officers, frequently in off-duty situations.

Perhaps the most stunning data on off-duty officers' use of firearms are included in a report that describes the 92 incidents in which Detroit police killed citizens from January 1, 1975 through June 30, 1979 (Hart 1979). Twenty (21.7%) of these incidents involved off-duty officers who killed 23 persons, excluding suicides. Among these were two burglars, one robber, and one murderer. One officer, however, killed his wife and himself; another killed his wife and their two children; two officers killed their husbands; another killed his estranged wife and himself; another killed his girlfriend; another killed his wife accidentally; another killed his ex-wife's husband and committed suicide two months later; three others killed four people (two of whom were armed) during barroom altercations; and three others killed three people (two of whom were armed) during street altercations.

Figures such as these have caused a rethinking of the traditional police wisdom that officers should be required to carry their guns at all times. In 1982 The International Association of Chiefs of Police (IACP) (Matulia 1982) promulgated a model policy which recommended that off-duty officers be permitted—but not required—to carry guns.[28]

Conclusions

On balance, and even though the available data are skimpier than we would like, it appears that the frequency of police use of deadly force is influenced heavily by organizational philosophies, expectations, and policies; that levels of community violence are marginal predictors, useful chiefly when organizational variables may be held constant (as in studying a single police jurisdiction); and that variations in law play a role in determining frequency of deadly force only when administrators abdicate their responsibility to see that propriety is not limited only by statutory definitions of criminal assault and homicide.

For this last reason, *Tennessee v. Garner* probably is not as sweeping as many suspect. By the time this case was decided, virtually all major police departments had adopted their own administrative policies that were at least as restrictive as the *violent* felon rule propounded by the Supreme Court. In his decision for the majority, in fact, Justice White made repeated suggestions that the Court's holding was not a major intervention into police administrative prerogatives because most large police departments already were in compliance. Indeed, the fact that Memphis itself had abolished administratively the *any* fleeing felon rule five years before the case

came to the Court (Memphis Police Department 1979) weakened seriously the city attorney's oral argument that the *any* fleeing felon rule was a valuable adjunct to the effectiveness of law enforcement. Thus it is likely that the major effects of *Garner* will be (and have been) felt in smaller police jurisdictions where, as Neilsen (1983) suggests, administrative rule making related to deadly force has been less frequent.

Still, although *Garner* itself will not revolutionize American law enforcement, the process leading up to it has altered dramatically the police community's view of the whole deadly force issue. As recently as 1980, for example, attendees at the annual IACP meeting voted "by a 4-to-1 margin reaffirming [the association's] support of laws and policies permitting police to shoot fleeing felony suspects." (*St. Louis Post-Dispatch* 1980). In the same year, the International Union of Police Associations passed a resolution seeking to remove Patrick Murphy "as President of a private corporation known as the Police Foundation and to boycott any organization or foundation that supports the Police Foundation" because Murphy had criticized "police officers' use of weapons," "notoriously accused our nation's police officers as the immediate cause of the riots that took place in the 60's," indicated that four police officers who had been acquitted in a Miami beating death (a verdict which sparked Miami's Liberty City riot) had committed the beating of which they were accused, and had "further stated that a restrictive shooting policy not only reduces police shootings of civilians but does not result in any increased danger to police officers or a rise in crime" (International Union of Police Associations 1980).

By 1982, however, IACP had promulgated a model policy on police use of force that would permit shooting at fleeing felony suspects only when "freedom is reasonably believed to represent an *imminent* threat of grave bodily harm or death to the officer or other person(s)" (Matulia 1982:164; emphasis in original). In 1983 IACP joined in recommending that the Commission on Accreditation for Law Enforcement Agencies adopt its present strict *defense of life only* standard for deadly force policies (1983:1-2). In 1984 the

Police Foundation's *amici curiae* brief against Tennessee and the Memphis Police Department in *Garner* was joined by "nine national and international associations of police and criminal justice professionals, the chiefs of police associations of two states, and thirty-one law enforcement chief executives" (Police Foundation 1984).[29] Equally significant, and contrary to past practice in cases of substantial constitutional issues involving the police, no *amicus* briefs were filed on the other side of the case. In 1985, when *Garner* was decided, IACP's executive director hailed it as a great step forward. This remarkable turnaround and disavowal of tradition and professional dogma was stimulated in large measure by research findings which suggested that the value of broad police shooting authority was overrated; rarely have researchers had such an effect on criminal justice policies and practices.[30]

Research regarding the people involved in incidents of deadly force by police generally shows that blacks and other minorities are overrepresented at both ends of police guns. Explanations for these disparities vary, but at least by my interpretation they typically involve embarrassing realities over which police have little control. Black citizens are overrepresented in the most violent and most criminogenic neighborhoods; individual black officers, who are still underrepresented in American policing generally, are far more likely than individual white officers to draw the most hazardous police duties in those same neighborhoods. Until these realities are altered, we can expect continuing minority disproportion in deadly force statistics no matter how stringently police officers' discretion is controlled.

This probability, I think, illustrates the central theme that may be drawn from all the research on deadly force reviewed in this essay. Police officers and the people at whom they shoot are simply actors in a much larger play. When police officers' roles in this play are defined carefully by their administrators and when the officers have been trained well to perform those roles, their individual characteristics mean little; the young cop, the old cop, the male cop, the female cop, the white cop, and the black cop all know what is expected of them, and they do it. When such clear expectations are not provided, officers improvise, and often we give their performances bad reviews. Yet because we put them on the stage in the first place, we also should criticize ourselves for failing to assure that they have been directed adequately.[31] When black children's roles are defined so clearly by the conditions in which so many are raised, we should expect that some will end their lives at the wrong end of police guns. We should not blame the police for that; we should blame ourselves for creating the stages on which so many black lives are played out.

Notes

1. Others with quasi-police functions (e.g., correctional officers and workers at mental institutions) typically bear a more limited version of this authority.

2. Although police also have used such lethal means of force as neckholds, other martial arts techniques, and even bombs, gunshots are far more frequent. Thus, for purposes of this essay, deadly force and shooting at human beings will be treated as synonyms.

3. By and large, writers in law reviews also appear to have left this subject alone until the mid-1960s (see the literature reviews in Geller and Karales 1981 and Sherman 1980).

4. Although we cannot assess easily the extent to which state deadly force laws may have been modified by court decisions, in 1985, 19 states had codified the *any* fleeing felon rule; four others had no statute but apparently followed the rule. Through statute or case law, 22 others followed some variety of the *violent* fleeing felon rule; the laws of the remaining states are unclear (see Fyfe 1986; Winter 1986).

5. The exception is Rodney Stark, who made the following comment on Robin's (1963) finding that Akron police were 45 times more likely than Boston police to have killed citizens: "[S]uch enormous differences in rates suggest either that the police in some cities are supermen, or that those in other cities are killers" (1972:65).

6. The lieutenant had intervened in a street altercation between the group of which the boy was a part and a building superintendent who apparently had sprayed them with a garden hose (National Advisory Commission 1968:36).

7. In a contemporaneous study of 45 of the 51 American police departments in cities with populations over 250,000, it was found that three forces had no written deadly force policies whatever and that in many other cases, deadly force policy consisted only of vague advice to use caution and good judgment (Cincinnati Police Department 1964).

8. See also, *United States v. Clark* (1887): Suppose, for example, a person were arrested for petit larceny, which is a felony at the common law, might an officer under any circumstances be justified in killing him? I think not. The punishment is altogether too disproportionate to the offense.

9. Under Tennessee law, 15-year-olds must be treated as juveniles unless they are accused of violent offenses, among which the law does not include burglary (Tennessee Code Annotated: 27-234 (1977)).

10. Readers who have not followed *Garner* might be surprised to learn that the case was decided on Fourth Amendment grounds rather than on an intuitively appealing Eighth Amendment argument of denial of due process/punishment without trial (see, e.g., Sherman 1980). During the 11 years of litigation between young Garner's death and the Supreme Court's resolution of his father's action, this argument was raised and rejected by lower courts on the grounds that punishment was a judicial rather than a police function. If that was true, reasoned, Garner's attorneys, their case was framed best in terms of the police function—arrest—and shootings to apprehend were cast as a form of seizure (see *Garner v. Memphis Police Department* [1979]).

11. The relevant Illinois law at the time of *Garner*, for example, included burglary under the "forcible felony" heading in which deadly force for apprehension was justified (Illinois Revised Statutes 1975). Also see Fyfe (1986) and Uviller (1986) for more detailed discussion of *Garner's* apparent effects on state law.

12. There also are many problems related to enforcement of criminal statutes governing police deadly force. Except perhaps in cases of money corruption, prosecutors typically are reluctant to charge the police, with whom they regularly work closely; grand jurors are reluctant to indict officers, and petit juries rarely convict (see Kobler 1975a, 1975b; United States Civil Rights Commission 1981:101-16).

13. After consulting and testifying in 100-odd civil cases emanating from police shootings, I see clearly that jurors are far more sympathetic to street police officers than to police chiefs. Jurors typically are very reluctant to place blame for bad shootings on officers who sit before them at defense tables day after day, in obvious agony over the tragedies to which they have been a party. Yet in their anxiety to right the wrongs done to victims of bad shootings, jurors are far less charitable toward abstract bureaucracies or toward police brass—who do not appear in court, or who testify briefly and leave—when plaintiffs' attorneys suggest that both police shooters and the persons shot have been victimized by police chiefs' failure to give officers direction in their most critical decisions.

14. In both Birmingham and Kansas City, Missouri, for example, police chiefs who promulgated restrictive shooting policies suffered severe criticism from segments of both their departments and the public (see, e.g., Sherman 1983).

15. Matulia's (1982:161) survey reported that as of 1980, 46 (86.8%) of 54 respondent police departments in cities with populations of more than 250,000 had administratively prohibited shooting at unarmed nonviolent fleeing felony suspects. An unpublished survey (Police Executive Research Forum 1982) of 75 police departments in jurisdictions with populations over 100,000 reported that 74 departments prohibited such shootings.

16. Perhaps the most puzzling of these discrepancies is that between the Horvath and Donahue (1982) figures for Detroit (79 fatalities between September 1, 1976 and August 31, 1981) and the most comparable data from Matulia (1985), which indicate 100 fatalities during calendar years 1976 through 1981. Because an earlier Detroit Police Department report (Hart 1979) counts 64 fatal shootings from January 1, 1976 through June 30, 1979 (as opposed to 67 in Matulia's data), it is probable that the Horvath and Donahue data are undercounted.

The reason that my New York data agree with the FBI's, I have long speculated, is that my work may be the source of the FBI's statistics. I collected the New York data in the table while I was a New York City police officer, and despite my insider's status, inquiries, and lengthy contact with every appropriate official, I never heard any word whatever that NYPD reported any data on police killings to the FBI. Indeed until 1971, NYPD's only internal repository for data on police shootings was operated on a catch-as-catch-can basis by the lieutenant in charge of firearms training. Nor does all my work agree with the corresponding FBI figures; during the *Garner* litigation, I was provided with data indicating that Memphis police had shot and killed 39 people during the eight years from 1969 through 1976 (Fyfe 1983). Matulia's (1985) data (which, in the case of Memphis, came exclusively from the Supplementary Homicide Report) indicate that Memphis police shot and killed 40 people during the seven years from 1970 through 1976.

17. Nor, with the exception of Texas, are intrastate variations such as these attributable in any significant measure to variations in community violence among the cities studied by Matulia. The correlation coefficients between public and police homicide rates in the states that include three or more of these cities (among which the law of police deadly force is a constant rather than a variable) are as follows:

State	n of cities	r	p
California	7	+.40	.18
Florida	3	-.53	.31
New York	3	+.13	.46
Ohio	3	+.49	.25
Texas	6	+.85	.01

18. It also is difficult at times to interpret the relationship between police policies and practices and deadly force rates. Matulia (1985:13), for example, reports positive associations between police homicide rates and the issuance of shotguns to officers, the use of on-duty weapons larger than .38 caliber, marksmanship awards, officer "survival" training, and simulator, stress, and physical exertion firearms training. To the extent that these variables may be related causally to shooting rates, however, the direction of causality is unclear. At this writing, for example, the Washington, DC area has experienced a rash of (largely drug-related) shootings of and by officers, and several police departments have responded by exchanging officers' .38 caliber revolvers for more potent 9-millimeter automatics (see, e.g., Yorke 1988:Cl). Aside from its merits, such a move is a reaction to increased violence between police and citizens, as (I suspect from my own experiences) are many of the training programs designed to assist officers in dealing with high levels of violence. In short, where extreme violence between police and citizens is not a problem, it is likely that there is no perceived need for big guns and the like. Consequently, Matulia's findings probably should not be read as a recommendation to eliminate specialized training in the interests of reducing violence between police and citizens.

19. Former Mayor Rizzo perhaps is best known for his advice that officers should "break their heads before they break yours." My favorite Rizzoism, however, dates from late 1979, when, in response to a question about a United States Justice Department suit against his administration and the Philadelphia Police Department, Rizzo commented on ABC-TV's *Nightline* that "when I became mayor, the Philadelphia Police Department had only one shotgun. Now we've got enough guns to invade Cuba and win."

20. Despite extensive review of PPD reports of all firearms discharges resulting in injury or death from 1970 through 1978, for example, I can find only two cases that resulted in departmental discipline against officers who had fired their guns while on duty. In one case an officer shot and killed his wife in a police station during an apparent argument over the disposition of his paycheck; the other resulted in the two-day suspension of an officer who had fired unnecessary shots into the air.

21. *Rizzo v. Goode* (1976), which had been brought by the brother of the present mayor of Philadelphia.

22. The policy (Philadelphia Police Department 1980) was promulgated on April 2, 1980. It authorizes officers to shoot in defense of life and, when no alternative exists, to apprehend fleeing suspects who officers know are in possession of deadly weapons that they have used or threatened to use, or who have committed forcible felonies. Of these last, PPD's position was as follows: Until forcible felony is defined by statute, the Police Department adopts the position that forcible felony includes the crimes of Murder, Voluntary Manslaughter, Rape, Robbery, Kidnapping, Involuntary Deviate Sexual Intercourse, Arson, Burglary of a Private Residence, Aggravated Assault Causing Serious Bodily Injury (Davis 1980).

23. Waegel (1984) suggested that an increase in PPD shootings followed the 1973 narrowing of the Pennsylvania deadly force statute. He concluded correctly that in the absence of commitment by police administrators, the law has little effect on shooting frequency. The analysis by which Waegel reached that conclusion is flawed, however, because the data available to him included only about two-thirds (459 of 744) of the incidents in

which PPD officers shot citizens during the period he studied (1971-1978). This gap is interesting in itself because it indicates that despite the best efforts of the Public Interest Law Corporation of Philadelphia (the source of Waegel's data) to monitor PPD police shootings, it did not learn of 245 incidents in which citizens were killed or wounded by the police. Yet despite its flaws, the trend of Waegel's work is correct. It supports the idea that the locus of control over police shootings is the chief's office, and that the law becomes a factor only when the officer's discretion is not guided more clearly by departmental philosophies, policies, and training. In Philadelphia during those years the law was not a factor because it was simply ignored.

24. As far as I have been able to determine, my doctoral dissertation is the only other published work that examines questions of subjects' race and departmental review of shootings. I found that the New York City Police Department reached negative findings (retraining, which approximates LAPD's "administrative disapproval" category; discipline; arrest; referral to mental health counseling) in 52 percent of the 221 incidents involving intentional shooting at unarmed persons from August 1972 through December 1975 (*n*=221), and that case dispositions did not vary with either officers' or subjects' race (see, generally, Fyfe 1978:399-480).

25. These data served as the basis for Garner's Fourteenth Amendment argument that blacks were denied equal protection under law because Memphis police used Tennessee's *any* fleeing felon statute against them, but typically refrained from doing so against whites. This argument was rejected by the trial court on the grounds that the rule was not employed exclusively against blacks, and that Garner Sr. could not show any evidence of racism in the specific case of his son's death. See *Garner v. Memphis Police Department* (1981). During appeals, the equal protection argument was addressed by neither the Sixth Circuit (*Garner v. Memphis Police Department* (1983) nor the Supreme Court, both of whom decided the case exclusively on Fourth Amendment grounds.

When one puts these decisions into the context of *McCleskey v. Georgia* (1987), a clear lesson emerges for social scientists and lawyers: statistics that suggest *patterns* of racial discrimination in decisions by the criminal justice system do not convince courts that decisions in specific cases are the result of discrimination. McCleskey employed University of Iowa professor David Baldus's statistical analyses to argue that he was the victim of racial discrimination in application of Georgia's death penalty statute. Like Garner's argument at trial, this claim was rejected by the Supreme Court on grounds that Baldus's analyses did not demonstrate specific racial animus in the case of McCleskey's death sentence.

26. Because of the fairly recent entry of females into police work, no meaningful comparisons exist yet between male and female officers' propensities to employ deadly force. In addition, the value of studies of the relationships between officers' characteristics and propensity to violence typically has been limited by the narrow ranges of most of these variables. Whether or not he shot justifiably, for example, the modal NYPD shooter from 1971 through 1975 was a 29-year-old, 5'11", married white male from a blue-collar background who possessed less than two years of post-secondary education, had a bright-normal IQ, had become a police officer in 1968 or 1969, and was assigned to a patrol car in one of the city's "high experience" precincts. None of this information distinguished him from the vast majority of the nonshooters with whom he worked.

27. Interestingly, the great racial disparities among rates of off-duty police shooting were not attributable entirely to disproportionate minority involvement in legitimate off-duty law enforcement situations. Just as blacks apparently encountered and fired in such situations six times as often as whites, they also suffered administrative or criminal penalties for shooting six times as frequently as whites. The experience of Hispanic NYPD officers was similar to that of blacks (Fyfe 1978:198).

28. In the Police Foundation's 1978 survey of the a administrative practices of 49 major police departments (Heaphy 1978) it was found that 24 departments (49%) required officers to carry guns while off duty. The next and more expansive survey of this type (Police Executive Research Forum and Police Foundation 1981:132-40) found that only 24.4 percent (30) of 123 respondent departments retained the off-duty gun requirement. The Chicago Police Department dropped its off-duty gun requirement on December 23, 1980. In 1981 the New York City Police Department, which effects about 185,000 arrests per year, conducted a study which found that off-duty officers (who account for about 100 firearms

discharges annually) made a total of 175 arrests during 1980. On the basis of this finding that off duty officers accounted for fewer than one arrest in 1,000—but for one shooting in five—NYPD dropped its requirement that officers carry firearms at all times while within city limits (*Law Enforcement News* 1981).

29. One of the joiners was the Academy of Criminal Justice Sciences. Two additional state police chiefs' associations agreed to join the brief too late to be included among signers.

30. This observation is tempered by the knowledge that increased governmental exposure to civil liability for failure to supervise police officers adequately has served also as a major stimulant to reform of deadly force policies and practices. Almost certainly, *Monell v. New York City Department of Social Services* (1978), in which the Supreme Court holds government entities liable when unreasonable policies and practices are proved to be the causes of constitutional violations suffered at the hands of individual agents, has had more effect on police operations than have any of the court's more celebrated rulings related to criminal procedure.

31. One area in which such direction apparently is needed involves police encounters with the mentally disturbed. During the 1970s, such events accounted for very small percentages of police shootings (1.6% in New York, Fyfe 1978:679; 0.6% in Chicago, Geller and Karales 1981:89). Since that time, however, I have received the impression that at least among shootings that result in controversy and civil suits against police, far higher percentages result from police encounters with mentally disturbed people. Apparently the deinstitutionalization movement of the last decade has created a major new problem for police (see Murphy 1986).

References

American Civil Liberties Union (1966) *Police Power vs. Citizens' Rights*. New York: American Civil Liberties Union.

American Law Institute (1931) 9 *ALI Proceedings* 186-87. (statement of Professor Mikell).

Baldwin, J. (1962) *Nobody Knows My Name*. New York: Dell.

Binder, A. and P. Scharf (1980) "The Violent Police-Citizen Encounter." *Annals of the American Academy of Political and Social Science* 452:111-21.

Binder, A., P. Scharf, and R. Galvin (1982) "Use of Deadly Force by Police Officers." Final Report Submitted to the National Institute of Justice, Grant 79-NI-AX-0134, December 1982.

Bivens v. Six Unknown Agents, 403 U.S. 388 (1971).

Blumberg, M. (1981) "Race and Police Shootings: An Analysis in Two Cities." In J. Fyfe (ed.), *Contemporary Issues in Law Enforcement*. Beverly Hills: Sage, pp. 152-166.

—— (1983) "The Use of Firearms by Police Officers: The Impact of Individuals, Communities and Race." Ph.D. dissertation, State University of New York at Albany. Ann Arbor: University Microfilms.

Boutwell, J.P. (1977) "Use of Deadly Force to Arrest a Fleeing Felon—A Constitutional Challenge."*FBI Law Enforcement Bulletin* 46:9-14.

Chapman, S.G. (1967) *Police Firearms Use Policy*. Report to the President's Commission on Law Enforcement and Administration of Justice. Washington DC: United States Government Printing Office.

—— and T.S. Crockett., (1963) "Gunsight Dilemma: Police Firearms Policy." *Police* 6:40-45.

Chicago Police Department (1980) General Order 80-20, December 23.

Cincinnati Police Department (1964) *Police Regulations Governing Use of Firearms Survey*, mimeo: April 22.

Clark, K.B. (1974) "Open Letter to Mayor Abraham D. Beame and Police Commissioner Michael J. Codd." Unpublished, New York, September 17, 1974.

Commission on Accreditation for Law Enforcement Agencies, Inc. (1983) *Standards for Law Enforcement Agencies*. Fairfax, VA: Commission on Accreditation for Law Enforcement Agencies, Inc.

Davis, A.J. (1980) Letter to Burton A. Rose of Peruto, Ryan and Vitullo, counsel for the Philadelphia Chapter of the Fraternal Order of Police, October 15.

Eastman, G.D. (1961) "Other Police Problems." In L. Holcomb R. (ed.), *Municipal Police Administration*. Fifth edition. Chicago: International City Management Association, pp. 422-454.

Florida Attorney General (1971) *Annual Report*. In Herman Goldstein (ed.), *Policing a Free Society*. Cambridge, MA: Ballinger, p. 127.

Friedrich, R.J. (1980) "Police Use of Force: Individuals, Situations, and Organizations." *Annals of the American Academy of Political and Social Science* 452:82-97.

Fyfe, J.J. (1978) "Shots Fired: An Analysis of New York City Police Firearms Discharge." Ph.D. dissertation, State University of New York at Albany. Ann Arbor: University Microfilms.

—— (1979) "Administrative Interventions on Police Shooting Discretion: An Empirical Examination." *Journal of Criminal Justice* 7:309-24.

—— (1980a) "Always Prepared: Police Off-Duty Guns." *Annals of the American Academy of Political and Social Science 452:72-81.*

—— (1980b) "Geographic Correlates of Police Shooting: A Microanalysis." *Journal of Research in Crime and Delinquency 17:101-13.*

—— (1981a) "Observation on Police Deadly Force" *Crime and Delinquency* 27:376-89.

—— (1981b) "Race and Extreme Police-Citizen Violence." In R.L. McNeely and, C.E. Pope (eds.), *Race, Crime, and Criminal Justice.* Beverly Hills: Sage, pp. 89-108.

—— (1981c) "Toward a Typology of Police Shootings." In J.J. Fyfe (ed.), *Contemporary Issues in Law Enforcement.* Beverly Hills: Sage, pp. 136-151.

—— (1981d) "Who Shoots? A Look at Officer Race and Police Shooting." *Journal of Police Science and Administration* 9:367-82.

—— (1982) "Blind Justice: Police Shootings in Memphis." *Journal of Criminal Law and Criminology* 73:707-22.

—— (1986) "Enforcement Workshop: The Supreme Court's New Rules for Police Use of Deadly Force." *Criminal Law Bulletin* 22:62-68.

—— (1988) "Police Shooting Environment and License." In J.E. Scott & T. Hirschi (eds.), *Controversial Issues in Crime and Justice.* Beverly Hills: Sage, pp. 79-94.

Gain C. (1971) "Discharge of Firearms Policy: Effecting Justice through Administrative Regulation." Unpublished statement, Oakland, CA, December 23.

Garner v. Memphis Police Department, 600 F.2d 52 (6th Cir. 1979).

Garner v. Memphis Police Department, Civil Action No. C-75-145, Memorandum Opinion and Order, slip op. (W.D. Tenn. July 8, 1981).

Garner v. Memphis Police Department, 710 F.2d 240 (6th Cir. 1983).

Geller, W.A. and K.J. Karales (1981) *Split-Second Decisions: Shootings of and by Chicago Police.* Chicago: Chicago Law Enforcement Study Group.

Goldkamp, J.S. (1976) "Minorities as Victims of Police Shootings: Interpretations of Racial Disproportionality and Police Use of Deadly Force." *Justice System Journal* 2:169-83.

Harding, R. and R. Fahey (1973) "Killings by Chicago Police, 1966-1970: An Empirical Study." *Southern California Law Review* 46:284-315.

Harring, S., T. Platt, R. Speiglman, and P. Takagi (1977) "The Management of Police Killings." *Crime and Social Justice* 8:34-43.

Hart, W.L. (1979) "Fatal Shootings by Police Officers." Unpublished report to the Detroit Board of Police Commissioners, October 22.

Heaphy, J.F. (ed.) (1978) *Police Practices: The General Administrative Survey.* Washington, DC: Police Foundation.

Horvath, F. and M. Donahue (1982) *Deadly Force: An Analysis of Shootings by Police in Michigan, 1976-1981.* East Lansing: Michigan State University.

Illinois Revised Statutes (1975) Chapter 38, Para. 2-8.

International Union of Police Associations (1980) *Resolution of July 15, 1980.* Washington, DC: mimeo.

Jenkins, B. and A. Faison (1974) *An Analysis of 248 Persons Killed by New York City Policemen.* New York: Metropolitan Applied Research Center.

Kania, R.R.E. and W.C. Mackey (1977) "Police Violence As a Function of Community Characteristics." *Criminology* 15:27-48.

Knoohuizen, R., R. Fahey, and D. Palmer (1972) *The Police and Their Use of Fatal Force in Chicago.* Chicago: Chicago Law Enforcement Study Group.

Kobler, A. (1975a) "Figures (and Perhaps Some Facts) on Police Killings of Civilians in the United States, 1965-1969." *Journal of Social Issues* 31:185-91.

—— (1975b) "Police Homicide in a Democracy." *Journal of Social Issues* 31:163-81.

Law Enforcement News (1981) "NYPD May Disarm Off-Duty. April 13:3.

Matulia, K.R. (1982) *A Balance of Forces.* Gaithersburg, MD: International Association of Chiefs of Police.

—— (1985) *A Balance of Forces.* Second edition. Gaithersburg, MD: International Association of Chiefs of Police.

McCleskey v. Georgia. — U.S. —, 95 L.Ed. 262, 107 S. Ct. 1756, 55 U.S.L.W. 4537 (1987).

Memphis Police Department (1979) *General Order 95-79, Deadly Force Policy,* July 16.

Meyer, M.W. (1980a) "Police Shootings of Minorities: The Case of Los Angeles." *The Annals* 452:98-110.

—— (1980b) *Report to the Los Angeles Board of Police Commissioners on Police Use of Deadly Force in Los Angeles: Officer-Involved Shootings*, Part IV. Los Angeles: Los Angeles Board of Police Commissioners.

Milton, C., J.W. Halleck, J. Lardner, and G.L. Abrecht (1977) *Police Use of Deadly Force.* Washington, DC: Police Foundation.

Monell v. New York City Department of Social Services, 436 U.S. 658 (1978).

Murphy, G. (1986) *With Special Care.* Washington, DC: Police Executive Research Forum.

National Advisory Commission on Civil Disorders (1968) *Report of the National Advisory Commission on Civil Disorders.* New York: Dutton.

National Center for Health Statistics (1967) *International Classification for Diseases, Adapted for Use in the United States* 8th Revision. Washington, DC: United States Government Printing Office.

National Commission on the Causes and Prevention of Violence (1969) *To Establish Justice, To Insure Domestic Tranquility.* Washington, DC: United States Government Printing Office.

Nielsen, E. (1983) "Policy on the Police Use of Deadly Force: A Cross-National Analysis." *Journal of Police Science and Administration* 11:104-8.

New York State Penal Law (1967).

Pennsylvania Statutes Annotated (1973).

Philadelphia Police Department (1980) *Directive 10*, April 2.

Police Executive Research Forum (1982) "Survey of Police Deadly Force Policies." Unpublished report, Washington, DC.

—— and Police Foundation (1981) *Survey of Police Operational and Administrative Practices 1981.* Washington, DC: Police Executive Research Forum and Police Foundation, 1981.

Police Foundation, joined by Nine National and International Associations of Police and Criminal Justice Professionals, the Chiefs of Police Associations of two States, and Thirty-one Law Enforcement Chief Executives (1984) *Amici Curiae Brief in Tennessee v. Garner.* United States Supreme Court 83-1035, 83-1070. Washington, DC: August 6.

President's Commission on Law Enforcement and Administration of Justice (1967) *Task Force Report: The Police.* Washington, DC: United States Government Printing Office.

Rizzo v. Goode, 423 U.S. 362 (1976).

Robin, G. (1963) "Justifiable Homicide by Police." *Journal of Criminal Law, Criminology and Police Science* (May/June): 225-31.

Rummel, B. (1968) "The Right of Law Enforcement Officers to Use Deadly Force to Effect an Arrest" *New York Law Forum* 30:749.

Scharf, P. and A. Binder (1983) *The Badge and the Bullet.* New York: Praeger.

St. Louis Post-Dispatch (1980) "The Police Chiefs on Deadly Force." Editorial, September 21: 16.

Sherman, L.W. (1980) "Execution without Trial: Police Homicide and the Constitution." *Vanderbilt Law Review* 33:71-110.

—— (1983) "Reducing Police Gun Use: Critical Events, Administrative Policy and Organizational Change." In Maurice Punch (ed.), *The Management and Control of Police Organizations.* Cambridge, MA: M.I.T. Press, pp. 98-125.

—— and R. Langworthy (1979) "Measuring Homicide by Police Officers." *Journal of Criminal Law and Criminology* 70:546-60.

Stark, R. (1972) *Police Riots.* Belmont, CA: Wadsworth.

Takagi, P. (1974) "A Garrison State in a 'Democratic' Society." *Crime and Social Justice* 5:34-43.

Tennessee Code Annotated (1977).

Tennessee v. Garner, 471 U.S. 1, 105 S. Ct. 1694, 85 L. Ed. 1 (1985).

Uelman, G. (1973) "Varieties of Public Policy: A Study of Police Policy Regarding the Use of Deadly Force in Los Angeles County." *Loyola of Los Angeles Law Review* 6:1-65.

United States v. Clark, 31 F. 710 (6th Cir., 1887).

United States Bureau of the Census (1974) *The Social and Economic Status of the Black Population in the United States.* Washington, DC: United States Government Printing Office.

United States Civil Rights Commission (1979) *Police Practices and Civil Rights Hearing Held in Philadelphia, Pennsylvania Volume 1, Testimony.* Washington, DC: United States Government Printing Office.

—— (1981) *Who is Guarding the Guardians?* Washington, DC: United States Government Printing Office.

Uviller, H.R. (1986) "Seizure by Gunshot: The Riddle of the Fleeing Felon." *New York University Review of Law and Social change* XIV: 705-20.

Waegel, W.B. (1984) "The Use of Lethal Force by Police: The Effect of Statutory Change." *Crime and Delinquency* 30:121-40.

Wilson, O.W. (1963) *Police Administration.* Second edition. New York: McGraw-Hill.

Winter, S.L. (1986) "*Tennessee v. Garner* and the Democratic Practice of Judicial Review." *New York University Review of Law and Social Change* XIV: 679-704.

Yorke, Jeffrey (1988) "P.G. Police to Boost Firepower." *Washington Post* February 21:C-1,C6.

31

Militarizing American Police: The Rise and Normalization of Paramilitary Units

Peter B. Kraska and
Victor E. Kappeler

Historically, the civilian (i.e., non-military) nature of American policing has been taken largely for granted. In this article, however, Kraska and Kappeler document the increasing use of heavily-armed police units outfitted in military garb, which they term "police paramilitary units." These police units not only look more like the military and employ quasi-military tactics, they also seem to have close ties to elite military units. Why do you think these kinds of units have become so popular lately? With increasing concern about foreign and domestic terrorism, do you think that we are destined to see even more of this police paramilitary activity? Do you see it as a benign development in police tactics or as an undemocratic aberration and potential threat to civil liberties?

Metaphors play a central role in the construction of and reaction to social problems: they act to organize our thoughts, shape our discourse, and clarify our values (Ibarra and Kitsuse 1993; Spector and Kitsuse 1987). Sociologists have documented the spread of the medical metaphor—defining social problems as "illnesses" to be "treated" by medical professionals—as an important trend in twentieth-century social control (Conrad and Schneider 1992; Conrad 1992). This attention to medicalization neglects other social problems metaphors, particularly the metaphor of war (e.g., the War on Poverty, the war on drugs). The ideological filter encased within the war metaphor is "militarism," defined as a set of beliefs and values that stress the use of force and domination as appropriate means to solve problems and gain political power, while glorifying the tools to accomplish this—military power, hardware, and technology (Berghahn 1982; Eide and Thee 1980; Kraska 1993). Militarism influences many dimensions of social life, especially in societies such as the United States that place high value on military superiority (Sherry 1995). Just as the medicalization of social problems becomes intertwined with social thinking and problem construction outside the medical profession so does militarization affect multiple dimensions of the construction of and reaction to social problems outside the armed services.

Recent developments illustrate the profound impact the war metaphor has on a critical dimension of governmental activity external to the armed services—the criminal justice apparatus. The military model is the framework for correctional "boot-camps," the much publicized Waco, MOVE, and Ruby Ridge incidents, and most significantly the "war on drugs." Politicians, the media, and government officials joined in fueling drug war hysteria during the 1980s, leading Congress and two presidents to transform drug war discourse into tangible militarized action. By the early 1990s, all branches of the military, including most state national guards, were becoming "socially useful" by involving themselves in both domestic and international drug law enforcement (Kraska 1993; Committee on Armed Services 1988). The Clinton administration and congressional supporters extended the police/military connection by mandating that the Department of Defense and its associated private industries form a "partnership" with the Department of Justice to "engage the crime war with the same resolve they fought the cold war" (National Institute of Justice 1995:35).

The military and police comprise the state's primary use-of-force entities, the foundation of its coercive power (Bittner 1970; Enloe 1980; Kraska 1994; Turk 1982). A close ideological and operational alliance between these two entities in handling domestic social problems usually is associated with repressive governments. Although such an alliance is not normally associated with countries like the United States, reacting to certain social problems by blurring the distinction between military and police may be a key feature of the post-cold war United States. With the threat of communism no longer a national preoccupation, crime has become a more inviting target for state activity, both internationally and in the United States:

> Perhaps the most striking feature of the modern epoch is the homogeneity of forms of physical coercion. Armed forces, police forces, paramilitary forces around the world make use of the same type of military technology. . . . With the help of advisors and training courses, forms of command, patterns of operations, methods of recruitment also bear a global resemblance. For the first time in history, soldiers and policeman from different societies have role in common with each other than the societies from which they come (Kothari et al. 1988:22; see also Gibson 1994; Nadelman 1993).

These developments signal not only a strengthening of the "criminal justice-industrial complex" (CJIC) (Christie 1994; Quinney 1975), but a growing collaboration between the CJIC and the military-industrial complex in the post-cold war era (Kraska 1993). Although it has escaped the scrutiny of most criminological researchers, a significant feature of this trend may be the movement not just toward the police-ization of the military but also toward the demilitarization of civilian law enforcement in the form of police paramilitary units (PPUs).

Ignoring Police/Military Connections

Police history, with its emphasis on the night-watchmen and British "bobbies," glosses over how civilian police often formed out of militia groups and military soldiers or, conversely, out of an acute fear of military control (Brewer et al. 1988; Enloe 1980;

Kraska 1994; Manning 1977; Weisenhorn 1995). Policing literature rarely examines police/military connections except when lamenting the poor decision made by policing's forefathers in choosing the traditional paramilitary police model (Angell 1971; Skolnick and Fyfe 1993). Speculating that the police could be anything but paramilitary denies the existence of the inherent bond—historically, politically and sociologically—between the police and military (Bittner 1970; Enloe 1980). Austin Turk (1982:21) makes clear this inherent connection in discussing the formation of civilian police forces in emerging states:

> As military dominance and jurisdiction are achieved in emerging governments, authorities consolidate their position by instituting a system in which internal control is accomplished by the process of policing instead of the more costly, more overt, and less efficient one of military control.

Scant attention has been paid, thus, to the emerging overlaps between police and military functions in the post-Cold War era (Kraska 1993). In the last decade most police academics have fixated on the professed turn toward community and problem-oriented policing. While transfixed on the "velvet glove," few have inquired into the possibility of a simultaneous strengthening of the "iron-fist" as a type of "backstage" phenomenon (Manning 1977; Crime and Social Justice 1983). Despite the overtly militaristic nature of U.S. police paramilitary units (PPUs), and their continued growth since the early 1970s, little academic research or discussion examines these units.[1]

Underlying the inattention paid to PPUs might be the assumption that they are sociologically and politically insignificant. Initially these units constituted a small portion of police efforts and were limited to large urban police departments. The constructed and publicly understood role of PPUs was confined to rare situations involving hostages, terrorism, or the "maniac sniper." Despite the camouflage of these common assumptions, there have been recent unmistakable signs of intensifying military culture in police departments. Although these units are highly secretive about their operations,[2] obvious expressions of militarism are found throughout contemporary policing in the form of changing uniforms, weaponry, language, training, and tactics (Kraska 1996). Manning (1995) insightfully criticized police research and scholarship for its growing apolitical orientation as it preoccupies itself with concerns of bureaucratic efficiency. An apolitical gaze not only accounts for overlooking these units but also for not labeling them with what might be misinterpreted as a politically charmed tag—"police paramilitary unit." It is important to demonstrate, therefore, that these units differ markedly from "cop on the beat" policing and differ little from other internationally recognized PPUs in Britain (Special Patrol Groups), Italy (the Carabinieri), Germany (the Grenz Schutz Gruppe 9), France (the Gendarmerie National) or the federal police paramilitary teams in the United States (FBI, DEA, and BATF).

Distinguishing Characteristics of PPUs

As opposed to traditional police, paramilitary units can be distinguished in the following ways. PPUs are equipped with an array of militaristic equipment and technology. They often refer to themselves in military jargon as the "heavy weapons units," implying that what distinguishes them from regular police is the power and number of their weapons. The weapon most popular among these units is the Heckler and Koch MP5 submachine gun; its notoriety originates from elite military "special operations" teams, such as the "Navy Seals." The MP5's direct connection to elite military teams, its imposing futuristic style, an agressive marketing and training program conducted by the Heckler and Koch corporation, and a host of hi-tech accessories such as laser sights and sound suppressers, all solidify this weapon's central place in police paramilitary subculture (Kraska 1996). Other weapons include tactical, semi-automatic shotguns, M16s, sniper rifles, and automatic shotguns referred to as "street-sweepers."

PPUs have an array of "less-than-lethal" technology for conducting "dynamic entries" (e.g., serving a search warrant). These include percussion grenades (explosive devices designed to disorient residents), stinger grenades (similar devices containing rubber pellets), CS and OC gas grenades (tear gas), and shotgun launched bean-bag systems (nylon bags of lead shot). "Dynamic entries" require apparatuses for opening doors, including battering rams, hydraulic door-jamb spreaders, and C4 explosives. Some PPUs purchase and incorporate a range of "fortified tactical vehicles," including military armored personnel carriers and specially equipped "tactical cruisers."

A PPU's organizational structure is modeled after military and foreign police special operations teams in that they operate and train collectively under military command structure and discipline (Jefferson 1990). These teams wear black or urban camouflage "battle dress uniforms (BDUs)," lace-up combat boots, full body armor, Kevlar helmets, and sometimes goggles with "ninja" style hoods. Team members place a high premium on group solidarity and view themselves as "elite" officers, a view supported and promoted by police management (Kraska and Paulsen 1996).

Traditionally, PPU work differed significantly from routine policing. The bulk of these units formed in the late 1960s and early 1970s to respond to civil riots, terrorism, barricaded suspects, and hostage situations. Today, it is all but impossible to differentiate most PPUs by their work, except that it tends to be what each department defines as "high-risk." High-risk activities are generally defined as those situations that require a squad of police officers trained to be use-force-specialists. These squads have an intensified operational focus on either the threatened or the actual use of collective force.[3]

Despite these distinguishing characteristics, PPUs could indeed be considered inconsequential and perhaps functional if they handled only the narrowly defined terrorist or barricaded suspect situations, were housed in the largest departments under tight control, and had little impact on the operations and culture of their departments. However, the authors' ethnographic studies revealed a different set of circumstances (Kraska 1996; Kraska and Paulsen 1996), raising numerous research questions amenable to a national police survey.

As elaborated in the conclusion, the findings in this research have theoretical importance, despite their descriptive nature. For example, some police scholars argue that we are witnessing the demise of the coercive dimension of policing in "high modern" times (Reiss 1993).[4] A backstage trend toward the militarization of the police has important theoretical implications in a time when most academic discourse centers on "democratic" developments in policing (i.e., community policing). The conclusion explores the irony in this incongruity, not by emphasizing the seeming contradiction between the militarization of police and community policing but, instead, by stressing the interconnections and possible symbiotic relationship between these two developments.

Methodology

We constructed a 40-item survey (98 variables) to examine the growth and normalization of military tactics and ideology among and within United States law enforcement agencies. The instrument sought basic demographic information on the responding police agencies, and included an option for respondents to list their identity and phone number. It also sought both descriptive and longitudinal data on the formation, prevalence, uses, and activities of PPUs as they relate to the U.S. military. Finally, we solicited attitudinal information regarding the respondents' rationales for using PPUs.

Our sampling frame was all United States law enforcement agencies, excluding federal agencies, servicing jurisdictions of 50,000 or more citizens and employing at least 100 sworn officers. This list yielded a population of 690 law enforcement agencies across the states, representing all the various political subdivisions of state and local government. Because we could not determine whether four agencies identified in our sampling frame existed, they were excluded from the mailing.

An initial mailing of the survey was sent to the entire population of police agencies in January, 1996. This mailing included a letter of introduction, along with a copy of the survey instrument. Because of the secretive and suspicious character of police agencies (Manning 1978; Skolnick 1966; Westley 1956) and the difficulty in researching highly sensitive topics associated with policing (Kraska and Kappeler 1995), the introductory letter was written on a recognized sponsor's letterhead. This letter was signed by the principal researcher (first author) as well as the director of the professorial organization that agreed to sponsor the research. It also noted the researchers' university affiliation.[5] The language used in the survey encouraged respondents to recognize the study as administratively oriented. This orientation, coupled with the authors' familiarity with PPU rhetoric and the promise of confidentiality and anonymity, likely provided a level of occupational comfort to the respondents.

Within four weeks, the first mailing yielded 413 responses, a 61 percent response rate. After approximately five weeks, a second wave of surveys was mailed to the remaining 281 non-respondents. The second mailing stressed the high level of participation among other law enforcement agencies and it urged cooperation from those departments without a PPU. After approximately 6 weeks, this follow-up mailing yielded an additional 135 responses for a total response rate of 79 percent.

The researchers selected 81 of the respondents that provided identification and telephone information for unstructured follow-up phone interviews. Forty agencies that used their PPU for proactive patrol work were selected at random; the remainder were called to have police officials elaborate on their responses. Each phone interview began with an introduction and a brief verification of the data provided on the written survey. We then explored the more sensitive and controversial aspects of PPUs. Interviews lasted between five minutes and one hour—the majority about 20 minutes.

Escalating and Normalizing PPUs

Of the 548 departments responding, 89.4 percent had a police paramilitary unit. Over 20 percent of those departments without a unit said they were "planning on establishing one in the next few years." Although most departments formed their units in the 1970s, the percentage of police departments with PPUs has grown steadily (see Figure 31.1). In 1982, about 59 percent of the police departments surveyed had a PPU. By 1990, this figure had increased to 78 percent, and by 1995 it reached 89 percent. The bulk of the newer units were from smaller municipalities and state police agencies.[6]

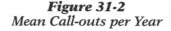

Figure 31-2
Mean Call-outs per Year

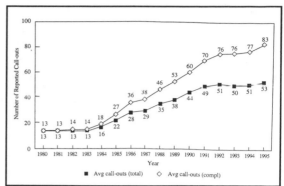

◼ Avg call-outs (total)   ◇ Avg call-outs (compl)

Figure 31-1
Year PPU Formed and Cumulative Growth

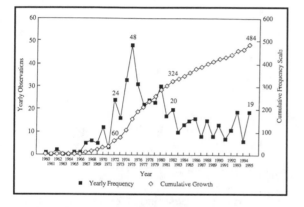

◼ Yearly Frequency   ◇ Cumulative Growth

Of course an increase in the number of PPUs, although an important indication of police militarization, means little without examining longitudinally the activities of these paramilitary units. Given the traditional role of PPUs, we might expect only a limited number of "deployments" in cases of barricaded suspects or civil demonstrations. Figure 31.2 reports on the mean "call-outs"— all emergency or high-risk deployments of the PPUs—for each of the years between 1980 and 1995. This graph depicts two sets of call-out data. The first includes all departments which provided call-out data for any of the years between 1980 and 1995 (marked as "total"). The second includes only those departments that had PPUs before 1980, and that provided complete data for all the years 1980-1995 (marked as "total").

Regarding the "total" data set, between 1980-1983 the mean number of call-outs was fairly constant and minimal, with about 13 call-outs on average per year, or approxi-

mately one PPU deployment per month. The level of police paramilitary unit activity more than doubled by 1986, almost tripled by 1989, and quadrupled by 1995. If we only include those departments that have had PPUs since 1980 (marked as "compl"), and that provided complete data from 1980-1995 (n=193), we find that the rise in paramilitary police activity is even more pronounced—a 538 percent increase.

This enormous growth in PPU activity documents an unprecedented yet little noticed phenomenon in U.S. policing—a dramatic increase in paramilitary policing activity. Moving from one call-out per month to four or five may only indicate a dramatic increase in the number of traditional PPU activities rather than normalization of these units into mainstream policing. Although we could not expect departments to provide data on the types of call-outs for every year, we did ask them for 1995 data on "barricaded persons," "hostage situations," "terrorist activity," "dangerous warrants," "civil disturbances," and "other activities." Of the total number of call-outs (n=25,201), civil disturbances accounted for 1.3 percent (n=3381), terrorist incidents .09 percent (n=23), hostage situations 3.6 percent (n=913), and barricaded persons 13.4 percent (n=3,880). Respondents reported that the majority of call-outs were to conduct what the police call "high risk warrant work," mostly "drug raids." Warrant work accounted for 75.9 percent (n=19,125) of all paramilitary activity in 1995.

Figure 31-3
Year PPU Began Warrant Work

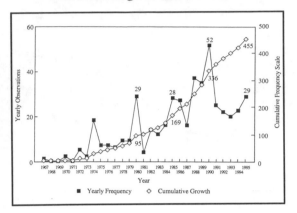

As shown in Figure 31.3, police using PPUs "proactively" for high-risk warrant work surged in the late 1980s and early 1990s. Phone interviews provided the researchers with insights into the significance of this phenomenon. Both large and small departments, with the exception of those few PPUs that have remained true to their original purpose (about 10 percent), save essentially the same account. The drug war of the late 1980s and early 1990s required the servicing of an unprecedented number of search warrants and a lesser number of arrest warrants. Rather than reactively responding to traditional crimes such as robbery, the police can go into the population and proactively produce cases against an almost limitless number of drug users and low-level dealers (Barnett 1987)—hence, the dramatic increase in "call outs." Most traditionally reaction-oriented PPUs enthusiastically accepted the new function of executing large numbers of warrants; man, PPUs now conduct between 200-700 warrants/drug raids a year.

According to our respondents, "warrant work" consists almost exclusively of what police call "no-knock entries." Generally a search warrant is obtained through either a police informant or a tip from a neighbor. After securing a warrant, the paramilitary unit conducts a "dynamic entry," generally on a private residence. Some departments claimed that these "drug raids" do not even require a warrant if the police have reason to believe that waiting for a warrant would endanger

lives or lead to the destruction of evidence.[7] As one commander described these operations, "our unit storms the residence with a full display of weaponry so we can get the drugs before they're flushed."[8] Some of the PPU commanders stressed that this type of proactive policing—instigated not by an existing high-risk situation but one generated by the police themselves—is highly dangerous for both PPU members and citizens.

A police official from a large southwestern police department explained: "In the early 90s we conducted 500 drug raids a year; things got way too dangerous and we cut way back." In this department, a team of ex-PPU members took over the warrant work after forming their own narcotics PPU. A specific incident led to this captain's negative view of drug raids:

> We did a crack-raid and got in a massive shoot-out in an apartment building. Shots were fired and we riddled a wall with bullets. An MP5 round will go through walls. When we went into the next apartment where the bullets were penetrating, we found a baby crib full of holes; thank god those people weren't home.

The interviewees also stressed that confiscating guns and money in these drug raids is as important as confiscating drugs. Several commanders noted how confiscated assets sometimes fund the purchase of new paramilitary equipment. It is critical to recognize, therefore, that doing "warrant work" is not just the perfunctory serving of a warrant subsequent to an in-depth investigation. Rather, it has become a proactive tool through which the police gather evidence and crudely conduct an investigation into suspected illegal activity. Marx (1988) has drawn considerable attention to police undercover narcotics investigations in the war on drugs. Few have noted this proactive policing tactic, perhaps more prevalent than undercover work, of PPUs conducting military-style investigatory drug raids on private residences.

These data demonstrate movement toward the normalization of paramilitary police groups. Another change that further substantiates the militarization of policing is patrol work. A recent article in a popular police magazine indicates just such a phenomenon. Police in Fresno, California pursue the goal of "proactive policing" by responding to what the article termed their inner-city "war zone" with a 40-man SWAT team, equipped with full military garb and weaponry. The objective of this full-time patrol-unit is to "suppress" the gang, drug, and crime problems. The article claims great success for this approach and sees it as an inevitable trend:

> The general consensus has been that SWAT teams working in a proactive patrol-type setting does work. Police officers working in patrol vehicles, dressed in *urban tactical gear* and armed with automatic weapons are here—and they're here to stay (Smith 1995:82; emphasis added).

Although we assumed the Fresno police department was an aberration, we still asked in the survey, "Is your department using the tactical operations unit as a proactive patrol unit to aid high crime areas?" Out of the 487 departments responding to this question, more than 20 percent (n=107) responded affirmatively. Using a PPU for patrol work was not limited to large metropolitan cities. Forty-seven percent (n=50) of the departments using their PPU for proactive patrol work served populations between 50,000 and 250,000; 20 percent (n=21) served populations between 50,000 and 100,000.

Figure 31.4 illustrates the year when each department began using its PPU for proactive patrol work. The graph shows a precipitous rise in normalizing paramilitary teams into patrol work. Since 1982, there has been a 292 percent increase (from 24 to 94) in the number of departments using PPUs for proactive patrol. Just since 1989, the number of departments deploying PPUs in this manner has doubled. As an indication of this trend continuing, 61 percent of the respondents agreed that: "Tactical Operations Units should be deployed to patrol high crime areas."

As Figure 31.4 shows, a few departments have used PPUs as patrol units since the late 1960s and early 1970s. Early PPUs sometimes engaged in "saturation patrol" of high crime areas, often in plain-clothes and unmarked cars. The question we needed an-

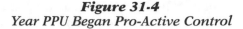

Figure 31-4
Year PPU Began Pro-Active Control

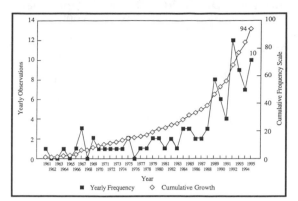

swered, and one that was too threatening to ask in the survey itself, was whether the PPU patrolled in full "tactical gear" like the Fresno police department.

Forty departments that answered affirmatively to the patrol question were randomly selected for telephone interviews. We asked about their garb, weaponry, and tactics. Different departments employ a variety of methods, ranging from full military-like, agressive patrol as found in Fresno (n=21), to patrol officers not dressed in full tactical gear but "slung with MP5s" (n=9), to PPU members in plain-clothes and standard police revolvers, carrying their full tactical gear and weaponry in car trunks (n=10). Some departments rotated these approaches depending on circumstances. One highly acclaimed community policing department described their latest approach:

> We're into saturation patrols in hot spots. We do a lot of our work with the SWAT unit because we have bigger guns. We send out two, two-to-four-men cars, we look for minor violations and do jump-outs, either on people on the street or automobiles. After we jump-out the second car provides periphery cover with an *ostentatious display of weaponry*. We're sending a clear message: if the shootings don't stop, we'll shoot someone [emphasis added].

Another commander described how his "progressive" police chief purchased a "SWAT bus" so that 30 tactical officers in full military gear could be deployed to "hot spots" throughout the city. "They geared up every night—30 officers every night for four months." One midwest police department that services a community of 75,000 people patrols in full-tactical gear using a military armored personnel carrier (termed a "peace-keeper") as their transport vehicle. The PPU commander described their approach as targeting:

> suspicious vehicles and people. We stop anything that moves. We'll sometimes even surround suspicious homes and bring out the MP5s. We usually don't have any problems with crack-heads co-operating.[9]

Two departments admitted they funded these very expensive operations with federal monies allocated for community policing programs—either by using these funds for overtime pay to PPU officers, or by hiring community policing officers and then transferring personnel to staff new PPU positions.

It is critical to note that several of the PPU commanders interviewed were shocked, and others displeased, to hear that other departments were patrolling in full tactical gear. One commander stressed that the practice not only would be offensive to the community he serves but, "operationally stupid. I realize some departments do that crap, it's just showing off—intimidation with no purpose." Another commander who disapproved of the practice did add that his PPU members repeatedly request to wear their black BDUs on patrol. As he put it, "I can't blame them, we're a very elite unit, they just want to be distinguishable."

The elite self-perception and status granted these police units stems from the high status military special operations groups have in military culture (Gibson 1994; Kraska 1996). Although the shared culture between the police and military seems obvious, little evidence supported the notion that these two use-of-force institutions were connected materially and operationally. However, field research uncovered a pattern of former and reserve soldiers intimately involved in police special operations units, as well as active-duty soldiers "cross-training" with paramilitary police officers (Kraska

1996). This survey, therefore, inquired into the training activities of PPUs and its connection to the U.S. armed forces. While "training" may seem to be a purely technical exercise, it actually plays a central role in paramilitary subculture (Gibson 1994). Training constructs and reinforces the "dangerousness" of the group's work, the importance of feeling and thinking as a team, the belief that this elite team is doing "real" police work (see Kappeler et. al 1994), and the "pleasure" that comes from playing out "warrior fantasies" (Gibson 1994; Kraska 1996). An entire "tactical" culture revolves around PPU training in which units from all over the United States, sometimes from other countries, join together in annual training competitions. Interagency training is also prevalent; our survey found that 63 percent of PPUs provide training to other police agencies.

With regard to PPU's material connection with the U.S. armed forces, departments were asked first to identify the sources of training—which were influential during the start-up period of their PPU. As seen in Table 31.1, almost 46 percent drew expertise from "police officers with special operations experience in the military." Similarly, 43 percent trained with "active-duty military experts in special operations." We then asked respondents to check those sources that currently provide training for the department's PPU. Table 31.1 shows that 30 percent of the departments received training from "police officers with special operations experience in the military," and almost 46 percent "trained with active-duty military experts in special operations."

Table 31.1
Past and Current PPU Connections to the U.S. Military*

Past Connection to Military	Yes	
	%	n
Police with Special Ops. Exp.	45.7	
Military Special Ops. Training	42.81	
Current Connection to Military	Yes	
	%	n
Police with Special Ops. Exp.	30.0	146
Military Special Ops. Training	45.7	222

Because 23 of the respondents wrote in the margin of the instrument that they train with either "Navy Seals" or "Army Rangers," we attempted to ascertain in phone interviews the extent and nature of this training. One respondent revealed the connection:

> We've had special forces folks who have come right out of the jungles of Central and South America. These guys get into the real shit. All branches of military service are involved in providing training to law enforcement. U.S. Marshalls act as liaisons between the police and military to set up the training—our go-between. They have an arrangement with the military through JTF-6 [joint task force 6]. . . . I just received a piece of paper from a four-star general who tells us he's concerned about the type of training we're getting. We've had teams of Navy Seals and Army Rangers come here and teach us everything. We just have to use our judgment and exclude the information like: "at this point we bring in the mortars and blow the place up."

During the late 1980s drug war, the Bush administration established several Department of Defense "Joint Task Forces" responsible for coordinating drug interdiction operations at the borders, abroad, and domestically (Kraska 1993). This arrangement required substantial overlap and cooperation between the military and civilian police forces, to the point of having the armed forces' elite special operations teams cross-train with U.S. civilian police forces.

Implications and Discussion: Emerging Trends in Formal Social Control

Our research found a sharp rise in the number of police paramilitary units, a rapid expansion in their activities, the normalization of paramilitary units into mainstream police work, and a close ideological and material connection between PPUs and the U.S. armed forces. These findings provide compelling evidence of a national trend toward the militarization of U.S. civilian police forces and, in turn, the militarization of corresponding social problems handled by the police.[10] The data also reveal a continuing upward trend in proactive paramilitary policing activities. Before attempting to make sense of these phenomena in a broader context, it is important to review some policy-specific dangers associated with the rise and normalization of paramilitary policing.

First, the militarism inherent in PPUs escalates to new heights the cynical view that the most expedient route to solving social problems is through military-style force, weaponry, and technology. Second, the heightened ethos of militarism in these "elite" police units is potentially infectious for the police institution; many police departments have created specialized PPUs for patrol, narcotics, and gang "suppression." According to some commanders, PPUs are also the testing ground for incorporating tactical equipment, such as percussion grenades, into mainstream policing. Third, despite the belief among tactical officers that PPUs enhance officer and citizen safety, numerous incidents and common sense raise questions about the dangerousness of these units to officers and citizens.[11] Contemporary PPUs do not just react to pre-existing emergencies that might require highly trained teams of police officers. Instead, most PPUs proactively seek out and even manufacture highly dangerous situations. Finally, paramilitary policing is not just an urban "inner-city" phenomenon. These units target what the police define as high crime or disorderly areas, which most often are poor neighborhoods, whatever the city's size.

A comfortable and certainly not illogical interpretation of this research is that contemporary policing is experiencing two parallel developments: a well-publicized movement toward community accountability, responsiveness, and problem-solving, and another backstage development toward militarization. This research, therefore, might be set aside as only uncovering a dark side of contemporary policing. The extent to which PPUs have been normalized into mainstream policing indicates otherwise. A police commander's description of his PPUs role in community policing accentuates this observation:

We conduct a lot of saturation patrol. We do "terry stops" and "aggressive" field interviews. These tactics are successful as long as the pressure stays on relentlessly. The key to our success is that we're an elite crime fighting team that's not bogged down in the regular bureaucracy. We focus on *"quality of life"* issues like illegal parking, loud music, bums, neighbor troubles. We have the freedom to stay in a hot area and clean it up—particularly gangs. Our tactical enforcement team works nicely with our department's emphasis on community policing [emphasis added].

This commander views community policing and militarized policing as linked symbiotically. Indeed, 63 percent of the respondents in this survey agreed that PPUs "play an important role in community policing strategies." Contemporary police reformers have asked the police to join together in problem-solving teams, to design ways to take control of the streets, to take ownership of neighborhoods, to actively and visibly create a climate of order, and to improve communities' quality of life (Bayley 1994; Goldstein 1990; Hoover 1996; Sherman 1995; Trojanowicz and Bucqueroux 1990; Wilson 1983, 1995; Worden 1996). Note how the PPU commander quoted above interpreted and implemented such "progressive" recommendations. Another self-proclaimed community policing chief provides a similar, although more blunt interpretation:

It's going to come to the point that the only people that are going to be able to deal with these problems are highly trained tactical teams with proper equipment to go into a neighborhood and clear the neighborhood and hold it; allowing community policing and problem oriented policing officers to come in and start turning the neighborhood around.

Both interpretations of community and problem-oriented policing are consistent with a historically embedded police ideology and practice. Indeed, police departments throughout the United States are reverting, with the support of reform-minded police academicians, to highly agressive tactics, many centering on precisely the paramilitary approach documented in this research

(Cordner 1996; Hoover 1996; Hoover and Caeti 1994; Lacayo 1996; Sherman 1992, 1994, 1995; Sviridoff and Hillsman 1996; Worden 1996; Worden et.al 1994)."[12] Three elements, then, are ideologically and pragmatically intertwined in an emerging form of policing: 1) the "war on crime and drugs" metaphor; 2) community and problem-oriented policing ideology; and, 3) the escalation and normalization of PPU activities.

Interestingly, the theoretical mortar troweled retroactively between these three elements is "routine activities theory" or what Sherman et al. (1989) calls a "criminology of place." Since the 1950s law enforcement has engaged in "pin-map" policing—conducting "saturation patrol" in those geographical spots with the most crime, or pins. Only recently, however, have we seen the academic and theoretical credentialization of this pin-map approach, along with a more sophisticated scientific discourse promoting the notion that the police need to "target aggregate populations," and social problems and spaces defined as criminogenic "hot-spots."[13] Considering the recent wave of U.S. Department of Justice research monies targeted for police crime reduction programs and the political penchant for "get tough" measures, it should not be surprising that some of the police action emanating from this "theoretical orientation" includes paramilitary drug raids and patrol tactics. Significantly, the resurrection of these efforts are often governmentally sponsored and touted in police academic circles as "scientific experiments" and "problem-solving" tactics (Hoover 1996; MacKenzie and Uchida 1994; Sherman and Erez 1995). Again, it takes little acumen to recognize how the metaphor of "war"—with its emphasis on occupation, suppression through force, and restoration of territory—coincides naturally with the "new science" of the police targeting and taking control, indeed ownership, of politically defined social spaces, aggregate populations, and social problems with military-style teams and tactics.[14]

On a broader level, this research demonstrates the necessity of widening our theoretical gaze to include the police institution's larger role, nationally and internationally, in wielding and maintaining state power, particularly as these processes relate to militarization. The converging trends of the militarization of police and police-ization of the military in the post-Cold War era renders Enloe's (1980:8) admonishment to social, political, and police analysis even more compelling: "the military and police in any state have to be considered in a common framework. Police and military analysts too often follow separate lines of inquiry; this blinds them to the mutually dependent relationship the police and military have in reality in any state." The streamlining of these two use-of-force entities raises questions about the taken-for-granted separation between the military and police as a tenet of U.S. democratic governance. C. Wright Mills (1970:246) expressed concern for what he called the newly emerging means of violence—referring to the military-industrial complex. The trends identified here, in conjunction with the escalation of the "crime control industry" (Christie 1994), may portend an inwardly focused and more subtle "emerging means of violence": a form of paramilitarized violence found in a rapidly expanding criminal justice-industrial complex, with both ideological and material connections to the military-industrial complex.

Notes

* A version of this paper was presented at the 1996 Academy of Criminal Justice Sciences Meeting in Las Vegas, Nevada. We would like to thank Louis J. Cubellis and Derek J. Paulsen for their assistance.

1. Stevens and MacKenna (1988) attempted a national study of SWAT units in 1986 but only obtained a 40 percent response rate. Their research focused on administrative issues, such as selection procedures and equipment use. Chambliss (1993) conducted field research on Washington D.C.'s Rapid Deployment Unit (RDU), documenting the repressive nature of this type of policing and its relationship to the crime control industry. *The Iron Fist and the Velvet Glove: An Analysis of the U.S. Police*, 3rd edition (Crime and Social Justice Associates 1982), written by the staff for the Center for Research on Criminal Justice at Berkeley, was the first to identify and critique the SWAT phenomenon.

2. Paramilitary units recently have become more visible in popular media. The television program COPS now periodically televises the work of paramilitary units in drug raids on private residences. The image of ninja-masked, paramilitary techno-cops also seems to be a growing theme in movies.

3. There is some confusion and controversy over Jefferson's (1990) use of the descriptor "paramilitary" in discussing police units and activities in the United Kingdom. Waddington (1993) charges Jefferson with an inexact "subjective" definition, while Hills (1995) so narrowly defines "paramilitarism" that paramilitary police activity only occurs when the police operate under the direct control of the actual military itself. At the risk of simplifying a complex debate, it seems to us that one must distinguish between indices of paramilitarism that contribute to labeling police units and their activities as "paramilitaristic," and those necessary factors that must be evident. In identifying a police unit and their activities as paramilitary, three necessary factors include: 1) the unit must be state-sanctioned, operating under legitimate state authority (we would exclude common "thuggery" exercised by a civilian paramilitary unit); 2) they must be trained and operate as a military special teams unit, such as the Navy Seals, with a strict command structure and discipline (or the pretense thereof); and 3) they must have at the core and forefront of their function to threaten or use force collectively, instantaneously, and not necessarily as an option of last resort (e.g., conducting a no-knock drug raid). Two contributing factors—military appearance and military weaponry—are critical in distinguishing paramilitary policing from standard policing, but they are not always necessary. For instance, many PPUs dress almost identical to military special operations teams. However, just as Navy Seals can dress-down into less militaristic or even plain-clothes and still operate as a paramilitary unit, so can police paramilitary unites when conducting activities as "tactical-patrol."

4. Chevigny (1995:263) provides evidence that today's police rely less on the use of force: "physical torture has been largely eliminated, and the use of deadly force has been greatly reduced over the last generation. A reduction in deadly force does not necessarily indicate, however, a reduction in police use of violence. Clearly, a more accurate indicator of whether the police are more or less often engaging in force with the intention of death would be the rate at which police fired shots at another person. These data are more difficult to access.

Geller and Scott (1992) report on these data for selected police agencies, finding that the rate at which police have discharged their weapons at people actually has increased in several departments during the late 1980s and early 1990s—coinciding with concerted police efforts in the drug war. With regards to PPUs and the use of deadly force, most highly trained and experienced PPUs have as a working credo "not to kill or be killed." This credo, as well as liability issues, probably explains the considerable interest in "less-than-lethal" technologies among PPUs. Expanding police use of force options is similar to correctional net-widening. Less-than-lethal technologies could reduce police use of deadly force, yet also expand the range of force options available to the police, and the situations in which these options are constructed as appropriate.

5. Sponsorship was limited to the use of the association's letterhead. The association did not provide any resources nor did it have any input into the project beyond its initial approval. Without the endorsement of a recognized law enforcement organization, the response rate would likely have been significantly lower.

6. Results from research just completed indicate an even more rapid growth in PPUs in smaller county and municipal police departments (departments serving populations between 25,000 and 50,000 with less than 150 officers). In 1985, 31 percent of these departments had a paramilitary unit; by 1995, 69 percent had a fully staffed paramilitary unit.

7. The PPU in Chapel Hill, North Carolina conducted a crack-raid of an entire block in an African-American neighborhood. The raid, termed "Operation Redi-Rock," resulted in the detention and search of up to 100 people, all of whom were African-American (whites were allocated to leave the area). No one was ever prosecuted for a crime (*Barnett v. Karpinos* 1995).

8. According to our interviews the majority of warrants served by PPUs are executed as dynamic, no-knock entries. While constitutional provisions of the Fourth Amendment are intended to constrain and limit the situations and methods used in police searches, courts have endorsed the use of PPUs to serve routine search and arrest warrants (Kappeler 1993). Courts are more than willing to issue "no-knock if necessary" warrants, particulary in cases characterized as drug-related (*Moss v. City of Colorado Springs*, 1989; *King v. Alarmon*, 1992). The case with which police can

obtain no-knock warrants and the almost unlimited "reasonable" justifications for deviating from the knock and announce requirement (*Collier v. Locicero*, 1993) partly account for increases in dynamic no-knock entries. The "if necessary" clause of the no-knock warrant has also given the police greater autonomy in how these raids are conducted. It is not uncommon for warrants to be issued based on fictitious police informants (*Streetman v. Jordan*, 1990; *Hevey v. Estes*, 1995), false or misleading information provided by police (*Williams v. City of Detroit*, 1994), or an officer's sole testimony concerning the detection of drug orders (*U.S. v. Riveria*, 1979). The growing list of exceptions to the Fourth Amendment's warrant requirement provides the police with near unlimited discretion in making the decision of whether to conduct a raid. Police now use the "administrative search exception" to the warrant requirement to conduct warrantless raids (*Hamilton v. Lokuta*, 1992). These raids often target locations deemed by the police to be community problems such as exotic dance halls, "drug-houses", private birthing clinics, or people the police previously, and often unsuccessfully investigated (*Hummel-Toner v. Strope*, 1994; *Hamilton v. Lokita*, 1992; *Turner v. Upton County, Texas*, 1990).

9. One PPU commander was overt about the intersection of militarism and racial bias in their paramilitary patrol work when he stated: "When the soldiers ride in you should see those blacks scatter."

10. We are not asserting that militarization is the only trend in policing, or even the predominant trend. As Manning (1995:609) states, "with . . . policing is fragmented and polyphonic, contains a variety of discourses, and symbolizes various aims and values."

11. Seven of the police departments surveyed had sharp declines in PPU activity in the last few years. We called these departments out of curiosity and they explained that there had been a controversy over the PPU killing or wounding innocent people, sometimes while at the wrong residence, or instances where team members were shot by "friendly fire." These departments' chiefs "temporarily" cut-back on using the PPUs proactively.

12. The former Police Commissioner of the New York City Police Department is probably the most vocal, and boastful, regarding its recent implementation of their "get tough on crime" approach. He ridiculed "liberal criminolo-

gists" who have claimed that aggressive policing cannot reduce crime (Lacayo 1996). In April 1996, NYPD launched a "3,000 officer offensive" to "crush drug trafficking and the drug business." (Kraus 1996:1). Referring to the widespread use of narcotics paramilitary police teams and paramilitary patrol units, one reporter noted: "this drug initiative is likely to look something like a military campaign."

13. Notice the similarities to what Feeley and Simon (1992) label the "new penology." Just as the modern U.S. prison apparatus moves toward focusing on controlling aggregate populations instead of individual offenders, so are the police and police experts emphasizing under the guise of routine activities theory, controlling aggregate populations (neighborhoods) and the criminalization of social space.

14. On March 28, 1996, ABC nightly news televised a 14-man PPU from Toledo, Ohio, based on a "tip from a neighbor," conduct a no-knock, dynamic entry on an average household (in other words, not a "crack-house"). With MP5s slung, and in full military garb, the paramilitary officers stormed the residence and aggressively threw people on the ground while ransacking the place for drugs. They found what they came for: less than an ounce of marijuana in one of the teenager's bedrooms. On the grounds of the Clinton Administration's Housing and Urban Development regulation termed, "one strike and you're out," the police and media were excited to report that the entire family was evicted. This program illustrates how even the regulatory aspects of community and problem-oriented policing can be intertwined with paramilitary policing tactics.

References

Angell, John E. 1971 "Toward an alternative to the classic police organizational arrangements: A democratic model." *Criminology* 9:185-206.

Barnett, Randy E. 1987 "Curing the drug-law addiction: The harmful side effects of legal prohibition." In *Dealing With Drugs: Consequences of Governmental Control*, ed. Ronald Hamowy, 73-102. San Francisco: Pacific Research Institute for Public Policy.

Bayley, David H. 1994 *Police For the Future*. New York: Oxford University Press.

Berghahan, R. 1982 Militarism 1861-1979. New York: St. Martin's Press.

Bittner, Egon 1970 The Functions of Police in Modern Society. Chevy Chase, Md.: National Clearinghouse for Mental Health.

Brewer, John D., G. Adrian; I. Hume, E. Moxon-Browne, and R. Wilford 1988. The Police, Public Order and the State. New York: St. Martin's Press.

Chambliss, William J. 1994 "Policing the ghetto underclass: The politics of law and law enforcement." Social Problems 41:177-194.

Chevigny, Paul 1995 Edge of the Knife: Police Violence in the Americas. New York: New York Press.

Christie, Nils 1994 Crime Control as Industry: Towards Gulags, Western Style. New York: Routledge.

Committee on Armed Services 1988 The Role of the Military in Drug Interdiction. Washington, D.C.: U.S. Government Printing Office.

Conrad, Peter 1975 "The discovery of hyperkinesis." Social Problems 23:12-21.

Conrad, Peter 1992 "Medicalization and social control." Annual Review of Sociology 18:209-232.

Cordner, Gary W. 1996 "Evaluating tactical patrol. In Quantifying Quality in Policing, ed. Larry T. Hoover, 185-206. Washington, D.C.: Police Executive Research Forum.

Crime and Social Justice Associates 1983 The Iron Fist and Velvet Glove: An Analysis of the U.S. Police, 3rd ed. San Francisco: Garret Press.

Eide, Asbjorn, and Marek Thee 1980 Problems of Contemporary Militarism. New York: St. Martin's Press.

Enloe, Cynithia 1980 Police, Military and Ethnicity. New Brunswick, N.J.: Transaction.

Feeley, Malcolm, M. and Jonathan Simon 1992 "The new penology: Notes on the emerging strategy of corrections and its implications." Criminology 30:449-474.

Geller, William A., and Michael S. Scott. 1992 Deadly Force: What We Know. Washington, D.C.: Police Executive Research Forum.

Gibson, James W. 1994 Warrior Dreams: Manhood in Post-Vietnam America. New York: Hill and Wang

Goldstein, Herman 1990 Problem-Oriented Policing. New York: McGraw-Hill Publishing.

Hills, Alice 1995 "Militant tendencies: 'Paramilitarism' in the British police." British Journal of Criminology 35:450-458.

Hoover, Larry T. 1996 Quantifying Quality in Policing. Washington, D.C.: PERF.

Hoover, Larry T., and Tory Caeti 1994 "Crime Specific Policing In Houston." TELEMASP Bulletin 1:1-12.

Ibarra, Peter, and John I. Kitsuse 1993 "Vernacular constituents of moral discourse: An interactionist proposal for the study of social problems." In Constructing Social Problems, eds. Gale Miller and James A. Holstein, 21-54. Hawthorne, N.Y.: Aidine de Gruyter.

Jefferson, Tony 1990 The Case Against Paramilitary Policing. Bristol, Penn.: Open University Press.

Kappeler, Victor E. 1993 Critical Issues in Police Civil Liability. Prospect Heights, Ill.: Waveland Press.

Kappeler, Victor E., Richard D. Sluder, and Geoffrey P. Alpert 1994 Forces of Deviance: Understanding the Dark Side of Policing. Prospect Heights, Ill.: Waveland Press.

Kothari, R., R. Falk, M. Kaldor, L. Ghee, G. Deshingkar, J. Omo-Fadaka, T. Szentes, J. Silva-Michelena, I. Sabri-Abdalla, and Y. Sakamoto 1988 Towards a Liberating Peace. New York: New Horizons Press.

Kraska, Peter B. 1993 "Militarizing the drug war: A sign of the times." In Altered States of Mind: Critical Observations of the Drug War, ed. Peter B. Kraska, 159-206. New York: Garland.

Kraska, Peter B. 1994 "The police and military in the post-Cold War era: Streamlining the state's use of force entities in the drug war." Police Forum 4:1-8.

Kraska, Peter B. 1996 "Enjoying militarism: Political/personal dilemmas in studying U.S. police paramilitary units." Justice Quarterly 13:405-429.

Kraska, Peter B., and Victor E. Kappeler 1995 "To serve and pursue: Exploring police sexual violence against women." Justice Quarterly 12:85-112.

Kraska, Peter B., and Derek Paulsen 1996 "Forcing the iron fist inside the velvet glove: A case study in the rise of U.S. paramilitary units." Presented at the Academy of Criminal Justice Sciences meeting in Las Vegas, Nevada.

Kraus, Clifford 1996 "NYC Police to start big drug offensive using new approach." Posted on World Wide Web, April 4: The New York Times Company.

Lacayo, Richard 1996 "Law and Order." Time Magazine January 15:48-56.

MacKenzie, Doris L., and Craig D. Uchida. 1994 Drugs and Crime: Evaluating Public Policy Initiatives. London: Sage Publications.

Manning, Peter K. 1977 Police Work: The Social Organization of Policing. Cambridge, Mass.: NM Press.

Manning, Peter K. 1978 "The police: Mandate, strategies and appearances." In Policing: A View From the Street, eds. P.K. Manning and J. Van Maanen, 7-32. Chicago: Goodyear.

Manning, Peter K. 1995 "Book Review: Forces of Deviance." Justice Quarterly 12:605-610.

Marx, Gary T. 1988 Undercover Policing: Police Surveillance in America. Berkeley: University of California Press.

Mills, C. Wright 1970 "The power elite and the structure of power in American society." In Power in Societies, ed. M. Olsen, 241-261. New York: McMillan.

Nadelman, Ethan A. 1993 Cops Across Borders: The Internationalization of U.S. Criminal Law Enforcement, University Park: The Pennsylvania State University Press.

National Institute of Justice 1995 "Technology transfer from defense: Concealed weapon detection." National Institute of Justice Journal 1:229.

Quinney, Richard 1975 Criminology. Boston: Little Brown.

Reiss, Albert J. 1993 "A Theory of Policing." Presented at the annual meetings of the American Society of Criminology, Phoenix.

Sherman, Lawrence W. 1992 "Attacking crime: Policing and crime control." In Policing and Crime Control, eds. M. Tonry and N. Morris. Chicago: University of Chicago Press.

Sherman, Lawrence W. 1994 "The Kansas City Gun Experiment." Update. Washington D.C.: National Institute of Justice, October.

Sherman, Lawrence W. 1995 "The police." In Crime, eds. James Wilson and Joan Petersilia, 327-348. San Francisco: ICS Press.

Sherman, Lawrence W., and E. Erez 1995 "Special issue on policing hot spots." Justice Quarterly 12:653-783.

Sherman, Lawrence W., Patrick R. Gartin, and Michael E. Buerger 1989 "Hot spots of predatory crime: Routine activities and the criminology of place." Criminology 27:27-56.

Sherry, Michael S. 1995 In the Shadow of War: The United States Since the 1930s. New Haven: Yale University Press.

Skolnick, Jerome H. 1966 Justice Without Trial: Law Enforcement in a Democratic Society,. New York: John Wiley and Sons.

Skolnick, Jerome H., and James J. Fyfe 1993 Above the Law: Police and the Excessive Use of Force. New York: The Free Press.

Smith, C.D. 1995 "Taking back the streets." Police Magazine: The Law Officer's Magazine 19:36-40.

Spector, Malcolm, and John I. Kitsuse 1987 Constructing Social Problems. Hawthorne, NY: Aldine de Gruyter.

Stevens J.W., and D.W. MacKenna 1988 "Police capabilities for responding to violent criminal activity and terrorism." Police Studies 11:116-123.

Sviridoff, Michele, and Sally T. Hillsman 1994 "Assessing the community effects of tactical narcotics teams." In Drugs and Crime: Evaluating Public Policy Initiatives, eds. Doris Mackenzie and Craig D. Uchida, 114-128. Thousand Oaks, Calif.: Sage Publications.

Trojanowicz, Robert, and Bonnie Bucqueroux 1990 Community Policing: A Contemporary Perspective. Cincinnati: Anderson Publishing.

Turk, Austin 1982 Political Criminality: The Defiance and Defense of Authority. Beverly Hills: Sage Publications.

Waddington, P.A.J. 1993 "The case against paramilitary, policing considered." British Journal of Criminology, 33:353-371.

Weisenhorn, Donald J. 1995 "Military model." In The Encyclopedia of Police Science, ed. William G. Bailey, 421-423. New York: Garland.

Westley, W. A. 1956 "Secrecy and the Police." Social Forces 34:254-257.

Wilson, James Q. 1983 Thinking About Crime. New York: Vintage Books.

Wilson, James Q. 1995 "Crime and Public Policy." In Crime, eds. James Wilson and Joan Petersilia, 489-510. San Francisco: ICS Press.

Worden, Robert E., "The effectiveness of street-level drug enforcement." In Quantifying Quality in Policing, ed. Larry T. Hoover, 131-152. Washington D.C.: Police Executive Research Forum.

Worden, Robert E., Timothy S. Bynum, and James Frank 1994 "Police crackdowns on drug abuse and trafficking In Drugs and Crime: Evaluating Public Policy Initiatives, eds. Doris MacKenzie and Craig D. Uchida, 95-113. Thousand Oaks, Calif.: Sage Publications.

Cases Cited

Barnett v. Karpinos, 460 S.E.2d 208 (N.C. App. 1995).

Bonner v. Anderson 81 F.3d 472(4th Cir. 1996).

Collier v. Locicero, 820 F.Supp. 673 (D.Conn. 1993).

Hale v. Townley, 19 F.3d 1068 (5th Cir 1994).

Hamilton v. Lokuta, 803 F.Supp. 82 (E.D. Mich. 1992).

Hervey v. Estes, 65 F.3d 784 (9th Cir. 1995).

Hummel-Toner v. Strope, 25 F.3d 647 (8th Cir. 1994).

King v. Marmon, 793 F.Supp. 1030 (D. Kan. 1992).

McGovern v. City of Minneapolis, 480 N.IV.2d 121 (Minn.App. 1992).

Moss v. City of Colorado Springs, 871 F.2d 112 (10th Cir. 1989).

Streetman v. Jordan, 918 F.2d 555 (5th Cir, 1990).

Turner v. Upton County, Texas, 915 F.2d 133 (5th Cir. 1990).

U.S. v. Riveria, 595 F.2d 1095 (5th Cir. 1979).

Williams v. City of Detroit, 843 F.Supp. 1183 (E.D.Mich. 1994).

Reprinted from Peter Kraska and Victor Kappeler, "Militarizing the American Police: The Rise and Normalization of Paramilitary Units" in *Social Problems* 44(1): 1-18. Copyright © 1997 by the Society for the Study of Social Problems, Inc. Reprinted by permission. ✦

32

Dragons and Dinosaurs: The Plight of Patrol Women

*Donna C. Hale and
Stacey M. Wyland*

The employment of women as patrol officers has been relatively commonplace for 30 years, and studies showing that women perform the job effectively have been available for twenty years. Nevertheless, as Hale and Wyland show in this article, women in policing continue to meet tremendous resistance, primarily from their male colleagues. Why is this the case? As you read this article, consider what changes should be made within police organizations to make them more hospitable to an increasingly diverse work force, especially women. Do you think it is the larger society that has to change first, or is the problem simply within the police culture? Also, what do you think should be the ultimate goal in the employment of women officers—50 percent of the force? More? Or less? Why?

This analogy for prospective women managers is also appropriate for women on patrol who for the past twenty years have been struggling for acceptance and recognition by their male peers and supervisors. Little did women in policing imagine that the videotape of Rodney King's beating by four Los Angeles Police officers would result in the Los Angeles City Council recommendation that more women patrol officers be hired. Unfortunately, it is often these serendipitous events that lead to the discovery of what we already knew in this case, that women are effective as patrol officers. The Christopher Commission's role in investigating the Rodney King incident was extremely important to the status of women on patrol because it resulted in illuminating the performance evaluation studies of the late 1970s that overall concluded that women are effective on patrol (Bloch and Anderson, 1974; Bloch, Anderson and Gervais, 1973; Craig, 1976; .Milton, Abramowitz,Crites, Gates, Mintz and Sandler, 1974; Sichel, Friedman, Quint and Smith, 1978). These findings, however, did not result in the acceptance of women on patrol. The organizational culture of policing as man's work has been entrenched since the nineteenth century and is very evident today in the attitudes of male peers and supervisors.

What *Time* reporter Jeanne McDowell describes (February 17, 1992) regarding the effective performance of women on patrol is not surprising. This information was reported at the time the performance evaluation studies were conducted fifteen years ago. It is ironic that the police organization has not accommodated the entry of women on patrol. Although the Equal Employment Opportunity Act and Commission have been in existence to ensure women's entry into patrol work, the organization has effectively kept the percentage of women on patrol below ten percent. The time has arrived to acknowledge that women can do patrol, and that they should not have to continually prove that they can do so.

The Christopher Commission "unearthed" these findings that women on patrol communicate effectively without using physical force. This discovery resulted in the city council of Los Angeles recommending that its police department increase female sworn officers to forty-three percent within the next seven years (*Time*, 1992: 72). In order to accomplish this feat, the police department needs to develop strategies to recruit and retain women as patrol officers.

Before discussing strategies to recruit and retain women in policing it is important to examine the research that supports the fact that women can do patrol work. Consequently, the first section of this article is referred to as "old wine in new bottles" because most of the information presented in the recent *Time* article is based on the performance evaluation studies of the 1970s. It is evident from this reexamination of the performance evaluations that the problem is not that women cannot do patrol work; the problem is the resistance that male police officers either as peers or supervisors hold against women doing what is considered "men's work"(Balkin, 1988; Bell, 1982; Milton, 1975; Golden, 1981; Charles, 1982; Lord, 1986; Martin, 1990; Price, 1985; Remmington, 1983; Jones, 1986). It is unfortunate that it takes the brutality of the Rodney King videotape beating to trigger a resurgence of the research substantiating that women can do patrol.

Old Wine in New Bottles: Are Women Better Cops?

Since the early 1970s, patrol women have struggled to be accepted as equals in what has traditionally been a male bastion—patrol. The resistance and hostility towards women is primarily based on stereotypes and myths regarding the ability of women to do what is considered a man's job (Bell, 1982). The literature on women in policing is replete with conclusions that women as patrol officers are not accepted by their male peers and supervisors. If women decide to remain in patrol, they experience and endure sexual harassment and discrimination. If they stay, women must find ways of coping or adjusting to the culture. Susan Martin (1979) has written extensively on the ways women have "adjusted" to the male world of policing. Perhaps her best known work is her description of the POLICEwoman and the policeWOMAN. Women have also resorted to litigation to secure their positions in policing (Hale and Menniti, 1993).

The aftermath of King's assault resulted in the establishment of the Christopher Commission. This is not new. A cursory examination of any introductory text on policing refreshes our memories of earlier studies conducted as a result of police misconduct. For example, the Wickersham and Lenox Commissions reports from the early 1900s; the Knapp Commission investigation of corruption in the New York City Police Department;

and the Kerner Commission that investigated reasons for rioting and destruction in American cities during the summer of 1967 (Inciardi, 1990: 301). Furthermore, it is interesting that although the Commission concluded that there were numerous causes [of the rioting and destruction], it specified "aggressive preventive patrol, combined with police misconduct in the forms of brutality, unwarranted use of deadly force, harassment, verbal abuse, and discourtesy as stimuli for the disruptions" (Inciardi, 1990: 302).

During the Christopher Commission's investigation experts testified that women are successful on patrol. Many of these experts' research substantiates the findings of the earlier performance evaluation studies of women on patrol that women could indeed accomplish the requisite dues of patrol.

The most significant contribution of *Time* reporter Jeanne McDowell was that her article reminded us what we already knew: women are effective at communication and calming volatile and potential violent situations. This information is a given: we have research that supports women are capable of patrol; what we need to do now is to keep these very capable women on the job. As McDowell (1972: 70) reported ". . . women constitute only 9% of the nation's 523,262 police officers. . . . After twenty years of meeting resistance by police departments, it is now time to examine the organizational culture of police departments and change the environment so women can be accepted as patrol officers.

Based on McDowell's report and the twenty-year-old research we know that: (1) women are better than men in talking people out of violence; (2) police work is not predominately violent; and, (3) physical size is irrelevant because violence is so little a part of police work. These same conclusions from the Washington, D.C. study are substantiated by those reported in *Time* (May 27, 1974) once again from a study in the nation's capital, there was little difference in the abilities of men and women to deal with violent, or potentially violent situations. Women were similar or equal to men in the percentage of arrests made that resulted in conviction, their attitude toward the public, the number of incidents they were involved in that required back-up support from other officers, the number of injuries they sustained on the job, and even the number of driving accidents they had.

And twenty years ago in 1972, *Time* (May 1: 60) reported that many police departments were assigning women patrol officers to do what was traditionally considered men's work handling domestic disputes. The reason for this change was that women appeared to be more successful at calming disputes. Over the years research by Kennedy and Homant (1983) indicated that victims of domestic violence believed female officers were more patient and took more time to deal with the conflict. These studies reported that female officers were more tactful and subtle, stayed longer, and were concerned about root causes of conflict. Women were described as having "a soothing and calming effect."

Also in 1972, *Newsweek* (October 23: 117) reported that the major objections to the entry of women on patrol in Washington, D.C., Boston, Miami and New York were: (1) women were presumed incapable of dealing with violent situations; (2) the chivalry factor; and (3) physical size. Effectiveness of women patrol officers was reported in handling family disputes, juvenile delinquency, shoplifting and drugs. Therefore, comparing these early articles regarding the effectiveness of women on patrol Keith McDowell's (1992) report twenty years later, it is clear that the conclusions regarding the effectiveness of women on patrol have not changed. Interestingly, however, in both articles the dissatisfaction with the uniform women were required to wear is similar. McDowell reports "[I]n most places it means wearing an uncomfortable uniform designed for a man, including bulletproof vests that have not been adapted to women's figures." The 1972 article discusses women on patrol wearing skirts and carrying their guns in their purses.

Before we leave this section, it is important to examine a classic article published in 1981 by Van Wormer and to briefly update her advantages and disadvantages of using men on patrol. Her first advantage was superior physical strength combined with stamina to subdue a suspect. Research now substantiates that although women do not have the same upper body strength of their male counterparts they can be trained to compensate for lack of strength (Charles 1981,1982). Earlier, Talney (1969: 50) pointed out that

> . . . it is not unreasonable to suggest that well-trained women officers could counter many kinds of disturbances and disorders which equally well-trained men could not . . . male officers are assaulted because . . . they represent a male authority figure which within the value system of many criminals makes them fair game. . . particularly if the encounter takes place in the presence of their peer group where such values are shared.

Talney (1969: 50) continues that female officers could avoid assaults because it is unheroic to assault a female . . . even a female police officer. "Furthermore, the public image of women facing unruly crowds could do much to swing public support to the side of proper police authority."

Van Wormer's second advantage was that men can handle long hours, nights, and rotating shifts. This is one area that women have difficulty with especially if they are single parents. In general, men do not encounter these problems because they have a spouse at home who is the primary caretaker of home and children.

The third advantage focuses on aggressiveness of men. Dranov (1985: 174-175) indicates that some male officers are unsure about the reliability of a woman partner to back them up. Lewis Sherman (1975:435) found that although females were less aggressive and tend to make fewer arrests than men, they were effective at patrol.

The final advantage is that males have related job experience, primarily military experience. This may have been true in the 1970s, but it would be interesting to examine this in 1993 to see if recruits are coming from the military, college campuses, or other blue-collar occupations? This is important for recruitment practices because it is necessary to learn just what the military experience has in common with police work. It may be that a college education is more beneficial, since officers spend the majority of their time providing services to the community. Finally, individuals may be attracted to police work because it does not require a college degree, but pays a higher salary than many other blue collar occupations.

According to Van Wormer, there are more complaints against men on patrol. The article by McDowell (1992) verifies that when the Christopher Commission investigated the Los Angeles Police Department after the King beating, it found "that the 120 officers with the most use-of-force reports were all men. Civilian complaints against women are also consistently lower. In San Francisco. . . . female officers account for only 5% of complaints although they make up 10% of the 1,839-person force."

Van Wormer points out that male officers provoke violence and are more physically brutal. This has been supported by the performance evaluation research that reported women on patrol as more effective in dealing with conflict because they rely on mediation and intervention techniques. Dranov's (1985: 21) response that "the ability to subdue someone is not as important as the ability to communicate intelligently reflects the overall consensus of the research that are effective." But, the comment by a deputy sheriff in southern California probably reflects many male's attitudes that physical size is more important than communication styles. The deputy sheriff stated "I don't care if a dame is Calamity Jane and can shoot a button off my vest. My biggest weapons are that I'm tall and pretty intimidating. These gals could only intimidate my little sister" (*Newsweek*, October 23, 1972: 117). As Katherine Perkins, Detroit police officer, pointed out "Any fool can shoot a gun. What you really need is intelligence and sensitivity—and that's what women bring to the job" (Dreifus, 1981: 58). This is similar to Elizabeth Watson's statement in the McDowell article that "intelligence, communication, compassion and diplomacy" (1992: 70) [are] required in policing.

Van Wormer stresses that women have a disarming affect and are better at public relations. Male officers often have poor reputations. Furthermore, male officers are not effective at questioning rape victims. Rape is a painful experience for female victims to report to male officers: and male officers may either be insensitive or feel uncomfortable with this type of case, similar to child abuse investigations. Historically, female officers were hired to deal with women as offenders and victims because of their gender. It was believed that women would more sympathetic/empathetic in these situations. It is interesting to note, however, that the English policewomen Lilian Wyles reported in her autobiographical account of her experience at Scotland Yard that male officers tried to shield policewomen from investigations regarding sexual offences. The reason cited was the belief that middle class women should be protected from these type of situations that may either sully or embarrass them.

Van Wormer's comments that male officers are reluctant to accept women on patrol and may overprotect them. This chivalry is a result of both stereotypes and socialization. Also, Van Wormer points out that historically women in policing have had more education than men. This is well documented in the early literature of policewomen in America. Men were hired because of their physical size; women were required to have higher education for their positions. In the early 1970s Perlstein (1972: 46) found that 35.3 percent of the women police in his study had higher educational levels. He concluded that more education results in less police authoritarianism.

To conclude this section on the effectiveness of women on patrol, it should be noted that in 1980 the Los Angeles Police Department doubled the number of its female officers. Commander Ken Hickman used this opportunity to complete his dissertation research by comparing the records of sixty-eight female cops hired to go out on patrol after 1980 with those of male officers hired at the same time. In an examination of 6,000 daily field activity reports he found that male-female teams were just as productive in initiating potentially hazardous calls as were male-male teams and the individual top initiators of potentially hazardous activities were female. He also found that recruit training officers rated men lower than women in tactics, initiative and self-confidence, writing and communication, and public contacts. Also, the I.Q.s of the female recruits were

higher and academically the women surpassed their male classmates in the police
academy. Assessing physical fitness and
height, Hickman found that these correlated
with success in the field for only four percent
of all police officers. Women officers got significantly more commendations from the
public. He found that both men and women
had similar numbers of complaints by the
public. Productivity levels were high for the
police women in the crime-ridden South Bureau. He also found that the females' communication skills were better and this was an advantage for them for them in domestic violence situations (Elias, 1984:17).

It is evident from this examination of the
performance evaluation research on women
on patrol that women can handle patrol
work. It is no longer necessary to debate or
discuss the effectiveness of women on patrol.
It is time, however, to address the greater issue of how women can unconditionally be accepted by their peers and supervisors. Twenty
years ago, Lewis Sherman (1973: 384, 393)
reported the benefits of hiring women patrol
officers as:

(1) a reduction in the incidence of violence
    between police officers and citizens;

(2) increased quality of police service be-
    cause women accentuate the service role
    of police work more than men;

(3) improved police community relations be-
    cause women are more visible than men,
    make more contacts, and citizens will as-
    sist police women upon request;

(4) police men can learn from the police
    women that an officer can be efficient
    without using force;

(5) police women more effective than police
    men in settling problems reported by
    women from low-income neighborhoods;

(6) a police department becomes more demo-
    cratic and responsive to the community by
    hiring personnel who are more repre-
    sentative of the community's population;
    and,

(7) lawsuits charging sex discrimination
    could be avoided by the police depart-
    ment that develops and implements job-
    related selection, recruitment and pro-
    motional standards and tests.

Lewis Sherman's (1975: 438) conclusion
that "the question of whether women could
perform general patrol duties was primarily
political rather than scientific [was evident]
from the very beginning." He points out that
"in many respects the enormous efforts that
have gone into evaluating the performance of
women have been a diversion from what has
always been the most genuinely important
question in police research what kind of person makes a good police officer? As he stated:

> Gender is not a relevant characteristic of
> that person. It is only a reflection of our
> prejudiced and conservative views that
> we should ever have thought it might be.
> The unassailable fact is that some women
> are good police officers and some women
> are not, just like men. Our quest still re-
> mains to define and measure a good cop-
> man or woman.

. . . The major problem for police departments is not recruiting women—the problem
is retention, because many police departments are locked in a "time-warp" that perpetuates the myth that only men can do
patrol. Although research clearly substantiates that patrol is primarily service, and
women can handle any physical problems requiring strength by using "karate, twist locks
or a baton instead of their fists" (McDowell,
1992), their male counterparts cannot accept
reality. Men still perceive police work as a
man's domain where women will only get in
the way, cannot be depended upon for backup,
or may get hurt. The expression "old habits die
hard" is evident. The nineteenth century ma-
chismo legacy is slow to die in the police organizational culture.

Recommendations for Recruitment and Retention

The major problems facing the recruitment and retention of women as patrol officers are the political, cultural and structural
systems of the police organization. Therefore, in order to change the milieu of policing
that is vested in traditions of machoism and
sexism, it requires a leader who takes the re-

sponsibility of slaying the dragons and replacing the dinosaurs who keep the old traditions alive and well. These changes require a "transformational" leader who will work to change both the political and cultural systems of the police department. To begin the change the leader first must develop a vision of women as patrol officers; next, mobilize the department to work toward achieving the new vision and lastly, institutionalizing the changes over time (Tichy and Ulrich, 1984: 344).

Tichy and Ulrich (1984: 345) state that before an organization will change there must be a "trigger" that indicates change is needed. Although for the past twenty years we have known that women are capable of performing patrol, it takes a horrific incident like the Rodney King beating to recognize the effectiveness of women on patrol. As discussed earlier, this incident led to the Los Angeles City Council's recommendation that the percentage of female patrol officers be increased to forty-three percent in the next seven years. The new police chief of the Los Angeles Police Department, Willie Williams, must create an agenda that requires improving police community relations in addition to hiring more female and minority police officers. He will need to rely on effective recruitment and retention strategies to change the orzanizational culture.

One area that must be addressed in hiring more female officers is how to retain them once they are hired. In general, women are kept out of male-dominated occupations by hostility, sexual harassment and male attitudes (Jacobs, 1989). The presence of women in a traditionally male domain is threatening and they are perceived and treated as outsiders. They are treated paternalistically and prevented from learning tasks that will later help with promotions, or with hostility, or both (Padavic and Reskin, 1990). Furthermore, Cockburn (1985), Dreifus (1980) and Hunt (1990) report the presence of women in traditionally blue-collar male occupations may challenge the men's "culturally-granted gender power" (Cockburn, 1985 in Padavic and Reskin, 1990: 617).

The Christopher Commission did not address how to deal with the resistance of the dinosaurs who believe women have no place on patrol. This resistance is based on three interrelated systems: technical, political and cultural. For example, technical resistance includes the uniforms that women wear. Even twenty years after the performance evaluation studies, improper fit of uniforms and bullet proof vests and size of handguns for women is still a problem. Another example of the technical aspects is the emphasis in the training academics on the physical testing as well as firearms training.

The political resistance in police departments is based on entrenched rules of patrol work established and maintained by the older male officers and supervisors. Especially evident in police departments are policies, or lack of policies regarding pregnancy and disability leaves for patrol women as well as flex shifts for women who have child care responsibilities. These policies also reflect the cultural aspect of the organization that resists changing the culture to accommodate the entry of women on patrol. Anecdotal information reveals that men become upset when women get special consideration because they are pregnant, or have child care responsibilities. Because of these responsibilities, women often move into administrative positions to have the more conventional shift of 8 a.m. to 5 p.m. Unfortunately, this removes the patrol women from the street where their visibility is important. Gender neutral shifts, flex shifts, child care programs and paternity leaves would improve the organizational culture for both male and female officers.

An examination of the litigation regarding sexual harassment and discrimination toward women on patrol reveals the hostility women have encountered. Simply stated, men do not want women on patrol (Hale and Menniti, 1993). In order for women to remain on patrol, the police leader must change the environment emphasizing that harassment and discrimination will not be tolerated. It must be clearly communicated that women will be hired in police departments and that if these policies are violated, recriminations will follow. The leader must make sure that all members of the department are trained regarding sexual harassment and sexual discrimination.

During the recruitment stage it is crucial to explain what the duties of a patrol officer are as well as preparing women for the resistance they will encounter. Timmins and Hainsworth (1989: 204) found that women police officers believed that although admission requirements were usually clear, many of the women were uncertain about why they were hired, what sex roles they should play as women cops; what problems they were likely to encounter, and what the police academy experience was supposed to do for them.

During the recruitment process police departments need to include female police officers as recruiters. Advertisements should depict women officers conducting patrol work as well as describing the department's policy of hiring, paying and deploying women the same as men (Sulton and Townsey, 1981). Once women are recruited, special workshop courses should be included in the police recruit training for both male and female recruits describing the stress of the job as well as explaining to both men and women officers that the evaluation research supports that women can do patrol. Also, in the recruit academy as well as later in-service training, time must be allocated to describing and discussing ethics and police work. Officers need to address issues of police violence and corruption through both presentation and discussion groups. In addition, training should include policies on sexual harassment and discrimination and explaining that these policies will be enforced. All these activities support the commitment that the police organization has to improving the organizational climate for both male and female officers.

Lastly, the changes regarding recruitment and retention of women on patrol must institutionalize the opportunity for promotion of qualified officers. This means that the existing performance evaluation/appraisal must be redesigned to reflect what patrol work is. It is also important that women patrol officers be trained by women patrol officers, or by men who are aware that women can do patrol work effectively.

These changes in the police organization will not take place overnight. They involve a major commitment by both the department's leadership and the local form of government to establish a police department that represents the community. Women as patrol officers should not have to encounter resistance by the peers and supervisors. Although dragons and dinosaurs die slowly; change must begin now. As Betty Friedan once said "A girl [sic] should not expect special privileges because of her sex but neither should she adjust to prejudice and discrimination" (Warner, 1992: 312).

The evaluation research reveals that women did not expect special privileges as patrol officers—they just wanted the opportunity to do the job. The role of the police leader is to change the technical, political and cultural resistance in the police department.

References

Balkin, Joseph. (1988) "Why Policemen Don't Like Policewomen." *Journal of Police Science and Administration*, 16(1): 29-38.

Bell, Daniel J. (1982) "Policewomen: Myths and Reality." *Journal of Police Science and Administration*, 10(1): 112-120.

Bloch, Peter B. and Deborah Anderson. (1974) *Policewomen on Patrol: Final Report*, Washington, DC: Police Foundation.

Bloch, Peter, Deborah Anderson and Pamela Gervais. (1973) *Policewomen on Patrol—Major Findings: Final Report, Volume 1*. Washington, DC: Police Foundation.

Charles, Michael T. (1981). "The Performance and Socialization of Female Recruits in the Michigan State Police Training Academy." *Journal of Police Science and Administration*, 9(2): 209-223.

Charles, Michael T. (1980). "Policewomen and the Physical Aspects of Policing." *Law and Order*, 28(9): 83-89.

Cockburn, Cynthia. (1985) *Machinery of Dominance*. London: Pluto.

Craig, G.B. (1976). *Women Traffic Officer Project: Final Report*. Sacramento, California: Department of California Highway Patrol.

Dranov, Paula. (1985). "The Lady is a Cop." *Cosmopolitan*, 199: 174-177, 213.

Dreifus, Claudia. (1981). "Why Two Women Cops Were Convicted of Cowardice." *Ms.*, 9(4): 57-58, 63-64.

Dreifus, Claudia. (1980). "People Are Always Asking Me What I'm Trying to Prove. . ." *Police Magazine*: 18-25.

Elias, M.K. (1984). "The Urban Cop: A Job for a Woman." *Ms.*, 12: 17.

None cited. (1972). "Female Fuzz." *Newsweek*, 80:117.

Golden, Kathryn. (1981) "Women as Patrol Officers: A Study of Attitudes." *Police Studies*, 4: 29-33.

Hale, Donna C. and Daniel J. Menniti. (1993). "Discrimination and Harassment: Litigation by Women in Policing." In *It's A Crime: A Critical Look at Women's Issues in Criminal Justice*. Edited by Roslyn Muraskin and Ted Alleman. Needham Heights, Massachusetts: Regents/Prentice-Hall.

Hennig, Margaret and Anne Jardin. (1977). *The Managerial Woman*. New York, New York: Pocket Books.

Hunt, Jennifer C. (1985). "The Logic of Sexism Among Police." *Women & Criminal Justice*, 1(2): 3-30.

Inciardi, James A. (1990). *Criminal Justice*. Third Edition. New York, New York: Harcourt Brace Jovanovich, Publishers.

Jacobs, Jerry. (1989). *Revolving Doors*. Stanford, California: Stanford University Press.

Jones, Sandra. (1986). "Women Police: Caught In The Act." *Policing*, 2(2): 129-140.

Kennedy, Daniel B. and Robert J. Homant. (1983). "Attitudes of Abused Women Toward Male and Female Police Officers." *Criminal Justice and Behavior*, 10(4): 391-405.

Lord, Lesli Kay. "Policewomen." In *The Encyclopedia of Police Science*. Edited by William G. Bailey. New York, New York: Garland Publishing, Inc., 491-502.

Lunneborg, Patricia. (1990). *Women Changing Work*. New York, New York: Bergin and Garvey Publishers.

Martin, Susan E. (1979). "Policewomen and Policewomen: Occupational Role Dilemmas and Choices for Female Officers." *Journal of Police Science and Administration*, 7(3): 314-323.

Martin, Susan E. (1989). "Women on the Move?: A Report on the Status of Women in Policing." *Women & Criminal Justice*, 1(1): 21-40.

McDowell, Jeanne. (1992). "Are Women Better Cops?" *Time*, 139(7): 70-72.

Milton, Catherine Higgs, Ava Abramowitz, Laura Crites, Margaret Gates, Ellen Mintz and Georgette Sandler. (1974). *Women in Policing: A Manual*. Washington, DC: Police Foundation.

Padavic, Irene and Barbara F. Reskin. (1990). "Men's Behavior and Women's Interest in Blue-Collar Jobs." *Social Problems*, 37(4): 613-627.

Perlstein, Gary R. (1972). "Policewomen and Policemen: A Comparative Look." *Police Chief*, 39(3): 72-74, 83.

The President's Commission on Law Enforcement and Administration of Justice. (1967). *Task Force Report: The Police*. Washington, DC: The US Government Printing Office.

Remmington, Patricia Weiser. (1983). "Women in the Police: Integration or Separation?" *Qualitative Sociology*, 6(2): 118-135.

Report of the National Advisory Commission on Civil Disorders. (1968). New York, New York: E.P. Dutton.

Reskin, Barbara F. (1988). "Bringing the Men Back In: Sex Differentiation and the Devaluation of Women's Work." *Gender and Society*, 2: 58-81.

Sherman, Lewis J. (1973). "A Psychological View of Women in Policing." *Journal of Police Science and Administration, 1(4): 383-394.*

Sherman, Lewis J. (1975). "An Evaluation of Policewomen on Patrol in a Suburban Police Department." *Journal of Police Science and Administration*, 3(4): 434-438.

Sichel, Joyce L., Lucy N. Friedman, Janet C. Quint, and Michael E. Smith. (January, 1978). *Women on Patrol: A Pilot Study of Police Performance in New York City*. Washington, DC: National Institute of Law Enforcement and Criminal Justice, Law Enforcement Assistance Administration, US Department of Justice.

Sulton, Cynthia G. and Roi D. Townsey. (1981). *A Progress Report on Women in Policing*. Washington, DC: Police Foundation.

Talney, Ronald G. (1969). "Women in Law Enforcement: An Expanded Role." *Police*, 14: 49-51.

Tichy, Noel M. and David O. Ulrich. (Fall, 1984). "The Leadership Challenge—A Call for the Transformational Leader." *Sloan Management Review*, 59-68. Reprinted in *Classic Readings in Organizational Behavior*. Edited by J. Steven Ott. Belmont, California: Wadsworth, Inc., 1989, 344-355.

Timmins, William M. and Brad E. Hainsworth. (1989). "Attracting and Retaining Females in Law Enforcement: Sex-Based Problems of Women Cops in 1988." *International Journal of Offender Therapy and Comparative Criminology*, 33(3): 197-205.

Van Wormer, Katherine. (1981). "Are Males Suited to Police Patrol Work?" *Police Studies*, 3(4): 41-44.

Warner, Carolyn. (1992). *The Last Word: A Treasury of Women's Quotes*. Englewood Cliffs, New Jersey: Prentice-Hall.

None Cited. (1980). "Women Cops on the Beat." *Time*, 115:58.

None Cited. (1972). "The Women in Blue." *Time*, 99: 60.

Wyles, Lilian. (1952). *A Woman at Scotland Yard*. London: Faber and Faber, Limited.